*To inspire ambition, to stimulate
the imagination, to provide the
inquiring mind with accurate
information told in an interesting style, and thus lead into
broader fields of knowledge-
such is the purpose of this work*

The New
BOOK OF KNOWLEDGE
Volume Three

Other Famous Works
of
Popular Instruction
by
the Same Editor

❖❖❖

PRACTICAL KNOWLEDGE FOR ALL
SIX VOLS.

NEW UNIVERSAL ENCYCLOPEDIA
TEN VOLS.

UNIVERSAL HISTORY OF THE WORLD
EIGHT VOLS.

THE SECOND GREAT WAR
NINE VOLS.

PEOPLES OF ALL NATIONS
TWO VOLS.

COUNTRIES OF THE WORLD
TWO VOLS

WONDERS OF THE PAST
TWO VOLS.

MANNERS AND CUSTOMS OF MANKIND
THREE VOLS.

OUR WONDERFUL WORLD
FOUR VOLS.

WORLD'S GREAT BOOKS IN OUTLINE
SEVEN VOLS.

MASTERPIECE LIBRARY OF SHORT STORIES
TWENTY VOLS.

MADE AND PRINTED IN GREAT BRITAIN BY THE AMALGAMATED PRESS, LTD.

SOME STRANGE INHABITANTS OF THE SEA

KEY TO COLOUR PLATE OVERLEAF

THE ocean waves, so monotonous in their restless, eternal dance, hide beauties more vivid and shapes more strange than any dry-land vista can show. There are gardens coloured like sunsets, lawns and parks of brilliant hues, and forests of tangled green and brown. There are mountain peaks and dark caves, and valleys so deep that not a ray of light ever reaches them.

On the following page is a scene such as you might observe if you were lying very quiet on a bank of sea moss off one of the West Indies islands, peering through the glass window of a diver's helmet. You see a flat Angel Fish (1) looking on like a submarine moon while a school of Blennies (3) swims into view. Between them a pair of Sea-Horses (2), gripping the kelp with their tails, are hoping their hungry foes will mistake them for bits of seaweed.

That red Sea Fan (4) seems to be a plant, but it is really a colony of tiny coral animals. Below it, the hideous Gurnard (5) is searching with its six feelers for food on the ocean floor. Those star-shaped " flowers " at the right (6) are animals too—Sea-Anemones. Let some passing creature brush against those " petals " and they will close up like a flash, and if the passing creature happens to be small enough it will be caught inside and eaten. At the left is a Sea-Urchin (7), protected, as it crawls mouth down along the bottom, by its sharp spines. In the corner, to complete the picture, lies a Mushroom Coral (8), stone-hard and beautifully fashioned.

The story of Fishes is told in pages 1296–1308

SOME STRANGE INHABITANTS OF THE SEA

Painting by Milo Winter

The fish world holds marvels of life and colour more astonishing perhaps than any to be found on land. Here the artist shows you a corner of this strange world of quaintly-shaped creatures in their bright-coloured surroundings. Overleaf there is given a key explaining the names of the fish. The story of Fishes is told in pages 1296–1308.

The NEW BOOK OF KNOWLEDGE

A Pictorial Treasury of Reading & Reference for Young and Old

Edited by
SIR JOHN HAMMERTON

COMPLETE IN EIGHT VOLUMES
Alphabetically Arranged

OVER SIX THOUSAND ILLUSTRATIONS
OVER 600 IN COLOUR AND GRAVURE

VOLUME THREE
DIA−GRAP

THE WAVERLEY BOOK COMPANY LTD.
Farringdon Street, London, E.C.4

HERE AND THERE IN THIS VOLUME

When you are just looking for ' something interesting to read,' this list will help. With it as a guide, you may wander through storyland, visit far-away countries, meet famous people of ancient and modern times, review history's most memorable incidents, explore the marvels of Nature and science—in short, find whatever suits your fancy at the moment.

HOW MANY QUESTIONS CAN YOU ANSWER?

Here are a few only of the unnumbered thousands which are answered in each one of our eight volumes. You can use this page as a test of your own knowledge, or you can draw up from it a set of ' posers ' with which to puzzle your friends. But odd scraps of knowledge are of little value compared with the result of organized study, and you should refer to the Study Outlines in the Eighth Volume for a reading guide.

COLOUR AND GRAVURE PLATES AND PAGES
IN THIS VOLUME

WHEN YOU ARE IN NEED OF READY REFERENCE

In using THE NEW BOOK OF KNOWLEDGE *as a work of reference, Volume Eight is indispensable. As regards its contents that particular volume is unique, for it is at once a complete Index to the preceding Seven Volumes and an Encyclopedia in itself. Its purpose is fourfold, as indicated below.*

(1) **Through the Year with the N.B.K.** Its opening section takes the form of a Calendar of the Year, giving for each day all the chief events and matters of interest, with references to the pages of THE NEW BOOK OF KNOWLEDGE in which full particulars concerning the event, personality, or other interest of the day may be found. By the intelligent use of this section (a) the young reader can have the daily delight of reading about topics that have special association with the particular day of the year on which he may be making his reference ; (b) father or mother can suggest what would be the most appropriate reading for the day ; and (c) the school teacher can set the lessons for the day with a genuine topical appeal.

(2) **Study Outlines.** This large and important section of the volume provides a simple method of study which should enable any of our young readers to become expert in using THE NEW BOOK OF KNOWLEDGE as an auxiliary manual of home study ; and thus what is learnt in school may be amplified, brought home more vividly, and more securely fixed in the memory.

(3) **The Fact-Index.** Actually this is in itself a complete Encyclopedia. In addition to providing many thousands of references to contents of Volumes One to Seven, it records many more thousands of facts in biography, geography, history, science, the arts, etc.,

that are not mentioned in its seven predecessors. Therefore, if you look in vain for any subject in the alphabetical order of Volumes One to Seven, turn to Volume Eight and you will almost certainly find it there.

It is a good plan, when using THE NEW BOOK OF KNOWLEDGE *as a work of reference,* **always** *first to look up any subject in the Fact-Index of Volume Eight.*

(4) **Thousands of Additional Entries.** In the main body of the work all important terms are explained as they arise ; but the scientist in every field of learning uses a "shorthand" of words and terms to convey a more precise meaning and to save repetition. Such words and terms are included in the Fact-Index so as to free the reading pages from a burden of thousands of brief cross-references which a more strict following of the full encyclopedic method would involve. When in doubt, therefore, about the significance of a term, *look it up in the Fact-Index* ; often you will find all the information you want there, but if further explanation is required the Fact-Index will give you page references to that more complete account in the main volumes. Remember that apart from its role as a never-failing source of recreative and entertaining reading, THE NEW BOOK OF KNOWLEDGE is designed to make your school and college learning of treble value by fitting that learning into its place in daily life.

KEY TO PRONUNCIATION

Most of the subject-headings in THE NEW BOOK OF KNOWLEDGE require no special indication of the way in which they should be pronounced. There are also many for whose proper pronunciation it is only necessary to know which syllable is stressed; in these cases the stress is shown *after* the syllable, thus, Armadil′lo. Where further guidance is necessary the following signs are employed.

ah = a as in father
aw = a as in ball
ê = vowel sound in fern, word, girl, curl
ow = vowel sound in now, bout
oi = vowel sound in noise, boy
Unmarked vowels have their **short sound,** as a in hat, e in bet, i in bit, o in not, u in but, oo in book
Marked vowels have their **long sound,** as in hāte, bē, bīte, nōte, tūne, bōōn

Vowels in italics have a slurred or obscure sound as in abet (*a*-bet′), recent (rē′-s*e*nt),con-form (k*o*n-form′), nation (nā′-sh*u*n), tailor (tā′-l*o*r)

th = first sound in thing, thank
th = first sound in the, that
zh = s in measure, leisure
g = hard g, as in good, girl
j = soft g, as in gem, ginger
kh = guttural in loch

LIST OF ABBREVIATIONS

The abbreviations most commonly used in this work are noted below; longer lists of abbreviations often met with in reading or conversation are given under the heading Abbreviations in Volume One and also in the Fact-Index that is contained in Volume Eight.

A.D., *Anno Domini* (in the year of our Lord, of the Christian era)
a.m., *ante meridiem* (before noon)
b., born
B.C., before Christ
C., Centigrade
c., *circa* (about)
Co., county, company
d., died
e.g., *exempli gratia* (for example)
etc., *et cetera* (and so forth)
et seq., *et sequens* (and following)
F., Fahrenheit
h.p., horse-power

i.e., *id est* (that is)
lb., pound, pounds (weight)
m., miles
MS., MSS., manuscript, manuscripts
oz., ounce, ounces
p.m., *post meridiem* (after noon)
Pop., population
Pron., pronunciation
q.v., *quod vide* (which see)
sq. m., square miles
St., Saint
U.S.A., United States of America
viz., *videlicet* (namely)
yd., yard

CRYSTALS *of* ROMANCE *and* COMMERCE

Out of a chance discovery made by children at play grew the great diamond industry of South Africa: securing fortunes for many and adding some extremely valuable glittering 'pebbles' to the world's display.

Diamond. One day some Boer children, playing on the banks of the Orange river in South Africa, found a very hard pebble that was brighter than any they had ever seen, and they ran to show it to their mother. It was nearly white and resembled a piece of lump alum, except that it was extremely heavy. There were bright spots on the surface where the outer skin was rubbed thin, and these spots shone as though there were a hidden light within. A few days later they showed it to a neighbour named Van Niekirk. He offered to buy it, but the children laughed at the idea and told him to " sell it and make his fortune."

From the original Cullinan diamond (the largest diamond known) a number of smaller stones were cut. It was more than twice the size of our illustration.

Van Niekirk took the stone to storekeepers in the towns near by. " It is a pretty pebble," they said, " but who will pay money for it? " Finally he gave it to a trader to sell for him. The trader sent it to a government agent, who said it was a diamond weighing 21 carats. Most of the diamonds we see in rings are only from one-half to one carat in weight. The governor of the colony paid £500 for it, and sent it to the Paris Exhibition of 1867.

People generally did not believe there were many diamonds in Africa. But Van Niekirk kept his ears open for stories of strange stones that were found; and two years later he learned that a poor shepherd boy had found an unusually large bright stone, which he carried around with him as a charm. Van Niekirk persuaded him to sell it for 500 sheep, 10 head of cattle, and a horse. This was unbelievable wealth for the poor boy, but it was not a tenth of the £11,000 that a Hopetown firm paid for it. It was a diamond of 83½ carats uncut and is now known as the Dudley diamond, having been bought by the 1st Earl of Dudley for £25,000.

When these finds became known there was great excitement not only in South Africa but all over the world, and diamond hunters came from every corner of the globe. One great diamond field after another was brought to light, and the mines were found to be the richest in the world. For many years South Africa produced 90 per cent of the world's supply, but the Belgian Congo, Gold Coast, Angola, Sierra Leone, South-west Africa, and Tanganyika are now important sources. British Guiana and Brazil supply a large part of the remainder of commercial diamonds, although diamonds in small quantities are mined in Borneo, India, Dutch Guiana, Australia, Sumatra, China and the United States.

For many centuries the diamond workings of India were the chief source of the world's supply, and some of the most beautiful and famous stones have come from that country. The Greeks, returning home after the invasion of India, in 327 B.C., probably brought the first knowledge of the precious gem to Europe. The diamond was held in awesome reverence, for it was supposed to have magical powers, being able to cure sickness and to bring good or ill fortune to its possessor.

The diamond is the hardest of minerals, its name being derived from the Greek word *adamas*, meaning " the unconquerable." It is the most prized of all precious stones because of its marvellous " fire " which flashes in every colour from brilliant blue to glowing red. This property is due to the strong dispersion of white light into its component colours as it passes through the diamond. Materials such as glass or colourless stones like rock-crystal (quartz) or topaz, which have low dispersions, show little " fire " even though they may reflect light brilliantly. Most diamonds are faintly coloured, blue, red and green being rare colours which add to the value of the stone. Some diamonds become phosphorescent in the dark after being exposed for a time to sunlight.

Scientists tell us that diamond is a crystalline form of the element carbon. One of the most common elements in nature, carbon exists not only in trees and plants of every kind, but is found in fossil form among the rocks of the earth's crust as coal seams. Diamonds, though relatives of our common coal, are believed to have been formed at much greater depths. They are found in vertical pipe-like masses of a rock called kimberlite composed of silicate minerals formed at

New York Times Photos
POLISHING A DIAMOND
Gripped in a holder, the diamond is held against an iron wheel or plate revolving at 2,500 revolutions per minute. The plate is fed with diamond dust and oil.

DEEP MINING FOR DIAMONDS IN SOUTH AFRICA

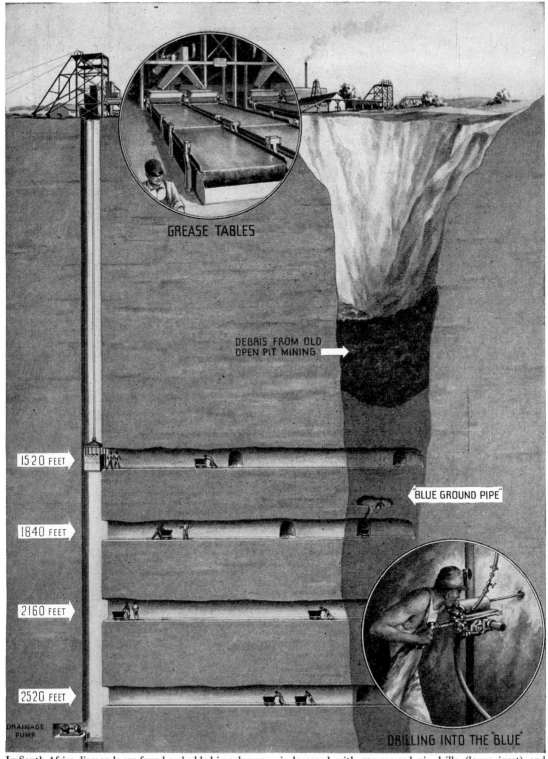

GREASE TABLES

DEBRIS FROM OLD
OPEN PIT MINING

1520 FEET

"BLUE GROUND PIPE"

1840 FEET

2160 FEET

2520 FEET

DRAINAGE
PUMP

DRILLING INTO THE "BLUE"

In South Africa diamonds are found embedded in columns of rock called 'pipes.' These extend deep into the earth, along channels which may once have been the vents of volcanoes. The rock in the pipes is called 'blue ground' from its colour. To extract it, a shaft is sunk and side tunnels are driven to the deposit. The material is loosened with compressed air drills (lower inset) and hoisted to the surface. After being softened by exposure to the sun and rain, it is crushed and washed, until only the heaviest particles remain. These are carried in a stream of water over vibrating iron tables coated with grease (upper inset). The diamonds stick to the grease.

SOME OF THE WORLD'S MOST FAMOUS DIAMONDS

The immensely valuable stones here shown are : the Koh-i-nur after its second cutting, 106 carats (1) ; after first cutting, 186 carats (5) ; Loterie d'Angleterre (2) ; Great Mogul, 287½ carats (3) ; Orlov, 199¾ carats (4) ; Regent, 140 carats (6) ; Duc de Toscane (7) ; Star of the South, 125 carats (8) ; Polar Star, 40 carats (9) ; Tiffany, after cutting, 125½ carats (10) ; before cutting, 287½ carats (18) ; Blue Diamond d'Angleterre (11) ; Sancy, 53¾ carats (12) ; Empress Eugénie, 51 carats (13) ; Scheik (14) ; Massuk (15) ; Pasha (16) ; Great Premier, before cutting (17).

high pressures and temperature; the pipes probably formed the feeders of volcanoes. The diamonds constitute only one part in fifteen million or more parts of the rock.

Where such primary deposits have been weathered away, the diamonds have been scattered in secondary or alluvial deposits such as river gravels. The most important primary occurrences are those in South Africa, and on these mining is carried on to great depths. The remaining African countries, as well as India and Brazil, derive their production from alluvial sources.

Many attempts have been made to manufacture diamonds synthetically. The French chemist Moissan dissolved pure carbon, prepared from sugar, in molten iron heated in an electric furnace at 5,500° F. and suddenly cooled the molten mass, subjecting the carbon to enormous pressure as the iron contracted. Tiny eight-sided crystals were obtained, but many chemists doubt whether these were true diamonds. J. B. Hannay, of Glasgow, succeeded in 1880 in making diamonds by heating paraffin and lithium metal in a sealed iron gun-barrel at dull red heat. The hydrogen from the paraffin combined with the lithium, while the carbon remained and crystallized under great pressure. Tiny diamonds made in this way by Hannay have recently been proved to be genuine

by X-ray crystallographic study at the British Museum of Natural History. Only a very small proportion of Hannay's experiments succeeded, and there appears to be little likelihood that diamonds can be manufactured on a commercial scale.

Besides its value as a gem, the diamond is of great use in the arts and manufactures because of its hardness. Small and inferior diamonds (bort), as well as black diamonds from Brazil (carbonadoes), are used in drill tips and saws for cutting rock, in lathe tools for machining metal, and in glass-cutters. Through diamond dies, fine wire is drawn to uniform size. Diamond dust is employed to polish gems and grind lenses. Three-fourths (by weight) of all diamonds mined are used industrially in one way or another.

Before being used as jewels diamonds must be cut and polished so they will sparkle by reflecting back as much as possible of the light that falls on them. First they are split or sawn, if necessary, then roughly shaped by mounting them in a lathe and holding a diamond-crowned tool against them as an abrasive. To cut and polish the many facets, the stones are firmly set in holders (" dops ") and pressed against the flat surface of a spinning iron disk carrying a paste of diamond dust and olive oil. For each new facet, the stone is set at a new angle in the dop. Several hours may be required to cut a single facet, and the utmost skill is needed to keep the angles of the facets symmetrical. The "brilliant" pattern has 58 facets, 33 above and 25 below. The "rose" pattern is flat below, with 12 to 32 facets above. In cutting and polishing to obtain the greatest beauty, half the weight of the stone may be lost. Antwerp and Amsterdam are the traditional centres of the diamond-cutting industry, but the craft has been developed in Britain in recent years.

The most noted historic diamond is the Koh-i-nur of the English crown jewels. There is a tradition that this beautiful gem was taken in 1304 from a rajah at Malwa, in whose family it had been an heirloom for centuries. It is believed to have been guarded with other treasures at Delhi until 1739, when it was carried off by the Persian Nadir Shah. Finally it was surrendered to the East India Company, whose directors presented it to Queen Victoria. Its weight in its Indian cutting was 186 carats, but after recutting in London in 1852 the weight was reduced to 106 carats.

The Great Mogul was the largest Indian diamond on record. It weighed 817 carats in the rough but was reduced to 287½ by unskilled cutting. It was seen by the French gem dealer Tavernier in Delhi in 1666, and may have been taken later by Nadir Shah. There has been no definite notice of it since Tavernier's time.

The Orlov was one of the Russian crown jewels. According to legend, it formed one of the eyes of an idol in a Brahmin temple and was stolen by a French grenadier and sold by him to an English sea captain. After passing through many hands, it came into the possession of an Armenian merchant, who sold it for £112,000 and a patent of nobility to Count Orlov, who gave it to Catherine the Great. This stone of 199·73 carats has been deposited in the Soviet Union diamond treasury.

The celebrated Regent or Pitt that weighed 410 carats in the rough was found in India in 1701. Legend says a slave miner stole it and gave it to a skipper who promised him free passage, then threw him overboard. Soon it was bought by Sir Thomas Pitt, governor of Madras. He sent the stone to London and there it was cut down to 140 carats. In 1717, he sold it to the French Crown, represented by the Duke of Orleans, regent. Later it flashed from the sword hilt of Napoleon, and after his fall, was placed in the Louvre.

The Excelsior, discovered in 1893 in Jagersfontein, Orange Free State, weighed 969½ carats. From this big stone were cut ten brilliants weighing 13 to 68 carats.

All other diamonds were outranked by the Cullinan, found in the Transvaal, in 1905. As big as a man's fist, it weighed 3,106 carats (1¼ pounds). In 1907 it was presented to Edward VII by the South African government, and in 1908 was cut into nine large and some 90 small stones. The largest, Cullinan I, or Star of Africa (530 carats), was set in the royal sceptre; and Cullinan II (309 carats), in the Imperial State crown.

The Jacobus Jonker (726 carats), named after the prospector who found it in the Transvaal in 1934, was sold to a New York dealer in 1935 for more than £150,000. The Vargas (726.6 carats), discovered in 1938 in the state of Minas Geraes, Brazil, was named in honour of Getulio Vargas, president of Brazil at that time. This blue-white stone was sent to New York and cut into 29 separate gems. In 1945 a 770-carat diamond was found in Sierra Leone, West Africa.

BEST BELOVED of ENGLAND'S NOVELISTS

Many years have passed since the pen slipped from Charles Dickens's dying hand, but still his novels enjoy a tremendous circulation and the characters he created are amongst the most vital in the whole gallery of fiction.

Dickens, CHARLES (1812–70). This most celebrated English novelist drew freely upon his own experiences for the characters and backgrounds of his stories, and so you can learn a good deal about his life by reading his books.

His father, John Dickens, was a clerk in the Navy Pay Office at Portsmouth at the time Charles was born in the suburb of Landport; two years later his work took him to London and in 1816 to Chatham. In 1821, through changes at the Admiralty, John Dickens lost his post, and from that time he was constantly in money difficulties. Like Mr. Micawber (in Charles Dickens's book David Copperfield), he was always confidently expecting something to "turn up," and as steadily going down in the world. While he was in a debtor's prison his family lived in a back attic of the London slums.

An odd, sensitive little fellow, whom his father at least knew to be a prodigy, Charles grew up with a sense of neglect and wasted talents, and in bitter humiliation. His mother taught him to read, he had some of the best books of imaginative literature, and during a few years of comparative prosperity he was sent to school. At 10, however, the family fortunes were at so low an ebb that he was put to work in a blacking factory. Two years later his father had a windfall in the shape of a legacy, and Charles was sent to school again. He then worked for a year or so in a lawyer's office, spending his leisure hours in reading in the British Museum and studying shorthand. Still working at his shorthand, he became in his 17th year a reporter at Doctors' Commons (a society of lawyers) and various police courts, and in 1831, at the age of 19, he was a Parliamentary reporter, with the reputation of being one of the quickest and most accurate in London.

At 24 he published his Sketches by Boz, and a year later The Pickwick Papers brought him fame and put him on the road to fortune. The rest of his life was an unbroken record of public success as a novelist, short-story writer, magazine editor, entertainer and social lion. His private life had been clouded by the unhappiness which culminated in the separation from his wife in 1856.

In 1857 Dickens moved to Gad's Hill Place, the house near Rochester, Kent, which he coveted as a small boy. In 1858 and again from 1861 to 1863, he gave many public readings from his books. In 1864 he was in a railway accident at Staplehurst, Kent. Though outwardly uninjured, he suffered a nervous shock that proved eventually to be serious. He occupied himself in the years between the accident and his death in giving readings in the United Kingdom and in America, which undoubtedly enriched but exhausted him. Then, in October 1869, he began the book he was never to finish—Edwin Drood. His health was failing, but he continued his writing up to the day before his death. He died on June 9, 1870.

Most of the characters in Dickens's novels stand out clear and sharp, not so much like living people as like living cartoons in a portrait-gallery of English personalities. A man becomes simply his most obvious virtue or fault, enlarged and illustrated. Some of his characters are ludicrous, some are grotesque, others are pathetic or very lovable; there is not one who fades into the background of

DICKENS AT HIS DESK

Charles Dickens was a prolific writer, and the fourteen longer novels which have made his name famous were written between 1836 and 1865. During those years he also produced minor works and was a magazine editor.

his surroundings for lack of clever, sharp pen-drawing. An observant reporter of life, not a smell or taste, a sight or sound, that could add to his word-pictures ever escaped Dickens. You may perhaps find him a little long drawn-out and hard to read at first. He runs into delightful little side-paths of description that have apparently little to do with the main narrative. But there is a big human story in every one of his books, and each of them is filled with the most original and unforgettable people.

Dickens's works include The Pickwick Papers (1836); Oliver Twist (1837); Nicholas Nickleby (1838–39); The Old Curiosity Shop (1840); Barnaby Rudge (1841); Martin Chuzzlewit (1843); A Christmas Carol (*q.v.*), The Chimes, and The Cricket on the Hearth (1843–48); Dombey and Son (1846–48); David Copperfield (1849–50); Bleak House (1852–53); Hard Times (1854); Little Dorrit (1856–57); A Tale of Two Cities (1859); Great Expectations (1860); Our Mutual Friend (1864–65); and the unfinished Edwin Drood.

A short adaptation from his Pickwick Papers follows, as a brief sample of Dickens at his best.

MR. PICKWICK *goes to* DINGLEY DELL

MR. PICKWICK was a stout, elderly English gentleman, who lived in lodgings in that London which Charles Dickens loved to describe. A bachelor with a good income, he was very neat in his dress. He wore the tightest of breeches, and gaiters buttoned up to the calves of his legs. He was clean-shaven and bald, and through the largest and roundest of spectacles his eyes twinkled and beamed on the world.

Everyone who knew Mr. Pickwick loved him for his kind heart and pleasant manners. They admired and respected him, too, for he was supposed to be a man of learning. He had written a paper on the ponds of Hampstead Heath, and on the habits of the tittlebat, or stickleback, a nest-building fish that lived in them. Really, you know, Mr. Pickwick was as simple and as busy about things that amused him as a child.

Mr. Pickwick thought he had a great mind and that he ought to use it for the public benefit. There were thousands of people in London who had never been outside of it, and all they knew of the country and towns around it was what they read in the newspapers. Mr. Pickwick felt that it was his duty

to face the perils of travel and investigate matters of scientific interest in other parts of England. As he liked good company he invited three friends to help form the Pickwick Club and join in his journeys.

He made a speech about it. With one hand under his coat-tails and the other waving in the air, Mr. Pickwick said there would be fame enough for all. He would make reports to learned societies. Mr. Tracy Tupman, who was fond of the ladies, could make a record of the times he lost his heart. Mr. Augustus Snodgrass, a romantic gentleman in a Roman-looking cloak, had always yearned to write poetry. He could put the beauties of rural England into verses that would never die. And the youngest of the four, Mr. Nathaniel Winkle, who had a taste for outdoor sports, could wear gorgeous hunting clothes and win fame as a sportsman.

All these gentlemen were just as simple as Mr. Pickwick. Every time Mr. Tupman made love to a lady, he got into trouble with her family or with a jealous rival. Mr. Snodgrass had the most poetic thoughts, but he never wrote any poetry. It was so dangerous for Mr. Winkle to carry a gun that he never learned to shoot. And Mr. Pickwick filled books with learned notes, but couldn't make head or tail of them afterwards, so he had nothing to report.

That is what makes the fun. The members of the Pickwick Club were simple, so they got themselves into the most ridiculous scrapes. They met the oddest people on their travels, had the funniest adventures, heard the strangest stories and believed every word of them. Sam Weller made a good deal of the fun. He was Mr. Pickwick's bright, talkative man-servant. There was Mrs. Bardell, the sentimental landlady who, through a very natural mistake, got Mr. Pickwick sent to the Fleet prison. And there was Mrs. Leo Hunter, who collected social lions; and that attractive scamp Mr. Alfred Jingle, who put Mr. Tupman in the shade as a lover; and the fat boy, Joe, who did nothing but eat and sleep.

At a military review the travellers met the Wardle family of Manor Farm—father, two daughters, a maiden aunt, and the fat boy Joe. They struck up such a friendship that the four Pickwickians were invited to spend some days at Manor Farm, Dingley Dell. The four travellers had rather an adventurous journey from Rochester, where they were then staying, to Manor Farm, for the horse Mr. Winkle was riding ran

From the drawing by Harry Furniss

ALFRED JINGLE

The unscrupulous Jingle led the Pickwickians into many awkward predicaments, but when Mr. Pickwick found the adventurer penniless in the Fleet prison, he befriended him and gave him a fresh start in life.

away when that gentleman had dismounted to pick up a whip, and the vehicle that Mr. Pickwick was driving was overturned. They finished the journey on foot, but this did not prevent them from receiving a very hearty welcome from Mr. Wardle and his family; and at Manor Farm they spent some pleasant days, though Mr. Winkle, in spite of his reputation as a sportsman, accidentally wounded Mr. Tupman at a shooting party.

On another day the host and his guests attended a cricket match between Dingley Dell and Muggleton, and here they met Mr. Alfred Jingle, whom they had last seen at Rochester. Mr. Jingle made himself so pleasant by his stories that he was asked to join the party, and he, too, spent some days at Manor Farm, a visit which ended when he eloped with the spinster aunt, the pair being hastily followed by Mr. Pickwick and Mr. Wardle.

Some time after, at the Christmas season, Mr. Pickwick and his friends accepted a second invitation to Manor Farm. They were accompanied by Sam Weller, who had now been for some considerable time in Mr. Pickwick's service. At three o'clock in the afternoon they reached the Blue Lion Inn at Muggleton. There they found Joe, the fat boy, who had been fast asleep in front of the taproom fire. He said he had a cart for the baggage and suggested that Mr. Pickwick and his friends should walk. Sam Weller remained behind to help with the luggage, which included—in addition to several portmanteaus and carpet bags—an enormous codfish and half-a-dozen barrels of oysters. He stowed the things rapidly into the cart while the fat boy stood quietly by watching him work with the deepest interest. They then got into the cart, and the fat boy asked, "Can you drive?"

"I should rayther think so," replied Sam.

"There, then," said the fat boy, putting the old horse's reins

From the drawing by Harry Furniss

MR. PICKWICK FINDS SAM WELLER

One of the most famous characters in the Pickwick Papers is Sam Weller, Mr. Pickwick's servant. Mr. Pickwick found him at the White Hart Inn, Borough High Street, London, where he was the 'boots,' and was so attracted by his ready wit that he forthwith engaged him. Here is the first meeting between the two. With Mr. Pickwick are Mr. Wardle of Dingley Dell and Mr. Perker, his lawyer.

in his hand and pointing up a lane. " It's as straight as you can go, you can't miss it." The boy then laid himself down and, with an oyster barrel for a pillow, instantly fell asleep.

Many young people were guests at the farm, for they had come to be present at the wedding of Miss Isabella Wardle, the host's daughter, and Mr. Trundle. They met the gentlemen from Rochester in the lane, and very hearty greetings were exchanged between them. When they reached the house the servants grinned with pleasure and the deaf old grandmother ceased to be cross when she saw the beaming face of Mr. Pickwick full of the spirit of Christmas. In a moment he was proposing to dance a minuet with the grandmother, and gently kissing the prospective bride. In the evening there were card games and much uproarious mirth, after which the party retired to bed to be ready for the wedding on the following day.

The wedding took place in the parish church of Dingley Dell, and Mr. Pickwick was one of those who signed the register. When the ceremony was over they trooped back to the farm for breakfast. Mr. Pickwick proposed the health of the bride and groom. It was drunk with cheers and tears, and the fat boy burst into such a loud blubbering that Sam Weller led him out. After the wedding feast the house party walked over the sparkling country for several miles. That was to give them an appetite for a hearty dinner. Then, with the carpets up in the spacious sitting-room, the fire roaring up the chimney, and the candles burning brightly, they began the dance. Mr. Pickwick wore silk stockings and dancing pumps.

" You in silk stockings? " cried Mr. Tupman.

" Why not, sir ? Why not? " Mr. Pickwick was a little warm, not to say heated. He led the delighted grandmother to the end of the room. The fiddles and harp struck up, the dancers saluted their partners and were off. For some hours the dancing continued, to be followed by a glorious supper downstairs.

On the following evening, Christmas Eve, the family assembled for games in the kitchen, for, as Mr. Wardle told Mr. Pickwick, such was their invariable custom. " Everybody sits down with us on Christmas Eve, as you see now—servants and all; and here we wait till the clock strikes twelve, to usher Christmas in and while away the time with old stories."

Mr. Wardle hung up from the ceiling of the kitchen a huge branch of mistletoe, whereupon Mr. Pickwick led the old grandmother beneath it and kissed her with the most respectful gallantry. This was the signal for that genial gentleman to be surrounded by a laughing group of young ladies and heartily kissed by every one of them. A game of blind man's buff followed, and then, after a game of snapdragon, they all sat down to a substantial supper with a mighty bowl of punch on the table.

The supper over, there was a call for a song, and Mr. Wardle in a good, round, sturdy voice treated the company to a Christmas carol, beginning I Care Not for Spring. This over, someone drew attention to the snow outside, and a remark made by the old lady, who remembered such a Christmas Eve many years ago, induced Mr. Wardle to tell the story of the goblins who stole the sexton.

We are going to stop here. As Sam Weller said when he wrote a letter to his sweetheart: " The great art o' letter writin' is to pull up sudden, so she'll vish there wos more." You can read all about that Merry Christmas, and other happenings, in the Pickwick Papers.—*Adapted from Charles Dickens's Pickwick Papers.*

Dictionary. There are many kinds of dictionary, but all are alike in having an alphabetically arranged list of words with their meanings, or definitions. The larger dictionaries, like the great Oxford English, are almost encyclopedic in range, giving the origin (etymology) of words and phrases, their pronunciation, and all their shades of meaning, with suitable quotations. An English boy or girl studying, say, French, usually buys a good French-English dictionary which gives the exact equivalents of words in both languages. Some dictionaries—also known as " lexicons," particularly when they deal with the Greek language—have special glossaries of technical terms, pronunciation of proper names, weights and measures, synonyms and antonyms, and so on. A detailed Biblical dictionary is called a concordance. The first real dictionary in English was the famous work on which Dr. Samuel Johnson laboured for eight years. This was published in 1755. (*See also* Encyclopedia).

Diesel Engine. Rudolf Diesel, a German engineer born at Paris in 1858, did not live to see the full development of the kind of engine which he patented in 1892. He died in 1913, before its wider possibilities were appreciated. Another quarter of a century was to elapse before Diesel engines were giving power to locomotives, ships, motor-cars and aircraft—besides serving as stationary power-plants.

The Diesel engine is an internal-combustion engine, in which the " working fluid "—some kind of gaseous mixture—is also the fuel which drives the machine. In a steam engine the working fluid is

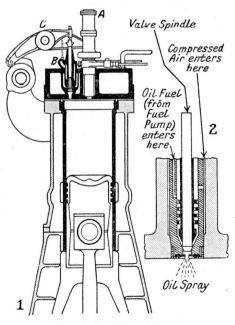

DIESEL ENGINE DETAILS
In the sectional view (1) of a Diesel engine in its original form, fuel oil is delivered by pump to A and sprayed in by compressed air ; air inlet valve, B ; cam and lever for valve operation, C. At 2 are shown details of fuel pump and oil-spray inlet.

of course steam; the steam is generated in a boiler by heating water with coal or oil fuel, and the working fluid is then led to the engine cylinders, there to propel the pistons and turn the wheels. In an internal-combustion engine the fuel is burned *inside* the cylinders, and the enormously expanded volume of gas then forces out the pistons. The principle behind all such engines is explained in our story of the Gas Engine. The petrol engine and the oil engine—this last named is used for engines which burn the gas produced from heavier oils than petrol —resemble the gas engine in general principles.

Diesel's plan was to use a much higher degree of compression than was customary in other internal-combustion engines, so that there would be no need for a spark or a flame to ignite the gaseous mixture inside the cylinders; the mixture would take fire and burn because of the heat generated by the compression as the pistons descended. He arranged to force the oil fuel into the cylinders right at the beginning of the explosion stroke, just as the compression was at its greatest. In order to do this, Diesel provided an air-compressor, driven by the engine itself, which charged a steel " air-bottle " with air at about 100 lb. per square inch pressure. Air from the bottle was led to the fuel injection nozzle and forced in a measured amount of oil at the right moment. To begin with, of course, this air-bottle had to be filled from some outside source. In later Diesels, compressed air was used to give the initial push to the pistons in the cylinders, so as to get the flywheel turning and to start the engine. In the first engines the wheel had to be pulled round by hand, until the fuel mixture ignited.

In starting the engine, air was drawn from the charged reservoir ; after that the engine itself kept the air-bottle full. Our diagram in page 1015 shows a cylinder as if cut through, and also the fuel-injection mechanism. Since the air in the cylinder was compressed to about 500 lb. per square inch, the engine had to be built more massive than other types of internal-combustion motors, and this fact for long was against its use for many purposes where the heavy weight was a drawback.

As a result another type, called the semi-Diesel, came into being. In this the oil is forced in separately by a pump, not along with the air; the compression inside the cylinders is lower than with the Diesel engine, and the fuel mixture has to be ignited by some outside means. One method was to have a " hot bulb " connected with the cylinder, into which air was compressed by the engine piston; this bulb was heated from the outside by a lamp, to start the engine, after which the machine itself developed enough heat to ignite the fuel at each explosion stroke.

Oil engines which ignite the explosive mixture by the heat generated by compression are called " compression-ignition " engines. (*See* Gas Engine; Oil Engine; Petrol Engine).

Digestion.

Any substance which will provide material for growth, for energy, and for repair of outworn tissue is a food, although its condition may need to be entirely changed before it can be so used by the living cell. This process of change of a substance into a form soluble in the fluids of the body, or in the case of fats into small globules, is known as digestion. The resulting fluid is ultimately brought into union with the cells —the miracle of life itself. The whole process of digestion can be completed accurately on a laboratory bench, but only the living tissue can absorb and " burn " material so prepared.

Food falls into five main classes: protein, carbohydrate, fat, mineral salts, and vitamins. Water is necessary for all processes of nutrition. The digestive tract of Man and animals of a similar type begins at the mouth and ends at the anus, various important organs along the route contributing essential secretions. In the mouth the teeth are responsible for cutting and grinding the food mass, and adequate chewing is the first step in good digestion and good nourishment. Inferior to the domestic hen, Man has no gizzard; and badly-bitten food asks for trouble, since there is no further mechanism for crushing it. The front, incisor teeth, are designed for cutting, and must not be used for grinding, which is the work of the back molar teeth, and work to which the incisors were not intended to stand up.

Any missing tooth should promptly be replaced by the dentist, for by its absence it kills its opposite number. A tooth keeps itself essentially sound by preening itself against its fellow. The bad chemistry resulting lower in the digestive tract from bad chewing is often associated with rheumatism.

While being chewed, the food mass is mixed by the tongue and teeth with the saliva, the first of the digestive fluids, running from small openings of the salivary glands into the mouth. It contains a ferment called ptyalin which as long as the food is alkaline changes starch into sugar. (Starch cannot be absorbed; certain sugars can.)

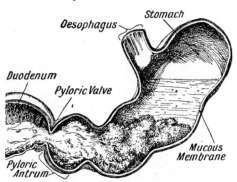

Oesophagus

Stomach

Duodenum

Pyloric Valve

Pyloric Antrum

Mucous Membrane

DIGESTION IN THE STOMACH
Food is liquefied in the stomach by the gastric juices, and thence, now known as chyme, it passes through the pyloric valve from the antrum into the duodenum, the first part of the small intestine.

Next, the food mass goes down the oesophagus, or food pipe, into the stomach, where the gastric juice takes over the task of grappling with meat and milk by its ferments of pepsin and rennin, acting in the presence of hydrochloric acid. The lower end of the stomach is guarded by a valve—the pylorus (Greek, gatekeeper), which opens from time to time under the control of chemical reaction, and allows the warm semi-fluid material to enter the small intestine (This first stage in digestion is illustrated above.) A light meal may take some three hours to leave the stomach; a heavy meal, six or seven hours. It is interesting to note that horse-radish, so commonly eaten with beef, increases that meat's digestion-rate in the stomach; and roast pork is aided on a quicker journey by apple sauce. This has been acted upon through-out the ages by diners who could not have known the facts. (Such findings, the result of observation merely, are known as " empirical.")

Alcohol is about the only substance absorbed by the stomach. That is why an alcoholic drink has so quick a result. It is immediately absorbed and carried by the blood stream straight to the brain cells, on which it acts. Water tends to go straight through the stomach into the intestine.

At this stage the food stream, now known as chyme, entering the small intestine is met within the first few inches by two important secretions—the bile and the pancreatic juice. The bile is secreted by that master-organ the liver, and is mainly stored before use in the gall bladder, a small receptacle adjoining it. Bile attacks fat, and by its antiseptic property resists putrefaction of the gut content. The pancreatic juice has powerful ferments, and, like a maid-of-all-work, sweeps up the remains of the digestion of fats, starch, vegetables and proteins. The picture of intestinal digestion is completed by a secretion from the walls of the gut, and by the presence of bacteria; some of these are friendly, changing poisonous material into harmless, and some are unfriendly, making foul smells.

Where True Digestion Takes Place

The fluid food stream, now known as chyle, is picked up by fine finger-like processes called villi projecting from the gut-wall, and also by the leucocytes, the white cells of the blood (which increase enormously after a meal, and which wander around picking up particles and engulfing them in their own substance before re-entering the blood vessels). Fats are meantime taken up by the lymph channels, and eventually all the nourishing food material finds its way into the main blood stream for distribution to the most distant needy cells—from the topmost hair to the nethermost toe-nail.

Peristalsis is the term used to describe the worm-like movement which passes onwards the contents of the gut. Specialised muscles run along the tube, and others around it, and while one contracts the other relaxes, thus allowing of progress for-ward—comparable with the method of progres-sion of an earth-worm. It is extraordinary how complete contact with the gut-wall must be; for that minute grain of calomel (often given as a medicine for liver trouble) never fails of its purpose, nor that small dose of vitamin in a capsule of its beneficent endeavour.

The stomach and small intestine are the sites of the gastric ulcer and of the duodenal ulcer, those disorders of which there is so much talk today. Their causes are not fully understood.

At the right side of the lower abdomen the small intestine merges into the large intestine. At this point is found that annoying structure the appendix, cause of so much disaster. Once upon a time it played a vital rôle as part of the digestive tract, as it does today in that of the horse; but the passage of thousands of years has altered its function and its structure, so that in the human it now remains but as a menace. It is a wormlike hollow tube a few inches long, its bore only large enough to let in particles of material, but too narrow to let them out; consequently they decay and set up inflamma-tion. This inflammation can cause indigestion at far-off stretches of the gut, and such disturbances do not always show their origin.

The appendix varies in the position it takes up, and its distress can be expressed only by its elbow-ing neighbouring structures. It is these variations of position, these variations of its cries for help, which underlie the great danger of appendicitis (inflamma-tion of the appendix); for the signs and symptoms are not constant. Moreover, if the appendix ruptures and causes peritonitis (inflammation of the peritoneum, the delicate outer coat of the intestine), the patient at once is in less pain because the pus in the appendix is no longer under pres-sure, and he mistakenly thinks that he is better—whereas he is now much more dangerously ill.

If the question of a diseased appendix ever arises, a surgeon and an X-ray examination will soon settle the matter. If it is indeed a case of appen-dicitis, removal of the appendix at the earliest convenient moment is the only wise decision. With modern methods, and with prompt attention, the removal of an appendix is hardly more dangerous than the removal of a molar tooth.

The large intestine (so-called because of its larger bore) rises to the height of the liver, crosses over, and descends on the left side to become continuous with the rectum—a straight piece of gut which terminates in the anus (a contracting ring). In its passage through the large intestine the food mass becomes more and more solid. As absorption is the essential work of the small intes-tine, so excretion is the essential work of the large gut, and the material, all nutritive value taken up, and added to by accretions of bacteria and various debris, is eventually pushed out through the anus as faeces (Latin, dregs ; residue). It is in this area that haemorrhoids or piles occur. These are small dilated blood vessels, most often caused through back pressure, due to constipation. For the most part prevention of the condition lies in regular soft motions. It is not generally realized that too fluid motions can also cause haemorrhoids, because they fail fully to dilate the anus and thus to exercise the blood vessels.

Diogenes (c. 412-323 B.C.). Once, it is said, Diogenes (pron. dī-oj´-en-ēz) was seen carry-ing a lantern through the streets of Athens in the daytime, and on being asked what he was looking for answered, " I am seeking an honest man." That is one of the many anecdotes told of this eccentric Greek philosopher.

Diogenes came to Athens from the Greek colony of Sinope, on the Black Sea. He adopted the philosophy of the Cynics, who taught that to attain wisdom and virtue one must give up all the pleasures of life, which stand in the way of self-mastery. So he got rid of all his possessions. He even threw away the wooden bowl he carried when he saw a boy drinking from the hollow of his hand. It is said that he lived in a tub (perhaps one of the great earthenware jars belonging to the temple of Cybele, or more probably a tiny mud hut jokingly called a tub by the Athenians), and in order to harden himself used to roll in hot sand in summer, and in winter embraced snow-covered statues.

At one time he made a voyage and was captured by pirates, who sold him as a slave in Crete. When asked his trade he replied that he knew no trade but that of governing men, and that he should be sold to a man who needed a master. He was sold to a master, who took him to Corinth to conduct the education of his children, and there Diogenes became famous.

At Corinth he met Alexander the Great, who asked him if there was any favour he could do him. Diogenes replied that the only thing Alexander could do for him was not to stand between him and the sun. Alexander was so struck with this answer that he said, " If I were not Alexander, I would be Diogenes." Diogenes died at Corinth, and a pillar was erected to his memory.

Dionysus. (Pron. dī-o-nī'-sus). Once—so the old story tells us—a beautiful youth, glowing with vigour and attired in bright garments, hired a ship to take him to Naxos; but the men, who turned out to be Tyrrhene pirates, steered in the direction of Asia, knowing that his beauty would command a good price in the slave markets of that continent. Scarcely had they bound the youth when the fetters dropped from his limbs.

" We have tried to bind a god ! " cried the pilot, as he beheld the miracle. " Let us hasten to restore this youth to the spot whence we took him, lest the immortals, for our impiety, afflict us with adverse winds and storms! " Heedless of these words, the pirates set sail for the open sea. But presently the ship stood still. Tendrils of ivy twined about the vessel, the masts and oars were turned into serpents, and strains of magic flutes were heard.

The terrified crew entreated the pilot to steer for the shore. But it was too late. The youth changed into a roaring lion and, rushing upon the captain, tore him in pieces. The sailors, maddened with terror, leaped overboard and were changed into dolphins. Only the pious steersman escaped this fate. The captive, resuming his true form, revealed himself as the great Dionysus, the god of the vine and the growing principle of Nature, whom the Romans called Bacchus.

This is but one of the many adventures that befell Dionysus during a time when he lived on earth and travelled from country to country, teaching men to cultivate the grape and to make wine. Often he rode in a chariot drawn by lions

and leopards, and was attended by satyrs, and bands of dancing women called Bacchantes. The satyrs, or fauns, were woodland deities, represented as half human, half goat—hairy creatures with pointed ears, flat noses, small horns growing out of the forehead, and with a tail like that of a goat or a horse.

Dionysus was the son of Zeus (Jupiter), the god of the sky, and of Semele, a goddess representing the earth. In his early years he was cared for by an aged satyr named Silenus, who remained one of his favourite companions. Dionysus was represented in works of art most often as a youth crowned with vine leaves or ivy, and wearing a fawn skin over his shoulders. His festivals were celebrated with processions, dances, and choruses, out of which grew the Greek drama. In Rome the Bacchanalia, or festivals of Bacchus, were celebrated with such excesses that they were forbidden in 186 B.C.

Disraeli, BENJAMIN, EARL OF BEACONSFIELD (1804–81). Benjamin Disraeli (Pron. diz-rā'-li) was a powerful and picturesque figure in politics, a master of biting phrase and telling gesture. In his day no one could be Prime Minister without wealth, and Disraeli was a poor man, who until his marriage in 1839 to Mrs. Wyndham Lewis, a widow of some fortune, was not qualified to lead the Conservative party. He had many other difficulties to overcome. His race, his Oriental trick of exaggeration, his passion for dramatizing himself, all seemed to stolid Conservatives to make him an outsider. But his ability, courage, and persistence carried him through all obstacles, and he came to be regarded as the founder of modern Conservatism.

In his early years Disraeli was handicapped by the fact that, though a Christian himself, he was the son of Jewish parents, his father Isaac D'Israeli (1766–1848) being well-known as a writer. Benjamin handicapped himself still further by his foppish dress. His speech and manner were as affected as his costume, and the first time he tried to make a speech in the House of Commons he was laughed down. " I shall sit down now," he shouted, " but the time will come when you will hear me ! "

Disraeli worked hard, studied the style of Parliamentary speakers, and gave up many of his peculiarities of dress and manner. And he had his

BENJAMIN DISRAELI
This drawing of Disraeli was made by W. Biscombe Gardner in 1880, a year before Disraeli's death, when he had been defeated at the polls and, at the age of 76, realized that his political career was finished. Four years earlier Disraeli had been created Earl of Beaconsfield.

reward, for his speeches were anxiously awaited, and the debates between him and his great rival Gladstone, the leader of the Liberal party, were some of the keenest that had ever been held in the House of Commons. Disraeli was especially clever at coining striking phrases. In 1846, when Sir Robert Peel, the Tory (Conservative) leader, abandoned the position of his party and advocated the repeal of the Corn Laws—a Whig measure — Disraeli declared that Peel had " caught the Whigs bathing and had walked off with their clothes ! "

Under his leadership the Conservatives no longer opposed all progressive measures, and in 1867 he persuaded them to " dish the Whigs " by carrying through a Parliamentary Reform Bill extending the right to vote even further than the Whigs (Liberals) had suggested. In 1868 Disraeli became Prime Minister as head of the Conservative party. His ministry fell within a year, but in 1874 he was again called to the Premiership, this time remaining in office for six years. As Premier he was much more acceptable to Queen Victoria than Gladstone was. Indeed, he won her affectionate friendship. With none other of her Prime Ministers was the Queen on terms of such familiarity. He himself explained this partiality by saying that " Gladstone addressed the Queen as if she were a public meeting, but he (Disraeli) addressed her as a woman."

Disraeli's foreign policy specially kindled the British imagination. He purchased for Great Britain from the bankrupt Khedive of Egypt his shares in the Suez Canal and so safeguarded England's route to India. He had Queen Victoria proclaimed Empress of India. He played a clever part against Russia in the Congress of Berlin (1878) blocking her progress in the Balkans and saving Turkey, and secured for Britain the administration of Cyprus. Queen Victoria rewarded him with a peerage. In the elections of 1880 the Conservatives were defeated and he retired to his estate at Hughenden, near High Wycombe, in Buckinghamshire, purchased in 1848. He died within a year thereafter, on April 19, 1881.

Disraeli's success as a writer was due largely to his political experience, for he was the first successful author of political novels. Some of the best-known of his novels are Vivian Grey (1826); Henrietta Temple (1836); Coningsby (1844); Sybil (1845); Tancred (1847) ; Lothair (1870); and Endymion (1880).

Keystone

DISTILLATION AT SEA

For use in lifeboats or on board ship if drinking water runs out, this still produces fresh water from the sea. It works on paraffin, solid fuel, or wood. Its inventor, Lieut. J. G. H. Goodfellow, R.N.V.R. (left), is seen demonstrating it to Admiral Sir Martin Dunbar-Nasmith, V.C.

Distillation. The only sure way of getting pure water is by the process called distillation. This consists simply in catching the steam from boiling water and cooling it until it turns back to liquid form. Water so obtained is pure, for the rising steam does not carry with it any of the solid impurities from the original water.

Any liquid, if you make it hot enough, will boil and give off vapour, which may be cooled and condensed in the same way as steam ; hence distillation finds many important uses. Chief of these is the process called " fractional distillation," employed in producing, among other things, petrol and paraffin from crude petroleum; and in making alcohol and perfumes.

Different liquids can be separated by fractional distillation because they boil at different temperatures. If you heat a mixture of water and glycerine, for example, the water will begin to turn to steam long before the glycerine becomes hot enough to give off its vapour, and you can collect and condense the water vapour, leaving the glycerine behind. In the same way, when petroleum is heated, the petrol will come away before the paraffin.

Diving. The deep-sea diver has to contend with intense cold, darkness, currents, and the pressure of the water above him. The air he breathes may be supplied by men in a boat above, slowly working an air-pump. For every 10 feet he descends he sustains an added water-pressure of nearly 4½ lb. over every square inch of his body. Hence he must descend carefully, not out-distancing the rate at which the pumps can supply the proper air-pressure, otherwise he may suffer great pain, bleeding at the nose, eyes and ears, and even loss of consciousness, or death. And he must ascend even more slowly, lest nitrogen bubbles form in his blood stream, causing extreme pain.

Divers in rubber suits do not, as a rule, work at lower depths than 300 feet, at which the water pressure is 133 lb. to the square inch. By using an armoured diving dress they can descend to considerably greater depths. In 1934 the American scientist Dr. William Beebe descended in a specially built chamber, called a bathysphere, to a depth of over half a mile, in order to study deep-water fish.

Perhaps the most interesting work of the diver is the salvaging of treasure and wrecked ships. From one Spanish vessel which sank off the Grand Canary Island in 160 feet of water, divers records, speaking-tubes, or telephonic apparatus. Air may be supplied from a pump above through a flexible tube entering the helmet. The exhaled air escapes either through another tube leading out from the back of the helmet, or through an ingenious valve arrangement.

Some suits are self-contained, making the diver independent of any connexion with persons above water. In one such, a compressed-air reservoir on the diver's back supplies him with air by a self-regulating apparatus. When he wishes to ascend he simply inflates his dress from the reservoir. In another form the air breathed is purified of carbon dioxide by passing through a suitable absorbent. The diver thus breathes the same air many times over. The oldest successful diving apparatus is the diving-bell, a big iron cylinder closed at the top and open at the bottom. When this is lowered into the water the air in it keeps the water out. Fresh air is pumped in from above, and a mechanism allows the used air to escape.

DONNING A METAL DIVING SUIT
The diver is seen, supported by an iron stand, waiting for the head-and-shoulder piece to be lowered over him. The two pieces are then screwed together by numerous strong bolts, making the whole absolutely watertight.

covered chests of gold worth nearly £100,000. Considerable results were achieved in the task of salvaging vessels sunk during the wars of 1914–18 and 1939–45.

In the construction of bridges, dams, under-river tunnels, and waterworks generally, divers survey for foundations, caissons, and pile-settings. Waterworks in large towns employ a diver constantly. Deep-sea divers are also used in several industries, as in fishing for pearls, corals, sponges, and shells, although native swimmers often perform such work without any equipment. Some of these natives can dive to great depths and remain under water two or more minutes.

Diving-dress may be flexible, for ordinary depths, or be made of jointed metal casings, like those illustrated in this page. In the flexible (rubber) dress the helmet is usually of copper, with windows of thick glass. Leaden weights are attached to the suit to enable the diver to descend more quickly, and the boots have lead soles to enable him to keep his balance feet downwards.

Divers communicate with fellow-workers on the ocean bottom and with attendants above by

DEEP-SEA DIVER GOING DOWN
In this aluminium alloy casing, weighing nearly half a ton, a diver can work comfortably at depths greater than 300 feet. Note the flexible joints (ball-and-socket type) and the mechanical ' hands.'

MASTERING *the* ART *of* DIVISION

*I*n this branch of Arithmetic the operations of Addition and Subtraction are
also employed, and they should already have been mastered. Both forms of
Division—the simple short and the long—are explained here.

Division. Dividing a number is separating
it into equal numbers. In the simplest form of short
division, one of the equal numbers is given, and the
problem is to find how many such are contained in
the number divided.

Example. How many 9's in 36 ?

The number to be divided is called the *dividend*.
In the above example 36 is the dividend. The
given one of the equal numbers into which the
dividend is separated is called the *divisor*. In the
above example 9 is the divisor. The result, or
number of times the divisor is contained in the
dividend, is called the *quotient*. In the above
example 4 is the quotient.

The carpenter makes a division sum when he
measures the wall with a 2-foot rule by dividing it
into equal parts of a given size (2 feet). As he
measures he says to himself, 2, 4, 6, 8, 10, 12, etc.
When he wishes to saw a board into equal lengths,
he marks off the distances in the same way, so as
to divide it into equal parts of a given length. He
then proceeds to count the number of parts so
marked off. But it is possible to avoid actual
measuring with a ruler, and also to find relations
that cannot be found by measuring spaces. This is
done by counting so as to measure one number in
terms of another. Thus a carpenter knows that a
16-foot board can be divided into 8 two-foot spaces
by counting 2, 4, 6, 8, 10, 12, 14, 16, and observing
the number of 2's. He measures 16 in imagination
and finds it 8 times 2. Examples follow.

1. A boy with 35 pennies wishes to find how many
books worth fivepence each he can buy. He counts
by 5's thus : 5, 10, 15, 20, 25, 30, 35 ; and notes
how many 5's he has counted. Thus he measures
the 35 by using the 5 as a measure. He finds that
where 35 is divided into 5's, it is seen to be composed
of 7 of them. In the same way, a line 35 inches long
if divided into 5-inch lines is found to be made of
7 such lines. So 35 of any thing divided into groups
of 5 of the same thing equal 7 groups. This is
expressed thus: 35 divided by 5 is 7, or 35 ÷ 5 = 7.

2. How many square yards of plastering are there
in 648 square feet of ceiling ? 648 ÷ 9 = 72.

3. How many gallons in 24 quarts of milk?
24 quarts ÷ 4 quarts = what number?

4. How many 4-inch strips can be cut from a
piece of ribbon two feet long? Only like quantities
may be compared by division. Hence we must
first convert the feet into inches (2 feet = 24 inches),
and state the problem thus : 24 inches ÷ 4 inches
= what number?

When a given number is divided into a number
of equal parts, the process involved is called Partition.
Examples follow:

1. If a 12-foot board is sawed into 3 equal parts,
how long is each part?

2. If Kenneth divides 12 marbles equally among
3 boys, how many marbles will each get?

Evidently the carpenter must divide the board
into thirds, and the boy must divide the marbles in
a similar way. However, he can distribute the
marbles one at a time. Let him give Martin,
Albert, and Henry each one, then each one more,
and so on until all are distributed.

Kenneth will give out 3 marbles each time round.
Each boy will receive as many as there are 3's in 12,
or 4. Hence we say one-third of 12 is 4, and by
knowledge of this and other similar facts the carpenter
is enabled to divide boards into a given
number of equal parts. Knowing that ⅓ of 12 = 4
(12 ÷ 3 = 4), the carpenter makes marks 4 feet
apart with the assurance that the marks for sawing
will prove to be in the right place.

Both kinds of division problems (Measure and
Partition) are worked by the same process of calculation.
Thus, if we wish to find how much ⅕ of
15 is (Partition), we may find it from knowing how
many 5's there are in 15 (Measure).

Imagine that the 15 units have been divided into
groups of 5. Call the units in each group A, B, C,
D, E. If they are distributed to 5 persons, the first
person will get the first unit from each group (the
A's), the second person the second unit (the B's),
etc., each person receiving 3; but each person
receives ⅕ of the total. Therefore, the statement
that ⅕ of 15 is 3 is true because the number of 5's
in 15 is 3. Therefore, any Partition problem may
be calculated by the same process as a similar
Measure problem.

Accuracy and speed in division are acquired in
these ways : (1) by mastering the fundamental
facts, or division tables; (2) by counting with as
few words in mind as possible; (3) by care in writing
each figure so that it falls directly in line with those
above or below it; (4) by mentally testing the
correctness of a figure in the quotient before writing
it; (5) by testing the final answer.

For practice in the fundamental facts involved in
uneven division, that is, when the divisor is not
contained an even number of times in the dividend
and there is a remainder, the following exercises
will be found helpful.

Find quotients:

2)‾4	2)‾10	2)‾16	3)‾9	3)‾27	3)‾33
2)‾5	2)‾11	2)‾17	3)‾10	3)‾29	3)‾35
4)‾12	4)‾20	4)‾36	5)‾25	5)‾30	5)‾45
4)‾13	4)‾23	4)‾38	5)‾27	5)‾34	5)‾48
6)‾42	6)‾54	6)‾36	7)‾21	7)‾49	7)‾63
6)‾47	6)‾59	6)‾40	7)‾24	7)‾52	7)‾69
8)‾24	8)‾40	8)‾72	9)‾36	9)‾54	9)‾81
8)‾27	8)‾45	8)‾79	9)‾41	9)‾62	9)‾89

There are two forms of division: short division
and long division. Short division is used in divid-

$$\frac{480}{2)960}$$

ing by a number of one figure. In this form of division only the figures in the quotient are written, as in the example shown. The rest of the calculation is carried in the mind.

Long division is used in dividing by a number

$$\begin{array}{r} 236\frac{4}{} \\ 21)\overline{4968} \\ 42 \\ \hline 76 \\ 63 \\ \hline 138 \\ 126 \\ \hline 12 \\ \overline{21} = \frac{4}{7} \end{array}$$

of two or more figures. Here, according to the usual custom, the result of each step is written down. The order of work followed is: (1) divide; (2) multiply; (3) subtract; (4) form a new dividend. Repeat these four processes until all the figures in the dividend have been used. In dividing 4968 by 21, 49 is divided by 21 and the number 2 written in the quotient. The product found by multiplying 21 by 2 (42) is written under the 49. This product is subtracted from the 49, giving the difference 7. The next number of the dividend, the 6, is then brought down to form the new partial dividend 76. The process is then repeated.

A second method is to place the quotient above the dividend and the remainder below it. Thus:

$$\begin{array}{r} 236\frac{4}{} \\ 21)\overline{4968} \\ 76 \\ 138 \\ 12 \end{array}$$

21 divided into 49 goes 2 and 7 over, so we place the 2 above and the 7 below. Bringing down the next figure, 6, we divide 21 into 76, and this results in placing 3 in the quotient and 13 in the remainder. Finally, we divide 21 into 138, and have a remainder of 12 or $\frac{4}{7}$.

To determine the true figures in a quotient,

$$32)\overline{176}$$

the first figures in the divisor and dividend are used as guides. In dividing 176 by 32, since 3 is contained in 17 five times, it is taken as probable that 32 is contained in 176 five times, and 5 is written in the quotient. In dividing

$$28)\overline{122}$$

by such a number as 28 it can easily be seen that 28 is nearly 30, so that it is better to use 3 as a guide in place of 2, and to think: since 3 is contained in 12 four times, it is probable that 28 is contained in 122 four times.

In dividing 246 by 39, we see that 39 is nearly

$$39)\overline{246}$$
$$48)\overline{374}$$
$$97)\overline{228}$$

40. Since 4 is contained in 24 six times, it is probable that 39 is contained in 246 six times. So in dividing 374 by 48 we think of 37 divided by 5, which is 7. In dividing 228 by 97, we think of 22 divided by 10, etc.

A figure in the quotient is known to be too large when the product is greater than the part of the dividend from which it is to be subtracted. It is known to be too small when the remainder is greater than the divisor.

In dividing, care must be taken to place the first

$$\begin{array}{r} 2010 \\ 821)\overline{1650210} \\ 1642 \\ \hline 821 \\ 821 \\ \hline 0 \end{array}$$

figure in the quotient directly above the last figure in the dividend used, and to place a figure in the quotient for each of the remaining figures in the dividend. Note that, in the example on the left, the first figure in the quotient is placed above the fourth figure in the dividend, and since 82, the second partial dividend, does not contain 821, a zero, or nought, is placed above the 2 in the dividend, and the new partial dividend 821 formed.

Find the quotients in these exercises by long division:

1.	$9072 \div 21$	15.	$32046 \div 49$
2.	$22050 \div 42$	16.	$68748 \div 63$
3.	$44667 \div 63$	17.	$195702 \div 78$
4.	$10086 \div 82$	18.	$291388 \div 97$
5.	$39831 \div 51$	19.	$15249 \div 39$
6.	$29756 \div 43$	20.	$435888 \div 48$
7.	$29757 \div 91$	21.	$143278 \div 142$
8.	$29408 \div 32$	22.	$267167 \div 369$
9.	$60152 \div 73$	23.	$1056852 \div 525$
10.	$22356 \div 81$	24.	$1686656 \div 395$
11.	$3074 \div 29$	25.	$2489592 \div 406$
12.	$33630 \div 57$	26.	$1217958 \div 1234$
13.	$15466 \div 38$	27.	$3839112 \div 4506$
14.	$79344 \div 87$	28.	$2875166 \div 574$

The usual test for division is to find the product of the divisor and quotient, adding the remainder if there is one. The result should give the dividend.

Docks. A really impressive idea of the immensity of the overseas trade of Britain, and of the importance of her mercantile marine, can be gained in the midst of the great docks at ports like London, Liverpool, and Southampton. The comings and goings of ships from and to all parts of the world, and the bustle and organization of loading and unloading, constitute one of the most wonderful pictures of human energy and enterprise to be observed in the world.

Before docks were built vessels had to get as near as possible to the shore of the port where they were loading or unloading, the goods then being carried to the shore in small boats or on men's backs. This meant that at low tide the ship was resting on the mud, while at high tide it was cut off from the shore. As trade and commerce grew and ships increased in size, better arrangements became vitally necessary.

The docks into which ships enter for loading or discharging freight are " wet " docks; we shall deal with " dry " docks later. Unless the entrance to the dock or basin can be closed watertight at will, the depth of water inside will vary with the state of the tides. In ports such as London, Liverpool or Le Havre, where there is a great range of tidal depth, the dock entrance is closed by huge gates, or by caissons (q.v.) when the tide level is sufficiently high. This holds back water and maintains sufficient depth in the dock for the big ships at all times.

Dock sides are built of massive masonry or concrete blocks. The quays may be constructed of pre-cast concrete monoliths which are somewhat like a honeycomb cell in shape, with a hollow centre. These may be sunk by placing cast-iron ingots called kentledge on top of them until the weight amounts to thousands of tons.

Dock gates resemble those used for canal locks. Caissons are moved into position across a dock entrance by sliding or rolling, and are housed, when the dock is open, in a recess at one side. Other types of caisson are floated into position to close the dock, and are then sunk by admitting water to the interior.

Adjoining the dock are great warehouses and sheds in which freight may stay until the railways can take it to its destination. Mighty cranes are ranged along the quays to lift merchandise or machinery into and out of the ships. Railway

HOW GREAT DOCKS WERE BUILT AT SOUTHAMPTON

Sir Robt. McAlpine & Sons; Topical; Fox

A mile-and-a-half quay, begun in 1927 and completed in 1933, was built of reinforced concrete monoliths (top), as extension to Southampton Docks. Each monolith weighed 5,000 tons, had a surface of 45 square feet, and was pierced by nine ' wells ' through which earth was brought up as the monolith sank into the ground. They were moulded in enormous wooden casings, as at left centre. At right centre, a view of the propellers of a giant liner in the King George V graving dock for cleaning. Lower, the liner Queen Mary enters the graving dock at Southampton.

A ship in need of repair is floated into the dock, the entrance is closed, and the water run out or pumped out; it may flow out on a falling tide. As the depth decreases, the ship comes to rest on keel blocks and bilge blocks which support it on an even keel. When the water has been got rid of, every part of the ship bottom is accessible for cleaning, painting or repairs.

A slip dock (used for smaller vessels) is somewhat similar, but the floor slopes downward through and beyond the entrance to form a slipway; on this slipway wheeled cradles are run out beneath a ship, running on rails. The vessel is then drawn up the incline by machinery, and the falling tide leaves it high and dry, ready for work to be done.

Keystone

FLOATING DOCK AT SOUTHAMPTON

Here riding high and dry and empty, this floating dock can be submerged to pick up a ship in need of repairs or other attention. The ship does not have to go to the dock: the latter may be towed out to sea where a disabled vessel is awaiting it. A ship is held upright by means of great timber supports when the floating dock is above sea-level again.

tracks run along the sides of the berths and quays, and connect with the main lines of the district.

Now to come to dry docks, of which the graving dock is the most important. Its name comes from the verb " to grave," or clean off accretions. This kind of dock is a basin or an excavated chamber closed at the sides and at one end; at the open end is a gate which can be closed and made watertight. (*See* illustrations of Southampton Docks in page 1023.)

" Floating " docks come into a class of their own, and in modern times have been built in ever bigger dimensions. Sometimes they are towed thousands of miles from the place where they have been built, to be installed at some oversea destination, and are thus of great value for naval purposes. A floating dock may even go out to sea to meet a disabled vessel that is unable to reach a port. This

Aerofilms

ONE OF LONDON'S MANY GREAT DOCKS

From the Tower Bridge to Tilbury there are huge docks on either side of the Thames which make London the greatest port of Britain. The total tonnage of the shipping entering and leaving the Port of London in normal times runs into several millions. This photograph shows the West India Docks, among the oldest and most famous. The West India Docks are on the Isle of Dogs, just opposite Greenwich, where the Thames makes a great U-shaped sweep.

kind of dock is like an enormous trough, with hollow floor and sides. It is sunk until its bottom is submerged deeply enough to permit a ship to float over and into it. Then the water is pumped out of the ballast tanks until the restored buoyancy raises the huge structure, with its burden, up above the sea-level. The dock now becomes, in effect, a graving dock, and can be used for similar purposes. All the machinery and power plant to work both it and the dock is housed in or on the hollow sides of the structure.

Dodo. (Pron. dō-dō). "Stupid" (in Portuguese *doudo*) was the name that Portuguese explorers gave this grotesque bird when, in 1507, they discovered it on the island of Mauritius in the Indian Ocean. It seems to have deserved its name, when changed circumstances confronted it, for long isolation in a land of no

British Museum (Natural History)
DODO : AN EXTINCT BIRD
Formerly inhabiting the island of Mauritius in the Indian Ocean, the dodo has been extinct since the 17th century. Its general appearance is shown in this expert reconstruction.

enemies had made it so clumsy that it soon succumbed, not only to Man but to the dogs, cats, pigs, and other creatures that came with him. By the aid of drawings made by artists accompanying the early explorers, some bones discovered in a marsh on the island of Mauritius have been set in an almost complete skeleton of the dodo, now to be seen in the Natural History Museum, South Kensington, London.

Scientifically, the dodo (*Didus ineptus*) was really a big flightless pigeon, but it had a round fat body, twice as large as a turkey's, with short legs which could scarcely support its weight. Its tail was a mere tuft of curly feathers, its wings were small and imperfect and of no use for flying, and its head was large, with a great hooked bill. On the neighbouring island of Rodriguez lived a similar bird, white in colour and called the "solitaire."

Man's FAITHFUL FRIEND and COMPANION

It has been said that a man's dog stands by him in prosperity and in poverty, in health and in sickness. He will kiss the hand that has no food to offer. When all other friends desert, he remains.

Dog. Among the many animals made use of by Man, the dog, his faithful friend, stands first of all. Long before there were any pictured records of Man's history, the dog was his tamed companion; his bones were even found with those of Stone Age Man. Scientists say that early men developed dogs for hunting purposes from the wild wolves of their particular regions. These were wolf-like dogs such as the Eskimos use today, or such as are shown us in Egyptian pictures over 5,000 years old. Most kinds of dogs that we know, however, have been developed within the last few centuries to meet Man's needs or his whims.

Dogs of today still have many queer little ways of reminding us of their wolfish ancestors. The hunting dog bays—a reminder of hunting wolves baying to keep the pack together. The dog howls at night—the ancestral habit of calling the pack. He sometimes howls, too, upon hearing certain music—does it remind him of the pack? He also turns round before lying down, because his ancestors had to do so in tramping down a flat sheltered bed in jungle grass or drifted leaves. And he buries his bones—even if it is only under a hearth-rug—just as his wild forefathers buried theirs in the wilderness in order to prevent their enemies sharing them. The dog has to thank his ancestors, too, for his marvellous sense of smell, acute hearing, keen eyes, sharp teeth, strong legs for running, muscular body covered with protective hair—all of which fit him for the active outdoor life which he loves, and for taking part with the hunter in the chase, a natural instinct in all dogs.

The Belgian poet Maeterlinck tells us that the dog is the one animal that can follow Man all over the Earth and adapt itself to every climate and to every use to which its master chooses to put it. Striking examples of the useful work a dog can do were shown to us in the wars of 1914–18 and 1939–45. The dogs "had a paw in the war" from the start—as rat killers, as Red Cross dogs for feeding and aiding the wounded, as sentinels, and as messengers. Then there are the specially trained dogs which will pilot a blind person through crowded streets, helping him to avoid obstacles and choosing the right place and time to cross a road (*see* illustration in page 160).

We all know what a difference there is in the looks of dogs. Compare, for instance, a 300-lb. St. Bernard, used for rescue work in the snows of Switzerland, with a tiny Pomeranian which can stand on your hand and weighs less than 2 lb.; or a tall greyhound with a little short-legged dachshund; or a shaggy Newfoundland with those queer little hairless, sausage-like dogs of Mexico or Africa. All of these have as many different ways of serving him as they have colours and sizes and shapes. Even the little toy dogs—the Pomeranian, poodle, pug, Maltese, Pekinese—have their uses as companions and house watch-dogs.

"The dog is something of an aristocrat, ready for sport, keen on the watch, but not over fond of work," says one writer. But we must not forget the sheep-dogs, so knowing and hard-working and useful. The Scotch collie, that wide-awake yeoman of the race, so loyal and intelligent, is now a favourite in every civilized land. When he has a flock of sheep to care for, he lives with them and for them, gathers them from the distant pastures, brings them to the fold when they are needed and will let no prowler meddle with them. It is wonderful to see a sheep-dog, at the sound of his master's whistle, scouring hill and dale, rounding up his flock—which may mean separating it from other sheep—guarding it, keeping it from straying or stampeding, and, finally, without losing any, bringing it safely home. Because of their remarkable sense of smell the collie and other sheep-dogs can trace and find sheep lost on the hills in snowstorms.

Eskimo Sledge-dog Teams

Most useful of working dogs are those of the Eskimos and other northern peoples—wolf-like dogs, which, in teams of a half-dozen or more, draw the sledges in the Canadian and Alaskan wilds. These hard-working animals, known as huskies, have played a noteworthy part in many Arctic and Antarctic explorations. Mastiffs, those huge, tawny, courageous fellows that are probably the oldest of all British dogs, were once used in warfare and hunting, and, in Roman times, for fighting in the amphitheatre.

The statuesque Great Danes were used for hunting wild animals in Northern Europe. Bulldogs, large-headed, strong-jawed, short-legged dogs of the mastiff type, remarkable for their courage, homely looks, and ability to " hang on," were used in olden times for boar-hunting and for the cruel sport of bull-baiting. Today, mastiff, Great Dane, and bulldog, and several others of their kind, are all excellent watch-dogs.

The aristocrats of the dog world are the hunting dogs. While every dog " knows with his nose," it is the bloodhound and the others of this class that have the most astonishingly keen scent. Like their wild ancestors, they learned the trick of following the scent of one animal through the confusion of many other smells, and learned, too, even to pick up a trail on the farther shore of running water.

The bloodhounds, good-sized tan or black-and-tan creatures, with sombre, wrinkled faces and long, floppy ears, were used in former times for tracking wounded animals. Now they are sometimes used by the police in tracking criminals. So remarkable is their power of scent, it is said, that they can follow a trail 30 hours after it is made.

Most of the hunting dogs are also splendid runners. One of the swiftest and most graceful is the tall, slender greyhound, called the " swallow among dogs." Greyhound racing is a popular organized sport. Another graceful runner is the borzoi, or Russian wolf-hound, which is tall and thin and noted for its wonderful silky coat—usually white with tan markings. There are many other hounds that are trained to chase the elk, gazelle, otter, deer, and other game.

One of the most popular hunting dogs is the fox-hound, a white and black-and-tan hound that has been used for centuries in the sport of fox-hunting. Large packs are kept in England for this purpose. The beagle and basset are smaller hounds that hunt hares and rabbits.

Pointers and Setters at Work

Among the staunchest allies of sportsmen we must not forget the dogs that help them to kill their game, or retrieve it after the killing. There is the pointer, who stands rigid when he scents the game (usually partridge, grouse, or quail), and points to it with his nose. The affectionate setter with his plumy tail and long silky coat is also useful in hunting feathered game. He was originally taught to indicate the

The Times

SHEEP-DOGS APPROACH THE CLIMAX OF THE ROUND-UP

Sheep-dog trials are held regularly in farming communities, and the spirit of competition is very keen. Here, two dogs have arrived at the moment when the sheep they are rounding-up have neared the mouth of the pen. Guided only by an occasional whistle or word from their shepherd, they will complete their wonderful exhibition by penning the sheep without one escaping or becoming unduly alarmed. Border collies, as seen here, are the dogs most often used

presence of birds by crouching or " setting," but now he is usually trained to " point." Various sorts of spaniels and retrievers—most of which are fond of swimming—are useful in bringing back to the hunter the game which he has shot.

The little dogs, too, do their share in the world of sport. Foxes, badgers, rabbits, rats, and other animals which seek refuge in ground burrows dread terriers—those smaller, usually shaggy, dogs of many varieties which, as their name suggests (from French, *terrier*, burrow) go to the earth for prey. They are bright, plucky, mischievous little rascals and do their work well, especially the killing of rats. From the short-legged Skye terrier, half buried in his own hair, and the bright, jolly fox-terrier, to the impetuous Airedale, these dogs are all knowing and self-reliant, and, if need be, will prove themselves " good sports " in every sense of the word.

About the most curious-looking dog is the German dachshund (which means " badger dog "), who can enter a badger's hole and drag out his prey. He is an affectionate and a plucky watch-dog, although his long, ungainly body and short, crooked legs will prevent him from ever becoming popular with people who like good-looking dogs.

Scientists class dogs in the family *Canidae* of the order *Carnivora*. More than 90 breeds are recognized by the Kennel Club, but the " world total " can scarcely be counted, since every land has its favourite, developed to suit the sports and tastes, or even the climate and terrain, of the country. There are wild dogs in some parts of the world, notably the dingo of Australia and the pariah scavenger-dog of the East. New breeds are produced by crossing known breeds to secure their good qualities for the created variety, as was done, for example, in the case of the Sealyham terrier. Hunting men have been very active in establishing new breeds, and many varieties of dog originate in cross-breeding to obtain special hunting qualities. In Great Britain and other countries dog breeders or fanciers band themselves together in associations to further the interest of the thoroughbred dog or of a particular breed. These associations are recognized by the ruling body, the Kennel Club, where a register of pedigree dogs is kept. Many breeders and owners exhibit at shows, the most famous of which is Cruft's, held in London. Dogs who have won certificates at three different championship

DOLPHIN : RELATIVE OF THE WHALES
Dark brown above and white underneath, the common dolphin (above) has a sort of beak, and the small fleshy back fin and horizontal tail show that it is a relative of the whales and not a fish.

shows are styled " champions." In Great Britain owners of dogs over six months old must take out a licence, which costs seven shillings and sixpence, and is renewable in January of each year. Shepherds are exempted, as are blind persons using trained dogs as guides. Every dog that appears " in public " must wear a collar, giving the name and address of its owner.

Doggett's Coat AND BADGE. Every year early in August the watermen of Thames-side gather to watch a race in which some of their fellows

DOGGETT'S RACE
In a quaint costume, the starter (above) of the race for Doggett's Coat and Badge gives his orders.

row from London Bridge to Chelsea. The prize for which they compete is a new coat and badge, known as Doggett's Coat and Badge after the man who first instituted the race. Thomas Doggett was an Irish actor, and it was in 1715 that he had the happy idea of offering this novel prize. He left a sum of money to provide a new coat and badge each year, so as to perpetuate the contest. It has been held every year (except during the war periods 1915–1919 and 1940–46) from his day to ours. The races for the years 1940–1946 were all rowed off in 1947.

Dolphin. Small relatives of the whale, these mammals are well known for the way in which they escort ships for miles across the sea, apparently delighting to leap out of the water and exhibit their swimming tricks. Probably because of their friendliness, no creatures of the ocean have been surrounded with more romance. The Greeks regarded the dolphin as a symbol of the sea.

It is easy to mistake a dolphin for a porpoise. The schools of porpoises described by many seafarers are in reality dolphins, for the true porpoise (*q.v.*) seldom ventures far from shore. Unlike the porpoise, the dolphin has a sharp, beak-like nose. Some of the so-called whales are also members of the dolphin family.

The common dolphin, *Delphinus delphis*, is 6 to 8 feet long, very dark brown or black on the back and white underneath. The tail is flattened horizontally instead of vertically like that of a fish, and the dolphin has other peculiarities of the whale family. It feeds upon fish.

Domesday. (Pron. dōōmz'-dā). In a glass case in the museum of the Public Record Office in London is to be seen the famous book known as Domesday Book or simply Domesday (Old English, *domesdae*, day of judgement), which is said to have received its popular name from the fact that it was looked upon as the final authority from which there was no appeal. Domesday is a

Humphrey Joel and Record Office

DOMESDAY BOOK

The illustration above is a photograph of a page of Domesday Book dealing with the lands of the Archbishop of Canterbury. Shown at the left are the two volumes of Domesday Book now in the Record Office in London. The binding is modern.

survey of the land of England, drawn up in 1086 by order of William the Conqueror (1027–87). The information required was obtained by sending officials into each county. From every village or manor came the priest and four villagers, and after interrogating them the officials noted down the facts. These were entered on rolls, and from these the book was compiled.

The book was intended by William to be a record of his fiscal rights, that is, of the income to which he was entitled, and the information collected was all directed to this end. He wanted to know how much each place could and should pay, either by way of geld or land tax, or rent or other dues. In each county the first entries are those of the king's own lands, then come those of the lands held by religious houses, abbeys, bishops, etc., then those of non-clerical owners of large estates and so on. Most of the entries state what the land was worth in the time of Edward the Confessor in 1066, what it was worth when its then owner received it, and what it was worth when the book was compiled. In each entry were given the amount of arable land, the number of workers, the number of plough-lands and oxen, and particulars about churches, mills, fisheries, and other items. There is also a good deal of miscellaneous information about local customs. The book is of supreme value for a study of the economic conditions and social history of the time.

Domesday was first kept in the royal treasury at Winchester. When the treasury was removed to Westminster, probably in the time of Henry II, Domesday went with it. Here it remained until the reign of Queen Victoria (1837–1901). The great book was printed and published in 1783, and photographic facsimiles have been issued for each county.

Dominican Republic. Occupying the eastern part of the island of Hispaniola or Santo Domingo, the second largest of the Greater Antilles, the Dominican Republic has an area of 19,332 square miles. Its northern shores are washed by the Atlantic Ocean and its southern by the Caribbean Sea. The western portion of the island is occupied by the Negro republic of Haiti. The island lies in the Tropics, but the heat is tempered by sea breezes, the temperature seldom rising above 90 degrees Fahrenheit. Four wooded mountain ranges cross the country from east to west, Mount Trujillo, 10,417 feet, being the highest peak.

Most of the land is very fertile, but the richest agricultural sections are in the north and east.

Agriculture is the most important industry, chief crops being sugar-cane, coffee, rice and cocoa. Large areas of forest yield mahogany, satinwood and dye woods. There are deposits of gold, silver, copper, platinum, iron, salt and petroleum, but the mining industry is comparatively undeveloped. Railways extend to over 800 miles, and there are about 2,300 miles of motor roads. The majority of the people are of mixed Negro and white blood, and the language is Spanish.

The capital of the republic is Ciudad Trujillo, founded in 1496 by Bartholomew Columbus, the brother of Christopher, and is the oldest surviving European settlement in the Americas. It was almost destroyed by a hurricane on September 3, 1930, except for a few historic buildings, including the 16th century cathedral of Santo Domingo. The city, rebuilt, has a population of 71,000.

Christopher Columbus discovered Hispaniola in 1492, and for more than a century Spanish rule was undisturbed. Then the French began to colonize the western shore, and by 1795 France had gained the whole island. In the early 19th century the Haitian Negroes drove out the French and took over complete control of Haiti and Santo Domingo, as the Dominican Republic was then called. In 1814 Spain again seized Dominica, but lost it in 1821. From 1822 to 1844 the Dominicans were under Haitian rule, but they gained independence in 1844, establishing a republic. In 1863, fearful of an invasion from Haiti, they asked for the protection of the United States, which was granted. Numerous revolts and periods of misgovernment led to the occupation of the republic by United States troops from 1916 to 1924. The population of the republic is about 1,850,000.

Dominoes. Invented in Italy in the 18th century, this game, which is played all over the world, varies considerably, but in Britain the " pack " consists normally of twenty-eight " cards," or pieces. Each " card " is usually an oblong of bone or ivory, divided into two parts with a line across the middle; each part has from one to six black dots or a blank. Thus the numbering runs from double blank to double six.

The game usually played is quite simple. The dominoes are first shuffled face downwards on the table, and each player draws one—the highest, or any double, winning the deal. They are then shuffled again and each player draws an equal number, any cards left being the stock, or pool. Playing a card is called posing. The leader who poses first may pose any card he likes, and those following him must do so according to what he posed. Thus, if he poses a card with one and three pips on its two halves, the next player can pose only cards having one or three pips, the ends whose pips agree in number being placed next to each other. The holder of a double is usually allowed to put his card across that with which it agrees, and he may have another turn; otherwise there is no rule as to the exact arrangement of the dominoes, and the custom varies widely. The player who first gets rid of all his cards wins the " hand," his score being the number of pips on the pieces still in the possession of his opponent or opponents.

During play, any player who cannot match the exposed numbers either calls " go," or draws from the stock until he can match, according to whichever convention is being followed.

Besides this simple game, there are others that are played with dominoes, of which Matador is perhaps the best. The aim in this game is always to pose a number that with the pips on the end of the card against which it is placed will add up to seven, instead of merely matching. Thus, five is placed next to two, six to one, three to four, and so on. A blank means that the end at which it shows is blocked, and play must continue at the other end only, unless someone can pose a matador, that is, a card whose pips add up to seven exactly, or a double-blank (which requires another matador to be played next it). Scoring is done in various ways in these games.

Some domino sets have up to nine pips, the double-nine then being the highest, while those used in other parts of the world may have very large packs of up to 150 cards, with correspondingly complex games.

Donegal. Although this county is geographically in Ulster, it is politically in Eire. It is also known by the old Gaelic name, Tirconnail. There are no large towns, but the scenery is wild and beautiful throughout its area of 1,860 square miles. Donegal has a deeply indented coast-line of about 165 miles, from Lough Foyle westward round Ireland's north-west corner to Donegal Bay. Not far from the coast are magnificent mountains, like Erigal (2,446 feet) and Blue Stack (2,219 feet). Stock-rearing and fishing are the chief industries; and Donegal tweed is woven in many places. Lifford, the county town, is practically a suburb of Strabane, on the Tyrone side of the river Foyle. The population of the county is about 136,000.

Dormouse. Famous on account of the length of its winter sleep, this little rodent (*Muscardinus avellanarius*) probably takes its name from

M. H. Crawford

DORMOUSE DISTURBED
The little dormouse has a great reputation as a deep sleeper, and indeed its very name refers to this habit. But this one looks lively enough as it peeps out of its nest of grass and newspaper. In the foreground is a partly nibbled Brazil nut, the remains of its interrupted meal.

the Latin *dormire*, "to sleep." In summer, it lives in trees and bushes, feeding on nuts and berries, and sits erect on its haunches like a squirrel when eating; it haunts especially hazel groves. It lays up a store of food for winter, and when cold weather comes it curls up in its nest and sleeps, usually from October to April, though on warm days it may wake, eat and fall asleep again. Dormice can be tamed and kept as pets, their big eyes, yellow-brown fur, and long tails making them very attractive.

Dorsetshire. The novels of Thomas Hardy (1840–1928), who was born near Dorchester, have made the scenery of this beautiful southern county of England familiar to many people. Dorset is situated between Hampshire on the east and Devonshire on the west, and its coast is washed by the English Channel. A peculiarity of the coast is the long and narrow Chesil Bank, a gravel and shingle ridge extending for 16 miles from near Abbotsbury to the so-called Isle of Portland, which is joined to the mainland by a causeway crossed by a railway connecting it with Weymouth.

Dorset has an area of 973 square miles, and is mainly a pastoral region, its chalk downs in the south and centre providing grazing for the Dorset and Portland breeds of sheep. The butter of the county is highly esteemed. Building stone is quarried in the south-eastern extremity, the so-called Isle of Purbeck, and at Portland. From Portland came the stones for St. Paul's Cathedral and other famous buildings.

The chief rivers are the Stour and Frome, the latter flowing to Poole Harbour, a vast, shallow tract of water whose shores are said to be 100 miles round. Dorchester is the county town. Other towns are Poole, Portland and Bridport. Weymouth, Swanage and Lyme Regis are famous holiday resorts. At Corfe Castle is one of England's most picturesque and impressive ruins. Besides Hardy, Dorset produced William Barnes (1801–86), the finest of all English dialect poets. The population of the county is about 239,000.

Dostoievski, FEODOR MIKHAILOVITCH (1822–81). Born at Moscow on November 11, 1822, Dostoievski (pron. dos-toi-ef'-ski) was the son of a military surgeon. He entered the army, but resigned after a few years' service to devote himself to literature. In 1846 appeared his first novel, Poor Folk, and he at once became a celebrity. Three years later he and some of his associates were arrested on a trumpery political charge and sentenced to exile in Siberia. They were told that they had been sentenced to death, and were actually lined up for execution before a firing party. This incident heightened his susceptibility to epileptic fits which had showed itself in childhood. His four years in Siberia were followed by three years in the army, after which he resumed his literary work, an embittered, suspicious, and taciturn man, imbued with a hatred of middle-class society and a profound understanding of the Russian lower classes, with whose lot he was fervently sympathetic.

In a succession of novels he gave expression to these feelings and furnished a graphic and terrible picture of his prison impressions. Already his work was acclaimed throughout Russia, but although he was producing with amazing fertility novel after

From a painting by V. G. Perov
FEODOR DOSTOIEVSKI
After Tolstoy, Feodor Dostoievski is better known in this country than any other Russian novelist. Crime and Punishment and The Brothers Karamazov are his most-read novels, and they rank high in the world's literature.

novel which rank among the finest in the world, he got deeper into debt, owing largely to his love of gambling, and fled to Germany to escape his creditors. Four years of feverish writing restored his finances sufficiently for him to return to Russia in 1871. A newspaper of his own, entitled An Author's Diary, gained him a position of influence, and his last years were passed in comparative prosperity. He died on January 28, 1881.

His genius blossomed first in his Letters from the Underworld (1864). From that time date his greatest works. In his earlier books one can detect the influence of Balzac, George Sand, and Charles Dickens, but after his Siberian experiences he underwent a profound change. The tremendous series of works begun with Crime and Punishment (1866); continued with The Gambler (1867), The Idiot (1868–1869), and The Possessed (1871); and ending with The Brothers Karamazov (1880), considered by some to be the greatest novel ever written, shows a power of expression perhaps never equalled.

Dover. Even in the days of the Roman occupation (A.D. 43–407) of Britain, Dover was one of the most important ports of the English Channel, for the opposite coast of France, at Calais, is here only 21 miles away. From the high chalk cliffs which tower nearly 400 feet above the harbour one may get a magnificent view of the French coast from Boulogne to Gravelines.

The most interesting building in Dover is the old castle, which occupies the site of a Roman fortress. The existing parts consist of the keep, 91 feet high, with walls about 20 feet thick, and several towers. In the grounds are the Pharos, a Roman lighthouse, and the ancient church of St. Mary de Castro, built of Roman bricks by the Anglo-Saxons. The public buildings include the modern town hall and, adjoining it, the Maison Dieu founded for pilgrims in the 13th century. Dover College is a large Public School for boys. The harbour works represent a massive line of masonry $2\frac{1}{2}$ miles in extent and enclosing 690 acres of water.

J. Dixon-Scott

DOVER HARBOUR OF WORLD RENOWN
One of the Cinque Ports, Dover stands on the Strait of the same name in the county of Kent. The harbour, with an area of 690 acres, is enclosed by the Admiralty Pier, the Eastern Arm and the Southern Breakwater. It was a great naval and military base in the First and Second World Wars and is the port of departure for a mail-packet service to France.

Dover, the chief of the Cinque Ports in medieval times, was an important naval and military base during the First and Second World Wars (1914–18 and 1939–45). During the Second World War the town suffered considerable damage from bombing raids by German aircraft, and even more from the shells of German long-range guns on the French coast, more than 2,000 shells falling on the town between August, 1940 and September, 1944. The clearance of demolished buildings in the Market Square led to the excavation of the Roman fort of Dubra. The population of Dover is 32,000.

Down. An eastern maritime county of Northern Ireland, Down stretches from Belfast and its lough in the North to the border of Eire in the South. It is a fertile area, 951 square miles in extent. The chief rivers are the Lagan, Bann and Newry ; mineral springs occur in several places. It produces oats, wheat and potatoes, and the manufacture of linen from home-grown flax is carried on. Fisheries and horse-breeding engage many people.

Downpatrick (population about 3,000) is the county town. Situated some 25 miles southeast of Belfast, it derives its name from a huge

W. Lawrence

DOWN: HIGHLANDS OF THE NORTHERN IRELAND COUNTY
Most of County Down is hilly, and in the south are the Mourne Mountains, which include the highest peak in Northern Ireland—Slieve Donard, rising to 2,796 feet. The range extends for about 40 miles. Two excellent motor roads serve this beautiful district. The principal industry of the county is agriculture : oats, wheat, flax, and potatoes being grown.

dun, or mound, in the neighbourhood, and from the fact that St. Patrick is said to be buried there. It has a cathedral and a number of holy wells. At the head of Strangford Lough is Newtownards, near which are Belfast's airport and a famous motor-racing track. It is in the beautiful Mourne Mountains, which rise (in Slieve Donard) to 2,796 feet, that Down has its greatest attraction. The population of the county is 211,000.

Downing Street. One of the places that visitors to London often insist upon seeing is Downing Street, and this turning off Whitehall is often crowded with sightseers who hope to catch a glimpse of the Prime Minister. For No. 10, Downing Street is the official residence of the Prime Minister. Next to it, at No. 11, lives the Chancellor of the Exchequer.

DOWNING STREET : NUMBER 10

Since the beginning of the 18th century Number 10, Downing Street, London, has been the official residence of the Prime Ministers of Great Britain. Sir Robert Walpole (1676-1745) was the first premier to live there. Meetings of the Cabinet are held in the Council Chamber at Number 10, and in times of crisis crowds collect in the street to watch Ministers pass in and out of the house.

The houses in Downing Street were originally built by Sir George Downing (1624–84), a statesman who served both Oliver Cromwell and Charles II, and it is from him that the street takes its name. Sir Robert Walpole (1676–1745) was the first Prime Minister to live at 10, Downing Street, and all his successors have followed his example, except Lord Melbourne, Sir Robert Peel and Lord Salisbury.

Downs. Amongst the most beautiful of English scenery in the southern half of our island is that of the two ranges of chalk hills which are known as the North and the South Downs. Although it is the latter range that springs first to our minds on mention of the Downs, it is not really so important as the North Downs. This range runs for a distance of 95 miles, starting at Farnham in Surrey, crossing that county and running on through Kent, to reach the sea at Dover. The highest point is Leith Hill (965 feet) near Dorking in Surrey.

The South Downs, starting at Petersfield in Hampshire, extend through Sussex to Beachy Head, a distance of 65 miles. The country between the two ranges is known as the Weald, and is for the most part rich and clayey. The South Downs are, in general, the more wild and bare, with great expanses of open country, grassland, and but few trees—usually beeches planted on prominent hilltops (*see* illustration in next page). They are also broken by numerous valleys and passes, through which rivers run down to the sea. Thus the rivers of Sussex—the Arun, Adur, Ouse, and Cuckmere—all break through these hills, just as the Wey, Mole, Darent, Medway, and Stour flow through the North Downs, northwards to the Thames or its estuary. Good pasture is provided by the short turf of the South Downs, which have given their name to a world-famous breed of sheep.

The name "Downs" is also given to the high chalk ranges of Berkshire and Wiltshire, even more spacious and bare than the better known ranges. And "The Downs" is a famous and important roadstead off Deal in the English Channel, a refuge for ships during heavy weather.

Doyle, SIR ARTHUR CONAN (1859–1930). The great detective character Sherlock Holmes first appeared in Conan Doyle's story A Study in Scarlet, in 1887. This acute and imperturbable master of deduction reappeared in three other novels—The Sign of Four (1890), The Hound of the Baskervilles (1902), and The Valley of Fear (1915)—and achieved world-wide fame as the hero of a series of mysteries which are related in The Adventures of Sherlock Holmes (1892, originally published in the Strand Magazine) and its four companion volumes of short stories. In Micah Clarke (1889), The White Company (1891), Rodney Stone (1896), and Sir Nigel (1906) Conan Doyle made excursions into historical romance, while The Lost World and The Poison Belt are two excursions into the

DOWNS: THE SUSSEX WEALD BENEATH THE SOUTHERN HILLS

The Times

One of the loveliest stretches of the English countryside is the South Downs (*see* article in the facing page). Here is seen the Sussex village of Poynings, at the foot of New Timber Hill. On top of the Downs, on the left, is one of the clumps of beech trees typical of these hills. The short turf provides pasture for sheep, and between the North and South Downs lies the rich land of the Kent and Sussex Wealds. Several rivers cut through the South Downs.

realm of fantasy. He was equally successful with short stories, especially those dealing with the adventures of Brigadier Gerard. After providing Sir Henry Irving (1838–1905) with an effective part in the one-act piece called A Story of Waterloo (1894) he wrote several successful plays, including The House of Temperley and The Fires of Fate, and adapted Brigadier Gerard and the Speckled Band for the stage.

Born at Edinburgh, on May 22, 1859, Conan Doyle was the son of one artist, Charles Doyle, nephew of another, Richard Doyle (who designed the cover of Punch), and grandson of a third, John Doyle, the cartoonist famous in his day as H. B. From 1882 to 1890 Conan Doyle practised as a doctor, but the success of his early novels caused him to abandon medicine. During the Boer War (1899–1902) he was physician with a field hospital, and in 1902 he was knighted. His History of the Great Boer War is a readable narrative, and during the First World War (1914–18) he wrote The British Campaigns in France and Flanders. For many years he was a leader in psychical research in England, and he published several defences of spiritualism. He died on July 7, 1930.

SIR ARTHUR CONAN DOYLE

Though Sir Arthur Conan Doyle is chiefly remembered as the creator of the great fictional detective, Sherlock Holmes, he also wrote a number of works with historical backgrounds. Conan Doyle was a qualified doctor and served during the Boer War (1899-1902).

Dragon. Long ago, according to an old legend, there dwelt in a distant pagan land a dreadful dragon. So mighty was this terrifying monster that the flapping of its great bat-like wings could be heard for miles around, and with a single blow of its claws it could fell an ox. Its snake-like body was covered with slimy scales, and on the tip of its pointed tail was a poisonous sting. From its nostrils came dense clouds of smoke and flame that brought death to everyone who breathed it.

Every year a girl was offered to it to appease it. One year the lot fell on Princess Sabra, daughter of the king; but she was saved by the valiant St. George, youngest and bravest of the seven champions of Christendom, who chanced to be riding in that far-off land in search of adventure. With his magic sword he slew the monster. Won over to the Christian faith by this deed of its champion the people were baptized, and the Princess was wedded to her deliverer. This is but one of the many dragon stories told in the lore of different countries.

For ages the dragon was the emblem of the former imperial house of China. The dragon of legend, whatever its particular shape and appearance, is always in essentials a lizard or snake. In the East, the home of huge, poisonous snakes, the dragon was in general an emblem of the principle of evil. In the sacred books of the Hebrews the dragon or serpent is the source of death and sin; this idea was continued in the New Testament and in Christian mythology generally, the dragon of Christian symbolism representing the devil and all his works. Classical legend has its Hydra, Chimaera, and other awful dragons, but also beneficent ones such as the dragon that guarded the apples of the Hesperides, and the snakes of the temples of Aesculapius (the god of medicine).

In the East Indies are the huge Komodo dragons (*Varanus komodoensis*), which inhabit Komodo island, in the Lesser Sundas. The largest living lizards, these creatures, exceeding 12 feet in length, may well have inspired Oriental legends.

Dragonet. A brilliantly coloured fish, the male dragonet (*Callionymus lyra*) is golden brown, striped with blue and yellow; the long, pointed first dorsal fin is yellow and pink, while the second dorsal fin, which stretches along the greater part of the back, is blue and yellow and green. The tail, too, is very bright. The female, however, is dull in colour. This fish occurs not uncommonly off the southern and western coats of Britain. Besides the common dragonet there is the spotted species (*C. maculatus*). This is smaller than *C. lyra*, and neither is more than a few inches in length.

A. S. Martin

DRAGON-FLY AT REST

Known also as 'horse-stinger'—though it has no sting and no connexion with horses—the dragon-fly is seldom seen in this position. Let a shadow fall across it when at rest, and the insect is off like a flash, chasing and catching small flies and other insects with remarkable agility.

Dragon-fly. These harmless and very beautiful insects have two marvellous compound eyes that are each really a large number of tiny eyes joined to make one great organ of sight; and each of these compound eyes, sticking out like bow windows, is almost as large as the head itself.

Martin Duncan

SMALL DRAGONET OF BRILLIANT HUE

To be found in deep water off Britain's southern and western coasts, this small fish—it is but a few inches in length—is noted for its gorgeous and variegated colouring, including the spiny fins and the tail. But this brilliance applies to the male only. The female dragonet is dowdy and dull.

There are two groups of dragon-flies, which together form the order *Odonata*: the dragon-flies proper, which keep their wings outspread when they alight—which is not often, for they seem tireless—and the slenderer-bodied damsel-flies, or demoiselles, which fold their wings along their backs. The latter forms all have long, slender, stiff bodies of dazzling colours, in steel-blue, purple, green, bronze, copper and silver-white. Their four long, narrow, silver-gauze wings are beautifully veined, and are often spotted with white or brown or blue. Some of the other dragon-flies, such as the common genus *Libellula*, have broader, flatter bodies and much less delicate wings. They all have strong jaws.

Dragon-flies live part of their life in the water and part on land. The eggs are laid in the water, and the young that emerge live there until they are ready to change to the adult form. These creatures are as ferocious in the water as the dragon-flies are in the air, feeding upon small water insects, and even very small fish. The underlip is jointed and very long, and bears at its tip a strong pincer. With this they reach out, grasp the food, and convey it to the mouth. When not in use this lip is folded back underneath the head. They breathe by sucking water through gills into the lower part of the body, where the oxygen is extracted by many little tubes. The water is forced out again, at the same time sending the nymph darting through the water in a series of jerks.

The adult insects feed upon gnats, flies and similar victims which they catch, at tremendous speed, on the wing. The dragon-fly is one of the greediest of insects, particularly when immature.

HOW THE DRAGON-FLY GETS ITS GAUZY WINGS

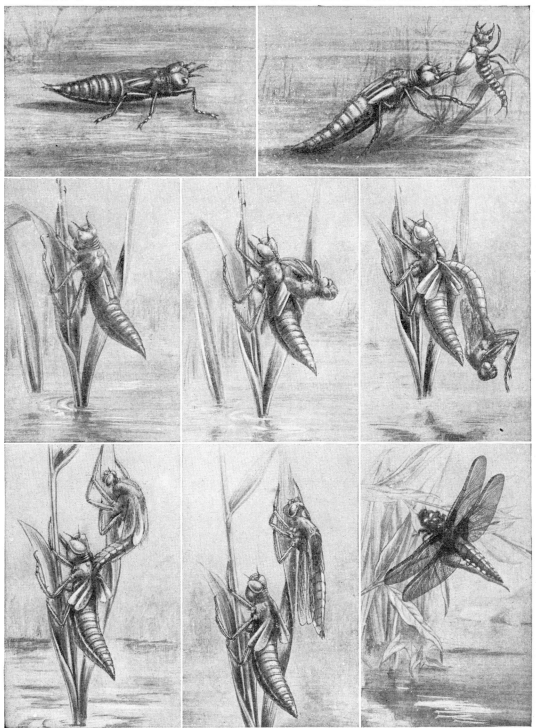

From a sluggish, drab-looking water-creature to a darting, colourful insect of the air, this transformation is wonderful. The female dragon-fly deposits her eggs in the water of a pond or ditch, and the small creatures that emerge spend the next few months crawling about the mud (top left). Their food consists of any other living water-creatures which they can catch and overpower (top right). When the time arrives for transformation to the winged form, the sluggish creature climbs the stem of a water-plant and there remains motionless for a time. Suddenly a split occurs down the creature's back and from the old skin there gradually struggles forth the four-winged dragon-fly as shown in the remainder of the pictures. When the wings have dried and become firm, it skims away in search of flying food—leaving the old skin a shrivelled relic of its early days.

SIR FRANCIS DRAKE

From an engraving by Hondius

Perhaps the most famous of all the Elizabethan sailors, Drake sailed round the world (1577-80), and was the founder of British naval supremacy. He died at sea on January 28, 1596, and his body was committed to the Atlantic Ocean.

Drake, SIR FRANCIS (1545 or 1539-96). To his countrymen, Drake was a hero. In the eyes of the Spanish, against whom he fought so successfully, he was a devil incarnate. Most celebrated of the English sea-dogs of Elizabeth's reign, Drake was the first Englishman to sail round the globe, and he took a leading part in defeating the Great Armada gathered by Spain to invade England in 1588.

Born near Tavistock in Devonshire, Drake grew up in a seafaring atmosphere. While still a boy he shipped as apprentice on a coasting vessel, and at the age of 20 he accompanied his cousin, the famous Sir John Hawkins, on a slaving voyage to Guinea on the west coast of Africa. Two years later he commanded a ship on another voyage, in the course of which the Englishmen were attacked by Spaniards in the port of Vera Cruz, Mexico, and lost all but two of their vessels. This disaster cost Drake nearly everything he possessed; moreover, the treachery of the Spanish authorities on this occasion, and their subsequent barbarity to their prisoners, were never forgotten or forgiven by Drake, and he determined to devote his life to a relentless war against Spain.

Drake gathered a band of adventurers together and made three successful voyages to the New World. He plundered Spanish settlements, destroyed their ships, and made a daring march across the Isthmus of Panama in 1572. From a high tree, he caught his first glimpse of the Pacific. His prayer that " Almighty

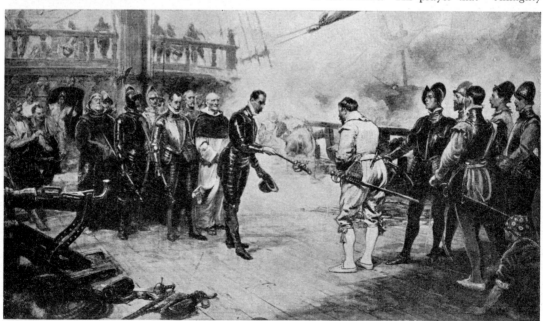

DRAKE RECEIVES THE SWORD OF DON PEDRO

Drake, though only second-in-command of the English fleet, played a great part in the defeat of the Spanish Armada, and the terror that his name inspired was a factor in the victory. A remarkable incident bearing out this fact is shown here. One of the Spanish leaders, Don Pedro de Valdez, met Drake's ship, the Revenge, in the course of the action. As soon as the Spaniard discovered his opponent was the redoubtable Drake he surrendered, though his vessel was much the larger. This painting by Seymour Lucas, R.A. (1849-1923), shows Drake on board the Revenge receiving the Spanish Admiral's sword, while the smoke of the great battle still eddies round.

God would grant him life and leave to sail an English ship upon that sea " was answered on his famous voyage round the world (1577–80).

On this voyage he set out with five vessels, intending to pass through the Strait of Magellan, near the southern extremity of South America, and explore the waters he had seen from the Isthmus of Panama. When the Strait was passed, Drake's ship pushed on alone; the other vessels had either turned back or been lost. Up the coast he went, plundering the Spanish settlements in Chile and Peru, and capturing unsuspecting treasure-ships bound for Panama.

He sailed northward, and claimed the California coast in the name of his Queen. To avoid braving the outraged Spaniards by returning the way he had come, he determined to emulate Magellan and return home by making a circuit of the globe. So he crossed the Pacific and Indian Oceans, sailed round the Cape of Good Hope, and reached England in September 1580. The magnitude of Drake's achievement and the courage which he displayed amply merited the acclaim which greeted him. Elizabeth shared richly in the treasure he brought, and honoured him by dining on board his ship and raising him to knighthood, although she knew this would infuriate the Spanish.

In the war with Spain which soon after broke out (1585), Drake won his crowning honours. After once more carrying death and destruction to the Spanish settlements in the West Indies, he led a daring raid into the port of Cadiz in southern Spain. Here he destroyed so many vessels that the great expedition which was being prepared for the invasion of England was delayed for a year. After thus " singeing the King of Spain's beard " Drake returned home in triumph.

When the Spanish Armada (*q.v.*) finally did come sailing up the English Channel (1588), Drake, as vice-admiral of the English fleet, played a chief part in the running fight of a week which drove off the Spaniards. On a final expedition against the Spaniards in the West Indies, Drake was taken ill and died on January 28, 1596.

The MAKE-BELIEVE WORLD *of the* STAGE

Here we trace twenty-five centuries of the drama—from its crude beginnings at the dawn of history in religious festivals to the superbly acted play on the revolving stage of the theatre of today.

Drama AND DRAMATICS. Drama of some sort or other is probably as old as civilization, but we owe the beginnings of the art, as we know it today, to the ancient Greeks. Early in their history these people had feasts to celebrate the two most important events of the year, the harvest and the spring-time—the time of plenty and the time of promise. At these festivals they did honour to Dionysus (Bacchus), the god of the vineyard, of trees and plants and fruitfulness. They worshipped this deity with song and dance and sacrifice, and processions and chants, at first made up on the spur of the moment, gradually became more or less fixed in form.

In certain forms of ancient Greek comedy the actors wore masks. This statue shows what they were like.

At the vintage-festival in the winter, bands of revellers marched riotously through the village chanting their crude choruses. In the intervals between the songs, the leader of the procession would exchange jests and banterings with members of the company or with the leaders of rival bands. The most striking of these dialogues would be treasured in memory, to be repeated the following year, until gradually they crystallized into genuine drama—the representation of a complete story by words and action. From these dialogues grew Greek comedy, so called from the Greek words *komos* (revel) or *kome* (village) and *aoide* (song).

The spring festivals took a different turn. At these times it early became the custom to tell in song and dance the chief episodes in the life of the god they were worshipping. Dressed in goatskins to represent the satyrs—beings half goat, half man, who attended Dionysus—they danced round the altar, reciting the god's adventures.

From this humble beginning sprang Greek tragedy, a creation of human genius which for moral grandeur, dramatic power and artistic perfection is equalled only by the greatest works of Shakespeare. Tragedy gets its name from the goatskins worn by the chorus, being formed from the two Greek words *tragos* (goat) and *aoide* (song). It is easy to see how, in course of time, the leader of the chorus would introduce passages of lively dialogue with the chorus, to extend and explain the narrative given in the choral odes. To arrive at genuine drama one step remained to be taken. Semi-dramatic narration must give way to the actual impersonation of the god, and of those, also, who shared in his adventures.

This step was taken about the beginning of the 6th century B.C. by Thespis, traditionally known as the father of Greek tragedy, who is said to have managed a company of travelling players. His innovation consisted in picking out a member of the chorus to play in turn the parts of all the prominent figures in the legend. This was the birth of true drama. Gradually the dialogues and choruses, at first hit off on the spur of the moment, took literary form. They were carefully worked out before the performance, and committed to memory by actor and chorus.

Thus the way was opened for the immortal trio—Aeschylus, Sophocles and Euripides—who established the drama as one of the noblest forms of literary art, and left the magnificent body of plays from which have sprung all later dramatic literature worthy of the name. Within a period of a little over 100 years each of these great men further unfolded the resources of the art.

Aeschylus (*q.v.*) introduced a second actor, thus making it possible to throw all the central incidents of a story into dramatic form. Also, he is said to have improved the mask worn by the actors and invented the *cothurnus*, or buskin, a thick-soled shoe used to increase their stature. Sophocles (*q.v.*) introduced a third actor, and gave the chorus a place of less importance.

The great contribution of Euripides (*q.v.*) was to "bring drama down from the skies." His predecessors represented the heroes, gods, and great legendary characters more than life-size. Euripides was the first realist in the drama, for he was content to paint men and women as they were, with all their defects and vices. He stripped the veil of idealism from the drama and humanized it, thus opening the way for Shakespeare and the other giants of modern drama.

Parallel with the development of tragedy went on the growth of comedy. From the jesting dialogues of the vintage-festival grew burlesques and parodies, plentifully provided with broad jokes directed against the men and fashions of the day. This is the character of Greek comedy as we see it in the plays of Aristophanes (*q.v.*), who made use of it for satires and burlesques against the men and the social conventions of his time.

Menander, the second great comic dramatist of the Greeks, whose work is known to us only in fragments and Latin adaptations, refined and developed the comedy form, and moulded it into something like the shape we have in the modern comedy of manners.

So great were the achievements of the Greek dramatists that the Romans could only follow in their footsteps. The chief Roman writers of comedy, Plautus and Terence, and their one great tragic poet, Seneca (who based his plays on those of Euripides), did little but imitate the Greek models. Scenes of Roman comedy were laid in Athens, and the characters had Greek names.

Both Plautus and Terence found their chief inspiration in Menander. Terence was content to translate or at the most adapt Menander's comedies. Plautus, aiming at a lower type of audience, dealt more freely with his original, and made his supposedly Athenian characters act and talk like the Romans of his own day.

Among the later Romans drama ran an inglorious course. The mixed populace of that time—the dregs of the vast Roman empire—had little mind for the severity of tragedy or the delicate fancy of comedy. They preferred the fights of gladiators and combats with wild beasts in the

WHAT IT WAS LIKE INSIDE A ROMAN THEATRE

The theatres of ancient Greece and Rome were open to the air, and no scenery as we know it was used. The illustration shows the theatre at Ostia, the port of ancient Rome. It dates from the time of Augustus, but was twice restored, the second time in the year A.D. 400. Above is a reconstruction based upon the existing remains. The back wall of the stage was ornamented with statues and columns, to form permanent scenery, and the auditorium rose in two main divisions from a mosaic-paved orchestra. An awning spread from poles protected the audience when the sun was hot.

arena, and the low buffoonery of the variety entertainment which they called the *mime.* So the influence of the rising Christian Church was naturally directed against the stage and all its works. The theatre was condemned and reviled, and dramatic literature passed from view for a thousand years.

Deprived of the great body of classical drama, the people of the Middle Ages began the process of developing a drama all over again. The harvest and springtime again were the inspiration of seasonal festivals, village games and dances. The maypole dance, which is still occasionally to be seen in rural England, is a survival of these sports on the village green. But the chief source of inspiration was again religion, as it had been in Greece. Drama was employed in the Church service itself at Easter and Christmas, to bring home in an easily understood form the birth and the resurrection of Christ. Little plays, dialogues and pantomimes (then a performance in dumb show) were devised to represent these and other incidents in the life of Christ.

The new dramatic art flourished throughout Europe, and reached its greatest development in England. After a time

A LONDON THEATRE IN SHAKESPEARE'S DAYS
Elizabethan theatres were very crude structures, with the actors playing on a raised stage and the audiences sitting in galleries or standing in a yard with but slight protection from the weather. This drawing shows the Globe Theatre at Southwark, by the side of the Thames, where Shakespeare's plays were acted in his own time.

the plays grew to such length that they could not be included in the regular service. Other Bible stories were added, with legends of the saints, and the performances were transferred to the churchyard and given in series. One play led to another, until these " Mysteries " and " Miracle plays," as they were called, expanded to long cycles. The York cycle includes 48 separate plays.

As these pieces became more elaborate the Church guilds and the guild organizations of artisans assisted in the performances, and gradually took them over altogether. Each guild would make itself responsible for a particular episode, and construct a wagon, consisting of a dressing-room below and a stage above. On Church festival days this wagon was dragged through the streets, halting at fixed points while the episode was played, over and over again, to the various companies of spectators. The costuming was often costly and realistic; devils were dressed in yellow and black to suggest the fires of hell. These Miracle plays continued to be very popular during the later 14th and throughout the 15th centuries. By 1550, however, their vogue had passed.

Along with these plays grew up another group —the Moralities. Instead of using Biblical and legendary characters for heroes and villains, they personified vices and virtues such as Hypocrisy, Heresy, Piety, Justice, Peace, and Truth. One of these plays, called Everyman, is often performed at the present day.

Into this crude, formless, artless folk-drama the Renaissance, or rebirth of classical learning, suddenly introduced a new inspiration. In the libraries of the monasteries, which were the only considerable storehouses of learning, scholars were beginning to rediscover the old Greek and Roman classics. The union of classical models with the subject-matter of the day produced the beginnings of modern drama.

France, England and Spain soon developed a vigorous national drama. In Germany, which was divided into small autocratic principalities and city states and was distracted by religious wars, national ideals were weakening through princely imitations of everything French, and there the drama developed late. Her great dramatists, Schiller and Lessing, belong to the 18th century. In England, Marlowe, Ben Jonson and Shakespeare; in France, Corneille, Racine, and Molière; in Spain, Lope de Vega and Calderon —these are the enduring names.

Shakespeare took the best from all ages and fused it into living, breathing, drama. What he did for tragedy and romantic comedy Molière did some sixty years later—for the comedy of manners.

After Shakespeare the English theatre declined rapidly. There are many scenes of beauty and power in the plays of Beaumont and Fletcher, Massinger, Ford, Middleton, Webster and others, but all these men fell far below their great predecessor in artistic and moral genius, and were—for all their great gift of poetry—mainly concerned with the workings of exaggerated passion. In one field alone was there progress—in polite comedy.

The opposition of the Puritans to the theatre, already pronounced, was deepened into bitter hostility by the merciless satire which the dramatists directed against them. In 1642, immediately after the outbreak of the Civil War, they closed the theatres and penalised all stage players.

Restoration Comedy

On the restoration of Charles II there was a wild reaction from Puritanism. Comic writers of genuine power, wit, and brilliance—Dryden, Congreve, Wycherley, Farquhar, Vanbrugh, and their contemporaries—poured out a flood of clever immoralities, the most brilliant examples of which included The Way of the World, Love For Love, and The Country Wife. These were brought to an end by the reawakened conscience of the people and the thunders of the famous pulpit orator, Jeremy Collier. From that day to the present the breach between the theatre and the Puritan spirit has remained.

During the 18th century no new plays of lasting value were brought out on the English stage until the time of Sheridan and Goldsmith. Goldsmith's She Stoops to Conquer, and Sheridan's The Rivals and The School for Scandal, are constantly performed. The 19th century, which saw the great struggle for democracy, the Industrial Revolution, new ideas in science and philosophy, witnessed, in its latter half, a real awakening of the drama.

Henrik Ibsen, father of the new drama which reflected the changing conditions of life during the 1860's and 70's, was a revolutionary inasmuch as he introduced living characters who, by the urgency of their problems and the reality of their dialogue, brought the drama into direct touch with life as lived by thousands of people. His influence on younger dramatists was considerable: notably on George Bernard Shaw, an Irish-born writer who rescued English drama from the conventional, insipid plays of the day. Shaw's brilliance as a playwright was built on paradox—a seemingly absurd statement enshrining a truth, though he used the propagandist methods adopted by Brieux in many of his earlier plays, of which the best-known was perhaps Candida. Like Ibsen he, too, was concerned with drawing attention to social wrongs, but instead of lecturing his audience he provoked laughter by his witty gibes and ironical situations. He had little in common with the Russian dramatists Ostrovski, Chekhov and Andreev.

Of these the most famous is Chekhov—a writer of great importance in the development of the drama. He wrote of the half-shades of emotion and showed the frailty of the human character set against the narrow provincial background of Russia before the Revolution. Later Russian playwrights such as Afinogenev and Simonov were drawn to the social movements of the time, and wrote of the changes that had taken place in Soviet Russia.

Celtic Literary Revival

Apart from Shaw and followers of his school, the Irish effected a change in English drama at the beginning of the 20th century. The Celtic literary revival, which centred round the Abbey Theatre, Dublin, directed by W. B. Yeats and Lady Gregory, produced such outstanding writers as J. M. Synge and Sean O'Casey. Synge's poetic play of Irish peasant life, The Playboy of the Western World, was the finest example of its kind. O'Casey's Juno and the Paycock, and The Plough and the Stars, based on the Irish Rebellion of 1916, carried on the tradition of fine writing. His later plays, Silver Tassie and Within the Gates, were expressionist, but in Red Roses for Me he returned to his earlier manner.

The " well-made " play, as the French characterized Sardou's type of drama, carefully and tautly constructed, thrived in the hands of Pinero in England and Sudermann in Germany. The plays of Rostand, Barrie, and Maeterlinck, on the other hand, turned sharply realistic portrayal to imaginative romanticism, enriched by symbolism. Most significant for the later writers of the 20th century, however, was the growth of naturalism, launched by Strindberg, with Hauptmann outstanding among its exponents. Naturalism arose from new conceptions of the importance of heredity and environment in the growth of character.

The expressionistic reaction to naturalism made less headway in France than elsewhere. Wit, fancy, sentiment, with now and then a serious touch, pervade the plays of Sacha Guitry and Bourdet. More serious were François de Curel, Paul Hervieu, Henri Bataille, J. J. Bernard, Jean Cocteau, and Lenormand. After the Second World War (1939-45) French dramatists turned to a more extreme form of dramatic expression, namely Existentialism

SHAKESPEARE AND CONGREVE AT THE 'OLD VIC'

J. W. Debenham

Coriolanus is a dramatic figure whose actions dominate the tragedy by Shakespeare which bears his name. Sir Laurence Olivier as the Roman hero (top) receives the blessing of his mother, Volumnia (Sybil Thorndike), and his wife, Virgilia, after his victory over the Volscians.

Restoration comedy—a direct reaction to the Puritanism of the Cromwellian period—is notable for its outspoken humour and verbal beauty. In the lower photograph, Ursula Jeans, in Congreve's Love for Love, exchanges witticisms with Jack Livesey, Dennis Arundell and Charles Laughton.

—a philosophy based on the study of various types of "existences." Jean Paul Sartre was the leader of this school. His Huis Clos (Vicious Circle) became world-famous and influenced such writers as Albert Camus. In Spain the drama remained more conservative. Among its leading exponents were the perfervid Echegaray, the sentimental Alvarez Quintero brothers, the Barrie-like Martinez Sierra, and the lively and versatile Benavente, who supplied a stage notable for its charm rather than for its novelty, ideas, or progress.

In Italy the stage was enriched by many new ideas. D'Annunzio set off the fires of his colourful voluptuous art; Pirandello, particularly in Henry IV, and Six Characters in Search of an Author, made the objective world waver in the uncertainty of Man's thoughts and dreams.

The most original experiments, particularly with expressionism, occurred in Germany and Austria, after the First World War (1914–18). Expressionism

holds that the outside world exists only as an expression, or projection, of the world of thought and feeling within the human spirit. Galsworthy and Pirandello experimented with this principle, and Oscar Wilde had voiced it long before the term expressionism was invented. But it remained for writers in the Germanic countries to carry it out to its logical conclusion.

Among the best of the expressionists in Germany was Ernst Toller, who had been embittered by his imprisonment for taking part in a revolution in 1919. Anti-war themes and revolt against the old social order also inspired Wedekind and Hasenclever, both of expressionistic technique. More eccentric and less talented were Kornfeld and Kaiser, weavers of fantasies seldom now performed.

In what was formerly Austria, Capek, the Czechoslovakian, produced the world-famous expressionistic play, R.U.R.; Molnár, a Hungarian, though chiefly facile and romantic, successfully employed expressionism in Liliom.

Expressionism had as its chief exponent in the United States the outstanding playwright Eugene O'Neill, whose plays The Hairy Ape and Emperor Jones were striking successes. O'Neill's plays were almost the only ones of their type to be at first readily accepted in England, where the advance guard of the drama was perhaps led as much by a few producers as by playwrights. Thornton Wilder's The Skin of Our Teeth carried the method still further. In England the work in collaboration of Christopher Isherwood and W. H. Auden, and that of T. S. Eliot— like Auden a writer of fine verse as well as a dramatist — was outstanding, and Eliot's Murder in the Cathedral (1936) was a really great play. Of the younger dramatists Christopher Fry was one of the most outstanding. J. B. Priestley turned from a modified form of expressionism in Johnson Over Jordan, 1939, to sociological plays such as The Linden Tree (1947).

Early in the 20th century various notable movements were started in repertory, that is, by theatres with a permanent company, depending on constant change of plays and not on a long run of a single play. Miss Horniman opened the Gaiety Theatre, Manchester, in 1908; Basil Dean started repertory at the Liverpool Playhouse in 1911, and Sir Barry Jackson at Birmingham in 1913. In 1914 Lilian Baylis (1874–1937) realized her ambition to pro-

SCENE FROM A SHAW PLAY
Adam, Eve, and the Serpent appear in this scene in Bernard Shaw's drama Back to Methuselah. In this play the author gives an astonishingly complete exposition of his biological, social, and political philosophy, and introduces characters ranging from Adam to the Prime Minister of the time when the play was written.

duce seasons of Shakespeare's plays and opera (in English) at the "Old Vic" in Waterloo Road, London — an ambition doubly realized with the opening of Sadler's Wells in 1931. In 1944 drastic alterations were made in the Old Vic's policy. A permanent repertory company was founded for performances of the classics at the New Theatre, London. In 1946 were founded an experimental theatre, a theatre school, and a children's theatre known as the "Young Vic."

Encouraging dramatists, reviving classics, and training actors who continue their careers on the London stage, the repertory movement has largely taken the place of the old provincial theatre, as well as of the large touring companies. There are usually enough serious playgoers in a town or district to support a small repertory theatre, as at Nugent Monck's Maddermarket Theatre at Norwich, where the performances, given chiefly by amateurs, are of the highest possible standard. Pro-

Strand Electric Co., Ltd.

CYCLORAMA ON COVENT GARDEN'S STAGE
This is one of the greatest developments of the modern theatre. Consisting of an elliptical sheet of some stiff material, it is placed right round the back of the stage ; and on to it the settings are optically projected. The effect is one of great spaciousness. Here you see the cyclorama being used at Covent Garden Opera House, London, for Wagner's opera, Das Rheingold.

ductions in the "little theatres" devoted to repertory include the whole range of dramatic fare, from the old moralities to the latest successes in the metropolitan theatres. New productions are a feature of most established repertory theatres and of the Malvern Festival, inaugurated in 1929 as a tribute to Bernard Shaw. The annual Edinburgh Festival, likewise, holds repertory performances of drama both old and new.

Staging the New Drama

Naturalism, expressionism, impressionism, and all the iconoclastic impulses in the modern mind which these loose terms vaguely convey, had quite as deep an effect upon staging, lighting, costume, scenic decoration, and all aspects of producing as they did upon the play itself. Such changes imply the growth in importance of the director, or *régisseur*. Footlights, and the old Italian notion of the proscenium arch framing the stage like a picture-frame, have been abandoned by many directors in favour of a stage in the midst of the audience, as in a circus, with floodlights, or light reflected from silk screens. In Wilder's Our Town the imagination of the audience supplied scenery, and stage properties—the performers acting on an empty stage and miming the action. Realistic scenery of the Victorian era has given place to permanent abstract settings, to beautiful and spectacular effects that suggest scenes rather than reproduce them realistically.

Experiments in the new stagecraft began shortly before and after 1900. Gordon Craig, an Englishman who worked in Russia and Scandinavia, and Adolphe Appia, an Italian-Swiss in Germany, were famous pioneers, and Max Reinhardt was soon adapting their ideas in his little Kammerspielhaus in Berlin. When his production of The Miracle was seen in London in 1911, English people began to realize that this new style, although a vulgarized

version of Craig's designs, was yet something very different from the "realistic" settings which were the usual background for contemporary plays.

Many European designers went to the United States during Hitler's dictatorship in Germany and Austria, and through their influence the American stage began to occupy a position formerly enjoyed by that of Berlin and Vienna.

The one great change following the First World War (1914–18) was the introduction of the unit-set —not actually a complete innovation, although it had long been forgotten—by which one basic background was used with a few alterations for the different acts. This in itself necessitated greater skill in lighting, which again led to the invention and adoption of the cyclorama, by which the scenic effects were optically projected on to the backcloth; and by 1936 this had become a permanent fixture in the latest theatres. Preceding the cyclorama was the revolving stage, a Japanese invention which reached us from Germany. It was used for the spectacular musical productions which became popular in London in the nineteen-thirties and also found useful for general purposes. In general, however, England, unlike the other homes of the drama, has long suffered from a lack of theatrical designers of great originality. Only in the revival of the ballet (*q.v.*) and a few isolated theatres did many opportunities arise for original and outstanding scenic work. The great advantage of the cinema over the "legitimate" stage, of course, lies in the realistic settings that can be employed. The films have now borrowed much of the "glamour" of the stage and have usurped the latter's general popularity, although the attraction of "flesh and blood" actors is such that it can never be entirely killed. The rapid progress of the Continental, as opposed to the English, stage may be attributed in large measure to the existence of the state-endowed theatre, which made playwright and producer independent of financial success. A beginning was made in England with a state-endowed opera and ballet at Covent Garden in 1945.

Amateur theatricals are very popular, and some notes of how to set about staging a show may prove of interest. First, do not be too ambitious in the choice of your play; bear in mind the limitation of your stage and the experience of your actors. Remember, too, that an audience comes, above all, to be entertained. A great deal depends on the stage-manager, who must be prepared to study the play from every angle. At the first rehearsal the play should be read through without any attempt at " dressing up." From then on every rehearsal should be on the stage, with the details settled as they arise. It is a good plan to devote a rehearsal to each act, or, if it is a short play, to each scene. Do not overlook those taking the smaller parts; these can make or mar the whole performance. At the dress rehearsal, of course, everything should be exactly as on the " first night."

A raised stage is an advantage, but may be ruled out for reasons of expense. In the same way, elaborate footlights, proscenium and scenery are not expected or desirable in amateur shows. A softly-lit stage, adequate curtain, and " wings " enabling the actors to make their entrances from the sides, are all that is wanted.

As for the acting itself, be natural. Come in on your " cues "— that is, at the end of the speeches previous to yours—as one would in real life, and work out appropriate gestures (particularly those with the hands) without appearing stilted or individual. Merge your personality in that of the character you are portraying, and keep to such elementary rules as facing the audience whenever possible, pitching the voice to reach every part of the auditorium. The British Drama League (9, Fitzroy Square, London, W.1) has developed and encouraged the art of the theatre, especially in the field of amateur dramatics.

There is no definite means of entrance to the career of actor, but perhaps the best way of beginning is a course of study at the Royal Academy of Dramatic Art (62, Gower Street, London, W.C.1), to which there are scholarships, and also an entrance test. Many actors have begun as child actors in pantomimes or similar productions, as in the child troupes which Italia Conti trained for so many years. Two London theatres have a school attached to them, viz. the " Old Vic " and Sadler's Wells. Other training schools include the Webber-Douglas, and the Embassy. Probably the majority of actors have " worked their way up " from the chorus or a " walking-on " part, but this is the most crowded and least secure " way in " to the theatre. An alternative is to secure a reputation as an amateur actor with one's local amateur dramatic society, or to enter a repertory company. The prizes both in salary and fame are great, but an actor's early years are usually a bitter struggle.

Draughts. (Pron. drafts). The first crude game of draughts was probably played by the Egyptians as long ago as 1600 B.C. Later the Greeks and Romans enjoyed the game, and more recently there have been French, German, Polish, Dutch, Scottish, and English versions of the game, which is called checkers in the United States.

The game is played with small round pieces of wood or bone, arranged in lines of battle on a square board divided into 64 alternating squares of black and white or black and red. (A chessboard can, of course, be used.)

Two players, using a set of 12 pieces each, direct the contest. The men of one player are coloured white (or red), and of the other black. The object of the game is to capture your opponent's men and remove them from the board.

The forces are drawn up on the first three rows of the black squares, on opposite sides of the board. Each side moves alternately, and the men may only be moved forward diagonally, to the right or left, to the next unoccupied black square. When the adjoining square is occupied by one of the enemy, and the next square in line is vacant, the player may "jump" his man over his opponent's piece to the vacant square, and remove the enemy's man from the board. Sometimes two or more jumps can be made in a single move. When a piece has penetrated to the last or king row of the enemy's line, it becomes a king (indicated by placing another draught on top of it). A king can move either forwards or backwards, but still only on the squares of the colour on which the game is played. When all the men of one side have been captured, or when the remaining men of that side are so blocked by the opposing forces that none of them can be moved without capture, the game is won by the player who has thus outgeneralled the other. Any game that cannot be played to a finish is counted as a draw.

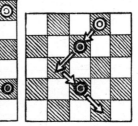

DRAUGHTBOARD PLAY

The diagram on the left shows the arrangement of the men on the draughtboard at the beginning of a game. That on the right shows a white ' man ' taking two of his opponents by jumping over them in the way indicated by the arrows.

Drawing. The first art to fascinate the young mind, drawing is one of the oldest of the arts, for primitive people were remarkably skilful in drawing animals on the walls of their cave-homes (see the examples in colour plate facing page 736). Moreover, drawing is the basis of architecture, sculpture and painting.

The word draw comes from Old English *dragan* meaning drag. So to draw is to drag a pointed instrument, such as a lead pencil, over a smooth surface, and thus leave a significant mark. The caveman no less than a great artist did this. Likewise the engineer, architect, shipbuilder, or tailor makes significant marks on paper. The art of all these

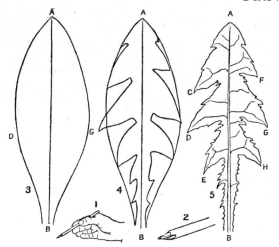

Above, you see : 1, how to hold a pencil, properly sharpened, and not as in 2 ; 3, 4, 5, stages in drawing a leaf (the letters A-H show corresponding points in the three stages). On the right, 1 shows the finished drawing of a crow, the earlier stages of which are seen in 2 and 3. The chief axes are drawn first, then outline and detail are added.

rests on drawing as a building depends on its foundation. Just what the drawing may be—sketch, portrait, plan or design—does not matter. Furthermore, all writing and numbering and musical notation are kinds of drawing. We learn to write by copying letters and drawing them over and over again.

As drawing is generally understood, it means the pictorial records which we make of the things our eyes see and our minds imagine. All artists draw, and afterwards paint upon their drawing as upon a framework or foundation. An architect draws the building he sees in his mind's eye so that masons, carpenters, and iron-workers may know exactly how to erect it.

The artist's kind of drawing is called free-hand, whereas the drawing of the architect and the engineer is known as mechanical. It is important to distinguish clearly between them. Free-hand drawing is done without the help of mechanical contrivances, such as rule, T-square, or compass, but mechanical drawing uses them, for its purpose is not creation or suggestion but exact information.

Free-hand drawing is done either as a preparation for painting or as an end in itself. Drawing which is done for its own sake is the more interesting. In kind, it is the same whether done by the beginner, or by master artists such as the Greek vase painters, or Leonardo da Vinci, Holbein, Raphael, Rembrandt and Albrecht Dürer.

There are two distinct varieties of free-hand drawing: pure outline, and outline

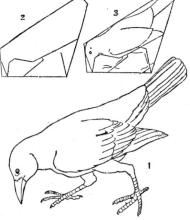

with shade and shadow added. The first never has been a favourite with the greatest artists. To this, the Greek vase painters are noteworthy exceptions. To see a subject in its total mass and various planes—which means the three dimensions, width, height and breadth—and differing degrees of distance, seems to be the almost universal way of master draughtsmen, whether in making the slightest sketch or in the finished picture.

The fact remains that beauty is often found in pure outline drawing. To see a good artist at work, or to understand a good drawing, is to realize that the outline and design are never really separated in the worker's thought. The Italian painter, Raphael (1483–1520), kept his outline pure by not confusing it with light and shade, though he almost never drew without putting them in at an angle to his outline, but not parallel with it. Drawing of this kind may at first seem crude or even careless. However, study of it will soon show that apparent carelessness is in reality expressive of the utmost conscious intention.

The Dutch artist Rembrandt (1606–69), often crossed and recrossed his light and shade lines until they made patches of lighter and darker tone. The edges fixed the shapes of the objects drawn, so that there seems to be nothing in his work which resembles in the least an outline. This leads to the question : What is a line ? What is its place in drawing ?

What do we really see when we look at an object, for example, an apple or a head ? The answer is, only the edge where the object leaves off and its background begins. Certainly we do not see a bounding line. The flesh of the cheek, the brown of the hair, the red and yellow of the apple simply cease, and whatever is behind—the background—begins. The truth is that Nature does not have a line in the sense in which we use the word. Man, in the infancy of the race, invented it just as he invented any other thing, such as language;

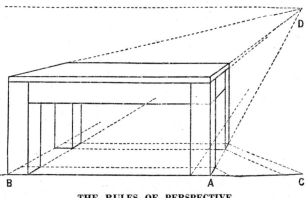

THE RULES OF PERSPECTIVE

To draw objects in three dimensions you must obey the rules of perspective. AB is the length of the table, AC its width, while D, where all the converging lines meet, is called the 'vanishing' point. The dotted lines are drawn first, and the outline constructed on them.

he felt the need to depict the shapes of things, actual or imagined. He wanted recognizable pictures. To make them he had to mark out their shapes from their backgrounds by line, which was a convention—a way, or a means—universally agreed on. There is one excellent rule to be followed in any of the branches of drawing: Take care of the spaces, and the lines will take care of themselves.

By means of foreshortening, an important principle in drawing, it is possible to suggest the actual size of an object when seen from any angle. A common illustration is that of a man with arm upraised shoulder high, pointing directly at you. A moment of careful study of such a picture will show you that the lines representing the arm and the hand are really much shorter than they would be if you saw the arm and the hand placed at right angles across the chest. You will also observe that although there is an actual shrinkage of the lines—that is, they take up less space—yet the actual size of the arm and the hand is accurately suggested to your imagination. This demands considerable technical skill in drawing.

Light and shade may be represented in drawing by a skilful use of lines. This process is called *chiaroscuro*, a union of two Italian words derived from Latin *clarus*, clear, and *obscurus*, obscure. An interesting effect of this technical feature of drawing is the impression that the object or objects are in relief, that is, certain parts seem to be higher than others; thus, the dimension of depth is suggested. Actually, of course, a plane, or flat surface, such as a canvas or a piece of drawing paper, has only two dimensional limits— these being breadth and height.

There is only one way to acquire appreciation of the beautiful art of drawing. Do some drawing yourself, and at all times watch Nature carefully; note her facts and the moods which they create in you. Furthermore, look carefully at all sorts of drawings—newspaper cartoons, illustrations, or famous drawings or copies of them. If we wish to appreciate drawing, we must learn to enjoy lines; to discover delicacy, vigour and beauty in them quite apart from the subject which, taken together, they create. Is a line evenly thick throughout its length? Is it varied for a discernible reason? Is it crumbly to represent weathered brick or stone? Does it flow uninterruptedly to represent the muscles of a man's leg? Does it end by returning on itself like a circus-master's whip, or does it stop in a little swelling like a drop at the

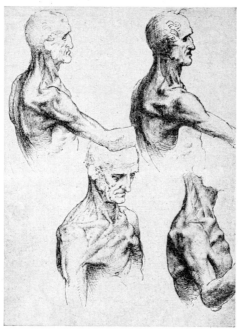

DRAWINGS BY LEONARDO
Like all great artists Leonardo da Vinci (1452-1519) made many studies of his subjects. These four drawings from his pencil are examples not only of his fine draughtsmanship, but of the great knowledge of anatomy which underlay his work.

end of a twig? Has it attributes such as these which make it, in itself, beautiful? Can you distinguish in the drawings of famous artists the characteristic line technique that gives their work much of its distinction, its originality?

The caricaturing of people, of animals, and of events is a special art, which is usually known as cartooning, and the comic strips and similar drawings in newspapers and magazines are called cartoons. Animated cartoons are produced by filming thousands of drawings one after another, producing, when projected on a screen, the effect of an ordinary moving picture. (An older meaning of cartoon is a preliminary drawing.) Caricature consists in the exaggeration of a person's characteristics, or of scenes and events, usually to make them appear ridiculous. It has proved a powerful weapon in politics.

Dredgers. Unless the approaches to our harbours, and the channels of our navigable rivers, were periodically dredged to clear them of the accumulated mud, silt and sand, they would soon become impassable to ships. Dredging is done by specially built vessels equipped with powerful machinery for digging out or sucking up the under-water soil and delivering it into hopper-boats which dump it where it can do no harm.

In some such dredgers the machines are not unlike those used for excavators (*q.v.*), comprising a big shovel or a grab let down into the water underneath the vessel, swept along to scour out the soil, and hoisted up to discharge into the hopper. The bucket or grab is fixed to the end of a dipping boom, which is lowered or hoisted by a derrick or some other type of crane. A cable draws the bucket forward into the material to be raised.

The grab looks like a gigantic clam-shell, with two scoop-like halves pivoted at the top; it is lowered, with jaws open, into the soil, rock, or other material and the two halves are then closed in on the material. Next, the grab is hoisted and brought over the hopper, where it opens its jaws again and discharges its load.

The bucket-ladder dredger comprises a long, ladder-like beam over which runs an endless chain to which digging buckets are attached. The beam works in a central opening in the vessel, which thus consists, for most of its rear part, of two portions separated by the central well. The beam is lowered until its buckets enter the soil to be lifted; the power is turned on, and the endless chain of buckets is set moving. The soil is discharged into

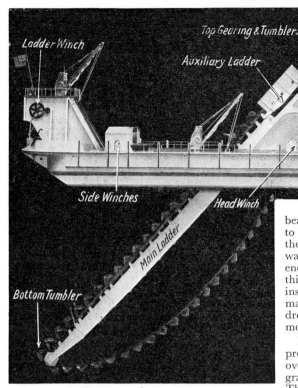

DREDGER'S MAIN MACHINERY
To keep clear the entrances of harbours and to deepen the water where docks are to be built dredgers are employed. Here is a model, showing the endless chain of buckets which lifts mud and sand for emptying into a hopper barge.

a hopper on the fore part of the vessel, whence it is delivered by chutes to a hopper-boat.

Where the soil is of a nature to be loosened and lifted as a watery mixture by suction, a suction-dredger can be employed. Instead of the ladder-

beam this lets down a big tube through the well to the bottom of the water; very powerful pumps then suck up the mud or sand. A strong jet of water is directed by rotating nozzles at the lower end of the suction tube to loosen the material; this jet is forced out of a separate pipe running inside the suction tube. Again, the dredged material is discharged first into a hopper on the dredger, and led by other chutes to the hopper-boat moored alongside.

For canal work a special type of dredger is used, provided with a long beam which can reach out over the canal bank and thus allow a bucket or grab to dump its load at the side of the waterway. The beam is supported by a floating platform moored between dredger and bank. A similar arrangement is used for a suction dredger, the delivery tube being taken out to one side on supports.

Another class of dredger is used for excavating mineral ores found in the alluvial deposits in rivers, or lakes. Examples are the gold dredgers of California, and the tin dredgers which dig out gravel from the bed of lakes in Malaya. Such ore deposits are the result of the natural breaking up of rock in long-past ages, and its carriage to its present

DREDGING FOR GOLD IN CALIFORNIA

Associated Press

Where gravel containing the ore is under water, dredgers are used to bring it to the surface. This one, part of a fleet of similar vessels, is in action in the Sacramento Valley in California. At the left, endless chains of buckets scoop up the gold-bearing gravel from the bed of a stream. At the right is a mound of spent gravel from which the precious metal has been removed. Vast amounts of gravel must sometimes be brought up to obtain even a small amount of gold.

sites by the swift-flowing current of rivers. This class of dredger is a floating metallurgical plant rather than a " vessel," and some of the separating and concentrating processes are carried out on the ore on board. Both bucket and suction types of dredger are employed. (*See* Excavator).

Dresden. Although primarily a commercial and industrial town—because of its position at the centre of a network of railways giving access to Austria, Czechoslovakia and all parts of Germany, and because of its trade on the river Elbe—yet Dresden, the capital of Saxony in Germany, was perhaps best known for its magnificent art treasures, libraries, and scientific collections, and for the manufacture of Dresden china at Meissen, a suburb. Its art gallery, called the Zwinger, built in 1711–22, was one of the finest of its size in the world.

With a history going back to the beginning of the 13th century, Dresden had been unusually free from war and devastation—save for a bombardment during the Seven Years' War (1756–63) and some damage done during the period in which it was Napoleon's centre of operations in 1813—until the Second World War (1939–45). The city was heavily bombed by Allied aircraft in February 1945, and six square miles of the inner part were laid in ruins. Many notable buildings were destroyed or severely damaged, amongst them being the Church of Our Lady, the former Royal Palace, the Opera House and the Zwinger Gallery. The population is about 454,000.

Drugs. The word drug is somewhat loosely used to describe any substance which has a definite effect on the body of Man or animals. Drugs fall into types according to this effect, and each of the animal, vegetable, and mineral worlds has contributed large groups. " Anodyne " describes a drug which eases pain; such are aspirin, phenacetin and, above all, morphia. Morphia is one of the most valuable drugs in the world, when it is remembered how much agony it has relieved. Aspirin and phenacetin, although they were originally prepared from the willow tree, are now manufactured at the laboratory bench, a by-product of coal-tar; while morphia is one of the active principles in opium which is got from poppy heads. Cocaine is another pain-easing drug.

Another great sub-division is the " hypnotic," which induce sleep. Of these, chloral and phenobarbitone are well-known examples. The pace and fret of modern life tend to sleeplessness, perhaps from over-fatigue of the brain, and the great manufacturing chemists have produced many substances of this class which ensure a good night with but little, if any, reaction next morning. The constant use of these hypnotics, however, is unwise as they tend eventually to spoil memory, concentration and attack. Anaesthetics comprise chloroform, ether and the like, quietening the brain cells so that the patient does not register pain. Their discovery and use are numbered among the real triumphs of modern medicine.

Some drugs are a definite antidote to a condition; one might instance quinine for malaria. Legend has it that long ago in an eastern jungle natives with malaria were left to die, with water in the great leaves of the cinchona tree placed beside them. Lapping the water, they recovered—because of the quinine it contained. Much medical material has been discovered like this ; " empirical " is the word used to describe such an observation made without proof, but found to be true. Colchicum, the principle in the bulb of the autumn crocus, is another such example. It is still our only cure for gout, we know not how or why. Digitalis, product of the foxglove, is still our best remedy for a weak heart. It, too, was the finding of " folk medicine " —of simple, undistracted minds blundering on to facts. Among modern drugs penicillin and the sulpha group spring to the mind, with streptomycin close on their heels. Between them they have revolutionised our treatment of wounds, boils and the like, pneumonia, some kinds of tuberculosis, and other diseases.

The term drug is used in a more narrow sense to describe a habit-forming medicine—i.e., a drug which when used a certain number of times causes the victim to long for more. The most common of these is alcohol, which is not a stimulant, as is commonly supposed, but a depressant. It acts by putting out of action the delicate brain cells which control finer judgement. These are the last to be developed and the easiest to disturb. Cocaine and morphia are the two chief habit-forming drugs, cocaine being much the quicker to enslave, and therefore the more dangerous on that account. Owing to their pernicious effect when used unwisely and without skilled prescription, drugs of this last-mentioned group are strictly controlled by law. (*See* Anaesthesia ; Antiseptics).

Druids. When the Romans conquered Gaul and Britain some 1,900 years ago, they found that the Celtic inhabitants were under the dominance of priests called Druids.

Little is known of the Druids, because they did not allow any of their lore to be written, but transmitted it all by word of mouth. Caesar records that the Druids of Gaul were judges as well as priests, sometimes sacrificing criminals to their gods. Britain was the headquarters of Druidism, although a general assembly of Druids was held in Gaul every year. The last serious stand of the Druids in Britain was made at Mona (Anglesey) in A.D. 61, when, according to Tacitus, the Romans under Suetonius Paulinus almost exterminated them and destroyed their sacred groves; the Roman general Agricola came into collision with them later in Anglesey, in 78. After being destroyed in Britain Druids were mainly heard of in Ireland, where tradition associates them with witchcraft and sorcery.

The Druids taught that the soul was immortal, passing after death from one person to another. The course of training was very long, sometimes lasting more than 20 years. The Druids were not a hereditary caste, and because members did not have to fight or pay taxes membership was highly prized. The Druids deemed the mistletoe sacred, and they usually held their strange rites in the heart of an oak forest. Anything that grew on the oak, especially the mistletoe, was looked upon as a gift from Heaven.

Wise in the lore of plants, animals and stars, they were magicians and astrologers of a sort. After the coming of the Romans their power declined. The many ancient stone monuments, circles, and dolmens scattered over the land they occupied were formerly ascribed to the Druids, but scientists now believe these to be even older.

Drum. A drum may have been the first musical instrument made by primitive Man, though some claim this distinction for the flute. Among savage tribes drums were, and still are, used on every occasion. They called the tribe together for battle, they beat the time for the dancers and the singers, and they played an important part in religious ceremonies. Among the ancient civilized nations we find several kinds of drum. The Egyptians used a small hand-drum; the Chinese had a large drum very much like our bass drum; and the Hebrews' favourite drum seems to have been a sort of tambourine.

The many shapes and sizes of drums, no matter where found, fall into three classes : first, those made of a single skin stretched over a frame which is open at the bottom, like the tambourine; second, a single skin on a closed vessel, like the kettle-drum; third, two skins, one at each end of a cylinder, like the bass drum.

Kettle-drums, or timpani, are the most important in a modern orchestra. Vellum, or calf-skin, is stretched over a hollow hemisphere of metal and held in place by a ring, which can be tightened or loosened by means of screws, thus making the pitch higher or lower. Kettle-drums were formerly played in pairs: one tuned to sound the " doh " of the scale, and one to sound the " soh," but often three or more are used in modern music. Three kinds of drumsticks are used: one with sponge tips for soft strokes, one with leather tips for medium, one with wooden tips for loud tones.

The bass drum and the snare, or side, drum do not produce sounds of any definite pitch. The

P. A. McCann

DRUMS OF THE JUNGLE

Some African Negroes play drums of various shapes and sizes made from skin stretched over a hollowed-out piece of wood, such as seen here with drummers of a West African king. Besides being beaten at dances drums are used for sending messages.

booming thud of the big drum is chiefly employed to mark rhythm or emphasize climaxes. The snare drum, so called because catgut strings or snares are stretched across the head to make the sound more brilliant, finds its chief use in military bands. In the orchestra it serves to emphasize crescendo passages. The tenor drum, midway between bass and side-drums, has no snares.

Messrs. Hawkes & Son

DRUMS OF DIFFERENT KINDS FOR BAND AND ORCHESTRA

In brass bands, military or civilian, drums play an important part. They are also used in large string orchestras. The five types shown here are (1) a Guards pattern side-drum, also used by other regiments ; on it are painted the regimental badge and the principal battle honours ; (2) a metal side-drum played in ordinary orchestras, showing the key used to tighten or loosen the vellum or calf-skin ; (3) cavalry kettle-drums, which are slung across the drummer's horse ; (4) an army regulation side-drum, made of wood ; (5) bass drum of the Grenadier Guards.

Dryden, JOHN (1631–1700). A mighty figure in English literature, Dryden stands out as a great critic, a great prose-writer, a great poet, and a great satirist. He became the literary dictator of his day. Even when old age had visited him with poverty, and his Roman Catholicism and political antipathies had earned him the disfavour of the government, he was unpersecuted and treated with respect. If not quite reaching the stature of Dr. Johnson in personality, he was the revered veteran of his profession.

Dryden taught that correctness, polish, and elegance, rather than originality, imagination and feeling, were the essentials of good poetry. He chose the regular heroic couplet as " fittest for discourse, and nearest prose." His age was an age of prose, and, although he exerted a great influence on the poetry of his own period and the one which followed, his most permanent influence in English literature has been rather in prose. Indeed, modern English prose style really begins with Dryden. Many of his lines are now used in everyday speech, as for example :

> None but the brave deserves the fair.
> Men are but children of a larger growth.
> Few know the use of life before 'tis past.
> Great wits are sure to madness near allied.
> Sweet is pleasure after pain.

Born in the village of Aldwinkle in Northamptonshire on August 9, 1631, he came of Puritan stock. His first important poem was an elegy on the death of the Puritan leader Cromwell, but he turned Royalist and welcomed King Charles II in 1660 with another poem, Astraea Redux. Later, he changed to the Roman Catholic faith, which he defended in an allegorical poem, The Hind and the Panther.

For a long time Dryden wrote only plays—bombastic, heroic tragedies and comedies which reflected the low moral tone of the day. He also wrote several personal and political satires, of which Absalom and Achitophel is the most powerful in English literature. He made translations from the Greek and Latin classics, notably of Virgil, and wrote a number of critical essays in the form of prefaces to other works. His odes, Alexander's Feast, Ode for St. Cecilia's Day, and Ode to the Memory of Anne Killigrew, are famous. He was Poet Laureate from 1670 to 1689. Just before his death, which occurred on May 1, 1700, he published his most engaging narrative poems, Fables, Ancient and Modern. In these poems he retold stories from Homer, Ovid, Chaucer, and Boccaccio. He was buried in Westminster Abbey.

Dublin. The largest city in Ireland and the capital of Eire is situated on Dublin Bay at the mouth of the River Liffey, on the east coast of Ireland. Dublin is the centre of Eire's Government and of the social and intellectual life of the country. On the north side of the Liffey are the huge, semicircular Bank of Ireland, the Irish Parliament House until the Act of Union with Great Britain in 1800, and the large group of buildings comprising Trinity College, Dublin's famous university founded in 1591. There is also the National University of Ireland. The best residential section, with fine squares and terraces, comprises much of the eastern half of the city.

Among the historic buildings the chief is Dublin Castle, originally built in the 13th century, and before the establishment of the Irish Free State in 1921 the headquarters of the British Government in Ireland. The Custom House, and the Four Courts, two fine buildings, were both damaged during the rebellion against the British in 1916. The Protestants have two cathedrals, St. Patrick's and Christchurch—the former associated with the British writer Jonathan Swift (1667–1745) who was its Dean—and the Roman Catholics have one. Other imposing buildings are the City Hall, the National Gallery, the science and art museum, and the national library. There is also the Abbey Theatre, headquarters of the national drama. Of the magnificent 18th century houses, Leinster House is now used for the Dail (Parliament), and Charlemont House for the gallery of modern art. Phoenix Park, nearly three square miles in extent, is the largest of the city's open spaces, and in the heart of the city itself is St. Stephen's Green (22 acres).

Dublin is not a city of great manufacturing activity, brewing, distilling, tobacco and biscuit manufactures

JOHN DRYDEN
Undoubtedly the greatest literary figure of his day, Dryden was a critic, poet, satirist and a writer of polished prose. He wrote a number of plays, but had no real gift for dramatic composition. This portrait of him by Sir Godfrey Kneller (1646-1723) is in the National Portrait Gallery, London.

Irish Tourist Association

DUBLIN'S MOST FAMOUS THOROUGHFARE

O'Connell Street, formerly known as Sackville Street, is the most famous thoroughfare in Dublin. Irishmen claim it to be among the six finest streets in Europe. Badly damaged in 1916 during the Irish rebellion against the British, it was rebuilt and renamed in honour of Daniel O'Connell, an Irish patriot who died in 1847. On the left of this photograph the columns are the front of the General Post Office. In the middle of the road is Nelson's Pillar.

being the chief industries. There is normally a large export trade in provisions and live-stock. It has been said that its most important exports are whisky, porter and playwrights. Since the rise of the Irish drama in the 20th century, many Dublin-born dramatists have become world famous, the foremost among these being Bernard Shaw, J. M. Synge, Sean O'Casey, W. B. Yeats and Denis Johnston.

In Easter week, 1916, there was a rising in Dublin. An Irish republic was proclaimed and a provisional government appointed ; but the insurgents were overcome after a good deal of damage had been done. There was again fighting in the city in April 1922, between the troops of the Irish Free State and Irish Republican irregulars. The population of the city of Dublin is 468,000.

Duck. Nature has been very good in clothing the ducks, for in addition to the closely packed outer feathers, they are provided with thick body-down that protects them from both wet and cold.

The webbed feet are set in the best position for swimming but not for walking ; that is why the duck has such an awkward waddle. Wild duck feed on insects, small water-creatures, grass, roots and seeds. They usually nest in undergrowth or in marshy ground, sometimes in trees. In the last case, when ready to leave the nest, the young birds are encouraged to " parachute " to the ground, and then in a family party are led to the water ; or the duck may carry them down, one by one, on her back. During the period when the dull-

coloured duck is breeding, the drake's (male bird's) plumage is also inconspicuous.

Numerous wild species of duck are found in all parts of the world, except the Antarctic continent, and they embrace forms adapted to all types of aquatic life. There are sea-going ducks, the structure of whose feet differs from that of pond ducks, which again are divided into surface ducks and diving ducks. The mallard (*Anas boschas*) as the common wild duck is frequently called (although the name is strictly applied to the drake only), is a surface duck, feeding by tipping itself up on end with head and neck under water and its tail in the air. This species is abundant over most of the Northern Hemisphere, and from time immemorial has furnished mankind with appetizing food. During the winter and spring the drake wears a head-dress of glossy green with purple lights ; his back is greyish-brown ; his wings, of the same colour, are banded with greenish-purple and white. The under-feathers are a lighter brown-grey. During the summer his dress is dusky-brown, like his mate's.

Other British ducks are the teal (*Anas crecca*), smallest of the family but one of the fastest in flight ; and the shoveller (*Spatula clypeata*), a species with a clumsy-looking, flattened bill round the edge of which are fringed bristles, which serve to sift its food from the mud.

The widgeon (*Anas penelope*) is another species of which numbers come to Britain from the far

B. Hanley; W. S. Berridge; A. R. Thompson; A. Brook

SOME DUCKS TO BE SEEN ON BRITISH LAKES AND RIVERS

Here are some of the very attractive ducks you may come across, chiefly in winter when their numbers are augmented by migrants from the north. At the top left is the pintail, with long, delicate tail feathers. At the top right is the tufted duck, a diver that breeds freely in London parks. At the lower left is the teal, one of the smallest and most handsome members of its family. At the lower right is the merganser, with a longer, more delicate bill than most.

north in winter. It may be known by its rich chestnut head with a buff crown and the broad white patch on its wings. The call of this bird is not a quack but a whistle. The tufted duck and the pochard are common divers, the tufted duck being frequently seen in the London parks.

Pintail is the name of another British species, and is aptly descriptive of the drake, for his two central tail feathers are very long and pointed ; they combine with a long neck and higher, squarer head than usual to give the bird a rather characteristic appearance.

Among the sea-ducks are various species of scoter, often seen off our shores in winter, as well as the eider, and, in North America, the canvas-back (*Nyroca vallisneria*). The name canvas-back was given because the greyish feathers of its back and sides are so compact as to resemble coarse canvas. Other sea-ducks of our British coast are the scaup duck and the sheldrake, of which the latter alone is a common breeding species. Where

there are sand-dunes it burrows for a nest—hence the sheldrake's other name of burrow-duck; it is a handsome bird and large for a duck.

The eider ducks (*Somateria mollissima*) are native to both northern Europe and North America. Their value lies in the down and the eggs they furnish. The duck pulls down from her breast and with it makes a padded " blanket " that completely covers the nest. Upon removal of the down and eggs she repeats the process, including the laying of more eggs. If the down-gatherers again empty the nest, it is said that the drake denudes his breast so that the nest may once again be properly fitted out with its soft blanket.

The domestic ducks of Europe and North America are descended from mallard stock. The White Aylesbury and White Pekin are Chinese ducks. There are, of course, numerous species maintained on lakes and ponds, such as the lovely harlequin ducks; and others are numbered among our winter visitors. The mergansers

MANDARIN DRAKE AND HIS DUN-COLOURED MATE

The mandarin duck is found in Eastern Asia, and the drake of this species is especially remarkable for its brilliantly-tinted plumes. One of the rear feathers on each side is turned upwards to form a fan upon the back, bright brown and purple in colour; and these same two colours are repeated on the mandarin's neck and breast. But the duck beside him is a dull brown bird.

A. Brock

The common wild duck, such as you see above, is often called the mallard, though this name is properly applied only to the drake of the species. The birds here are either females or young males, probably in winter dress; by next spring the young drakes will be as finely plumaged as their own father with lovely greys and greens. But the females, as is usual wi members of their tribe—an example is the mandarin duck se overleaf—retain their somewhat sombre colours throughout li

and goosanders are a small group of fish-eating ducks, the beak, which is long and comparatively slender, being equipped with indentations on the inside to enable the ducks to grip their victims. They have striking and beautiful plumage—both sexes being usually crested ; and they are chiefly winter visitors to Britain. All the ducks, with the geese and swans, comprise the order *Anseres*.

Duckbill. It has a beak like a duck, hair like a cat, and a tail like a beaver. It has four legs and webbed feet. It lives both on land and in the water, lays eggs and hatches them like a bird, but

W. S. Berridge
DUCK : AN EIDER DRAKE
Except for the breast, which is a pinkish-yellow, the plumage of the eider drake (above) is black and white. The female is not nearly so distinguished, being mainly dull brown.

feeds its young with milk! This creature, which is also called the duck-billed platypus and is perhaps the strangest of all living things, is found only along the streams of south-eastern Australia and of the island of Tasmania. It is a good swimmer, diving to the muddy bottoms in search of water insects and worms which it roots out with its bill, but moves awkwardly on land.

Its den, built far back in the bank of a stream, usually has two openings, one under water, the other concealed by weeds above the surface. There the female builds her nest and hatches her eggs, usually two in number, and there she nurses her young. The young first develop teeth, but these soon fall out to make way for the tough, horny plates with which the adult chews its food. The male duckbill has on its hind feet grooved spurs connected by long tubes with poison glands situated near the thighs. The poison closely resembles snake venom, but appears to be seldom used. The voice of these curious animals is like the growl of an angry puppy; but they are exceptionally timid, rarely showing more than their nostrils above the water.

A land-dwelling relative of the duckbill (*Ornithorhynchus anatinus*) is the *Echidna*, or spiny ant-eater, several species of which are natives of the Australian region. This creature has quills like a porcupine and a long, slim beak. It also lays eggs and nurses its young, but the eggs are incubated in a pouch on the underside of the mother's body.

The duckbill and the spiny ant-eater are grouped in a special division, the *Monotremata*, and are looked upon by scientists as modern survivals of ancient forms of life, produced while Nature was evolving the mammals, the birds and the reptiles of today from the simple primitive animal types which existed millions of years ago.

That these creatures should be found only in the Australian region is explained by the fact that these lands became separated from their neighbours early in the history of mammals.

Dumas, ALEXANDRE (1802-70). Nearly every critic who has written of this French novelist and dramatist has qualified his praise. One says that Dumas's novels are " outside literature "; another that his writings are careless; yet they all agree that for charm, movement, clever dialogue and brilliance of style he is unsurpassed.

Alexandre Dumas (pron. dū-mah) was born on July 24, 1802, at Villers-Cotterets, a town 50 miles from Paris. His pictures reveal a smiling face surrounded by a mop of black hair; his lips are

thick, showing his likeness to his grandmother, who was a Negress. His schooling was not of much consequence, and after his family had procured for him a humble government position in Paris he overcame his lack of knowledge by means of wide reading.

His first great success was a play called The Court of Henry III, produced in 1829. Perhaps the greatest work he ever wrote is the novel The Count of Monte Cristo, 1844-45. The astonishing thing about Dumas's work is its bulk. He told Napoleon he had written 1,200 volumes. The

E.N.A.; Dorien Leigh
DUCKBILL : A WEB-FOOTED ANIMAL
One of the queerest of living creatures, the duckbill or duckbilled platypus (above) is a very primitive type of animal found only in south-east Australia and on the island of Tasmania. At the right, one is sitting on its nest built at the end of a tunnel in the bank of a stream.

number cannot be much smaller, and clearly could not have been produced without considerable help; no single writer could produce that amount of manuscript. Dumas employed various assistants, who provided him with skeleton romances on plans he himself had drawn up, and he then proceeded to rewrite the whole thing. Nor did Dumas always hunt for fresh material; he often borrowed from Shakespeare or anyone else he fancied. He defended his method by saying that " the man of genius takes his material where he finds it, and he doesn't steal but conquers."

Naturally, the scores of novels which he produced were uneven. Undoubtedly one of the best is The Three Musketeers, with its two sequels, Twenty Years After and The Vicomte de Bragelonne. In this series he follows the fortunes of D'Artagnan, a Gascon soldier, and those of Aramis, Porthos, and

THE TWO DUMAS—FATHER AND SON

These two photographs show a father and son both famous in French literature. On the left is Alexandre Dumas, novelist and dramatist, whose remarkable romances have caused him to be recognized as one of the greatest narrative writers in the history of literature. On the right is his son, Alexandre Dumas, the younger, who was the author of a number of plays.

Athos, D'Artagnan's three faithful friends. In addition to the books mentioned perhaps the most familiar of the novels of the elder Dumas, at least to English readers, are The Queen's Necklace, Taking the Bastille, Chicot the Jester, and The Black Tulip.

Dumas's personal history was a stormy one. Intrigues, politics, debts, great wealth, exile, and honours followed in rapid succession. He died at Dieppe on December 5, 1870.

His son, Alexandre (1824-1895), achieved a place in literature chiefly as a dramatist. His tremendous power of emotional characterization swept his audiences off their feet. His plays contain lively and brilliantly witty dialogue, combined with intensely dramatic situations, and he was singularly fortunate in his interpreters. La Dame aux Camélias (The Lady of the Camellias), his best-known play, was long the favourite role of the great French actress Sarah Bernhardt. After his plays his most impressive achievement was the publication of two political pamphlets, Nouvelle Lettre de Junius, and Lettres sur les choses du jour.

Dumbartonshire. Few counties in the whole of Scotland can compare with Dumbartonshire for beauty and variety of scenery. Not only is it bounded by Loch Lomond, the " queen of Scottish lakes," which is 23 miles long and five miles broad, but it has also two of the finest sea-lochs on the west coast of the country, and beautiful mountains, glens, and woodlands.

The sea-lochs are Loch Long and Gare Loch, both offshoots of the estuary of the river Clyde, which traces the county's southern boundary. Loch Long, 17 miles in length, separates the county from Argyllshire, and with Gare Loch, eight miles in length, forms the peninsula of Roseneath. The rivers, except the Clyde, are all small, the largest being the Leven and Kelvin. The Leven is noted for its salmon fishing. The highest mountain is Ben Vorlich (3,092 feet), in the extreme north.

The southern portion of the county is given over to agriculture. Cattle and sheep rearing, engineering and ship-building are important industries; cotton goods, glassware and machinery are manufactured; there are bleachfields and dye-works. Coal, iron and slate are the principal minerals.

The county town, Dumbarton (population 22,000) stands on the Leven near its junction with the Clyde estuary. Near Renton was born Smollett (1721-71), the novelist. The area of the county is 246 square miles, and the population 159,000.

Dumfriesshire. Separated from Clydesdale and Teviotdale by a natural barrier formed by the Southern Uplands and the Cheviot Hills, this southern county of Scotland has many memories of the Scottish king, Robert Bruce (1274-1329) and the poet, Robert Burns (1759-96), and of the Border wars and the risings of the Jacobites (supporters of the right of James II and his descendants to the throne of Great Britain) in 1715 and 1745.

Covering an area of 1,072 square miles, Dumfriesshire has a somewhat barren and undulating surface, becoming mountainous in the north and north-east, the highest summits being White Coomb, 2,695 feet, and Hart Fell, 2,651 feet, both on the Peeblesshire border. The Annan, Esk and Nith, three picturesque rivers well stocked with salmon and trout, flow into the Solway Firth. The chief lakes are Lochs Skene and Urr.

About one-third of the area is under cultivation, and large numbers of sheep and cattle are reared. Salmon and trout fisheries are important. Minerals found include coal, limestone and lead.

Keystone

DUNDEE BESIDE THE FIRTH OF TAY

Lying on the north bank of the Firth of Tay in the county of Angus, Dundee is situated at the point where the river is spanned by the Tay bridge (above). This structure carries the double-track main railway line and is more than two miles long. It was opened in 1887 to replace an earlier bridge which had been blown down in a great storm in 1879 while a train was crossing it. The city has some of the most extensive hemp and flax factories in the world, and is noted for its marmalade. Dundee is also a considerable port, the harbour extending for about two miles along the river.

Dumfries, the county town (population, 25,000) manufactures tweeds and hosiery, and here Burns, the great Scottish poet, is buried. Ecclefechan was the birthplace of the historian Thomas Carlyle (1795-1881). Moffat is noted for its medicinal springs. Near the Cumberland border is Gretna Green, once famous as the scene of runaway marriages. The estimated population is 82,000.

Dundee. Fourth largest city of Scotland, Dundee is in the county of Angus, on the North shore of the Firth of Tay, which is spanned by the 3,593 yards long Tay bridge (*see* picture above). The city is the centre of the Scottish jute industry.

Other industries include engineering, shipbuilding, dyeing and fruit preserving. The harbour extends for two miles along the river, with a dock area of 38 acres. The population is 162,000.

Dunkirk. Standing on the Strait of Dover close to the Belgian frontier, Dunkirk is one of the chief ports of France. Normally it exports the coal of Belgium and north-east France, and the manufactures of the adjacent industrial region. Shipbuilding is carried on; other industries include the manufacture of machinery, soap and shipping accessories. There are oil refineries, saw mills and flour mills. A cross-channel train ferry service connects Dunkirk with Dover.

In March 1947 a 50-year treaty between France and Great Britain was signed at Dunkirk, binding those two countries in alliance for mutual protection against German aggression.

Dunkirk (French, *Dunkerque*) owes its name to the fact that it was founded in the 7th century as a small settlement around a church on the sand dunes, *Dunkerque* meaning Dunechurch. Taken and retaken by Spain and France in turn, the town was in English hands from 1658 to 1662, when it again became French. During the First World War (1914–18) it suffered severe damage from Germans bombs and shells.

After the withdrawal of the British Expeditionary Force from Dunkirk in 1940 during the Second World War (1939–45) the port was occupied by the Germans and was frequently bombed by the Allied air forces. In September 1944 the rapid British and Canadian advance across France and Belgium isolated the German garrison, which held out until May 11, 1945. The port was reopened in August 1946.

DUNKIRK ON THE STRAIT OF DOVER

One of the chief French ports in normal times, Dunkirk suffered severely during the Second World War (1939–45), as can be seen from this photograph taken in 1946. The port was occupied by Germans in June 1940 and was frequently bombed by Allied aircraft.

DELIVERANCE *achieved by* VALOUR

During the Second World War many thousands of men of the British Expeditionary Force, and Allied troops, were withdrawn from battle in France—to re-form and re-arm in England. Here we outline those tremendous days.

Dunkirk, EVACUATION OF. The fleet that began to assemble off Dunkirk, in those last days of May 1940, must surely have been the strangest, most motley gathering of craft that a British admiral ever commanded. There were destroyers, cargo boats, fishing boats, yachts, motor-boats, even pleasure-boats from the Thames. For the call had gone out that every small craft was needed urgently. From every port and seaside town along the east and south-east coasts of England, from the London docks, Hull and Lowestoft, Burnham-on-Crouch (the Essex yachting centre) and the Norfolk Broads, the astonishing flotilla set out across the North Sea under a clear blue sky to face the German guns and bombers off the flat, sandy coasts of Belgium and Northern France.

The task of this extraordinary gathering, which the Royal Navy's Dover Command controlled, was nothing less than to evacuate the British Expeditionary Force, which with its French and Belgian allies was being desperately hard pressed by the numerically superior German armies.

Armoured Divisions Broke Through

Let us look back at the course of the fighting from the Germans' invasion of the Netherlands and Belgium on May 10, 1940. It early became clear that the German strength had been sadly underestimated by the Allies. While German forces pressed down from the North, their armoured divisions broke through the French line just north of the Maginot Line and drove a wedge between the two halves of the Allied force, one defending Paris and the Channel ports, the other withstanding the onslaught in Flanders.

The British Commander-in-Chief Lord Gort and the French General Weygand tried desperately to join up the two halves of their forces; but the task became hourly more hopeless. The Germans seized Boulogne, then Calais, despite the stubborn defence of the British troops there; and by May 25 the B.E.F. (British Expeditionary Force) was isolated in a roughly triangular area, its apex at Douai, its base along the coast from near Gravelines in France to Nieuport in Belgium. The apex was held by the French 1st Army, the flanks by the British; and at the north-east corner the gallant remnants of the heavily-hit Belgian army still held a 20-mile sector. The only British armoured division was outside this isolated area.

By May 26 it was realized that this triangle was too large to be held by the force within it. Plans had to be made to reduce it, to defend a perimeter that could be manned adequately by the troops available. The possibility of a retreat, and indeed of something worse, was fully understood by the British Government. On the morning of May 26 the Secretary of State for War (Mr. Anthony Eden) sent a telegram to General Gort making this clear, and including these words :

" . . . in such conditions, only course open to you may be to fight your way back to West, where all beaches and ports east of Gravelines will be used for embarkation. Navy will provide fleet of ships and small boats, and R.A.F. will give full support." In other words, it might be necessary to evacuate the Continent, leaving the Germans victorious on the battlefield.

Any chance that remained of saving the situation, of beating off the German attacks, joining the severed halves of the Allied armies, and holding at any rate the greater part of France, vanished when, at midnight on May 27-28, the Belgians laid down their arms. The British Commander-in-Chief had no more than an hour in which to man a 20-mile gap in his line against the German armoured forces advancing on Nieuport. The 4th Division and a force of men of the Royal Navy were rushed into the gap and, fighting desperately, held up the German attack. Had the Germans broken through and advanced along the coast, there would have been an end of the plan to evacuate the B.E.F.

General Gort proposed to withdraw his forces into a bridge-head some 15 miles long and less than 10 miles deep, stretching along the coast from a point between Gravelines and Dunkirk as far as Nieuport. The western end was to be held by the French, the centre and eastern end by the British, with a strength of three corps. Once within the perimeter they would destroy bridges and blow up dikes to inundate the surrounding country.

Hard-pressed and Exhausted Troops

On May 27 the British began to retire from their positions. At first the French commander had refused to take part in the operation, saying his troops were exhausted. Only a personal appeal by Lord Gort won him over; and it then became necessary to arrange for the French to be evacuated as well as the British. This the British Government agreed to.

The only quays or piers available for ships of any size were those in Dunkirk itself. Most of the troops proceeded to the flat, sandy beaches at La Panne, Bray Dunes, and Malo-les-Bains. One beach was allotted to each corps, and one to the French. General Headquarters was established at La Panne.

The troops that began to pour into the bridge-head were utterly exhausted. They had had to fight every inch of the way and to march long stretches, for the streets of Dunkirk would have been swamped by all their transport. The roads leading to the coast presented an astonishing sight: on the verges and in the fields that flanked them lay every kind of British vehicle, disabled and abandoned, while the roadsides were littered with broken wooden cases, gas-capes and all sorts of small military stores.

The Germans harassed the withdrawal unceasingly with artillery fire and air bombing. The dive-bomber was then still a new weapon, and a terrifying one. By May 28 Lieutenant-General Sir Ronald Adam, whom General Gort had taken

THE EVACUATION FROM DUNKIRK : A STIRRING EPISODE IN BRITAIN'S HISTORY

No greater test of stubborn courage and iron discipline can be imagined than the long wait under fire and bombing on Dunkirk beaches, while an improvised armada of little ships and big ships took on board some 330,000 British and French troops who had fought their way back to the sea. This painting by Charles Cundall, A.R.A., portrays one phase of this grim operation, which lasted from May 26 to June 2, 1940.

To face page 1056

British Official

HOMEWARD BOUND
FROM DUNKIRK

UNDAUNTED by their grim ordeal on the shell-torn beaches of Dunkirk, these men of the British Expeditionary Force crowd to the rail of the transport which is taking them to Britain, for a final glimpse of the French coast smothered under the smoke of war. They represent but a handful of the hundreds of thousands who were rescued from death or imprisonment, and brought home for re-equipping and re-arming—the nucleus of Britain's new armies which, four years later, won decisive victories which led to peace.

To face page 1057

from the command of 1st Corps to organize the embarkation, reported that the docks were virtually unusable. The inner harbour was blocked for ships of any size, and few of the seriously wounded could be taken off. The naval plan had not yet come into operation—and there were 20,000 men waiting to be embarked. Dunkirk itself was in flames. There was no water in the town, and little on the beaches.

By May 28 the perimeter had been manned, mostly by artillery. Two days later the last weary infantry had stumbled in, the bridges were blown, the dikes breached, and the perimeter was closed. The naval plan began to function on May 29, and the incredible assembly of little ships appeared off the coast. Shelled, bombed, and machine-gunned without rest, the British soldiers waited patiently, courageously, and good-humouredly on the beaches for their turn to embark. They stood in lines on the sand and up to their waists in the sea until the boats came to take them off. There was no panic, no fighting for places; it was, as one observer described it, " as orderly as a bus queue." First 3rd Corps went, then 2nd Corps, then 1st Corps. By midnight on May 30-31, some 80,000 of the British troops within the bridge-head had been evacuated.

It seemed that the German dive-bombers had the sky to themselves. But the R.A.F. was there— deep inland striving to beat off the Luftwaffe formations before they reached the coast, and out at sea protecting the over-loaded boats as they struggled home.

General Gort was ordered to hand over his command as soon as his force amounted to less than the strength of one corps. He was too valuable a commander to risk losing. On the evening of May 31 he handed over to Major-General the Hon. H. R. L. G. Alexander (later Lord Alexander, q.v.) and at two o'clock the next morning General Gort sailed for England.

The operation was nearly completed. At midnight, June 2-3, General Alexander and the Senior Naval Officer (Captain W. G. Tennant, R.N.) cruised along the beaches in a motor-boat to make sure that no British soldier remained, then turned for home. Only the wounded, and those who covered the last stages of the retreat, fell into enemy hands.

Of the force that had retired into the bridge-head, 80 per cent were taken off. There were evacuated 211,532 British officers and men, with 13,053 wounded, and 112,546 Allies, nearly all French. Some of the boats, returning over and over again to run the gauntlet of German fire, never completed their last run to England; others brought home many whom the German machine-guns had killed or wounded as they stood on the decks. But the miracle had been accomplished. The flower of the British Army, threatened with annihilation, was snatched from the very jaws of the enemy—to fight again—to fight and, this time, to conquer.

Durban. The premier port of the Union of South Africa, and having the only good harbour on the coast between East London in the Cape of Good Hope and Delagoa Bay in Portuguese East Africa, Durban is the largest city in the rich province of Natal. The harbour, over eight square miles in extent, lies in a fine land-locked bay called Port Natal. Through the port pass the imports for the gold centres of the Transvaal and the Orange Free State; it is also the headquarters of a whaling industry. Durban is a great residential centre, with

South African Railways and Harbours

DURBAN: GREAT PORT OF THE SOUTH AFRICAN UNION

Third largest city in the Union of South Africa, Durban is on a land-locked bay on the coast of the province of Natal. West Street, a thoroughfare in the heart of the city, is shown in this photograph. On the right is the clock-tower of the General Post Office. On the left, in the foreground, part of the City Hall can be seen. Durban's harbour, with an area of eight square miles, and including a large dry dock, ranks as one of the finest in the southern hemisphere.

DÜRER'S CRAFTSMANSHIP
Dürer's St. Jerome in his Study (above), uniting superb craftsmanship with religious intensity, is a masterpiece of copper engraving. The self-portrait (right) is in the Munich Art Gallery.

the Berea ridge, a delightful district, in the background. Rickshaws, drawn by fantastically dressed Zulus, still ply for hire in the streets. The population is about 338,800, of whom 125,000 are Europeans.

Dürer, ALBRECHT (1471–1528). One of 18 children of a goldsmith in Nuremberg, Germany, Dürer (pron. dūr′-er) was born on May 21, 1471. His father, Dürer has told us, took special delight in him, " Seeing that I was industrious in working and learning, he put me to school; and when I had learned to read and write, he took me home from school and taught me the goldsmith's trade."

But Albrecht was more interested in drawing and painting than in goldsmith's work. So at 15 he entered the studio of a painter. His apprentice days over, Dürer travelled in Germany and Italy, and became famous for his portraits and other paintings. What is more important, he was turning out a number of examples of the art of engraving (q.v.). This art was still in its infancy. Men had only just begun to realize its vast possibilities. Paintings were expensive, and only the wealthy could possess them. Here was an art which made it easy to produce and spread among the people pictures telling the stories of sacred and classical history, and driving home for the multitudes who could not read the points in religious and social discussions. The engraver's art especially attracted Dürer, and he carried it to its highest point of perfection by his skill and imagination. He helped to set the model of engraving for all time.

The character of the man is well brought out in his own words: " Attentively regard Nature and take her for your guide, and do not depart from her, imagining that you will fare better by yourself. Truly, Art is hidden in Nature. Never think to do anything better than God has done it, for your power is pure nothingness compared with the creative activity of God." Dürer died on April 6, 1528.

Dürer was remarkably industrious. His own list of his works totals 1,254 pieces. Of his paintings, The Adoration of the Magi (Uffizi Gallery, Florence) is among the best known. The Life of the Virgin, a series of 21 cuts, and The Apocalypse, rank among his best woodcuts. The Knight and Death, Melancolia, and St. Jerome in his Study are considered the greatest of all engravings on copper. For beauty and accuracy his coloured drawings of plants and small creatures are unsurpassed.

Durham. On the north-east coast of England, between Northumberland on the north and Yorkshire on the south, Durham has an area of 1,015 square miles, with about 32 miles of coast washed by the North Sea. The River Tyne forms much of its northern boundary. Its southern boundary is traced by the River Tees, while the Wear and Derwent run through the county.

The most important industry is coal-mining, others being shipbuilding and the production of chemicals, glass, woollens and earthenware. There are also numerous blast furnaces, iron works and machine shops. Large quantities of ironstone, millstone, granite, and lead are obtained. Sheep farming is carried on, and Durham is also noted for its horses and shorthorn cattle. Besides the ports of Sunderland, Stockton-on-Tees, the Hartlepools, Jarrow and South Shields, the large towns include Gateshead and Darlington.

The county town of Durham (population 19,000) stands on the River Wear and is famous for its cathedral, one of the noblest in the land and magnificently placed above the river. Begun in the 11th century, it is largely Norman (*see* illustration in page 723). The castle is a fine building and the city has a university and a public school. The university was founded in 1832 and was originally intended for the training of Church of England clergy. In 1908 it was divided into two parts, one at Durham and the other at Newcastle. That at Durham is still mainly concerned with training candidates for the Anglican ministry, while the Newcastle division contains a school of medicine. The population of the county of Durham is 1,486,000.

Dwarfs. Very tiny persons are known as dwarfs, and the term is particularly applied to those under four feet in height. A dwarf may belong to the pygmy tribes of Central Africa or the Far East, or he may be a freak of Nature. There have been many dwarfs in history who, combining intelligence with a diminutive appearance, have found favour in the Courts of Royalty. Queen Mary I (1516–58) had a dwarf two feet high named John Jervis. Jeffery Hudson, who until 30 was only 18 inches high, was introduced to Charles I (1600–49) in a model of a pie. In more modern times, the most famous dwarf was the American, Charles Stratton, known as General Tom Thumb, who was exhibited in London in 1844 and again in 1857. He was 31 inches high and his wife was only one inch taller.

Dyes. Almost as old as food and clothing are the colourings used to make clothes beautiful. Since early times people have used dyes and stains, and have gone to infinite trouble and expense to get

DWARF TOM THUMB
Charles Stratton, an American, popularly known as General Tom Thumb, was exhibited in London about a hundred years ago. He was only 31 inches high. Here he is in Napoleonic costume.

them. Some of the natural dyes, from plants and animals, were in use probably 4,000 years ago.

Natural dyestuffs abound everywhere, yet those which give vivid, beautiful and lasting colours are not numerous, and they early became prized articles of commerce. Such was the precious Tyrian purple (really a crimson), which yielded immense wealth to the ancient city of Tyre. This was made from a Mediterranean shell-fish a thousand years before Christ, and later dyed the robes of Roman emperors and chief magistrates. Such, though less costly, were indigo, madder, turmeric, and later, cochineal and morin, the latter a yellow dye from the wood of a tree grown in South America and the West Indies.

Today Man's instinctive love of colour has built up great industries, for colours of infinite variety are now made cheaply and plentifully in factories. Indigo, once obtained only from plants, is now made from a coal-tar product, and is chemically identical with the plant product. (*See* Coal-tar).

For long, practically all dyes were made from natural organic substances. No one dreamed that they could be made from inorganic substances. But in 1828 Friedrich Wohler showed that organic compounds could be synthesized in the laboratory. In 1856 an Englishman, William Henry Perkin, when attempting to make artificial quinine from coal-tar, obtained a mauve substance from aniline, a coal-tar derivative. Aniline had first been isolated from indigo, and was so called from " *an-nil*," an Arabic word meaning the indigo plant. Perkin's mauve colouring was the first aniline dye. From this beginning the making of synthetic dyes grew rapidly. Germany was the first to see its possibilities, and before the First World War (1914–18) German chemists held the secrets of hundreds of processes for making dyes. Hence they had practically a monopoly of dye manufacture. The blockade of Germany during the war crippled the textile industries of America, Great Britain, and other countries. Before the war Great Britain had imported a large part of her dyes, and of the materials for making dyes. British manufacturers met the emergency, and soon made dyes equal to those of German origin. Now Britain produces most of her dyestuff requirements.

The first dyers were no doubt housewives, who dyed with woad, oak-galls, and other native vegetable substances the stuffs that they had spun and woven. Egypt, Persia and India early perfected the art. India especially was the source of many of the best dyes until modern times. Indigo was the " Indian dye " to the Greeks and Romans. The dyers' art, at least commercially, was largely lost in Europe from about the fall of the Roman Empire until the Moors planted madder in Spain, and returned Crusaders revived dyeing in Northern Italy. Thence the art spread to France, Flanders, Germany and England. The discovery of America gave the world many new dyes, particularly cochineal, logwood and fustic. When the route around the Cape of Good Hope was opened up, larger quantities of dyestuffs were imported into Europe from India. Desperately but vainly did the European woad-growers fight the importation of the " devilish drug " indigo ; but time had in store its revenges on the lordly indigo planters.

Not every colouring substance is a dye ; for a dye, unlike a paint or a stain, becomes physically or chemically incorporated in the fibres of the dyed material and is not removed by ordinary washing processes. Dyes are of several kinds. Substantive dyes colour the fabric (e.g. cotton) by mere immersion in an acid or an alkaline bath. For dyeing with " mordant " dyes, such as alizarin, the fabric is treated with a metallic salt (e.g. alum), the " mordant," which forms an insoluble compound with the dye. Vat dyes, such as indigo, are applied in a soluble colourless form, and later oxidised to the insoluble coloured form. Ingrain colours are actually made on the fabric, which is immersed first in one and then in another chemical solution. It is believed that dyes, and some other organic substances, absorb light of some colours, and are therefore coloured, because they contain atoms linked by shifting double bonds (*see* our story of Chemistry), which have vibrating electrons.

How Patterns are Produced by Dyes

Dyes are applied to raw stock, to the spun yarn, or to the woven fabric. " Discharge " processes treat the fabric so that it will discharge a portion of the dye to produce a white polka dot or other figure. Block dyeing, an ancient colour art still in use, gives beautiful results; in this method the dye is stamped on the paper or fabric from a hand-carved wood block.

" Resist " processes, by which a portion of the fabric is protected from the action of the dye, are exemplified in the batiks in which artists take so much interest. Batik printing has been skilfully practised in Java for perhaps 2,000 years ; a coating of wax is put on the parts of a pattern that are to be protected from the dye before immersing the cloth in the colour, and repetition of the process makes several colours possible. Sometimes screens of bolting cloth, on which the design is marked with a special dye-resisting paint, are placed above the material to be dyed.

Dyes are closely related chemically to many other coal-tar products, and, in time of war, dye-making factories can be used for making explosives. Synthetic dyes are of several kinds—acid, basic, phenolic, aniline, and others—and in each class there are many colours. Silk, wool, cotton and rayon require special dyes, each with a wide range of colour. Some materials, such as leather and fur, present special problems of dyeing. In some dyes, as in indigo, the peculiar structure giving the colour is so modified in the process of preparation that when the cloth is taken from the dye bath it is white and becomes coloured only when exposure to air oxidizes the dye. Many dyes require complex chemical processes for their formation ; indigo, the most used of all dyes, had been the subject of chemical research for years before it was put on the market in 1897 as a synthetic product.

Dynamite AND NITROGLYCERIN. One of the most powerful explosives in common use, nitroglycerin was discovered in 1846 by the Italian scientist, Ascanio Sobrero. It is made by treating glycerine with a mixture of concentrated nitric and sulphuric acids. It was used at first as a headache remedy, under the name " glonoin." It proved too difficult and dangerous an explosive for practical blasting purposes until Alfred Nobel of Sweden began his experiments in 1862 near Stockholm.

Nobel's brother was blown to pieces during the tests, and Nobel was forced to move his laboratory to a barge anchored in the middle of a lake. Then a ship loaded with nitroglycerin blew up off Colon, Panama, and most of the nations of the world forbade their vessels to carry it. But the Swedish chemist refused to abandon his labours, and in 1866 he was rewarded by the invention of dynamite. This is today one of the commonest of the high explosives, and enables Man to blast away masses of rock and other obstacles with comparative safety.

Dynamite consists of a mixture of the liquid nitroglycerin with some absorbent substance giving it a solid form. The absorbent used by Nobel was kieselguhr or diatomite, a kind of earth formed by the flinty skeletons of countless millions of tiny fossil plants known as diatoms. Later, wood pulp, sawdust, charcoal, plaster of Paris, and many other substances came to be used. Perhaps the most powerful form of dynamite is the " blasting gelatine " devised by Nobel in 1875. This contains nitrocotton colloidally (*see* Colloid) dissolved in nitroglycerin, and is waterproof. Many dynamites use ammonium nitrate mixed with nitroglycerin.

Ordinary dynamite is usually made in the form of " sticks " from one to two inches in diameter and about eight inches long. These are contained in brown paper wrappers coated with paraffin to keep out moisture. If a small quantity of dynamite is set on fire, free from pressure, jarring or vibration of any kind, it will burn ; but if the least blow strikes it while burning, such as the fall of a pebble, it will explode with great violence. Dynamite is usually set off with a detonator or blasting cap. (*See* Explosives ; Glycerine).

Dynamo. This is a name originally given to a class of electrical machines which are also referred to as generators (and, in the case of alternating current or A.C. machines, as alternators). All the electricity which runs your train or trolleybus, lights your house, and does a thousand things from heating the bath-water to milking the cows on the farm where your milk comes from, is provided by these dynamos which convert mechanical energy into electrical energy by the process of electromagnetic induction (*see* Electricity ; Magnetism), which was discovered and developed by Faraday.

Fig. 1 illustrates the principle. A loop of wire is connected to a galvanometer, and one side of the loop lies between the poles of a permanent magnet. If the loop is moved up or down it will cut through the lines of the magnetic field of force produced by the magnet, and the galvanometer will indicate a momentary " kick " of current, flowing in one direction or the other, depending on whether the conductor is moving upwards or downwards.

We want more than a momentary " kick " of electricity— we want a steady flow, so we bend the

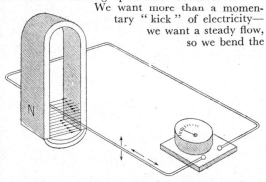

DYNAMO : THE PRINCIPLE

Fig. 1. One side of a loop of wire connected with a galvanometer lies between the poles of a permanent magnet. When the loop is moved up and down the galvanometer will register a momentary ' kick ' of electricity.

wire into a smaller loop and rotate it between the magnet poles, as shown in Fig. 2. Since one half of the loop is travelling upwards and the other half downwards, at any given time, they cut the magnetic field in opposite directions; but, since they are on opposite sides of the loop, the two e.m.f.s (electro-motive forces) will be added together.

Since the loop is rotating we cannot fasten the ends to any fixed point, so we must have some form of sliding contact to make connections to an external circuit. We could have a pair of metal " slip rings " with metal " brushes " rubbing on them ; but in Fig. 2 we use what is called a commutator (the original name given to a reversing switch). This consists of one ring or tube, split into two halves (insulated from one another), with one end of the wire loop connected to each half. The two brushes rest upon this ring at opposite sides.

The reason for this is as follows : Imagine that the loop is in a vertical position, midway between the two poles. As it starts to rotate, one half (or one conductor, if we are considering them as two conductors in series) is moving downwards and

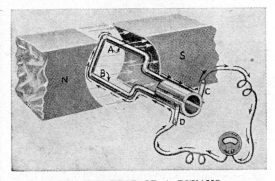

THE PRINCIPLE OF A DYNAMO

Fig. 2. In a direct current generator or dynamo the chief parts are the field magnets (N and S) ; the armature (A B) ; and the split cylinder called the commutator (C and D), from which the brushes collect the current. Light arrows show the direction of the magnetic lines of force ; black arrows indicate the path of the current through the circuit.

cutting the magnetic flux in one direction, while the other is cutting it in the reverse direction. After half a revolution the conductor which was moving downwards is now moving upwards, and cutting the flux in the reverse direction. If, then, we used two slip rings the direction of the direction in the external circuit would reverse—the machine would generate an alternating current. The commutator, however, reverses the connexions to the outside circuit every half revolution so that, although the current in the loop continually alternates or reverses, the current in the outside circuit is always in the same direction.

Now, although we have the elements of a direct current dynamo, the power produced by such a simple machine (with one loop or coil) is very small—in fact it would need a fairly delicate instrument to measure it. How can we make our dynamo give a larger output ?

The voltage produced by a dynamo is governed by three things—the number of lines of force produced by the magnet; the speed at which the conductors cut the lines, and the number of conductors which we connect in series, so that their e.m.f.s add together. We start, then, by making our magnet large and powerful, and put an iron " core " in the centre of the coil to make an easier path for

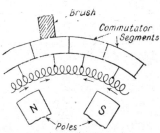

CURRENT PICK-UP

Fig. 3. As the commutator segments of a rotating armature come into contact with the brush, current is taken from the dynamo in a single direction, irrespective of the periodic reversal.

the magnetic flux. Instead of a simple loop we use a coil of many turns, running at a high speed.

Actually, we use more than one coil. A single coil as shown in Fig. 2 has one part of its revolution (where the coil is vertical) when neither side is cutting through the flux, so that no e.m.f. is generated. Thus the current in the external circuit, although uni-directional (i.e., it does not reverse), is not steady but drops to zero twice every revolution. We use, then, a number of coils distributed around, so that at least one of them (usually more) is cutting the magnetic flux at some time. If more than one coil is used our simple two-part commutator is no use, and we must have one in which the number of parts (segments, as they are called) is equal to the number of coil-ends which we have in our winding. The principles of commutation, however, remain the same. (*See* Fig. 3).

A modern armature (as the rotating part of the dynamo is called) consists of an iron drum, built up of thin stampings or laminations. Around the outside are a number of slots, in which the coils lie, carefully insulated, and wedged into position (*see* Fig. 4). The reason for building the body or core out of thin sheets instead of a solid lump of iron is, that if a solid lump were used it would itself act as a conductor cutting the magnetic flux, and what are known as " eddy currents " would be induced in it. These currents would not only

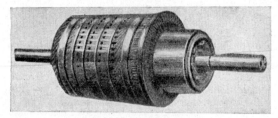

DYNAMO'S ARMATURE

Fig. 4. In the drum type of armature the coils are laid in longitudinal slots. The drum itself is built up with thin sheets of iron so that it will not act as a conductor cutting the magnetic flux and so become very hot.

waste most of the driving power but would cause the armature to get very hot in a comparatively short time. Some of the early machines, built before these principles were fully understood, did get red-hot from this cause.

The commutator is made up of a number . of shaped copper bars, with mica insulation in between; the brushes—which in the earliest machines were actual brushes of tinsel or copper gauze— are now made of carbon held in spring brush-holders and attached to a "rocker" so that they can be moved slightly backwards or forwards, to select the best spot for running without any sparking.

Except for very small generators (such as motor-car magnetos, cycle dynamos, and the like) permanent magnets are very seldom used in dynamos, their place being taken by an electro-magnet (see Magnetism), which is energised by a separate supply of current (separate excitation), or by a small portion of the current generated by the machine itself (self-excited).

The original horseshoe-shaped magnet is not often used nowadays, most magnets being of the ring pattern with pole pieces on the inside, as shown in Fig. 5. There is less "magnetic leakage," and this shape of magnet gives a more compact and neater machine, which can be totally enclosed to keep out dirt and moisture. The number of poles is not limited to two, and 4, 6, 8, 12 and even more are used. Most machines nowadays have smaller magnet poles in between the main ones ; the small ones are called commutating poles, or interpoles, and help to produce sparkless commutation—they have no effect on the voltage produced by the machine. A typical direct current or D.C. dynamo is shown in Fig. 6.

In A.C. dynamos, or alternators as they are termed, there is no need for a commutator ; and, for a simple single-coil machine, two slip rings would be used. From Fig. 1, however, you will see that it is only " relative " motion between the magnet and the conductor which is necessary. It would make no difference if the conductor stood still and the magnet moved. This being so, and there being no need for a rotating commutator, it is easier to build an alternator " inside out," as it were. The coils are wound in slots on the inside of

a ring structure known as the stator (also made up of stampings) and the " field magnet " revolves.

There are two main classes of alternator. Where they are to be driven by a low-speed engine they are of large diameter and short length, with a rotor or field magnet having a large number of poles arranged round a wheel—in fact, they are often called " flywheel alternators."

Where they are to be driven by high-speed steam turbines (up to 3,000 revolutions per minute) they have a stator of comparatively long length and small diameter, and the rotor has two or four poles only (according to speed), and resembles a direct current or D.C. dynamo armature, having the field winding sunk into slots so that the outer surface is smooth, and will not cause a great deal of " windage " (air friction) losses at the high speed at which it rotates.

The prime mover, as the driving force is called, may be a steam turbine, a slow-speed steam engine, a gas or oil engine, or a water turbine. In the last case, the alternator is often laid on its side, with

RING-SHAPED MAGNET

Fig. 5. Besides the four poles in this field magnet there are two interpoles, which prevent sparking.

the driving shaft vertical, and the water turbine in a pit below ; this type is called an umbrella alternator, a term which well describes it (see Hydro-Electric Installations). Whatever form of power is used, the major amount of it is taken to overcome the magnetic drag due to the electrical load on the machine. There are small losses due to the windage already referred to, losses due to mechanical friction in the bearings, and electrical losses caused by the resistance of the windings, and by the power taken to excite the field magnet system.

Since a field magnet cannot be excited with alternating current a separate small dynamo is used, often driven from the main shaft. This is termed an exciter. In some large machines (alternators are built up to 60,000 kW.), for ease of control this exciter is itself excited by an even smaller one which is termed a service exciter.

Messrs. Bruce Peebles & Co., Ltd.

DYNAMO OF MODERN DESIGN

Fig. 6. Since a field magnet cannot be excited with alternating current, a small separate dynamo is sometimes used for this purpose ; but modern dynamos, such as the one shown here, are usually self-exciting.

E

Eagle. From time immemorial the eagle, no matter what its species or where its habitation, has been known as the king of birds. Its extraordinary powers of flight, the majesty of its appearance, and the wild grandeur of the scenery in which it builds its eyrie or nest, have made it the universal emblem of might and courage from the most ancient times. Five thousand years ago the Sumerians of the city-kingdom of Lagash, in the Euphrates valley, in what is now known as Iraq, used the spread eagle (eagle with outstretched wings) as the symbol of their power.

Eagles are found throughout Europe, Africa, Asia and North America and are members of the hawk family. They are supposed to attain great age, and are not mature until they are several years old. Their nests are structures of sticks, sometimes six feet across and tremendously thick.

The golden eagle (*Aquila chrysaetus*), one of the most widespread species and the sole surviving British representative, is a mountain-loving bird. It is found in Europe and Northern Asia, and in the United States from Mexico northward. Its plumage is brownish in colour, the feathers of the head and neck appearing golden in the sunlight. It attains a length of about three feet, and up to seven feet in spread of the wings. In Scotland it feeds principally on hares, and grouse, ducks, and similar birds, but will occasionally attack a lamb or young fawn.

Often placed in a quite accessible position on some cliff edge, the golden eagle's eyrie consists of an enormous mass of sticks, which is added to every time the nest is used again. Each pair of birds appears to have several eyries, which are occupied in succession, so that one may be used only every third or fourth year. Sometimes, but not commonly, the nest is in a tree. Heather, moss and grass are the lining of the great stick-platform, and the bird seems to have a marked preference for the wood rush (*Luzula*). Like most birds of prey, the golden eagle is continually adding green branches, sprays of plants and other green material to the nest so long as there is either egg or young bird in it.

The egg of the golden eagle is white, with brownish, purplish, or even violet-coloured spots and blotches. The sole clutch of each season consists normally of two, occasionally of three, eggs, and if the first are destroyed, others are not laid. The young eaglets are covered with white down, and great care appears to be taken with their food, the liver of the victims being at first their sole diet.

The method of hunting employed by the eagle is a soaring flight, followed by a bomb-like drop upon the prey. There is no pursuit, and for this reason, amongst others, the bird was not used in the old days of falconry, although a few golden eagles, even in recent times, have been trained to fly "from the fist."

The sea-eagles are also widely distributed. They are found in most parts of the world, with the exception of South America. They feed largely, but not solely, on fish, and usually nest in high trees. The bald-headed eagle (*Haliaeetus leucocephalus*) is peculiar to North America, and is the national emblem of the United States. It gets its name from the whiteness of its head, for the original meaning of the word bald was white (preserved also in the word piebald).

One of the most remarkable things about the eagles is their so-called third eyelid, a membrane which, while not impairing the bird's sight, is drawn over the eye to protect it from the glare of the sun at high altitudes (*see* illus. in page 438). In ancient mythology the eagle was the bird of Jupiter (supreme god of the Romans), and came to stand for earthly power and dominion. Hence it was adopted by the Roman emperors, and eagles made of silver or bronze were carried on long poles by the Roman standard-bearers. A two-headed eagle was the emblem of the old Austro-Hungarian empire, as it was also of the Russian Tsars. Under Napoleon I (1769–1821) and Napoleon III (1808–73) the

Capt. C. W. B. Knight

GOLDEN EAGLE ALERT
Sole surviving British representative of all the eagles, this bird gets the name ' golden ' from the feathers of the head and neck, which appear to be that colour when seen in the sunlight. Its wing-spread may be as much as seven feet, and its length three feet.

BLEAK HOME-LIFE OF THE EAGLE

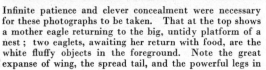

A. Brook and Capt. C. W. B. Knight

Infinite patience and clever concealment were necessary for these photographs to be taken. That at the top shows a mother eagle returning to the big, untidy platform of a nest ; two eaglets, awaiting her return with food, are the white fluffy objects in the foreground. Note the great expanse of wing, the spread tail, and the powerful legs in position for 'landing.' At the lower left both parent birds are at home, one with a beakful of material to add to the nest. At the right, the white fluffy eaglets have reached the stage when they can try a first flight from the bleakly exposed nest, or eyrie. With all their troubles ahead of them, they will learn to hunt their own prey.

French soldiers carried eagles—a bronze, gilded and crowned bird placed on the end of a pole instead of flags. The lectern in church takes the form of an eagle because—so some say—the eagle is the natural enemy of the serpent (symbol of evil) ; the two wings represent the two Testaments. Others, however, say it is because the eagle is emblematic of St. John.

Ear. The word ear wakens in the mind an image of the shell-like appendage on the head of Man, or the long ones flapped by a donkey. These and all their variations in other animals represent the most simple part of the mechanism of hearing. They are an apparatus for catching and concentrating sound, comparable to the horn of the old-fashioned gramophone. Real hearing—the interpretation of sound—takes place in the auditory, which is the hearing, centre of the brain; just as sight, the interpretation of things seen, of visual images, takes place in the sight centre of the brain.

Following the course of a wave of sound, the latter is caught by the outside structure and runs along the ear-passage until it strikes the drum, a thin, tough, pearly-coloured membrane blocking its path. On the inner side of the drum in the middle division of the ear three very minute and very delicate bones are arranged (they weigh perhaps a hundredth part of a sixpence). These still bear the names given to them by the old anatomists because of their vague resemblance

BALD-HEADED EAGLE
This bird is the eagle adopted as the emblem of the United States of America, where it is one of the least rare members of its group. It gets its name from the whiteness of its head, which looks bald as it gleams in the sunlight.

to a Hammer, Anvil and Stirrup. (In Latin the Malleus, Incus and Stapes.) These structures vibrate in response to the wave of sound, and these vibrations are passed on.

The middle ear, as it is called, is connected with the throat by two minute tubes, the Eustachian tubes, so fine in bore that a pig's bristle cannot traverse them. These allow of the air pressure being equal on both sides of the drum so that in normal conditions it is not hindered in its function by being pulled or pushed by differing air pressures.

Then comes the most difficult part of the ear to understand, the inner ear. There is first to be considered the so-called " bony labyrinth," which is a group of tiny connected chambers and passages in the temporal bone. These are filled with a liquid called " perilymph." In two places these chambers, and consequently the perilymph, are separated from the middle ear only by small, thin membranes. One of these tiny apertures is called the *fenestra ovalis*, or " oval window," and the inner end of the chain of bones fits in there. When the bones vibrate they move the liquid in the inner ear.

The next thing to consider is the " membranous labyrinth." This consists of thin-walled, flexible tubes and peculiar enlargements suspended in the bony labyrinth and surrounded by the perilymph. These tubes are filled with liquid called " endolymph." At certain places on these membranes the nerve-fibres or tiny

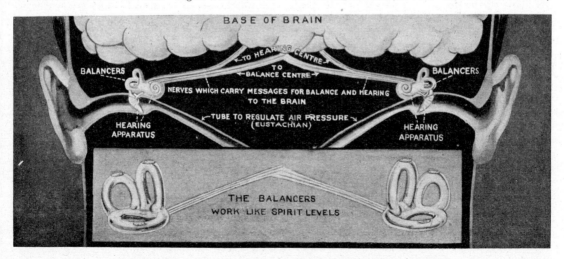

HOW THE EAR IS CONNECTED WITH THE BRAIN

When a sound enters the ear, it strikes those little shell-like drums and sets them vibrating. The vibrations are passed on to the set of nerve-fibres, which carry them to the hearing centres in the brain. The Eustachian tubes open downwards into the throat, and keep the pressure on both sides of the drums equal, so that they can vibrate freely. The curled tubes marked ' balancers ' have nothing to do with hearing ; they maintain the sense of balance. The enlarged picture at the bottom shows how they are filled with a liquid which flows backwards and forwards as the head is dipped.

individual strands of the auditory nerve have their endings, which seem to be essentially very delicate hairs suspended in the endolymph. When the endolymph vibrates these hair cells are stimulated, nerve currents or impulses are aroused in the nerve-fibres and travel back to the brain, and arouse or stimulate the hearing area.

The vibrations of the air, or physical sound, do not reach the brain at all. It is the nerve currents or impulses that stimulate the brain. The nerve currents are aroused by the vibrating liquid; this is set going by the chain of bones, and these by the sound waves. But every stage in the process corresponds in respect to time, intensity and number of vibrations with the original sound.

How, then, can one hear so many different tones ? It is believed that the inner ear is so constituted that each pitch of a tone stimulates only one nerve-fibre. For example, if we strike middle C on the piano, one fibre would take the message to the brain, and arouse the sensation of middle C. If we strike another string, another fibre records the sound. Different animals have differing sensitivity to sound. Few humans can hear the high-pitched squeak of a bat ; and many lower animals have a keener hearing than has Man.

Where the Sense of Balance Originates

In addition to the " cochlea " (which is the name of that part of the inner ear by which sounds are recognized), there are the " semi-circular canals " and related parts. These also have sensory nerve-fibres ending on them. But they have nothing to do with hearing. Their function is to give information as to the position of the body and to give vital aid in maintaining balance.

Wax in the outer-ear passage is a frequent and simple cause of deafness. It is interesting that a fine film of wax which can hardly be observed through a special instrument—a little tube carrying a small electric lamp—can render its victim completely deaf; whereas large lumps of wax which yet allow the air to carry vibrations to the drum cause little disability. Wax should be softened by dropping oil into the ear passages before being

syringed out by a trained hand. Recurring troublesome wax always implies some septic focus in the sinuses, teeth or throat, and this septic focus should be sought out and treated by a doctor.

Real deafness is a social problem now getting much-needed attention. It may not seem true, but it is nevertheless so, that a deaf man is more cut off from his fellows than is a blind man. Such deafness can arise from two main causes : changes in the bones and drum, or changes in the nerve of hearing and centre of hearing. The first can be helped by various ingenious inventions which magnify the vibrations ; and where these fail or the nervous mechanism is at fault, lip reading— the recognition of spoken words by the movements of the lips—is a happy solution. A child may be born deaf through some defect in all this complicated mechanism, when he will be dumb—because speech is acquired by imitation. But again the expert teacher comes to the rescue and the child not only eventually lip-reads but speaks.

Causes of Temporary Deafness

In modern life hearing is often temporarily affected after travelling by aeroplane, the pressure of the upper air driving the ear-drums inwards. That is why wads of cotton wool are offered for plugging the ears. This condition also occurs in blockage of the Eustachian tubes, perhaps by inflammation, when air cannot get through them to equalise pressure on either side of the drum. A doctor may advise the inhaling of cool steam from a kettle well-off the boil; only steam can reach the minute interior of the tubes.

In earlier days the middle ear was the scene of many tragedies, germs invading it by way of the Eustachian tubes or from the blood and lymph streams, and finding their way into the hollows of the surrounding bone (" inflammation of the mastoid ") and possibly to the brain. Surgery was then the only and not always successful remedy against deafness or death, but now penicillin and the sulpha group of drugs seldom fail to control the situation. Ear troubles, of any kind, demand prompt recourse to a doctor for advice and treatment.

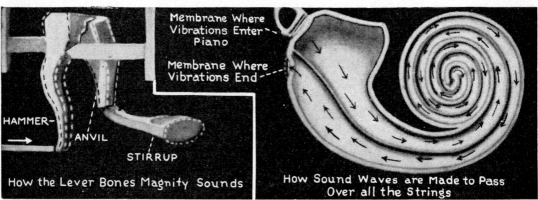

Membrane Where Vibrations Enter Piano

Membrane Where Vibrations End

HAMMER-

ANVIL

STIRRUP

How the Lever Bones Magnify Sounds

How Sound Waves are Made to Pass Over all the Strings

HOW THE EARS 'HEAR' AIR WAVES

Behind the ear-drum are tiny bits of living machinery, which do most of the work of ' hearing.' On the left are three delicate bones. The ' hammer ' bone receives pulsations from the ear-drum, and sets the ' anvil ' vibrating, which in turn passes on the motion by a lever action to the ' stirrup ' bone. The foot of the stirrup bone fits into an opening in the inmost ear, as ' piano,' as seen at the upper edge of the right-hand diagram. The vibrations set up in the stirrup are carried, as shown by the arrows, through a delicate fluid over the ' sounding strings ' of that snail-shell coil, which is called the ' labyrinth.' These strings, or nerve-ends, transmit the message to the brain.

Whirling PLANET on which WE LIVE

At first a mass of white-hot vapours and molten solids, our Earth has had many slow and some violent changes in its form and surface. Its early story, as outlined here, is a fascinating one.

Earth. As we all know, the earth has taken a tremendous time to come to its present form, and indeed at first our planet was once " without form and void." There was neither land nor sea, neither mountain nor solid earth, still less any sign of life. It was only after many millions of years that the earth was ready for any living thing of any kind at all.

Our earth is, of course, one small member of one of the myriad systems of the universe. As far as the earth is concerned, the important members of the solar system are the sun and the moon. It is the sun which, by the power of gravitation, holds the earth in its course, while the moon is our " satellite," travelling round the earth as the earth travels round the sun. Originally, the earth was just a whirling mass of white-hot vapours and molten solids, and it took millions of years to reach the infinite variety of life and surface that it shows us today. The slow processes of cooling and solidification had to proceed to that point when the first life appeared—minute forms which we could not call either plant or animal—existing most likely in the seas, certainly in water. Then sprang up the first green plants, making possible animal life in all its different forms. But we must allow for another great gap before the primitive forms were followed by such creatures as sponges, starfish, insects, lobsters; the earliest backboned animals, fish were the first creatures to get this great improvement in body-building; then the first amphibians, that is, creatures at home both in water and on land, the ancestors of our frogs, toads, and newts; next the reptiles, which are represented today by our crocodiles, tortoises, snakes, and lizards; and, finally, the birds and the mammals—that is, all the hairy-coated four-legged creatures—and Man, with his erect posture and large brain space in the skull.

Each kind of creature, as it developed, had to fit the changing conditions around it or else give way to others in the struggle for life. So a great many creatures occupied the earth for a time and then passed away from it, and sometimes they were succeeded by creatures resembling them, but better fitted to live on the earth.

Thus, very many years ago, the great mammoths and mastodons vanished and made room for the elephant, one of the most intelligent mammals; and very many races of men, of whom there is no written history, lived and died before Man had become sufficiently intelligent to invent an alphabet and leave a record of what he had learnt to help those who came after him.

Nobody has ever been much more than a mile below the earth's surface, but scientists can guess what the inside of the earth must be like. It probably consists of a central core surrounded by "shells" or zones. The central core, which may be some 4,000 miles in diameter, does not transmit some

earthquake waves which are known to pass through every form of solid matter. Because of this, geologists contend that this central core must be plastic, or even liquid matter. It probably consists of metals (chiefly iron) at a white heat, enormously compressed by the weight of the outer shells. The shell immediately encasing the core forms the main mass of the earth and is known as the barysphere, or heavy sphere. It surrounds the core to a depth of 2,000 miles, so that the combined diameter of core and barysphere is about 8,000 miles. The barysphere is composed of heavy basic (alkaline) rocks at red heat, which are kept solid and rigid by the high pressure from without.

Surrounding this mantle is the lithosphere, or rocky crust, which is estimated to be from 25 to 30 miles thick. Geologists tell us that this crust, which forms only about one part in a hundred of the earth's mass, may be composed of a layer of

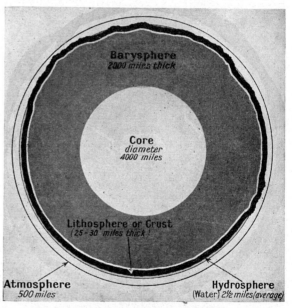

THE EARTH'S FIVE DIVISIONS

According to scientific deductions the centre of the earth is either plastic or liquid and consists of white-hot metals, chiefly iron and nickel. Next to this is the barysphere, comprised of dense basic rocks at red heat, from which a crust of granitic rocks has separated. Even the deepest mines penetrate only the top skin of this crust or lithosphere.

basalt beneath a layer of granite, with a veneer of sedimentary rocks like sandstone or chalk on top. Radioactive substances in the granite layer keep it very hot, and it is this heat, not the heat of the deep interior, which shows itself in volcanic activity.

Above the lithosphere we get the oceans, seas, lakes, and rivers, which collectively form the hydrosphere. For the purpose of our diagram the

THE MAKING OF THE MOUNTAIN MASSES OF THE EARTH

The upper illustration shows the vast masses of primeval rock that were of the greatest importance in the building of the world. Throughout geological time these primeval highlands have
seldom been beneath the sea, and their formation helped to prepare the earth for Man. In the
course of ages the debris that was washed down the slopes, and volcanic upheavals from below,
formed the continents as we know them today (lower picture).

vapour it did cover it entirely. If it had continued to do so, we can see that the earth would then have had a very different history. But the earth is always shrinking, the interior more quickly than the solid crust, and while it was still young, and shrinkage was going on most rapidly, the crust would have to adjust itself to the smaller interior.

Everyone knows how an apple changes after it has been picked some time. It begins to become dry and to lose size, and the skin, which has become loose, wrinkles itself in order to fit the apple. In much the same way, while the crust of the earth was still thin it crumpled everywhere to keep pace with the lessening bulk inside. Thus the surface would become divided into land and water, but the arrangement would certainly be very different from that which exists today. Later on, when the crust was thicker, the crumpling took place only in the weaker areas, and as shrinkage went on great portions of it sank and formed shallow depressions. As a result the earth today is a globe slightly flattened on four faces, and these hollows are filled by the four great oceans.

Whether the four great hollows have always existed, causing the distribution of land and water to resemble that of the present day, is not certain. What is certain is that many parts of the earth have been dry land at one time and sea at another. Nearly all England, for example, has been many times covered by the sea, and then uplifted again.

The arrangement of land and water has much to do with making the globe habitable (see Ecology). Lands are fertile only if they get sufficient moisture, and the oceans are the reservoirs which send them their water supply by means of rain-bearing winds. Since the winds are drained of their moisture as they pass over land, any country situated too far from the sea is a desert. A much larger proportion of the land surface of the globe would be habitable if land and sea occurred in comparatively small areas than

hydrosphere is shown as a sort of shell of an average depth of 2½ miles. Above all lies the atmosphere, a gaseous envelope possibly 500 miles thick in which the air gradually thins out.

The separation of the earth into these five divisions was completed when the earth solidified. Since then conduction of heat from the interior has been so slow that little change has occurred there. Near the surface, though, external factors must have worked great changes.

As the rocky crust formed and cooled, the water which had been present in vast quantities as vapour in the earth's envelope of gases became liquid and filled the hollows in the surface. These became the ocean basins, and the higher regions became the continents. Thus the divisions into land and water took place, roughly five-sevenths being water and the remaining two-sevenths dry land; around the globe the envelope of gases formed the atmosphere.

There is enough water in the oceans to cover the whole globe if the surface were made even; it is quite possible that when it first condensed from

would be the case if all the land formed one vast continent and the water one vast ocean.

If we speculate about the appearance of the infant earth, when its crust had solidified and cooled sufficiently to allow the water in the atmosphere to condense upon its surface, we may imagine a tumbled confusion of hills and valleys still warm and moist; warm, stagnant seas, not yet salt, not yet ruffled by the winds we know today; and, wrapping it around, an atmosphere laden with carbon dioxide and so thick with clouds that it could scarcely be penetrated by the sun's rays. Under this cloud-screen the temperature would vary hardly at all, day or night, summer or winter. It would be a grey earth under such a sky, with no sunshine to bring out the colour of the rocks.

Not an atom of living green would be visible, for no life, as we know it, could exist when the first crust was hardening out of molten matter. It would take ages of preparation before the earth could be fit for the most primitive form of such life. Before it appeared, the original rock surface would have to be broken down by destructive agencies existing and working from the beginning, and rebuilt into new rock layers, under whose pressure the hardening of the deeper-seated rocks would go on.

As the shrinkage of the globe continued, more rapidly in the interior than in the outer layers, cracks would be formed in the crust, some parts of it would sink, and the added pressure on the softer rocks beneath would drive them to escape, becoming liquid as the pressure was removed, through the vents, in volcanic eruption. Once on the surface they would be exposed in their turn to the same destructive agencies as the older rocks.

Running water was already at work. Acid gases were present in the atmosphere; and when the sun could penetrate the screen of clouds it would start the winds blowing, the waters circulating, and all the forces of erosion. All that was necessary for the fashioning of the earth and the development of its life was already in existence. But the germ of life had still to appear, and the preparation was long before the earth was fit to receive it. This preparation and the development as we see it today have taken perhaps a thousand million years.

The substance of living things is a jelly-like material called protoplasm, which is not found except in living bodies. All forms of life must have developed from a drop or grain of this simplest of living material.

It is possible that living matter arose in favourable conditions from matter that was not living—very, very long ago, but after the earth had passed through those stages when life could not exist. At the present day we know forms of protein which behave in some respects like living, reproducing matter, and in others like non-living, crystalline material, and it is possible that there were innumerable stages between the non-living material of protoplasm and the living jelly, even as innumerable forms of life have arisen from the first living protoplasm-grain. If it be true that life came from the lifeless matter of the earth's crust, then it is in a literal sense true that Man is made of the dust of the ground, since he is the highest point of the many-branched tree of life that sprang from it.

What were probably the conditions on the early earth that led up to the day when life was born?

The surface was warm and moist and, because of the thick cloud-screen round it, its temperature would vary little. While the earth was hot enough to give out light, various chemical compounds would be created which would readily break up and form new ones. When the water was condensed upon the surface of the earth it would contain materials dissolved from the earth's crust and also from the atmosphere. This water would saturate the mud along its shores, which, being moist and warm, would provide a home for the living jelly.

The sun, from which comes all the energy—by which we mean power to do work—existing upon our earth, would provide the energy needed for the breaking up of chemical compounds and the uniting of their elements to form new ones, and thus very simple living matter might rise, developing by slow stages into protoplasm. (*See* Biology; Geology).

Earthquake. More earthquakes occur in Japan than in any other country. About three shocks a day are recorded on the average, though

EARTHQUAKE DESTRUCTION IN TOKYO
One of the most disastrous earthquakes of modern times was that which occurred at Tokyo, Japan, on September 1, 1923. Nearly three-quarters of the city was destroyed, and uncontrollable fires swept through the ruins. The total number of victims was never known, but 33,000 people perished in one area.

EARTHQUAKE-STRICKEN QUETTA

Royal Society of Arts

A particularly severe earthquake devastated Quetta, in the province of Baluchistan, Pakistan, in 1935. The town was almost completely destroyed, and the death roll was estimated at 40,000. This is the main street before the clearing-up had started.

most of them are very slight. Earthquakes are common also in a belt which crosses Southern Europe and Asia and passes along the west coast of the Americas.

For some time scientists thought that nearness of the sea had some connexion with earthquakes, but, in fact, most earthquakes are due to "faulting." The rock formations of the earth, down to great depths, sometimes break, and the parts on opposite sides of the fracture slip. This slipping movement is known as a "fault." Thus the east slope of the Sierra Nevadas in the United States is the result of a fault, the west side having risen while the east sank. The slip along a great fault does not all take place at once. Rather, there is a repetition of small slips. Though the amount of slipping at one time is

slight—a few inches or a few feet—the vibrations set up spread far and wide, and sometimes result in much destruction. Another cause of earthquakes is volcanic action. You know what would happen to a steam-filled boiler if there were no safety-valves on it. Volcanoes have to make their own safety-valves, and the creation of an outlet often causes earthquakes.

Even a small shock may cause serious disaster. When shocks are violent, buildings are destroyed and fires are started almost at once, owing to the breaking of gas pipes and electric cables. When an earthquake movement causes the sea to recede from the coast, the returning wave sometimes rises to 60 or 80 feet. Submarine earthquakes usually cause huge waves that carry destruction far inland. In the Lisbon, Portugal, earthquake of 1755, waves 60 feet high drowned many thousands. At Arica, a port of Chile, on the west coast of South America, in 1868, warships were said

HOUSETOP HAVOC

In June 1931 earthquake tremors were felt all over England and, as this photograph shows, were severe enough to dislodge chimney-pots at Bridlington, Yorkshire.

to have been carried two miles inland by the force of a great earthquake wave.

Scientists use instruments called seismographs for registering and measuring earthquake vibrations. The main feature of this instrument is a steady pendulum, unaffected by the earth's tremblings, which marks a line on a rotating drum. When the earth trembles, the drum does so also, and the line traced becomes uneven. Seismology, or earthquake science, is of great importance in engineering. The Panama Canal was built across the isthmus rather than across Nicaragua partly because the chosen site is freer from earthquakes than Nicaragua. By studying the force and character of shocks, architects and engineers are able to construct buildings, dams, and locks in such a way as to withstand shocks which might otherwise destroy them.

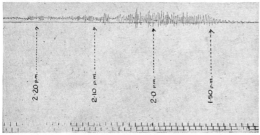

EARTHQUAKE DETECTOR

Scientists use an instrument called a seismograph (top) for registering earthquake vibrations, which are recorded on a rotating drum. The record, or seismogram, of an earthquake in the Philippine Islands is shown (lower), with the duration and time of the shocks; the instrument was in London, 10,000 miles from the upheaval.

Earthworm. "The earth without worms," wrote the great naturalist Gilbert White of Selborne in Hampshire (1720-93), "would soon become cold, hard-bound and void of fermentation, and consequently sterile"; and, indeed, we may well call the earthworm "Nature's ploughman," nearly always at work, piercing and loosening the soil and making it more fertile. Charles Darwin estimated that an acre of garden has on the average about 53,000 earthworms, through whose bodies some 10 tons of soil pass annually.

Some tropical species of earthworms reach four feet in length, but British species are measured in inches. The surface of the earthworm's body is provided with tiny bristles, which help in crawling and in burrowing. The body is divided by furrows into a number of rings ; those in front are larger than those in the middle, and those behind are flatter : which, incidentally, enables one to distinguish the front from the tail end.

The earthworm, although its outward appearance is so simple, is wonderfully constructed. It is provided with digestive, circulatory, and nervous systems; but it is without eyes. The digestive system is a muscular tube running through the body, having a crop and gizzard in its course. The food consists of animal and vegetable matter (such as leaves) mixed with soil. The food is digested and taken into the system and the earth voided again. In this way the worm is continually moving the soil about. Thus do worms bring vegetable mould to the surface, throwing up their familiar " worm-casts." New generations of earthworms come from eggs.

Earwig. That this insect creeps into people's ears and bores a way to their brain is just a silly story. It eats animal and vegetable matter, and its custom is to spend the daytime hidden in some dark cranny: hence one may find an earwig inside a broken or decaying apple, or inside a large flower-bud.

The family life of the earwig is interesting. The female guards and cares for her numerous young, which emerge from eggs in about 15 days, and which look just like herself, only smaller and paler, until they are big enough to fend for themselves. So quickly does she breed that she may have a new family on her hands before she has finished bringing up the previous one. As for the earwig's formidable looking pincers, at the end of its tail,

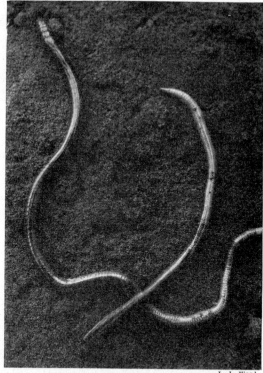

J. J. Ward

EARTHWORMS UP FOR AN AIRING
In very dry weather, earthworms go deep down into the soil where there is moisture. Similarly, in frosty weather they keep well away from the surface. When the top soil is reasonably moist they frequently emerge. But seldom is one found far from the entrance to its burrow.

the insect uses them for folding up its wings and tucking them away under the little leathery wing-covers. The pincers of a male are curved; those of a female are straight. Earwigs belong to the order *Dermaptera*. The common earwig of Britain is *Forficula auricularia*. It flies mostly by night.

J. J. Ward

EARWIG : MOTHER AND GROWING FAMILY
Unlike most insects, which lose all interest in the eggs the moment they are laid, the female earwig (left) tends both eggs and young (centre). The eggs take about 15 days to hatch, and the young earwigs are at first very pale, almost silvery, in colour. As they increase in size, so they discard their tight outer skins in a series of moults. The one on the right has almost slipped out of its old skin—seen bunched round the pincers. Note the cloak-like wing-covers.

LIFE and LANDS EASTWARD in AFRICA

Three European Powers—Great Britain, France and Portugal—have possessions along the east coast of Africa. Once regarded as a paradise for big-game hunters, we learn here how important these lands have become commercially.

East Africa. Included in this immense portion of the continent of Africa are British East Africa, consisting of Kenya Colony and Protectorate, the Uganda Protectorate, Tanganyika Territory, and the islands of Zanzibar and Pemba; British and French Somaliland; the two former Italian colonies of Eritrea and Somaliland ; and Portuguese East Africa or Mozambique.

Kenya Colony extends from the Indian Ocean to Lake Victoria and Uganda, the territories on the coast rented from the Sultan of Zanzibar forming the Protectorate. It is bounded on the north by Abyssinia and the former Italian Colony of Somaliland, and on the south is Tanganyika Territory. It has an area of 225,000 square miles. Agriculture is the most important industry, the main producing areas being in the highlands of the interior, where flax, coffee, maize and wheat are grown. A start was made in 1946 on the intensive and large-scale production of ground-nuts. The mineral resources have not yet been fully explored, but include silver and salt. Nairobi is the capital. The population of Kenya Colony is estimated at 3,940,000.

The Uganda Protectorate is still partly governed by native chiefs and kings under British supervision. The leading tribe is the highly intelligent Baganda. They are Christian. The Uganda railway extends from Mombasa in Kenya to Kampala, the commercial centre of Uganda. The Protectorate includes the course of the Nile from Lake Victoria to Nimule, on the frontier of the Anglo-Egyptian Sudan. Part of its western boundary is formed by the Belgian Congo. Of the area of 93,981 square miles, 13,610 square miles are covered with water. This includes part of Lakes Victoria, Albert, and Edward, and the whole of Lakes George, Kioga, and Salisbury. The chief product is cotton. Coffee, chillies, oil-seeds, tobacco, hides, tin-ore and ivory are also exported. Extensive experiments in agriculture are being conducted from the British administrative headquarters at Entebbe. The country is covered with a network of motor roads and there is a government transport service on those not served by private enterprise. The estimated population is about 3,900,000.

At the end of the First World War (1914–18) the former German colony of East Africa was divided between Great Britain and Belgium under mandates of the League of Nations. The British portion, renamed Tanganyika in 1920, occupies 620 miles of coast line between Kenya Colony and Mozambique, extending inland to Lake Tanganyika and the Belgian Congo. The area is roughly 360,000 square miles, great lakes accounting for about 20,000 square miles of this. The high pasture lands of the interior feed great numbers of cattle and sheep, mostly owned by the natives. There are about 5,600 square miles of valuable timber. Chief exports are sisal, cotton,

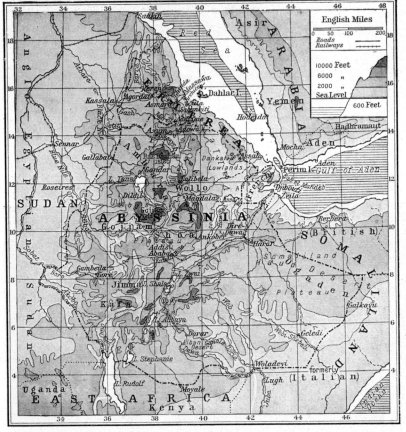

EAST AFRICA'S NORTHERN LANDS
Much of the northern part of East Africa is barren, but the interior of Abyssinia is very fertile. Somaliland is peopled by wandering tribes who are continually seeking fresh grazing grounds. Abyssinia, Eritrea and part of Somaliland belonged to Italy until 1941, when Abyssinia was restored to its Emperor, and the rest freed by the Allies.

coffee, ground-nuts, hides, and copra. In 1946 a scheme was introduced for the production of ground-nuts on a large scale. The territory produces gold and diamonds. There are over 22,000 miles of motor roads and about 2,000 miles of railways. The estimated population of Tanganyika is 5,500,000.

Portuguese East Africa, or Mozambique, lies to the south, and fronts the French island of Madagascar across the 300 miles' breadth of Mozambique Channel. To the west are Northern and Southern Rhodesia, and to the south lies the Union of South Africa. Mozambique has an area of 297,654 square miles. The chief products are sugar, maize, cotton, copra, sisal and gold. The capital, Lourenço Marques (population 43,000), is on Delagoa Bay, a highly important harbour. It is connected by rail with Pretoria, the Transvaal capital, and is the chief outlet for that rich mining region. The population of Mozambique is over 5,000,000.

By her conquest of Abyssinia in 1936, Italy created an East African Empire. Eritrea and Italian Somaliland had been Italian colonies for some time. But they were greatly extended to include portions of the old Abyssinia. The whole of this vast area was very undeveloped, but the Italians built roads, wireless stations, and harbour works, including a new port at Assab in Eritrea. During the Second World War Italy's East African Empire was conquered by the Allied Forces, the Italians surrendering in 1941. Eritrea and Italian Somaliland then came under a British military administration until 1950.

In March 1950, Italy again took over the administration of Somaliland under United Nations trusteeship for 10 years, at the end of which time the country would become independent. In December 1950 the United Nations decided that Eritrea was to become a self-governing country in federation with Ethiopia by September 1952.

Eritrea lies along the shores of the Red Sea. Its barren, sandy lowlands are inhabited by nomadic peoples who cultivate the land. Potash, skins, and salt are principal products. The population is about 600,000. Italian Somaliland has a very long coastline, but only one real port—Mogadiscio. In the south is the Jubaland region, which was handed over from Kenya in 1925. Cattle rearing and agriculture are the main occupations of the Somalis. The population is over 1,000,000.

The small colony of French Somaliland (area 9,071 square miles) lies between Eritrea and British Somaliland; the capital is Djibouti.

British Somaliland is a Protectorate, 68,000 square miles in area. The natives are nearly all wanderers by nature, although one or two largish towns have been developed along the coastal strip under British rule. The capital is Berbera (population 20,000). The population of the Protectorate is 700,000.

EAST AFRICA AND ITS DIVISIONS

Easter. The name Easter may come from that of the ancient Anglo-Saxon goddess of spring Eastre, in whose honour a festival of spring was held in the month of April. It is from these old-time pagan festivals that many of our Easter customs have come. Easter also contains survivals of the Passover feast of the Jews, observed in memory of the exodus from Egypt.

One of the oldest of Easter customs is exchanging coloured eggs as symbols of the Resurrection of Jesus Christ. From time immemorial eggs have been used to represent the new birth of the springtide. Easter has been celebrated as a Church

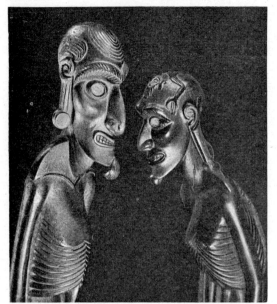

Bech & Macgregor

EASTER ISLAND ART
That the former inhabitants of the volcanic Easter Island in the South Pacific possessed a high degree of craftsmanship is evidenced by these two wooden figures, now in the British Museum, London.

festival since the very early days of the Christian Church. It is known as a movable feast, because it is not always held on the same date. The Church Council at Nicaea, in Asia Minor (A.D. 325), decided that Easter should be celebrated on the first Sunday after the first full moon after the vernal equinox (March 21). But the calculation of the date is very complicated, and most of us are content to take it from those who work out the calendar year by year.

Easter is the climax of a series of special days of observance instituted by the early Church. Lent is the fast of 40 days which ends with Easter. The first day of Lent is Ash Wednesday, named from the custom of strewing ashes over the head as a sign of penitence. Palm Sunday is one week before Easter, and commemorates the triumphant entry of Jesus into Jerusalem. On this day many

churches are decorated with palms. Palm Sunday, following Passion Week, opens Holy Week, in which are observed Maundy Thursday, commemorating the last supper of Christ with the disciples; Good Friday, commemorating the crucifixion; and Holy Saturday, on which in the Catholic Church the first Easter Mass is held, and which closes Lent.

Easter Island.
In the South Pacific Ocean 2,300 miles west of the coast of Chile lies the little speck of land known as Easter Island. It belongs to Chile, and was for a time a convict station but was made into a national park in 1935.

Today it supports scarcely more than 300 Polynesian natives, yet upon it are stone ruins which tell of a bygone civilization the origin and fate of which are utterly unknown. Chief among the ruins are great stone platforms upon which lie the remains of gigantic statues. In near-by quarries half-cut figures stand, just as they were when the workmen laid down their tools long ago.

The heads of the big grey images, one of which is 37 feet high, were cut flat to receive crowns made of reddish stone. A number of these crowns have been found in the quarries and near the platforms. The ruins also include remains of

EAST INDIES : CHAIN OF FERTILE ISLA
Lying between Asia and Australia is the group of islands known as the Malay Archipelago
East Indies. In olden days European countries obtained their spices from those lands, and
to capture the valuable spice trade that the Portuguese, Dutch and English established them
in the East Indies. After the Second World War (1939–45) the Netherlands East Indies,
included the islands of Sumatra, Java and Madura, obtained self-government from the

From Scoresby Routledge:
The Mystery of Easter Island

EASTER ISLAND
Huge stone faces, one measuring 37 feet, are scattered about Easter Island, but what race carved them long ago has not been discovered, nor have the inscriptions been deciphered.

large stone houses which command views of the sea. While other islands of the Pacific have somewhat similar remains of ancient builders, the ruins of Easter Island alone bear traces of picture-writing. The meanings of these pictographs scientists have tried in vain to unravel. Examples of these sculptures are to be seen at the British Museum in London. Easter Island is roughly triangular in shape, with a volcanic peak at each corner. Its area is 50 square miles. Its discovery on Easter Day in 1722 is credited to the Dutch Admiral Roggeveen.

East Indies.

Stretching eastward for nearly 4,000 miles from the south-east coast of Asia, on past the northern coast of Australia, lies the largest group of islands in the world, known variously as the Malay Archipelago, the East Indian Archipelago, and the East Indies. It

VEEN THE INDIAN OCEAN AND CORAL SEA
ablished the United States of Indonesia. A curious feature of the groups is the Wallace Line (named after the British scientist A. R. Wallace, 1823–1913), because the wild life to the west of it is Asiatic and that to the east is of the Australian type. The diagram in the top right-hand shows how the East Indies (here blacked-in) would appear if superimposed on the United From the western tip of Sumatra to the eastern tip of New Guinea is about 4,000 miles.

includes the Moluccas, New Guinea, Java, Borneo, Sumatra and the Philippines.

Among the larger islands, Sumatra has an area of 165,000 square miles; New Guinea about 320,000 square miles: and Borneo, about 290,000 square miles; Celebes is larger than Ireland and Scotland combined; Java, about the size of England; and Luzon (in the Philippines), somewhat larger than Ireland. Besides these, there are hundreds of smaller islands, many of great beauty and fertility. A deep strait separates the islands of Bali and Lombok, just east of Java, and while the plants and animals of Bali are Asiatic, those of Lombok are Australian.

One of the remarkable features of the archipelago is the large number of active and extinct volcanoes which commence in Sumatra, extend to the Sunda Islands, and then continue northward through the Philippines, forming a rough horseshoe. The Equator passes through the centre of the archipelago. In normal times the exports include rubber, sugar, spices, tobacco, various gums, coffee, tea, petroleum, copra and tin.

The East Indies are the rich spice islands sought by Columbus, Vasco da Gama, and other explorers. Many tales had reached the European countries of these wondrous islands, and their dream was to share in these riches. Early in the 16th century Portuguese adventurers finally reached the island of Sumatra. Soon after that explorers from other European nations made their way to the islands, and wars for their riches were waged by England, Portugal, and the Netherlands.

The Dutch managed to retain possession of the Netherlands East Indies, which comprised five large islands—Java, Sumatra, most of Borneo, Celebes, and the western half of New Guinea—and thousands of small ones. During the Second World War (1939–45) the Japanese overran and occupied these islands, and after the surrender of Japan to the Allied nations in August 1945 the native inhabitants of the Netherlands East Indies demanded a large amount of self-government.

Fighting broke out between the Dutch and the Javanese and continued intermittently for about two years, but in November 1946 an agreement was signed between the Dutch and the native leaders which provided for a Netherlands-Indonesian Union. In late 1949 the Netherlands East Indies (with the exception of Dutch New Guinea) became an independent republic known as the United States (later Republic) of Indonesia, the Netherlands handing over all power to the Government of the new State.

The British Colony of North Borneo occupies the northern part of the island of Borneo and includes the island of Labuan. On the north-west coast of the island is Sarawak, which from 1841 until 1946, when it became a British Colony, was ruled by white rajahs under British protection. The eastern half of New Guinea is under the Australian Government, and is divided into the Territory of Papua (the south-eastern portion) and the Territory of New Guinea (the north-eastern region).

The Philippine Islands were acquired in 1899 from Spain by the United States, and during the occupation of the islands by Japanese forces (1941–45) in the Second World War the people assisted the American troops, rendering considerable service to the Allied cause. In view of this they were granted independence by the United States in 1946 as the Republic of the Philippines.

Ebony. The chief characteristic of this valuable wood is its jet-black colour. This, combined with durability, hardness, and the readiness with which it will take a high polish, makes it prized for ornamental cabinet work and for inlaying. The black keys of the best pianos are made of ebony, as are knife-handles and other small articles.

P. M. Synge

EAST INDIES : JAVANESE FISHERMEN
Standing on small rafts, these natives of Java are casting nets at shoals of small fish swimming in shallow water. Fish and rice are the two main articles of diet of the Javanese, who are of Malay stock. This island of Java, which is about the size of England and is one of the world's richest tropical areas, is included in the Republic of Indonesia.

MARVELLOUS SPECTACLE OF THE SUN IN ECLIPSE

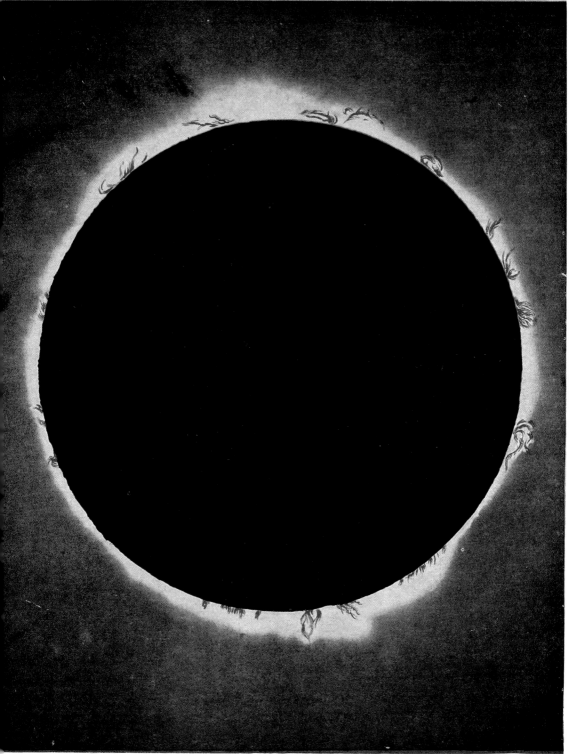

ring a total eclipse the orb of the sun is obscured by the moon for only a few minutes, so that astronomers have merely that ef period in which to make observations and take photographs.   This photograph was taken at Giggleswick, in Yorkshire, during total eclipse of June 29, 1927.   The vivid fiery prominences are tongues of flame shooting out from behind the eclipsing moon.

TOTAL AND PARTIAL ECLIPSE OF THE SUN

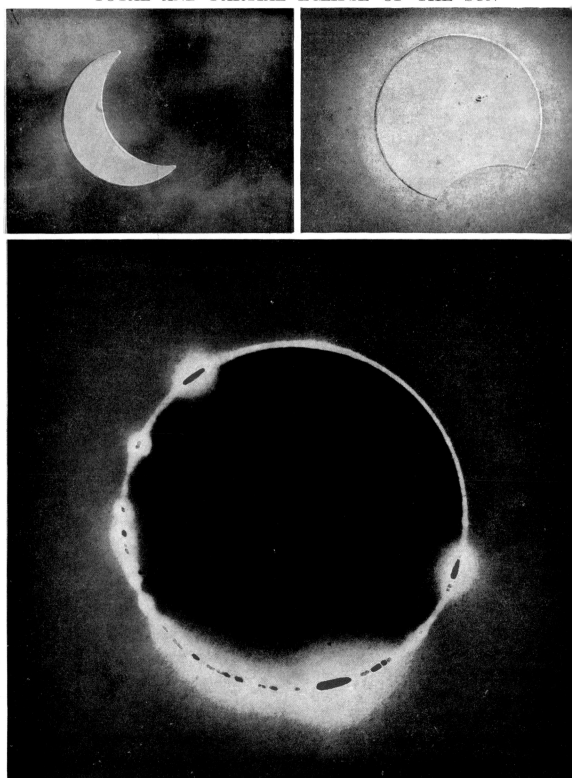

The lower photograph, taken by Dr. R. L. Waterfield at Camptonville, California, during the eclipse of April 26, 1930, shows cur; knobs of light on the outer rim of the sun. These are known as Baily's Beads, because they were first observed by Francis B (1774–1844). Top right, a partial eclipse of November 1929; top left, a phase of the 1927 eclipse, which is depicted over)

Painting by J. W. Waterhouse; Walker Art Gallery, Liverpool

ECHO IGNORED BY THE YOUTH NARCISSUS

According to the old Greek legend, Echo was a nymph who fell in love with the beautiful youth Narcissus, who became enamoured of his own reflection in a pool and never ceased gazing at it. Echo slowly pined away from unrequited love until there was nothing left of her but her voice, which you can hear repeating your words if you call out in a valley. In another tale she is stated to have refused the love of Pan, who caused her to be torn in pieces, only her voice remaining.

Of the numerous tropical trees which produce this hard black timber, the most important is the ebony tree of the southern part of the sub-continent of India and Ceylon, which yields logs of up to three feet in diameter. Only the heart-wood is used, for the sap-wood underneath the bark is white. Trees of western Africa and the East Indies also produce fine ebony. The West Indian ebony is a small tree or shrub, its trunk rarely more than four inches in diameter, with dark brown wood.

Most ebony trees belong to the genus *Diospyros*. The scientific name of the southern Indian variety is *Diospyros ebenum;* it is distinguished from other species by its jet-black charred-looking bark. The Coromandel ebony (found in the East Indies) is *Diospyros melanoxylon.*

Echo. Nearly all ancient peoples had poetic stories about the echo. According to the old Greeks, Echo was a mountain nymph who was once the companion of Hera (Juno). Having displeased the goddess, Echo was changed into a being who could not speak till she was spoken to, and then could only repeat the last word that had been spoken. She pined away for love of the youth Narcissus, until there was nothing left of her but her voice. According to another legend she refused the love of Pan, who caused her to be torn in pieces by shepherds, only her voice remaining.

No one really knew what an echo was until scientists discovered that sound travels in waves, just as water and light travel. If a wave of water is stopped by a cliff it is thrown back into the sea. If a sound-wave is stopped by a cliff or wall, it is thrown back to our ears; but the sound very seldom comes back just as it was made. Sometimes the echo repeats the sound several times. This is caused by successive rebounds from several different objects, placed at varying distances from the observer. If you stand about 100 feet from the deflecting surface you hear only the final syllable of what you call. If you take your stand farther back, more syllables may be heard, only much more faintly, of course. Sir Isaac Newton used the echo in a corridor at Trinity College, Cambridge, to measure the speed at which sound travels. Standing at one end of the corridor he started a group of sound-waves by stamping his foot. These waves were thrown back by the wall at the far end of the corridor. By timing the interval between stamping his foot and hearing the echo, he learned how long it took the sound to travel down the corridor and back. He calculated the velocity of sound, but incorrectly. We know today that sound travels at the rate of about 1,100 feet a second—at ordinary temperature and altitude. It is a peculiarity of many public buildings that speakers cannot be properly heard by all because their remarks are drowned on the way by their own echoes. (*See* Sound).

Eclipse. The primitive Northmen thought the sun and moon were pursued by two enormous wolves, who now and then very nearly succeeded in devouring our chief sources of light. Even till recent days the Chinese believed a solar eclipse was caused by a great dragon attempting to swallow the sun. On such occasions they would set up a terrific din to frighten the monster away.

The facts are not so romantic, though we might almost say that the sun and moon and earth are playing hide and seek with one another. A solar eclipse occurs when the moon gets between the sun and earth, obscuring the sun from our view. A lunar eclipse is caused by the shadow which the

If you were floating in space some thousands of miles from the Earth this is how an eclipse would appear to you. The Moon has come in line with the Sun and casts down its conical shadow on the Earth. Complete darkness occurs in one comparatively small circle—in this case in the middle of the Sahara Desert. Partial darkness extends over a much larger area. In a total eclipse of the Sun by the Moon the diameter of the Moon's shadow cast upon the Earth averages about 150 miles and sweeps across the Earth from west to east with great rapidity. The longest time a total eclipse of the Sun by the Moon can be visible at any place is a little over seven minutes.

earth casts on the moon when the earth is between the moon and the sun.

Imagine a straight line drawn through the sun and earth and extending beyond the earth on the other side. If the moon in its monthly trip around our planet always passed directly through this line, first on one side of the earth and then on the other, we should see two eclipses every month—one of the sun and one of the moon. But the moon moves in an orbit which is tilted somewhat away from the orbit made by the earth in its annual journey round the sun, and for that reason, eclipses are rather rare.

There may be as many as five of the sun and three of the moon in a year, or there may be no eclipses of the moon and only two of the sun. In many cases, of course, these eclipses are only partial, and from a single spot on the earth it is not likely that a total solar eclipse will be observed more than once in 300 years. But since a total lunar eclipse is visible over half the earth's surface at once, everyone has a chance of seeing several during his lifetime.

It is little wonder that primitive people were frightened by a solar eclipse. For a period—sometimes as long as seven minutes—the earth is plunged in darkness, the stars flash out, flowers close up, birds go to rest, and cattle in the field become restless and terrified. Round the edges of the moon can be seen numerous rose coloured prominences, while shooting still higher—extending upwards a million miles or more from the surface of the sun—are streamers of pearly white which constitute the corona.

A solar eclipse is of supreme interest to astronomers, and leads many of them to travel long distances to points from which it is observable, taking their instruments with them and hoping for a clear sky. Observations of eclipses have led to many discoveries. That of 1868

ECLIPSE OF THE SUN NEARING COMPLETION
One of the most impressive sights is an eclipse of the sun, but the period during which the earth is in almost complete darkness lasts only a few minutes. This photograph was taken during the total eclipse of June 29, 1927, which was visible in England. There will not be another total eclipse which can be observed from England until 1999.

resulted in the detection of helium in the sun 27 years before it was found to be a constituent of one of the rarer earths, cleveite; while at the eclipse of May 1919 a Greenwich party verified Einstein's theory of relativity according to which light is attracted by the sun and deflected from a straight path. Much information about the physical nature of the sun has also been obtained during total eclipses, because only when the sun is obscured can its atmosphere be studied.

Ecology. Though this is one of the younger branches of biology (q.v.), some of its principles were clearly set out as long ago as the time of Charles Darwin. He explained how a farmer, by supporting a number of domestic cats, could increase his pasture crop of red clover ! The cats would kill field mice; this would save the life of many humble-bees, whose nests and grubs would otherwise have been devoured by the mice. There would be more humble-bees at work visiting and fertilising the clover flowers, a task for which they alone are fitted.

The more thoroughly the blossoms were fertilised, the more seed would be produced, and so on.

Of course a good clover crop does not depend on bees alone, and if we were to look more closely into this little problem we should find that many more kinds of denizens of our meadows were involved, as well as the birds in the trees around. In fact, the plant and animal inhabitants of any region form a community in which the balance of Nature depends on a nice adjustment of the whole. Man, in trying hastily improvised measures to rid himself of one pest, may import some kind of animal or insect into the region—and find he has saddled himself with a worse pest.

For many years farmers and scientists have disputed whether rooks, for example, did more good than harm, although they admittedly raided growing crops. Bird lovers have urged that rooks should not be slaughtered indiscriminately; some investigators, by examining the crop and gizzard of thousands of rooks killed, have sought to prove that the enormous numbers of insects eaten gave the birds a claim to be considered friends of the farmer. A government inquiry was even held on this question—and could not give a verdict either way. This all goes to show what a complicated business is the balance of Nature.

Ecology, then, treats of plant and animal communities, and seeks to show the relations of living things to the region they inhabit. It investigates chains of cause and effect, like the cat-mouse-bee-clover example just given. It suggests ways in which we can read Nature's secrets more intelligently, and can apply our knowledge to make the forces of Nature serve us more effectively.

Each kind of plant or animal life is suited to the region where the organism lives—the kind of soil, the amount of moisture and light, and the varying temperatures and seasons. Moreover, each of them is living there because, for the time being at least, it is able to hold its own among its neighbours. Some very slight change—such as the felling of many trees in the area, or the destruction of many birds—may have astonishing results. A violent storm which kills many migrating birds or insects on the wing, or a succession of late frosts which kills insect grubs, or a shortage of food, may likewise upset the balance for the time being.

Restoring the Upset Balance of Nature

A few years ago both cougars (" mountain lions ") and deer were abundant in the Grand Canyon National Park of the U.S.A. and in the near-by Kaibab National Forest. Because cougars preyed on the deer, hunters were allowed to shoot cougars in the Kaibab until they had destroyed almost all. Then, with their natural enemy gone, the deer increased so rapidly that the herbage and foliage of the Kaibab were not sufficient to support them. They stripped the trees of all the leaves and twigs they could reach, and did great damage in the Grand Canyon Park as well.

Eventually the deer grew feeble, and their young were not strong. At last it was necessary to let the hunters now shoot the deer ·to reduce their number until the feeding grounds would be ample to support the remainder. The cougars, on the other hand, were now protected in the hope that they would multiply and carry on again their role of maintaining Nature's balance—by killing off weakly deer which, because of their less vigorous condition, would be likely to produce poor breeding stock similar to themselves.

Sufficient has been said to make it clear that ecology is one of the most interesting, and one of the most important, branches of biology. Our colour plate graphically portrays how heat and moisture may influence the plant and animal life of a region.

Economics. Thomas Carlyle called it " the dismal science," yet there should be nothing dismal about the story of how we and all the other people in the world get our living. For that is really the subject-matter of economics, or political economy as it used to be called. It is concerned with the bread-and-butter activities of mankind. The text-books may still assert that economics is the science of wealth, but economics today is concerned with much more than what is regarded as wealth in popular speech. To " wealth " one might add the word " welfare," for economics treats of the material welfare of human beings.

As such it cannot but be of interest to everybody. It tries to give answers to such questions as: How is wealth—useful goods and services of any and every kind—produced, distributed, and consumed ? Why are the few rich and the many poor? Why should a policeman get more pay than a farm-labourer? Are big businesses better than small? Where does money come from, and who decides how much each shall get? What causes unemployment? These are just a few of the thousands of questions with which the economist is concerned, and to answer them properly would require the rest of this volume. Here we can only outline briefly the principles which are necessary to understand simple economic problems.

We all need food, clothing, and shelter; and the simplest way of getting these things would be for each of us to grow our own food, weave our own clothes, and build our own houses. Such, indeed, is the custom among some primitive peoples to this day. But the standard of living desired among civilized peoples calls for more than this.

We desire delicacies and nice clothes, comfortable beds and well-furnished houses, electric light, telephones, motor-cars, restaurants, well-paved streets, churches, theatres, books, and other things which each one cannot produce for himself. We have machinery which does the work of many men, but which no one person can afford to own for his private use alone. We have water companies and railway lines whose value depends upon the fact that they serve the needs of a great many people at once.

Labour Exchanged for Goods or Services

So we have arrived at what is called " division of labour," a state of society in which each person confines himself to doing certain things and exchanges his labour or its products for goods produced or services rendered by others. The shoemaker makes shoes, the baker bakes bread, and each gets the other things he needs by barter or by selling his goods for money and then buying what he needs. Sometimes the " division of labour " goes so far that a person spends all his working time at one small operation, repeated over and over again.

We may divide the history of any commodity into three parts : production, consumption, and distribution. The mining of iron ore, the manufacture of machinery, the growing and harvesting of wheat, the grinding of the flour, the making of bread—these are all obvious examples of " production." But the railway and the grocer's shop are also engaged in production in the economic sense, for although they do not grow or manufacture anything they actually " produce " a part of the value by placing the commodity at your door. The final " consumption " comes, of course, when (let us say) you eat the bread; but there are also earlier stages, as when the wheat was consumed in making bread. These stages are called " productive " consumption.

The most difficult and complicated of the three divisions is the " distribution " of wealth created by production. Wealth here means " anything which has the power to satisfy our wants and which cannot be obtained without effort." In the sense in which economists use the term, a pound of wheat, a pound

ECOLOGY: INFLUENCE OF HEAT AND LIGHT

Great heat with heavy rains produces the kind of forest shown here. At the right we see a primitive native settlement typical of this environment. Here men must fight against excessive vegetation and a too abundant insect life.

Here the red and blue bars at the left show great heat with very little rain—the conditions that create a desert. Only around the rare water holes can life of any kind exist, and the oasis is the centre of all human activity.

The plant-animal balance is at its best where rain and heat are moderate. It is in this type of environment that farming prospers and most of the world's food is grown. Here too the most vigorous civilization flourishes today.

Scanty rainfall in a temperate zone usually means treeless plains with meagre water-courses, like the old buffalo ranges of the Western United States. These now support cattle and sheep, but without irrigation farming is difficult or impossible.

ECONOMICS—THE SCIENCE OF EVERYDAY LIFE

Fox; Topical; British Railways; Leica

Economics is concerned with every human activity that affects production and trade, and the principal economic problem for any community is how to make the best use of its labour and resources in order to satisfy the wants of the people. The economist must acquaint himself with such widely different work as that done by the coal miner (1) and the stenographer with her typewriter (2).

In Throgmorton Street (3), seen here crowded with men discussing the day's affairs, is the London Stock Exchange, whose business involves many problems of economics. The work and pay of such citizens as stevedores (4) who load and unload ships' cargoes, the engine-driver on the footplate of a locomotive (5), and the ploughman preparing the land for sowing (6), must also be considered.

To face page 1081

of flour, a loaf of bread, are all objects of wealth, and in this case the amount of wealth is measured by the price paid for the loaf, the flour or the wheat.

Let us ask ourselves what types of agencies take part in the production of wealth, as represented in this case by the loaf of bread. The answer given by economics is : land, labour, capital, and organization or management. The root of all wealth is in *land*. It is the source of all the raw materials of production. It yields the iron ore and the wheat crop; it provides the site for the mill and the factory. The landowner's share of the product is usually called " rent."

The next great agency in wealth production is *labour*. Without labour, wealth cannot be created out of natural resources. But we must not think of it as manual labour alone, for the railway managers and the foremen are as truly labourers in the economic sense as the men who actually plough the field and load the flour into the lorry. In either case the labourer's share of wealth is measured in " wages."

The third element, *capital*, may be defined as " the results of past labour or enterprise accumulated by thrift or abstinence." When a person acquires a share of wealth either he may use it in buying things he desires, or he may deny himself this satisfaction and save it. In the latter case, that share of wealth may become capital, and be used in production.

Capital includes tools, machinery, buildings, raw materials; and out of it are paid wages and all other expenses incurred in the period between the beginning of production and the receipt of pay for the product. Money is merely one form of capital, and that not the most important. Capital's share from the production of wealth is called " interest "; in other words, interest is the price that men pay for the use of capital.

Organization, or *management*, the fourth and last agency in the production of wealth, is the one which unites all the others and puts them to work, so to speak. We might have land, we might have men ready to labour, we might have capital ready to be used—yet nothing would be produced unless they were brought together in some definite undertaking. This task is performed by the organizer—the *entrepreneur*, as he is called by the old French economists—or what we should usually refer to as " the business man."

He is the one who conceives the productive project, who obtains the land, hires the labour, procures the capital, and sometimes takes the risks. His share in the production of wealth is called " profits," and consists of whatever may be left over from the sales of the product after rent, wages, and interest have been paid. If the project has been a good one, the profits may be large; but if misfortune attends it he may get nothing for his pains and may even lose money.

Now for a word of history. One of the earliest groups of political economists was that of the " Mercantilists " (16th and 17th centuries), who believed that gold and silver were the chief forms of wealth. The " Physiocrats " of the 18th century held agriculture to be the chief source of a nation's wealth, and denounced the restrictive measures by which their predecessors encouraged manufactures and commerce. The Wealth of Nations, a book published in Great Britain by Adam Smith in 1776, laid the foundations of the more modern science, and gained for its author the name of " the father of political economy." T. R. Malthus's writings on the laws of population, and David Ricardo's on the Iron Law of Wages both advanced the " classic " school of the science. John Stuart Mill's book Principles of Political Economy (1848) long remained the standard treatise from this point of view. Since that time a host of British, French, German, Austrian, Italian and American writers have dealt with the subject from less abstract and more historical points of view, and have profoundly modified and humanized the teachings of this science, which formerly was rather dreary.

The EQUATOR COUNTRY of AMERICA

*E*cuador takes its name from the Spanish word meaning equator, and it is
situated on that imaginary line around the earth. Why, though on the
equator, the climate of the greater part is temperate is explained here.

Ecuador. (Pron. ek'-wa-dōr). Situated on the west coast of South America, with Colombia to the north and Peru to the south, Ecuador affords a vivid contrast to the parched coastal regions of its southern neighbour. This arises from the fact that the Antarctic current, whose cold waters prevent the evaporation of the sea water to form rain, is suddenly turned westward by the bulging coast of Peru. The coast of Ecuador, therefore, enjoys abundant rains, and its broad plains are covered with dense forests and rich soil. Ecuador has the only considerable group of navigable waterways and the only important gulf —the Gulf of Guayaquil—on the whole Pacific coast of South and Central America.

A 287-mile railway journey to the north-east of Guayaquil, the chief seaport of the republic (population, 160,000), climbing the Andes to a height of 9,000 feet, brings the traveller to the capital, Quito, one of the strangest cities in the world. Although Quito (population 150,000) is within 15 miles of the Equator, its great height gives it a climate of perpetual spring. One season is so like another that planting and harvesting go on side by side. The mountain pass which gives entrance to the fertile plain of Quito is guarded by a group of snow-clad peaks. Here stands the majestic Chimborazo (20,702 feet), and near by is Cotopaxi (19,613 feet), the loftiest active volcano in the world.

Ecuador's climates—for it has several varieties— are arranged in vertical belts. Above the tropical lowlands lie the plateaux enclosed between the eastern and western ranges of the Andes, where it is always spring ; higher still unbroken winter makes life almost impossible. On the eastern slopes of

ECUADORIAN INDIANS OF THE WILD INTERIOR

When babies are taken out of doors in Ecuador they are carried in a shawl slung over their mother's shoulder (left). By this means the parent's hands are left free, and she knows her child is safe while she is working.   On the right is a Jivaro hunter, a member of a tribe inhabiting the little-known forested country of south-eastern Ecuador. Dressed only in a cotton waist-cloth, he has bamboo tubes in his ears as ornaments, and a necklace of white buttons.

H E. Anthony, American Museum of Natural History

Like some of the natives of Borneo and Malaya, the Jivaros use blow-pipes, and here is a hunter taking aim. For small game the ammunition consists of sun-baked pellets of clay; to kill large animals, cane darts with poisoned tips are used.   The poison kills very quickly, but does not spoil the meat for eating.   The Jivaros are also head-hunters, and it is difficult for a young Indian to find a wife unless he can display a captured head as proof of his bravery.   Among the Zaporos, who are neighbours of the Jivaros, it is a courtship custom for a young man to throw down before the lady of his choice some game that he has killed.   If she picks it up and cooks it, she accepts him.

the Andes and in the valleys of the Amazon river system are tropical forests and swamps, where the heat and humidity are dangerous to any but the Indians.

In the fertile lowlands of the coast cocoa beans, cotton, vegetable ivory (or corozo nuts), fibre for Panama hats, coffee, sugar-cane, tobacco, rice, maize and tropical fruits grow. Higher up, on the temperate plateau, grow wheat, oats, maize, barley, potatoes and other vegetables, but only enough for home consumption. The resources of the prolific forest region of the eastern lowlands are largely undeveloped; here are vast supplies of rubber, vegetable ivory, dyewoods, and cinchona bark from which quinine is made.

The country is known to be rich in copper, iron, lead and coal. Gold is mined, and oil-fields are worked. Development of the mineral and agricultural resources has been held back by the lack of communications. Only about 700 miles of railway have been laid, the chief being the picturesque and difficult line connecting Guayaquil and Quito.

Ecuador possesses the Galapagos Islands, lying on the equator 730 miles to the west, embracing a territory of 2,868 square miles with a population of about 2,000. They have strategic importance, since they lie directly in the path of vessels approaching the Panama Canal from Australia. Their chief interest arises from the study made of their natural history by Charles Darwin, the English scientist. They are the home of a giant tortoise that can carry several men on its back.

Underwood

ECUADOR'S MOUNTAIN CAPITAL : QUITO
Standing over 9,000 feet above sea-level and surrounded by volcanic peaks, Quito (pron. kē-tō) has suffered repeatedly from earthquakes, many of the old buildings being damaged or destroyed. The city was an Indian capital long before it was captured by the Incas of Peru in 1470.

Hundreds of years before the Spanish conqueror came Ecuador was inhabited by a race of unknown antiquity—a semi-civilized people who built roads, palaces, and temples of stone, wrought household implements of pure gold, filled teeth with gold as skilfully as any modern dentist, and who have left mysterious memorials of their art in groups of great carved stone chairs, beautifully designed and ornamented. Long years before the Incas founded their wonderful empire this prehistoric race built its cities and temples on the heights of Ecuador, and then vanished, no one knows how or when or why. (*See* Incas).

Conquered in 1534 by lieutenants of the Spanish adventurer Pizarro, the country was administered under the Spanish viceroyalty of Peru. From 1809 to 1822 there were several efforts to shake off Spanish rule, culminating in 1822, when one of the generals of Simon Bolivar (*q.v.*) the " liberator of South America," finally defeated the forces of Spain. Ecuador was at first incorporated with Venezuela and Colombia, but became an independent republic in 1830. The area of the republic is estimated at 275,000 square miles. The population is about 3,200,000.

Eddington, Sir Arthur Stanley (1882–1944). British astronomer and philosopher, this scientist's Report on the Relativity Theory of Gravitation (1918) and Space, Time and Gravitation (1920) are contributions of outstanding value to physics. His reputation with the general public was based upon his charm as a lecturer and his remarkable powers of explanation which made his later books—Stars and Atoms (1927), The Nature of the Physical World (1928), Science and the Unseen World (1929), The Expanding Universe (1933), and New Pathways in Science (1935)—extremely popular with the ordinary reader.

Eddington was born at Kendal on December 28, 1882. He left Owens College (now Manchester University) to enter upon a brilliant mathematical career at Trinity College, Cambridge. He was appointed chief assistant of the Royal Observa-

Elliott & Fry

SIR ARTHUR EDDINGTON
Known to the public through his popular books on scientific topics, this British astronomer became chief assistant at Greenwich Observatory in 1906, was appointed Director of Cambridge Observatory in 1914, and was knighted in 1930.

tory at Greenwich in 1906, and rapidly established his reputation as one of the ablest mathematical astronomers of his day. Taking up the post of Plumian professor of astronomy at Cambridge in 1913, he was appointed director of the University observatory in 1914 and also made a Fellow of the Royal Society, the premier scientific society in the United Kingdom. In 1928 he won the Royal Medal of the Royal Society. President of the Physical Society, 1930–1932, he was knighted in 1930 and invested by the king with the Order of Merit in 1938. He died on November 22, 1944.

Eddystone Lighthouse. Extraordinary difficulties had to be overcome by John Smeaton, who built the third Eddystone lighthouse in 1759, knowing the fate of its predecessors. The first was destroyed by a hurricane in 1703, after only three years; the second was burnt down in 1755.

The Eddystone rocks lie in the English Channel some 14 miles south-west of Plymouth in Devonshire, right in the track of ships; therefore the importance of a warning beacon can be imagined. Smeaton's lighthouse, which was 95 feet high, stood from 1759 to 1877, when it was considered to be unsafe. The present lighthouse was built in 1882 by Sir James Douglass, 40 yards from the site of Smeaton's structure, the upper parts of which are preserved on Plymouth Hoe. It contains 4,688 tons of stone, has nine rooms, and is 168 feet above water level.

Eden, GARDEN OF. In the Bible we read how " the Lord God planted a garden eastward in Eden, and there he put the man whom he had

formed. And out of the ground made the Lord God to grow every tree that is pleasant to the sight, and good for food; the tree of life also in the midst of the garden, and the tree of knowledge of good and evil." Adam, the man whom God had created,

EDDYSTONE LIGHTHOUSE
Erected on a reef 14 miles south-west of Plymouth, Devonshire, the present Eddystone Lighthouse was completed in 1882. It was the fourth built on those rocks. The lantern gives two flashes every 30 seconds, and the light is visible at a distance of nearly 18 miles.

Walker Art Gallery, Liverpool

EDEN : ADAM AND EVE EXPELLED FROM THE GARDEN

Vividly depicted in this painting by the British artist A. T. Nowell (1862–1940) is the expulsion of Adam and Eve from the Garden of Eden, punishment for their sin in disobeying God's commands. The forlorn misery of the First Man and his wife and the pity of the guardian angels for their fall are well expressed.

was put in this garden to tend it and keep it. And he was told that he might eat freely of every tree in the garden except one, the tree of the knowledge of good and evil. Later the Lord made a woman, Eve, to be Adam's wife. Tempted by the serpent, Eve tasted the fruit of the forbidden tree, and persuaded Adam to eat of it also. To punish them for their disobedience God expelled them from the Garden, to labour for their bread and become the first parents of Mankind.

Such is the Biblical story of the Garden of Eden. Similar legends have been traced in the early literature of the Babylonians, and in much later times the English poet Milton (1608–74) dwelt upon the idyllic life of Adam and Eve in the Garden of Eden and their expulsion in his great epic poem called Paradise Lost (*see* Milton). Scientists have tried to determine the locality of the Garden of Eden, and one conjecture places it on the Persian Gulf ; another, in the western part of the Nile delta.

Eden, ROBERT ANTHONY (born 1897). Few politicians manage to enter the British Cabinet before they are 40 years old, a feat which was

Topical

ANTHONY EDEN

Entering Parliament in 1923 when in his 24th year, Mr. Eden was Foreign Secretary from 1935 to 1938, Secretary for War in May 1940, and again Foreign Secretary, 1940-1945 under the Premiership of Mr. Winston Churchill.

accomplished by Mr. Anthony Eden, who became Foreign Secretary in December 1935. The second son of Sir W. Eden, he was born on June 12, 1897, and was educated at Eton and Christ Church, Oxford, where he distinguished himself in Oriental languages. He was in the Army during the First World War (1914–18), and in 1923 was elected Conservative M.P. for Warwick and Leamington. Made Under-secretary for Foreign Affairs in 1931, he was Foreign Secretary from 1935 to 1938. On the outbreak of the Second World War in September 1939, he became Secretary for the Dominions.

When Mr. Churchill succeeded Mr. Neville Chamberlain as Prime Minister, in May 1940, he appointed Mr. Eden Secretary of State for War. As such he announced the evacuation from Dunkirk and the formation of a Home Guard. In December 1940 Mr. Eden was again appointed Foreign Secretary, holding office until the defeat of the Churchill Government at the general election of July 1945. He retained his seat in Parliament. A volume of his speeches, entitled Foreign Affairs, was published in 1939.

Edinburgh, PRINCE PHILIP MOUNTBATTEN, DUKE OF (born 1921). The son of Prince and Princess Andrew of Greece and a great grandson of Queen Victoria, Prince Philip was born at Corfu on June 10, 1921. He was brought up by his uncle Lord Mountbatten, being educated at Gordonstoun, Scotland, and the Royal Naval College, Dartmouth. From 1940 he served in the Royal Navy. He became a naturalised British subject in 1947, taking the surname Mountbatten, and his engagement to Princess Elizabeth was announced on July 10, 1947. He was created Duke of Edinburgh by the King, and married Princess Elizabeth at Westminster Abbey on November 20, of the same year. (See Elizabeth.) In 1950 he was promoted lieutenant-commander and given the command of a frigate.

Edinburgh. (Pron. ed'-in-bur-o). The Castle Rock, a bold precipitous height of 430 feet, dominates the capital city of Scotland, just as the Acropolis dominates Athens. This circumstance, together with the city's in-

THE DUKE OF EDINBURGH

Here we see the Duke of Edinburgh going in to bat in a village cricket match. A good player and a keen sportsman, he was President of the National Playing Fields Association from 1948, and President of the M.C.C. 1949–1950.

tellectual and political prominence, makes Edinburgh's title of The Athens of the North more appropriate than such nicknames usually are. The rock is surmounted by a massive medieval castle, which was the ancient seat of the Scottish kings. In the precincts of the castle is the noble Scottish National War Memorial to those who fell in the First World War (1914–18).

From this height can be seen one of the finest panoramas in all Europe. On three sides the rock drops sheer to the valley below. To the east along a narrow ridge runs The Royal Mile (the Lawnmarket, High Street, and Canongate) to the Palace of Holyroodhouse, on the edge of King's Park, with Arthur's Seat (820 feet) behind. In Holyroodhouse once dwelt unhappy Mary Queen of Scots and others of the Scottish royal line. Our Royal Family still stay there on occasion.

To the south of the Royal Mile lies the quaint Old Town, familiar to readers of Scott's romances. At the foot of Castle Rock to the north are the beautiful Princes Street

F. C. Inglis

EDINBURGH SEEN FROM THE CASTLE ROCK

One of the largest cities in the United Kingdom in extent, Edinburgh measures over 11 miles by eight. In the centre of this photograph is Waverley Station, on the left of which is the colonnade of the National Gallery. Facing us above the railway tunnel (in the foreground) is the Royal Academy. In the distance on the right is part of the Old Town. In East Princes Gardens (left) is the monument to Sir Walter Scott (1771–1832) in the form of an open Gothic tower with a statue of the novelist within. To the left of the memorial is Princes Street, one of the finest thoroughfares in the world.

Gardens, sharing the ravine with the railway and Waverley Station; and beyond them rises the New Town, with its massive modern buildings and splendid commercial thoroughfares. Princes Street, bordering the Gardens on the north, is regarded as one of the finest streets in Europe.

Reminders of a long and illustrious past everywhere meet the visitor's eyes. In Queen Mary's room in the Castle was born James I of England (1566). Queen Margaret of Scotland died in 1093 in the chapel which bears her name—the oldest building in Edinburgh. In Holyroodhouse are many relics of Queen Mary; a brass plate in the vestibule of her audience chamber marks the spot where her favourite Rizzio was assassinated. In St. Giles' cathedral (built 1385–1460) John Knox, the Scottish Protestant reformer, often preached; and not far away is the house where he lived. The city tolbooth, or prison, that stood near St. Giles's church has been pulled down, but the tolbooth in the Canongate still stands.

The City, or Mercat, Cross, whence royal proclamations are made, is near the cathedral. Other buildings of note are the national gallery and the royal academy, the national library and the register house, and famous schools, including Edinburgh Academy, Heriot-Watt College, the Royal High School, George Watson's College and Fettes College. The University, founded in 1583, is one of the most famous in Europe. The buildings occupy the site of Kirk o' Field, scene of the murder of Darnley, husband of Mary Queen of Scots. In Lauriston Place is Heriot's Hospital, a fine 17th century building founded by George Heriot (1563–1624), and close by is the Greyfriars Church where the National Covenant was signed in 1638. The episcopal cathedral is dedicated to St. Mary. The fine monument erected in memory of Sir Walter Scott stands in the East Princes Street Gardens, and consists of a 200-foot Gothic spire of red sandstone, in whose niches are statues of the famous characters in Scott's writings. Under the canopy is a marble statue of Sir Walter, with his dog.

Edinburgh, despite its nickname Auld Reekie, or old smoky, is not a great manufacturing centre. Brewing, printing and glass making are its chief industries. There was a walled settlement on Castle Rock before Roman times. In the 7th century, when the Angles of Northumbria seized it, it was named after their king, Edwin, and they erected the first fortress to occupy the Castle Rock. In the 10th century the town was seized by the Scots, becoming the Scottish capital in 1060.

The Edinburgh Festival of music and drama held annually since 1947, and lasting for three weeks

EDINBURGH CASTLE ON ITS ROCK
Seen from the Old Town, the Castle stands high above the city. In the chapel Queen Margaret of Scotland died in 1093, and in the apartments of Mary Queen of Scots, King James I of England was born in 1566. The Scottish National War Memorial to those who fell in the First World War (1914–18) is built on the summit of the Rock.

D. McLeish

of August and September, attracts visitors from all parts of the world. Performances of plays, music, ballet and films are given. The population of Edinburgh, which is the county town of Midlothian, is about 475,000.

Edison, THOMAS ALVA (1847–1931). Edison was the busiest, happiest, most interested boy in the village of Milan, Ohio, in the United States, where he was born on February 11, 1847, of mixed Dutch and Scottish descent. At school, where he spent only three months of his life, he passed for a dunce. His wise mother, however, understood her son, and he gained a valuable education through following the promptings of his unchecked curiosity. At 10 years of age his favourite study was chemistry.

When only 12 Edison worked as a newspaper boy on long-distance trains, but somehow found time to print a little newspaper and start a laboratory in one of the carriages. Then one day some chemicals

Painting by John Cameron

EDISON IN HIS WORKSHOP

Born at Milan in Ohio, United States, in 1847, Edison had almost no regular education, but that did not stop him from becoming one of the greatest inventors of his time. In this painting he is seen working in his laboratory, where he carried on experiments long after he had become wealthy and famous.

and transmitted the prices of shares on the Stock Exchange. For this and other inventions he received £8,000. With the money the young genius started a laboratory and factory in Newark, New Jersey, U.S.A., for the manufacture of electrical and other apparatus. But before he was 30 his health failed, and he gave up his factory for a laboratory at Menlo Park, New Jersey, where he devoted his time entirely to invention.

Not all of his inventions were made easily. Some he worked on for years and spent a fortune in perfecting. The phonograph, long-distance telephone, incandescent electric light, microphone, railway signalling, alkaline storage battery, cinema—these are a few of the big inventions which owe much to Edison. The incandescent electric light made him rich, but took years and vast expense to perfect. In 1915 he received the Nobel prize for physics. He died on October 18, 1931.

Education. When people use the word "education" they are usually thinking of what boys and girls are taught in school. An educated man is one who has spent years of his youth in the class-room, while an uneducated man is one who has had little in the way of schooling, perhaps because he had to go out to work when still a boy. We talk of people who have had a technical or grammar school education, and of others with a university education.

But we are using the word in a narrow sense if we suppose that education is a matter of one's early years only. True, etymologists tell us that the word comes from the Latin verb *educare*, which means to bring up (children); but it also is related to *educere*, to draw out, and so we have the idea of continual drawing out of the powers with which we are naturally gifted. In this sense, education is a process which goes on as long as we have breath in our bodies. For most people their schooldays finish when they are in their teens, but their education is never really completed. All through life they are learning—from books, from the observation of Nature, from their varied experiences, and their contacts with their fellow men and women. All these influences affect the way in which we think and feel and act.

It was Gibbon, the great historian, who wrote that "every person has two educations, one which he receives from others and one, more important, which he gives himself." But though we "live and learn," the foundations of the knowledge we gain in our grown-up years are laid in the school. Many

set fire to the carriage. The guard threw out young Edison's things at the next station, and the youthful chemist too, with a box on the ear. This, unfortunately, left him permanently deaf—an affliction which, however, Edison often called a blessing in disguise, since it relieved him of many distractions.

In saving the life of a station-master's baby the boy won a friend who taught him the trade of telegraph operator. He soon became skilful in sending and taking messages, and at 15 he was in charge of an office. He was determined to know how the instrument worked, so he experimented with an old battery in his father's cellar until he really understood it.

Edison's first invention was a telegraph repeater, by which a message is transmitted or relayed to a second line which repeats it at a slower rate. Then he began to experiment on the problem of sending more than one message at a time over the same wire. At 21 he devised a machine which recorded

a man in later life has deeply regretted the hours he wasted in class and has wished he could once again be sitting at his desk learning algebra and geography, physics and history. At the time he thought that it was all so dry and useless, but when he became a man he found that even the most out-of-the-way item of information had its usefulness. The education we get later from life is all the richer and fuller for a really sound education in our youth.

The world has little place nowadays for the uneducated man. Time was when the " three R's," as reading, writing, and arithmetic were called, were sufficient to allow a man of ordinary intelligence to hold his own. Not so today. The man or woman who knows *how* to read, but has no knowledge of *what* to read, who can listen without understanding, and who acts on the first impulse, with no idea of weighing the pros and cons—such a person is a danger to himself and to others. So it is that in most countries the State makes sure that every citizen goes to school for a period of years.

The Ministry of Education is an important Government department, with headquarters in Belgrave Square, London. It supervises public education in England and Wales, and has at its head a Minister usually a member of the Cabinet.

The LONG LINE of ENGLISH EDWARDS

*E*leven English Kings in all have borne the ancient and honoured name of Edward, though the last was entitled Edward VIII—because the first three reigned in pre-Norman times when Kings bore no numbers.

Edward. KINGS OF ENGLAND. Eight English sovereigns have borne the name Edward since the Norman Conquest of 1066, and three before that event.

Of the earlier, or Anglo-Saxon, Edwards, EDWARD THE ELDER (ruled 901–24) was the son of Alfred the Great, and distinguished himself by reconquering from the Danes a large part of England which at Alfred's death still remained in their hands. He ruled as far north as the Humber, and his overlordship was acknowledged by the Kings of Northumbria and Scotland.

EDWARD THE MARTYR (ruled 975–78) was murdered outside Corfe Castle in Dorset, at his step-mother's suggestion in order to bring her son Ethelred the Unready (978–1016) to the throne. He was long reverenced as a saint and martyr.

EDWARD THE CONFESSOR (ruled 1042–66) was the son of Ethelred, and was the last of the Anglo-Saxon kings, for after his death came England's conquest by William the Norman. Edward was noted alike for his weakness as a ruler and for his piety as a man. His great legacy to his people was Westminster Abbey, in London.

EDWARD I (born 1239 ; ruled 1272–1307) belongs to the offshoot of the Norman line which we call the Plantagenet, and which came to the throne (1154) in the person of his great-grand-father, Henry II. He was one of the greatest rulers England ever produced.

Becoming king at the age of 33, Edward accomplished three things of great importance. He united Wales and England (1284) by conquest, though actually this conquest applied only to the northern part of the principality, the power of the border lords being little affected ; and from his reign dates the use of the title Prince of Wales for the heir to the British throne. Secondly, Edward helped the development of Parliament and of constitutional government by calling the Model Parliament (including not only the higher clergy and peers but also knights and people from the towns) of 1295, and by distinctly recognizing the principle that no new or extraordinary taxes should be levied without the consent of Parliament. Of equal importance was his reorganization of the laws of England ; and by the close of his reign both the English system of law and courts and the English constitution were fully established.

Until 1289 the care of his French possessions, then limited to Gascony, absorbed much of his attention. For the rest of his life his main concern was Scotland. His chief failure grew out of his effort to unite Scotland with England—an attempt checked by Wallace at Stirling in 1297. Edward's victory at Falkirk (1298), his greatest military feat, only subdued the Scots, who were outnumbered.

Edward I was a fine-looking man, with fair hair and ruddy cheeks. He was so tall that he was nicknamed " Longshanks," but he was well-knit and athletic. He prided himself on his truthfulness, and adopted as his motto " keep faith " (*pactum serva*).

EDWARD II (born 1284; ruled 1307–27) was the unworthy son of Edward I. He had the tall stature and fine appearance of his father, but mentally and morally he was a weakling, and was constantly under the influence of some designing favourite. With such a man on the throne it is easy to understand why the reign was one of disorder and disaster. Yet one benefit resulted. Things grew so bad that in the end Edward

British Museum
EDWARD THE FIRST'S GREAT SEAL
Edward I revived the customs of the legendary King Arthur, and had his own Round Table at Kenilworth Castle, Warwickshire. On his Great Seal he is depicted in armour on his charger.

FOUR EDWARDS OF ENGLAND IN SCENES FROM THEIR LIVES

After a long siege Calais in France surrendered to Edward III in 1347, and in the top left picture, dating from the 15th century, some of the principal citizens are making their submission. The painting by Daniel Maclise (1806–70) at the top right depicts Edward IV (1442–83) and his Queen watching Caxton's printing press at work. Caxton (c. 1422–91) was the first English printer and publisher. Edward V, who succeeded Edward IV in 1483, and his brother were imprisoned in the Tower of London by their uncle, the Duke of Gloucester, and subsequently murdered; the painting of the princes by the French artist Hippolyte Delaroche, at the lower left, is in the Louvre, Paris. Edward VI, the delicate boy who reigned from 1547 to 1553, is seen with his councillors in the picture at the lower right, by the late Paris (1839–93).

was forced to give up the throne, and Parliament's control of the country was thus strengthened.

The defeat of the English forces by Bruce at Bannockburn (1314) compelled Edward to recognize the independence of Scotland. In 1326 Edward's enemies planned a widespread revolt. They easily captured the king, with whose weakness and folly the whole land was disgusted. Then in January 1327, Parliament declared Edward II deposed, and set in his place his young son Edward III. Eight months later the deposed king was brutally murdered.

EDWARD III (born 1312; ruled 1327-77) was only 15 when his father was overthrown and he himself made king. He proved himself a chivalrous knight rather than a great king. He gained temporary glory but no lasting profit through prolonged fighting in Scotland and in France, where he began the Hundred Years' War.

The chief results of his reign were internal. The English people became more conscious of themselves as a nation distinct from the French. There was increased use of English in the government and in the literature of the day. The war also compelled the king to summon Parliament frequently in order to secure from it money to meet his great expenses, and so it increased in importance. During Edward's reign a terrible plague, known as the Black Death, wiped out from one-third to one-half of the country's population, and caused great social and economic changes, the effects of which lasted for centuries.

EDWARD IV (born 1442; ruled 1461-83), the first of the Yorkist kings, grew up in the midst of the struggles between the two great houses of York and Lancaster which is known as the Wars of the Roses, the Yorkists taking a white rose as their badge and the Lancastrians a red one. He became leader of the Yorkist party through the death of his father Richard, Duke of York, at the battle of Wakefield (1460), triumphed over the Lancastrian Henry VI, and secured the throne largely through the support of his powerful cousin, the Earl of

Russell & Sons, Southsea

EDWARD VII, ' THE PEACEMAKER '

Prolonged efforts to maintain peace in Europe earned for Edward VII the title of Edward the Peacemaker. He helped to establish a deep understanding between France and Britain, and his diplomacy averted war between Norway and Sweden in 1905. He is seen here with his eldest grandson, Prince Edward, who became Edward VIII.

Warwick, later called the Kingmaker. But Edward soon offended Warwick by marrying against the latter's wishes, and by placing his wife's relatives in positions of influence at court. Warwick finally went over to the side of the Lancastrians; and, though for a time he forced Edward to abandon England and take refuge in Flanders (1470), Edward proved himself more than a match for his enemies in the end. He returned to England, defeated and killed Warwick in battle at Barnet, Herts (1471), and reestablished himself on the throne. Immediately he caused the weak-minded Henry VI to be murdered; and some years later he also brought about the death of his own brother, the Duke of Clarence.

Edward showed much ability as a ruler, and was popular till his end. He won back for the kingship much of the absolute power lost to Parliament by the Lancastrian kings, did much to restore the country to a settled condition, encouraged trade and patronized such men as Caxton, who was the first English printer.

EDWARD V (born 1470; ruled 1483) was the son of Edward IV, and was nominally king from April to June, 1483. His uncle, Richard of Gloucester, got himself appointed Protector, and soon afterwards the king, then only 13, and his younger brother were shut up in the Tower of London and disappeared. Probably they were murdered by order of their uncle, who had himself crowned king as Richard III. In 1674 some bones of two children were found in an old chest under a staircase in the Tower, and buried in Westminster Abbey. The bones were exhumed in 1933, and examination proved that the remains were those of the princes.

EDWARD VI (born 1537; ruled 1547-53) belonged to the house of Tudor, which came to the throne on the death of Richard III in 1485. He was the son of King Henry VIII by his third queen, Jane Seymour, and became king at the age of 10. First his mother's brother, the Duke of Somerset, and then the Duke of Northumberland controlled the government. The young king was well educated, and great things were expected from him, but he died of consumption in July 1553. Under Edward VI the English Church, which had ceased to recognize the authority of the Pope, made great strides towards Protestantism.

EDWARD VII (born 1841; ruled 1901–10) was in his sixtieth year when he became king. He had married Princess Alexandra of Denmark in 1863, and before his accession was continually before the British public as the most active member of the royal family, owing to Queen Victoria's retirement during her long widowhood. Edward VII was a man of unusual social gifts and worldly experience, and as king his course was marked by tact and judgement. In the realm of diplomacy he used his intimate knowledge of Continental courts to the full, devoting his influence to the task of strengthening England's position in Europe. His strong French sympathies persuaded him to urge on the *entente* (understanding) with France; he visited President Loubet officially in 1903, and the visit was returned later in the year. Again, the Anglo-Russian agreement of 1907 was greatly strengthened by his visit to Russia in 1908. The wisdom of these steps is still a matter of controversy, and there is little doubt that Germany began to feel that she was being isolated in Europe. But King Edward was not blind to her state of mind, and his official visit to the Kaiser in 1909 temporarily mitigated the growing tension in Anglo-German relations, and helped to stave off open conflict. King Edward VII died of heart failure, following bronchitis, on May 6, 1910.

EDWARD VIII (ruled 1936) was nearly 42 years old when he became king on his father's death, January 20, 1936. Born at White Lodge, Richmond,

Surrey, on June 23, 1894, he was the eldest son of George V and Queen Mary, then Duke and Duchess of York, and was given the names of Edward Albert Christian George Andrew Patrick David. In 1907 the Prince entered the Naval College at Osborne, and there and at Dartmouth he was trained as a naval cadet. In 1912, having left the Navy, he entered Magdalen College, Oxford, as an undergraduate, and for nearly two years he remained at the University. During the First World War (1914–18) the Prince, as an officer of the Army, was constantly on active service. During the years between the end of the War and his accession to the throne, the Prince travelled very widely, but he also found time to discharge many public functions at home, and certainly no former heir to the throne had ever gone about so freely and so frequently among his future subjects in all parts of the Commonwealth and Empire.

On January 20, 1936, the Prince became King and Emperor, taking the title of Edward VIII. Towards the end of the same year he expressed the desire to marry an American lady, Mrs. Wallis Warfield Simpson. His ministers at home and in the Dominions did not consider that his choice was in keeping with the dignity and traditions of the Crown. Mrs. Simpson had already been married twice, and her second divorce had not yet been made absolute. Edward, however, was determined to proceed with the proposed marriage, and on December 10, 1936, he abdicated.

He was succeeded on the throne by his younger brother, who had been known as the Duke of York, and became King George VI. The first act of the new king was to create his brother Duke of Windsor. The Duke married Mrs. Simpson in France on June 3, 1937.

Eel. Though we all know that it is not a snake but a fish, the Greeks wondered a good deal about the eel, and the philosopher Aristotle said that eels "from the entrails of the sea." In England the idea persisted for years that eels developed from horse-hairs that had fallen into the water !

The fact is that freshwater eels spend from four to eight years of their life in small ponds and ditches or lakes and large rivers. Then, at spawning time, they make their way to the sea. The eggs are laid far off in the depths of the Atlantic ocean, and then the old eels die.

The first clue to the mystery was the discovery about 150 years ago, in the waters of the Atlantic and Mediterranean, of creatures with tiny heads and ribbon-like bodies, transparent as glass. They were long supposed to be a kind of fish new to science. But during the latter half of the 19th century several experimenters found that these small creatures, kept in aquariums, turned into young eels.

With this fact to help him, a Danish scientist, Johannes Schmidt,

Imperial War Museum

EDWARD VIII AS PRINCE OF WALES
During the First World War (1914–18) Edward VIII, then Prince of Wales, served in France and Italy on the British General Staff. He is here seen in Italy chatting with a French officer. After his abdication his brother, who had succeeded him as King George VI, created him Duke of Windsor.

began in 1905 to track down the secrets of the eel. Before his death in 1933 Professor Schmidt had made six cruises, covering more than 40,000 miles, and had dredged up from the ocean depths the answer to the puzzle.

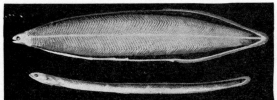

THREE STAGES IN AN EEL'S LIFE
The grown-up freshwater eel in the lower picture is shown about one-sixth its actual size. The baby eel at the top shrinks considerably at a later stage in its transformation and assumes the form shown in the centre photograph ; both are life-size.

When the time approaches for the adult eels to go to the spawning grounds they put on an extra layer of fat and the skin takes on a silvery colour. Presently they start towards the sea—wriggling overland if there is no other way to reach the salt water. Then out into the Atlantic they swim, gradually going deeper and deeper. At last they reach the warm waters of the Sargasso Sea in a tract south of the Bermudas and about 900 miles east of the American coast. There in the blackness, 3,000 feet down, the females lay their millions of eggs and the males fertilise them. Then the grown eels die.

Within a few days the glass-like baby eels, a quarter-inch long, hatch from the eggs. Each carries a tiny drop of oil, which floats it upward toward food and sunshine. At first it simply drifts, feeding with needle-sharp teeth on the microscopic life at the surface. Then it begins to grow, and when it is about three inches long it commences to shrink : the thin body shortens, turns pink and becomes round—much the shape and size of an ordinary wooden match. Gradually it takes on the regular eel shape—narrow head, undershot jaw, long body, with two fins near the throat, and a continuous narrow fin running from the middle of the back round the end of the tail, to the middle of the stomach. As soon as the young eel has gone through this transformation it starts its journey to fresh water. The distance from where the eggs were laid to their destination in Europe, where the young eels will complete their growth, may be as much as 4,000 miles. The wonder of it all is not lessened when we realize that some of the eels will be impelled, by a mysterious instinct, to wriggle beyond the banks of the river which at last they enter from the sea and take an overland route to a freshwater pond

or lake or muddy ditch remote from the coast. Professor Schmidt showed that there are similar breeding places for the eels of Africa, Asia and Australia.

Though they are filled with exceedingly fine bones, eels are delicious food. They are usually caught with set lines, traps, or eel-pots, as they travel downstream to the sea. They will eat almost any animal substance, dead or alive, and thus do much damage in trout streams.

The common eel (*Anguilla vulgaris*) is usually between 18 inches and three feet in length. The great conger eel grows sometimes to six feet or more, often weighing 30 to 40 lb. It is excellent to eat.

Egg. While the very lowest single-celled creatures reproduce by simply splitting in two, birds, most reptiles, fishes and insects, reproduce by eggs. Such eggs have always a protective covering containing the life-germ of the young and a supply of food—the yolk—to nourish it until hatching time.

Birds' eggs, and those of crocodiles and certain turtles, are provided with a rigid shell. But most of the reptiles have eggs covered with a tough elastic membrane, like parchment. The eggs of

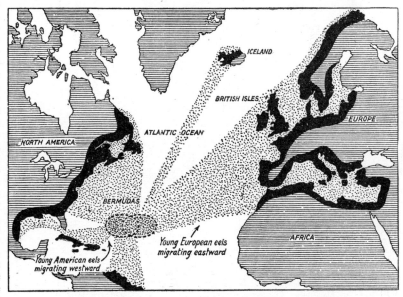

EELS' LONG TRAIL TO AND FROM THE ATLANTIC
For many years the life-history of the common freshwater eel was a complete mystery, but it is now known that their breeding-grounds are in the Atlantic, south of the Bermudas. There the eggs are laid. The young eels whose parents came from Europe then swim back thousands of miles to fresh water in the homeland; the young American eels move off in the opposite direction, as indicated above.

EGGS IN UNFAMILIAR FORMS AND SIZES

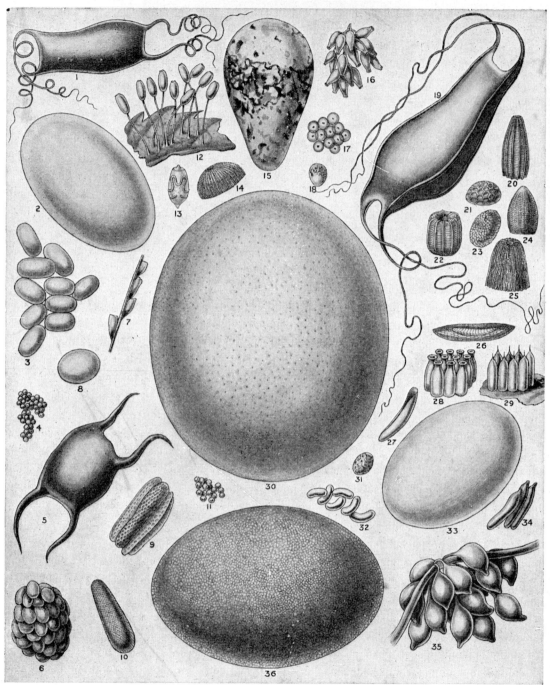

There is astonishing variety in the design of eggs. Some are oval; some have points and even tendrils; some are in clusters; some are set on stalks. 1, Dog Fish. 2, Crocodile. 3, Grass Snake. 4, Salmon. 5, Skate. 6, Whelk. 7, Head Louse. 8, Duckbill. 9, House Fly. 10, Flesh or Blow Fly. 11, Snail. 12, Lace-wing Fly. 13, Walking-stick Insect. 14, Cotton Worm Moth of the United States. 15, Guillemot (sea bird). 16, Purpura (shellfish from which purple dye can be obtained). 17, Frog. 18, Creeper (bird). 19, Shark. 20, White Butterfly. 21, Copper Butterfly. 22, Tortoiseshell Butterfly. 23, Blue Butterfly. 24, Milkweed Butterfly. 25, Queen of Spain Butterfly. 26, Malaria Mosquito. 27, Stable Fly. 28, Wheel or Pirate Bug of the U.S. 29, Alder Fly. 30, Ostrich. 31, Grasshopper. 32, Leaf-cutter Bee. 33, Python. 34, Snake Fly. 35, Cuttlefish. 36, Emu. In addition to the variety in appearance which these pictures (not drawn to scale) show, there is a greater difference in size between many of the eggs than is apparent here. For instance, the ostrich egg, in the centre, is about six inches long and weighs three pounds; most of the insect eggs are no bigger than a pencil point. The dangers to which eggs and young are exposed determine the number of eggs laid; some fishes lay millions of them at a time.

fish, toads, frogs, salamanders, are usually surrounded by a jelly-like substance, which often binds them together in masses. Those of certain sharks are contained in strange, horny, flexible cases; while those of the octopus are produced in clusters, like b e r r i e s attached to a stalk.

The only egg-laying mammals are the duckbill (q.v.) and the spiny ant-eater. The members o f o t h e r orders of animals vary greatly in this r e s p e c t. Some snakes, lizards and fish bring forth living young, others lay eggs.

Reptiles, as a rule, leave their eggs to be hatched by the warmth of the ground, but some snakes guard theirs in the coils of their bodies. Australia, which produces the duckbill, produces also birds which hatch their eggs like reptiles. They are called the *Megapodes*, and are the only birds which do not "brood" or incubate their eggs. The brush turkey of East Australia, for instance, simply scratches up mounds of earth and leaves, lays its

EGG-STEALING LIZARD

Various birds, animals and reptiles steal eggs to eat. This lizard has just robbed a nest and is hurrying off to partake of its meal in safety. The mongoose is fond of eggs, and so are the jay and curlew.

eggs in the mound, and waits for the heat generated by the sun and decaying vegetation to hatch them.

The egg-laying habits of insects present, perhaps, the greatest variety of safeguards employed for their protection. Some, like the bees and wasps, place their eggs in specially constructed combs or cells; others, like the ichneumon flies, plant them in the bodies of other insects; the gall-flies bury them in plant tissues. Mosquitoes and gnats lay their eggs in the form of little rafts that float on the surface of still and stagnant water. Spiders usually safeguard their eggs by surrounding them with tiny silky bags, which may be suspended in some protected place or carried about.

Many varieties of eggs are eaten besides those of poultry. In tropical countries turtle eggs may form part of the diet of the shore-dwelling natives. Fish eggs, under the name of "roe," or salted and prepared as the "caviare" of the sturgeon, are recognized delicacies the world over.

The WONDERLAND *of* FATHER NILE

Many believe that civilization began in the narrow valley, hemmed in by the desert, that is Egypt. Here is an account of the country as it is today; the romantic story of its past is described in pages 1113 to 1121.

Egypt. Out of Egypt's total area of about 383,000 square miles, only 13,600 square miles, an area less than half that of Ireland, are habitable. This is chiefly in the Nile valley, a narrow strip of country hemmed in by the Arabian desert on the east and by the Libyan desert on the west, and varying in width from two to 120 miles. This fertile valley is a gift of the river. Without the Nile, which for centuries has deposited rich alluvial mud upon the sand, Egypt would be desert.

In Upper Egypt are people who have never seen rain. At Cairo, 100 miles from the sea, there are only four or five showers a year. Yet the Nile valley is everywhere productive, and the dwellers on the lower Nile get three harvests a year. The

Nile valley is not only a garden. It is also a museum. Before Abraham was, before Moses, before Ur of the Chaldees, before Christ or Caesar, Egypt was the seat of a mighty civilization, cultured, mature and rich.

It is possible to travel today quite luxuriously by sleeping-car a n d river steamer from the mouth of the Nile to Gondokoro (S u d a n) near its source. Along the banks are to be seen the best of modern irrigation works, and by way of contrast the slender, brown-skinned *fellahin* (peasants) irrigating the land with the *shadoof*, a primitive water-raising d e v i c e. Beside the Nile are the oldest monuments in the world, the ruins of great temples, the Pyramids and the Sphinx.

The Arabian desert on the east (not to be

Extent.—Area of Egypt, about 383,000 square miles; population, about 17,423,000.

Physical Features.—The Nile, about 3,500 miles long; the fertile Nile valley, varying from 2 miles or less to 120 miles in width; the Libyan and Arabian deserts; the fertile province of Fayum; the delta of the Nile; Sinai Peninsula.

Engineering Features.—Suez Canal, 100 miles long, across Isthmus of Suez; Assuan Dam, on the Nile, 1¼ miles long, 147 feet high; barrages (artificial bars on the Nile to increase the depth) at Esna, Assiut, Zifta. Railways: more than 4,000 miles.

Chief Cities.—Cairo (1,307,000 population), Alexandria (682,000), Port Said (126,000), Tanta, Mansura, Assiut.

Products.—From the Fayum and Lower Egypt, cotton, rice, Indian corn, wheat, barley, clover: from Upper Egypt, cereals and vegetables.

History.—Rise of Egyptian civilization between 5000 and 4000 B.C.; the Pyramid Age, 3000-2500 B.C.; Egypt's wide empire, 1580-1150 B.C.; Age of the Ptolemies (Greek rulers), 323-30 B.C., followed by Roman rule; since A.D. 641, Mahomedan; British occupation begun in 1882; tribute to Turkey ended in 1914; independent kingdom, 1922; entry into League of Nations, 1937. In Second World War (1939-45) Egypt remained neutral, but joined the United Nations in 1945.

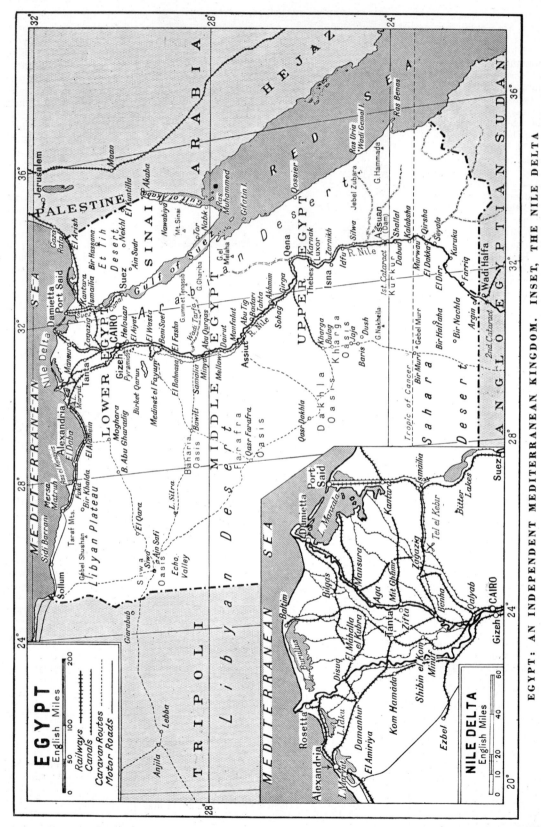

EGYPT: AN INDEPENDENT MEDITERRANEAN KINGDOM. INSET, THE NILE DELTA

a land of flowing streams, and abounds in oranges, peaches, pomegranates, olives, figs, and grapes, besides cotton, sugar and cereal crops. It is also famous for its roses.

From Wadi Halfa, the southernmost point of Egypt proper, on the Nile to Assuan is a two nights' river journey down-stream. Between these two places the river widens into a lake a mile wide with rocky islands showing here and there with palm trees growing straight out of the water. This is the result of the great dam built at Assuan for the purpose of storing the Nile waters. At Assuan the real Nile valley begins. Limestone cliffs, rising in places to 1,000 feet from the valley floor, begin to open out, leaving sometimes a few yards of bank on either side of the river, sometimes 30 miles of it. The crops are onions and sugar, food and fodder.

At Esna is the first of the Nile barrages, a masonry structure which piles the water up, not to dam it completely but to force it through irrigation canals and ditches and on to the fields along the river. Just beyond, the cliffs open out to form

Dorien Leigh

NILE BOATS UNDER SAIL

Fitted with large triangular sails, dahabiyehs or Nile boats are familiar sights on that river. This is a cargo boat. Larger ones, with excellent accommodation, are used for the conveyance of passengers and as houseboats by tourists. The Nile is still the chief means of communication in Egypt, though there are more than 4,000 miles of railway.

confused with the desert of the same name in Asia) rises in a series of step-like plateaux to lofty mountains bordering the Red Sea. Here dwell scattered groups of nomad Beduin or Arabs, and here are the remains of mines from which the ancient Egyptians drew their gold.

Here and there are dry river beds known as *wadis*, and in the rare thunderstorms these carry torrents which cast boulders about like pebbles. The wind sweeps over the desert so mercilessly that not even sand is left upon much of its rocky surface. In some districts of the Libyan desert, however, to the west of the Nile, are immense crescent-shaped sand-dunes that creep onwards at the rate of about 50 feet a year, burying everything in their path. The Beduin fears the fierce sandstorms of this region, though he knows well how to protect himself by wrapping his head in his blanket and crouching in the shelter of his camel. In the Libyan desert are five large oases, made fertile by underground water. Kharga, the southernmost, is reached by a railway, and supports a population of 8,000 upon crops of dates, rice and cereals.

The Fayum is one of the most fertile provinces of modern Egypt. It occupies a depression in the Libyan desert into which the engineers of the Pharaohs 4,000 years ago drew off the waters of the Nile in years of great flood. Today the province is

A. W. Cutler

EGYPT'S SETTLED BISHARIN

Normally a wandering people, who are continually moving their camels, sheep and goats to fresh pastures, some of the Bisharin have a permanent settlement at Assuan, where they live in huts built of sun-dried mud (above). They are a slim wiry race, whose home is in the Nubian Desert.

EGYPT NEW AND OLD
The harbour at Port Said, the northern gateway
to the Suez Canal, is thoroughly modern. To
irrigate their land Egyptian peasants still use
a method (left) that is many centuries old.

a wide double bay, the plain of Thebes.
Here are temples and cliff tombs, and in
the distance the Colossi of Memnon.

From Girga to Assiut is the Coptic
centre of Egypt. Here are the two great
Coptic monasteries, the White and the
Red, founded in Roman times. The
Copts, whose name is a corruption of the
Greek *Aiguptioi* (Egyptians), are the same
race as other people of Egypt, but are all
Christians. Their language is descended
from the ancient Egyptian, and the Coptic
Church is one of the earliest forms of
Christianity. They number about a
million and furnish a large proportion of
the traders and artisans.

Lower Egypt or the delta of the Nile
begins a little to the south of Cairo. This
region is watered by 300 miles of the Nile,
which here flows in two main branches
emptying into the sea at Rosetta on the
west and Damietta on the east. The landscape is vivid green, and crossed by such
a network of irrigation canals that in
summer little water is left to reach the
Mediterranean through the natural channels of the Nile. All the larger cities of
Egypt—Cairo, Alexandria, Port Said and
Tanta—are in the delta.

More than 60 per cent of the 17,400,000
inhabitants of Egypt are agricultural
labourers. The government is the ultimate proprietor of the land, getting a large

EGYPTIAN PEASANTS OF THE NILE VALLEY

Dorien Leigh

Though most of the Egyptians are Mahomedans many of the peasant women, like the one above, do not veil their faces. Except in the desert, where the camel is more at home, donkeys are widely used in Egypt as beasts of burden and for riding (left).

Dorien Leigh

Among the poorer people the women of Egypt have to work hard. One of their tasks is to fetch water from the Nile, which is their sole source for cooking and drinking. Here is an evening scene on the bank of the river, where one woman has brought her ox for a drink and a bath. Receptacles for water are balanced on the head. Drinking polluted water is the cause of much sickness amongst the Egyptians, who do not always take the trouble to boil it.

Few manufactures are carried on in Egypt, but there are numerous cotton mills. Calico and other coarse cotton cloths are made, and Egyptian handwoven silk shawls and draperies are often very beautiful. The Egyptians have a process of tanning practised only by themselves, and they produce an excellent quality of morocco leather. They are noted for the making of pottery, their ornamental woodwork, sometimes inlaid with pearl and ivory, their vessels of hammered brass and copper, and gold and silver ornaments. Cigarettes are manufactured at Cairo and Alexandria; and perfumes, including attar of roses, are produced at Cairo and in the Fayum. Mills are found in every part of the country which grind maize and other grains for home con-

proportion of its revenue from the land tax. Nearly 60 per cent of the land under cultivation is in holdings of 50 acres or less, and more than 60 per cent of the land-owners get their entire living from an acre or less of land. Irrigation is practised on something more than two-thirds of the 6,000,000 cultivated acres, and two or three crops are obtained every year, mainly of cotton, wheat, maize, rice, barley and vegetables.

The peasants live in close-packed villages but the better return which their land is bringing them under scientific irrigation and the introduction of schools are gradually making their lot less miserable.

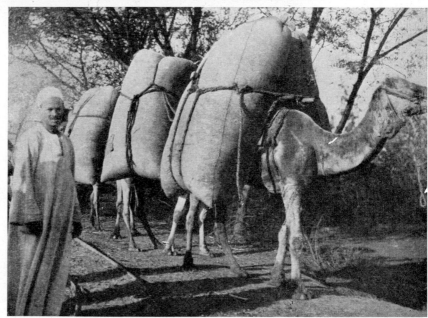

Dorien Leigh

EGYPT'S WEALTH : COTTON AND WHEAT

Egyptian cotton is noted for its excellent quality, and much of the country's prosperity depends on that crop. In some places camels are used to carry the bales of cotton on the first part of their journey to the mills. Wheat ranks next to cotton in importance, and the upper picture shows a harvest being winnowed by tossing it into the air so that the wind blows away the chaff, leaving the grain to fall to the ground.

sumption. Rice-milling, sugar-refining and soap-making are other important industries. The salt marshes in the Delta have been reclaimed to increase the acreage of rice.

Conquered by the Turks in 1517, the modern history of Egypt may be said to begin with Mehemet Ali, an Albanian leader, who co-operated with the British (1801) in driving out from Egypt the French under Napoleon. The Turkish Sultan made him Governor of Egypt in 1805, and the present Egyptian royal house is descended from him. Mehemet repaired and improved the irrigation systems, which had been badly damaged during long years of internal strife. He introduced standards of European civilization, and started the cotton industry in Egypt. All this he achieved by ruinous taxation and forced labour on public works. He also reformed the navy and the army.

In 1856 Said Pasha, son of Mehemet, granted Ferdinand de Lesseps the concession to build the Suez Canal, which was completed in 1869. Said's successor, Ismail, in 1867 secured the title of *Khedive* or Prince from the Turkish sultan. Ismail sold the khedival share of the Suez Canal finances and control to the British government for a huge sum, but his extravagances left the Egyptian treasury in such a bankrupt condition that in 1876 England and France took over international control of Egypt's revenues. In 1879 the Sultan of Turkey ousted Ismail as khedive and placed his son, Tewfik, on the throne. Tewfik was unable to control the resentment of the Egyptians against the interference of the Europeans. Massacres of Europeans in Alexandria aroused the European powers, and late in 1882 the British landed troops in Egypt. Britain's rule in Egypt dates from the

EGYPTIAN DESERT POLICEMAN

In the towns of Egypt foot and mounted police perform much the same duties as European police, but parts of the desert have also to be patrolled, especially against smugglers. This work is done by armed policemen mounted on camels, like the one above, which are trained for riding.

Royal Air Force, Official (Crown Copyright)

FLOOD-TIME IN THE NILE VALLEY

There being only a very light rainfall in Egypt the fertility of the country has always depended upon the annual flooding of the Nile, which also created the conditions favourable to the development of an early civilization. The floods reach their height in October, when the river spreads over much land that is dry in summer. Here the Nile is shown at its highest, when the villages, built on slight rises in the ground, are isolated by encircling water.

victory of the British over Arabi Pasha in the battle of Tel-el-Kebir in September 1882.

Rebellion in the Sudan retarded stabilization of the Egyptian government. An army of 10,000 Egyptians was wiped out in 1883 near El Obeid by the rebel leader Mahomed Ahmed, the Mahdi or Prophet of Sudan. General Gordon was killed in Khartum in 1885 after the long siege of that city,

EGYPT'S HUGE DAM AT ASSUAN
H. J. Shepstone
Designed for irrigation purposes and flood control, the dam across the Nile at Assuan was made 30 feet higher during 1931–34 to enable it to hold back more water. It is a mile and a quarter in length, and the work that had to be done before the foundations could be laid is shown in page 959. There is a channel at the western end to allow vessels to proceed up or down the river.

and not until 1899 was the Sudan finally pacified, and established as the Anglo-Egyptian Sudan under control of the British and Egyptian governments.

Egypt prospered almost from the start of the British administration. It was still nominally part of the Turkish empire until 1914, but after 1882 it was governed by Great Britain, who appointed officials to advise the khedive, as the ruler was called, and kept an army in the country. In 1914, when Turkey took the side of Germany in the First World War (1914–18), Egypt was annexed

by Great Britain, and this state of affairs continued until 1922, when it was made independent, with the khedive, who since 1914 had been called the sultan, as its king. This independence was qualified by the fact that, in order to protect the Suez Canal and to look after the Sudan, Britain continued to maintain an army in the land. The Egyptians, or some of them, began to demand complete independence, and the nationalist party, called the Wafd, became very active. Early in 1936 King Fuad, who had come to the throne in 1922, died, and his young son Farouk succeeded him.

Full sovereignty came to Egypt with the conclusion of the Anglo-Egyptian Treaty of Alliance in August 1936. The following year the kingdom was admitted to the League of Nations. The British undertook to withdraw all their forces from the country as soon as the Egyptians were strong enough to take over the defence of the Suez Canal. In the meantime Britain was to maintain 10,000 soldiers and 400 airmen on Egyptian territory.

Britain began to reinforce her Egyptian garrisons on the outbreak of the Second World War (1939–45). Nevertheless, when Italy declared war on France and Great Britain, in June 1940, Italian forces were able to force their way some distance into Egypt. The Egyptians determined to remain neutral, while giving their British allies, and later the Americans, all the facilities they needed. Alexandria became the principal Mediterranean base of the Royal Navy, and British military depots and airfields were established in many places in the Suez Canal zone (notably at Tel-el-Kebir) and in the desert west of Alexandria.

A German and Italian force penetrated to within 70 miles of Alexandria in the summer of 1942, but they were hurled out of Egypt four months after they had entered it. Alexandria, Cairo, and Ismailia were several times bombed by enemy aircraft. Just before the end of hostilities Egypt declared war against the Germans, thus gaining the right to become a member of the United Nations and to have a voice in the disposal of the ex-Italian colony of Libya.

In 1945 the Egyptians asked for a revision of the 1936 Treaty (which was intended to last for 20 years), requiring not only the immediate evacuation of British troops from Egypt but also Britain's withdrawal from the Sudan. Negotiations dragged on without agreement being reached, and several times there were anti-British riots in Cairo and

SHIPPING IN THE DESERT AND AT PORT SAID

Paul Popper

At the Mediterranean end of the Suez Canal is Port Said (lower), founded in 1859 as a coaling-station. Here ships at the entrance must wait their turn to pass through the canal, only one vessel at a time being allowed to proceed in either direction. Craft appear to be steaming over the sand (top) where the waterway traverses the desert. The canal, 103 miles in length, connects the Mediterranean with the Red Sea. It is 34 feet deep and 197 feet wide.

Alexandria. British forces were withdrawn from those cities in the spring of 1947, but a small force remained in the Canal Zone.

Egypt has always strongly supported the Arabs against the Jews in Palestine, where the two races came into conflict over the ownership of the country. While Great Britain was in control of Palestine (1917–48) the fighting between the Jews and Arabs was in the nature of guerrilla warfare. But when in May 1948 Britain surrendered the mandate that she held originally from the League of Nations and withdrew her armed forces from Palestine, open warfare broke out between the Jewish and Arab armies, and Egypt sent a small force into southern Palestine to assist the Arabs.

What are they like, the people of Egypt? They are handsome and slender, their colour varying from olive in the Nile Delta to coppery brown in the Upper Nile area. They speak a form of Arabic, and are mostly of the Mahomedan faith. Generally courteous and dignified, they can sometimes be very excitable. The men wear a white or coloured *galabieh*—a flowing, full-skirted gown—with a turban or fez. The women dress in black.

All Egyptian children must go to school between the ages of seven and 12. Many of the elementary and secondary schools are run by the Government. There are two universities: the University of Fuad I in Cairo, founded in 1908, and the University of Farouk I in Alexandria, dating from 1943.

Though the Egyptians do not indulge in active sports, which are confined to the very rich, it is interesting to observe that an Egyptian, Amr Bey (who later, as Amr Pasha, became the Egyptian ambassador in London) was during the 1930's the

Paul Popper

SKYSCRAPER OF ALEXANDRIA
Much of the latest architecture in the principal cities of Egypt is impressive in appearance, as witness this towering block of flats and shops in Alexandria, the chief seaport and commercial capital of the country.

finest squash racquets player in the world. After the Second World War another Egyptian, M. Karim, won the squash racquets British Open Championship.

The *fellahin* or peasants prefer to spend their leisure more restfully. You will often see them sitting outside the coffee-houses playing their favourite *tric-trac*, a form of backgammon; and they delight to foregather in the public baths and talk. They are fond of music, and some of their tunes, especially those heard in the mosques and the Coptic churches, are very ancient. The Egyptians are great eaters of sweet cakes and pastries, and drinkers of strong, sweet coffee, with which they sip a glass of cold water.

Egypt's importance rests on her geographical position, for the Suez Canal lies wholly within Egyptian territory. Control of this vital waterway is in the hands of the British and French, but their concessions from the Egyptian Government, which permit them to hold this control, are to expire in 1968, and Egypt has announced that the concessions will in no circumstances be renewed. That will mean that all British shipping passing through the Canal to her Dominions and Colonies in the East will have to pay canal dues to Egypt. If Great Britain were involved in war, Egypt would wield a power out of all proportion to her strength, because she would control the shortest sea route to Australia and the East.

Central Press

BY THE SWEETWATER CANAL
Extending between the Nile at Cairo and the Suez Canal is the Sweetwater Canal, in which this peasant girl is washing clothes. At one time girls in Egypt did not go to school, but in 1933 attendance was made compulsory for them between the ages of seven and 12.

LIFE AND ART OF ANCIENT EGYPT

E.N.A.

On the cliffs facing Thebes and the valley of the Nile the temple in which Queen Hatshepsut was buried rises in three terraces, the upper two of which are seen above. The temple is partly built, partly hewn out of the solid rock. Queen Hatshepsut, who may have been the princess of Egypt who adopted Moses, was one of the most enlightened rulers of history, and reliefs in this temple record her expedition to Punt (region south of Egypt) and Sinai.

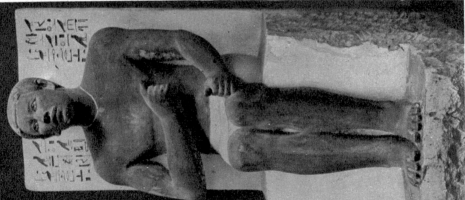

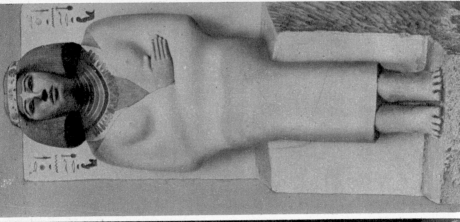

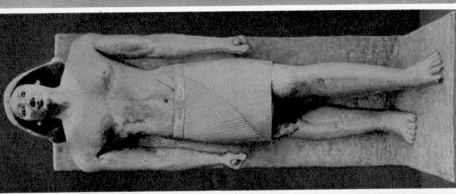

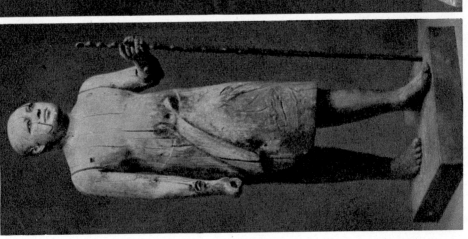

EARLY EXAMPLES OF EGYPTIAN SCULPTURE IN WOOD AND STONE

Ancient Egypt produced many sculptors whose achievements may challenge comparison with those of the great modern masters. Four of the finest examples of sculpture which excavators have discovered are reproduced above. From left to right they are: A life-like wooden statue of a Fifth Dynasty official which was found in his tomb at Sakkara; a painted limestone statue of Ra-nefer, a priest of Memphis during the Fifth Dynasty, also discovered in his tomb at Sakkara; next is a statue of the lady Nefert from the necropolis at Medum; it is of painted stone, the flesh being yellow and the dress white; the fourth figure is a statue of a pharaoh's son, the husband of the lady Nefert, falling in date roughly between the Third and Fourth Dynasties. The red-brown colouring of the flesh indicates that he spent much of his time in the open air.

ROCK-HEWN COLOSSI OF ABU SIMBEL SEEN BY MOONLIGHT

One of the most impressive Egyptian temples is in Nubia (part of the Anglo-Egyptian Sudan), though this is far from the seat of the kings of ancient Egypt; this fact affords proof of Egypt's cultural and political influence over comparatively distant lands in Africa. Of this wonderful temple every detail is hewn out of the living rock of the sandstone cliffs that bound the Nile. It is called the temple of Abu Simbel, and the entrance is flanked by four 65-feet-high colossi of Rameses II, its builder. Two of them are seen above, photographed by the light of the moon.

AN EGYPTIAN QUEEN ASCENDS TO HER COUCH

The kings and queens of ancient Egypt were attended by many slaves and did nothing for themselves, and their every movement was surrounded with pomp and ceremony. The Italian artist, Fortunino Matania (born 1881), here shows the consort of Tutankhamen escorted to her couch by slave girls carrying long-handled fans. The steps that lead up to it and the couch itself are fine examples of the elaborate ornamentation and skilful carving of ancient Egypt. Every detail of this picture is carefully copied from objects found in the tomb of Tutankhamen.

FUNERAL POMP AND CEREMONY OF A PHARAOH

As we may guess from their magnificent tombs, the funerals of great persons in ancient Egypt were carried out with stately and splendid rites. Death was to the Egyptians a time less of mourning than of rejoicing, for they believed that after it the soul, and the body, continued to live in a finer land. Above we see the mummy of a pharaoh (right) being ferried across the Nile, towed by a boat (left) containing relations and professional mourners.

so that the dead king should not be alone and unattended in his after-life there was buried with him everything he would need after death, including his slaves. The four oxen in this picture that are drawing the shrine which has been taken off the boat after crossing the river will also be sacrificed at the entrance of the tomb. Behind the bier follows a mighty throng of the dead king's subjects of all classes, led by the priests, who wielded great power.

RUIN OF A GREAT KING'S GATEWAY AT KARNAK

D. McLeish

Named after Ptolemy III Euergetes, who lived and ruled in the middle of the third century B.C., this magnificent portal or ' propylon ' stands in the avenue leading to the temple of Khensu at Karnak. It is covered with beautifully carved reliefs, which show the king praying and making sacrifices to the gods of Thebes in thanks for his conquest of the Seleucid (Macedonian) ruler of Syria. The monument, though not so grand or impressive as some of the earlier ones, still has much of the massive dignity that is associated with ancient Egyptian architecture.

WONDERFUL COLONNADE OF THE LUXOR TEMPLE

D. McLeish

Described as the most beautiful colonnade in Egypt, what a magnificent sight it must have been when first completed, fresh from the hands of the architect and artist, its lovely contours glowing with colour under the tropic sky and framed with verdure and waving palms! The seven pairs of columns are about 52 feet high, and at each side are colossal seated figures of Rameses II. Compare this colonnade with the other at Luxor in page 1112. After the introduction of Christianity, the temple, about 284 yards in length when completed, was converted into a church.

CLUSTERED COLUMNS AROUND A TEMPLE COURT BUILT BY EGYPT'S GREATEST KING

The work of its actual founder, Amenhotep III (c. 1400 B.C.), this is one of the most magnificent remaining portions of the great temple at Luxor. It is a vast unroofed space, measuring 49 by 56 yards, with a double row of columns forming a colonnade on three of its sides and the pillars of the temple portico (right) on the fourth. These columns, though battered through 34 centuries by the forces of Nature, still furnish an outstanding example of artistic conception and architectural skill, and are extremely graceful in their porportions; they represent clusters of papyrus reeds, with papyrus buds as their capitals. Later Pharaohs, including Rameses II, made additions to this temple.

When the PHARAOHS ruled in EGYPT

Modern excavations have thrown a bright light on the dim days of Egypt's beginnings, some thousands of years before our era began. Indeed, we know almost as much of its life then as of some primitive tribes of the present day.

Egypt, ANCIENT. Let us take a steamer up the Nile to read the story, going back 6,000 or 7,000 years, that its tombs and monuments have to tell. Nowhere else in the world can we find so complete a history of Man's progress for so long a time, and nowhere else can we trace so fully the links in the chain which led him up from barbarism.

The Nile valley was the chief cradle of the earliest civilization, in the days when men first learned to erect buildings more permanent than mud-daubed huts, and to work metals and make written records. The hot drifting sands and rainless atmosphere of Egypt have also preserved the remains of that civilization in greater abundance than those of any other early people. In burial pits of the late Stone Age, scooped out in gravel beds below the sand, we find the bones of Egyptian peasants and chiefs who died more than 6,000—some scientists think 10,000—years ago. By their side lie stone implements and pottery, which tell us that though they had not learned the use of metals, they were skilled at moulding and baking clay into vessels to hold food and drink. Pictorial records show local chieftains controlling the irrigation ditches and collecting taxes of grain and flax. Fragments of linen, small stores of barley and wheat, vase-paintings of boats with oars and sails, give us further glimpses into their life.

Stop for a moment to think how ancient these records are. Think back 2,000 years to the shadowy figure of Queen Cleopatra, last of the ancient rulers of Egypt. How long ago that seems ! But 2,000 years before Cleopatra Egypt was already an ancient empire with 1,400 years of known, written history !

Go back to about 4000 B.C. and we reach the time when some unknown Egyptian discovered strange metallic beads melted from the copper-bearing rocks with which he had banked his camp fire, and so those Egyptians learned the use of metals. Go back another thousand years—to about 5000 B.C.—and we find them irrigating their fields of flax and wheat, weaving linen and making pottery—though their only tools were of stone and bone, and their only houses were wattled mud huts.

It is only within the last few years that archaeologists have discovered these things by uncovering the burial pits of four, five and six thousand years ago. A whole science, called Egyptology, is now devoted to this study.

Tombs of later dates show us how the ancient Egyptians learned to make paper from the papyrus

plant, how they developed their early picture-writing into alphabetic writing, how they learned to mould bricks, cut stone and carve statues. We find paintings, pottery, jewels, tools, wooden chairs and papyrus books, and even their bodies; for their mummies are so perfectly preserved by embalming that we can compare their features with the portrait statues of their kings.

Much of this marvellous story would still be a sealed book to us if it had not been for the famous Rosetta stone (an illustration of this appears in page 1118), which gave scholars the key to the long-forgotten hieroglyphics (picture characters). This is a thick slab of black basalt, measuring three feet nine inches by two feet four and a half inches, discovered by Napoleon's soldiers while digging trenches near the Rosetta mouth of the Nile in 1799. On it is inscribed a record in honour of one of the kings of Egypt in 195 B.C., written in two languages —in Greek, which was then the official language of the government, and in Egyptian, both in the ordinary Egyptian characters and in the ancient sacred hieroglyphics. By comparing the Greek translation with the Egyptian texts an ingenious

EGYPT AND THE FERTILE CRESCENT

Well-watered and cultivated, the valley of the Nile and the Fertile Crescent of Western Asia were the homes of Man's earliest civilizations. From Egypt culture spread across the sea to the island of Crete, thence to Greece and the lands bordering the Aegean Sea.

French scholar named Champollion was able to begin the reconstruction of the Egyptian language.

Why did the Egyptians take such pains to preserve their bodies, their records, and the objects of their everyday life? The answer is in their religion. " The Egyptians," wrote the Greek historian Herodotus, " are the most religious of all men." They believed, as the Christian does, that the soul lived on after death, and thought it would be judged by the great god Osiris. They also believed that the soul could return to the body, and eat the food and drink prepared for it and read the sacred texts. So their earliest pharaohs or kings built themselves great brick-walled tombs in the ground, and by 3000 B.C. they had begun constructing enormous pyramids of polished granite and limestone, some of which survive to this day.

ZOSER, PYRAMID BUILDER
At Sakkara in Upper Egypt is the step-pyramid, even more ancient than the more famous group at Gizeh. The builder was King Zoser (c. 3000 B.C.), and this statue of him was found buried near by.

KING IP
Known as the Scorpion, Ip was probably the earliest monarch of Egypt's First Dynasty (c. 3400–3200 B.C.).

Let us make our first stop at Thinis, near Abydos about 350 miles south of Cairo. Here was born King Menes, who united Upper and Lower Egypt about 3400 B.C. We know that a thousand years earlier, in 4241 B.C. — the first event in history to which we can give an exact date— the dwellers in the Nile delta invented a yearly calendar with 12 months of 30 days each, and five feast days at the end to make out the full 365. This is very much like the calendar we are still using. But the shifting silt brought down by the Nile has buried the remains of the early delta civilization, and we have to begin our story of civilization in Ancient Egypt far to the south.

At Thinis are several underground brick-walled tombs, one of which may be that of King Menes himself. Ivory and ebony tablets and inscribed jewels tell of the histories of these earliest kings.

The second great chapter in Egyptian history opens at the royal city of Memphis, about 12 miles south of Cairo. The city was destroyed by the Arabs in the 7th century, and has long since crumbled into dust. Nothing remains but a few blocks of granite, sculptured fragments, and rubbish heaps. The colossal pyramids still stand which the ancient dwellers of Memphis built to protect the bodies of their kings. These vast edifices of masonry extend more than 60 miles along the Nile. Each pyramid marks the last resting place of one of the pharaohs of the Pyramid Age, which was from about 3000 to 2500 B.C. The chamber hidden deep within each of these piles once housed a royal mummy, bedecked with jewels, and costly raiment. But robbers opened the majority of the sarcophagi (stone coffins) ages ago and stole any articles of value.

Near the site of Memphis stands the oldest surviving building of masonry, the step-pyramid of King Zoser, erected not much after 3000 B.C. This earliest pyramid was really a series of flat tomb structures built one on top of the other in diminishing sizes, but it suggested the form.

Not more than 100 years later (2900 B.C.) King Khufu (or Cheops) was building the Great Pyramid in the cemetery of Gizeh opposite Cairo. It covers 13 acres, each side being originally 755 feet long, and the height 481 feet. It contains 2,300,000 blocks of limestone. Herodotus says that 100,000 men spent 20 years building it, and modern archaeologists believe it may have taken even longer.

Scarcely less gigantic is the neighbouring pyramid of King Khafra (Chephren). Before it stands the great Sphinx, long a riddle. Now it is known that the Great Sphinx of Gizeh was the portrait head of Khafra, attached to the body of a lion.

Around the pyramids of the kings stand small flat-topped tombs of nobles and members of the royal

AGRICULTURAL SCENES IN ANCIENT EGYPT

Dating from the 18th Dynasty (1580–1350 B.C.) this painting from a tomb depicts a herd of cattle, having been numbered and divided into groups of five, being driven off by the herdsman. This is a kind of fresco, painted on a thin layer of plaster. On such decorations we largely rely for our knowledge of daily life in ancient Egypt.

The prosperity of Egypt has always depended on water from the Nile and on the industry of peasants cultivating land on the banks of the river. This series of reliefs from the tomb of a nobleman named Ti, who lived about 5,400 years ago, shows scenes at harvest time. Men and donkeys are setting out for the fields (first row). Grain is being tied into sheaves (third row) before being packed into nets and loaded on to donkeys (second row), who carried the harvest to the threshing floor, where they trampled it (bottom) to separate the grain from the ears.

house. As the pyramid had its temple, endowed with an income from many towns, so the tombs of the nobles had their chapels, where the priests served dinners of many courses for the mummy. Here, too, are the pyramid texts—prayers and incantations supposed to help the dead. Later generations prepared a collection of these charms and numerous copies have been found. The name Book of the Dead has been given to this collection of texts, some copies of which are splendidly illustrated. The chapel walls are often painted with scenes depicting life on the estate over which the noble once ruled. You see his herds of cattle, and watch the peasants hoeing and ploughing and planting. You see also craftsmen working at their trades. Here is the coppersmith hammering a saw out of a strip of tempered copper; and there the lapidary grinding out of diorite—a stone as hard as steel—bowls so thin they let the light through, or inlaying turquoise into golden vases. Here also is the goldsmith making richly wrought jewelry; and the potter turning clay vessels on a potter's wheel and baking them in closed clay furnaces as tall as a man.

Glass, too, was made and used to glaze tiles, or fashioned into vases and bottles. Here, too, are women weavers making gossamer fabrics of linen, tapestries for the pharaoh's palace or awnings for the

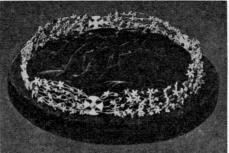

From Dahshur (Cairo Museum)

OLD EGYPTIAN DIADEM

Beautiful jewelry was made by the ancient Egyptians, and this exquisite diadem belonged to Princess Khnumuit, daughter of Amenemhet II (1935–1903 B.C.). It is of blue flowers with cornelian centres attached to a gold filigree.

noble's roof gardens. Men are gathering papyrus reeds in the Nile marshes to split and paste together into strong double sheets of pale yellow writing paper. Shipbuilders are making the typical Nile vessels with curving hulls, and cabinet-makers are busy upon chairs and couches to be overlaid with precious metals, inlaid with ebony and ivory, and cushioned with soft leather. On another wall we find a scene in the market-place. Coins had not then been thought of so the people are literally trading by barter. The cobbler offers the baker a pair of sandals in return for a cake, and the carpenter's wife gives the fisherman a little wooden box in exchange for some fish.

In the Pyramid Age art was developing as well as industry. The painter had learned to observe life and use brilliant colours. The portrait sculptor could make marvellous likenesses in stone or wood, coloured to the life and with eyes of rock crystal. The temple standing near the pyramid of Khafra shows us what progress the Egyptians of the Pyramid Age had made in the art of building. It is a splendid hall of granite with massive square pillars supporting the roofs which covered the three aisles. Openings in the walls admitted light.

The Pyramid pharaohs were rich and powerful. Their treasuries consisted of storehouses and

From a model in the Metropolitan Museum, New York

MODEL OF A GIGANTIC HALL IN EGYPTIAN THEBES

Except the Pyramids, the largest buildings in the whole of ancient Egypt were undoubtedly those of the Temple of Amen or Ammon at Karnak where the city of Thebes once stood. This temple took several centuries to build, but the huge hypostyle (having the roof supported on pillars) hall, of which a reconstruction of the central part is seen here, **was erected during the reigns of three pharaohs of the 19th Dynasty—Rameses I, Seti I and Rameses II (c. 1300 B.C.). The hall measured 338 feet by 170 feet, and the central columns were 69 feet high and 33 feet in circumference. The human figure standing beside the fourth column from the right gives an idea of the immensity of the temple**

PHARAOH ON HIS WAY TO THE TEMPLE

At Karnak was the magnificent temple of the god Ammon, which was one of the greatest of Egypt's architectural achievements. To this sacred shrine the Pharaohs went with music and numerous attendants. Here the Pharaoh, enthroned on a litter borne on the shoulders of slaves, has entered the courtyard through the archway between the two obelisks in the background, and the procession is making its way to the temple. The people are prostrating themselves, because their ruler was regarded as sacred and because he was supposed to represent the whole nation when he worshipped. The queer looking figures of animals in rows on either side are sphinxes with rams' heads, the ram being symbolic of Ammon. At first a local god of southern Egypt, Ammon grew in importance when the Thebans became masters of the north, until he came to be regarded as the supreme deity.

granaries, for taxes were paid in grain and live-stock, wine, honey and linen. At the central offices armies of clerks were kept busy with their reed pens and papyrus rolls, recording taxes paid. These pharaohs also sent donkey caravans to the Sudan for ebony, ivory, ostrich feathers and fragrant gums ; and ships went to Phoenicia and through the Red Sea to the coast of East Africa.

The first great age—the age of the Pyramids, or Old Kingdom—of Egyptian civilization lasted about 500 years. A new epoch begins about 2500 B.C., when the great nobles became powerful enough to wrest many privileges from the pharaohs, each ruling vast estates much as the barons did in the Middle Ages of Europe. To study this period we must sail about 200 miles up the Nile to the great cliff tombs where the feudal lords are buried.

Much of the contents of the tombs at the island of Elephantine, at Bersheh, Beni-Hasan, and Siut, have been moved to museums for study and safe keeping. For example, story-books, telling of ship-wreck and of wanderings and adventures in Asia; tales of old magicians; songs and poems in praise of the pharaoh, and a few works of science, including the oldest known medical book, a papyrus roll 66 feet long. In the tombs at Dahshur were found the jewels of the princesses, among them a diadem of little flowers exquisitely wrought on gold (*see* illus-tration, page 1116).

The pharaohs of this epoch built irrigation works, and dug a canal from the north end of the Red Sea to the nearest branch of the Nile. This served the purpose that the Suez Canal does nowadays. They also kept a standing army and conquered Nubia as

KEY TO EGYPTIAN MYSTERIES
Found at Rosetta in Lower Egypt in 1799, the Rosetta Stone provided the key to the deciphering of the inscriptions on Egypt's ancient monuments. It was set up at Memphis in 196 B.C. to commemorate the coronation of Ptolemy V, and the text was written in Greek and two Egyptian scripts.

far as the Second Cata-ract (near Wadi Halfa), thus adding 200 miles of the Nile to the kingdom of Egypt.

The feudal period was at its height from 2000 to 1800 B.C. After-wards Egypt seems to have been ruled by a line of foreign kings, the Hyksos, or shep-herd, kings. Little is known of them except that they came from Western Asia.

About 400 miles above Cairo the Nile valley suddenly widens and on the west bank are the two colossal statues long known as the Colossi of Mem-non, but actually figures of Amenhotep III.

The Louvre
AKHNATON
Reigning in about 1375 B.C., Akhnaton gave up the worship of Ammon for that of the sun.

Here is the plain of Thebes, site of the greatest period of Egypt—from the 16th to the 12th century B.C.—when the government was no longer a little valley kingdom, but an empire ruling from the Euphrates in Asia (Iraq) to the Fourth Cataract of the Nile (about 60 miles north of the present town of Abu Hamed). The modern centre of the plain is Luxor, with its double row of columns along the Nile, its hotels, and the Arab village creeping up into the temple precincts. To the north-east lies Karnak; this tangle of vast temples is approached from the Nile by a broad avenue of ram-headed sphinxes. Karnak contains the greatest colonnaded hall ever erected. The columns of its central aisle are 69 feet high, and 33 feet in circumference (*see* illustration in page 1116). This one hall covers as much space as the cathedral of Notre Dame in Paris. Near by stand sculptured figures cut from a single block 80 or 90 feet high. Sculptures in relief tell of Egyptian wars in Asia. Here for the first time the horse is represented in sculpture, and so we are able to fix the date when it began to be used in Egypt.

Within the precincts of Karnak and the many other great temples of ancient Egypt once dwelt an army of priests, who supervised not only religious practices, but also much of the daily life of the people. They were powerful because it was be-lieved that they had magical powers. All learning was in their hands alone.

Some of these Theban tombs remained unopened for many centuries, and many of them have been left just as they were when discovered. Through guarded doors you may pass through chambers and corridors to the room where the mummy lies in its sarco-phagus, surrounded by furniture and jewelry.

One of the most sensational discoveries in the his-tory of archaeology was made here in 1922–24, when a party uncovered the tomb of Tutankhamen, the Pharaoh who ruled about 1350 B.C. In it was found the most magnificent collection of Egyptian antiquities ever brought to light, for no thieves had found it. The extraordinary beauty and workman-ship of the bewildering mass of objects found here gave the world a new idea of Egyptian artistry.

Among the priceless treasures were four chariots, richly carved and ornamented with gold, ivory, and coloured glass; several large ceremonial gilt couches, bedsteads, chairs and stools; a throne, covered with gold and silver and inlaid with semi-precious stones; and boxes containing clothing, mummified foods and other articles. And in the inmost chamber, in an exquisitely decorated coffin under a huge double canopy blazing with beaten gold and precious stones, lay the mummy of the king himself.

Another memorable find occurred in 1905, when the tomb and temple of Queen Hatshepsut were dug out of the sands. She was the first great woman of history, living about 1500 B.C. In the temple wall paintings one may read her whole story from birth.

Hatshepsut's successor, Thothmes III—the Napoleon of ancient Egypt—also becomes a real person for us. In his reign of more than 50 years, he conquered much of western Asia and made one

Egyptian Exploration Society

QUEEN HATSHEPSUT

The first great woman ruler in the history of the world, Queen Hatshepsut (who reigned about 1500 B.C.) was looked upon in the same light as a male pharaoh. In this relief from her temple at Deir el-Bahri she is represented as a man.

of his generals governor of the Aegean islands. For some reason he erased the name of Queen Hatshepsut from the monuments wherever he could and walled up her great obelisks, one of which is still standing at Karnak.

Of this period is the young king Akhnaton, son of Amenhotep III and father-in-law of Tutankhamen. He abandoned the ancient belief in many gods (polytheism) and tried to convert his people to the belief in one god (monotheism).

The number of deities in the Egyptian religion was prodigious, for at first every village seems to have had its own god or gods. Gradually most of the deities of the smaller communities had been forgottten, and there remained only the great gods of the principal cities.

These were usually worshipped under the form of some animal, and in some places animals of these sacred classes were mummified after death. Vast cemeteries of mummified cats have been found at Bubastis,

British Museum

EGYPTIAN SOCIAL GATHERING AND ENTERTAINERS

In the days of the greatest splendour of the Egyptian empire magnificent entertainments were held amongst the upper classes ; music and dancing played an important part, just as they do today. Married couples (lower) are waited on by slaves (apparently single men and women were kept apart from the other guests). In the upper picture are two dancing girls and a group of musicians, one playing a form of flute. These pictures are tomb paintings.

TUTANKHAMEN'S SHRINE AND LAMP

In the innermost treasure-house of the tomb of Tutankhamen was found a carved and gilded shrine of surpassing loveliness (left). Four goddesses keep watch with outstretched arms. On the right is an ornate lamp, with a figure of the pharaoh visible only when the wick is lit.

Ptah, a craftsman and artist (like the Greek Hephaestus) and one of the creators of the world.

For these cults Akhnaton attempted to substitute the adoration of the power of the sun. The old worship at Karnak being too strong, he moved his capital to Amarna. There in a sculptor's ruined workshop has been found a portrait statue showing him as having the beautiful face of a dreamer. At Amarna also were found the famous Tel-el-Amarna letters — baked clay tablets inscribed with cuneiform (wedge-shaped) characters— from the kings of western Asia to the pharaoh. These show

and crocodiles, lizards, bulls, ibises, and other animals were similarly treated at various places and times.

Chief among the Egyptian deities were the falcon-headed sun-god Ra, worshipped in later times as Ammon-Ra; Osiris, judge of the lower world, incarnated on earth in the sacred bull Apis; Isis, sister and wife of Osiris, represented by a cow;

us how the northern territory in Syria was being taken by the Hittites coming in from Asia Minor, and the southern by the Hebrews drifting in from the desert. The Hittites possessed weapons of iron, while the Egyptians had only bronze.

But before the Egyptian empire fell, it flared up in one final blaze of glory under Seti I and his son

PALACE FURNITURE IN TUTANKHAMEN'S TOMB

One of the most important finds in the history of Egyptian archaeological research (usually called Egyptology) came in 1922–24 when the tomb of King Tutankhamen (died 1353 B.C.) in the Valley of the Kings at Thebes was dis- **covered and explored. The royal tombs of Egypt always contained a variety of personal possessions, such as the furniture from his palace found in the antechamber of the vault (above), buried with the mummified body of the king.**

the belief of the Egyptians in an after-life beyond the tomb we owe most of our knowledge of that ancient people. These uisite figures—half life-size—were found when the tomb of Mehenkwetre was opened in 1920. They had stood there, erect wide-eyed, for 4,000 years, ready to serve their master in the other world with the food and drink in their baskets.

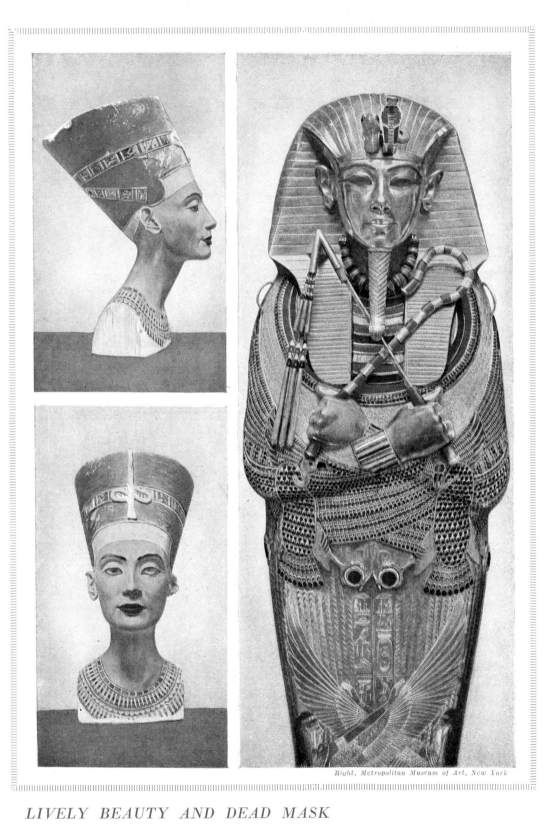

LIVELY BEAUTY AND DEAD MASK

These remarkable relics of Egypt 1300 years before Christ reveal exceptional artistic merit. The two photographs left show a bust of Nefertiti, Queen of the Pharaoh Akhnaton. It is of painted limestone, and was found in the workshop of the sculptor at Akhetaton. On the right is the casket of pure gold, magnificently worked, containing the mummy of Tutankhamen, Akhnaton's son-in-law.

GOLD-ENCRUSTED STATUE OF TUTANKHAMEN

When the tomb of Tutankhamen, who reigned from 1358 to 1353 B.C., was discovered during excavations in 1922–4, two statues of the pharaoh were found in the ante-chamber. The one shown here is a perfect example of ancient Egyptian art. It is carved in wood, and gorgeously adorned with a head-dress and ornaments of beaten gold. It stands seven feet in height.

Metropolitan Museum of Art, New York

The models found in the old Egyptian tombs illustrate every phase of life in the age of the Pharaohs, and those on this page represent boats that once navigated the Nile. Those shown above are typical fishing craft, made by binding together bundles of reeds covered with pitch, and they are towing between them a sieve net. On the right is a sailing vessel with the crew hoisting the one broad sail, and the look-out at the prow holding a fender to be used in the event of a collision.

EGYPTIAN ARTISTIC GENIUS
Throughout the history of ancient Egypt portrait sculpture was the one branch of art in which superb skill was repeatedly displayed. This head demonstrates the artistry of the Theban sculptors, expressing the dignity of old age.

British Museum

and scientific capital of the world. That beautiful city, however, has lain buried for many centuries far beneath the busy modern city of Alexandria, so perhaps the best way to get a glimpse of the last great chapter of Egypt's long history is to travel still farther up the Nile to the island of Philae, above the great dam at Assuan. The Ptolemies left many temples, new or remodelled, along the Nile, such as that at Edfu, but none more exquisite than the temple of Isis at Philae, which is now under water the greater part of the year.

After the death of Cleopatra, who was the last of the Ptolemies (*see* Cleopatra), Egypt became a Roman province. At first Christians were persecuted, but later Alexandria became a great centre of Christian leadership. Rome regarded Egypt merely as a valuable granary and burdened the natives with cruel taxes. Among others, there were grain taxes, sales taxes, poll taxes, and inheritance taxes. Three centuries of Byzantine misgovernment followed the rule of Rome and left the Egyptians in a mood to welcome the Saracen conquest (641 A.D.), which came nine years after Mahomet's death. Ever since that time the creed of Mahomedanism has prevailed in the land of the pharaohs.

Rameses II, the most famous of the pharaohs. From the delta to the great rock temple of Abu Simbel in Nubia, where colossal portrait statues of him look down from the cliff, his name is upon almost every building. He was the greatest builder of all the rulers of Egypt (*see* illus., page 1107).

Rameses II reigned for 67 years, from about 1292 to 1225 B.C., waging long wars in Asia which restored much of Egypt's lost prestige there. He may have been the pharaoh who so grievously oppressed the Israelites, as we read in the Bible.

Egypt was now to be the conquered instead of being the conqueror. The country was subdued by the Assyrians in the 7th century, and by the Persians in the 6th. It remained a Persian province until 332 B.C., when Alexander the Great seized it.

Alexander's conquest meant for Egypt a new great age, for under Ptolemy I—the Macedonian general who took Egypt as his share after the death of Alexander—and his descendants it was again ruled as an independent country. From Alexandria, the harbour city which the Ptolemies made their capital, their fleets ruled the seas from the Indian Ocean to the Hellespont. They reconquered Palestine and southern Syria, and made Alexandria the commercial, literary

D. McLeish

EDFU'S TEMPLE DEDICATED TO HORUS
Begun by Ptolemy III in 237 B.C., that at Edfu in Upper Egypt is the most complete Egyptian temple in existence. Shown here are the Court and the Great (West) Pylon, which date from the reign of Ptolemy XIII (died 51 B.C.). In this court was an altar on which offerings were made to Horus, the sun-god.

Einstein, ALBERT. Born of German-Jewish parents at Ulm, near Württemburg in Germany, on March 14, 1879, Albert Einstein's boyhood was spent in Munich, where his father owned an electro-technical works, but Albert later went to school in Switzerland. As a youth he attended lectures at the University of Zürich, at the same time teaching mathematics and physics to support himself. In 1901 he became an examiner of patents in the Swiss patent office, but this did not prevent his devoting all his spare time to the study of theoretical physics. Here began the series of remarkable scientific papers which were to revolutionise physical thought, and which were soon to elevate their author to the foremost rank of eminent scientists. The first suggestions of his new theory of relativity were published in 1905.

Having, in the meantime, become a Swiss citizen Einstein was in 1909 appointed to a special professorial post at the University of Zürich, and in the next four years he took up similar positions in Prague, Berne and Leyden. The special position of Director of the Kaiser-Wilhelm Physical Institute, in Berlin, was then created for him. Here he was free to devote all his time to research, without any of the normal routine duties and interruptions of a professorial post. The development of his general theory of relativity was carried out here, papers being published on this subject in 1915.

By the 1920's, Einstein had achieved worldwide fame, which can be judged by the many honours conferred upon him. Elected a Foreign Member of the Royal Society, he was awarded the Nobel Prize for Physics in 1921, besides receiving honorary degrees from diverse universities. In the early 1930's he visited England and America, and it was while in America that the anti-Jewish Nazi government of Germany deprived him of his post as Director of the Kaiser-Wilhelm Institute. He then settled in America and became a professor in the Institute of Advanced Study at Princeton

ALBERT EINSTEIN
Made famous in 1919 by his prediction as to the bending of light from the stars, which was verified by the British solar eclipse expedition, Einstein is best known for his theory of relativity. As a recreation he enjoys playing the violin.

University, New Jersey. There he continued to work on his unified field theory, which attempts to co-ordinate relativity, gravity and electrical force in one all-embracing theory. He was also an active member of the small group of scientists who persuaded the U.S. government to go forward with the atomic bomb project early in the Second World War (1939–45).

The theory of relativity, for which Einstein is most famed, has had the greatest influence on modern physics, both theoretical and experimental. By the end of the 19th century physics had reached the stage when most natural phenomena could be accounted for by drawing some analogy between them and an easily-conceived mechanical model. As an example of this, light was thought to travel as a wave-motion in some medium, the " luminiferous ether," much as water is a necessary medium for waves to travel along a water surface. The various physical properties of this luminiferous ether were calculated, and then came the problem, " Is the Earth moving through the ether, and is the ether fixed in position with respect to any part of the Universe?" Experiments failed to detect any flow of ether through any part of the Universe, which circumstance the older physics could not explain; and it was only with the advent of the relativity theory that such experiments were shown to be meaningless. The more fundamental fact emerged that it is not always possible to explain physical facts on a mechanical basis; and that, in any experimental measurements, the effect of the relative position of the experimenter has a great effect upon the results he gets. Although the basic concepts and a great part of the mathematical reasoning of the theory are quite simple, the results are far-reaching. The variation of the " mass " of a body with its speed, one of the predictions, is of widespread application in atomic and nuclear physics. The equivalence of mass and energy (*see* Atom), another outcome of Einstein's theory, enables us to calculate the energy to be derived from annihilating atoms, as happens naturally in the Sun, or artificially in the release of atomic energy.

Einstein was one of the first to grasp the significance of Planck's quantum theory (*q.v.*) of radiation; whereby light is regarded as being emitted in little packets of waves. He applied the idea to explain the then recently discovered phenomenon of photoelectricity (*q.v.*), in which electrons are shot out of metal surfaces when certain types of light fall on the metal. The complete agreement obtained between his theory and the experimental results provided strong evidence for the truth of the quantum theory.

Professor Einstein's remarkable genius as a scientist has not prevented him from displaying keen interest in other affairs. He has a sensitive and imaginative mind and is an accomplished violinist. He is married and has three children. His passionate belief in peace and human welfare have recently expressed themselves in his efforts urging the international control of atomic energy, one of the fundamental necessities, he believes, for world unity in the future.

Eire. In 1937 the name of the Irish Free State, which consisted of the 26 southern Irish counties, was changed to Eire, and the State was declared to be independent. This was the culmination of a long struggle which had been waged with Great Britain for self-government.

In April 1916 an insurrection against British rule took place and a Republic was declared. The rebellion was suppressed, but the armed struggle between Great Britain and Southern Ireland was renewed in 1919 and continued until 1921. The independence of Ireland was reaffirmed in 1919 by the Irish National Parliament, which was not recognized by the British Government. In 1926 an Act was passed by the British Parliament, under which two Parliaments were set up for two parts of Ireland under the titles of Southern Ireland and Northern Ireland. Northern Ireland accepted this; but the rest of Ireland, having already proclaimed a Republic, ignored the Act.

In December 1921 a Treaty was signed between Southern Ireland and Great Britain, under the terms of which Southern Ireland accepted Dominion status for the time being under the name of Irish Free State. The Irish people were not satisfied, and in 1937 complete independence was proclaimed and the name of the state changed to Eire. In 1949 the country left the Commonwealth to become an independent republic. (See Ireland).

Eisenhower, GENERAL DWIGHT DAVID (b. 1890). " I regard him as one of the finest men I have ever met." Such was the verdict of Winston Churchill, Britain's war leader, on the American General Eisenhower; and the words must have found an echo in many hearts when, in June 1945, cheering throngs saw him go to London's Mansion House to receive the Freedom of the City of London. On the same day he was decorated with the Order of Merit, the first American ever to be so honoured. Russia bestowed on him its highest military honour, the Order of Victory.

This great general, who had led the Allied forces to victory in Africa and in Europe in the Second World War (1939–45), was born in Denison, Texas, on October 14, 1890. He became a Second Lieutenant in 1915, and in 1918 he was entrusted with the organization of a tank training centre, which he commanded until 1922. He had wide staff experience between 1929 and 1935, and was responsible for America's plans for industrial mobilization in case of war. From 1935 to 1940 he was assistant military adviser to the Commonwealth (now the Republic) of the Philippines.

In June 1942 he arrived in England, with the rank of Lieutenant-General, to command the U.S. forces in Europe. Five months later he was in North Africa, where he directed the tremendous operations against the Germans and Italians in North Africa, Sicily, and Italy. In December 1943 he was nominated Allied commander-in-chief of the forces which were to liberate Western Europe. In February 1944 he was appointed head of the Supreme Headquarters, Allied Expeditionary Force (S.H.A.E.F.). His own government promoted him to the rank of General of the U.S. Army, equivalent to a British Field-Marshal, and King George VI created him an honorary G.C.B. (1943).

Under his direction the Allied liberating armies swept the Germans out of France, out of Belgium, and back across the Rhine, until on May 8, 1945, the Germans were crushed between the Western Allies and the Russians and forced to surrender un-

GENERAL EISENHOWER

Keystone

As Supreme Commander of the Allied Expeditionary Forces, 1944–45, General Eisenhower was one of the greatest leaders of the Second World War. He returned to Europe in 1951 to organize and command the armies raised in Europe under the terms of the North Atlantic Treaty.

conditionally. He commanded the U.S. forces of occupation in Germany until November 1945, when he returned to the United States to take up the duties of Army Chief of Staff. In 1947 he resigned from the army to become President of Columbia University, New York, but in December 1950 he resumed his military career on appointment as Supreme Allied Commander, Europe, under the terms of the North Atlantic Treaty of 1949.

Eisteddfod. (Pron. ās-te*th*'-vod). Welsh for a session or sitting, this word is used to denote the national bardic congress of Wales, held every year to encourage singing and music and maintain the Welsh language and customs.

Meetings of this kind have been held for very many years—indeed, since before the Christian era —but the present name was not applied to them before the 12th century. They seem to have been held regularly till about the end of the 17th century, when the custom fell into disuse for some 130 years. After the Napoleonic wars at the beginning of the 19th century there was a general revival of Welsh national feeling, which led to the resumption of the annual Eisteddfod. It has been held almost annually ever since. The Gorsedd, with its bardic rites, was originated in 1792 to take the place of the Eisteddfod, but it is now incorporated in it.

During the Eisteddfod, which lasts three or four days, contestants—bards, they are called—compete for medals and prizes for poetical, musical, and prose compositions, for the best choral and solo singing, for singing with the harp, and for the best playing on the harp and other instruments. The whole festival reflects the Welsh love of music, for the

Welsh are the most musical of all the peoples of Britain; and the bard who wins a high prize at the Eisteddfod is something of a national hero.

The Gaelic Mod, held annually at Oban or Inverness or some other Scottish town, is a more recent institution than the Eisteddfod, but is intended to serve much the same purpose, i.e., to encourage music, especially national or folk music, and the use of the Gaelic language.

Elbe, RIVER. (Pron. el'be). Having its source on the Czechoslovak side of the Riesengebirge, or Giants' Mountains, the Elbe traces a course of 150 miles before it reaches the German plain on its north-westerly course to the North Sea. The total length of the Elbe, which is Germany's second river in importance, is 725 miles, of which about 525 miles are navigable. Of its many tributaries the most important are the Vltava and Ohre (in Czechoslovakia), and the Mulde, Saale, and Havel (in Germany), and there is a system of canals linking it with the Oder, Spree and Trave. The cities and towns standing on its banks include Hamburg, Dresden and Magdeburg. An interesting invention is the great towing chain laid along the bottom of the river for 400 miles, from Hamburg to Aussig in Czechoslovakia, along which vessels travel. Vessels simply loop it up over revolving drums on their decks, thus pulling themselves along.

Elder. Usually about 10 feet in height, the elder bears clusters of white blossoms, and following the small fragrant flowers come the heavy clusters of dark purplish berries that may be made into a spicy and very tasty elderberry wine. The name of the common elder is *Sambucus nigra*.

The dwarf elder (*S. ebulus*), a local species, seldom exceeds four feet in height. The leaves consist of from five to eight pairs of lance-shaped leaflets, each about six inches long, and are crowned in July or August by flat clusters, botanically known as cymes, of pink and white flowers.

Eleanor of Castile (died 1290). The daughter of Ferdinand III of Castile, she married in 1254 Edward, son of Henry III, later to become Edward I of England. During the Barons' Wars Edward sent his wife to France for safety, but when he was victorious at Evesham, Worcestershire, in 1265 he brought her back to England. She accompanied him on a Crusade to the Holy Land in 1270. In 1272 Henry III died, and in 1274 Edward I and Eleanor were crowned at Westminster Abbey, London. Thus began one of the most important reigns in English history (*see* Edward I).

Eleanor is remembered for the original way in which Edward paid tribute to her after her death. She died on November 28, 1290, at Harby, in Nottinghamshire, and Edward brought her body to be buried at Westminster. At the places where her body rested on the journey the king erected crosses—at Lincoln, Grantham, Stamford, Geddington (Northants), Hardingstone, near Northampton, Stony Stratford, Woburn, Dunstable, St. Albans, Waltham, and, in London, at Westcheap and Charing. Only those crosses set up at Geddington

M. H. Crawford

ELDER TREE : BLOSSOMS AND BERRIES

Britain's summer-flowering elder of wayside and hedgerow was at one time held in special esteem for the wine which can be made from its abundance of purplish berries (lower right). These follow the flat clusters, or cymes, of fragrant white blossoms (top right). In contrast with the attractive appearance of an elder tree or bush in flower or in berry is the strangely unpleasant odour given out by the leaves and shoots when bruised. The many superstitions connected with the elder arise perhaps from the somewhat gloomy appearance of the tree when it is not in flower.

Northampton and Waltham now remain. All are in an excellent state of preservation. The cross now standing in Charing Cross station yard was designed by Sir Charles Barry and set up in 1863, the original one having been destroyed by the Puritans in 1647, together with that in Cheapside (as Westcheap is now called).

Electric Clocks. When we talk about electric clocks, it is important to distinguish between the various types. Some clocks are electrically wound, otherwise they have springs or weights to drive them, and rely for timekeeping on a pendulum or a balance wheel. They have a small electric motor which is switched on automatically every so often to re-wind the springs or weights, and are not really electric clocks at all.

Other clocks rely for their timekeeping on an ordinary seconds pendulum (*see* Clocks) which is "electrically maintained." There are no weights or springs, but there is an electro-magnetic apparatus by means of which the pendulum itself switches in some arrangement for imparting a tiny impulse regularly to keep the pendulum swinging. If you have read our story of Clocks you will know that this idea, of making the pendulum do some work, is quite foreign to the old established principles on which clockmakers worked for ages—of leaving the pendulum free of interference as far as possible.

But modern methods of instrument making are so accurate and precise that the extra work which the pendulum is required to do adds so little to its burden that very accurate timekeepers can be constructed on what is known as the "impulse-pendulum" system. Modern science has produced electric clocks so accurate that they can be used in observatories for timing the records of stars and planets. But such clocks are costly.

In factories comprising many buildings of many floors, and in large office blocks, it is a convenience to have all clocks synchronised from a master clock, and all showing the same time. A master clock on the impulse-pendulum system is generally used, connected electrically to a large number of dials in other rooms or buildings. The master clock is installed in some place free from vibration or other disturbance. It has a long pendulum, delicately poised, to which is attached a slight hook-shaped member which engages, at every swing to one side, with a fifteen-toothed "count-wheel." At every alternate swing the wheel is thus advanced one tooth; at the end of fifteen advances it has completed a revolution, and a lever on it trips a gravity arm which closes electrical contacts and lets an impulse from batteries go to the secondary clocks.

For greater accuracy the master clock, of special design, is relieved of the count-wheel mechanism, which is installed in a second clock called a slave. The pendulum of the master clock is "free," and gets its impulses by the falling of a tiny lever released by the slave clock at each half minute; the lever falls upon a small wheel mounted on the free pendulum, and in rolling off this wheel it gives a little push to the master clock's pendulum. At the same time this action sends a synchronizing signal to the slave clock, which keeps this clock in step with the master. It is from the slave clock that the impulses are sent out which work the many dials of clocks in other places in the building.

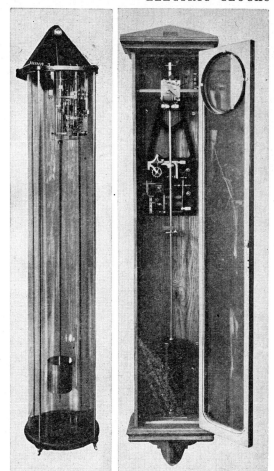

Science Museum, London

IMPULSE PENDULUM CLOCK

The Shortt 'free pendulum' clock (left) controls a slave clock (right), keeping it in synchronism with itself. At regular intervals the slave sends an impulse by electricity to the master clock, so releasing a lever which falls by gravity and imparts a tiny push to the free pendulum.

These room clocks consist only of a dial with a pair of hands, a train of wheels, and an electro-magnet; the magnet, by attracting a hinged iron armature at every impulse received, advances the minute hand by a ratchet one half-minute every time the master clock sends out an impulse. By this system it is possible in, say, a large factory, to have clocks in each department which all show the same time, and require no winding or regulation.

Most of the clocks commonly known as electric clocks are of the synchronous type. As you know, most houses are supplied with alternating current (*see* Electricity). This is kept at a standard frequency of 50 cycles per second. If, then, we can make a simple electric motor which keeps exactly in step with the alternations, and gear it up to a pair of clock hands, we have a clock which needs only to be plugged into the mains and set to the right time to keep on showing the exact time, so long as the electricity supply neither fails nor varies.

The principle of the simplest type of synchronous motor is shown in Figs. 1A, 1B and 1C. A small

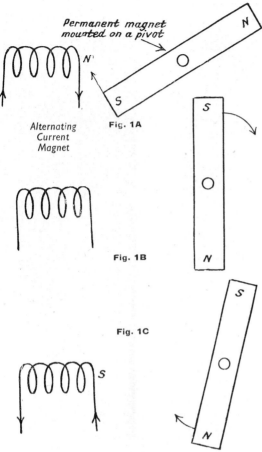

Permanent magnet mounted on a pivot

Fig. 1A

Alternating Current Magnet

Fig. 1B

Fig. 1C

PRINCIPLE OF SYNCHRONOUS CLOCK
In Fig. 1A the A.C. magnet is attracting the N. pole of a pivoted permanent magnet. In 1B the rotating magnet has shot past into a new position where there is no magnetic flux from the A.C. magnet ; but it continues its movement and comes under the influence of the A.C. magnet again, so continuing to rotate (1C).

" permanent " magnet is mounted on a spindle so that it can rotate about its centre. Near by is fixed an electro-magnet which is fed from the A.C. mains so that it keeps changing its polarity with the reversals of the current, giving a North pole for the positive half of the cycle, and a South pole for the negative half. (*See* Electricity ; Magnetism).

In the position shown in Fig. 1A the magnetic flux from the A.C. magnet is giving a N. pole, thus attracting the S. pole of the permanent magnet. As this reaches the A.C. magnet the flux is already dying away, and the rotating magnet, no longer attracted, will shoot past by its own weight to the position shown in 1B, where there is no flux at all from the A.C. magnet. Slightly past this position (1C), the A.C. magnet is building up a S. pole, thus attracting the N. end of the rotating permanent magnet. This continues every time that the current changes, so that the rotating magnet keeps exactly in step with the supply frequency—it is a true synchronous motor. You can quite easily see that it cannot run either faster or slower—if it got " out of step " there would be no force to make it go ; in

fact, it would be pulled backwards and would stop. Actually the commercial clock is not quite so simple. You could make a clock with a single magnet, but it has disadvantages—for one thing, it runs at a very high speed. If the rotating magnet has to make one complete revolution for each cycle of current, it must run at 50 revs. per second, or 3,000 revs. per minute. This not only requires more gearing to bring it down to 1 rev. per hour (the speed of the minute hand), but the high-speed gearing is apt to be noisy and to wear rather quickly. If we added another A.C. magnet so that the rotating magnet only had to move $\frac{1}{4}$ of a rev. to change from one polarity to another (instead of $\frac{1}{2}$ rev.) the speed would be halved, i.e. 25 revolutions per second.

If we were to put 50 poles on the A.C. magnet, the speed would be only 1 rev. per second. Most clocks of this type have several pairs of poles, which are arranged something like the way they are shown in Fig. 2 (page 1127). The poles are spaced like teeth in a saw, and are all excited by one A.C. coil; there is no need to use a separate coil for each pole. Twin rotating permanent magnets are used, and you will see that the rotor only has to move a comparatively short distance for each cycle.

How an Electric Clock is Started

Clocks of this type are not usually self-starting, but require a flick from a starting knob to spin the rotor up to about the correct speed, or a little above, when it drops into step of its own accord. Self-starting clocks *are* made, but many people prefer, however, that the clock should stop altogether in the event of an electricity failure, rather than have it resume operations an hour or so later. Self-starting clocks are usually made with a small indicator which shows when the clock has been stopped at some time. This prevents anyone being misled, as they might be if a clock, having stopped for some while, started again without giving any indication of the stoppage having taken place.

Of course, synchronous electric clocks are absolutely dependent upon the frequency for their accuracy, and the real " clock " is the " frequency master " we describe later. The supply frequency must be kept absolutely correct, since even the tiniest error in the speed of the rotor will add up to a considerable amount in the course of a few hours, and the greatest

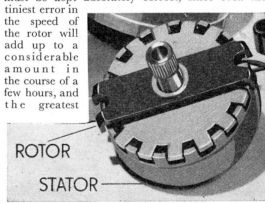

ROTOR

STATOR

ELECTRIC CLOCK : SYNCHRONOUS TYPE
The synchronous clock is kept going by mains current ; the number of current alternations per second governs the rate and time-keeping of the clock. Here are seen the rotor and stator. Compare with diagram in page 1127.

possible care is taken to ensure accurate control. The "frequency master" at the power station takes the form of a double clock with two seconds hands on the same spindle, one being driven by a synchronous clock from the mains, and one by a very accurate pendulum clock. Both pointers move together, and the slightest error in the frequency which the station is keeping shows up as a difference in their position, and thereupon can be promptly corrected.

At the electricity generating stations arrangements are made to correct the frequency regularly, so that our synchronous clocks are put right if there has been any divergence from the proper rate over any given period.

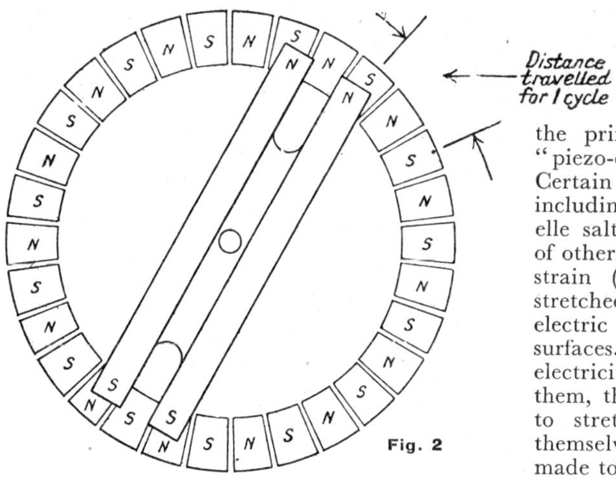

There is, in addition, another type of electric clock, which, however, is not seen in houses. It is used where the utmost accuracy is required, such

Fig. 2

SYNCHRONOUS CLOCK MOTOR

This represents a practical clock motor, in which the rotor has thirty poles and there are twin rotating permanent magnets. Compare the diagram with the photograph of an actual clock rotor and stator in page 1126.

as in astronomical time measurements at observatories. This works on the principle known as "piezo-electricity" (*q.v.*). Certain mineral crystals, including quartz, Rochelle salt, and a number of others, if placed under strain (*i.e.*, squeezed or stretched) produce minute electric charges on their surfaces. Conversely, if electricity is applied to them, they can be made to stretch or compress themselves, and can be made to vibrate at an exceedingly high frequency, which remains remarkably constant. The vibrations can be counted by electrical or electronic methods and used for time-keeping. Standard clocks of this type are, of course, far too delicate and expensive to be brought into general use, but are ideal for astronomical use where an error of a second a year is important.

LIFE FORCE *of the* MODERN WORLD

For centuries a mystery, then for long nothing but a scientific plaything, electricity came into its own during the 19th century. Today the civilized world would slow down to a stop without it.

Electricity. Rub a fountain pen, a stick of sealing wax, or similar material on dry flannel, or fur, and it will attract and even pick up little pieces of paper or other light objects. That is the simplest experiment in electricity, and it was first carried out by a Greek called Thales in about 600 B.C., who used amber. It was, however, nearly 2,000 years later that William Gilbert of Colchester, repeating these experiments with a number of substances, coined the name "electricity" from the Greek word for amber, *elektron*. Gilbert published in 1600 his work On the Magnet, Magnetic Bodies and the Great Magnet of the Earth, paving the way for all later systematic experiments on electricity.

The feeble electric charges produced by this method were increased by Von Guericke in 1660, who made the first frictional machine, consisting of a ball of sulphur rotated by hand; and by the invention of the "Leyden jar" about 1750, a device was made for storing or accumulating larger charges than had previously been possible.

In 1752, Benjamin Franklin made his famous kite experiment when, by obtaining sparks from a damp kite string during a thunderstorm, he showed that lightning flashes were due to clouds becoming charged with electricity of the same kind as that obtained by friction.

Galvani, in 1785, discovered what was then thought to be a different kind of electricity when he observed that some newly-dissected frog's legs twitched when hung by a copper hook on an iron railing. It was, however, left to Alessandro Volta to show that the electrical effect was produced by dissimilar metals in contact with one another, and he produced the "Voltaic pile," the forerunner of the primary batteries which you use in your electric torch. Such "galvanic currents," as they were then known, were thought to be unconnected with frictional electricity.

A Dane by the name of Oersted found, in 1821, that a galvanic current passed through a wire near to a compass needle caused the needle to move, showing that a magnetic field of force was set up around a current-carrying conductor. Michael Faraday reversed this procedure and produced a current in a conductor moving in a magnetic field. More important than this, however, was Faraday's demonstration that all "kinds" of electricity—frictional, galvanic, animal (*i.e.* electric shocks obtained from certain fishes), thermo-electricity (derived from heating the junction of two dissimilar metals), and electricity induced by a magnetic field were, in fact, the same "force." He recognized, however—and this still holds good—two different states, electricity in a state of rest or "tension," and electricity in motion. The study of these two states are classified as electrostatics and electro-dynamics.

Think of a small tank of water perched up on a high tower. A pipe leads to within a few feet of the ground. Depending upon the height of the tower—and thus the "head" of water—there will be a very high pressure at ground level. If the pipe bursts, the tank will be quickly discharged—there is a high pressure but only a small quantity of water. In a similar way, an electrostatic charge which accumulates on a rubbed body has a high pressure, or potential or tension or voltage as it is variously called, but the quantity of electricity is small—not sufficient to produce a current flow for any length of time. Even a lightning flash, which has a voltage high enough to jump hundreds of yards, and a current high enough to melt sand, only lasts a few millionths of a second.

Now think of water flowing through a large pipe on the ground. The head may be small—perhaps only a few feet, but there is a steady flow of water through the pipe, and that flow may be made to do useful work.

"*Voltage*" and "*Current.*" A volt is the unit of electrical pressure or difference of potential between two electrified bodies. To give you some sort of a mental "yard-stick" so that the name "volt" means something to you, an ordinary torch battery is from $1\frac{1}{2}$ to $4\frac{1}{2}$ volts, a car lighting battery is from 6 to 12 volts, and the standard voltage for electricity supply to your house is 240 volts. Trams and trolley-buses are usually run at 600 volts, as are electric trains, although 1,500 volts is occasionally used. The main transmission lines of the Grid operate at 132,000 volts, and other lines are operating at 264,000.

The rate of flow of a current is measured in amperes or amps. An ordinary "hundred-watt" lamp takes about $\frac{2}{3}$ amp. and an electric kettle, toaster, or iron, about 2 amps.

Power and Energy. Power is measured in watts, which is the product of the voltage and the current. Thus 1 amp. at 100 volts would be 100 watts, as would 10 amps. at 10 volts. Since the watt is rather a small unit, we often speak of kilowatts (a thousand watts) and megawatts (a million watts).

Energy is measured in watt-hours, which is the product of power and time. A one-kilowatt electric fire left on for one hour would use a kilowatt hour or Board of Trade unit of electrical energy, and the same amount would be used if four such fires were "on" for fifteen minutes.

Conductors and Insulators. A material which will allow electricity to pass freely through it in all directions is known as a conductor of electricity, while one which will not so behave is known as a non-conductor or insulator. There is no such thing as a perfect conductor. Even silver, the best material of all, offers a certain resistance to the flow of current—*i.e.*, a certain proportion of the electrical energy carried by a conductor is lost in overcoming the friction of the electrons (*see* Electron), and reappears in the form of heat energy.

Think once again of the water-pipe. To pump a certain quantity of water through a pipe requires a certain pressure. Some pressure will be lost because of friction between the water and the pipe, which will depend upon three things—the length and diameter of the pipe, and its inner surface. To pump a quantity of water through a small pipe obviously requires more pressure than to pump the same quantity through a large one; and a rough pipe will offer more friction than a smooth one.

In the same way, if an electric current is passed through a conductor, there will be a certain voltage drop across it, depending upon its resistance. This will vary with its length; its cross-sectional area (a thin wire has a higher resistance than a thick one); and its material. An iron wire, for example, has nearly six times the resistance of a copper wire of the same size, copper being the next best conductor to silver, and the most frequently used.

Resistance is measured in *ohms*, named after Georg Simon Ohm, a Bavarian, who carried out the pioneer work and stated, in 1827, what is now known as Ohm's Law, that *the current in a circuit is equal to the voltage divided by the resistance*, or $I = \dfrac{V}{R}$ from which we see that if a 10 ohm resistance has 20 volts applied across it, the current will be $\dfrac{20}{10} = 2$ amps. In the same way, 200 volts with 100 ohms would give 2 amps. I is the usual symbol for "current."

There is no such thing as a perfect insulator or non-conductor, since all substances conduct slightly. In general, most non-metallic substances (except carbon) are either poor conductors or practically non-conducting. This does not mean that they are suitable for use as insulators—an insulating material is chosen for other properties such as mechanical strength, freedom from moisture absorption, in addition to being a non-conductor. Examples of good insulating materials are dry air, ebonite, rubber, paper, oil, paraffin wax, silk, cotton, porcelain, glass, mica, and many plastics.

The Electric Circuit. The early experimenters in frictional electricity found that if they electrified different materials they obtained different effects. A glass rod, for example, would attract an electrified amber rod, whereas it would repel another electrified glass rod. This led them to the opinion that there were two kinds of electricity—vitreous and resinous, later termed positive and negative, since they were of opposite "sign." If a body is given equal charges of positive and negative electricity, it is found that it possesses no charge at all—the two neutralise one another.

Benjamin Franklin, about 1750, proposed the first reasonable theory of electricity, which is now known as the one-fluid theory. He said that electricity was an invisible weightless fluid, which existed everywhere. If a body, by rubbing got more than its share of the electric fluid, it was positively charged ; if less, then it was negatively charged. Think of two tanks each containing equal amounts of water. If water is pumped from one to the other, then the tank with more water represents a positively-charged body, while the other—deficient in water—represents a negatively-charged body. If the two are now connected by a pipe, water will flow from the full tank to the other, until both are equally full once more. In the same way electricity is regarded as flowing from the positive—or point of high potential—to negative—or point of low potential.

Franklin's theory provided such a convenient explanation of so many problems that is is still—for practical purposes—in use. We now know (*see* Electron) that a so-called positively-charged body is one which is actually short of negatively charged electrons; and that a negative charge is due to an excess of electrons. Thus any flow is, actually, a

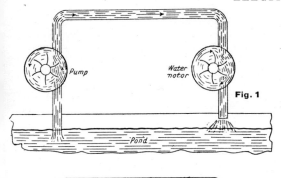

Fig. 1

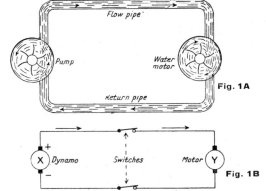

Fig. 1A

Fig. 1B

WATER AND ELECTRIC CIRCUITS

The pump in Fig. 1 sucks water from a river, raises its pressure or 'head,' and pumps it to a water motor ; after turning the motor the water, its energy spent, returns to its source. In Fig. 1A, the water flows in a closed circuit. The electrical analogy to Fig. 1A is seen in Fig. 1B: a dynamo and electric motor replace the pump and water motor.

flow of negative electrons from negative to positive. Nevertheless, all practical electrical science is founded on the rule that a current flows from positive to negative—from a point of high potential to a point of low potential. We must be quite clear in our minds about this, or we shall get confused.

The electron theory is accepted—electrons *are* negative, and they *do* flow from negative to positive. But it is much more convenient to regard an electric current as flowing from positive to negative. We still say that the sun rises—we know quite well it doesn't, and that it is the earth revolving that makes it seem to " rise." If a number of people are forming a human chain, passing buckets of water from a pond to a fire and the empty buckets back again, one can just as easily say that they are passing empty buckets (or buckets filled with air) from the fire to the pond.

An electric current, then, flows from a point of high potential to a point of low potential. On its way it can be made to do useful work. There must be a continuous conductor to take it to and from its

load. The complete path is termed a circuit and, once again, we call into play a hydraulic analogy to help us to understand it.

In Fig. 1 a pump, driven by some source of power (not shown) sucks water from a river, raises its pressure or " head " and pumps it through a pipe to a water motor, where the energy of the water is converted into mechanical energy, and the low-pressure water is returned to the river. In Fig. 1A instead of the water being taken from, and returned to, the river, a return pipe is installed, so that there is a complete closed circuit.

A corresponding electrical circuit is shown in Fig. 1B. X represents a source of electrical energy (say a dynamo) and Y a load, which may be a motor if mechanical power is required, or may be a lamp or a resistance if it is desired to convert the electrical energy into light or heat. The direction of current flow is indicated in the diagram; switches are also shown in both positive and negative conductors. Since there must be a complete path for the current, it is only necessary to open a connexion on either lead to cut off the current, and a switch is merely a way of interrupting the circuit.

Series and Parallel Circuits.—Figure 2 shows two different methods of connecting more than one piece of apparatus in a circuit. In this case, for simplicity, a dynamo is shown supplying two similar lamps, but the principles are the same no matter what kind of things you use, or how many there are of them. In A, the lamps are connected in series—the same *current* flows through both, one after the other, and they divide the *voltage* of the circuit between them. In B, they are connected in parallel—each has full circuit voltage across it, but the total current flowing in the circuit is divided between them. In each case the dynamo output is taken to be 100 volts, 1 amp. For series connexion, therefore, lamps would be rated at 50 volts, 1 amp. ; for parallel connexion at 100 volts, $\frac{1}{2}$ amp. The wattage of both the dynamo and the lamps is the same in both cases.

Series circuits are not often used for lamps. It is not possible to switch off one lamp only and, with a number of lamps, the voltage required becomes dangerously high. The lamps in your house, and the plugs for vacuum cleaners and the like are all wired in parallel.

Short Circuits.—Any circuit of very low resistance which by-passes the main circuit is called a short circuit, since the electricity will pass through it in preference to the full resistance of the load (Fig. 2B). The " short " may be due to a wrong connexion; to an accident, such as a nail being driven through the two conductors; or to the insulation becoming

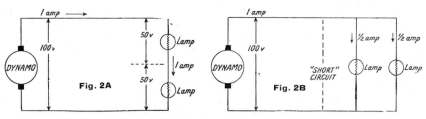

Fig. 2A

Fig. 2B

SERIES CIRCUIT AND PARALLEL CIRCUIT

In a series arrangement the current goes through the two or more lamps or appliances one after the other, fed by the same pair of conductors : the total voltage is halved. In a parallel circuit each lamp or appliance has its own conductors and takes current at full voltage from the supply.

frayed or worn away, and the conductors allowed to touch one another. This may have very serious effects. If, for example, the resistance of the "short" is 1/10th of an ohm, the current will increase (Ohm's law again) from 1 amp. to 1,000 amps.

We have already seen that the passage of a current causes heating. Now, a conductor which will carry 1 amp. without becoming even warm, will melt in a fraction of a second at 1,000 amps., and probably cause a fire. Hence, in electrical work we always have some form of protection against short circuits, and the "fuses" near your meter are one of the forms of protection. A fuse is a short piece of wire, thinner than the main conductor—a weak link in the chain—which will melt before the conductor gets overheated, and can be easily replaced. Another method is to have an automatic switch called a "circuit breaker" which trips or opens as soon as a short circuit occurs.

Alternating Current. Up to now, we have only considered electricity at rest and flowing steadily in one direction—*direct current* or "D.C." The majority of electrical machinery used nowadays, however, works on *alternating current* or "A.C." In this, the current flow stops and reverses many times per second, and a given point will be positive at one instant and negative at the next. It may be a little difficult to understand how, if this occurs, the electricity can ever "get anywhere" if it rushes backwards and forwards at this rate. Perhaps it will be easier to understand if we think of water.

In Fig. 3, two cylinders fitted with pistons, cranks, and flywheels, are coupled together with pipes as shown, both pipes and cylinders being filled with water. If one flywheel is turned, the piston moves, forcing water out of the cylinder on one side and pulling it into the cylinder on the other side. The water so displaced will be forced through the connecting pipes and move the other piston, so driving the second flywheel by means of the crank. Yet

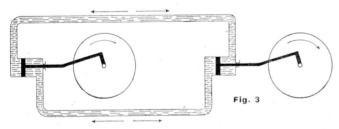

ALTERNATING CURRENT : MECHANICAL ANALOGY

If one flywheel is turned, water is pushed out of one side of one piston and sucked in at the other side ; water thus displaced is forced around the circuit to the other cylinder and will move that piston. Note that there is no continuous circulation of water ; it merely moves backwards and forwards in the same pipe. (See also Fig. 3A).

there is no continuous circulation of the water—it merely keeps on moving backwards and forwards in the same pipe, although at any instant there is the effect of a continuous flow.

The way in which the flow of water varies in each pipe is shown in Fig. 3A and is exactly the same shape as an alternating current wave. It starts at zero (dead centre of the crank), rises to its maximum speed of flow at $\frac{1}{4}$ revolution; slows down and stops again at $\frac{1}{2}$ rev. (dead centre); then reverses and flows the other way, reaching a maximum negative value

at $\frac{3}{4}$ rev.; and stops once more at the conclusion of a rev. It then repeats the "cycle," as it is termed.

In alternating current work, the number of times per second that the cycle is repeated is known as the frequency, and varies from 50 cycles per second in the standard electricity supply (although frequencies as low as 16 2/3 cycles are occasionally used for electric trains), to 30,000,000,000 (thirty thousand million) cycles per second in some forms of radio work.

Polyphase Circuits. The simple A.C. circuit just dealt with, known as a single-phase circuit, while

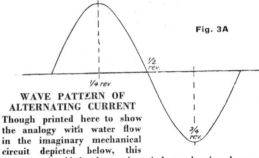

Fig. 3A

WAVE PATTERN OF ALTERNATING CURRENT

Though printed here to show the analogy with water flow in the imaginary mechanical circuit depicted below, this diagram should be borne in mind as showing how an alternating current rises to a maximum in one direction (wave-crest), and then drops to zero before again rising.

A complete 'cycle' is represented in the diagram.

quite satisfactory for many purposes, is not ideal. Referring again to Fig. 3A, we see that there are too many zero points where no power is being transmitted. There is no continuous flow of power. This could be remedied partly if we added another set of pistons and cylinders at right angles to the original pair in Fig. 3. We now see that when the first set are at dead centre, the other set are producing the maximum "push." This is, in effect, what is done in electrical machinery to produce what is known as two-phase current. It has the disadvantage that four conductors are usually necessary.

If now, we put three cylinders at each end (Fig. 4), spaced at 120 degrees to each other, we find a perfectly workable arrangement is possible using not six, but three pipes, and getting a remarkably even turning effort. The power-flow diagram is shown in Fig. 4A, from which it will be seen that when the flow in one pipe is at zero, one of the others is rising to a maximum, and the other is falling.

In three-phase A.C. work something of this sort is done. There are, as it were, three electrical systems on one machine, each displaced by one-third of a cycle from the other two. The system has many advantages (chiefly in connexion with the transmission of power and the running of motors), and is very widely used.

Methods of Producing Electricity. Strictly speaking, we do not "produce" or "generate" electricity—we merely convert some other form of energy into electrical energy, and there are various ways of doing it, some of which are more efficient than others.

Static Electricity. The most elementary—and inefficient—method of producing static electricity

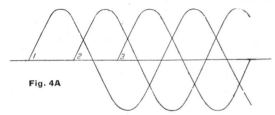

Fig. 4A

to repel each other and refuse to lie flat in the weaving process. In fact, the engineer devotes much ingenuity to getting rid of static charges.

Batteries.—Electrical energy can be produced from chemical energy in a *cell*, or *battery* (as a number of cells is called), and the earliest currents were so produced in Volta's " pile." The chemical action which produces an electric current is dealt with under Battery, and it is sufficient to say that

is by means of the rubbing process already referred to at the beginning of this story. Various experimenters have designed machines which would enable larger charges to be produced, these operating either by plain friction or by " electrostatic induction," the principles of which are shown in Fig. 5. If a ball B having equal charges of positive and negative is brought near to a positively-charged ball A, the positive charge on A will tend to attract the negative charges in B and repel the positive, since " like " poles repel each other.

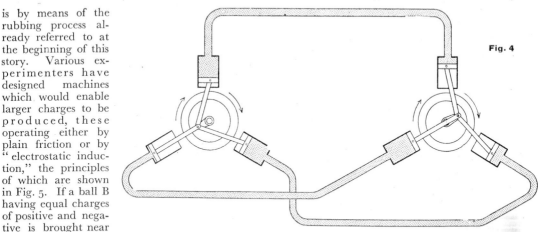

Fig. 4

ELECTRICITY : SIMPLE ILLUSTRATION OF POLYPHASE CURRENT
The mechanical analogy of a water circuit with two ' pumps,' shown in page 1130 has a jerky motion, with many points where no power is being transmitted. If three cylinders were used at each end, spaced at an angle of 120 degrees to each other, a more even turning movement would result. When the flow in one pipe is at zero, that in another is rising and another is falling.

If, then, B is touched with the hand, the positive portion of the charge will leak away to earth, leaving B, when it is removed from the neighbourhood of A, with a negative charge. Ball B, now being negatively charged, can be used to induce further positive charges on other uncharged bodies. This principle is used in a number of machines, the best-known of which is the Wimshurst.

Static electricity is generated when a jet of steam plays upon metal surfaces. The effect usually passes unnoticed in the majority of cases ; (*e.g.* in railway locomotives the loco is " earthed " through the rails, and the charges can leak away to earth). In the case of steam road wagons with rubber tyres, however, it will be noticed that there is always a chain hanging down on the ground, to ensure earthing, and severe shocks are occasionally experienced if this chain is removed.

Static charges are frequently a considerable source of trouble. The rubber blankets used in hospital operating theatres have caused fatal accidents owing to static charges accumulating with friction, causing a spark which has exploded ether vapour. The friction of petrol passing through a rubber hose has caused explosions, due to sparks igniting petrol vapour. Hospital blankets are now made of a special non-insulating rubber; and petrol pipes are lined with metal, for earthing purposes. The damage caused by lightning is too well known to require mention. In paper mills and printing works, static charges cause sheets of paper to cling together, or to curl up and jam in machinery. In textile mills, like charges on textile fibres cause fibres

a cell usually consists of two dissimilar electrodes and an " electrolyte " solution. One of the elements (frequently zinc) dissolves in the electrolyte, and requires renewing from time to time.

The Leclanché cell (*see* page 375), as used for bell ringing and similar duties, utilises a zinc rod as one electrode, the other being a carbon plate packed round with a mixture of crushed carbon, and a depolariser known as manganese dioxide. Ammonium chloride, frequently known as "sal-ammoniac " is the electrolyte. The familiar dry cell (*see* p. 376), as used in hand lamps and torches

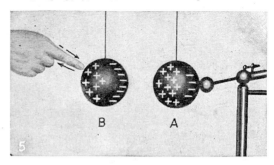

B   A

ELECTROSTATIC INDUCTION
If a ball, B, having equal charges of positive and negative electricity, is brought near to a positively-charged ball, A, the positive charges on A will tend to attract the negative charges on B, and to repel the positive charges on B. By then touching B with the hand, the positive part of the charge on that ball will leak away to earth. This leaves B, when it is taken away from the neighbourhood of A, with a negative charge only.

is a modified form of the Leclanché cell, with the zinc formed into a case surrounding the remainder of the cell, and a " jelly " type of electrolyte, instead of a thin liquid.

Secondary batteries, in which electrical energy is transformed into chemical energy, and back again, are discussed in page 377.

The voltage of the average primary battery is about 1½–2 volts per cell, and if higher voltages are required, it is necessary to connect a number of cells in series. Primary batteries are not a practical proposition for the production of large amounts of power, owing to the trouble required to maintain them in good condition, their bulk and weight for the output obtained, and the expense of the active material (*e.g.* zinc) which is consumed.

Electro-Thermal Processes.—It is possible to transform heat energy directly into electrical energy by heating the junction of two dissimilar metals (e.g. copper and iron). The thermopile consists of a number of such thermocouples joined together in series, so that their voltages are added together. This principle has no practical value for the production of large amounts of power, but it is frequently used as a thermometer. Since the voltage produced increases with the temperature of the junction, a small thermocouple, used with a sensitive measuring instrument, will measure temperatures too high for the ordinary mercury thermometer; by the use of long connecting wires, it will allow temperatures to be measured at a control panel some distance away from the hot spot.

Electro-Magnetic Induction.—This is the most important method of all for generating electricity, and is the basis of all modern electrical machinery, from the giant " alternators " which supply electricity to the whole of the country, to the tiny motor in the toy train which runs on miniature rails around the nursery floor.

We have already referred to Oersted and his discovery that a current in a conductor produced a magnetic " field of force " (*see* Magnetism) which would affect a compass needle, thus showing that magnetism and electricity were not two separate sciences, but were inter-related. In 1825 the first electro-magnet was produced by a scientist named William Sturgeon (1783–1850), who showed that by taking a horse-shoe of soft iron and winding a coil of wire round it, a current passed through the wire would produce a very powerful magnetic field.

CURRENT POLARITY

Compass needle here shows the presence of electric current in a wire brought near the needle.

Faraday reversed Oersted's experiment, using his famous ring (*see* Transformer) ; he showed that a magnetic field induced a current in a conductor *if the field were changing*. Thus, the lines of force or magnetic flux must be growing (switching on the electro-magnet) or collapsing (switching off), or the conductor must be moving in the field so as to cut through the flux. The first two only gave a momentary " kick " of current, but the last one would give a continuous current so long as the conductor could be kept moving in the magnetic field.

Faraday's first generator was a copper disc, rotating between the poles of a permanent magnet, and from this has grown the large family of electro-magnetic machines known as dynamos, generators, and alternators which are explained under Dynamo, for converting mechanical energy into electrical energy; and the equally large family for performing the reverse operation, which are described under the heading Motor.

Capacity and Condensers.—An insulating material, as we know, will not conduct electricity—or will pass such a tiny amount that we can disregard it. The reason it will not conduct is that its electrons are more firmly attached to its atoms, and cannot pass on easily to the next atom to form an electric current. They try to, however. Think of a sealed tin box with a tube on each side. If you blow into one side, air comes out of the other. If, now, you stretch a thin rubber sheet across the centre of the box, dividing it into two compartments, and then blow again, what happens? The rubber sheet stretches and bulges, forcing some air out of the other side, so that at first it seems as though you were still blowing straight through. As the sheet stretches more and more, however, it becomes harder and harder to blow, until you can force no more air in at all. If you take the tube out of your mouth, the air rushes out again, fast at first, then slowly, until, when the rubber sheet is no longer stretched, the air flow stops altogether.

If you take two unconnected metal plates with an insulating substance or dielectric in between, you have what is known as a condenser. If you apply a source of electricity " across " the plates —by connecting two wires from a battery to the plates, positive to one and negative to the other— a current will flow which rapidly dies away when the condenser is " charged." If, now, the source of electricity is removed, and the two plates joined together by a wire, a current will flow in the reverse direction until the condenser is discharged. (A simple condenser is shown in Fig. 6.)

You can think of the two condenser plates as the two halves of the box, and the dielectric as the rubber sheet. Just as we strained the sheet by blowing, so we strained the dielectric by applying a voltage across it. We tried to make it conduct, and it stored up a charge in itself. When the strain is relieved the stored-up charge is returned.

Just as the capacity of the box to store air depends on the size of the box, so the capacity of a condenser depends on the size of the plates. It also depends on their distance apart—the nearer they are the larger the capacity (*see* Fig. 6); also on the material of the dielectric. Just as a very " stretchable " rubber sheet will allow you to store more air in the box, so a dielectric with a high " specific inductive capacity " or " dielectric constant " will allow the condenser to take a greater charge for the same voltage applied to it. A mica dielectric, for example, will give about seven times the capacity of an air film of equal thickness.

Condensers usually consist of a number of metal plates interleaved to get the maximum capacity into a given space, although any arrangement of two conductors with a dielectric in between—two cores of a cable, for example—will act as a condenser. " Variable " condensers (as used in a radio receiver) have an arrangement for altering the amount of overlapping of the plates, thus altering the capacity.

The unit of capacity is termed a *Farad* (after Faraday), and a condenser of 1 Farad will allow a charging current of 1 amp. to flow for 1 volt applied across it. This unit is very large, and it is more usual to speak of microfarads (one millionth of a farad) or even micro-micro-farads (one millionth of a microfarad).

You may often hear it said that "a condenser will stop D.C. but will pass A.C." A condenser will not let *any* current pass through it, unless you raise the voltage so high that the dielectric is broken down or punctured. (Just as you would burst the rubber sheet if you blew too hard, so you can break down any insulation if the voltage is high enough.) A condenser with a punctured dielectric is, of course, short-circuited.

If you remember Fig. 3, where we compared A.C. with water pumping backwards and forwards in a pipe, you will realize that a condenser on A.C. would be charged and discharged every time the current reversed, and thus the current *seems* to pass right through it.

Inductance.—The work of Faraday told us about electro-magnetic induction. There is, in addition, a property known as "self-induction" or *inductance*. The magnetic field set up by a current in a conductor will not only induce a current in a neighbouring conductor (when the first current is rising or falling), but will induce, in the second current, a back voltage tending to oppose the change in current producing it. This effect is far more pronounced in the case of a coil of wire, or an iron-cored electromagnet, than it is in a single straight conductor; its action is, of course, to oppose the flow of current when it is first switched on, and to prevent the flow stopping when it is switched off. In effect, it is rather like the electrical equivalent of the inertia of a heavy flywheel—the current in an inductive circuit takes a lot of starting and a lot of stopping.

On direct currents, inductance only has any effect when switching on—when the current takes some time to reach its full value as decided by the resistance of the circuit—and on switching off, when it tends to make the switching operation difficult by refusing to stop when the switch is opened, and forming an *arc* or flame, between the switch contacts.

On A.C., however, the effect is to oppose each reversal of current, so that it reduces the current below its normal value and appears to add to the resistance of the circuit. This apparent resistance (which causes no heating and is due to the inductance only) is known as *reactance*; the combination of inductance and resistance is known as impedance. A coil which is used to limit currents on A.C. circuits by reactance only is known as a reactor,

choking coil, or choke, because it has a throttling effect upon the current. The inductance of a coil is measured in henrys—named after J. H. Henry (1797-1878), an American scientist—and a coil which gives a back voltage of 1 volt for a change in current of 1 amp. per second has an inductance of 1 henry.

Detecting and Measuring Electricity.—The earliest device for detecting the presence of static electricity was the pith ball electroscope, which consisted of a tiny ball of wood pith (being one of the lightest substances obtainable) hung upon a silk thread. A charged body would produce attraction, thus

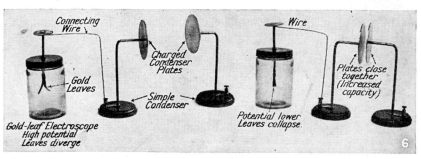

ELECTROSCOPE USED TO SHOW 'POTENTIAL' DIFFERENCE

Electric pressure between charged bodies varies as their distance apart. Potential difference between the condenser plates above is high when the distance is great, and is registered by divergence of the gold leaves of the electroscope (left). Decrease of distance, without alteration of charge, results in lower potential, registered by collapse of the leaves (right). The amount of electric charge a condenser will carry depends on the area of the plates and on the nature of the dielectric, as well as on their distance apart.

demonstrating the presence of electric charges. Another device was the gold leaf electroscope (Fig. 6) consisting of a pair of leaves of thin gold foil suspended by a wire (inside a glass jar, to prevent air currents disturbing the leaves). When charged electrically, the gold leaves (being connected to the same wire and thus receiving the same charge) repelled each other, thus diverging and indicating the presence of a charge by remaining diverged, until the charge leaked away or was neutralised by a charge of opposite sign, when they collapsed again. The gold leaf electroscope is still in use for static experiments.

A much more recent instrument frequently used in electro-dynamics for measuring voltages, is the electrostatic voltmeter. This takes many forms, but the basic principles are the same. The instrument is fitted with two sets of light metal plates, one set being fixed, and the other allowed to move. The two sets are connected to opposite sides of the system, and when a voltage is applied to them, they attract each other. The moving set are restrained by a spring, and carry a pointer which moves over a graduated scale; and the movement of the pointer can indicate directly the voltage that is applied.

Two other electrical effects are used in measuring instruments—the thermal effect of a current and the magnetic effect. As you know, when a metal is heated, it expands in proportion to the amount its temperature is raised. If then, we take a thin wire, fix one end, and fasten the other to a pointer moving over a scale, and pass current through the wire, the amount of expansion and, consequently the value of the current, will be shown by the

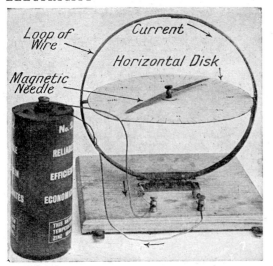

ELECTRICITY : A GALVANOMETER

Fig. 7. The current in the wire loop produces an electro-magnetic field, the intensity of which is measured by the deflection of the magnetised needle. This is the principle of the galvanometer, though there are several types.

movement of the pointer. This, the hot-wire type of instrument, has a number of uses in electrical engineering.

The electro-magnetic force of a current can be measured in various ways. The simple *galvanometer* (of which the principle is shown in Fig. 7) is one. Other types are used—for example, the d'Arsonval or moving coil galvanometer uses a tiny coil and a large magnet. The coil is suspended between the poles of the magnet, and carries a mirror which reflects a beam of light on to a scale some distance away, thus giving the effect of a very long pointer which weighs nothing at all, so that the moving system can be made very light and sensitive.

Galvanometers will thus detect the presence of a current—they can be made to give an absolute measurement of its value if they are calibrated, or compared with some known standard. For ordinary everyday use, however, we require something which will give us a direct measurement without any calculation, and there are many different direct-reading instruments which are self-contained and read directly in amps. (ammeter or ampere-meter), in volts (voltmeter), in watts (wattmeter) and in ohms (ohmeter). All vary greatly in details, but all operate on either electrostatic, electro-thermal, or electro-magnetic principles.

It is also possible to measure a current by its electro-chemical effect, by weighing the amount of, say, silver or copper which is deposited in a given time (*see* Electro-chemistry; Electroplating), but this is not a practical method for everyday use.

Electric Light. When you press the electric light switch, do you ever think that this simple action turns on a brilliant flood of light at a smaller price than your grandfather paid for the dim light of a guttering candle? We are so accustomed to taking this gift of science for granted that we can hardly believe that it was only in 1879 that Edison in America, and Swan in England, simultaneously developed the incandescent electric lamp.

Before this, the only commercial form of electric lighting was by the electric arc, which consists of an arc or flame, burning between two carbon rods which have their ends nearly touching, and the other ends connected to a source of electric power. The current which passes through the rods is conducted across the gap by a cloud of white-hot carbon vapour, and the light comes partly from this, and partly from the intensely hot ends of the rods. The light given is very powerful, and the carbon arc is still used in searchlights, cinematograph projectors, and similar applications, where an intense, concentrated light is required.

Arc lamps were at one time largely used for street lighting. They have two chief disadvantages: the carbons burn away rapidly and require constant renewal and attention, and it is only possible to make the lamps in large sizes—they cannot be used in small units for lighting rooms. It was the need for " the subdivision of the electric light," as the early workers called it, that led to the development of the parallel circuit, and the incandescent lamp.

You will remember that in the article on Electricity we saw that a current passing through a resistance produced heat. In the incandescent lamp, as produced by both Edison and Swan, a thin carbon " filament " made from carbonised cotton or bamboo was heated by the passage of a current to a bright yellow heat, being enclosed in

Sylvania Electric Products, Inc., New York

ELECTRIC LIGHTING

A modern development of the ' discharge ' lamp, fluorescent lighting (above) gives shadowless illumination, with complete absence of glare. This floor in a big office block affords a striking example of fluorescent strip lighting.

a glass bulb from which all air had been exhausted, so that the filament should not burn away. The first house in England to be lighted with Swan's lamps was that of Sir William Armstrong, at Cragside, Northumberland, in 1880. The efficiency of the carbon lamp was very low by present-day standards, taking about 3 watts of electricity to produce the equivalent of one candle-power.

The incandescent lamp as we know it today has a filament made of tungsten ; the filament is thinner than human hair, and is coiled up into a small spiral. In lamps known as the " coiled-coil " type, this tiny spiral is itself wound into another coil. The filament is held by support-wires made of molybdenum, which are sealed into a glass stalk called the " pinch," which protrudes inside the bulb. From the end supports go leading-in wires which carry the current from the cap to the filament. These leading-in wires are made of copper-coated nickel-iron where they pass through the glass bulb, since this material expands under heat by the same amount as glass, and does not lead to cracking as would occur if the rates of expansion were different. Early metal-filament lamps operated in a vacuum, like the carbon lamps. In a vacuum, however, although the filament cannot oxidise or burn away, it tends to evaporate above a certain temperature, being deposited as a blackening on the inside of the bulb. This limits the temperature at which the filament can be operated, and led to the introduction of the gas-filled lamp. In this, an inert gas replaces the vacuum, and this allows a higher filament temperature (and so a higher light output) without evaporation. The gases most used are nitrogen and argon, although in miner's cap lamps, where the maximum efficiency is desired, a gas called xenon is used, but this is too expensive to make it worth-while in ordinary lamps. In the smaller sizes, gas filling of any sort produces no worth-while increase in efficiency, and vacuum lamps are still used.

It has been stated that in 1939 there were more than 13,000 different types and ratings of lamps made, varying from lighthouse lamps of 10,000 watts rating to tiny lamps no bigger than a match-head for surgical work.

Greater efficiency can be obtained from incandescent lamps only by running their filaments hotter and hotter, and no materials exist at present to enable this to be done without shortening their life too much. This has led scientists to turn their attention to new principles in lighting, and the results are to be seen in a number of " discharge " and " fluorescent " lamps.

In a discharge lamp, the light comes from an actual luminous discharge between two electrodes in an atmosphere of mercury vapour, sodium

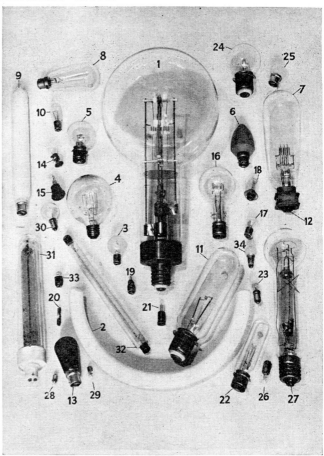

The Lighting Service Bureau, E.L.M.A.

ELECTRIC LAMPS IN MANY FORMS
Some of the many types of electric lamp are shown. 1. Lighthouse. 2. Architectural. 3. Motor-car Head. 4. Class B Projector. 5. Aircraft Landing. 6. Gothic Candle. 7. Shutter Signalling. 8. Tungsten Vacuum. 9. White Sprayed Tubular. 10. Exciter for Sound Film. 11. Signalling. 12. Special Pre-focus Cap for Positive Clamping. 13. Coloured Pygmy Sign. 14. Hand Signalling Lamp. 15. Fluorescent Lamp Thermal Starter. 16. Horizontal Burning Projector. 17. Miner's Cap Lamp. 18. Exciter Lamp with Pre-focus Cap. 19. Naval Gunsight. 20. Telephone Indicator. 21. Army Gunsight. 22. Class A.1. Projector. 23. Miner's Hand Lamp. 24. Aircraft Landing. 25. Bus Lamp. 26. Miner's Cap Lamp Double Filament. 27. Mercury/Tungsten. 28. Lens Type Flash Lamp. 29. Car Indicator Lamp. 30. Mines Shaft Examination. 31. Sodium. 32. Double-ended Tubular. 33. Tank Lamp. 34. Miner's Hand Lamp.

vapour, or neon gas. By a process of ionisation (*see* Electro-Chemistry) the vapour or gas becomes conducting, and the passage of the current " excites " it until it emits light. Most people are familiar with the bluish-green mercury vapour lamps and the orange-coloured sodium lamps installed for street lighting, as well as with the reddish neon tubes used for advertising purposes. Both mercury and sodium are very efficient (sodium in particular), and they give a high output of light for the power consumed, though many things in their light do not show natural colours.

As we explain in the article on Colour, white light is made up of all the colours of the rainbow, from violet to red, each colour being light of a different wavelength or frequency. Light of frequency above the violet (ultra-violet) or below the red (infra-red) although present in sunlight is not visible to the eye. Mercury vapour lamps are particularly rich in the ultra-violet, which are of course, no use for seeing with.

There are a number of chemical substances, called phosphors, which possess the power of changing the wavelength of light. When " excited " with invisible ultra-violet, they send out visible light of various colours, this being known as " fluorescence." If, then, we mix phosphors of various colours in the correct proportions we can get white light—or, indeed, any colour we wish—and that is what is done in the fluorescent lamp. It consists of a long tube of glass which is coated inside with the correct mixture of phosphors, and fitted with an electrode at each end. The tube is exhausted of air, and filled with argon and a small amount of mercury. When a discharge takes place between the electrodes, the ultra-violet rays produced cause the phosphor to emit a brilliant light which, in the " daylight " type of tube, matches natural daylight from a north sky.

These tubes probably represent the lighting of the future as far as the home is concerned, and they have been used for street lighting with considerable success. Many people believe, however, that high-power street and industrial lighting will be carried out with discharge lamps (non-fluorescent) having improved colour-correction. This type, known as the " compact source " lamp, consist of an arc—not burning between carbons in the open air, but between tungsten blocks inside a quartz envelope or bulb, containing a small amount of mercury with other substances to give good colour correction. Lamps of this type have been made in powers up to 10,000 to 25,000 watts.

Electro-Chemistry.

This is the name given to the branch of science which deals with the production of chemical changes in substances by means of electricity. The method by which a current is carried through a liquid, for example, is quite different from its passage through a metallic conductor, which conducts by the handing-on of free electrons. A liquid conducts by what is known as ionization.

" Ions " (which means " wanderers ") are atoms which have gained or lost electrons. As you will know from reading the articles on Atom and Electron, an atom is electrically neutral—it has equal amounts of positive and negative charge. If it gains an electron, it becomes negatively charged, and is known as an anion (short for " anode-seeking ion ") while if it loses an electron, it becomes positively charged, and is known as a cation (short for " cathode-seeking ion "). The current is carried by the wandering of these ions through the liquid, so that the passage of the current results in the splitting-up or decomposition of the liquid, this being known as electrolysis.

The diagram in page 1137 shows what happens in an electrolytic cell (a vessel in which electrolysis takes place). Two terminals known as electrodes dip into the liquid, which is known as the electrolyte. The positive (known as the anode) is the one where the current enters the cell (i.e., where the electrons leave); while the other (negative) is called the cathode. Let us suppose that the electrolyte is hydrocholoric acid which, as you

probably know, is made up of hydrogen and chlorine. The two break up, the hydrogen ion losing an electron and becoming positively charged (a cation). It is attracted towards the cathode, where it collects another electron, turns into a plain hydrogen atom, and bubbles away. At the same time the chlorine anion does the same thing at the anode, and is released as an atom of chlorine.

The decomposition of an electrolyte into two gases is perhaps the simplest example of the process. If other substances are decomposed the general principles are the same. Metals and hydrogen tend, in general, to form positive ions, and to be attracted to the cathode; and, at the same time as the ions carry the current across the cell, the electrolyte is decomposed. If the substances formed are solids, they may be deposited at the bottom of the cell as a sludge or precipitate, or they may be deposited on the cathode. If, for example, a solution of copper sulphate is used with a copper anode, the copper will be converted into positive ions, and will be deposited on the cathode as free copper; the sulphate ion (or sulphion) will be attracted to the anode and, as it is released, will combine with the copper of the anode to form copper sulphate. The outward effect of this is not to split up the electrolyte, but to transfer material from one pole to another, and this is made use of in electro-plating (q.v.).

We can think of the operation of a battery to produce electricity by chemical action as electrolysis in reverse. Do not forget that a battery is supposed to *give* current, so we think of the anode as the negative pole and the cathode as the positive. At the anode, some of the atoms go into solution and release electrons, thus becoming positive ions, and being attracted to the cathode. The electron released at the anode travels out through the external circuit to which the battery is connected, and reaches the cathode, where it combines with one of the cations which have travelled through the solution to meet it. This forms a neutral atom once more, so that, in effect, electricity is produced at the expense of the anode, which is dissolved.

The voltage produced by two metals used as a battery depends on their position in a list called the electromotive series, which shows the relation between the various metals, in the order of their readiness to release electrons. (*See* list at side of column.)

Lithium
Potassium
Sodium
Barium
Calcium
Magnesium
Aluminium
Manganese
Zinc
Chromium
Cadmium
Iron
Cobalt
Nickel
Tin
Lead
Hydrogen
Copper
Arsenic
Bismuth
Antimony
Mercury
Silver
Palladium
Platinum
Gold

Conduction through gases is also by ionization, which usually occurs by particles colliding. A free electron meets a gas atom, and collides with it, knocking off an electron. This leaves us with a positive ion, and two free electrons which are now free to collide with other atoms and form further positive ions; or, by attaching themselves to an atom, to form negative ions. This effect is used in discharge and fluorescent lamps. (*See* Electric Light).

Electrolysis:

This is the splitting-up of chemical substances by an electric current. Large industries have grown up around this process.

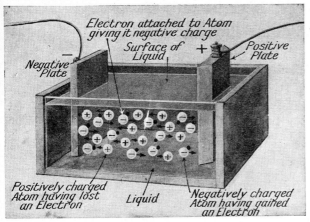

Electron attached to Atom
giving it negative charge
Surface of
Liquid
Positive
Plate
Negative
Plate
Positively charged
Atom having lost
an Electron
Liquid
Negatively charged
Atom having gained
an Electron

ELECTROLYTIC CELL

The flow of an electric current through a liquid is shown here. Ions
from the cathode plate gain an electron, while those from the anode
lose one. The result is dissociation of the atoms of the liquid and
deposition of the solids. *See the article in the opposite page.*

which is used for the production of aluminium,
magnesium, zinc, copper, chlorine, and caustic
soda, amongst others. Electrolysis is, for example,
the only practical process for producing aluminium
on a commercial scale, and is the cheapest method
for manufacturing chlorine and caustic soda, which
are produced simultaneously by the electrolysis
of salt water. The use of electrolysis has made it
possible to produce the metal magnesium from the
magnesium salts found in sea-water.

To produce materials by electrolysis in the large
quantities necessary in modern industrial plants
requires very heavy currents (10,000 amps. or
more), and immense amounts of power are used,
so that electrolytic plants have to be built where
electricity is cheap, and are best situated where it can be produced from
water power. (*See* Aluminium).

Unwanted electrolysis often occurs.
Gas and water pipes, for example, are
often attacked and eaten away by stray
currents from tramways and electric
railways using an "earth return."
On a smaller scale, the use of copper
hot-water pipes in many houses with
a galvanised (zinc-coated) iron tank
forms a battery, and many cases have
occurred of the tanks being eaten away.

The remedy which heating engineers
use for cases of this sort, where iron
is attacked, is to fit zinc "protector
slabs" near the part which is likely to
be attacked. Zinc, being higher in
the electro-chemical series, will transfer
the attack to itself, and will itself be
eaten away, thus saving the iron. The
protective zinc slabs are replaced from
time to time.

Electrolytic meters have been used
for measuring direct-current supplies.
The amount of mercury which is
deposited from a solution is a measure
of the ampere hours of electricity
passing through the meter.

Electron: THE THEORY. When a
rod of copper and one of zinc are dipped
into a jar of copper sulphate solution, and
the free ends are joined to the terminals of
a galvanometer by means of a wire, the
galvanometer needle swings over in one
direction. If the terminal connexions are
reversed, the needle moves in the opposite
direction. The early experimenters were
quick to realize that something must be
moving along the wires to produce these
effects, and they named it the "electric
current." Further, they said that this
"fluid" flowed from the copper, along the
wire, to the zinc.

Later, in 1897, J. J. Thomson showed
that when electricity flowed in a low-
pressure gas the current was carried by
material particles of very light weight, and
from the direction in which they were flowing
he concluded that they must be negatively
charged. It was soon realized that the movement of these *electrons*, as they were called,
constituted the electric current in the wire,
too. If, now, metals contain free electrons which are
capable of moving in a certain direction to give an
electric current, where did they originally come
from? The answer was provided by Niels Bohr
(*q.v.*) who put forward the theory that electrons are
a fundamental constituent of all matter, and that
atoms are like miniature solar systems, with a central
Sun or nucleus, surrounded by rapidly revolving
electrons. The nucleus must be positively charged
to balance the negative electronic charges. The
number of electrons spinning round the nucleus,
or the "atomic number," as it is known, determines
how the atom will behave chemically. Metallic
atoms are those which have their outer orbital
electrons only weakly attached. They tend to leave

A. G. Arendt

ELECTROLYSIS : MAKING CHLORINE

Brine (a solution of sodium chloride) in these cells is split up by an electric
current into chlorine gas and metallic sodium. The sodium is deposited
on the steel cathodes and then dissolves in the electrolyte to form sodium
hydrate. The anodes of the cells are of carbon.

the parent atom and drift about inside the metal, to be swept along if an electric potential is applied.

The electrons spinning round the nucleus of an atom tend to arrange themselves in groups, usually of eight. If an atom has only seven electrons in its outer " shell," it will try to gain an electron from another atom. If this other atom is a metal, with one loosely-attached outer electron, the transfer will take place, and the two atoms will then be said to have combined chemically. The arrangement of these extra-nuclear electrons in the atom, which gives the clue to its chemical nature, was worked out in 1913 for a large number of elements by H. G. J. Mosely, a brilliant young experimenter who was killed in the First World War (1914–18).

The electrons in an atom all have their separate elliptical orbits, round which they move. According to the quantum theory (q.v.) only certain paths in space are allowed for these orbits, but the electrons may jump from one allowed orbit to another. The energy change in such a jump is given out as light of a definite wavelength, and by observing the sort of light which a glowing gas emits we can gain a great deal of knowledge about the atoms in the gas. The study of spectroscopy, which entails the analysing of these radiations into their separate wavelengths, is a powerful aid in finding out atomic structure.

Electrons may be pulled out of a metal into a vacuum, where they are free to move unhindered. This happens in the radio valve and in similar devices. It was by performing experiments on these free electrons that their charge and mass, two fundamental physical constants, were determined. The electron weighs only $\frac{1}{1800}$ part of the mass of a hydrogen atom, which explains why it can be made to move about so quickly. (See Atom; Electricity; Electronic Devices).

Electronic Devices. Electronics is the name given to a branch of electrical engineering which makes use of various devices in which electron flow occurs without a complete metallic circuit (i.e., across a vacuum or through a gas).

The simplest of such devices is the ordinary two-electrode valve or diode (see Thermionic Valve), where a hot cathode emits a stream of electrons which are attracted to an anode maintained at a positive potential compared with the cathode. This results in a current which will flow through the vacuum in one direction, but not in the other ; the valve has, as it were, a rectifying action, and will suppress one half of an alternating-current wave, and allow the other half to pass.

Another device is the three-electrode valve or triode which also is described under the heading Thermionic Valve. In addition to the anode and cathode, this is fitted with a " grid " which controls the flow of electrons between cathode and anode, rather like a small child turning a large tap or valve and controlling large amounts of power. A small variation in the grid potential has a comparatively large effect on the anode current, so that the valve has an amplifying or magnifying effect. By arranging several valves so that each anode operates on the grid circuit of the next " stage," the amplification is multiplied, and it is quite easy to magnify very weak " input signals " by a million times or more.

There are several valve devices which, instead of utilising a stream of electrons in a vacuum, conduct by ionization (q.v.) of mercury vapour contained in the valve. The thyratron is a gas-filled triode of this type. In this, the potential applied to the grid determines the point where the electron stream to the anode commences but, when it has once started, cannot stop it until the current wave itself dies down to zero. It has, in fact, a " trigger " action—it can fire the gun, but the bullet must then go on until it stops of its own accord or is stopped in some way.

Mercury Arc Rectifiers in Use

The mercury arc rectifier is a kind of gas-filled diode, using a pool of mercury as a cathode, with anodes of graphite. It has a rectifying action like a diode, but works on a very large scale (hundreds of amperes) in place of the milliamperes (thousandths of an ampere) handled by the ordinary vacuum diode. It is used for converting alternating current to direct current on power systems, and has three, six, or twelve anodes, operated from a three-phase supply. (See Electricity).

Another electronic device for somewhat similar service is the ignitron. Unlike the plain mercury arc rectifier, which is kept burning while in use (since starting takes several seconds), the arc in an ignitron is struck separately for each half-cycle of current which passes, the process of " firing " the tube taking only a few millionths of a second.

Another electronic device of considerable importance is the photo-electric cell, in which (see Photo-electricity) a stream of electrons is produced by light rays striking what is known as a " photo-sensitive " cathode, so that a beam of light can control an electric current.

Finally, we have the cathode-ray tube. A funnel-shaped glass tube has its large end (or " screen ") coated with a fluorescent compound (see Electric Light) which produces a glowing spot where it is struck by a high-speed beam of electrons. This beam is produced by a hot cathode (as in an ordinary thermionic valve), which is mounted at the other end of the tube. In the neck of the tube is what is known as an " electron gun " which speeds-up the electrons from the cathode and focuses them as a glass lens focuses a light beam. " Deflector coils " or " deflector plates " are fitted between the gun and the screen, and either attract or repel the beam so that the end of the beam moves around all over the screen, producing a spot of light wherever it strikes. By connecting these " deflectors " to electrical circuits, the beam will move around like a pointer and tell us what is happening in these circuits. It will trace out a wave-form, or draw a diagram ; or, if the correct signals are applied, it will " paint " a moving picture in a series of light and dark spots.

Modern science and industry have, then, a collection of electronic devices. We can rectify current from A.C. to D.C.; we can magnify minute currents many thousands of times; we can use tiny currents to " trigger off " large amounts of power, turning heavy currents on and off in a fraction of a second. We can translate the variations of a beam of light into an electric current by the photo-electric cell; and by the use of the cathode ray tube we can observe what takes place in an electric circuit, by making a " transient " current write its own signature by the movement of an electron beam on a fluorescent screen.

Now, what can these remarkable devices do for us ? The answer is—practically anything. First and foremost, they are applicable to all kinds of automatic control. The principles underlying automatic control are simple. We must have something which will tell us what is happening (the " input signal "), which is compared with what we want to happen (the " reference value "). If there is any difference, it must operate to change what is happening until the input and the reference signals balance each other, and the difference disappears.

Imagine a bath-tub with a tap where both hot and cold water come out mixed, from the same spout. To control the water to a certain temperature, you turn on both taps, and put your hand under the spout. The nerves of your skin tell your brain whether the water is hotter or colder than your brain wants it to be. Your brain then tells the muscles of your other hand whether to turn the hot tap up or down, until the water is at the temperature that your brain wants it to be. You are acting as an automatic control— a very inaccurate one, it is true, since your hand can only tell the temperature of the water very roughly. If you wanted to be more accurate, you would hold a thermometer under the tap. Even then, the thermometer column would have to move—one way or the other—before you could begin to correct the temperature of the water.

Automatic Control of Temperature

The electrical resistance of practically all metals increases as they get hotter. If, then, we place an insulated wire in the water stream, so that it becomes hotter or colder as the water does, and connect the wire in an electric circuit, the current in that circuit can be made to indicate the temperature of the water; since the resistance of the wire will change with the temperature of the water. But the change is a very small one, so small that it could only be detected with a very sensitive instrument. If, however, we balance the current in the wire against another current (the " reference "), and magnify the difference by means of a valve amplifier, we can use the magnified output current of the amplifier to trigger the firing point of a thyratron, and apply the output of the thyratron as the supply to an electric motor geared to open or close the hot tap. This would give us control of our water temperature to a hundredth of a degree. No one wants to use complicated and expensive apparatus like this for their bath-water, but something of this sort might be absolutely necessary for an industrial process where accurate temperature was essential.

Automatic control of timing is another duty which electronic devices can carry out where other methods fail. If you were asked to switch on a current for exactly 30 seconds and then switch off again, you could time it with a watch. Given a high-grade stop-watch you could time down to about one second. But if you were asked to time it for one-hundredth part of a second (one half-cycle) you would find it impossible—you could not time such a small interval. Now, when a condenser (*see* Electricity) is connected across a source of electricity, a current flows into it until the condenser is " charged." This charging is not instantaneous but takes a certain definite time, depending upon the capacity of the condenser. The rise in voltage as the condenser becomes charged is a measure of time.

If then, we apply this to the grid of a thyratron arranged to " fire " at a certain voltage, the thyratron will be triggered off when the voltage has risen to this chosen figure—i.e., when the condenser has been charging a certain time. By altering the firing voltage of the thyratron we can alter the timing. This principle, with the thyratron arranged in its turn to fire an ignitron, is used in the automatic timing of spot-welders (*see* Welding), where extreme accuracy in the measurement of small time intervals is required.

Practically all automatic operation can be analysed into the control of time, temperature, voltage, speed, or position. Speed control does not only mean keeping an electric motor at an absolutely constant speed although this, of course, can be done with great accuracy. It also includes more difficult operations such as varying the speed of a motor winding, say, a reel of cloth or steel strip. Thus, although the diameter of the reel increases continuously, the control mechanism will keep an absolutely constant tension on the material being wound, so as to avoid tearing or kinking.

Position control, as its name indicates, is the control of the position of one thing by the position of another. A heavy gun, for example, can be coupled by position control so that it will follow the slightest movement of a sighting mechanism situated at some considerable distance away. The principles involved are the same as for any other form of automatic control. When the " driver " and " driven " mechanisms point in the same direction, a state of balance exists in the various electrical circuits making up the control system. Moving the " driver " gear produces an unbalanced state, which applies power to move the " driven " object until balance is restored.

Then there is the important part played by photo-electric cells in automatic controls, from counting articles passing down a chute (or trains passing in the Tube railways) to " watching " for paper breakages on printing machines. These and other applications are explained in the story of Photo-electricity.

Electro-Plating. In the story of Electro-Chemistry it is explained how it is possible to deposit metal, from a solution of a suitable metallic salt, on to the cathode of an electrolytic cell. It is more than a century since the first patent was issued for the deposition of silver as an ornamental coating on to " base " metals, and the process of electro-plating is now used very largely for the finishing of all sorts of manufactured articles, either for decoration or for protective purposes, to prevent rust and corrosion. Nickel and chromium are used for items varying from bath taps to motor-car radiators. Cadmium and zinc are used for providing a rust-resisting coating to steel bolts and nuts.

A fairly recent development is the so-called " hard chromium " process, by which a comparatively thick coating of chromium is plated on to worn parts of machinery to restore them to their original size, and engine cylinders are sometimes treated by this method. Drills, edged tools, and m ulds for plastics are also faced with this metal to take advantage of its extreme hardness, and to give a long working life.

Plated deposits are extremely thin—the "comparatively thick" deposit of chromium means only about one-thousandth of an inch. A normal plating, such as is used on a bath-tap, would be about one fifty-thousandth of an inch thick.

Although almost every plater has his own particular "bath," and methods differ widely in detail, the general principles are the same. In most cases anodes of the metal to be deposited are used; these become dissolved in the solution to take the place of the metal being deposited on the cathode, so that the plating solution, or electrolyte, remains at its original strength. In other cases (chromium plating, for example) this is not possible, and lead anodes are used, the solution becoming weaker as plating continues.

Plating is often done in two or more steps. Iron articles, for example, which have to be nickelled are usually copper-plated first; and chromium plating is often put over a first coating of nickel. In automatic plating, the articles are conveyed from one bath to another by an endless chain.

Plating methods "in reverse" have come into use in the last few years for what is known as "anodising" aluminium. The article is put into a kind of plating bath with a suitable electrolyte, but is itself made the anode of the cell. The result is to form a hard "skin" of aluminium oxide which is highly resistant to corrosion, and can be dyed in various ornamental colours if required.

Electrotyping.
The principle of electro-plating is used in producing electrotypes for printing. By this process copies of type pages and illustrations are made in copper (sometimes nickel) to be used on the printing press, thus saving the wear of the originals.

A wax mould is first made of the type or engraving to be reproduced. After being dusted with graphite to make it a conductor of electricity, this mould is suspended in the bath, usually consisting of a solution of sulphate of copper. The process proceeds as in electro-plating, until a thin copper plate is formed over the wax. As soon as this plate is as thick as a stout sheet of paper it is removed from the bath, separated from the wax mould, and strengthened by a backing of type metal, which is applied by melting and pouring it on the back of the copper plate until it is about $\frac{1}{4}$ to $\frac{3}{8}$ inch thick.

Books are printed for the most part from electrotype plates, because of their durability; newspapers use stereotyped plates, made by taking a reverse mould of the type page and casting a replica in type metal.

Elephant.
In past ages various species of mammoth roamed over the northern hemisphere. To-day there are but two representatives of this family of giants—the African and the Asiatic or Indian elephant. Both have several varieties. Elephants are the largest and most powerful of living land animals, yet in captivity they are docile, patient and faithful servants of Man, quick to learn and to obey.

Moeritherium

Palaeomastodon

Tetrabelodon

Mastodon
(Anancus Arvernensis)

Elephant (Elephas Jeffersonii)

ELEPHANT'S ANCESTORS
It took hundreds of thousands of years for the elephant to develop to something approaching its present size. At the top left is its remote pig-like ancestor of Eocene times; then came the Palaeomastodon, Tetrabelodon and Mastodon, all increasing in size, until there appeared Elephas Jeffersonii of the Pleistocene or Ice Age, which resembled our elephant.

ELEPHANTS' DELIGHT
Wild or tame, all elephants are fond of water, and at least once a day they like to have a bath, spraying the water over themselves with their trunk, or sprawling on their sides. They will also indulge in a sand or dust bath when opportunity offers.

for weeks; individuals have been known to remain on their feet for five years.

The elephant is an excellent swimmer, and instances are recorded of animals swimming continuously for six hours in water more than 30 feet deep. Elephants cannot leap and never have all four feet off the ground at a time. Normally, the elephant is timid and docile, but when enraged it can become very dangerous. When about to charge an enemy it utters loud trumpetings, rolling up its sensitive trunk as a measure of precaution. When pleased it squeaks or purrs softly. Rage is expressed by a roar, suspicion by rapping the trunk on the ground and emitting a volume of air with

The African elephant is the larger, attaining 11 feet in height. The Asiatic never exceeds 10 feet. The African elephant has larger ears and its forehead is convex in contrast to that of the Asiatic, which is concave. The trunk of the African species appears regularly ridged, and the margins of the extremity form two finger-like lips; that of the Asiatic elephant is smooth and tapering, with but one lip. There are also other distinctive differences, and so some zoologists have classed these elephants as separate species.

The range of the African elephant (*Elephas africanus*) is limited to the interior of the African continent; but the Asiatic (*Elephas asiaticus*) is not confined, as its alternative name might imply, to the sub-continent of India. It is found wild in Ceylon, Burma, Siam, Cochin-China, Sumatra and Malaya.

The habits of the two species are similar. All elephants are social, and herds numbering from 10 to 100 or more, usually led by females, are found in forests in the neighbourhood of streams, although they move into open country during the rainy season and even ascend high mountains. " Rogue " elephants are males living outside the herd; they are usually bad-tempered and often dangerous.

Elephants frequently migrate with the change of seasons to find better feeding grounds. Like horses, they sleep either standing up or lying down and usually in the middle of the night or in the heat of the day. In captivity they may not lie down

Dorien Leigh

YOUNG ELEPHANT AND MOTHER
The long hair that sparsely covers the bodies of young elephants at birth soon wears off, because their mothers so frequently stroke them with their trunks. If a youngster does not behave it receives a sound slap from the parent's trunk. A female elephant is very dangerous when she has a family, which she guards with great care.

ELEPHANTS AT WORK IN A BURMESE TIMBER YARD

Teak is a very heavy wood, and in Burmese teak forests and timber yards elephants trained to the task are employed to move the great balks. A mahout, or keeper, sits on the elephant's back and directs it with his voice or with blows from an iron goad. When a load has to be pulled, the elephant may be harnessed to it. The animals, however docile, will not work during the hottest hours and they very soon get to know when it is time to knock-off for the day.

a sound like tin-foil crinkling. Wild elephants use branches of trees to brush away flies, or, lacking foliage, they throw grass or spout water over the body. An elephant's skin is very sensitive.

In India elephants are regularly employed in heavy work. They haul logs and lift and carry timbers or boxes of merchandise. An elephant is capable of carrying half a ton over level country. In hauling heavy loads a regular harness is employed, consisting of a leather collar round the neck to which a dragging rope is attached. Elephants are also sometimes harnessed to wagons or ploughs. For riding, a padded saddle is usually placed on the back of the elephant, and on this is bound a box called a howdah, to carry from two to six passengers. The driver or mahout sits astride the elephant's neck. In Siam and Ceylon white (albino) elephants are held sacred.

So great is the mother's care that a baby elephant rarely dies. When on the march, mothers and young go in advance, but if an alarm is sounded they immediately fall back and the old males go to the front. The young elephant returns the mother's affection in full.

In India elephant drives take place about every 10 or 12 years, the object being to replace stock that may have died while in captivity. For several weeks before the elephants are due to be captured a small army of beaters goes through the forest and jungle, to drive the animals to the areas where they will finally be rounded up. When everything is ready for the last stage of the drive, a terrific noise is set up by the beaters and their helpers, in

STOCKADE FOR ELEPHANT ROUND-UP

To capture elephants in Ceylon natives build a keddah, or stockade, with a long V-shaped approach, the tip of the V leading into the enclosure. Beaters surround a herd and drive it towards the pen, into which the animals run, the entrance then being closed. Outside, men with poles (above) stand prepared to prod captives who may attempt to break out.

order to stampede the animals in the right direction. Soon they are driven into the selected stockade or enclosure, and then forced to enter an inner enclosure, where they are tied up.

Since early times elephants have been killed for their ivory tusks, and at one period more than 40,000 African elephants were killed every year for this reason. Until comparatively recently elephants were regarded as fair game by big-game hunters, but now their indiscriminate slaughter is discouraged by the governments concerned. Today special licences are necessary for elephant " shoots," and they are granted very sparingly.

Elgar, Sir Edward William (1857–1934). Although Elgar was no revolutionary in musical form there is a stamp of individuality about his compositions that is none the less real for all its elusiveness. That his compositions are worthy of a very high place in the annals of English music is undoubted.

SIR EDWARD ELGAR
Outstanding British composer of the early 20th century, Elgar's oratorio The Dream of Gerontius won him fame in 1900.

Elgar was born at Broadheath, near Worcester, on June 2, 1857. His parents were Roman Catholics, his father being organist at St. George's Roman Catholic Church at Worcester. He was largely self-taught as a musician, although he learned much from his father (whom he succeeded as organist at St. George's in 1885), from the cathedral services at Worcester, and from the Three Choirs Festivals. In 1889 he married, and moved to London. The Froissart Overture (1890); The Black Knight, for chorus and orchestra (1893); and King Olaf and The Light of Life (both 1896) were produced with some success. By this time Elgar, who having found little encouragement in London had moved to Malvern in 1891, was beginning to receive critical attention, and in 1899 came his Enigma Variations, which established his reputation.

He now turned to choral work on a large scale. The Dream of Gerontius, produced at Birmingham in 1900, did not at once receive the recognition it deserved, but proved a great success at the Lower Rhine Festival at Düsseldorf in Germany. This German appreciation caused its revival at Worcester two years later and in London in 1903, these performances establishing it as the finest imaginative choral work written by an Englishman and one of the great choral works of all time. The Apostles and The Kingdom, two more oratorios, followed in 1903 and 1906. Meanwhile, Elgar had been knighted in 1904, in which year the first Elgar Festival was held at Covent Garden, London. Next, Elgar turned to instrumental and orchestral work. His first symphony (Manchester, 1908) enjoyed an immense success, equalled by that of the violin concerto (1910) and the second symphony.

This was virtually the end of Elgar's productive period, although other pieces, including the Falstaff Overture, were produced with success ; many earlier works, such as the Pomp and Circumstance marches, the overtures Cockaigne, Sea-Pictures, and others, were revived. His patriotic song, Land of Hope and Glory, may almost be regarded as the National Anthem of the British Commonwealth. Elgar was awarded the Order of Merit in 1911—the first musician to gain that honour—and was made Master of the King's Musick in 1924, receiving a baronetcy in 1931. He died on February 23, 1934.

Elgin Marbles. (Pron. el'-gin.) In many ways the world of today is far in advance of the world of a thousand, or even a hundred, years ago. Nevertheless, there is at least one department of the fine arts in which the masterpieces of one

ELGIN MARBLES BROUGHT TO ENGLAND FROM ATHENS
Among the chief treasures of the British Museum in London are the Elgin Marbles, which once formed part of the frieze of the Parthenon, Athens, and were brought to England to save them from destruction. The portion in the photograph, showing a rider about to mount, is typical of the excellence of the conception and the perfection of execution.

ancient civilization remain supreme and unrivalled by anything in the modern world, and that is Greek sculpture. Nothing that has been chiselled from marble during all the centuries of the Christian era, and in all the countries of the world, can at all compare with the sculptures of Pheidias, the Athenian, who was born about 490 B.C.

Is it not, then, a very wonderful thing that the finest surviving masterpieces of the greatest of the Greek sculptors have survived about 2,400 years, and are today treasured in London, where in normal times they may be seen on any day of the week by any visitor to the British Museum ?

When the ancient Greek civilization was at the height of its power and glory, one of the ways in which it sought to express its love of the beautiful was by the erection and adornment of magnificent temples. Amongst the noble buildings set up in

Athens during this period the most important was the Parthenon, which was built between 447 and 438 B.C. It was a temple of the virgin goddess Athena (Minerva). Its site was a fortified hill of rock called the Acropolis (q.v.).

The Parthenon was of the style of architecture known as Doric. It was surrounded by a colonnade with eight lofty columns at each end, and 17 on each side. The building was 228 feet in length, 101 feet in breadth, and 66 feet high. It contained a statue of Athena Parthenos, which has since perished, as well as other public treasures, and was used as a place of worship.

The sculptures used in beautifying the temple were of three distinct types. In the gables which surmounted the columns on the east and the west ends there were magnificent groups of statuary, that on the east representing the birth of Athena,

British Museum

ELGIN MARBLES CARVED WITH SCENES OF ANCIENT GREECE

Consisting largely of sculptures by Pheidias (c. 490–432 B.C.) and other famous Greek artists, the Elgin Marbles were removed from Athens in 1801–03. The lower section shows a group of magistrates conversing while waiting to take

their place at the head of a procession to the goddess Athena. At the top are Greek knights on prancing horses, and although the carving is not more than $2\frac{1}{4}$ inches at its deepest the illusion of horsemen riding abreast is complete.

and that on the west the contest of Athena with Poseidon (Neptune) for the possession of Attica (district of ancient Greece).

Along the summit of the columns on each side of the temple there was another series of decorations, each consisting of a block of marble about three feet square on which were sculptured figures in bold high relief. Then along the top of the outer wall of the cella, or temple, within the colonnade, was a frieze in low relief, representing the Panathenaic Procession, the great festival of the Athenians (*see* pictures pages 1143, 1144).

The Parthenon was undoubtedly one of the most beautiful buildings ever erected by Man, and even as a ruin it is one of the wonders of the world. It is with the surviving relics of its best statuary—now known, together with others from the temple of Nike Apteros (Wingless Victory) at Athens, and various antiquities from other parts of Greece, as the Elgin Marbles—that we are chiefly concerned.

When Lord Elgin was appointed British Ambassador to Turkey in 1799, the Parthenon was in a state of ruinous decay. Greece was then part of the Turkish Empire, and the Turks had very little interest in the care of these monuments of Greek art. Lord Elgin, who was intensely interested in Greek art, began to make plaster casts of many of the remaining sculptures. Enthusiasm grew as the work proceeded, and before long he conceived the even more ambitious project of rescuing the actual statues and other sculptures from further mutilation and spoliation by transferring them to England.

The enterprise and influence of Lord Elgin enabled him, in 1801, to secure from the Turkish Government authority to excavate among the ruins of the Parthenon. Soon Lord Elgin, his assistants, and three or four hundred workmen were hard at work. Statues were lowered from the pediment; metopes and slabs of the frieze were removed; houses built on the rubbish were purchased, pulled down, and their foundations explored.

In a little over a year 200 boxes filled with sculpture were ready for shipment. But several years of disappointment were to pass before these treasures found a permanent home in England. The Napoleonic wars were in progress, and in

1803, on being recalled from Turkey, Lord Elgin was detained by the French and confined in Paris. It was not until 1812 that the sculptures at length arrived in England. Finally, Parliament agreed to purchase the Elgin marbles for the nation, the price paid being £35,000.

Eliot, GEORGE (1819–80). Under this masculine name, Mary Ann (or Marian) Evans became famous as one of the world's greatest novelists. Born in Warwickshire, she grew to womanhood on the beautiful old estate of Arbury Hall, of which her father, Robert Evans, was the manager. Thus she gained that intimate knowledge of English rural life which forms the background of several of her novels.

National Portrait Gallery, London

FAMED AS 'GEORGE ELIOT'

Like some other women novelists Mary Ann Evans chose to write under the name of a man, and she is remembered better as George Eliot, the author of The Mill on the Floss, than by her maiden name or as the wife of J. W. Cross. This portrait is from a drawing by Sir Frederick William Burton (1816–1900).

Called from a girls' Methodist school at Coventry by the death of her mother, Mary Ann Evans at the age of 17 became the sole companion and the housekeeper of a father of narrow mind and Puritanical strictness. In one way this was a fortunate circumstance, for, obliged to educate herself, she followed her own bent for the classical languages, German, Italian, music, philosophy, science, and ancient and modern literatures. Thorough in everything, she made herself a woman of wide and varied scholarship; but years of loneliness left their mark.

She was not unknown when, at the age of 30, after her father's death, she went to London as assistant editor of the Westminster Review, for she had already contributed critical papers to that magazine and translated scholarly works from the German. So she was welcomed in the most distinguished literary circle. But in a group which numbered Spencer, Carlyle, and J. S. Mill, George Henry Lewes alone suspected that the genius of this intellectual but modest country woman was remarkably creative, and urged her to write fiction. Her subsequent relationship with Lewes—which she regarded as marriage although Lewes's first wife was not divorced—shut her out from all society but his and that of a small group of faithful friends.

Mary Ann Evans herself had so little confidence in her powers and was so sensitive that she published her Scenes of Clerical Life under the *nom de plume* of " George Eliot." The stories, which were first published in Blackwood's Magazine, met with a most enthusiastic reception. They showed what a remarkable knowledge she had of country life and interests. The author was assumed to be a man; and she did not disclose herself until the next year, when her novel Adam Bede won her lasting fame.

To the end George Eliot's personal life was one of struggle and painful experiences. While she sustained with dignity and courage a difficult situation of her own making, she suffered from adverse criticism to a tragic degree. She never recovered from the shock of Lewes's death, which occurred in 1878. Two years later George Eliot

married John Walter Cross, but she died in the same year, on December 22, in London, at 4, Cheyne Walk, Chelsea.

The scenes of George Eliot's novels are laid almost entirely in four Midland counties of England—Warwickshire, Staffordshire, Derbyshire and Lincolnshire. Her principal works are : Scenes of Clerical Life (1858); Adam Bede (1859); The Mill on the Floss (1860); Silas Marner (1861); Romola (1863); Felix Holt (1866); Middlemarch (1872); Daniel Deronda (1876).

The 'VIRGIN QUEEN' of OLD ENGLAND

Men living in Elizabeth's reign thought of it as a second Golden Age, so blessed was England then with great adventurers, statesmen, and poets. They knew full well, too, what they owed to the queen they called Gloriana.

Elizabeth (1533–1603). The long reign (1558 to 1603) of the Virgin Queen was one of the most important in the annals of English history.

Modelled by the artist Nicholas Hilliard (1537–1619), this head of Queen Elizabeth was made some years before her death in 1603.

Elizabeth established England as a Protestant kingdom, she saw the country well on the way to become mistress of the seas, and in her reign occurred the greatest burst of literary activity the world has seen since the days of ancient Greece.

Elizabeth, the daughter of Henry VIII (1491–1547) and Anne Boleyn, was brought up under the cloud of her mother's execution and her father's dislike; she was finally recognized in his will as heir to the throne after her half-brother Edward and her half-sister Mary.

During the Catholic reaction under Mary, who was herself a Catholic, Elizabeth's known friendship for Protestants caused her to be imprisoned in the Tower of London, and she was charged with a plot against the unpopular Mary. She survived this danger, and at the age of 25, on the death of Mary, was summoned to the throne amidst the rejoicings of the Protestants and of many moderate Catholics.

Elizabeth possessed rare natural qualities which had been sharpened by hard schooling in the world of men and books. In her puzzling and contradictory character may be seen her mother's vanity and uncertainties of temper, the caution and prudence of her grandfather, Henry VII, the pride and charm of manner that early made Henry VIII irresistible, and that lack of feeling that characterized all the Tudors.

In her youth Elizabeth was striking and attractive. Her figure was tall and well proportioned, she had a broad, commanding brow, a fine olive-tinted complexion, hazel eyes and a wealth of auburn hair. She had also remarkable physical vigour, could hunt all day, dance or watch masques and pageants all night, and, when necessary, apply herself to official

duties. She was masculine in her coarseness of word and action, and carried stinginess to the extreme. Carefully trained under the best teachers of the day, she spoke French with ease, knew a little Greek, and could speak with an ambassador in Latin, if necessary. Her letters and speeches show a superb command of English. She was an excellent musician, but cared little for literature or art.

Elizabeth's first step as queen was to restore the Protestant Church practically as it had been under Edward VI (1537–53). For the next 30 years, aided by well-chosen counsellors, she struggled to maintain England's independence from foreign control and to settle the religious differences that split the nation. Yet a large Catholic party in England was plotting to put Mary Queen of Scots (1542–87) on the throne in place of Elizabeth. They sought the aid of the Pope, France and Spain. Elizabeth strove to hinder these plans by pretending that she was going to marry either the king of Spain or some French prince. To make trouble for her enemies, she aided the Protestant Netherlands when they revolted from Spain, and also helped the Scots when they went over to the Protestant cause.

As a result of this change in Scotland, Mary Queen of Scots was compelled to flee across the English border, where she fell into the hands of Elizabeth's officials (1568). Elizabeth's advisers urged her to have her rival executed in order to safeguard her own position. Not until 19 years had passed, and the King of Spain was gathering a great fleet to invade England, did Elizabeth yield to this advice and sign the death-warrant of the Scottish queen on the ground of a plot against her life.

Defeat of the Spanish Armada

Now took place the most glorious event in Elizabeth's reign—the defeat of the Spanish Armada (1588). All England gathered itself to meet the foe. Yet Elizabeth was the last to believe that the Armada was coming, and was so mean in fitting out and provisioning the English Navy as almost to risk defeat and prevent the victory from being as complete as it was. (*See* Armada, Spanish).

By this victory England entered upon her great career of sea-power and colonization. The Englishmen of that day felt a new sense of power which found expression in the writings of a group of brilliant men whose works have shed undying glory on the reign of Elizabeth. Supreme among these was Shakespeare (1564–1616). In some famous lines from his play King Richard II new pride in and love for England are finely expressed—

This royal throne of kings, this sceptred isle,
This earth of majesty, this seat of Mars,
This other Eden, demi-paradise,
This fortress built by Nature for herself
Against infection and the hand of war . . .
This precious stone set in the silver sea.

Exploration and commerce had much to do with the making of England's supremacy at sea. The country ceased to be insular, looked outward and beyond, and a rosy optimism seemed to develop in the race as never before.

Elizabeth early set about adding to her naval force, and all through the 45 years of her reign adventurers assisted her with their private vessels. They were, in a word, pirates, even though their owners or other folk interested in them were highly respected members of society. There may have been patriotic reasons, but the chief motive seems to have been profit. In some of the expeditions not officially undertaken to punish her enemies, the sovereign was not above having a financial interest, and when Elizabeth invested money she always expected, and usually got, a handsome return. Thus we find ships belonging to the Navy taking part in the shameful but profitable slave-trading expeditions of such adventurers as Sir John Hawkins.

Perhaps nothing in the sea history of the period better reveals the grasping character of the shrewd woman who presided over the destinies of England than an incident which took place in 1592. Some ships owned by the Earl of Cumberland, a seaman of ripe experience with a liking for expeditions, fitted out at his expense, together with others belonging to Raleigh and the Hawkins family, fell in with the Portuguese ship Madre de Dios. Unfortunately, a little English naval vessel which the enemy ship could have " swallowed " happened to be present, and Elizabeth claimed and secured the greater part of the profit made from the sale of the rich East Indian cargo. It is stated that the wonderful array of silks, spices, carpets, and other goods captured so aroused the enthusiasm of the London merchants who saw them that the prize had no little influence on the formation of the East India Company that laid the foundations of our Indian Empire.

Though Elizabeth never married, her suitors were numerous, and she kept them dancing attendance until she was an old woman. Perhaps her heart was most deeply touched by Robert Dudley, Earl of Leicester, Master of the Horse, handsome and clever, husband of the ill-fated Amy Robsart. Her next favourite was the equally ill-fated Earl of Essex, whom Elizabeth alternately loved and scolded, seeming to care for him much as a mother

QUEEN ELIZABETH PAYS A STATE VISIT

Surrounded by her court, Queen Elizabeth is here shown by a contemporary artist seated on her ' carrying throne,' which somewhat resembled a sedan chair, arriving on a visit to the home of her cousin Lord Hunsdon. He is carrying the Sword of State before the Queen, and on his right is her wise old counsellor Lord Burghley (1520–98), whom she made Secretary of State. On Burghley's right, and with his head turned towards him, is Lord Howard of Effingham, who was Lord High Admiral from 1554 to 1573. His son was one of the admirals who led the English fleet against the Armada.

ELIZABETH DOOMS MARY QUEEN OF SCOTS

Painting by Julius Schrader

Two dramatic episodes which will always be remembered in English history occurred in Queen Elizabeth's reign (1558–1603). These were the defeat of the Spanish Armada and the execution of Mary Queen of Scots. Mary was imprisoned by the Scottish nobles in 1567, but the following year she escaped to England—where she was a captive for 19 years, Elizabeth fearing that Mary might become the centre of a Roman Catholic plot to supplant herself on the throne. Such a conspiracy, called the Babington plot, was discovered in 1586, and Mary was tried for complicity in it and sentenced to death. Here an artist has depicted the scene when Lord Burghley at last persuaded Queen Elizabeth to put her name to the death-warrant.

cares for a spoiled child. Yet, when he was condemned in 1601 for armed rebellion, Elizabeth forced herself to sign his death-warrant.

The religious question, the defeat of the Armada, and the flourishing of literature are the things we think of chiefly as marking the reign of Elizabeth. Not less memorable, however, are the hundreds of important laws—on shipping and commerce, roads and industry, poor relief and agriculture—which shaped the policy of England for more than two centuries after she and her advisers were in their graves. In fact, the reign of Elizabeth marked the passing of the main features of the Middle Ages and the birth of modern England.

Elizabeth's vanity, her fondness for dress, her love of flattery and attention, often made her appear ridiculous in her old age, yet she was ruler of England to the last. Not the least of her achievements

' GLORIANA ' OF ENGLAND
Painted by an unknown artist, this picture from the National Portrait Gallery, London, shows Queen Elizabeth when middle-aged and at the height of her power. In her right hand she holds the Tudor rose.

was the fact that at her death she aided the peaceful accession of her relative, the Scottish king, the Protestant son of Mary Queen of Scots, who became James I of England, and so brought about the permanent union of England with Scotland.

Elizabeth, QUEEN CONSORT (born 1900). Gracious charm, gentleness, an extraordinary power of putting others at ease, a kindly look—these are a few of the items that go to make up the winning personality of Queen Elizabeth. Her world-famous smile gained her the name of the Smiling Duchess; she will go down in history as the Smiling Queen.

Elizabeth Angela Marguerite Bowes-Lyon was born at St. Paul's Walden Bury, near Welwyn, Hertfordshire, on August 4, 1900, the third daughter of the Earl of Strathmore. On her father's side she traces her descent to Sir John Lyon of Forteviot,

WHEN QUEEN ELIZABETH LAY DYING
Now in the Louvre, Paris, this painting by the French artist Paul Delaroche (1797–1856) shows the scene at Richmond Palace, Surrey, when Queen Elizabeth was dying. Taken ill at the end of February 1603, her condition rapidly became worse the following month. She refused all medicine and would not take to her bed, lying on the floor on cushions, with the Lords of the Council and ladies of her Court in attendance. She died on March 24, 1603.

The Associated Press Ltd.

ELIZABETH, QUEEN-CONSORT

In April 1923 Lady Elizabeth Bowes-Lyon (later Queen Elizabeth) married the Duke of York, who succeeded his brother Edward VIII on the throne in 1936, as King George VI. Here the Queen is seen at the State opening of the South African Parliament at Cape Town in February 1947.

who in 1372 married Lady Jean Stuart, daughter of King Robert II of Scotland, and received from the King the thanage (barony) of Glamis, which has remained in the family ever since. On her mother's side she descends from Elizabeth of York, daughter of Edward IV and consort of Henry VII.

As a girl she lived chiefly at St. Paul's Walden Bury, though for three months in each year the family migrated to Glamis Castle, in the county of Angus, Scotland, and there were occasional visits to Streatlam Castle in Durham, another of her father's seats, and to London. During the First World War (1914–18) Glamis was used as a hospital, and her radiant presence did much to cheer the wounded men. In 1923 she was betrothed to the Duke of York (afterwards King George VI), the wedding taking place on April 26 of that year at Westminster Abbey. A daughter, Princess Elizabeth, was born in London on April 21, 1926, and a second daughter, Princess Margaret Rose, was born

at Glamis Castle on August 21, 1930, the first member of the Royal Family to be born in Scotland since a younger brother of Charles I.

As Duchess of York, Queen Elizabeth became widely known to the country by the performance of many public duties. In 1927 she accompanied her husband on an extensive Dominion tour, which culminated in the opening of the Commonwealth Houses of Parliament at Canberra in Australia. She was crowned Queen Consort in Westminster Abbey on May 12, 1937.

In September 1938 she launched the liner which bears her name. The support received by the British Commonwealth from the North American continent during the Second World War (1939–45) owed much to the visit paid by the royal couple to Canada, Newfoundland and the United States in May–June 1939.

Her Majesty's charm of manner, ready sympathy and understanding have endeared her to everyone. During the Second World War she broadcast at different times to the women of the British Commonwealth, of France and of the U.S.A., and was Commandant-in-Chief of the Women's Navy, Army and Air forces. In February–April 1947 she and the King, accompanied by the Princesses, paid a state visit to the Union of South Africa. On April 26, 1948 the King and Queen celebrated their silver wedding anniversary by attending a service of thanksgiving at St. Paul's Cathedral, London.

Elizabeth, PRINCESS, DUCHESS OF EDINBURGH. The elder daughter of King George VI and Queen Elizabeth was born at 12, Bruton Street, the London residence of the Earl and Countess of Strathmore, the Queen's father and mother, on April 21, 1926, and was christened Elizabeth Alexandra Mary. The Princess is heir presumptive, not heir apparent, to the throne, which means that if a son were born to the King and Queen he would succeed to the throne before Princess Elizabeth.

She was educated at home under the direction of the Queen, and in addition to the usual subjects she studied economic and constitutional history and the trend of political developments. A good horsewoman and a fine swimmer, she is an excellent pianist and keenly interested in the drama.

Princess Elizabeth joined the Girl Guides in 1937 and the Sea Rangers in 1942, and was appointed honorary Colonel of the Grenadier Guards by the King in 1942. She was granted a commission in the Auxiliary Territorial Service in March 1945. Her 21st birthday was celebrated in South Africa while she was on tour with her parents, and she marked the occasion by a broadcast to the British Commonwealth in which she dedicated her life to the service of that Commonwealth.

On November 20, 1947, at Westminster Abbey, London, she married her third cousin, Lieutenant Philip Mountbatten, an officer of the Royal Navy and formerly entitled Prince Philip of Greece and Denmark. The bridegroom had been created Duke of Edinburgh by the King the day before. On November 14, 1948, a son was born at Buckingham Palace, and was christened Charles Philip Arthur George. As Prince Charles of Edinburgh he was second in succession to the throne. A daughter, Princess Anne Elizabeth Alice Louise was born on August 15, 1950, at Clarence House, London.

PRINCESS ELIZABETH ON HER WEDDING DAY

Planet News

At Westminster Abbey, London, on November 20, 1947, Princess Elizabeth, heir presumptive to the throne of Great Britain, was married to her second cousin the Duke of Edinburgh, who had received the Dukedom from King George VI on the day before the wedding. An officer in the Royal Navy, he had at one time borne the title of Prince Philip of Greece and Denmark. This photograph was taken in Buckingham Palace after the ceremony.

Elm. Most people think of only two kinds of elm in Britain, the common elm (*Ulmus campestris*) and the wych elm (*Ulmus montana*), but there are more than half a dozen distinct species growing wild in our country, as well as hybrids and introduced forms in parks and gardens. But it is by no means easy to distinguish the species.

The common elm has quite small, broad leaves, rough above and downy along the veins below; those of the true wych elm are very rough above and large, with prominent veins. In lusty saplings they often have two subsidiary points, one on either side of the main apex. Then there are the smooth-leaved elm (*U. nitens*), whose leaves are usually narrower in proportion to their length than those of other species, and smooth, often shining, above; the Cornish elm, native in the south-west of England, a tall, small-leaved type; the

Wheatley elm, narrow and pyramidal, ideally suited for town-planting without ever needing pruning; and the Dutch elm, with large, coarse leaves. Among less common varieties are the cork elms, whose shoots have prominent " wings " of cork.

It is a curious fact that the English elm, although probably native, produces seed only scantily in Britain, mostly spreading itself by means of suckers (shoots arising at a distance from the trunk, from the tree's roots); the true wych elm, however, produces seed very freely—as you may often see in the north, where this tree is common—and it has no suckers. The fruits, called samaras, are oval, the actual seed being in the middle of the surrounding wing; in great brown bunches, they are very conspicuous in early summer. Elm wood is tough, strong and durable, when kept permanently wet or permanently dry; it is commonly used for coffins, and sometimes for furniture. A modern seasoning system known as reconditioning renders it suitable even for fine panelling, but it is otherwise inclined to warp badly.

Ely, ISLE OF. Though lying within Cambridgeshire, the Isle of Ely for some purposes ranks as a separate county and has an area of 372 square miles. Ely, the best-known town, is a cathedral city standing on the left bank of the Ouse, 15 miles north of Cambridge. Nearly 900 years ago the Benedictine abbey that replaced the 7th-century monastery founded by Etheldreda (*c.* 630–679), a daughter of the King of East Anglia, was the refuge for some time of the English leader Hereward the Wake, who had continued to resist the Normans under William the Conqueror (1027–87).

Etheldreda's monastery housed both monks and nuns, and stood till 870, when the Danes destroyed it. Hereward's refuge was founded a century later, and in 1083 the present magnificent cathedral was begun by Abbot Simeon. This beautiful church, a cruciform building 537 feet long and 180 feet across the grand transepts, has been added to at various times since it became the cathedral in 1109. The nave and west front were added in 1189; the choir dates from the 14th century, when the octagon tower and lantern were also built out of the remains of the tower, which fell in 1321. The Lady Chapel was finished in 1349. The bishop's palace is a picturesque building, and the city has some interesting old houses. The population of the Isle of Ely is 81,000; that of Ely, 8,500.

Embroidery. The art of ornamenting fabrics with needlework is called embroidery. Most ancient nations apparently knew how to embroider, and some of their work has been preserved to this day. The sandy soil and dry climate of Egypt have preserved examples of embroidery which were worked more than 3,500 years ago; the earliest of these are now in the Cairo Museum, Egypt. Some of the early Egyptian embroidery was worked on

H. Bastin; British Museum (Natural History)
ELM TREE AND LEAVES
One of the tallest of British trees, the common elm often reaches 100 feet in height. The bark is rough and twisted, and the leaves have finely toothed edges. In the top photograph leaves of the common elm are shown at 2, those of the wych elm at 1. At 3 are leaves of the hornbeam, sometimes confused with the elm.

leather in a form of mosaic. Similar work on leather has been found among the primitive tribes of Central America.

The ancient Greeks practised embroidery, and the Romans termed the art "painting with the needle"; many famous Roman writers allude to the embroideries on tunics and other garments. Strangely enough no examples have been found near Rome, though embroideries found elsewhere, especially in Egypt, show Roman influence.

The people of the Orient excel in embroidery today as they did centuries ago. In China and in Kashmir the art has suffered little change in either style or design. The delicacy of workmanship and gradation of colouring, particularly of the Chinese work, are exquisite. The embroidery of Japan is very similar in character to that of China, but

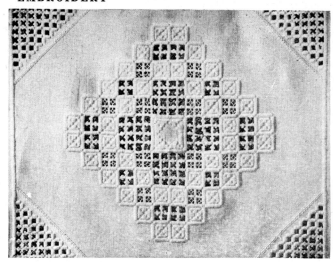

the stitches are generally more loosely worked and are more fanciful. In working a scene, stitchery is frequently allied to painting to secure variety in the effect. Persian work has been confined chiefly to the decoration of hangings and to carpets (particularly prayer rugs).

With the advent of the Christian era the art of embroidery in Europe began to change in design, and to a great extent was influenced by religion. Even on garments scenes from the Gospels were depicted. Naturally, church vestments and hangings were embroidered; some of the early ecclesiastical work is still preserved and provides, in some cases, a pictorial contemporary history. Women of the upper classes spent much of their time in embroidery, especially in working wall hangings.

One of the most famous pieces of embroidery of the Middle Ages, which pictures the life and dress of those far-off times, is that known as the Bayeux Tapestry (*see* Bayeux), a strip of linen 231 feet long, which contains 72 scenes, embroidered in coloured wools, telling the story of the Norman Conquest.

From about the end of the 12th century distinct national styles began to develop. In most cases the embroidery on domestic articles has not survived, so that the history of the art has been chiefly traced in the church embroidery. In England embroidery has been a favourite way of occupying leisure hours for many centuries.

In the 13th century English embroidery was noted throughout Western Europe.

During the Tudor period the garments of the rich were lavishly embroidered in silks and in gold thread. About this time a variety of embroidery known as "black work" was popular; it was done in black silk on linen, either white or unbleached. Another kind of work of the period was done in wools and silks on an open-mesh material, closely worked and completley covered with embroidery. This work is called petit-point, the name given to it in France; it was used for hanging tapestries, screens, chair and stool seats. French embroidery is notable for the grace of its design,

EMBROIDERY OF THREE KINDS

The top photograph shows a design for a table runner in Hardanger work on loosely-woven linen. The beautiful design in the centre picture is executed in Renaissance work, which relies on buttonholed bars to emphasize the design. The lower illustration is a linen table-mat embroidered in punch work.

often a combination of floral and scroll forms. In the Netherlands, the various schools of painting influenced the embroiderer's art; it seems evident that, for some of the larger tapestries, painters were commissioned to create designs for the embroiderers. Hungarian, Rumanian, and Swiss peasant embroideries are famous, and are usually on fine muslin or linen, in bright colours. The Armenian embroideries are fine and colourful peasant work. Smocking and drawn-thread work are often features of peasant embroidery. Some of the finest smocking is to be seen in the specimens of English

EMBROIDERY : AN EXAMPLE OF CROSS-STITCH
Coloured threads were used for this border design, which is worked in cross-stitch. Old embroideries of this kind were done on very fine linen. For modern work specially woven cloth, with rounded threads, or canvas, is used. Cross-stitch is one of the simplest forms of linen embroidery and was very popular in the 16th century.

embroidery of the 18th and 19th centuries, and the various stitches in these are still copied extensively.

In Germany, during the 13th and 14th centuries, some fine pieces of ecclesiastical embroidery were worked, depicting figures of saints. Much later German work was floral in design and rather bold.

Styles of embroidery which are often copied include the following: Broderie Anglaise, though chiefly characterized by eyelet work, both rounds and ovals, is often composed partly of solid stitches to suit the design. Real Madeira work consists of circular eyelets worked in groups. Renaissance work has the outlines of a design in buttonholing, and the pieces connected with buttonholed bars, under which the material is cut away. Richelieu work is similar, but the connecting bars are buttonholed, woven, and rolled, and are ornamented with picots. Venetian embroidery has buttonholed edges and bars, the inside of the design being filled in with fancy stitches and fillings, such as those used in needle-made laces.

Danish hedebo work is linen decorated with openwork designs overcast and the material cut away at the back; open spaces are crossed with threads, and these in turn are overcast or rolled. It is combined with open lace stitches worked as a background independent of the linen background, as this latter is afterwards cut away. Italian quilting is a type of raised work; the material on which the actual stitches are worked is backed with carded wool, and a design is outlined with small running stitches.

Linen embroidery has two varieties: that done on counted threads, and embroidery worked over a design which has been transferred to the material irrespective of lines. Cross-stitch is the simplest of

the counted work. Hardanger work is done on a loosely-woven canvas where the threads can be counted. Punch work is executed in loosely-woven linen (though it is often worked on finer materials such as silks) to produce a drawn-thread effect without the actual drawing of threads; it is sometimes called Rhodes embroidery, or fillet work.

Embryology. We are all familiar with the eggs of moths and butterflies, of birds and reptiles ; and we know that the young organism develops within the egg until it arrives at a stage when it can begin its separate existence. We know, too, that within the ovary (or egg-chamber) of a plant the fertilised cell grows which is later to become a seed. Both the egg and the seed are embryos, immature organisms. In higher animals the egg-cell continues its growth and development within the mother, and makes its entry into the outside world only when it has become fitted by growth to go on with an independent life. In some animals, those we know as marsupials, the young creature when born must still pass a period of growth within the mother's pouch.

Embryology is the branch of Biology which studies the reproduction and development of plants and animals before they begin a separate existence. The best way to approach it is by way of plant biology, to which our articles on Botany and Plant

EMBRYO INSIDE AN EGG SHELL
This diagram shows how a chicken's egg is made up. BL, original cells of embryo ; WY, white yoke ; YY, yellow yoke ; V, yolk membrane ; F, layer of fluid albumen (' white ') ; D, dense albumen enclosing the yolk with preceding envelopes (in this envelope, D, are incorporated the ends of CH, the supporting membranes) ; W, body of the albumen ; C, somewhat denser layer of albumen, surrounded by a fluid layer ; M, outer and inner shell membrane separated at A, air chamber ; S, shell.

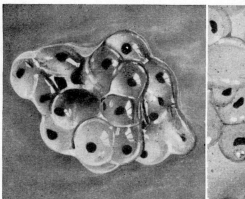
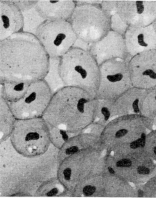

M. H. Crawford

FROG EMBRYOS IN JELLY-LIKE EGGS

From masses of frog spawn laid during spring in ponds and ditches come tadpoles that will develop into miniature frogs before summer. Left, the embryos show through the 'jelly' as big black dots. At the right, the dots have elongated, and these queer, wriggling specks of life will presently be swimming free as tiny tadpoles.

Life will furnish an introduction. All life begins as a cell, so that the study of embryology is that of the growth and development of the original cell as it divides and multiplies to form the embryo. The cells arrange themselves in layers to form tissues and, later, organs ; by the end of the embryonic period, which differs in length for different animals, the original cell has become a complex organism ready to take its place in the outside world.

Life and nourishment, in the egg such as that of a fowl, are provided by food stored up beforehand; the seed of a plant has a similar store surrounding its germ cell. Animals which do not lay eggs, but bring forth their young alive, must nourish and sustain the developing embryo by supplies of their own blood passing to the embryo through a life-line which is broken only when the young creature comes out into the world. Some classes of animal (mammals) continue to nourish their young with the mother's milk for a period after that; while birds feed the naked fledgings until the latter have grown feathers and are able to fend for themselves.

Early ideas of the way in which the embryo grew and developed were very confused. For long it was thought that the young animal existed already formed within the egg but was exceedingly tiny. Development, it was believed, was merely the growth and expansion of the minute creature to its greater size. Then K. E. von Baer (1792–1876), the father of modern embryology, showed that all the tissues and organs come from cell-layers, or germ-layers. One layer gives rise to nerves, another to skin or feather or fur, from a third come the internal organs, bones, etc. This is the germ-layer theory.

Others scientists broke down the rigid line that was supposed to separate vertebrate and invertebrate animals (those with backbones and those without), and showed how higher types had been developed from simpler ones. The chick, and for that matter Man himself, in the embryo has gill clefts like a fish, which the fish uses for passing out water through its gills to extract the oxygen. These

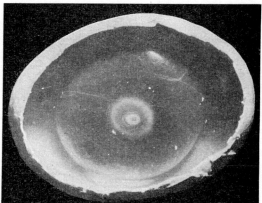

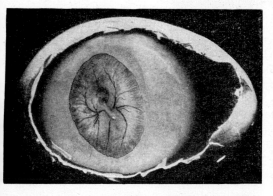
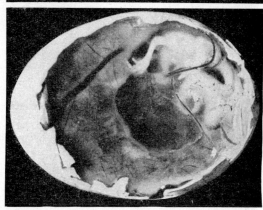

THREE STAGES IN THE EMBRYOLOGY OF A CHICK

Portions of shell have been broken away to enable us to see something of what goes on inside a hen's egg whilst the chick is developing. The upper photograph on the right shows the embryo just forming on the surface of the yolk. In the lower left-hand picture the blood-vessels are spreading on either side of the heart—which is the organ first formed. Some days later the chick is well formed ; in the right-hand photograph a leg is visible at the top, and the rest of the young bird-to-be is curled neatly around. Soon the young chick will be pecking its way out and giving its first chirp.

disappear in the land animals as the embryo develops, but they give clues pointing to the time when perhaps these creatures, too, were water-breathers. Thus, in a way, embryology retraces life's history, contributing important evidence in support of the belief that the higher animals have been evolved from simpler ones. (*See* Biology; Cell; Evolution).

Emerald. Among the oldest precious stones used by Man, emeralds were known to the Egyptians as early as 1650 B.C. Emerald mines were worked for Alexander the Great (356–323 B.C.) by Greek miners. Cleopatra (69–30 B.C.) also obtained supplies of these gems. The Spaniards took large quantities from Peru after their conquest of that country in the 16th century; but the position of the mines was kept a close secret, and has never since been discovered. At the present time the chief sources of supply are parts of South America, and the Ural Mountains in the Soviet Union.

In olden times the emerald was supposed to possess magical qualities—it drove away evil spirits, and cured such diseases as epilepsy and dysentery; the superstition that green is unlucky may perhaps deter many people from wearing these stones.

Emerson, RALPH WALDO (1803–82). Emerson ranks among the most powerful and profound of American thinkers; and he is still powerful in that his thoughts stir vigorous movement in the minds of his readers. He is not among the most widely read authors of today, but he has been a strong influence in moulding the ideas of the past hundred years.

His ancestors were Puritans who went to New England in 1635. Eight of his ancestors were ministers of New England churches. His father died when the boy was eight years of age, leaving the family poor. Emerson went to Harvard in 1817, and on leaving college taught in his brother's school and then entered the Unitarian ministry.

Through all his early years Emerson had been a quiet, unobtrusive, self-contained person. For the first 30 years of his life he seemed destined to follow peacefully in the footsteps of his ministerial ancestry. But underneath the quiet exterior was a steadily growing resolve which was to separate him from the Church, and he resigned his position as minister.

For a time he did not find himself. His young wife died in 1832, and Emerson's health broke down. He travelled to Europe, and visited England where he met most of the great men of letters of the day: Landor, Coleridge, John Stuart Mill, and, above all, Carlyle, whom he admired more than any of them.

To understand Emerson's aloofness from men and events one must grasp his way of thinking. He believed that great truths come to us by intuition— that is, that they come to us unbidden. Furious

RALPH WALDO EMERSON
American poet, essayist and philosopher,
Emerson was first a teacher and then a
Unitarian Minister before entering upon his
career as a writer and lecturer.

striving avails us nothing; truth comes gently and unawares. Most modern philosophers do not agree with Emerson; they think that truth may be reasoned out. Besides, they are interested in the working out of truth in relation to human life, while Emerson was always on the alert for the first dawning. He never finishes, but is always beginning, and his beginnings have been inspirations to the people of two continents.

In the matter of style Emerson is supreme for his power of saying much in few words, of so phrasing his thoughts that they sparkle and glow. Every sentence seems as good as the one it follows. This is true of his poetry as well as his prose—that is, the power of stating truth in sharp relief. He began writing for The Dial in 1840 and edited it for two years. The first series of those Essays by which he was to become most widely famous was published in 1841, and a second series followed three years later. In the autumn of 1846 he revisited England on a lecturing tour, delivering a series of addresses on Representative Men—Plato, Swedenborg, Montaigne, Shakespeare, Napoleon and Goethe. The volume containing these addresses was published in 1850. In 1856 the fruits of his observation during his stay in England were embodied in English Traits. As writer and lecturer he came to take his position as the chief leader of American thought of his generation. His successive works including Society and Solitude (1870) and Letters and Social Aims (1876), met with the same cordial welcome from readers on both sides of the Atlantic.

Emerson married a second time in 1835, and when his home — the old Manse, at Concord, Massachusetts — was burned down in 1872, a popular subscription was made and the funds used to rebuild it. He died on April 27, 1882, and was buried in the famous cemetery of Sleepy Hollow near by.

Emery. In outward appearance emery has nothing in common with the sapphire and other precious stones to which it is related. It is a heavy, non-transparent, dull substance, like a fine-grained iron ore, ranging in colour from reddish-brown and grey to blue-black. It is found in large boulder-like masses in Asia Minor and on Naxos and other islands of the Greek archipelago.

The rock is made ready for use by breaking it into lumps and crushing these to powder in stamping mills. As emery is one of the hardest natural substances the powder is used for cutting and polishing many kinds of stone; until other abrasives such as carborundum were made artificially there was no rival to emery. When used for polishing metals it is spread on some kind of surface to form emery-paper, emery-cloth or emery-sticks. Emery wheels, used for grinding, are a mixture of emery-powder and some cementing substance.

Emery is an impure variety of the mineral corundum, which is chemically an oxide of aluminium. The beautifully coloured crystalline varieties of corundum are known as sapphires, oriental rubies, oriental topaz, and other precious stones. Corundum in cruder forms is used like emery for grinding and polishing.

Emotion. Feelings which we experience in our everyday life are referred to as emotions—such as love, hate, fear, anger, joy and sorrow. Psychologists (scientists who study the human mind) have paid much attention to emotion, beginning with the lower animals. A cat chased by a dog spits, arches its back, displays a bushy tail, unsheathes its claws, and glares at the enemy through widened pupils. On the trail of a mouse it displays a lithe eagerness, and creeps toward its prey with tail swishing and muscles tense.

Emotion in human beings is much more complicated, but it is similar in many ways to emotion in animals. The angry infant who throws himself out of his cot, the boy or girl in school who flushes and stammers, the football player who clenches his fist and suddenly attacks the referee—all these are under the influence of emotional states. All such emotions involve unusual excitement and, unless kept under control, give rise to actions which are more or less unplanned, or irrational.

Everyone is familiar with the outward physical signs of emotion. The person in a sharp attack of anxiety breaks out into perspiration. The angry person reddens and then turns pale. The frightened child trembles. At the same time disturbances are taking place within the body. The blood pressure rises; the pulse beats faster; breathing is more rapid and uneven; the normal processes of digestion are halted; even the supply of blood has been directed from the stomach and towards the trunk muscles and into the arms and legs. The adrenal, or suprarenal, glands, which sit like tiny cocked hats on top of each kidney, pour an increased supply of adrenalin into the blood. This speeds the heart beats, changes the chemical composition of the blood, diminishes the poisons caused by fatigue, increases the rate at which blood clots.

We can easily see the usefulness of these reactions in certain situations. The changes in breathing, blood pressure, and pulse rate are of great assistance to the man who faces sudden danger and must fight for his life or seek escape. The adrenal glands, working at high speed, prevent his feeling fatigue; and if he should happen to be wounded, the prompter clotting of the blood helps the injury to heal. Emotion, then, may be regarded as Nature's way of equipping us to meet emergencies.

In calmer times, too, emotion plays its valuable part in enriching life. Our friendships, our enjoyment of music or poetry or trees or flowers are, in large measure, emotional. Our love of country, or loyalty to school or football team, have a strong emotional quality. The desire to achieve great things is closely related to emotion. During intense excitement we sometimes have inspired strength, and can accomplish things deemed impossible.

But emotions have their unfortunate aspects. Though emotion aids the man who must fight or run for his life, in modern civilization most problems cannot be met by fighting or running away, but must be solved by calm reason. Clear thinking is hindered by emotional stress; it is doubly hard to reason calmly when we are stricken with fear. Again, each strong emotion seeks expression in physical activity, such as fighting when we are angry, and running when we are frightened. If they are denied these outlets, they may become physically harmful.

Emotions are sometimes organized into patterns called complexes, which may cause great difficulty. A common type of complex is the phobia, or abnormal fear, such as the fear of high places, open spaces (agoraphobia), or close rooms or tunnels (claustrophobia), or of certain kinds of animals. Emotions which have been allowed to drift into wrong channels may find expression in the form of outbursts of rage, irritability, needless worry, or extreme shyness.

Emu. (Pron. ē'-mū). Closely related to the cassowary, this running bird lives on the plains of Australia and is a member of the *Ratitae*, or

Australian National Travel Association
EMU AND CHICKS
To make up for its lack of the power to fly, the emu has powerful running legs—and with them can deliver a swift succession of kicks capable of crippling or killing a dog, or similar enemy, that may approach too close to its black-and-white striped chicks.

flightless birds, its scientific name being *Dromaeus novaehollandiae*. The emus have no "cap" or "helmet" such as the cassowaries wear, and are really more likely to remind you of the ostrich than of anything else. But the plumage is heavy and dull brown in colour, and has no ornamental value. The bird stands about five feet high, ranking next to the ostrich in size. Its food is exclusively vegetable, consisting of fruits, roots and herbage. It may be tamed, and breeds easily in captivity. It lays nine to 13 dark green or bluish eggs, nearly as large as ostrich eggs, in a cavity scooped in sandy soil.

Enamel AND ENAMELLING. The extraordinarily delicate examples of "cloisonné" ware in the jeweller's window, the beautiful glazed decoration of cups, plates, and vases carefully preserved in museums, much of the dazzling white equipment of our bathrooms, granite ware, the shining blue and white kitchenware, and the dials of our watches, are all examples, despite their different appearance, of the art of enamelling.

Enamelling means coating a base of metal, pottery, or other mineral substance with finely powdered glass and then heating it until the particles melt and form a glaze. Enamelling as an art has a long history. The ancient Egyptians and Assyrians used enamelled bricks of wonderful lustre in the walls of their palaces. They also used enamel in the decoration of jewelry. The Greeks and Romans were masters of the art, employing it both in jewelry and as an accessory of sculpture. In Ireland and England numerous ancient enamel ornaments have been dug up, including jewels, pins, harness plates, and other objects, of many different colours. Ancient shields and helmets were studded with enamel coloured to resemble coral and precious stones. Some old crowns have enamel ornamentations. Evidences are many that the art early existed also in Persia, Asia Minor, southern Russia, China, Japan and India. Today the Japanese are especially famous for enamel work.

One of the most beautiful of enamel wares is the cloisonné ware previously mentioned. Thin metal strips are soldered to a base (usually of the same metal) to form a design. The little cells thus outlined are then filled with enamel pastes of various colours—bright hues for flowers, green for leaves and branches, black for shadows, and so on. The piece is then baked, or "fired," several times until the enamel has been built up to a sufficient height. When the last firing is safely over, there follow weeks of polishing with pumice stone under running water. During this process the rough surfaces become smooth and shining until the finished work manifests itself as a thing of great beauty in colour and design.

Another form of inlaid enamel is champlevé, which is made by cutting little grooves in the metal itself—usually it is bronze or some other metal less precious than gold—to form the design, and filling these grooves with the enamel. A considerable portion of the metal is usually left as a background for the enamel design. Many of the valuable and beautiful old Chinese enamels are champlevé.

In the later Middle Ages artists began to make painted enamels. In this form a coat of enamel is fused over a metal surface, and a design is painted on this background with enamels of various colours. Numerous firings are necessary before the work is completed. Many beautiful plates, bowls, pitchers, salt-cellars, candlesticks and miniatures in enamel are to be seen in museums and private collections; and some gorgeous transparent enamel windows have been placed in cathedrals. Perhaps the finest examples of painted enamels are those produced at Limoges, France, which are distinguished for their elaborate detail.

Apart from enamelling as producing beautiful ornaments and jewelry, an offshoot of the process in modern times has given us durable and cleanly cooking utensils—enamelled "hollow-ware," as the trade term goes. A whole host of household utensils and other articles is coated with vitreous (glass-like) coatings which can be washed clean with water. Table tops, gas cooker parts and those of electric cookers, are formed of steel and then enamelled blue, grey and white, as the case may be; the coating resists heat. Baths and washbasins are often made of sheet steel, again with a glossy and easily-cleaned enamel coat. Baths and basins are also made of earthenware and then given a vitreous glazed covering like that put on to other pottery articles, but "enamel" really presupposes a metal base to the article.

Materials to form the enamel coating are finely pulverised and ground so that when

British Museum

ENAMEL WORK OF THE CELTS
In ancient Britain the art of enamelling was practised with great success by the Celts. Numbers 1, 2 and 4 are very early specimens of the period prior to the Roman conquest of Britain in A.D. 43. Number 3 is a gold and silver pin set with amber.

SOME OF THE EXQUISITE WORK BY ARTISTS IN ENAMEL

Some of the many possibilities for variety of treatment which may be obtained by enamelling are shown in these three fine specimens of the craft. On the platter, or dish, at the top is a beautiful representation of The Last Supper, done in painted enamel on a copper base by the French artist Jean Raymond in the second half of the 16th century. The jar (lower left) is a modern specimen of Japanese cloisonné work. In cloissoné the design on the porcelain is outlined in metallic bands; the final process is a lengthy polishing with pumice. The wine pot with a handle (right) is of enamelled copper. The platter and the wine pot are in the Victoria and Albert Museum at South Kensington, London; the jar is in the Metropolitan Museum of Art, New York City.

melted the liquid will flow smoothly without lumps. The metal utensil or other part is chemically cleaned, and then dipped into the enamel—or the liquid is applied to it. Mottled effects are obtained by first applying a background colour and later stippling or dappling this with a grey or blue-grey tint to produce the familiar marbled or granite-like effect. Parts which for some reason or other are not to be coloured are masked off; another colour later follows, to coat the parts thus covered. Enamelled name plates and advertising signs are made in a similar way.

The enamel-coated parts have to be fired in an oven to fix the coating and make it durable. It is this which distinguishes true enamelled ware from enamel-painted articles, which are merely dipped into or sprayed with a glossy kind of paint.

Encyclopedia. In form this book is an encyclopedia, as it covers subjects from A to Z. Not until the 18th century was the alphabetically-arranged book of general knowledge given the name of encyclopedia (the " e " spelling is preferable to the diphthong " æ "). An important early work was the Cyclopaedia: or Universal Dictionary of Arts and Sciences of Ephraim Chambers (d. 1740), and it was a translation of this that formed the basis of Diderot and D'Alembert's famous Encyclopédie (published 1751-72). This vast compilation consisted of 33 volumes, including supplements and plates, and its expression of political opinions aroused much controversy in contemporary France. The first edition of the Encyclopædia Britannica, published in Edinburgh about the same time, was a compromise between the alphabetical and scientific arrangement of subjects. Other famous English encyclopedias are Chambers's and The Universal (founded by Sir John Hammerton). The greatest names among Continental encyclopedia-makers of modern times are, perhaps, Larousse in France and Meyer in Germany.

Energy. When we say that someone is " full of energy" we usually mean that he is a hard worker. The scientist uses this term energy, too, but he restricts its meaning to something a little more definite, and to something which he can measure. He defines it as the amount of work that a body can do by virtue of the state in which it exists. For example, the weights in a grandfather clock possess energy, for they can do work in making the hands go round. Gunpowder possesses energy, for it can propel a bullet through the air at a high speed; and the bullet, in its turn, possesses energy, as we know from the damage that it is capable of doing when it strikes an object.

In the example of the clock weights, let us suppose that they weigh one pound and that in the course of time they fall through a distance of one foot. The work done by them in falling is then said to be one foot-pound. Work is always measured by the product of a force (in this instance, the force of gravity acting on the clock weights), and the distance through which the force is applied. Energy is measured in the same units. The energy possessed by the weights before they fell was due to their position, and so is termed *potential* energy. The energy of a moving bullet, on the other hand, is acquired by virtue of its speed; this type of energy is known as *kinetic*. We could measure the kinetic

energy of the bullet by finding the work done in bringing it to rest. It can easily be shown that this kinetic energy of a moving body is proportional to the square of its speed. This means, for example, that a train moving at 60 miles an hour possesses four times as much energy as one travelling at 30 miles an hour. (The speed is doubled, the energy quadrupled.)

Energy is transformed from one form to another quite easily. Think of a clock pendulum moving backwards and forwards; when it is momentarily at rest at the top of its swing it possesses potential energy. As the pendulum swings down, this energy is gradually turned into kinetic energy, or energy of motion; and, on the other side of the swing, potential energy is stored up again. If the pendulum were perfectly frictionless the motion would go on indefinitely. As no pendulum can be made frictionless, some of the available energy is lost, and this makes us ask where it could have gone. The answer is that the heat produced by friction (*q.v.*) in the bearings must be another kind of energy.

Energy Cannot be Created or Destroyed

It was in the late 18th century, before scientists had divined the true nature of heat, that a Count Rumford (1753–1814), while superintending the boring of cannons at the Munich arsenal, made measurements on the heat produced in the process. He found that by using a blunt borer, he could generate enough heat to boil the water in a large oak box, without at the same time removing an appreciable amount of metal from his cannon. The heat generated was only dependent on the amount of work done by the horse which turned his lathe, and from this he formed the opinion that heat and mechanical work were interchangeable forms of energy. It was left to a Manchester scientist, James Joule (1818–89), to make accurate measurements on the amount of heat equivalent to unit amount of work.

Having established the fact that heat was a form of energy it was then possible to formulate a general law, that of the Conservation of Energy. This states that *energy cannot be created or destroyed*, but only changed from one form to another. To illustrate how this applies to a practical case, consider the way in which we get heat energy in our homes from an electric fire. First of all, coal is burnt in furnaces. This releases chemical energy which is transformed into heat. The heat boils water in the boiler tubes and steam from them goes to drive turbines, where part of the heat energy is transformed into kinetic energy of motion. The kinetic energy is then turned into electrical energy by the dynamos, and we release the heat energy once again in our electric fire. As well as the heat we get some light from our fire, and this indicates that light is yet another form of energy. It is by means of light, and other radiations, that energy can be transferred across the vast expanses of empty space without being used up anywhere in the process.

It is interesting to note that heat is nearly always the last form of energy produced in any transformation. This heat goes to warm up the Earth's atmosphere very slightly, and it is then incapable of being used any more to do useful work. Although energy is never lost we must distinguish between the two kinds of energy, *available* and *unavailable*.

Our only real supply of available energy, on this Earth, comes from the Sun. The chemical energy obtained from coal was originally due to the absorption of sunlight by vast prehistoric forests, which stored up the energy as they grew. Water-power is derived from the Sun's energy, too, since it is due to the evaporation of water from low-lying places and subsequent condensation of the vapour, as rain, on high places. Likewise every other source of energy can be traced back to the Sun. Where, then, does the Sun get its energy?

The answer was provided partly by observing the kind of light given off by the Sun, but mainly was due to a drastic change in ideas as to the relationship between mass and energy, brought about by Einstein's Relativity theory. The Laws of Conservation of Energy and Conservation of Mass can be lumped together as one Law of Conservation of Mass-Energy; that is, it is possible, in some circumstances, for matter to be annihilated, with the formation of an equivalent amount of energy. An enormous quantity of energy can be derived from the destruction of a very small quantity of matter, and this is what is going on in the Sun. Hydrogen atoms are being turned into helium atoms, by a rather complicated cycle of events, and in the process the Sun is computed to be losing weight at the rate of four million tons per second!

The realization of a similar annihilation of matter on the Earth, with the release of enormous energy, was accomplished as a result of many years' research by atomic scientists. In the atomic bomb, and in the new atomic " piles," uranium atoms are split up into smaller components whose total weight is less than that of the original uranium. The change in mass is released as energy, and the reactions repeat themselves, so keeping it going until all the atomic " fuel " is used up. (*See* Atom; Chemistry).

'This BLESSED PLOT . . . this ENGLAND'

To most of the readers of this book England is the Homeland, the land above all lands in their affection and esteem. Yet how little we usually know of the England that lies beyond our own town and district!

England. Though he may never express them in words, every native of England harbours such thoughts as those put into John of Gaunt's mouth by Shakespeare in his play Richard II:

This happy breed of men, this little world,
This precious stone set in the silver sea
Which serves it in the office of a wall . . .
This blessed plot, this earth, this realm,
  this England. . . .

The centuries have left their enduring mark on the land and its people in the form of age-old tradition, a deep inbred loyalty and wholesome respect for law and order.

Go into the little village church, ivied and lichened, grey with years. History stares at you from the escutcheon nailed above the door; the stone seats beside the entrance have provided rest for generations of tired folk. The bells whose ropes dangle from the rafters of the tower have tolled for generation after generation of true Englishmen; perchance they gave warning of the Spaniards' coming in their great Armada. The recess beside the altar speaks eloquently of a primitive rite, a more ancient Church. The brasses upon the chancel floor show knights clad in armour such as the Crusaders wore, and dames in stately steeple-hats. Upon the walls a Tudor squire and his lady, beruffed in starched magnificence, kneel to pray surrounded by their children. From this pulpit all the winds of theological opinion have blown since the days of the Reformation, and where now are the square pews were once ranged the medieval worshippers. As for the churchyard, the bones of the village fathers lie deep, pressed heavily, layer upon layer, in one rich mould of human soil. They sleep in their hundreds beneath the boughs of the trees which sheltered them when they came for archery practice after church service, within hail of the green over which they danced as youngsters when time-honoured revelry greeted the return of May.

But the story of England's past belongs to a later chapter. Here we are concerned with the land as it is, and so we proceed to take what may be called a bird's-eye view.

Geographically, England is the chief of the divisions of the British Isles, and forms an irregular triangle whose greatest side is only 430 miles. Along the Welsh border are low mountains. But even the Cheviot Hills, which separate England from Scotland, and the Pennine Range which runs southward into England and is called its backbone, seldom rise above 2,500 feet. In the south-west, the Mendip Hills (highest, 1,067 feet), the Cotswolds (1,100 feet) and Dartmoor (2,039 feet), though containing tracts of wild and desolate country, are the nearest approach to mountains.

In the main, England is a fertile and well-watered land, with a climate neither very cold in winter nor very warm in summer. The

Extent.—Greatest from north to south, 430 miles; greatest from east to west, 370 miles; coast-line more than 2,000 miles. Area, 50,337 square miles. Population, 37,916,000.

Natural Features.—Low rolling country, broken by the Pennine Range in the north (highest point is in the Cumbrian Mountains: Scafell 3,210 feet), and the Downs and Devon hills in the south and south-west. Principal rivers: Tyne; Humber (tributaries—Trent and Ouse); Welland, Nene and Great Ouse; Thames; Avon; Severn and Wye; Mersey. Climate, mild with little variation.

Products.—Wheat, barley, oats, hay and forage crops, fruit, potatoes; cattle, sheep, pigs, poultry, horses, dairy products; herring, haddock, cod and other fish; coal, iron, tin and clay; textiles, ships, aeroplanes and motor-cars, iron and steel manufactures (including cutlery and machinery), chemicals, clothing, pottery and hardware.

Cities.—London (estimated population of Greater London in 1938, 8,700,000); Birmingham (1,001,000); Liverpool, Manchester (over 500,000); Sheffield, Leeds, Bristol (over 400,000).

numerous navigable rivers afford excellent harbours and there is a great wealth of minerals—tin in the southwest, immense coalfields in the centre and north, and some iron. Nowhere is the sea more than 100 miles distant—inviting seamen to voyage forth.

Despite the amazing growth of population—it increased by approximately 16 million in the 60 years 1871-1931, until there are now about 750 people to each square mile—and the development of industry and transport, the greater part of England is still unspoilt countryside, with some of the finest agricultural land in the world.

Sport & General

A FOX IS THE QUARRY

One of the most colourful scenes of English country life is the meet of a fox-hunt. Here, people have gathered at Quainton, Buckinghamshire to see the Bicester Hunt ; the Master (left) and the hunt servants are wearing the traditional pink coats.

more regular in outline and drier in climate than the west, is washed by the North Sea, and in places is being slowly worn away by it. The principal inlets on this coast, from which the fishing fleet goes out to the Dogger Bank and the other North Sea fishing grounds, are the mouths of the Tyne and the Tees; the Humber estuary, into which flow the Trent and the Yorkshire Ouse; the Wash, an extension of the low-lying Fens; and the estuary of the Thames, London's sea gateway.

The south coast, from the South Foreland to the Lizard and Land's End, is broken by several harbours, notably Portsmouth Harbour, South-

Much of the course of England's history may be traced to her insular position, though even the Atlantic is now no barrier to an aeroplane, and only 21 miles separate England from France, her nearest Continental neighbour, at the Strait of Dover. The east coast, which is, generally speaking, ampton Water, and Plymouth Sound. Half-way along, beyond the chalk cliffs of Kent and Sussex, is the Isle of Wight, geographically within the county of Hampshire. Headlands include Dungeness, Beachy Head, Selsey Bill, and Portland Bill. Southwest the coast becomes high and rugged. Devon

Fox

SHEEP AND THE TRANQUIL BEAUTY OF THE COTSWOLDS

Forming the western boundary of the central plain of England, the Cotswolds are rolling, down-like hills, dotted with small woods and rising generally to about 600 feet— to more than 1,000 feet at Broadway in Worcestershire.

The spacious hills provide excellent grazing for large flocks, and here we see a round-up of sheep near Winchcombe in Gloucestershire. The villages are noted for their cottages of grey stone, which is a distinctive feature of the Cotswolds.

CHEDDAR GORGE THROUGH THE MENDIP HILLS

World Press

There is no more impressive sight in England than the Cheddar Gorge in Somerset, a narrow pass two miles long through which a road winds between limestone cliffs. It was formed, through long ages, by water wearing away the rocks. Caverns run deep into the hills of this awe-inspiring gorge, and in some of them stalactites and stalagmites are reflected in water, producing wonderful effects, as is shown in the colour plate facing page 732. The Mendips, a chain about 25 miles long, contain other caves, among them Wookey Hole (*see* illustration in page 733).

LOVELY CASTLE COMBE IN WILTSHIRE

Claimed by many to be the loveliest village in England, Castle Combe is in Wiltshire, close to the Somerset border. It contains old buildings with gabled fronts and mullioned windows—a striking contrast to the densely packed industrial cities, such as that illustrated below.

important commercially as the Thames or the Trent, and its source actually lies in Wales. North of Wales we come to the Mersey, at the mouth of which is Liverpool; between Cumberland and the south of Scotland is the Solway Firth. The actual boundary between England and Scotland is the valley of the Tweed and the Cheviot range.

To the west of the Pennines, in the north-west corner of England, are the Cumbrian mountains, standing sentinel over the beautiful Lake District. Our pictures include several of this picturesque area. Windermere (10½ miles long) is the largest lake. In Yorkshire, the biggest county in England, is a great area of bleak moorland.

The hills of southern England are lower and have a more gradual slope than those of the north. The Cotswolds and the Chilterns, both favourite districts, lie largely in Gloucestershire, Oxfordshire and Buckinghamshire. In Somerset, farther south, are the Mendips and the Quantocks. Then, between London and the south coast, are the rolling North and South Downs (*q.v.*), and

(which includes Lundy Island) and Cornwall, with the outlying Scilly Isles, form a rocky peninsula.

On the west the Bristol Channel forms the estuary of the Severn, which is Great Britain's longest river (220 miles). It is, however, not so

BIRMINGHAM, MIGHTY INDUSTRIAL CITY OF THE MIDLANDS

The second city in England, Birmingham in Warwickshire, has a population of more than one million. As a great manufacturing centre it pays one of the penalties of prosperity, for on most days of the year it is covered with a canopy of smoke from hundreds of factory chimneys. This aerial photograph was taken on a day when a high wind had blown away the smoke, and so we are given a fairly clear idea of the extent of this great industrial city.

physical features of England are indicated in the map of the British Isles facing page 584. This map of England and Wales shows the English counties, chief towns, railways, canals and steamship routes.

WHERE WHITE CLIFFS GUARD ENGLAND'S COAST

J. Dixon-Sco

The white cliffs of Albion are the first scene to spring to many a foreigner's eye when he thinks of England, for they seem—to Englishmen as well—to symbolize the sturdy individualism and rugged independence of the English character. One can easily understand why the returni exile's heart rejoices when he sights again the white wa of his homeland at Dover, where the great chalk headla of the Shakespeare Cliff (seen above) juts out into the s

To face page 118

between them lies the Weald of Kent. Salisbury Plain, and the Wiltshire downs, may be regarded as a westward extension of these chalk downs.

The low-lying plains of England may be divided into three main areas : the eastern, including the Vale of York, the Fens, and East Anglia (Norfolk, Suffolk and Essex); the central, covering most of the Midland counties; and the western, from Lancashire to the Severn basin.

There were once huge forests in England, but the most important of the few remaining are the New Forest in Hampshire and the Forest of Dean in Gloucestershire. Dartmoor and Exmoor were once extensively forested. There are still many beautiful stretches of woodland and parks, but much

queer shops and old timber-built houses make it one of the most picturesque of English cities.

In Manchester—like Liverpool, a city of Lancashire—we reach the metropolis of the great cotton industry. Through its huge ship canal, which connects the city with the Mersey and Liverpool, making Manchester practically a sea-port, come steamers laden with bales of raw cotton from the United States, the sub-continent of India and Egypt, to be sent on to Oldham, Bolton, Preston, and other neighbouring towns to be spun and woven into cotton goods. Why should the Lancashire region be given over so largely to cotton manufacture ? The answer is to be found partly in its moist climate—the wettest in all

Fox

FAMOUS SEASIDE RESORT NEAREST TO LONDON

On the Essex bank at the mouth of the Thames estuary, Southend-on-Sea is 36 miles to the east of London. It has a pier more than a mile and a quarter long—the longest in England—which is traversed by an electric tramway. Up and down the Thames estuary passes an enormous volume of shipping serving the Port of London, which stretches from Tilbury, about 13 miles west of Southend, to the heart of the City. Nowhere in England are you far from the sea ; and to this the country owes its even climate, the sea keeping air warm in winter and cool in summer.

of the latter is private ground belonging to great landowners. Apart from the Lake District, England is almost devoid of lakes, although the Broads of East Anglia cover a fair-sized area.

Let us follow a visitor who has just landed at Liverpool, one of the greatest commercial cities. At its long grey docks he will see ships from Africa and Australia, from China, from the sub-continent of India and from South America—indeed, from every great port in the civilized world. If it is summer, he will want to see something of the country before going to London, and will turn aside perhaps to visit quaint old Chester on the river Dee, near the border of Wales. Once a Roman camp, its medieval walls follow on three sides the line of the old Roman walls; while its

England—favourable to cotton-spinning, and partly in the coalfields of the near-by Pennine Chain.

If you were to fly over England in an aeroplane you would see a vast smoky district stretching from Cardiff in Wales to the river Tyne on the north-east coast, and on the west coast to Glasgow and the Clyde district of south-west Scotland. Blacker, smokier, more crowded than anywhere else in this "Black Country" would appear the district about Manchester; for here are the richest coal-fields, and, therefore, the greatest factories, because fuel is easily obtainable. Along the Trent in Staffordshire are great pottery works.

Not far away, where iron and coal are found close together, is Birmingham, in the counties of Warwickshire and Worcestershire—greatest

G. P. Abraham

Rocky heights, turbulent waterfalls and tranquil lakes constitute what is known as the Lake District in North-West England. Wastwater in Cumberland, seen here in the distance from Great Gable, is the deepest of the lakes. It is some three miles long and about half a mile wide. The altitude of Great Gable is 2,950 feet. The highest of the mountains is Scafell Pike, reaching 3,210 feet, at the eastern end of Wastwater; it is also the loftiest peak in England. This picturesque region extends from Cumberland into Westmorland and part of Lancashire.

BY WOODED HILL AND PASTURE FLOWS THE WYE

J. Dixon-Scott

A specially beautiful stretch of English countryside is in the Wye Valley, with its wooded hills and rich pastures. Here the landscape is in extreme contrast with the rugged panorama of the Lake District in the facing page. The Wye rises in Plynlymmon, on the borders of Cardiganshire and Montgomeryshire, and flows into the estuary of the Severn just below Chepstow in Monmouthshire. Among the lovely places on the river is Symond's Yat, Herefordshire, where the Wye flows round the base of a hill 740 feet high. Also on the Wye is the famous ruin of Tintern Abbey.

metal-manufacturing centre in England. Also in Warwickshire is Coventry, which makes motor-cars and all kinds of machinery. Sheffield, 75 miles to the north of Birmingham, in the south of Yorkshire, has similar advantages, making it the world's centre for cutlery. In this same busy region are others of England's great industrial cities—Huddersfield, Halifax and Bradford, with their world-renowned woollen mills; Leeds, a centre of the cloth industry and also a city were heavy machinery of all kinds is turned out.

A little north of the industrial area of Lancashire is the beautiful Lake District. Here is the country

archbishop, has the largest and, perhaps, the grandest of all English Gothic cathedrals. Hull, on the Humber, owes its importance to its fisheries and extensive commerce, as does Middlesbrough to the neighbouring iron-field; and Lincoln, some 50 miles south of Hull, presents a cathedral which historically is more interesting than York's.

Lichfield cathedral, in the Staffordshire city of the same name, is one of the smallest, but also one of the loveliest of these old churches; and Ely, with its massive Norman towers, rising in the great fen district of Cambridgeshire—now drained and cultivated—is one of the most majestic and impressive of these shrines. (This and other cathedrals mentioned are pictured in pages 721-728). Not far from Ely is the university town of Cambridge, with its historic halls; it ranks in educational importance with the university at Oxford, on the upper Thames, 76 miles to the south-west.

Perhaps the most significant development in English industry after the First World War (1914-18) was the movement of manufacturing activities to the south-east, particularly in the London area. Let us now sail down the broad estuary of the Thames, with its ships coming and going on the world's commerce, and turn southward about Kent to skirt the beautiful and historic shores of the southern coast. In Kent the Anglo-Saxons landed in the 5th century, and there at Canterbury St. Augustine (d. 604) founded England's mother church.

PEACE OF THE NORFOLK BROADS
Windmills are a conspicuous feature of the Norfolk Broads, the one here being beside the River Ant, not far from Ludham bridge. Large stretches of water lying mainly in Norfolk, partly in Suffolk, the Broads are wide parts of certain rivers, of which the Ant is one, rather than actual lakes. Yachtsmen and others enjoy the calm waters.

The Times

made famous by Wordsworth, Coleridge and Southey, sometimes called the " Lake poets."

As we approach the Scottish border we find a reminder of Britain's early history in the remains of the old Roman wall, built by the Emperor Hadrian (A.D. 76-138), stretching from a point west of Carlisle to what is now the busy city of Newcastle-on-Tyne, in Northumberland—a distance of 73½ miles. Many miles of this great wall still stand, shorn it is true of more than half its original 20 feet of height, but still a carriage road in width striding over hill and down dale. Newcastle is only one of the great towns whose shipyards have meant so much to England's commerce.

Less than 20 miles south of Newcastle is the wonderful old city of Durham. Here stands the famous old cathedral which is the finest existing example of a Norman Romanesque church. As we travel southward we come upon many more of these picturesque cathedral cities, each with its own individual character. York, the seat of an

In Sussex, once the kingdom of the South Saxons, William and his Normans first set foot on their great invasion in 1066. Then, in Hampshire, as we have seen, is the harbour of Southampton Water and, off Spithead, the great naval station of Portsmouth. Inland, in Hampshire lies Winchester, the capital of England in Saxon days, and in Wiltshire is the cathedral city of Salisbury.

In picturesque Devonshire we come to Plymouth, another famous seaport. The whole length of the English Channel, from the Strait of Dover to Land's End in Cornwall, has been the scene of stirring episodes in English naval history, from the time of Drake down to the present day. Up the west coast, where the Avon flows into the broad Bristol Channel, is Bristol, once the chief port of western England. Everywhere, indeed, in England we come upon traces of a historic past, vistas of scenic loveliness, evidences of commercial greatness. (*See also* British Isles ; English History ; United Kingdom; and the articles on the countries and the chief cities).

G. P. Abraham

Lake District of Cumberland and Westmorland provides of the finest scenery in England. Here we see Grasmere, of the most notable of the lakes. Across the lake can be Helm Crag, a rocky hill rising to a height of 1,279 feet above the surface of the waters. In the village of Grasmere, beside the lake, the poet Wordsworth lived for fourteen years. Great efforts have been made to preserve the Lake District from defacement, and large areas have been purchased for the nation.

F. Frith

WHITE CLIFFS FRINGING THE BLUE WATERS OF THE ENGLISH CHANNEL

The great chalk-mass of the South Downs runs from just north of Portsmouth, in Hampshire, until it terminates at the sea between Seaford and Eastbourne, in Sussex, Beachy Head being the eastern extremity. West of Beachy Head, also, there are chalk cliffs, much lower, but of great beauty. They form the succession of headlands seen above, known as the Seven Sisters. The headland in the foreground is Seaford Head, almost as impressive as Beachy Head itself.

W. F. Taylor

AT MOORINGS IN THE UPPER REACHES OF THE THAMES

It is possible to go by boat from Kingston-on-Thames to Oxford, and along the 91 miles journey we pass scenery of a quiet beauty typical of southern England. Above is a scene at Halliford, Middlesex, only 21 miles from London. A branch of the main stream makes a backwater in which pleasure craft are moored. On either side of the river are meadows, interspersed here and there with riverside houses, whose gardens, running down to the stream, are generally a blaze of colour in the summer months.

H. W. Nicholls

OLD SALTS REPAIR THEIR NETS

At many seaside places where the fishing boats are drawn up on to the beach such a scene as this may be met with. Above high watermark is a row of sheds in which the nets are kept, and these three old fishermen, sitting in front of one, are repairing the nets damaged on the last fishing trip. The sea takes a heavy toll of their gear.

S. H. Nicholls

THE VILLAGE SMITH AT HIS ANVIL

Motor-cars and motor-tractors have not quite driven horses from the English countryside, and teams still draw the wagons or plod patiently in front of the plough. The village blacksmiths, therefore, still make and fit horseshoes, though many of them find it necessary to turn their skill at the anvil in other directions.

F. Deaville Walker

IN A CORNISH FISHING HARBOUR

One of the most picturesque villages of Cornwall is Polperro. It lies on the south coast, near Looe, at the foot of cliffs 400 feet high, and is approached by a narrow gorge. On the side of the cliff are clustered stone-built cottages rising one above the other, and beneath them lies the little harbour for the pilchard-fishing boats.

ENGLAND'S MASTERS *of the* BRUSH

Though England has produced few ' old masters ' in the generally accepted sense, there are English painters of world renown, and there is a recognizably British school, notable for portraiture and landscape.

English Art. Long before painting as we know it today came into existence two other branches of pictorial art were highly developed in Europe: illumination and mural decoration. Illumination flourished especially in Britain. As far back as the 8th century English artists were producing fine illuminated manuscripts, especially at Canterbury. Most of these men were monks, and most of their work consisted in the illumination of the borders and headings of religious works, or Bibles. There are many styles in this type of work, the earliest of them influenced by Byzantine art; but the most important British illuminations of the 8th century were those of the Irish School, whose finest productions, the Book of Kells, the Lindisfarne Gospels, and the Book of Durrow, rank among the world's masterpieces of illumination.

National Gallery, London
Sir Thomas Lawrence (1769–1830) painted this portrait of Princess Lieven.

In England the Anglo-Saxon school attained its greatest perfection in the works of the Winchester School, whose masterpiece is the late 10th-century Benedictional of St. Aethelwold. The 12th century produced the Anglo-Norman School; at Winchester, Bury St. Edmunds, and elsewhere in the south and east were produced fine manuscripts, many of which show those weird beasts and fantastic creatures which one is apt especially to associate with the word illumination. This school was succeeded in the next century by a completely new one, which reached Britain from France, and which was in tune with the general development of Gothic art in that country. To the late 14th century belongs the famous Bedford Book of Hours, in which initials are filled with little portrait medallions of several hundred celebrities of the time.

Masters of Miniature Painting

While English art, as seen in illuminated manuscripts and the miniatures that accompanied and illustrated them, could compete on equal terms with anything then produced on the Continent, there was another branch in which the English were soon to become the greatest masters—that of miniature painting as we now know it.

The English miniaturists, however, were profoundly influenced by the work of Hans Holbein (*q.v.*), who spent many of his most fruitful years in this country. Holbein died in 1543; and four years later our first great artist of miniatures was born, namely, Nicholas Hilliard (1547–1619). His work shows the influence of Holbein, in early examples especially, but the influence of English illuminators is seen in the delicacy of decoration and ornament which is far removed from the sombre, almost stark simplicity of Holbein. Hilliard enjoyed royal patronage under Queen Elizabeth and James I, and he ranks as the first of our native painters whom we can call a master.

Hilliard was succeeded by many other men who became famous for their miniature portraits. They include the Olivers, father and son, and the Hoskins, father and son, of whom the elder, John Hoskins (d. 1664), taught Samuel Cooper (*c.* 1609–72), greatest miniaturist of all. His miniatures are real portraits; indeed, contemporary critics averred that, if enlarged to life size, they would appear to have been painted that size—high praise for paintings which occupied, at the most, only six or seven square inches. Many of Cooper's works are in the national collection at the Victoria and Albert Museum, London.

In Cooper's day there were many other fine exponents of this art, including his own brother Alexander. But it was not until after the middle of the next century that another great miniaturist appeared, in the person of Richard Cosway (1742–1821). He had many imitators, conscious and unconscious, and as miniatures are very often

Courtesy of the Duke of Devonshire
ILLUMINATION MASTERPIECE
In England the art of illuminating the borders and headings of religious books reached nearest perfection in the works of the Winchester School, whose masterpiece, shown here, is the late 10th-century Benedictional of St. Aethelwold.

unsigned it is extremely hard to tell which are his work; at one time any really excellent miniature of his period was attributed to Cosway. His contemporaries include George Englehart (1750–1829), the Hones, and the Plimers.

So far we have been dealing only with illumination and miniature painting, arts which exist to a certain degree at the present day, for illumination in recent times has been truly represented by the black-and-white decorative work of engravers such as Eric Gill, John Farleigh, and Robert Gibbings, and the " decorations " of Rex Whistler. Very little is known about any other type of painting in Britain prior to Stuart times, and still less about the painters. There are, however, a certain number of more or less well-preserved paintings (frescoes) on the walls of churches—and a few on screens and other objects—scattered all over the country. Among the earliest of these are 12th-century paintings at Canterbury. To the next century belong those at Winchester, and the 13th-century roundel in the Chapel of the Bishop's Palace at Chichester. This last painting shows the Virgin and Child, and although we have no notion who the artist might have been there is no doubt that it is our finest medieval painting.

In the 13th century, too, lived Matthew Paris, the author and illustrator of important historical works. The many pictures in his books, notably heads and full-page, full-length drawings of the Virgin and Child, show that he was original and had great artistic ability.

To find good paintings of definite date we must now pass directly to the end of the 15th century, when the walls of Eton College Chapel were decorated with a series of paintings of the Miracles of the Virgin. They seem to have been executed, in part at least, by one William Baker. Art experts can trace in these paintings something of the style of the Winchester school of illuminators, and the same influence may be discerned in the portrait of Lady Margaret Beaufort in the National Portrait Gallery, London, done about 1485.

Holbein and His Successors

But such examples as these are few and far between; a notable work by an unknown master is the Wilton Diptych (in the National Gallery). Holbein was monopolizing court painting during the early 16th century, and he succeeded, later in the same century, by Flemings such as Sir Anthony Mor and Hans Eworts (anglicized as Eworth). John Bettes is a name that stands out, since we have a single very Holbeinesque portrait by this artist in the National Portrait Gallery. Other portraits were almost all done by men from the Netherlands, not only in Stuart times but well into the 18th century. Not unnaturally, as they settled in Britain, or at least spent much time here, these men were influenced by their surroundings, but even so the names of Daniel Mytens (c. 1590–1642), Cornelius Janssen (1593-1664), Marcus Gheeraerts (c. 1561–c. 1635), alone bespeak their foreign origin. Van Dyck, too, reaching England in 1632, and working here a great deal, had tremendous influence.

Two more painters of such type are Lely (whose real name was Peter van der Faes) (1618-80) and Kneller (1643-1723). Both were fine painters of portraits in the grand manner, Lely especially showing the influence of Van Dyck; and both were good technicians. A figure deserving mention is that of William Dobson (1610-46), whose early death cut short a career of great promise. Another of whose work we have material evidence is Robert Walker (c. 1600–c. 1660), who painted portraits of Oliver Cromwell.

Slightly later come William Riley (1646-91) and J. M. Wright (1625-70), a Scot. Both these painters, who are represented in the National Portrait Gallery, show some originality. After their time came a gap in which we find only the rather solitary figure of Sir James Thornhill (1675-1734), the mural decorator of the dome of St. Paul's, who also worked at Greenwich, in Hampton Court, and in many other large buildings in and near London. But Thornhill is chiefly remembered in connexion with our first great native artist, William Hogarth (1697-1764), for Hogarth

A SEVENTEENTH CENTURY BEAUTY

Sir Peter Lely, a Dutchman who settled in England in 1641, established himself as one of the leading portrait painters of his time. This example of his work, in the National Portrait Gallery, London, was long thought to be a picture of Nell Gwynn, favourite of Charles II, but this is now disputed.

not only studied under Thornhill but eloped with his daughter !

Hogarth was influenced more or less equally by the Dutch and the Italians in his subject-matter (many of his works are documents on the life of his age), which was completely new in a country such as England, yet robustly British in his technique and use of colour. From the layman's point of view, the greatest gift Hogarth brought to painting in England was that of life and light, for the difference between his lively, colourful and brilliantly drawn scenes from real life and the estimable, but dull, portraiture which had long stood for painting in Britain is tremendous; his own portraits, too, are a great advance on previous work. Hogarth did not have a very wide influence, even on those painters who studied under him. Joseph Highmore (1692–1780) is spoken of as one painter who shows this influence.

National Gallery, London

PHAETON AND PAIR BY STUBBS

During the 18th century a notable school of English sporting painters arose, of whom the finest was George Stubbs (1724–1806). In this Phaeton and Pair, which combines his favourite equestrian subject with a charming portrait, he shows himself an excellent draughtsman and a fine artist. A painting such as this is specially useful to the student of period costumes.

From the time of Hogarth the names of English painters become more and more numerous. Thomas Hudson (1701–79), for example, was a good portrait painter, but he can only be considered here as the master of Reynolds and Gainsborough; in this capacity he had a wider influence on the development of the English school than through his own works. Another man whose work influenced Reynolds was a Scot, Allan Ramsay (1713–84), himself also a portraitist of great merit. Especially famous as a painter of women, he was court painter from 1767 until his death. His finest work is in the galleries of Edinburgh.

Now we come to Sir Joshua Reynolds (1723–92), considered by many to be our best portraitist. For all his faults—and they are not a few—Reynolds stands foremost among members of the British school, not only for the tremendous influence which he had on his art in this country, or merely through his excellence as a painter, but also as a great man.

One noteworthy point about Reynolds was his perpetual willingness to learn; indeed, it is true to say that his art went on improving as he grew older. He was, essentially, a painter of men, and of intellectual men at that. On the whole, the finest of his portraits are perhaps the series of literary celebrities of his time, men who were his friends as well as his sitters; his portraits of Dr. Johnson, Boswell, Sterne and others are amongst the finest examples ever done of this type of art. His women were dignified, beautiful, but often lacking in humanity. As a painter of children he excelled; one such portrait is reproduced in page 1186.

Reynolds, ever a keen student, gained hints from all the great painters whose work he knew and examined, and thus, indirectly, he widened the knowledge of all who followed him. He himself was at first influenced by Allan Ramsay, but later Allan Ramsay was learning from him. In his book, Discourses on Painting, Reynolds imparted much sound advice which is still of value to students of art. As part-founder of the Royal Academy, and its first president, he had an enduring influence on the " business " side of British art.

Gainsborough's Artistic Vision

It was unfortunate that Reynolds experimented with all manner of pigments and mediums, and so ruined many of his greatest works for posterity. In this, as in many other respects, he differed from his great rival, Thomas Gainsborough (1727–88). As to which was the greater painter, argument will be endless ; but while there is no doubt that Reynolds had a more marked influence on the development of the British school, it is equally certain that Gainsborough was the more imaginative artist. This is perhaps not unnatural, when we consider that he had none of the advantages of travel and social contact which were part of Reynolds's life. Gainsborough was largely self-taught, as his fine landscapes, founded on his own intimate knowledge of Nature, show; and although he spent a certain amount of time copying the old masters, he certainly did not use them as did Reynolds. He had, besides, much more of the traditional artistic temperament, a fact which is shown in his love of music and in his choice of friends. Technically, Gainsborough was not always superior to Reynolds, but he used purer colour and his brushwork was more subtle. Moreover, most of his pictures maintain the same high standard throughout, for he did not rely upon assistants to put in the draperies, backgrounds, and other less interesting parts of his portraits. In fact, the landscape background, of great importance in a Gainsborough painting, reflects the mood that is shown in the sitter's face.

Before turning to the landscape school, which Gainsborough also largely inaugurated, we must note some followers of the two masters of the English portrait school. Foremost among them were Romney, famous for his pictures of Lady Hamilton—he did over 60—and Raeburn, renowned for his magnificent portraits of Scottish notabilities. George Romney (1734–1802), having early incurred the hostility of Reynolds, never exhibited at the Academy, yet he was sufficiently successful to be a thorn in the side of the president of the Academy. His great quality is a certain soft, warm charm which he imparts to his portraits, especially those of women and children. Something of Romney's warmth is also to be seen in the female portraits of Sir Henry Raeburn (1756–1823), a Scot who lived and worked almost entirely in his own country. It is as a painter of men, however, that Raeburn, with his vigorous style, strong colour, and straightforward manner, is chiefly famous.

The last great painter of the English portrait school was Sir Thomas Lawrence (1769–1830).

Something of an infant prodigy, at the early age of 25 he was a full Academician. He was a notable painter of women and children, and, above all, a deft and ingenious draughtsman; but he tended to make all his sitters look almost inhumanly sweet. As the most influential portrait painter of his time, however, he had many followers, while among his rivals was John Hoppner (c. 1758–1810).

Hoppner, admittedly a disciple of Reynolds, painted many charming portraits, which have also retained a value far beyond their artistic worth. Other followers of Reynolds were Francis Cotes (1725–70); James Northcote (1746–1831); John Opie (1761–1807); and the Rev. Matthew William Peters (1742–1814), all good portraitists.

For many years the art of the mezzotint had been practised by the Dutch engravers, Lely especially inspiring some fine works. But in the 18th century men such as Valentine Green (1739–1813), John Raphael Smith, Bartolozzi and others produced many superb reproductions of the work of artists already described, as well as of our great landscape painters. Mezzotinting has survived to modern times, although only in isolated instances; Sir Frank Short was perhaps the finest modern worker in this particular medium.

The English landscape school owes a great deal to Gainsborough, who was perhaps the first of all landscape painters to paint Nature as he saw it, without adding classical buildings and other accessories, and who always thought of himself as a landscape artist. The other great early English landscape painter was also a portraitist of some skill. This was

National Gallery, London

A SELF-TAUGHT ARTIST PAINTED THIS

Born in Norwich, Norfolk, in 1768, John Crome delighted to paint the scenery around that city. A self-taught artist, he spent most of his early life as a painter of inn signs, and was about 40 years of age before he produced his first great picture. He holds a high place among English landscape artists. No one has reproduced so faithfully the countryside of East Anglia. This Moonlight on the Marshes of the Yare is a typical example of his work.

Richard Wilson (1714–82), one of the most original of British artists. His landscapes show the influence of a visit to Italy, but before this he had done some brilliant portraits. At his best, as in his glorious views of Snowdon, Cader Idris (in the National Gallery), and other Welsh hills, Wilson, neglected during his lifetime, is a great artist. He achieved a great deal towards a true rendering of the "atmospheric" quality of a scene, and at the same time kept close to Nature, a feature not present in the work of any previous artist of this kind. The influence of Claude Lorrain and Poussin is visible in his work, but he excelled them in many respects, and his own influence on Crome and Turner was also considerable.

Contemporary with Wilson were other landscape painters, such as Samuel Scott (1710–72), who depicted chiefly marine subjects and also recorded the London of his day; and from now onwards such artists enjoyed more prominence. Most of them were water-colourists, such as Paul Sandby (1725–1809), who is sometimes considered to be the "father of British water-colour"; Alexander Cozens (c. 1698–1786), and his son, John Robert Cozens (1752–97), who did some superb Alpine landscapes; and Thomas Girtin (1775–1802), a great painter who, in spite of his short life, had a tremendous influence on his art. From Girtin we can follow the whole sequence of the development of water-colour painting through Cotman (q.v.), David Cox, de Wint, Rowlandson (q.v.) and others, to the present day.

More important, however, since we are concerned mainly with oil painters, is John Crome (1768–1821), leader of the East Anglia or Norwich school. A self-taught artist, he was born in Norwich, the son of a journeyman, and spent his early life chiefly as an inn-sign painter, and later copying engravings. His interest in painting led him to study the works in those collections to which he could obtain access, and as these contained largely Dutch paintings it was not unnatural that his work should be influenced in that direction. Not until he was about 40 did he produce his first really great painting. He earned money by teaching drawing, founded the Norwich Society for exhibiting paintings, and went but little outside his native town.

Crome holds a high place in the history of landscape painting. Like other English landscape artists he observed and drew Nature at first-hand, especially the country of East Anglia. Yet by the middle of the 19th century Crome's pictures were forgotten, and it is said that the famous view of Mousehold Heath, now in the National Gallery, was purchased at one time for a few shillings. Crome's works, one of which is seen in page 1180, reflect his own peaceful life, which in every way was a contrast to that of our next subject, Turner.

J. M. W. Turner (1775–1851), considered by many to be the greatest of all English painters, and certainly one of the world's greatest landscape artists, was probably born in London. He led a strange, solitary life. (See the article on Turner, J. M. W.). As a painter, Turner was primarily interested in the effect of light, especially in his more impressionistic works, with their nebulous, fiery colour, and brilliant intensity. If we start with his earlier works and then consider the glorious masterpieces of his later days, we can easily recognize the various stages of his work.

Turner travelled a good deal—his pictures of Venice are justly celebrated—and wherever he went he added something to his style. His earlier works, with their more sombre hues and less vivid atmospheric effects, are simple enough, and no one can fail to be impressed by the power and the observation with which he could paint the sea—better, perhaps, than anyone who has ever lived. To see his colour at its most striking, and to see the best of the phases in which he so clearly anticipates the Frenchmen of the end of the century, we must examine his later water-colours.

Very different from Turner is John Constable (1776–1837), who continues to have a far greater popularity, since he is the more easily understood. Constable painted the scenes we can see any day in the country, and that is why he has such a wide appeal, and why his work is perhaps the most popular of all landscape in reproductions. Constable was the first British artist to achieve Continental fame. Yet Constable—like Crome, and unlike Turner— did not achieve early brilliance. Even at the age of 40 he was only beginning to feel sure of himself. Perhaps this was because he deliberately set out to be a "natural painter," to reproduce the scene as accurately as possible. We are fortunate in having a very complete and valuable series of Constable's paintings and sketches which show the artist's entire development, from his early efforts to his most complicated manner. These are in the

National Gallery, London

A SCULPTOR'S PAINTING
Better known as a sculptor, Alfred Stevens (1817–75) was also a fine portrait painter ; this picture of Mrs. Leonard Collmann has been described as one of the most beautiful portraits by an English artist in Victorian times.

Victoria and Albert Museum, a visit to which will make it clear why he is considered the forerunner of the French Impressionists.

Another rather isolated figure in the story of the English school is R. P. Bonington (1801–28), a fine painter of sea- and land-scape who was influenced by Constable, and who, had he lived longer, might have achieved real greatness. He showed also considerable French influence, and was himself influential in France, where he spent much time.

We must go back a little to pick up the threads of yet another type of British art, that of the " conversation piece," for the most part showing groups or families, indoors or out. Among the earliest painters of the conversation piece was Arthur Devis (1711–87), whose naïve figures have a certain distinction. Then there was John Zoffany (1733–1810), who did many good groups and portraits, and was influenced by Hogarth. In yet another aspect of the British school we have the painters of sporting scenes, of men and horses, of whom George Stubbs (1724–1806) is the most notable representative. His groups have much of the " conversation piece " atmosphere. This leads us to pure " *genre* " pictures (*i.e.* the portrayal of ordinary life), such as those of George Morland (1763–1804), who painted in the country inns and blacksmiths' shops, and whose work, coarse, good-humoured, and full of virility, is widely known through engravings. Similarly, Francis Wheatley (1747–1801) is remembered by his famous Cries of London series.

One of the most remarkable artists of all time was William Blake (1757–1827). Men whom he influenced were Edward Calvert (1799–1883) and Samuel Palmer (1805–81). A friend of Blake's was the great illustrator and draughtsman, John Flaxman (1755–1826). Another fine draughtsman, but of a very different type, was Alfred Stevens (1817–75), who ranks as the first of the " modern " painters—as opposed to " old masters." He painted some fine portraits, but his name is almost unknown except as a sculptor. He was influenced especially by Michelangelo, and it has been said of him that he alone of artists in his day and country caught the spirit of the Italian Renaissance. He is followed by G. F. Watts (1817–1904), who painted both portraits and ambitious allegorical themes. Watts is often associated with the Pre-Raphaelites, though neither he nor several lesser painters of a rather similar style, such as Lord Leighton (1830–96), Sir Lawrence Alma-Tadema (1836–1912), and Sir Edward Poynter (1836–1919), can be classed with them.

The original members of the Pre-Raphaelite brotherhood were Sir J. E. Millais (1829–96), Holman Hunt (1827–1910), and D. G. Rossetti (1828–82). Constituting a deliberate revolt against the decadent conditions of art at the time (1849), they had a considerable influence, not merely directly on painting, but also, indirectly, on applied arts, especially through William Morris (1834–1906), who was more designer than painter, and to whom a revival in good book production is largely due (*see* Morris, William). Other names sometimes linked with the Pre-Raphaelite Movement were those of Ford Madox Brown (1821–93), and Sir Edward Burne-Jones (1833–98).

William Etty (1787–1849) falls into no particular group. He is our finest painter of the nude, and was strongly influenced by the Venetians. Contemporary with him are *genre* painters such as Sir David Wilkie (1785–1841), William Mulready (1786–1863), and William Powell Frith (1819–1900), famous for his Derby Day. Sir Edwin Landseer (*q.v.*) was the most popular artist of his time.

While the Pre-Raphaelites were flourishing, J. M. Whistler (1834–1903) was beginning to puzzle the public by his Impressionist paintings, which showed considerably the influence of Japanese art, then entirely unknown in England. It was the

Tate Gallery, London

WHISTLER'S SUPERB ARTISTRY
Born in the United States in 1834, Whistler settled in London in 1863. His distinction as a painter is due chiefly to his sense of colour, his exact placing of objects and economic use of detail. Old Battersea Bridge—a night scene on the Thames—is perhaps one of his loveliest works.

PORTRAIT BY ORPEN
One of the most brilliant portrait painters of the early
20th century, Sir William Orpen exhibited Le Chef de l'Hôtel
Chatham (above) at the Royal Academy Exhibition of 1921.
Orpen was knighted in 1918, and died in January 1931

Walter Judd, Ltd.

titles of Whistler's works, as much as their content,
that upset the stolid British public and critics alike,
for he gave them what appeared to be musical
names—Arrangements, Nocturnes, etc. Later, as
an etcher, he did even greater work ; his finest etchings are those of the Thames, and of Venice.

In spite of Whistler, the Academicians continued
to produce " problem pictures " such as those of Or-
chardson (1835-1910)—the majority of these being
the heirs of the anecdotal or " every picture tells a
story " school, immensely popular during the mid-
19th century—dull portraits, seascapes and landscapes. But at the newly-formed New English Art
Club and the International Society less conventional works (inspired by French Impressionistic
models) were being exhibited, and by 1910, when
post-Impressionism became a leading movement,
the masters of the modern English School were all
fairly well established. An American, John Sargent
(1856-1925) was famous for his brilliant, though
sometimes superficial technique ; and, like him,
William Strang (1859-1921), a portrait and subject
picture painter, showed the influence of Manet.
Mention must be made of Charles Conder (1868-
1909), who derived from Watteau and Fragonard,
and who was perhaps the world's finest painter of
silk fans; Charles Wellington Furse (1869-1904), a
painter in the grand manner of outdoor pictures ;
and Aubrey Beardsley (1872-98), a true genius in
black and white, largely influenced by the Japanese.
Two important influences were the Glasgow and
Newlyn Schools. The former gave us James
Crawhall (1861-1913), whose small output includes some of the finest studies of birds and animals

ever done; and Sir John Lavery (1856-1941), a very
fine portrait painter, as well as many others. The
Newlyn School included, among others, Henry Tuke
(1858-1936), a painter of seascapes and nudes.

The greatest master of the modern English
School, P. Wilson Steer (1860-1942) was a real
Impressionist at first, but in the landscapes for
which he is best known he also showed the influence
of Turner and Constable, with whom many would
class him as a landscape painter. A reproduction
of his " Richmond Castle " appears in page 1191.
Similar in many ways to Wilson Steer, though a
less inspired artist, was Henry Tonks (1862-1937),
a portrait painter who also did delightful " conversation pieces." The Impressionist technique, too,
was exploited by Sir George Clausen (1852-1944).

Other painters who were prominent before the
First World War (1914-18) were Sir William
Rothenstein (1872-1945) and Walter Richard Sickert
(1860-1942). The former, influential as a teacher
and notable as a writer besides, achieved many
fine portrait-drawings, and a large number of oils.
Sickert, an experimenter in many styles, has had a
great influence on English painting, himself having
developed from Impressionism. An artist whose
work has been more appreciated abroad than at
home, where he is best known as an etcher and
mural decorator, is Sir Frank Brangwyn (b. 1867).
He made a break with the trends we have noted,
with his vigorous drawing, rich colour, and romantic
outlook. Sir Charles Holmes (1868-1936), who was
among the first to exploit the possibilities of the
so-called " industrial landscape," Sir Arnesby
Brown (b. 1866), famous for landscapes with cattle,

National Gallery, London
NEVINSON'S REALISM
Noted for his versatility, C. R. W. Nevinson (1889-1946)
emphasized the horrors of mechanical destruction in his
starkly realistic pictures of the First World War (1914-18).
His La Mitrailleuse (The Machine-gun) is a grim study of
French soldiers in a trench.

National Gallery. London

NEW TESTAMENT SCENE BY SPENCER

Born at Cookham-on-Thames, Berkshire, in 1892, Stanley Spencer made the scenery of his native village the setting for works from the New Testament, such as his Nativity, painted in 1912, and Christ Bearing the Cross (above), 1920. He shows sacred characters in contemporary dress, and has exceptional powers of design.

The members of the Camden Town Group which later became the London Group, included Harold Gilman (1876–1919) ; Spencer Gore (1878–1914) ; Charles Ginner (b. 1879), Henry Lamb (b. 1885); Duncan Grant (b. 1885) ; and Percy Wyndham Lewis (b. 1884), who invented " Vorticism," the English version of Cubism. This last is only one of the many " isms " in modern art, all of which have had adherents in Britain. An early disciple of his was William Roberts (b. 1895), whose unusual style has always added interest to his powerfully painted groups. Of sculptors, Henry Moore (b. 1898) was one of the most prominent. His work and that of Frank Dobson (b. 1888) and Jacob Epstein (*q.v.*) are described in the article on Sculpture.

Coming now to a group of painters whose work is of contemporary importance, we find first the brothers John and Paul Nash. Paul Nash (1889–1946), the better-known, was a fine landscape artist, and as the founder of the short-lived "Unit One" he was very influential. John Nash (b. 1893) is also a painter of many fine outdoor subjects. Included in " Unit One," and perhaps the most discussed British painters

and Sir D. Y. Cameron (1865–1945), a famous etcher, are other notable artists of the 20th century.

The modern British School has produced three great portraitists. The first is Ambrose McEvoy (1878–1927), whose portraits show a great interest in light, and have a cleanness of colour and a general air of brightness which in themselves are signs of the new century. They differ widely from those of Sir William Orpen (1878–1931), one of the most successful portrait painters of his day. Besides his portraits Orpen did many other excellent paintings, especially the fine series in the Imperial War Museum, London. As the third of this group we have Augustus John (b. 1879), one of our greatest " *bravura* " painters (those noted for brilliant or ambitious execution). John excels in portraiture. Before the First World War (1914–18) he did some superb etchings, which a few critics were prepared to hail as the greatest, in their way, since Rembrandt. This side of his work is not generally appreciated, however, and it is for such paintings as his Mme. Suggia, in the Tate Gallery, that John is best known. An example of his work appears in page 1192.

Painters whose work aroused much discussion during the years between the First and Second World Wars included Christopher Wood (1901–29), who worked in Brittany and Cornwall; Mark Gertler (1892–1939) ; and C. R. W. Nevinson (1889–1946).

of recent years, were Ben Nicholson, Edward Wadsworth, Matthew Smith, and John Tunnard. The former is the son of William Nicholson (1872–1949), one of the " Beggarstaff " brothers, who with James Pryde (1869–1941) brought about a revolution in poster art, and who became famous for his portraits and still-lifes. Ben Nicholson (b. 1894) concerned chiefly with surfaces and planes, has a quality which marks his paintings as genuine and valuable contributions to British art. Edward Wadsworth (b. 1889) is also a Surrealist. The work of Stanley Spencer (b. 1892) is chiefly allegorical in subject matter; unlike many of his contemporaries, Spencer is interested in his subject, not merely in painting. He is remarkable among his contemporaries for having devoted most of his time to depicting scenes from the New Testament, notably Resurrection Day, in the Tate Gallery, though he dresses his characters in the clothes, and puts them in the scenes, of his native country. He, like the Nash brothers, was greatly influenced by the First World War. The younger British painters influenced by Bonnard and Vuillard, belonging to the Euston Road Group, had a simplicity of approach to natural form untouched by intellectual analysis.

Our strength in water-colour painting and other branches of art, and many of the artists, are discussed under their own headings.

PRICELESS GEMS OF ENGLISH ART

w portraits of husband and wife are so successful as
s, in which William Hogarth (1697–1764) has delight-
ly shown us the famous actor David Garrick (1717–79)
d his wife. Hogarth's paintings, apart from their
at artistic merit, are valuable to students of his times
for the wealth of detail in costume and furnishing which he
always supplies. This painting suffered somewhat from
the artist's temperament, for, when his sitter criticised
the work, Hogarth in a fury disfigured Garrick's face in
the painting, the damage being only party repaired later.

National Gallery

Although Sir Joshua Reynolds (1723–92) was primarily a painter of straightforward portraits, and was at his best when dealing with men of his own age and type, he produced some of his loveliest work when his subjects were children. He had, evidently, some way of putting his small sitters quite at their ease, and in this lovely study the master has caught to perfection the unconscious beauty of a little girl. But the artist's endless experimenting led to the use of materials which have deteriorated (as in the foreground, here), and so we are that much the poorer

GAINSBOROUGH'S FAMOUS 'BLUE BOY'

The story goes that Thomas Gainsborough (1727–88) painted his Blue Boy, here seen, because Sir Joshua Reynolds had proclaimed his opinion that there could be no successful picture of which the main mass was blue. Gainsborough determined that he would prove to his rival that a fine picture in blue was possible. He dressed up his young sitter, Jonathan Buttall, in a blue suit and produced this masterpiece. Done about 1774, it was sold in 1921 to a collector in America, the price being said to be £150,000.

REALISM IN A LOVELY CONSTABLE LANDSCAPE

John Constable (1776–1837) painted The Cornfield in 1826. It is one of the best known of English landscapes, for reproductions of it are to be seen everywhere. The secret of its popularity, like that of many of Constable's works, is probably to be found in the straightforward natural treatment of an absolutely English scene, which brings home to everyone who sees it the brightness and shadow of the country lane, the sun gleaming on the wheat, and the village with its church beyond. Constable's work was as much admired and copied in France as in England.

TWO MASTERPIECES OF MARINE PAINTING

It is interesting to compare the work of John Sell Cotman (1782–1842) with that of John Crome (1768–1821), because both painted East Anglian landscapes. Crome's Moonlight on the Marshes of the Yare is in page 1180, and at the top is Cotman's Wherries on the Yare, with its smoothly constructed pattern in simple masses of colour. This looks strangely simple beside the lower picture, which is one of the masterpieces of J. M. W. Turner (1775–1851)—Ulysses deriding Polyphemus. A typical work in Turner's later manner, it fairly glows with colour.

TYPICAL WORK INSPIRED BY THE PRE-RAPHAELITE MOVEMENT

Founded in 1848 by the artist William Holman Hunt (1827–1910), the purpose of the Pre-Raphaelite Brotherhood was to further a return to the simpler and more natural ideals of painting which were in vogue before the days of Raphael (1483–1520). Leaders of the movement, besides Hunt, were J. E. Millais (1829–96) and Dante Gabriel Rossetti (1828–82). Dante's Dream, seen here, was painted by Rossetti in 1870–71 and is in the Walker Art Gallery, Liverpool. Attention to detail, accuracy of description and truth to Nature were three of the points which the Pre-Raphaelite Brotherhood sought to make in every picture, all displayed in this typical work. The models for most of Rossetti's female figures were his own sister, the poetess Christina Rossetti, and his wife, formerly Elizabeth Eleanor Siddal, whom he married in 1860.

THE ENGLISH SCENE BY OLD & MODERN MASTERS

The work of our first great landscape master Richard Wilson (1714–82), and that of Wilson Steer (1860–1942) are seen here. At the top is Wilson's lovely View in the Wye Valley, which is in the National Gallery, London, and shows well that artist's spirit of quietude and reflection. Such are the breadth and largeness of atmosphere of this painting that it is surprising to learn that it is quite a small picture. Wilson Steer, influenced by Constable and painting in the Impressionist manner, produces an altogether different, more lively and exciting effect in his Richmond Castle (lower). This is in the Tate Galley, London. Steer was awarded the Order of Merit in 1931.

FROM AUGUSTUS JOHN'S VIGOROUS BRUSH

For all its simplicity, both of subject and of treatment, you cannot help feeling that this is the work of a fine painter. It is Augustus John's The Orange Jacket, a typical example of his best work. The strong colouring, simple drawing, and brilliant handling of light and shade are features in which he always excels, and which have helped to make him perhaps the best-known modern painter in Great Britain. Augustus John (born 1878) was elected Royal Academician in 1928 but resigned 10 years later, being re-elected in 1940. He received the Order of Merit in 1942.

The STIRRING STORY of OLD ENGLAND

This continues the history of the English from where the article Britain left off (page 574) down to the Act of Union of 1707, which united England and Scotland. The United Kingdom is dealt with separately in these volumes.

English History. England is less than one-fourth the size of France and only a little larger than Newfoundland. Yet consider her greatness! Did England become great because of her geography, or of her soul? Did she conquer the physical facts around her, or was she made by them? The secret of England's greatness is that she used the facts of her history and geographical situation to build up her great power.

Phoenician merchants from the Mediterranean came in galleys rowed by slaves chained to the oars—through the narrow Strait of Gibraltar, up the Spanish coast, and on to a little-known land only 21 miles across the sea from Gaul (modern France). There they found strange, wild, blue-eyed people, dressed in hides, with shields of skin so thick and hard that an arrow could scarcely penetrate. These people wore leather sandals and leggings, and stained their bodies with a blue weed called woad. They belonged to the race which we call Celts (Kelts). They themselves were styled Britons and the island Britain (*q.v.*).

What the Phoenicians wanted especially from Britain was its tin, so necessary in making the bronze tools and weapons used in that distant age. Greek merchants from Marseilles (in southern Gaul) also visited Britain, and the Romans learned of it. Julius Caesar (55 and 54 B.C.) was the first Roman to lead an expedition to these shores, and he did so because the Britons were continually crossing the narrow waters of the English Channel and helping the Gauls, whom Caesar was then striving to conquer. His first landing was not far from the white cliffs of Dover.

When Julius Caesar came on his second expedition he penetrated up the Thames to a muddy village where the Celts lived in thatch-roofed cabins by dank swamps and thick forests, near what is now London. It was not until nearly 100 years after Caesar (A.D. 43) that the Emperor Claudius sent an expedition which began the real conquest of the island. Only the southern half was actually conquered and organized as a Roman province. To keep back the savage Picts and Scots of the north, the Emperor Hadrian (A.D. 122) built a great wall across the narrow neck of the island from Solway Firth to Wallsend-on-Tyne in Northumberland.

South of the Roman Wall, the Romans built roads and walled cities.

They taught the Britons how to grow oats and barley and wheat, and the upper classes became Romanized. For more than 300 years the Britons were under the civilizing influence of the Romans.

During this time soldiers and traders introduced the Christian religion, and here and there arose its chapels. Then about A.D. 407 the last of the Roman legions withdrew, for Rome was now in conflict with hordes of Teutonic barbarians.

Left to themselves, the Britons found they had well-nigh forgotten how to fight, and were unable

INVADERS OF ENGLAND'S SHORES

When the Romans held England they left as their mark well-built roads, many of which have survived until the present day. Here the brush of the artist has shown some of those who have travelled the Roman roads : the British chieftain with his coat of skins, the Roman legionary, the Saxon thane, the Dane with his horned helmet, and the Norman knight.

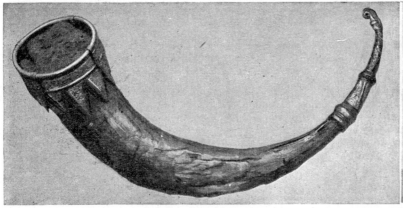

British Museum

DRINKING-VESSELS OF SAXON ENGLAND

The Teutonic races who conquered Britain were great beer-drinkers. The bronze-mounted drinking-horn (left) was found in the burial-mound of a great chief at Taplow, by the Thames. Probably he had to drink up his ale or mead at a single draught, for it was difficult to lay the vessel on the table unless it was empty. Such vessels were made from cows' horns, and were often two feet long. The bronze stoup on the right was found at Long Wittenham, Berkshire

to unite under a single government. When their old enemies the Picts and Scots began to attack them, they were in despair. From the Continent came heathen sea-rovers of the German tribes—Angles and Jutes and Saxons—beginning their conquests about A.D. 449, when the brothers Hengist and Horsa landed in Kent. In the course of the next 250 years the newcomers possessed themselves of the whole of Angle-land, or England (Engel-land), so named from the invading Angles.

Two centuries later (A.D. 829) the scattered English kingdoms were for the first time united into a single kingdom, soon to be made illustrious by the name of Alfred (see Alfred the Great). Danish raids and settlements troubled the land for over a century, but Alfred checked their advance and his successors reconquered the territory in which these Northmen had settled. In the 11th century there was a second wave of Danish conquest, and, under Canute (q.v.) and his two sons the whole of England was for a quarter of a century under Danish rule. But presently the old Saxon line was restored in the person of Edward the Confessor (c. 1005–66).

Then in 1066 came the Norman Conquest. William of Normandy, claiming that he had been promised the throne of England, defeated and killed the elected King Harold at the battle of Hastings, and conquered the country. Half the land was divided among William's followers. Everyone who received or kept land directly from the king (the barons) had to swear allegiance to him and supply him with soldiers. This is known as the Feudal System. But in the next 150 years the Normans became English. The old laws and customs and language of the Anglo-Saxons triumphed over the Norman-French, though considerably changed. By that time the Plantagenet kings, descended from the Conqueror's granddaughter, were reigning.

The kings never made new laws or managed to get money in new ways without consulting a Council of the leading men—a Saxon fashion. When King John (1167–1216) tried to do otherwise the powerful barons made him set his seal to Magna Carta (1215), which meant that no one, not even the king, had a right to break the law, or to change it without the Council's consent.

Later the Council became Parliament. Members elected to represent the bigger towns and the

By permission of the British Academy
SAXON KING AND HIS THANES

This illustration, purporting to represent 'Nimrod the mighty hunter,' actually shows an Anglo-Saxon king among his courtiers. It is taken from a manuscript copy of some religious poems by Caedmon, the Anglo-Saxon poet, whose story is given in page 650.

Everywhere, except among the Celts in Wales and Scotland, the Latin language, Roman civilization and the Christian religion practically disappeared. A Teutonic speech and Teutonic institutions—brought with them by the invaders—took their place. Christianity was soon introduced again, chiefly by Augustine and his companions, who landed in Kent in the year 597.

counties or shires were summoned to attend it, as well as the greater barons whose right to attend was already established by custom. This change was made by Edward I in 1295. Soon after that, Parliament (*q.v.*) was divided into two bodies, the House of Commons and the House of Lords. The Hundred Years' War with France (1338–1453) and the Wars of the Roses (1455–85) are described in separate articles.

When Columbus in 1492 discovered the West Indies for Spain, the Tudor king Henry VII (1457–1509) was on the English throne.

The English, a nation of sea-rovers, with harbours on the Channel, on the Humber, on the Thames, on the Bristol Channel, had the love of the sea and the love of freedom in their souls. They were born seafarers, and seized upon the opportunities offered by the New World. London, although a great mart for traders, was little more than a small town sprawling on both sides of the Thames; Liverpool was a village; Bristol was a seafaring town of perhaps 10,000 people.

In 1588 something else happened in Europe to change this little island's destiny. England defeated the great Spanish Armada (*see* Armada, Spanish) through the leadership of those very sea-rovers, who already, in the person of Sir Francis Drake, had explored distant oceans and sailed around the world.

This left England mistress of the seas. The sea was her wall against forays and wars which devastated continental Europe. Her greatness was dependent upon her sea power; and in her sons was the passion for freedom of a race that had learned to fight and die for the liberty of their land.

Wars and persecutions of Protestants on the Continent were driving the suffering peoples abroad; and to many of these, under the influence of her own adoption of Protestantism, England became a place of refuge. Flemings had already come from the Netherlands and taught the English the arts of weaving, lace-making, metal work and watch-making. Exiled French Huguenots carried to England the secrets of French manufactures—and hatred of their king, Louis XIV (1638–1715). Jews from as far east as Constantinople established themselves in England in the days of Cromwell, who tolerated their re-admission and helped to make London a centre of banking.

At the death of Queen Elizabeth in 1603 England had attained a position of great prosperity, and she added to her strength by uniting with Scotland in 1603, in which year Elizabeth was succeeded by James VI of Scotland, the great-grandson of Henry VIII's elder sister Margaret. King James, who ascended the English throne as James I, sometimes tried to ignore Parliament, though a wholesome

From a painting by Herbert Bone

DANISH SEA-ROVERS SIGHTED OFF THE ENGLISH SHORE

To our ancestors, the Danish and Norsemen sea-rovers of the 8th, 9th and 10th centuries were destructive enemies of the peaceful life which the Saxons preferred. Every summer the Saxons maintained a specially careful watch around their coast, for it was then that the Danes made their raids and had to be stopped from gaining a footing on English soil. In this painting a Danish fleet has appeared offshore, and Saxons are gathering to repel the raiders.

DEATH OF HAROLD, THE LAST SAXON KING

Pierced through the eye by a Norman arrow, King Harold fell at Hastings in 1066. He might have won this battle, but he had just had to deal with the Norsemen at Stamford Bridge, and his earls failed him in the hour of England's need. William the Conqueror's victory was commemorated in the Bayeux Tapestry, of which this illustration is a portion events of that time were worked into it by order of William's half-brother Odo, bishop of Bayeux. *See page 378*

fear of being driven to fighting kept him from over-stepping the limits of English endurance. But he destroyed the basis of mutual goodwill between the Crown and the people, which had been the foundation of the Tudors' apparently despotic authority.

Charles I (1600–49) reaped the bitter fruits of his father's acts. The Parliaments of the Stuarts were only too ready to quarrel with the monarch. Charles gave them grounds for this by entrusting the direction of policy to his favourite, George Villiers, Duke of Buckingham; by standing on what he regarded as his legal rights of raising

revenue without the sanction of Parliament; and by repressing religious toleration, enforcing his will through the Star Chamber and High Commission.

In 1628 Parliament compelled the king to accept the Petition of Right, but this failed in its precise purpose—the accurate definition of the royal pre-rogative (the king's rights and privileges). Eleven years of arbitrary rule without Parliament were ended in 1640 by rebellion in Scotland, which regarded itself as quite independent of England.

The Long Parliament, instead of aiding him against the Scots, proceeded to force the king to accept the abolition of the arbitrary courts and the loss of the disputed prerogatives. The attempted arrest by the king of five members of Parliament on January 4, 1642, failed. The king left London, and after months of futile negotiation with Parliament the Civil War opened in August 1642.

After some indecisive fighting and skirmishing the army of the Parliament was reorganized by Oliver Cromwell and won the great victory of Naseby on June 14, 1645. Charles surrendered to the Scots, who had associated themselves with the cause of the Parliament, in May 1646; was handed over by them to the Parliament in February 1647

British Museum

MAGNA CARTA : FOUNDATION OF ENGLISH LIBERTY

Magna Carta was something more than a treaty forced upon a tyrannical king by his discontented barons. It was the document which decided the principles on which Britain has been governed ever since. The lower illustration is a copy of part of the document. Above it is a fragment of the original, with King John's seal on it. John did not 'sign' the charter, for he could not write ; he put his seal to it—at Runnymede, in Surrey, on June 15, 1215

MEDIEVAL SCHOOLROOM: AND WAT TYLER'S END

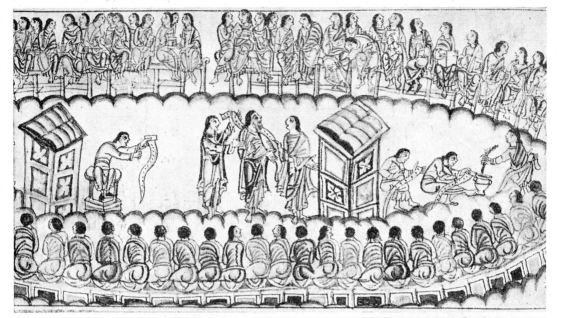

Trinity College, Cambridge; Johnes, Froissart's Chronicles

When King Richard II (1367–1400) met Wat Tyler and his rebels at Smithfield, London, on June 15, 1381, Tyler's attitude towards the king (centre foreground in lower illustration, wearing a crown) was so threatening that William Walworth, Lord Mayor of London, struck him with a dagger, though this contemporary print from a French manuscript shows Walworth using an immense sword. According to history Walworth did not kill Tyler, who was despatched as he lay on the ground by John Sandwich, one of the king's squires. In the top picture, Eadwine, a monk of Christ Church, Canterbury, gives us a glimpse of a 12th century English schoolroom.

and was carried off into the custody of the army on June 3 of that year. From his place of confinement he intrigued with his own supporters and negotiated with three separate groups—the chiefs of the Parliament, those of the army, and the Scots— each of whom now had different objects in view. His attempt to escape to France, coupled with Cavalier (supporters of King Charles) insurrections, and a Scots invasion in 1648, gave the army complete control in England, and determined its chiefs that the king's death was necessary. He was tried and condemned to death, and was executed on January 30, 1649.

England was now proclaimed a Commonwealth. The Scots recalled the prince who was the rightful Charles II, but the Common-

ARK ROYAL
Lord Howard of Effingham's flagship when he led the British fleet against the Spanish Armada in 1588 was the Ark Royal, seen in a contemporary woodcut.

wealth could not have the claimant to the throne of England seated on the throne of Scotland. A war with the Scots culminated in Cromwell's victory at Worcester (September 3, 1651), but Charles made his escape from the country. The remnant, or "rump," of the Long Parliament, which had constituted itself the ruling body by its own authority, sought to transform itself into a permanent government, but was forcibly ejected by Cromwell in April 1653; and from that time Cromwell was virtually absolute ruler.

Cromwell's government was necessarily despotic, but it strove at least to be as just as the circumstances permitted, while his vigorous foreign policy made England feared on the Continent.

With Cromwell's death in 1658 came chaos, and it was with general satisfaction that Charles II was recalled to the throne in 1660.

But the Restoration did not mean the triumph of the Stuart idea of monarchy. The country intended Parliament to be predominant,

British Museum

JAMES I AND HIS PARLIAMENT
King James the First is seen enthroned in the House of Lords. The old engraving shows that at that time the Commons were separated from the Lords only by a barrier, the top of which is just visible in the foreground. Earls, barons and bishops are grouped around the Chancellor's seat, which is vacant and placed in front of the throne.

CHARLES THE FIRST AND HIS EXILED SON'S RETURN

British Museum

On May 26, 1660, Charles II (son of Charles I) landed at Dover after his long exile. According to the English diarist, Samuel Pepys (1633–1703), he was welcomed by General Monk who helped to put Charles on the English throne and later was created Duke of Albemarle in recognition of his services. This contemporary print shows that Charles was accorded an enthusiastic reception; a modern treatment of the same incident is given in page 1207.

In 1648 there appeared a pamphlet entitled ' Discours du bon et leial subject ' (Discourse of a good and loyal subject) which contained this picture of Charles I in the House of Lords. Behind the king on the right is the Chancellor, on the left is the Treasurer. The official on the left holding the crown is the Grand Chamberlain, and on the right is the Constable with a sword. A herald wearing a tabard with the Royal arms is in the right foreground.

James II (1633–1701) with "all the cards in his hands," but he did not know how to play them. The loyalty of the country was turned first into uneasiness and then into grim hostility. When James alienated ardent Royalists and fervent Churchmen by arbitrarily suspending or overriding the law in order to help the Roman Catholic Church, men of every party joined in calling to their aid his Protestant son-in-law, William of Orange.

William landed in Tor Bay, Devonshire, on November 5, 1688. James took flight, and on February 13, 1689, William and Mary were proclaimed king and queen of England, having accepted the Declaration of Right which laid down what were to be in future the fundamental limitations of the power of the Crown—limitations which were put forward as the historic right of the people.

JAMES II'S FLIGHT TO FRANCE

Succeeding his brother Charles II in 1685, James II soon made himself unpopular by his attempts to aid the Roman Catholics ; and in 1688 Parliament invited William of Orange to take the throne. James fled to France, and this engraving by Romeyn de Hooghe (c. 1646–1708) shows him embarking at Whitehall.

and with regard to legislation and taxation the king found that it was neither to be cajoled nor overridden. And Parliament, rendered by the Puritan rule of the Commonwealth intensely hostile to Puritanism, proved no less hostile to Roman Catholicism, much to the surprise and disappointment of Charles, who had promised himself and his cousin, Louis XIV of France, the restoration of the Roman Catholic Church.

Under the mask of frivolity Charles concealed an invincible determination to avoid openly fighting with Parliament, but to make himself entirely independent of it by secretly selling himself and his country to the King of France. For 25 years he successfully deceived statesmen, courtiers, politicians, both English and foreign, and the King of France. On March 28, 1681, with Louis XIV's money in his pocket, he dissolved his last Parliament at the moment when its leaders imagined that he was fast in their grip. In 21 years he had built up a standing army sufficient for his purposes. In the following years he obtained virtually absolute control over the Parliamentary elections.

Charles had secured the succession to his Roman Catholic brother, James. His death left

Scotland followed suit, with the result that the crown remained united.

The accession of William, the lifelong enemy of Louis XIV, carried England into the midst of international politics. The ascendancy of the English navy, long disputed by Holland and now for a moment challenged by France, was decisively established with the battle of La Hogue in 1692. The right of Parliament to fix the course of the succession to the throne was won. The State system of finance was reconstructed by the creation of the National Debt and the Bank of England.

William died on March 8, 1702, at the moment when England was about to be plunged into the War of the Spanish Succession (1702–14). He was succeeded by Anne, the second daughter of James II, under whom that war was fought out to its end. But another issue had arisen. Scotland demanded a permanent union with England upon terms which would be agreeable to herself. On May 1, 1707, the Act of Union came into effect. From that hour the history of England as a sovereign State is merged in the history of Great Britain. In this book it will be found under the heading of United Kingdom.

National Portrait Gallery, London

QUEEN ANNE

Born in 1665, Anne married Prince George of Denmark in 1683. This portrait by Michael Dahl (1656–1743) shows her at the age of 30, with her son William, Duke of Gloucester. *See* also illustration in page 164.

The first people from the Mediterranean to trade with England were the Phoenicians. Their country was the narrow land, north of Palestine, between Mount Lebanon and the sea. Their skill as shipbuilders and navigators gave them a supremacy over all rivals in seaborne commerce ; they alone among seamen passed out of the Mediterranean, and by the 5th century B.C. they had coasted along France and Spain and had even penetrated as far as the Baltic. In their voyages they discovered the ' Tin Islands '—the Scilly Isles and Cornwall—and traded with the early Britons. In this picture by Lord Leighton (1830–96) Phoenician merchants are bargaining with a Cornish family.

KING ALFRED THE GREAT IN THE DANISH CAMP

From the painting by Bone

Many legends and stories have centred round the name of Alfred the Great (849–901), and one of them tells how he himself spied out the strength of the Danes. Disguised as a minstrel and carrying a small harp, he penetrated into the Danes' camp and wandered about entertaining them with his simple songs. The Danes were so delighted that they were loath to let the king go, but when at last he got away he knew the strength of the Danish army and the plans of its leaders. Returning to his own people he gathered a fresh army and defeated the Danes in battle.

VICTORY AND DEFEAT OF THE DANISH INVADERS

After their landing in East Anglia the Danes gradually forced their way westward. This painting by the Danish artist Lorentz Frolich shows the sacking of Tavistock by the invaders in 997. The magnificent Abbey was burned; the people were robbed of their goods and livestock, and many were carried captives to the Danish camp. Five years later the long-suffering English retaliated in a great massacre of the Danes in Wessex.

While the Danes were in England there was frequent fighting between them and the English. Manchester, which was originally a Roman fort, became an early English settlement, but was taken by the Danes. Years of strife followed until in 923 the Danes were finally driven out. The fighting during the expulsion is shown in this painting by F. Madox Brown (1821–74). From the window of the house a woman is pouring boiling water on the fleeing enemy, for though the weapons of those times were primitive no device that could injure the foe was neglected by the defenders.

THE CONQUEROR GRANTS LONDON ITS CHARTER

After the defeat and death of Harold at Hastings in 1066, the people of London acknowledged Norman William as king. At this ceremony of homage to their royal master, 'William the Bishop and Gosfrith the Portrieve' are receiving the new London charter from the Norman Conqueror. William's wife, the princess Matilda, of the Anglo-Saxon royal line, being a descendant of Alfred the Great, is on his right.

KING JOHN ACCEPTS MAGNA CARTA

The foundation of English liberties was the Great Charter which was drawn up after years of revolt and fighting between the barons and King John, and was based on the series of demands that the barons had presented. On June 15, 1215, John met the barons at Runnymede, a meadow between Windsor and Staines, and accepted their demands. This illustration shows King John just before the charter was sealed.

ILL-FATED CHARLES STANDS ON THE SCAFFOLD

From a painting by E. Crofts

Charles I's trial, condemnation and beheading followed in quick succession in January 1649. As at his trial, so in his last hours he displayed remarkable dignity. He crossed from St. James's to Whitehall, and at the execution stepped on to the scaffold from a window of the Banqueting Hall. Troops were assembled in front, and behind them stood the sorrowing people, who were too far away to catch the last words of the king. In the picture, the executioner is waiting while Charles converses with Bishop Juxon to whom he entrusted his last mysterious message, 'Remember!'

TRIUMPH AND FAILURE OF THE LAST STUART KINGS

After many years of exile Charles II landed at Dover, when his restoration had been made possible by the Declaration of Breda. The king set sail on a warship, the Naseby, renamed the Royal Charles, on May 24, 1660, and landed at Dover on May 26. This engraving, after Benjamin West, shows General Monk receiving Charles on his landing.

The arrest, trial and acquittal of the seven bishops in 1688, and the rumour that James II was trying to impose on the people as his son a child who, it was said, had been brought into the palace in a warming-pan, finally turned public opinion against the last of the Stuarts. Leaders of all political parties combined in offering the crown to William of Orange, Stadtholder of Holland, James II's nephew and son-in-law. William accepted, and this picture by E. M. Ward shows the scene in the Palace of Whitehall when the news of his landing was broken to James.

'GLORIOUS REVOLUTION' AND 'ACT OF UNION'

Though he was hailed as a deliverer from the tyranny of James II, William's succession to the throne of England, brought about by the 'Glorious Revolution' of 1688, was approved only after long discussion in Parliament. This engraving shows the presentation of the crown to William, beside whom sits Mary, his wife and joint Sovereign.

Commissioners from the two kingdoms of England and Scotland drafted the Articles of Union and finished their work in 1706. By the Act of Union of 1707, the Scottish parliament was abolished. Henceforth Scottish representatives were to be sent to Westminster, 16 to the Lords and 45 to the Commons. Scotland, however, retained its own laws and courts of justice. By separate acts, incorporated with the Act of Union, it was provided that the two Churches should remain independent. In this illustration Queen Anne is shown in council, receiving the Articles of Union.

English Language.

There is an old saying in Europe that Italian is the language to use when you want to sing, French when you want to make love, and English when you want to do business. English is good for many other uses besides business. Indeed, it is one of the richest languages spoken today, with more variety than almost any other, and it is spread over a greater part of the earth's surface.

English is made up, like the people who developed it, of many national inheritances and foreign importations, and its history and growth make a very interesting study. Have you ever dug a hole beside a stream and seen the different layers you find as you dig—sand and gravel and small stones one above the other? If you look well into the English language you will find that it was formed in much the same way.

Of course, the words are all mixed together, so that often in a single sentence you will use words that come from all the different layers. If you say, for instance, "My mother received a good telegram," you have used words from four different sources. "Mother" is a very old word and comes from the original Indo-European root language; "received" is a word of Latin origin; "good" is a Teutonic or Anglo-Saxon word; and "telegram" is from the Greek.

English is classified as a Teutonic or Germanic language. This is not because more of our words are Teutonic, but because the Teutonic words are the framework of the language, the connecting words and the simple, fundamental names of ordinary things. So that, in spite of the fact that only one-fourth of our words in the dictionary are Teutonic, in ordinary speech about four-fifths of the words we use are Teutonic. Another reason is that we put our words together with the grammatical construction of the Teutonic languages.

For Common People and the Rich

After the Teutonic words the most important are the words of Latin origin, which have come to us either from the Latin direct, or through the French or Italian or Spanish, but especially the French. These words have a different feeling from the Teutonic words when you know them. They are more polished, more stylish—you might say more precise. The Normans, who spoke French, came over and conquered England and ruled over the Teutonic people, the Anglo-Saxons, who lived here. So it came about that the words the common people used stayed Anglo-Saxon or Teutonic, and those of the wealthy or ruling classes became Latin.

For instance, as long as a sheep was alive and was tended by the shepherds, who were common people, it was called by the Teutonic word "sheep," but as soon as it was cooked and came on the table of the noble classes, it became "mutton," a French word. In the same way, "cow" is Anglo-Saxon, and "beef" is French; "hog" is Anglo-Saxon, and "pork" is from the language of the conquerors. The influence of the Church, the classical Renaissance of the 16th century, and the later coining of scientific terms from the Latin greatly increased this element in English.

One great advantage which English has over many other languages is the ease with which it forms new words out of old by simply joining them together, as in "rainfall," "railway," "backslide," "outcome," "daisy" (from "day's eye"). It is also rich in prefixes and suffixes which can be added to existing words to modify their meaning.

Thus we form nouns by the use of such suffixes as -ness, -dom, -age, -tion, -ment, -or, giving us such words as "wickedness," "kingdom," "breakage," "accusation," "amazement," "actor." The suffixes -al, -ic, -ous, -able, -ful, etc., are used to form adjectives, as "critical," "pedantic," "famous," "approachable," "tuneful." The prefixes anti-, pro-, re-, inter-, un-, and a host of others enable us to make such useful words as "antiseptic," "Pro-German," "reclassify," "intermarry," "unnecessary."

In general, the words of Latin origin are not so strong or so full of meaning as the Teutonic words. For instance, the Anglo-Saxon "friendship" has its Latin equivalent "amity," which means just the same thing, but it is a pale word and not nearly so good for most purposes. In poetry, where the colour of words is very important, Anglo-Saxon words are usually better than Latin words. But the Latin words have the advantage of being more exact.

From Many Places for Many Uses

The Greek words are much fewer in number and are largely scientific words, like "geology." We have a number of Dutch words, particularly about the sea, like "schooner"; Scandinavian words (mostly from the old Danish conquest), like "earl," "window," "egg," "husband," "sky"; a few American Indian words, like "tomahawk"; a good many from the Arabic, like "alcohol" and "algebra"; and an assortment of odd words such as "alligator" (Spanish), "tea" (Chinese) and "orange" (Persian). We have a few words invented to describe new things, like "television" and "aeroplane." Others, like "buzz," "splash," "cluck," are imitations of the sound of things. Some words are names of people, like "sandwich," which came from the Earl of Sandwich, who is said to have been too busy gambling to eat regular meals, and "boycott," from the name of the Irish land agent who was its first victim.

The language of the old Britons was Celtic, and traces survive in modern Welsh, still the tongue of Wales. When the Romans conquered England they introduced a certain number of Latin words in the three centuries that they ruled the island. When the Anglo-Saxons came over from the north of Europe they brought with them their own Teutonic language, which is the basis of English, with some admixture of Celtic and Latin from the conquered inhabitants. The earliest written examples of this Anglo-Saxon language are from the 7th century.

The periods in the development of the English language are called Old English (or Anglo-Saxon), Middle English, and Modern English. Old English was spoken until about A.D. 1100, and was very highly inflected—that is, it had a complicated system of grammatical changes to indicate case, number, person, tense and the like. Middle English was spoken from about 1100 to about 1500, and was much less highly inflected; and Modern English, which has developed since 1500, has lost its inflexions almost entirely. In Modern English there has been an almost entire disappearance of the forms in er and en which were earlier used as plurals. In Middle English, for example, the plural

³ T 3

of "eye" was "eyen." "Oxen" and "children" are almost the only survivals of this form.

There have always been—and are today in fact, though now they are only dialects—three varieties of English spoken in England: Northern, Southern, and Midland English. Northern English was important in the very early days and later developed into the Scottish dialect, such as you find in Robert Burns's poems. Southern English was the most important in the Old English period, especially under King Alfred. Modern English developed

out of Midland English in the Middle English period. Chaucer, who wrote in Midland English, and the Authorized Version of the Bible and the English Book of Common Prayer did much to set Modern English in the form it now has.

A modern system, devised by C. K. Ogden, known as Basic English, simplifies the language for the foreigner by reducing the vocabulary to 850 essential words and a few simple rules of grammar. Words and phrases of Latin derivation are avoided, those of Saxon origin being used instead.

Our GOLDEN STORE of PROSE & POETRY

From Chaucer to Shaw the sky of English literature is studded with stars to which all the peoples of the world look with admiration. Here is a guide to this national treasury of which we are all heirs.

English Literature. Nearly 1,500 years ago, when the Angles and Saxons still lived in Jutland and along the North Sea shores, and spoke a Teutonic language that no one can read now without special study, English literature was born in what we would now term humble circumstances.

In the middle of the 5th century these peoples —the Anglo-Saxons— came to Britain, conquered the Celtic inhabitants and drove them westward into Wales. They brought with them tales in verse sung by wandering minstrels. Beowulf, one of these anonymous tales of heroic adventure, was written down by some unknown scribe, and thus becomes the first landmark in English literature. The first poet whose name has come down to us was Caedmon, a labourer in St. Hilda's monastery at Whitby, Yorkshire, who made a metrical translation of parts of the Scriptures about the year 670. The greatest prose writer in Anglo-Saxon was King Alfred, who translated Latin books for his people and started the Anglo-Saxon Chronicle. Among his translations is an English version of Bede's Ecclesiastical History.

The Normans, who conquered England in 1066, brought with them the French language. But being of the same original stock as the English they gradually united with them, and the language of the country became English modified and enriched by French. Wycliffe's translation of the Bible (1380), the most important prose work of the 14th century, set a standard of English prose and made it the people's language of religious thought. During those years while the language was forming, the old Welsh legends of King Arthur became popular, chiefly through the Latin writings of Geoffrey of Monmouth. To the same century belongs The Vision of Piers Plowman, by William Langland.

In 1623 appeared the first edition of Shakespeare's works, and on the title page was this picture of the Elizabethan poet.

Geoffrey Chaucer (1340?–1400) is England's earliest great poet. He belongs to the springtime of English poetry. His best-known work, Canterbury Tales, gives us pictures of people who lived in England then, all journeying on a pilgrimage in April, telling stories to pass the time, while—

. . . smale fowles maken melodye
That slepen all the night with open eye,

and the fresh and charming English countryside blossoms around them in all its beauty.

The years of the 15th century, after Chaucer, though they showed in England no important writings, were a busy time of preparation. All Europe was awakening to the renewal of classical learning, for the Greek and Roman literature lost to western Europe for nearly 1,000 years was now brought to light. The invention of printing, brought to England by William Caxton in 1476, made it possible to spread books and knowledge far and wide. The world was growing larger, for that century saw the beginnings of the age of voyages of exploration and geographical discovery. Other men were seeking truth in religion, and the Reformation was being prepared.

In England the New Learning was represented by the famous Dutch scholar Erasmus (who came to England in 1497); by John Colet, the learned and lovable Dean of St. Paul's; and by Sir Thomas More. More's Utopia, though written in Latin, reflects English thought about society and religion. The Reformation enriched the English language, for William Tyndale's translation of the Bible helped to fix the standard of English speech and literary style. There was little new poetry in that time, but Caxton's printing press spread the works of Chaucer and other native poets of genius. Caxton printed, too, Sir Thomas Malory's Morte d'Arthur, an English prose translation of Arthurian legends compiled from French sources. In the lowlands of Scotland lyric poetry was written, the best by William Dunbar ; and this Scottish strain, with its warmth of feeling and love of Nature, was a powerful influence on the writers of a later day.

All these new influences—renaissance of learning, religious reformation, travel, discovery, invention— worked slowly but decisively on English literature. Then, in Elizabeth's reign (1558–1603) they flowered in the most wonderful creative period in the history of English writing. Poems, ballads, masques

NOAH'S ARK IN A SAXON BOOK

To Caedmon, Anglo-Saxon poet of the 7th century, are attributed the Biblical poems which were collected about A.D.1000 in the Caedmon Manuscript. Here is Noah's Ark, drawn like a Saxon warship by the 11th century illustrator.

and pageants, the ancient classics and new romances and verse forms brought home by travellers in Italy, stories of voyages, books of religious reform, the Bible in English—all supplied inspiration, and England became a land of poets.

Edmund Spenser's Faerie Queene finely embodies the freshness, and beauty of the age. It is a long story-poem of the adventures of the Red Cross Knight and other knights who personify the virtues fighting against evil.

For centuries the drama had been growing up gradually, through the "mystery," "miracle," and "morality" plays presented to teach the people Bible stories, the lives of saints and the moral virtues. The real English drama began to appear in the later 16th century. One of the early playwrights, Christopher Marlowe, whose most famous works are Tamburlaine the Great, and Doctor Faustus, was probably the greatest pioneer in English literature, and Shakespeare owed much to him.

Shakespeare, the greatest dramatist of all time, " touched life at all points," and something of what he saw and felt went into his plays. King and queen and peasant, wise man and fool, of his own time and of the past, walk before us. We sound the depths of human tragedy in Hamlet and King Lear; revel in fairyland in A Midsummer Night's Dream; laugh uproariously with Falstaff in The Merry Wives of Windsor, and wonder at the peaceful beauty of The Tempest. Shakespeare touches every emotion and speaks to all times and nations. Through him England reached its supreme poetic expression.

After Shakespeare's death drama and poetry greatly declined. Ben Jonson wrote carefully wrought plays and lovely songs; Beaumont and Fletcher were dramatists with flashes of extreme vigour and beauty; but none had the precious gift of supreme genius.

The times of James I and Charles I, in which the Elizabethan impulse greatly persisted despite the rising tides of Puritanism, produced many beautiful lyrics, such as those of Herrick, Lovelace, and Suckling. George Herbert, Henry Vaughan, Abraham Cowley, and George Wither found inspiration in religion. The most important prose writer of the period, the one who still speaks to us as forcefully as he did to those in his own time, was Francis Bacon, whose Essays will " live as long as books last," as he himself foretold.

The Puritan standards in religion, morals and government, which had been gaining power, at last prevailed in the Civil War (1642–1648) between Crown and Parliament. In the main the Puritan age which followed was more favourable to the development of prose than of poetry, for philosophy, religion and government were constant subjects of thought and controversy. Yet, though the age was one of argument and contention, it produced Milton, who stands next to Shakespeare in the galaxy of the greatest English poets.

In his early poems, like Il Penseroso and L'Allegro, Milton's genius is more akin to the spirit of the Elizabethan age than to that of his own time. In his Areopagitica (on the freedom of the Press) and other prose writings, he serves the cause of liberty. In his magnificent epic poem Paradise Lost, written in the noblest of blank verse, he expresses the Puritan spirit at its loftiest and best.

Another great Puritan, who stands with Milton as a representative of the age, was John Bunyan, the nonconformist preacher who wrote Pilgrim's Progress. This story of Christian's journey from the City of Destruction to the heavenly country is an allegory full of meaning and charm. It has been translated into more languages than any book save the Bible. Three quaint books of the time, sometimes read now for their wisdom and pleasant fancy, are Robert Burton's Anatomy of Melancholy, Sir

ILLUSTRATION TO SPENSER'S POEM

Dedicated to Sir Philip Sidney (1554–86), English soldier and poet, Edmund Spenser's Shepheardes Calendar, published in 1579 under the pen-name of Immerito, contains illustrated poems for each month, the picture above belonging to February. Spenser is best known as the author of the Faerie Queene.

A COMMAND PERFORMANCE OF SHAKESPEARE

In Queen Elizabeth's time the Sovereign and the Court never visited the theatres, which were the haunts of pickpockets and breeding-grounds for the plague and other ills. Instead, as sometimes nowadays, command performances were given before the Queen at her palace. This purely imaginary conception shows William Shakespeare reading a scene from one of his plays to Elizabeth. Her reign was the most wonderful creative period in English literature

Thomas Browne's Religio Medici, and Izaak Walton's fascinating Compleat Angler, the latter having been called " The Bible of Fishermen."

With the return of the Stuarts in 1660, and the removal of Puritan restraints, some forms of literature showed a natural reaction. The drama especially reflected the loose living and frivolity of the court life. The more serious poetry and prose underwent great changes. Writers felt less and had less to say; so they gave less attention to *what* they said than *how* they said it, emphasizing especially directness of style.

John Dryden, " the greatest man in a little age," led in the new poetry. His Absalom and Achitophel is the greatest political satire in the language. Dryden also wrote plays, but his great influence has been through his critical essays, which helped to form modern prose style. Samuel Butler's Hud-

ibras was a fiercely satiric poem against Puritanism. In their diaries, Evelyn and Samuel Pepys give " the very taste and colour of life " in their times.

There were also far-reaching developments in science, and the Royal Society was incorporated in 1662. Sir Isaac Newton's Principia began a new age in science, while John Locke's Essay Concerning the Human Understanding opened new fields in philosophy as his Essays on Government opened new fields in political thought.

In the early 18th century, under Queen Anne, standards of personal and political morality were low, and there was very little left of the old Puritan loftiness of purpose. Writers were weak in feeling and imagination, and turned largely to satire and criticism. But they laid increasing emphasis on perfection in literary form, developing a beautifully polished prose style. Because of this, the period is one of the great

National Portrait Gallery

JOHN MILTON

One of the greatest English poets, Milton became blind in 1654. Here he is shown after he had suffered this infliction. His daughters and friends read to him, and took down at his dictation Paradise Lost and Paradise Regained.

ages in the history of English literature. Alexander Pope was the outstanding poet, brilliant in satire and criticism. In his Essay on Criticism, his Rape of the Lock, his savage satire The Dunciad, and his verse translation of Homer, he used the rhymed couplet (then considered the perfect verse, for irregularity and lack of smoothness were counted barbaric faults).

But the reign of Anne was pre-eminently an age of prose. The most original writer of the day and one of the most powerful satirists of all time was Jonathan Swift, author of Gulliver's Travels, which bitterly and mercilessly holds up to scorn Man's faults and weaknesses. The periodical essay as developed by Addison and Steele was a new form of writing, which was the ancestor of the modern novel, magazine, and newspaper.

These two men wrote for the Tatler and the Spectator essays on English life, morals and manners, ridiculing gently the failings of the age and bringing a cultivation and good breeding into clubs, coffee-houses and homes. Sir Roger de Coverley, the English country gentleman, immortalized in a group of the Spectator papers, is a well-loved character. Addison's kindly humour and elegance make his essays delightful reading.

The tone of Addison's work is one evidence of changes working in morals and literature. There was warmer feeling in religion, and great emotional preachers like Whitefield and the Wesleys soon were reaching the working classes. Interest in romance and Nature reappeared, in the period 1740–80, in Macpherson's professed translation of the epics of the Gaelic Ossian, and in Bishop Percy's collection of old ballads, the Reliques of Ancient English Poetry. Love of Nature animated the poems of William Collins, James Thomson, and Thomas Gray, author of the Elegy in a Country Churchyard. Oliver Goldsmith's Deserted Village has both beauty and feeling, and his play She Stoops to Conquer is full of robust humour.

The character studies of Addison and Steele, the stories of Daniel Defoe, author of Robinson Crusoe, and the revived interest in old-time romance pointed the way to the new form which today provides the greatest part of our literary pleasures: the novel. Pamela (written in the form of letters), by Samuel Richardson, heads the list. Henry Fielding, Oliver Goldsmith, Laurence Sterne, and Tobias Smollett all added valuable elements to the new literary type, and their novels served as models for those that followed. Goldsmith's Vicar of Wakefield (1766) remains popular.

Above the literary life of the time towers the substantial figure of Dr. Samuel Johnson, great conversationalist and arbiter of literature, compiler of the Dictionary, and author of Lives of the Poets, Rasselas, and many periodical essays; but his personal influence was far more potent than his writings. With Sir Joshua Reynolds, he founded a famous literary club, of which the statesman Burke, Goldsmith, Boswell, the historian Gibbon, and the actor Garrick were members.

Johnson's style was ponderous and full of large, resounding words. His emphasis on classical severity and dignity retarded the development of the freer spirit of romanticism with its bold origin-

DR. JOHNSON READS GOLDSMITH'S ' BEST-SELLER '
Often the impecunious Goldsmith (centre) could not pay his rent, and here we see his landlady presenting her overdue bill. She has called in the sheriff's officer to arrest him, but Dr. Johnson (left) has discovered the manuscript of Goldsmith's The Vicar of Wakefield, which he is going to take to a publisher, so that Goldsmith's difficulties will—temporarily—be solved.

ality and rejection of ancient precedents. Happily (since the man himself is more interesting than his works) we have a remarkable biography of him by his friend and admirer James Boswell.

The standards of the early 18th century could not endure at a time when men were thinking of freedom, when governments were changing, and the people were making themselves heard. The French Revolution had a powerful influence on literature. Love of liberty animated all who thought deeply. Literature revolted from its old limitations and found free expression in thought and feeling.

William Blake and William Cowper were forerunners of a new outburst of poetry and prose. From

PERCY BYSSHE SHELLEY

Shelley's remarkable gifts were first seen in full maturity in Alastor or The Spirit of Solitude, which appeared in 1816. This portrait was painted in 1819, when Shelley was 27— three years before he was drowned at sea off Leghorn.

National Portrait Gallery

Samuel Taylor Coleridge wrote only a few truly great poems, but those few are unexcelled for imagination, penetrating vision and melody. His Ancient Mariner stands alone in magical rendering of the supernatural and fantastic. The unfinished poem Kubla Khan has haunting lines.

The spirit of revolt that is the outstanding characteristic of the time appears in most intense form in the poetry of Byron. Don Juan, Childe Harold, and other fiery poems exercised immense influence on the younger writers of his day.

Most ardent of the young poets of liberty was Percy Bysshe Shelley. His longer poems soar into a spiritual region which his contemporaries found disturbing. But today all can enjoy such exquisite lyrics as The Cloud and the Ode to the West Wind. Like his own Skylark,

> Higher still and higher
> From the earth thou springest
> Like a cloud of fire.

The other poet of this group was John Keats, whose early death Shelley mourns in Adonais. Keats was deeply moved by the passionate love of beauty for its own sake. Such short poems as On a Grecian Urn or To a Nightingale have unsurpassed beauty, and contain such music as—

> . . . hath
> Charmed magic casements opening on the foam
> Of perilous seas in faery lands forlorn.

In the same romantic age Scott created the historical novel. His Waverley Novels—Ivanhoe, The Heart of Midlothian, and others—were the favourites of the period and were read all over Europe. Another novelist was Jane Austen, one of the first to write, in Pride and Prejudice, Emma, and Persuasion, of the day-to-day events of quiet, undramatic lives.

Scotland, whose poets had long loved Nature and freedom, came Robert Burns, singing the new brotherhood and democracy, as in the line " A man's a man for a' that! "—and the love of Nature, the tender sentiment, and the rollicking humour of his race, in such poems as To a Mouse, The Cottar's Saturday Night, and Tam o' Shanter. Another poet of Scotland was Sir Walter Scott, who put stirring border tales into poems like The Lay of the Last Minstrel.

Greatest of all the Nature poets was William Wordsworth, who better than anyone else leads one to understand meanings hidden beneath Nature's outward forms. He spoke eloquently in his meditative short poems, and in his sonnets—as the one beginning "The world is too much with us, late and soon."

National Portrait Gallery

WILLIAM WORDSWORTH

Benjamin Haydon (1786–1846), artist friend of Keats and other romantic poets, painted this portrait of William Wordsworth in 1842, when the poet was 72. Wordsworth succeeded Southey as Poet Laureate in 1843, and died in April 1850.

Thomas De Quincey wrote voluminous essays in a beautiful and elaborate style. Most lovable of essayists is Charles Lamb, author of the gentle, whimsical Essays of Elia. He and his sister Mary retold Tales from Shakespeare.

By the time Queen Victoria came to the throne a new age was producing new writers. The idea of evolution changed the outlook of science and philosophy and affected religious thought. The spread of democracy was reflected in the poetry and prose of the time. The two chief poets were Alfred Tennyson and Robert Browning. Tennyson wove Arthurian legends into the Idylls of the King, rich in meaning and imagery, melodious in language. In Memoriam and Locksley Hall mirror the religious and scientific spirit of the day. Browning wrote stirring narrative poems, character analyses, dramas, and love poems. His wife, Elizabeth Barrett Browning, wrote the love poems entitled Sonnets from the Portuguese.

The restraint of Greek art and the mental stress of the modern age were present in the poetry of Matthew Arnold. The pre-Raphaelites, under the leadership of William Morris and Dante Gabriel Rossetti, turned their backs on the present and addressed their poetry to the past. Delicious music and a philosophy of pleasure were the essence of the rich poetry of Algernon Swinburne. Matchless among prose authors for clear, forcible, picturesque studies of great men was Macaulay. Thomas Carlyle spoke directly, flamingly, to arouse people to thinking, in his Sartor Resartus and Heroes and Hero Worship. John Ruskin, Matthew Arnold, and aesthetic Walter Pater form a group of critical writers of the first rank.

Prose fiction was now the chief art form, and innumerable novels were written. Charles Dickens, author of Pickwick Papers and David Copperfield, with his humour, pathos, and understanding of human nature, is one of the best-loved authors. William Makepeace Thackeray, the keen but kindly satirist of Vanity Fair and The Newcomes, is scarcely less a favourite. Middlemarch, Silas Marner, and the other novels of the woman novelist, George Eliot, all have their problems and serious purpose. Anthony Trollope left a long series of novels depicting with wit and fidelity life in the clerical and " county " society of his day. Literary heir of Thackeray was George Meredith, whose brilliant novels, such as The Egoist, illuminate the social scene with sharpness and pungency. Irresolute readers called Meredith's epigrammatic, condensed, flashing style " unintelligible " and " obscure."

The great figure of the period was Thomas Hardy, over whose novels broods a dark, inescapable fate— the fate imposed on Man by his own nature, by all the forces of land, sea and sky. The power of environment, the clutch of the past, wring sheer tragedy out of the lives of Tess of the D'Urbervilles, Jude the Obscure, and all the other stumbling heroes and heroines of Hardy. In The Dynasts he showed immense power as a poet.

Robert Louis Stevenson had a lighter touch, marked by a sedulously polished style and a won-

THOMAS HARDY
Novelist, poet and dramatist, Hardy studied architecture before he began writing novels and stories which portrayed rural life in Wessex with remarkable realism. He was awarded the Order of Merit in 1910 and died in January 1928. He was nearly 70 when he wrote his masterpiece, The Dynasts.

derful gift for story-telling. Kidnapped, Catriona, Treasure Island, are swinging tales of adventure; the unfinished Weir of Hermiston (completed by Sir Arthur Quiller-Couch) is among the finest of his stories; such essays as Virginibus Puerisque, short stories and fantasies as The Sire de Maletroit's Door and Will o' the Mill, and his verses for children never fail to charm.

All the ingredients of popularity were manifest in the swift, bright tales of Rudyard Kipling, in his marching or mocking verse, in The Jungle Books, favourites of children. His imperialism is seen at its best in his descriptions of Britons at work in distant territories. Of supreme importance in the development of the short-story and novel is the work of Henry James. He brought profound analysis to bear on almost everything he wrote, and in such meticulously planned novels as The Wings of the Dove, and The Golden Bowl, he anticipated later 20th-century methods.

Changing views of the social order have sifted the dust of theory, propaganda and sociology over much of 20th-century fiction. H. G. Wells began as a writer of highly imaginative scientific romances, and ended as an inexhaustible evangelist of social theories, a fountain of ideas, suggestions, conjectures. His Outline of History, intended to establish a new attitude towards history rather than to present new facts, had a tremendous vogue.

The " what's-wrong-with-the-world " theme also animated the novels of John Galsworthy. The Forsyte Saga is a series of novels about one family, in which he sketches an upper stratum of English life. Arnold Bennett struck many a neat blow at human stupidity and pride in his memorable The Old Wives' Tale. Joseph Conrad let the reader make what he liked of the moving pageant of the world, set down as if by magic on the pages of his sea tales, his narratives of political intrigue, and his glowing stories of the tropics; this Pole wielded a foreign tongue with a power which few Englishmen have equalled. Fantasy of a delicate sort charmed readers and audiences in the stories and plays of Sir James Barrie. Maurice Hewlett accomplished the difficult feat of making historical characters live in his romantic novels of the past.

No writer impressed his age more strongly than did Bernard Shaw, whose stinging prefaces to his plays pricked any remnant of Victorian smugness. An Irishman of equal wit but of a very different stamp was George Moore. His exquisite prose suggests both music and fine embroidery. Whether he made use of a political or religious idea, or whether he chose a historical theme, he produced a work of art in a severely simple and almost flawless English—The Brook Kerith, The Untilled Field, The Lake, and other works.

A third remarkable Irishman, James Joyce, created in Ulysses what has been called the most influential single work of the 20th century. One of the most brilliant philologists, Joyce devised word-coinages to express the subconscious desires of his characters. Finnegan's Wake extended the manner adopted in Ulysses, which records 24 hours in the life of a Jewish salesman in Dublin by means of the " stream of consciousness " device initiated by Henry James, and brought to so fine a pitch of sensitivity by Virginia Woolf in her To the Lighthouse, Mrs. Dalloway, and Between the Acts.

Among the most outstanding talents developed in the 20th century, D. H. Lawrence stood out as an explorer of the darker reaches of the soul. He infused a gnawing vitality into the strange, obsessed novels he wrought out of his sick, unhappy life. Katherine Mansfield was a genius, cut short by death, who in such fragments as Bliss showed powers akin to Chekhov. Popularity came to Sir Hugh Walpole for his story-telling instinct, easy style, and for his faithful portraiture of certain easily-recognizable types of character. Among his many popular works the Rogue Herries series is perhaps the best-known. A fine study of Anglo-Indian relations appeared in E. M. Forster's A Passage to India, a novel created slowly and thoughtfully by a mind unvitiated by too great facility. His earlier works, A Room with a View, and Howard's End, were landmarks in the art of the novel.

Aldous Huxley, who satirized fashionable London life of the nineteen-twenties in Point Counterpoint, later turned to mysticism. Though W. Somerset Maugham achieved fame by his plays, it is probably for his novels that he will be remembered, of which the most distinguished were Of Human Bondage, The Moon and Sixpence, and the Razor's Edge. One of the novelists who were inspired by the First World War was R. H. Mottram.

When realism and psychological analysis bear too heavily upon the reading public, it is on such stories as The Constant Nymph, by Margaret Kennedy,that popularity descends. Other successful novelists were Rebecca West, Compton Mackenzie, Charles Morgan, Francis Brett Young, L. A. G. Strong, Howard Spring, Sheila Kaye-Smith, Graham Greene, H. E. Bates, A. J. Cronin, James Hilton, Elizabeth Bowen, E. M. Delafield and Ivy Compton-Burnett.

GEORGE BERNARD SHAW *Vandyk*

George Bernard Shaw became a fearless opponent of sham and hypocrisy. With their satiric comments on life and character, the plays of this Irish dramatist won him a world-wide reputation.

J. B. Priestley, author of The Good Companions, attained wide popularity with both novels and plays.

Poetry of the period developed a somewhat bewildering interest in startling experiments in new forms; and even while such poets as A. E. Housman and John Masefield (made poet laureate in 1930) clung to the old forms, their subject-matter and points of view were essentially new. Housman's A Shropshire Lad echoes long in the mind, and Masefield's The Everlasting Mercy and The Widow in the By-Street shocked the conservative by the beauty they lent to sordid themes.

T. S. Eliot led the modern symbolist school: his The Waste Land aroused a storm of controversy over its startling form and obscure content ; East Coker was one of his finest works, and he became the leader of an important school. As a dramatist he was widely appreciated. Murder in the Cathedral, and Family Re-union, were fine examples of his philosophy. To his school, too, belonged W. H. Auden, and Stephen Spender. Richard Aldington, with Images Old and New, was an " imagist."

The war note was, of course, to be heard in much poetry of the nineteen-twenties and forties. Rupert Brooke and Wilfred Owen were young poets who lost their lives in the First World War. Siegfried Sassoon, Robert Graves, and Robert Nichols survived to condemn war in verses of bitter realism. Of the most distinctive poets of the Second World War, Sidney Keyes (1922–43) occupied an important place.

Robert Bridges, poet laureate, 1913–30, showed extraordinary technical power in creating subtle rhythms and in depicting Nature. James Stephens played new tunes on old Irish tales, and Padraic Colum and W. B. Yeats likewise developed Irish themes. Sir William Watson was a poet in the great tradition, a master of true eloquence. Edith Sitwell, from her earlier Sleeping Beauty, to her mature Song of the Cold, showed the wealth of the poet's mind. Her brother Sacheverell was also a poet of distinction.

A number of novelists and essayists also wrote excellent verse, including G. K. Chesterton, Hilaire Belloc, Walter de la Mare, and Alice Meynell. Chesterton and Belloc led in the field of the witty, provocative, controversial essay, and Max Beerbohm in the gently malicious parody, essay, and caricature. A later and more pungent use of the essay was seen in the work of George Orwell, who also wrote Swift-like satires in fiction form. Different aspects of satire appear in the novels of Rose Macaulay and Evelyn Waugh.

In the varied field of non-fiction writing, T. E. Lawrence's Revolt in the Desert, later published in full as The Seven Pillars of Wisdom, stands out as a work of great merit. Lytton Strachey infused new life into the art of biography with his Eminent Victorians and Queen Victoria. His aim was to portray historical characters critically, dispassionately and without bias. Philip Guedella and a host of others followed him in this field. Sir Osbert Sitwell's autobiography Left Hand, Right Hand appeared in several volumes, giving a brilliant picture of personalities and society from Edwardian times up to the Second World War.

Brilliant essays and criticism, as well as fiction, came from the pens of John Cowper Powys and his brother, Llewelyn Powys. Literary critics of distinction were George Saintsbury, W. P. Ker and Sir Edmund Gosse. The most widely-read historian was G. M. Trevelyan whose English Social History was popular during the nineteen-forties. The work of the learned George Santayana, born in Spain, who lived for many years in the United States before taking up residence in England, may properly be classified as belonging to English literature, which is enriched by his beautifully written critical studies. The age is too close to us to allow a reasoned judgement whether any modern writer is truly great, or to know what names will be the most outstanding.

Engraving.
The simplest form of engraving is the one used for making visiting cards; the name and address of a person are *cut into*—this is the meaning of the word engrave—the polished surface of a copper plate. Now, if we rub an inked pad over the surface of the plate, the hollows where the engraver's tool made an incision will be filled with ink; we next wipe off the ink from the surface of the plate, leaving the pigment in the hollows. A card is placed over the plate, and both are forced together in a press: the ink in the engraved lines on the copper is printed on to the card, leaving the rest white. You will probably have reasoned out that the design which the engraver cut on the plate would have to be made in reverse, right to left, so that the finished writing, when printed, would read from left to right.

Engraving is used to ornament plate and jewelry, and engraved name-plates and memorial tablets are also common. But it is in its use for reproducing designs and illustrations that engraving is chiefly notable. The method we have described, of cutting the design into a flat surface and then printing from the ink left in the hollows when the surface is wiped clean, is known as *intaglio* printing—from Italian words meaning " cut in." Another method, which is just the opposite, is to cut away the parts of the plate which are to show white in the print, and to leave the lines of the design standing up higher to catch the ink. Such a plate or block is said to be in *relief*. The big types used to print posters are made in this way, the letters being cut on wood. In order to make our description complete we must mention

ENGRAVING: A MASTERPIECE BY ALBRECHT DÜRER

As a painter the German artist Albrecht Dürer (1471–1528) was not a supreme genius, but as an engraver on wood and copper he has never been surpassed. It is to the superb engravings he produced at Nuremberg, Germany, in the last few years of the 15th and the beginning of the 16th century that he owes his enduring fame. The illustration shows a characteristic specimen of his work. It is entitled St. Anthony, and the city in the background is Nuremberg.

a third method of producing a printing surface—that used in the art of lithography.

Lithography means printing by stone. Originally, blocks of fine-grained stone were used as the printing surface, but today sheets of some metal such as aluminium are chiefly employed, since they can be bent around a cylinder, and used for the faster process of rotary printing. Moreover, they are of course much lighter, easier to store, and can be made with a uniform and regular quality—which was impossible with natural stone. The design to be printed is drawn on the stone with a greasy crayon or pencil; the surface of the stone is kept wetted with water, which ensures that only the parts which have the design in grease-crayon will then take the coat of greasy ink which is now applied. A sheet of paper laid on the stone and pressed down on it will take the design.

Such a printing surface is flat—neither cut into nor raised in parts. So the name for this method is *plane* or *surface* printing. Ordinary printing from type or from blocks is termed *letterpress* printing; the letters, or the parts of the illustration to show on the paper, are raised above the surface, like those of the wooden poster type we mentioned earlier.

Before going on to describe the various kinds of engraving used by artists for producing an original work we will mention photo-engraving, used to make the printing blocks for the illustrations you see in our volumes. A photograph of a drawing in simple lines is made; the "positive" of this photo is printed by light exposure on to a sheet of zinc or copper. By a photo-chemical process the design lines are then made resistant to the acid used for "etching" away all the parts that are to show white in the print on the paper. Thus we have a printing block in relief, with the design lines left standing.

But suppose we wish to make a photo-engraved block of a photograph, or of a "wash drawing," which has various shades of light and dark and is not merely shaded by lines or hatching? We must then use the *half-tone process*. In this the drawing or the original photograph is photographed, but this time a glass screen ruled with fine lines which cross one another in a mesh or network is interposed between the original photograph and the camera lens. So the photo thus taken has on it a picture of the original, with a fine network of lines crossing it over every part. The effect is to break up the surface of the picture into groups of dots. These are light ones far apart

in the lighter portions of the picture; and dark ones close together in the dark portions. The positive of this half-tone negative is printed down on to a copper plate, and etched as before described. If you look at any of our half-tone illustrations through a pocket lens you will see the dots made by ink which was caught on the raised parts of the printing block.

Etching spares the engraver the task of cutting away metal with his tools, but it is really a distinctive art, with qualities very different from "line engraving." In engraving, lines and depressions are cut on copper plates with the burin, which gouges out a V-shaped line. The burr left by the burin at the sides of the cut are removed by another tool called a scraper. Thus the essential feature of an engraving proper is a very clean line.

In *drypoint* a zinc or copper plate is used, and is incised with a very hard steel pointed tool, which is drawn towards the artist, leaving a burr on one or both sides of the cut. The burr is not removed in drypoint, but gives warm, soft lines in the print, very different from the clean and clear-cut lines left by the burin. Another difference from engraving is that in the latter process the burin is pushed away from the artist. He bears lightly on the tool at the start of an incision, and lessens the pressure again as he nears the end of the line; thus the middle portion is deeper and holds more ink than the shallower, finer ends. Albrecht Dürer and later engravers used drypoint to give finishing touches to etching, as well as employing drypoint alone for their works.

In the making of etchings the copper plate is covered with a " resist "—some mixture of beeswax and other materials which melts when warm and hardens when cold, and which resists the action of the etching acids. The dry ground is usually smoked over a flame to give it a black coating of soot, on which the design can be lightly indicated with a pencil. Then the etcher takes his needle and cuts away the ground along the lines of the picture, but not cutting the metal itself. Next the plate is immersed in the acid bath (nitric or hydrochloric acid) until the biting has gone far enough, when the acid is washed off and the plate cleaned.

In printing an etching the artist may discriminate by leaving more or less ink on some part of the plate; or he may even rub one part cleaner than the rest to give a particular effect. The press used is something like a mangle, with the copper plate and the paper resting on a flat bed which travels

FOR ENGRAVING

These are engraving tools: A, a graver, or burin, with which the lines are cut; B, the scraper, with which the burr is removed.

THE COPPER AND THE PRINT
In making an engraving the line is obtained by cutting away the metal. On the left is a stippled engraving on copper of a sketch by G. Morland (1763–1804), and on the right is an impression from the plate.

ETCHING MADE BY REMBRANDT

This reproduction of an etching made by the Dutch artist Rembrandt (1606–69) is a self-portrait, only four first impressions of which exist. In etching, the plate is coated with a 'resist' of wax, through which the design is cut ; then acid is used to bite lines into the copper.

surface is sprinkled with powdered resin, which is made to stick on by warming. The resin gives a grain to the surface and does away with sharp lines and dots, imparting a rich texture, which contrasts with the colder effect of half-tone reproductions.

In printing by photogravure, the etched cylinder is made to revolve in a trough of greasy ink; the surface is scraped automatically by a sharp blade which leaves ink only in the depressions produced by the bite of the acid. Next, the cylinder comes in contact with another one, covered with rubber, and leaves its inky impression on a sheet of dampened paper fed between the two cylinders. The rubber covering forces the paper against the inked cylinder. In flat-plate photogravure the process is similar. By these methods modern printing technique is able to produce illustrations resembling original engravings and etchings.

Wood engraving (in relief) was the earliest method of illustrating printed books, and such engravings were a substitute for the hand-painted initials and miniatures which made medieval manuscripts such works of beauty. Albrecht Dürer and Hans Holbein were masters of this art. Long before their time, however, the Chinese were using wood blocks for stamping designs and pictures on paper and silk. Relief engravings are made usually on a slab of boxwood or cherry, the lines of the design being left standing up and all the parts which are to be white being cut away. The artist himself might do the cutting, after drawing the design; or he might leave this task to a woodcutter. The process thus described is *black-line* engraving.

In *white-line* engraving (or the making of " woodcuts "), the cutting is done on the end grain of a piece of boxwood and the design is reproduced in white by cutting into the wood. Various mechanical effects are got by the use of tools which produce a hatched or shaded result. As an art, wood engraving continued in favour after its general use for book and newspaper illustration ceased with the invention of photo-engraving.

under the mangle roller as the latter turns. The pressure forces the plate into the paper and leaves a typical " plate-mark " at the edges of the plate.

The line engraver gives more accurate details, but the etcher has more freedom of line and shading; often the two are combined, the line work being done on the plate after it has been bitten; or drypoint completes the etching with softer tones.

Etching was probably invented early in the 15th century, and many of the greatest artists have practised this process. Van Dyck and Rembrandt were especially interested in it, the latter being probably the most important figure in the whole history of this art. Later many leading artists tried their hand at it, but its great revival in the 19th century was due to Sir F. Seymour Haden and J. A. M. Whistler. Great modern etchers include Sir Frank Brangwyn, Sir Muirhead Bone, Alphonse Legros and Anders Zorn.

As a parallel to the method for making printing blocks by the relief process, described earlier, we have the *photogravure* process for reproducing pictures by the intaglio method. A sensitized paper is exposed photographically under a black-and-white positive made without a screen. This carbon tissue is transferred, after exposure, to a copper plate or cylinder. The parts which are to be white have been hardened and made acid-resistant by the action of light; the other parts can be etched through on to the metal to form the depressions corresponding to the engraved or etched lines of an artist's plate. But before the cylinder is etched, the

Entomology. This word comes from two Greek words : *entomon* meaning insect, and *logos*, science. Entomologists tell us that insects, the study of which occupies their time, are our chief enemies in the modern world, so that this is really a very important science. And when it is learned that a single species of insect may cost a country hundreds of thousands of pounds in damage every year, it becomes obvious that entomology is worth studying. The men and women who work to keep insects at bay are called economic entomologists; other scientists, of course, occupy themselves with various other branches of entomological work.

From a practical point of view, entomology concerns everyone who grows any kind of plant, from the gardener whose roses are attacked by green-fly to the fruit-grower whose thousands of acres of oranges or apples are beset with their particular pests. There is a special branch of the science which deals with the insects that live on goods in warehouses. There is practically nothing in the way of soft goods and foodstuffs, from leather and tobacco to dried ginger and flour, which is not attacked by some insect, and occasionally warehouses are literally crawling with caterpillars and beetles. Many firms have special staffs of men who occupy their whole time on these problems, and governments spend large sums of money in entomological research and insect control.

Enzymes. This is the name applied to a chemical ferment produced by living cells of plant or animal, playing an important part in growth, digestion, and most other life processes. An unripe apple is very different in taste from one that has been ripened; enzymes have brought about the change. A cut apple exposed to the air turns brown; an enzyme of oxidation has been at work. The action of yeast and bacteria is due largely to the enzymes they produce.

In the article on chemistry you can read about catalysts—substances that promote the interaction of other chemicals without becoming part of them. Thus it is that the presence of platinum promotes the union of oxygen and hydrogen to form water. Enzymes act in the same way with organic substances; they are the catalysts of the organic world. The body produces many kinds of enzymes, each of which has its own specialised task. Thus, in digestion, ptyalin, found in saliva, is concerned with the conversion of starch into sugar; the pepsin of the gastric juice grapples with fibrous tissue, reducing it to an absorbable entity (*see* Digestion). Every cell in the body contains enzymes, both for transforming food into cell substances and, when the cell's life is over, for eventually dissolving the cell itself.

In plants, too, enzymes are busy. The yeast plant secretes two enzymes, invertase and zymase. Invertase first is active in reducing sugar to less complex form; then zymase steps in to complete the change of sugar products into alcohol and carbon dioxide. Exceedingly small quantities of an enzyme can play on a large mass of material, and they can stimulate very rapid chemical reactions. On chewing a piece of bread, it sweetens almost immediately in the mouth, an example of the enzyme ptyalin, just referred to, at its quick work.

Up to the present the complex and unstable nature of enzymes has foiled all attempts to determine their chemical composition, but it is certain that they are essential factors, in growth and in nutrition, in life and in death. They may have some function in the processes of thought. And it may be

that sleep is a rhythmic cessation of their activities in certain brain cells, and that unconsciousness under an anaesthetic depends similarly on their being temporarily put out of action.

Epictetus. Man must find happiness within himself, this Greek Stoic philosopher taught, and not in his surroundings. "No one is a slave whose will is free," he declared. The name Epictetus (pron. ep-ik-tē'-tus) is the Greek for "acquired," and denotes his servile condition, for he was taken as a slave to Rome. His real name is unknown. He was born in Phrygia, Asia Minor, about A.D. 60, and in Rome became acquainted with the Stoic philosophy, which taught that virtue was the highest good, irrespective of pleasure or pain. After he gained his freedom Epictetus began to give lessons in philosophy.

About A.D. 90 the Emperor Domitian banished all philosophers from Italy, and Epictetus went to Nicopolis, in Epirus, Greece, where he opened a school. He continued to teach the doctrines of Stoicism, until the time of his death. He wrote nothing, but talked in a familiar way with his pupils concerning the conduct of life. Arrian, the Greek historian, his favourite pupil, took down much of his teaching, which is preserved in two treatises— the Discourses, and the Enchiridion (Handbook).

Epicurus. (341–270 B.C.). "Let us eat, drink, and be merry, for tomorrow we die." This is the phrase commonly used to sum up the philosophy of Epicurus (pron. ep-i-kūr'-us). But it gives a very extreme and mistaken view of his ideas; and the fact that in modern language the word Epicureanism is so often used to indicate addiction to sensual pleasures, and particularly to indulgence in eating and drinking, still further shows the common misunderstanding of his principles. Epicurus certainly taught that pleasure is the aim of life, the only happiness; but for him pleasure was the absence of pain and worry; it was a habit of mind, not the excitement or exuberance of a moment. No pleasure, he said, is bad in itself, but only the pleasure in freedom from pain is a true good. Understood aright, the desire for pure pleasure leads to a desire for righteousness and virtue; the virtuous Man alone is happy.

The founder of the school of philosophy known as Epicureanism came of Athenian parentage and was born in Samos, an island in the Aegean Sea. He taught in various places in Greece, and, settling in Athens in 306 B.C., founded a school in his garden, where he and his followers lived a life of the greatest simplicity. Among his chief disciples was the Roman

Ny Carlsberg Museum, Copenhagen
EPICURUS
The teachings of the Greek philosopher Epicurus (founder of a school of philosophy in Athens) are often misunderstood. According to him pleasure was the absence of pain and worry, not merely sensual enjoyment.

poet Lucretius (c. 98–55 B.C.), whose great poem De Rerum Natura (On the Nature of Things) embodies the main teachings of the Epicurean school of philosophy.

Epstein, JACOB (b. 1880). Some people consider the works of this sculptor are strange, and even difficult to understand, yet cannot help being impressed by them, one way or another. In London are some of his most famous works, such as the relief of Rima on the memorial to W. H. Hudson (British author and lover of birds) in Hyde Park, and the famous Night and Day, on the London Transport building at St. James's Park Station. But these are large works, and do not show Epstein at his best, for he is more of a modeller than a sculptor, as is clear from his magnificent portrait busts in bronze.

Jacob Epstein was born in New York, of Russo-Polish parents, and he studied widely before settling in London in 1905. In 1908 he was commissioned to execute large works on important buildings. His later works, such as Adam (1939) and Jacob and the Angel (1942) still rouse critics and public alike to a frenzy of abuse or enthusiasm, although no longer to such a pitch as was reached on the appearance of his Christ (1920), and Genesis (1931).

Equinox AND SOLSTICE. Twice a year—once about March 21 (called the vernal equinox) and again about September 23 (called the autumnal equinox)—the Sun is in the plane of the Earth's equator. The name (from Latin aequus, " equal," and nox, " night ") is derived from the fact that the length of the night then exactly equals the length of the day all over the Earth, since the Sun's rays on these dates fall upon the Earth perpendicular to its axis of spin.

At the vernal equinox the Earth has completed one-quarter of its revolution about the Sun, and at the autumnal equinox three-quarters. Because the Sun then appears to be over the equator, the equinoxes are popularly spoken of as the dates on which " the Sun crosses the Line." Equinoctial storms are supposed to accompany the event.

The solstices ("standing still of the Sun") come at the other quarters of the Earth's revolution—the summer solstice (about June 21) when the Earth's N. pole is tipped towards the Sun, and the winter solstice (about December 22) when the S. pole is most inclined towards the Sun.

" Precession of the equinoxes " is the term applied to the slow advance from east to west of the equinoctial points, or the points at which the equator and the ecliptic intersect each other. The change is so slow that it takes in the neighbourhood of 25,800 years to make a complete shift around the ecliptic. (See Earth ; Sun).

Erasmus, DESIDERIUS (1466?–1536). An ardent religious reformer, Erasmus by his writings purged the Church of its abuses and outworn traditions; he returned to the Bible itself and to the early Fathers for his conception of Christianity. He has been much criticized for the part he played in the Reformation and for his attitude towards the German religious reformer Luther (1483–1546).

EPSTEIN AND ONE OF HIS BUSTS
No artistic works of recent years have caused such differences of opinion as the sculptures of Jacob Epstein, who was born in New York in 1880 and settled in London in 1905. He is seen here with a bust, Roma II, a characteristic example of his portraiture in bronze.

" Erasmus laid the egg, and Luther hatched it," it was said. The truth is that Erasmus was a man of letters, not a theologian; he was not the stuff of which religious zealots or martyrs are made. While conscious of the faults of Roman Catholicism he always remained a Catholic, and while acknowledging the need of religious reform, he clearly saw the dangers that would inevitably follow extremist efforts in that direction.

Erasmus was born either at Rotterdam or at Gouda on October 28, probably in 1466, a son of Gerard de Praet of Gouda, and he became a priest in 1492. After holding several minor posts, and studying in Paris (in 1496), he was persuaded to visit England. Here he became the friend of Thomas More and Colet. In 1500 he returned to Paris, resolved to devote his life to study. He revisited England in 1506 and 1509, and was appointed professor of Greek at Cambridge, and there he wrote the famous satire on clerical abuses and human follies called Moriae Encomium (Praise of Folly), and completed his work on the New Testament. For some time he led a wandering life, until in 1521 he settled at Basle. From 1529 to 1535 he lived at Freiburg in Germany, whence he returned to Basle, where he died on July 12, 1536.

Erasmus was one of the most industrious scholars that ever lived. Of his editions of classical works the most important is Terence (1532). His reputation was established by his Chiliades Adagiorum (Thousands of Adages), published in 1508, a collection of over 3,000 Greek and Latin proverbs relieved by apt comments and lively anecdotes. His greatest service to theology was his edition of the New Testament (1516), a Greek text with a

Latin translation, his superb treatment of which entitles him to be called the pioneer of Biblical criticism. The Enchiridion Militis Christiani (Dagger or Manual of the Christian Soldier), 1502, is an attack on formal religion, and the Colloquia (Conversations), 1516, is a series of dialogues on topical subjects, and especially a castigation of the vices of priests and others of the period in which he lived.

Ericsson, JOHN (1803–89). Born in Vormland, Sweden, on July 31, 1803, this Swedish - American engineer showed a mechanical bent very early. From 1820 to 1827 he was an engineer in the Swedish army. Arriving in England, he built, with John Braithwaite, the " Novelty," a locomotive which was beaten by Stephenson's " Rocket " in the Liverpool and Manchester Railway competition of 1829. Ericsson was occupied with various inventions, chiefly marine engines, up to 1836, when he brought out a marine screw propeller, and won a British government award of £5,000. In 1838 he designed the engines and propeller used by the first vessels to cross the Atlantic in regular steamship service.

In 1839 he went to the United States, becoming a naturalized citizen of that country in 1848. Turning his attention to armour for warships and improvements in marine engines, he designed in 1861 the first armoured turret ship, the Monitor, for the United States navy. Ericsson died in New York on March 8, 1889, and the following year, at the request of the Swedish government, his body was sent to Sweden, where it was buried.

Eritrea. Bounded on the east by the Red Sea, on the north by the Anglo-Egyptian Sudan, on the south-west by Abyssinia, on the south by French Somaliland, this region of East Africa

Giraudin

DESIDERIUS ERASMUS
Though his part in the Reformation antagonized both Protestants and Catholics, Erasmus (1466–1536) did more than any other scholar to advance intellectual liberty in Europe.

has an area of 15,754 square miles. The chief town is Asmara, and the principal port Massawa. Along the coast the climate is very hot and moist, but the uplands are comparatively cool. Products include hides, ostrich feathers, palm nuts and salt.

Italian forces occupied Eritrea in 1889; and in 1936 the territory became part of Italian East Africa, which was taken by Allied forces in the Second World War. After the war Eritrea was administered by the British. In December 1950 the United Nations decided that Eritrea should become a self-governing country in federation with Ethiopia by September 1952. The population is about 850,000.

Ermine. A quick, restless and bloodthirsty little animal is this member of the weasel family, *Mustela erminea*, better known in Britain as the stoat. It has a slender body, about 10 inches long, and short legs. It runs swiftly, climbs and swims well, and feeds on smaller animals and birds, being a great enemy of rats and rabbits. It is found in Europe as far south as the Alps, and in Asia and North America.

In summer the fur is red-brown above and yellowish-white underneath. In cold countries the fur in winter changes to white, except the tail, which has a black tip. This fur is the ermine formerly used in the linings of the robes of kings and queens and still used for the robes of judges in England. The white colour is the symbol of the purity which should attach to the office of judge.

Eskimo. When explorers first reached the Arctic lands of North America, they found the Eskimos living much as some of them do today. Then, as now, they were scattered all along the shores of Labrador and the north coast of America, on the Arctic islands, on Greenland, and on a part of the Siberian coast of Asia. They are closely allied to the natives of the Aleutian Islands, off the Alaskan coast ; and may be of the same stock as the American Indians, whom they resemble in their straight black hair, obliquely set eyes, and brown skin. A tribe of blond Eskimos was discovered by Stefansson during his 1910–11 expedition on Coronation Bluff, far inside the Arctic Circle.

Although they are so widely scattered Eskimos are extraordinarily alike in language, habits, and appearance. Some tribes, in districts farthest south, have adopted many civilized ways from the white

M. H. Crawford

ERMINE : THE STOAT IN WINTER DRESS
The brown summer coat of the stoat turns white in winter with the exception of the black tip of the tail. In Britain this change takes place regularly in Scotland and northern England, but is rare farther south. Ermine fur is little used except for official robes. Skins for commercial purposes come from Alaska and Siberia.

people. They learn readily and show marked intelligence. Generosity, hospitality, and friendliness to strangers are characteristic traits of this primitive race. Warfare is almost unknown among them.

Although the Eskimos cover such an expanse of territory they probably do not number over 40,000. Their villages are small, with from 25 to 200 inhabitants. There is no chief, and no form of government. Each tribe has its own territory. Sometimes all the people of a village will be found living in a community igloo—a dome-shaped hut made of snow. Most of the Eskimos of West Greenland, Labrador, and Southern Alaska have accepted Christianity. Not all Eskimo tribes are uncivilized. In the south-west of Greenland, for instance, they have had some contact with Europeans for nine centuries or so, the Norsemen under Eric the Red

Vilhjalmur Stefansson

ESKIMOS' WINTER HOME OF SNOW BRICKS
In the Arctic regions it is vitally necessary to have a home that is warm and really wind-proof. Eskimos of the mainland and islands of Northern Canada build igloos—dome-shaped structures made of blocks of compressed snow, with an opening at the top to let out smoke. Chinks between the blocks are packed with snow, which quickly freezes solid. The interior is unlined.

having colonized part of that area at about the time of the Norman invasion of England.

Esperanto. Of the many attempts that have been made to invent a universal language, Esperanto is by far the most important. It was the work of Dr. Zamenhof (1859–1917), a Polish oculist, who presented it to the public in 1887,

Danish Legation

ESKIMOS IN THEIR FRAIL KAYAKS AND LARGE UMYAKS
To a certain extent Eskimos are a seafaring race, for they are largely dependent on the sea for food and, in summer when the ice and snow have gone, for communication. To the male Eskimos of Greenland a kayak is an essential possession for fishing and for hunting seals. Kayaks are here seen in the foreground ; behind them is an umyak, which is usually called the woman's boat because women travel in, and often form the crews of, these large transport craft.

the name Esperanto coming from the Spanish for "hope." It uses sounds and words common to many European languages. The grammar is very simple. Here is a stanza from a poem by its founder, with an English translation:

Sur neutrala lingva fundamento,	On a neutral lingual foundation,
Komprenante unu la alian,	Understanding one another,
La popoloj faros en konsento	The peoples shall form in agreement
Uno grandan rondon familian.	One great family circle.

Essay. It was in the tower of an old castle in France, not far from Bordeaux, in the month of March 1571, that the first essay was written. Michel de Montaigne, a cultured Frenchman, had retired there to forget the cares of the busy world and to read and meditate in quiet. A desire to preserve his memories and clarify his reflections led him to write. He called the little book, which he began at this time and published in 1580, Essais—meaning "attempts" or "trials." The term essay, which was soon adopted in England, thus suggests that the author is merely touching upon the subject in hand, and not treating it in detail; giving short, pithy comment rather than a complete and formal discussion, as in a treatise or monograph.

Unlike the novel or the short story or the drama, the essay does not aim at creating characters and through them telling a story. It speaks directly to the reader, giving the author's views on customs or happenings or people, on art, on books, or on life in general. It may teach, argue, persuade, arouse emotion, or merely amuse.

Though French in origin, the essay form appealed especially to the English. After Montaigne, an Englishman, Francis Bacon (1561–1626), was the next great writer of essays. He called his essays "certain brief notes set down rather significantly than curiously," and spoke of them also as "dispersed meditations." As a matter of fact, his essays are written with painstaking care. They are more formal and less personal than those of Montaigne.

When magazines and newspapers began to be published in the 18th century, the essay became especially popular. In the 19th century came one of the most delightful of essayists—Charles Lamb (1775–1834), who, though he hid under the pen-name of Elia, revealed his whimsical, lovable personality as few writers have done. The British historian Lord Macaulay (1800–59) wrote essays of a very different type. They are carefully organized and noted for the clearness of their style and choice of words. Macaulay's essays—that on Milton, for example—may be taken as typical of the formal essay, just as Lamb's Essays of Elia are representative of the familiar or informal essay. Of the essayists who followed, some leaned towards one type and some towards the other. Hazlitt, Leigh Hunt, Carlyle, Ruskin, Thackeray, De Quincey, Matthew Arnold and Stevenson are among our greatest essayists.

The essay, it should be noted, is essentially a prose form. Alexander Pope's works entitled Essay on Criticism, and Essay on Man, in verse, are poetic treatises, not essays; the same writer's Moral Essays, however, have the substance, though not the form, of essays.

Essen. Twenty miles north-east of Düsseldorf in Germany, Essen is the centre of the Ruhr industrial area and before the Second World War (1939–45) was the headquarters of the German coal and heavy armament industries. The vast Krupp works were at Essen, where, besides guns and other weapons, locomotives and various kinds of machinery were produced. An important railway and canal shipping centre, during the Second World War it was frequently bombed by the Allied Air Forces, the Krupp works being put out of action and much of the city destroyed. Essen was captured by United States troops on April 9, 1945, and after the war was included in the British zone. The population in 1939 was 660,000.

Essex. One of the south-eastern counties of England, Essex is separated on the south from Kent by the River Thames, is bounded on the north by Suffolk and Cambridgeshire, on the west

Underwood

ESSEX : ST. MARY'S CATHEDRAL AT CHELMSFORD
Made the cathedral of the new bishopric of Essex in 1914, St. Mary's Church, Chelmsford, was completed in 1424. The original building stood until 1800, when workmen opening a vault undermined the walls and the body of the church collapsed. It was restored in 1800–3. Chelmsford, the county town, is in the valley of the Chelmer, 30 miles north-east of London.

ESTHER THE JEWESS IS CROWNED QUEEN OF PERSIA

Painted by the Spanish artist José Villegas (1848–1921), this picture was inspired by the Biblical story of Esther, who became the queen of King Ahasuerus (*c.* 519–465 B.C.) of Persia. The Jews, and especially Mordecai, Esther's cousin, incurred the hatred of Haman, the chief Minister of Ahasuerus, and Mordecai begged the queen to save her people from a massacre. This she managed to do, Haman being hung on gallows he had had erected for Mordecai.

by Hertfordshire and Middlesex, and on the east and south-east by the North Sea. Its low, flat seaboard is nearly 100 miles long, and is indented by shallow creeks. Inland the surface is undulating, rising in the north-west to nearly 500 feet. The area of Essex is 1,530 square miles.

Harwich is the chief seaport, with steamer services to the Continent; and the county contains a number of popular seaside resorts, including Southend, Frinton, and Clacton. There is little manufacturing away from the London area, though brewing is an active industry at Romford, and agriculture and oyster rearing are the chief pursuits. There are large motor works at Dagenham, and Tiptree is famous for its jam.

Chelmsford is the county town. There are the populous boroughs or urban districts of Colchester (with important Roman remains and the ruins of a Norman castle), Walthamstow, Ilford, Leyton, East Ham, West Ham, Barking, and Romford. Tilbury, included in the Port of London, is an increasingly busy port. Rivers include the Thames, Lea, Crouch (with the yachting centre, Burnham), Stour, Blackwater, Colne, Chelmer and Roding. Epping Forest, about 6,000 acres, is a public possession. The population of the county is 1,755,000.

Esther. In a story from the Book of Esther in the Old Testament we are told how the mighty king Ahasuerus of Persia (Xerxes, son of Darius I) chose from among all the maidens in his kingdom the one he deemed fairest to be his queen. This was a Jewess named Esther, although the king knew not who were her people or her kindred. Her father and mother were dead, and she had been brought up by her cousin Mordecai.

Shortly after Esther became queen a great disaster threatened her people : a haughty man named Haman had been raised to the highest office in the kingdom, and he demanded that all should bow down before him. Mordecai refused to bow down, and for this Haman hated him so that he wished to destroy not only Mordecai but all the Jews. The king allowed Haman to have his own way in many of the affairs of state, and Haman issued a decree that on a certain day all Jews throughout the kingdom should be slain.

When Mordecai heard the news he begged Esther to intercede with the king on behalf of the Jews. To this end, she invited Ahasuerus and Haman to a banquet, after which the king learned that Mordecai had at one time frustrated a plot to seize Ahasuerus. In gratitude, the king directed Haman to honour Mordecai by leading him through the city on the king's own horse.

The next day Esther again invited the king and Haman to a banquet, at which Ahasuerus told her that any request of hers would be granted. His queen asked that her own life and those of her people might be spared. The king, who was unaware of Haman's plan, demanded to know who threatened her and the Jews. Esther told him it was Haman—and the king gave orders that Haman was to be hanged on the gallows that he had set up for Mordecai's execution.

Estonia. One of the Republics of the Soviet Union, Estonia is bounded on the north by the Gulf of Finland, on the east by the Leningrad region of the Russian Soviet Federal Socialist Republic, on the south by Latvia and the Gulf of Riga, on the west by the Baltic Sea. It has an area of 18,353 square miles. Except in the south-east, where it is hilly, the country is flat, with many lakes, streams and marshes.

ESTONIAN PEASANT WOMEN
In the Soviet Republic of Estonia the winters are severe, and large supplies of wood have to be sawn up to keep the stoves burning day and night. The women help in this work as well as in the fields, agriculture being the main industry.

Agriculture is the chief industry, with stock-breeding next in importance. Manufactures include iron, steel, machinery, cement, cotton, paper and spirits. Tallinn, connected by railway with Leningrad, is the capital and chief seaport.

Little is known of the early history of Estonia. At the beginning of the 13th century it was conquered by Danes and Germans. For some time the land was divided between Sweden and Poland, then in 1629 it was united as a Swedish province. In 1721 it was won for Russia by Peter the Great from the Swedes. After the Bolshevik Revolution of 1917, Estonia became an independent republic.

In the autumn of 1939 Russia made demands on Estonia for naval and air bases and occupied two of the Baltic islands; in August 1940 the country became the 16th Republic of the Soviet Union. In 1941, during the Second World War (1939–45), Estonia was occupied by German forces, which were driven out by Russians in 1944. The population of Estonia is 1,120,000.

Ether. The "luminiferous (light-carrying) ether" was the name given by 19th century scientists to the medium in which light, and all other electro-magnetic radiations, are propagated. To see why it was deemed necessary for such a medium to exist, we must first know a little about the nature of light. In olden times the ancient Greeks believed it to consist of rays projected out of our eyes when we looked at something. Newton thought that it was composed of high-speed particles shot out from a luminous body. More recent evidence shows that light can be regarded, for most purposes, to be a kind of wave motion, which travels at a speed of 186,000 miles per second through empty space, and at a somewhat lower velocity when going through transparent matter. (*See* Light).

You can study wave motion by dropping a stone into the middle of a pond and watching the ripples which spread out in ever-widening circles from the centre. The waves all travel at a uniform speed, and the distance between successive wave-crests is the same. This distance is known as the wavelength. If, now, you float a cork on the surface of the water, you will find that it bobs up and down as the waves go by, but it does not travel along with them. This shows the essential feature of wave motion; namely, that it is a way in which energy of motion can be transferred from one point to another without the intervening medium actually moving with the wave. Another kind of wave motion, the propagation of sound through air, illustrates this truth well. When we hear a noise the sound waves are not accompanied by a rush of wind, as we would expect if the medium moved in the direction of the wave.

If light is some kind of wave motion, it is natural to inquire what the waves are like, and what are the properties of the medium in which it travels. A brilliant Victorian physicist, Clerk-Maxwell (*q.v.*), solved the former problem. From the work done by Faraday (*q.v.*) on the relation between electricity and magnetism, he showed that it would be possible for an electro-magnetic wave to exist: and, further, Clerk-Maxwell calculated its velocity in empty space. This was before the velocity of light had been directly measured; and when, some years later, H. L. Fizeau (1819–96) performed the experiment, the agreement between the two velocities was exact. The electro-magnetic theory of light was thus completely vindicated.

Electro-magnetic waves are rather hard to imagine since, instead of a water surface bobbing up and down, we have an electric field which varies in strength periodically, accompanied by a magnetic field, also varying but lying in a direction at right angles to the electric field. Both electric and magnetic fields are mutually at right angles to the direction of propagation of the wave, and one cannot exist without the other.

These electro-magnetic waves are found in a variety of forms, according to the size of their wavelength. We are familiar enough with radio waves, which can have a wavelength of anything from a fraction of a metre to thousands of metres. Infra-red, or heat rays, come next in scale of magnitude, and visible light has the even smaller wavelength of about one two-thousandth part of a millimetre. Ultra-violet light, X-Rays and Gamma Rays have successively shorter wavelengths but they, like all the other types of radiation mentioned, are electro-magnetic in character. The scale of wavelengths, or " spectrum," is essentially a continuous one, there being no definite line of demarcation between one type of electro-magnetic wave and another.

What, now, of the medium in which these waves travel? It must obviously fill a vacuum, and pervade all matter in which light travels. The ether, as it was called, could have various properties, such as elasticity and density, assigned to it, and it was regarded as a sort of elastic, jelly-like, weightless substance. Scientists firmly believed in its physical existence until measurements were made, at the end of the 19th century, on the speed at which the Earth was drifting through this ether. Obviously the ether must be at rest with respect to one of the heavenly bodies moving about in space, but it could not be stationary with respect to all of them at the same time. The experiments all gave negative answers. No ether drift could be detected.

Does Ether Really Exist?

The dilemma into which scientists were thrown as a result of these negative experiments was overcome by Einstein (q.v.), who introduced his Relativity Theory in 1907. He showed that, according to the new theory, all such experiments designed to measure ether drift were bound to fail in the end. The reasons leading to this remarkable statement are difficult to explain without invoking the aid of mathematics, but are connected with the fact that all experimental measurements are transmitted to their human observer by means of a light wave. When we try to make objective measurements on another light wave, complication is sure to result.

Although the existence of a physical ether was thus challenged, the electro-magnetic theory of light still holds good. This is because it can be expressed as a mathematical equation, and does not really need a physical picture to support it. All modern physics goes to show that it is not sufficient to draw an analogy between two natural phenomena to " explain " them. Comparing light waves with water waves does not really explain either; the mathematical equation governing the wave motion is the only reality. However, as it is difficult to think entirely in terms of mathematics, we first have to conceive in our mind some kind of mechanical model, to explain the processes that go on; but then we must be careful not to take the resulting analogy too far. The ether is a convenient word to use for picturing a light wave in motion, but its existence is not a necessity to the physicist who develops the mathematical theory.

As it happens, light has been found to behave in some ways like a material particle, as Newton long ago conceived it. For instance, light can " collide " with an electron, changing its direction and energy. The light particle is termed a " photon," and of course no ether is necessary for this to travel through. Here we see a further proof that the use of pictorial conceptions to explain physical facts is bound to have a flaw in it, and that the mathematical laws governing them are the only ultimate reality. (See Light ; Relativity).

Ether (DIETHYL OXIDE). This is a colourless volatile liquid, with a pleasant odour, often used as an anaesthetic to prevent the patient from feeling pain during a surgical operation. Ether boils at such a low temperature ($35°C$) that it may be rapidly vaporised by blowing through it a current of air ; during this experiment so much heat is absorbed that crystals of ice form on the outside of the jar containing the ether—a miniature refrigerator.

Valerius Cordius, in 1540, described the preparation of ether from alcohol and sulphuric acid, a reaction which is still used during the manufacture of ether, and which may be represented in simplified form as follows :

$$2 \ C_2H_5OH \qquad (C_2H_5)_2O \qquad .. \qquad H_2O$$
$$\text{alcohol} \qquad\qquad \text{ether} \qquad\qquad\qquad \text{water}$$

Being a good solvent for fats, resins and other organic compounds, ether is not only used as an anaesthetic but serves many other purposes. Mixed with alcohol it is used to dissolve guncotton (nitrocellulose) to make collodion, of value for forming a protective skin over chilblains, wounds and ulcers.

We have so far only mentioned ordinary ether. To the organic chemist the term " ether " is a general name for a whole family of organic oxides. When we speak of ether we generally mean diethyl ether, but there are other ethers, including dimethyl ether (a gas), methyl ethyl ether, ethyl propyl ether, and vinyl ether.

Ethiopia. When the Arabs conquered northern Africa in the 8th century they scornfully gave the name Abyssinia (from the Arabic word *habesh* or *habeshi*, meaning " mongrel ") to the rugged part of ancient Ethiopia where many mixed Christian tribes took refuge. The modern inhabitants naturally resent the word, and the name Ethiopia is returning to general use. The word Ethiopia is derived from the Greek *aithein*, to burn, and *ops*, face, and was originally applied to all countries inhabited by persons of dark brown or black colour. (See Abyssinia).

Ethnology. This word, derived from two Greek words, *ethnos*, meaning " race " and *logos*, " science," and its fellow term, ethnography, describe the study and the distribution of the races of Man. They are both branches of anthropology, which is the name given to the general study of Man. In the ethnological sections of a museum are articles showing the habits and customs and mode of life of various peoples, generally in such a way that similarities and differences between adjacent races can be compared and contrasted. Ethnographers map out the distribution and migrations, past and present, of the various races of mankind. Much work in these sciences has been done by travellers and explorers.

Etiquette. (Pron. et′-i-ket). The code of good manners called etiquette governs our behaviour in social intercourse as well as in our business life. It teaches us how to conduct ourselves at the table; the usages to be followed by the host and hostess and guests at a dinner party or other entertainment; the correct clothes to be worn by a man or woman at a formal dinner, ball, or reception, and at an informal luncheon or tea. It teaches the correct usage in introducing people to one another—for instance, that a young person should be presented to an older one, and a man to a woman.

Etiquette sets forth certain forms for formal invitations and for accepting or refusing them, certain forms of address for business correspondence, and others for social correspondence. In fact, etiquette prescribes a thousand and one little niceties of behaviour which go to make up the conventional " good manners " that rule in any given society. The groundwork of etiquette is always thoughtfulness for others, courtesy, and a gracious manner.

Table manners are of the greatest importance, and a lack of them is inexcusable. Sit right at the table; do not slide down on your spine or sprawl forward on your elbows. Lay your napkin across your lap; don't tuck it in your collar. Don't fidget with your knife and fork, drum with your fingers, or tap your foot on the floor. Don't make a noise when eating and drinking, or take enormous bites. When eating bread with a meal don't bite into a whole slice, but break the bread into suitable pieces. It is usual, however, to bite into a whole sandwich.

When having soup, fill the spoon from the edge that is farthest from you, and take the soup from the near side of the spoon, not from the tip. If soup is served in cups it is customary to use a spoon for the first part and drink the remainder from the cup. When you have finished eating, drop your napkin unfolded beside your plate.

An important thing to remember about behaviour in the street and in public places is not to interfere with others or to draw attention to yourself. When

a gentleman meets a lady it is she who should smile or speak first. A gentleman lifts his hat to women. If a gentleman wishes to talk with a lady it is correct to turn and walk in her direction. And when he is walking with a lady, a gentleman lifts his hat to anyone she recognizes, whether known to him or not. The lady, however, does not recognize his friends unless they are known to her also. A young man should raise his hat on meeting elderly male acquaintances and persons of importance. When a gentleman is with a lady, he walks between her and the road. A gentleman who enters a vehicle with a lady helps her in and follows her. In leaving he gets off first and helps her down.

The kind of behaviour required in a well-conducted schoolroom is expected in church, theatre, concert- and lecture-hall, libraries, and art galleries. A lady should take off her hat whenever she sees that other ladies have done so. In church it is bad manners to look at a watch or to leave before the service is finished. One may leave a theatre or concert, quietly, between the acts or numbers—never in the middle of one.

Except when in the company of intimate friends, don't talk about yourself or your activities. Don't interrupt people, or help anyone to tell a joke. Remember the words of King Arthur to his knights: " Speak no slander, no, nor listen to it." A malicious story may not be true; it is certainly unkind, and it should not interest you. Rebuke scandal by silence and by changing the subject. Talk of things and ideas, not persons, except interesting public persons like politicians, actors, authors, artists, and musicians, whose talents give wide pleasure. Be brief, be merry and bright. Draw out other people, and be more ready to listen than to talk. Intelligent listeners are scarce and popular. If asked to sing, play, tell stories, or join in a game, do so.

In making an introduction the gentleman is always presented to the lady, and the younger lady to the older. It is sufficient simply to mention the two names, as " Mrs. Miller, Mr. Jones "; but it is rather more dignified to say, " Mrs. Miller, allow me to introduce (or present) Mr. Jones." The people who meet are not required to say anything—a smile and bow are sufficient. It is perfectly good form, however, to say, " How do you do, Mr. Jones? " On being introduced people shake hands or not, as they choose. Two men usually do so. It is the usual custom at evening parties for guests to converse freely with those nearest without previous introduction.

Etna, MOUNT. On the eastern coast of the island of Sicily in the Mediterranean Sea, 200 miles south of Mt. Vesuvius, towers the volcano of Etna—older, much higher and grander in its eruptions (though less frequent) than Vesuvius. More than 80 eruptions of Etna are on record, the earliest about 476 B.C. In A.D. 1169, about 15,000 inhabitants of the neighbouring town of Catania were destroyed, and in the eruption of 1669 some 20,000 perished. In

E.N.A.

ETNA : SNOW-CAPPED VOLCANO
Up to about 3,000 feet the lower slopes of Mount Etna in Sicily are well cultivated and thickly populated, despite the fact that there have been more than 80 recorded eruptions. The latest major eruption was in 1928, when the town of Mascati was completely destroyed.

1792 there was an eruption which lasted for a whole year; that in 1892 lasted six months. There was a destructive eruption in 1928. Over a dozen have occurred in the past century.

In spite of these terrors, villages and farmhouses nestle on Etna's flanks. The mountain rises through three zones—the cultivated region, of about 2,000 feet, where date palms, bananas, oranges, lemons, olives, figs and almonds are grown; the wooded region in the middle, with forests of chestnut, cork, beech, pine, maple and oak; and the desert region, beginning at about 6,300 feet, a waste of black lava and ashes, snow-covered through a large part of the year.

ETON COLLEGE QUADRANGLE

D McLeish

Buildings of dark red brick form three sides of this quadrangle, which is known to Etonians as School Yard, the Chapel occupying the fourth side. Facing us is Lupton's Tower, dating from 1517 and a monument to Roger Lupton, Provost of Eton, 1503-35. On the right is the entrance to the Chapel, completed in 1480 and built on a stone platform to avoid floods

An observatory, 9,075 feet above the sea, was built there in 1880, and is the highest inhabited house in Europe, being 1,000 feet higher than the shelter on the Great St. Bernard in the Alps. The summit of Mt. Etna is about 10,750 feet above the sea; its base is 90 miles round. Much of the world's sulphur is secured from the craters of this mountain, which the Sicilians call Monte Gibello.

Eton. On the north bank of the River Thames, Eton is in the county of Buckinghamshire. Its fame is due to its college, which is acknowledged to be the most famous English public school in the world.

The "King's College of Our Lady of Eton beside Windsor" was founded by Henry VI in 1441. Most of the original structure still stands, but the college in modern times has far out-grown its ancient buildings, and new ones have been added from time to time. Many famous men, including royal princes, have been educated at Eton. Speech-day, the chief annual celebration, is held on June 4. On St. Andrew's Day, November 30, there takes place the wall-game, a kind of football, which is just one long scrimmage, played along the base of a high wall. The population of the town is about 4,000.

Etruscans. In Italy, long before the days of Rome's greatness, there dwelt a people far advanced in civilization and culture—the Etruscans, or Tyrrhenians as they were called by the Greeks. The "mystery race" of Italy, they rose to prosperity and power in the 7th century B.C., and then vanished completely. The Etruscans taught Rome much of her art and science, and they gave her many of her social, religious, and political customs and institutions. But the language of their inscriptions has been only partially deciphered, and only in the few remains of their ancient buildings and monuments—most of all, in their tombs—can we read their puzzling, fascinating story.

As they are depicted in the paintings on the walls of their tombs, the Etruscans were a short, thick-set people, liking garments of graceful lines and bright colours. Their religion was sombre and mysterious, and they dwelt much on the life after death. Otherwise they were fond of good living, games and amusements, dancing, music and the theatre. The women were noted for their jewelry; many specimens, as well as mirrors

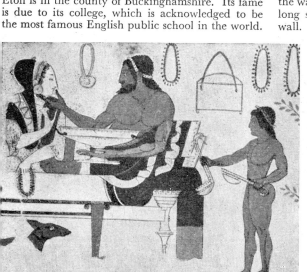

ETRUSCAN FAMILY SCENE

From Weege Etruskische Malerei

Much of what is known about the Etruscans has been learned from paintings on the walls of their burial chambers. Here husband and wife are reclining before a table, while the servant on the right proffers two ladles and a wine strainer.

of polished bronze, have been found in their tombs. Weapons and other implements, vases and statues of stone, bronze, and terracotta show that the Etruscans were skilled craftsmen. But most of their work was imitations of earlier Greek craft.

It is thought that the Etruscans were a seafaring people from somewhere in or near Asia Minor. As early as 1000 B.C. they settled in Italy, in the district corresponding roughly to modern Tuscany, which was then known as Etruria. At one time their rule embraced the greater part of Italy, including Rome. Driven from Rome about 500 B.C., the Etruscans sought power in other fields. They already controlled the commerce of the Tyrrhenian Sea on the west coast of Italy, and they strengthened their naval power by means of an alliance with Carthage against Greece. But in 474 B.C. their fleet was destroyed by the Syracusans of Sicily, and from then onwards their power rapidly declined. The Gauls overran their country, and their fortress of Veii fell to Rome after a 10 years' siege (396 B.C.).

Etymology. The investigation of the origin and meaning of words is termed etymology and includes the branch of philology, or the science of language, concerned with this process. The word etymology is derived from—or, in other words, its etymology is—the Greek words *etymon*, meaning true, and *logos*, science.

Etymology as a science did not become possible until a knowledge of Sanskrit (old sacred language of the Hindus) was introduced into Europe by Sir William Jones (1746–94). This led to the study of the formation of the Indo-European languages and the establishment of certain fixed principles of sound-change which governed the changes in the form of a word in different languages.

Eucalyptus. Among the world's tallest trees is a variety of eucalyptus, native to Australia. All the eucalyptus family are valuable gum trees. Their tall white stems often rise 60 or 70 feet above the ground without a branch. This group includes more than 350 species, ranging from giant trees down to small bushes.

The wood is very tough and durable, and is used for ship construction and wharf-building because it resists decay in the water. It takes a high polish, and so is valuable for interior furnishing. Certain eucalyptus trees yield a gummy sap, from which tannin is obtained. The inner bark of some species consists of very tough and long fibre, used for rope-making, paper, and thatch. The leaves, which in many species turn edgewise to the sun, furnish the eucalyptus oil used in medicine for its germ-killing and stimulating properties.

The name eucalyptus comes from two Greek words meaning " well covered," referring to the abundant foliage. Because this enormous leaf-area enables them to evaporate into the atmosphere the vast quantities of water absorbed by their roots, eucalyptus trees are often planted in swamps, which they help to drain. It is this faculty for drying up mosquito marshes, rather than their pungent odour, which has won for them their reputation as safeguards against malarial mosquitos.

The eucalyptus genus belongs to the family of myrtles. Among the most common species are the blue gum, valuable for its timber; the manna gum, valued for the nectar of its white blossoms of which bees are very fond; the jarrah tree, most used for ships and docks; the peppermint tree noted for its oil; and the swamp mahogany specially noted as a reclaimer of swampy lands. The tree makes itself a home in California where 70 species have been adopted for their beauty and utility.

Eugenics (Pron. ū-jen'-iks) Two thousand years ago the Greek philosopher Plato (427–34 B.C.) asked: " If care were not taken in the breeding, would not your dogs and birds greatly deteriorate And what if the same principle holds of the human species? Today we are asking the same question.

Eugenics (from the Greek *eugenes*, meaning well born) as a science dates from the last quarter of the 19th century, when the term was coined by Sir Francis Galton (1822–1911) in his book, Inquiries into Human Faculties. He defined the science a

EUCALYPTUS TREE : FRUIT, FLOWERS AND LEAVES
The extremely small seeds of this useful tree mature within the cup-like fruit shown at the top left ; below it are the fruit, flowers and leaves as they grow on the tree. The giant eucalyptus at the right is of the kind known as the Red Gum.

" the study of the agencies under social control that may improve or impair the racial qualities of future generations, either physically or mentally." Practically, this simply means control of the unfit—the feeble-minded, diseased, and criminal. Segregation of the feeble-minded and those otherwise physically unfit is much advocated.

Euphrates, RIVER (Pron. ū-frā'-tēz). After the Nile, the Euphrates, a river of Iraq, is probably the most famous stream in history. It rises in north-east Turkey and flows south, breaking through the Taurus Mountains in a succession of rapids and cataracts for about 40 miles. At Kurna the Tigris joins it, and the combined stream with the new name of Shatt-el-Arab empties itself by several arms into the Persian Gulf, about 1,700 miles from the source of the Euphrates. It is navigable for small boats for nearly 1,200 miles, and steamboats ascend it to its junction with the Tigris.

In ancient times, by a system of canals and embankments, the river was used for irrigating the country as the Nile is used in Egypt, but the works were not kept up. Today there is little to suggest the fertility and culture of 5,000 years ago. The Euphrates is mentioned in the Bible as one of the four rivers of the Garden of Eden. The city of Babylon was situated on its banks and Nebuchadrezzar, who was King of Babylon from 604 to 561 B.C., had locks and dikes made to enable large vessels to sail up the river as far as the city. The river figured prominently in the Mesopotamian campaign of the First World War (1914–18).

Eurhythmics. (Pron. ūr-ith'-miks.) About 1910 the Swiss professor E. J. Dalcroze opened a school of eurhythmics with the intention of simplifying the teaching of music. The purpose of his system was " to create by the help of rhythm a rapid and regular current of communication between brain and body." Eurhythmics, as we now know it, is regarded as a system of rhythmical exercises, used simply for self-expression, for the treatment of nervous diseases in children, and for teaching the development of a sense of rhythm. Eurhythmics is useful for a groundwork in dancing, as a means of obtaining exercise, for helping one to understand music, teaching how to breathe correctly and for keeping nerves as well as body in good trim. Numbers of schools teach this system all over the world.

American Colony, Jerusalem

EUPHRATES : RIVER OF WESTERN ASIA
Rising in Turkey, the Euphrates is joined by the Tigris at Kurna in Iraq, the combined stream under the name of Shatt-el-Arab flowing into the Persian Gulf. The Euphrates has no large modern cities on its banks ; but ancient Babylon stood beside it.

EURIPIDES
Athenian tragic dramatist, Euripides (480–406 B.C.) was credited with 90 plays, of which 18 survive ; he was a master in the handling of the tender and pathetic.

Euripides (480–406 B.C.). Tradition says that this great Greek dramatic poet was born on the day of the Greek naval victory over the Persians at Salamis, whither his parents had fled for refuge. In his youth Euripides (pron. ūr-ip'-i-dēz) was a famous athlete, and a painter, but soon began writing for the stage.

He presented his first play at the age of 25, but did not take the prize offered for the best tragedy until he was 39. He wrote over 90 plays, and won the first prize five times. He was in advance of his time. He questioned the popular idea of religion, and he drew real men and women instead of gods and demi-gods or idealized human beings of heroic stature. This is why the Greek philosopher Aristotle (384–322 B.C.) calls him " the most tragic " of the poets, for his plays, being the most human, were also the most moving.

The tragedies of Euripides are more frequently performed on the modern stage than those of any other Greek poet. Among the 18 plays that have survived are Alcestis, notable for its picture of woman's devotion; Medea, regarded as among his masterpieces; Hippolytus, the tragic love story of Phaedra; Hecuba; The Trojan Women; and Electra.

Taking a BIRD'S-EYE VIEW *of* EUROPE

Though smallest but one of the continents, Europe has an importance and interest out of all proportion to its size. Here, briefly, are described its geographical features. Details are in articles on the individual countries.

Europe. Packed into Europe's small area are most of the great nations of the world. By making a series of short journeys every day it would be possible to hear a different language daily for several weeks, and to visit the cities and battlefields where most of the history of the world has been made for the past 2,000 years.

Nor is any region of the world more delightful, in normal times, for the traveller. Rapidly the scene changes from the woods and green fields of England to the carefully cultivated valleys of France; from the mountain pastures of Switzerland, knee-deep in flowers, to the olive groves and vineyards of Spain and Italy; and from the canals and windmills of the Netherlands to the deeply cleft fiords of the coast of Norway.

Europe has been the favoured continent of civilization. It has no such barriers of desert and mountain as Asia (of which it is in reality a western prolongation), no such vast distances, no such extremes of temperature. It lies entirely outside the tropical zone and almost wholly outside the frigid zone. Its average elevation above the sea is the lowest of any continent except that of Australia. These two advantages, combined with the warm winds blowing from the Atlantic, give it the mildest and most genial climate of all the land masses in the same latitude, as well as a wide distribution of rainfall.

Half the secret of the even temperature of this continent lies in its sea-coast—more than 23,000 miles long. Besides being a long coast it is largely a western one. This means that the warm west winds from the ocean give the western parts of the continent a much warmer climate than is the lot of those in the east.

Let us travel round the coast of Europe, starting at the south-east. The first feature is the little Russian peninsula of the Crimea reaching down into the Black Sea. Then, sailing through the Bosporus at Istanbul, the Sea of Marmara, and the Dardanelles, we must travel far to the south to skirt the Balkan peninsula, at the end of which is Greece. Continuing westward, the Italian peninsula is reached, and then, sailing the last half of the length of the blue Mediterranean, we arrive at the Iberian peninsula, comprising Spain and Portugal. This is the second largest of all the peninsulas of Europe. It is so broad and high that, except for the low-lying rim, it has a Continental rather than an oceanic climate, i.e. it is very hot in summer and very cold in winter. Continue through the Strait of Gibraltar, round Portugal, across the Bay of Biscay, through the English Channel, and into the North Sea, and presently there appears the peninsula of Denmark jutting north from Germany. Just opposite is the Scandinavian peninsula, the largest of all.

The long, deeply-indented sea-coast has encouraged commerce by rendering communication easier. At first it is surprising to find that most of the larger seaports lie well inland. Hamburg is 75 miles up the Elbe, and Bremen is about 50 miles up the Weser. Amsterdam lies at the end of a sea canal, Rotterdam some distance up the Rhine, and Antwerp at the head of the estuary of the Scheldt. Hull on the Humber, and London on the Thames, are both some miles from the sea. So it is with Rouen on the Seine, Nantes on the Loire, Bordeaux on the Garonne, Oporto on the Douro, Lisbon on the Tagus, and Seville, which is not less than 70 miles inland, on the Guadalquivir. It is no accident that these ancient ports lie so far inland. Their founders established them at the highest fordable point to which the tides reached, in order to serve the commerce of both banks, and to make them less vulnerable to attack.

The Mediterranean, unlike the Atlantic, has no great navigable rivers flowing into it. The Ebro, the Rhône, and the Po are the only large rivers discharging into it from Europe. Of these the Rhône is too swift, and the others are at certain seasons too shallow for sea-going vessels. Nor would the Mediterranean river ports—if there were any—have the advantage of tides enjoyed by Atlantic ports, for Mediterranean tides are slight.

The ports of the Black Sea are of comparatively little importance, with the exception of Odessa in the Soviet Union, although into it flow four navigable rivers—the Don, the Dnieper, the Dniester and the Danube. The Danube is the second river of Europe, and forms the great highway between Central Europe and the East. The Caspian receives the largest river of Europe, the Volga, which is navigable for 2,260 miles of its 2,500, but it is icebound in winter. This fact, together with that of its emptying into the land-locked Caspian, makes it suitable only for local traffic. The Pechora, flowing into the Arctic Sea, and the Dvina into the White Sea, are icebound for more than half the year, and only during the summer months can timber, furs and grain

---

Extent.—North to south, 2,400 miles; east to west, 3,000 miles; area about 4,000,000 square miles. Population, estimated at about 500 million.

Mountains.—Northern system, including mountains of Scotland and Scandinavia (highest point 8,540 feet); southern system, including Pyrenees, Alps, and Carpathians, with Apennines and Balkans as offshoots (highest point, Mt. Blanc, 15,782 feet). The Ural Mountains (highest, about 5,540 feet) and Caucasus Mountains (Mt. Elbruz, highest peak in Europe, 18,470 feet) separate Europe from Asia.

Rivers and Lakes.—Chief Rivers: Rhine, Elbe, Oder, Vistula, Dvina, and Pechora flowing northward into the North Sea, Baltic, or Arctic Ocean; Rhône, Po, Danube, Dniester, Dnieper, and Don flowing south into the Mediterranean, Adriatic, or Black Seas; Volga and Ural flowing south into the land-locked Caspian Sea. Largest lakes: Ladoga, Onega, and Peipus in Russia, Wener and Wetter in Sweden, with numerous smaller lakes in Finland and in the Alpine region in the heart of the Continent.

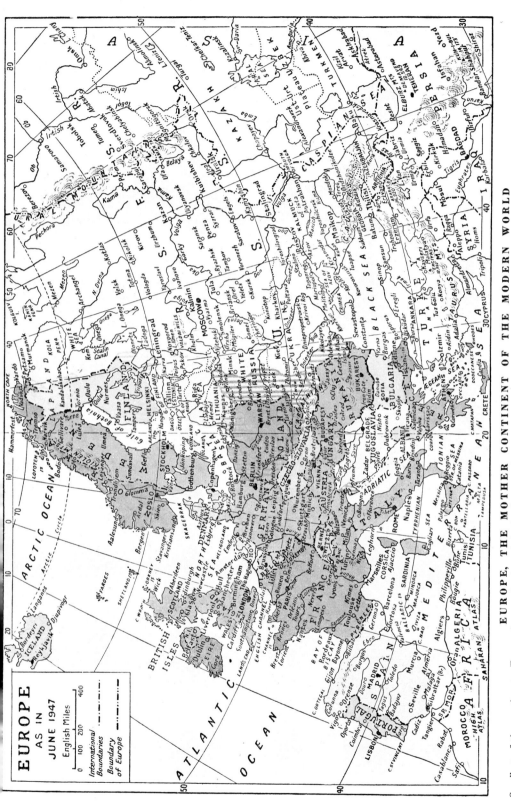

EUROPE, THE MOTHER CONTINENT OF THE MODERN WORLD

Smallest of the continents, Europe is a projection of the land mass of Asia, the two continents together being known as Eurasia. The boundary between them is based on ancient Russian political divisions and is roughly determined by the Ural Mountains. Territorial changes arising out of the Second World War (1939–45), which are indicated by vertical stripes, are not final, and can only be considered official after the signing of the Peace Treaties.

To face page 1252

be brought to Archangel for export. A series of canals has, however, considerably improved river communication in Soviet Russia.

Europe's long sea-coast creates industries of its own as well as promoting commerce. Fishing ports dot nearly its entire length, and the fishing fleets push far out into the open sea—to Arctic Iceland and the distant Banks of Newfoundland. In the Baltic and North Seas the fisheries appear to be practically inexhaustible.

The curing of fish is an important industry. Olive oil and sheet-tin for tinning sardines are among the largest imports of Norway; and smoked, salted or pickled cod, salmon and herring are produced in large quantities. Kippers and Yarmouth bloaters (forms of herring) from Great Britain, and anchovies and sardines from the Mediterranean and the Atlantic coast of Spain and Portugal, are exported to many countries.

How would the continent of Europe look if we could see its whole extent as a great panorama stretched out before our eyes? Imagine that we are far above the Alps—the roof of Europe—in an aeroplane and are equipped with binoculars powerful enough to see any part of the continent.

First, look straight down. Under our feet lie the snow-capped peaks of the Alps, rising from valleys dotted with lakes and green patches of mountain meadows. This magnificent range, from 10,000 to 15,000 feet high, is one of many ranges of rugged mountains of southern Europe.

To the south in Italy we see the Alps falling steeply to the low fertile Po river basin, the plain of Lombardy. This is perhaps the most productive region of Europe. On both sides of the Po valley the Alps thrust out long fingers to the south-east—jagged ranges, but not so high as the central mountains. One of these, the Apennines, forms the backbone of Italy, reaching far into the Mediterranean and nearly joining Europe and Africa by way of the island of Sicily. On the eastern side of the Adriatic Sea lie the Dinaric Alps, continued by the huge, broken, sprawling mass of highlands which make up the Balkan peninsula, the Balkan mountains pushing east to the Black Sea, and the Pindus range dividing Greece.

The mountains of the eastern wing of the Alps are prolonged north-eastward across the Danube by the grand sweeping curve of the Transylvanian Alps and the Carpathians, which circle round the northern and north-eastern edge of the plain of Hungary. In this mountain-girdled basin fields of wheat, maize, flax and rye alternate with treeless steppes where horses, sheep and cattle graze. The lower basin of the Danube, separated from the Hungarian plain by the gorge of the Iron Gates, is a far-stretching expanse of treeless plain. There the Rumanians raise their wheat and maize and pasture extensive herds.

In the far distance—2,000 miles away to the north-east—is the long low range of the Urals, which forms 1,200 miles of the boundary between

IN THE NETHERLANDS SHIPS SAIL ABOVE THE FIELDS

Some typical sights of the Netherlands are shown here. They include dikes to keep back the sea and to furnish banks for the canals, which are so vital a part of the country's transport system, and tree-lined roads like those in the distance in the top left-hand corner. Beyond the crowded canal are partially-flooded marshlands. The windmill by the farm in the right foreground is one of very many. On many Dutch farms stables and cowsheds are built on to the house, so that the farmer can tend the animals without having to go out into the open.

Europe and Asia. These are old worn-down hills, the mere stumps of mountain ranges that once rose steep and high, reaching from the Arctic Ocean almost to the Caspian Sea.

Nearly the whole of the Russian plain between the Carpathians and the Urals is covered with enormous grasslands and fields of wheat and other grain, potatoes and sugar-beets, alternating with woods and marshes. In the far south, near the Black Sea and the Caspian, the plain becomes a treeless steppe, pasturing the herds of wandering inhabitants. Around the margin of the Caspian, in the basin which that sea once occupied, the soil is so filled with salt that few plants will grow.,

In the far north, next to the icy Arctic Ocean, the plain takes the form of the swamps called

North Sea. If we could look down through the waters to the ocean bottom we should see that the North Sea is far shallower than the rest of the Atlantic. In fact, the North Sea is a drowned plain which once rose above the surface of the ocean and joined the British Isles with continental Europe. This whole region has now sunk so far beneath the waves that only the high plateaux and tops of the mountains still remain uncovered, forming the British Isles.

Now look back to the great Russian plain—the granary of Europe. Notice how it continues westward along the Baltic, forming the fertile lowlands of the Soviet Republics of Estonia, Latvia, Lithuania, and of Poland. Farther on it forms the northern half of Germany, with the Danish peninsula jutting north. The plain is then continued to the south along the North Sea, forming the Netherlands and the lowlands of Belgium—much of it so low that it is actually below the sea-level and is only prevented from being drowned like the rest of the old North Sea plain by an elaborate system of dikes.

In north-western France the plain spreads out, forming the fertile Paris basin. On it goes, southwards, past the plateau of Brittany— once a part of the chain of mountains that ran all the way in a great semicircle through the British Isles to Scandinavia —again expanding to form the wine and wheat district of the Garonne valley. Here is the formid-

Polish Embassy

EUROPEAN BISON PRESERVED IN POLAND

Two or three thousand years ago the European Bison, which is smaller than the North American species, was common in many parts of the Continent. Now only a few herds remain, in the Caucasus Mountains, Russia, and in Poland. The Polish herds, which suffered severely during the First and Second World Wars, are preserved in national parks (above) by the Government.

tundras, which never thaw for more than a yard or so below the surface; below that, the ground is permanently frozen. Here grow only mosses, lichens, dwarfed trees—many only a few inches high—and a few other hardy plants.

Following the line of the Arctic Ocean to the west, the plains continue right up to the forest-covered hills of Finland between the Arctic Ocean and the Baltic Sea. The surface of Finland is dotted with hundreds of lakes amidst the forests. Further west the upland of Finland rises into the broad highland mass of the Scandinavian peninsula, which reaches south between the Gulf of Bothnia and the Atlantic. The mountains of Sweden and Norway have been worn down through the ages into a series of broad plateaux dotted with clear blue lakes. On the west coast the sea has entered the old valleys, making the steep-walled fiords.

Follow the line of the Scandinavian peninsula south-westward to the British Isles across the

able barrier of the Pyrenees, the rugged range which completely shuts off the Iberian peninsula from the rest of Europe, except around its flanks. On the other side of the Pyrenees are the dry and barren plateaux of Spain, traversed by chains of mountains and bordered by narrow strips of lowlands along the coast. Portugal is mildly hilly, with extensive flat areas.

We have now viewed the whole of the continent of Europe, and noted its most important natural features, except the central highlands that slope north and west from the Alps. Now look north-west, across the Rhône. The central highlands here are the treasure-house of Europe. They contain most of the great iron and coal mines on which the industrial prosperity of Europe depends ; and they are rich in other kinds of minerals, as well as in water-power and timber. Although Europe is the smallest of the continents, with the exception of Australia, it is the most densely populated. It

Known as the Piz Bernina, this Alpine height, 13,295 feet above sea level, is in south-east Switzerland, near the Italian frontier, its northern slope overlooking the Upper Engadine Valley. Climbers in the foreground are contemplating the final hazardous ascent to the summit, which is considered the most difficult in that region. The Alps are of great importance to Europe, because in summer their melting snows feed the rivers which water the fertile plains of France, Germany, Italy and Austria; and their swift-flowing streams generate electricity for the railways of Switzerland and Italy. Although Switzerland is generally regarded as the Alpine country of Europe, the mountain system to which is given the comprehensive title of Alps extends west into France (where is the highest peak, Mont Blanc), east into Germany and Austria, and south into Italy.

The number and beauty of the pinnacles and the delicate tracery of the stonework of the cathedral at Milan, Italy, make it one of the most magnificent buildings in the world. Built of brick faced with white marble, it was founded in 1386 but was not completed until the beginning of the 19th century. Here we see how elaborately the flying buttresses (*see* Architecture) have been ornamented. There are 98 spires on the church and more than 4,000 statues. The cathedral covers an area of 14,000 square yards and is capable of accommodating a congregation of some 40,000 persons. After St. Peter's in Rome and the cathedral at Seville, Spain, it is the largest church in Europe. Milan stands in the plain of Lombardy, and is the industrial capital of Italy.

has a total population of about 300 million—more than half as much as Asia, and nearly twice that of North and South America combined.

Comparatively few wild animals still remain in Europe. Reindeer roam parts of the far north, and the last remaining European bison are preserved in the national parks of Poland and in the Caucasus Mountains. Some of the wilder forest regions harbour wild boars, bears and wolves. The lynx is found in Sweden and Norway. The chamois still exists in the mountains of central and southern Europe. Deer and other game preserves are numerous.

A large part of Europe was once covered with forests; but centuries of reckless destruction ex-hausted the timber over many thousands of square miles, and this so seriously affected climate and irrigation owing to the loss of the power of the forests to preserve moisture that governments now replant and look after forests systematically.

Europe falls into three main climatic divisions: (1) the Mediterranean region, where the summers are dry and hot and the winters mild and rainy; (2) the east, where most of the rainfall comes in the summer and where the differences of tempera-ture between summer and winter are great; and (3) the west, where the rainfall is distributed throughout the year and the seasonal changes in temperature are only comparatively slight.

The DRAMA of EUROPE'S HISTORY

For thousands of years Europe has been the scene of tremendous events—of battles which spelt the doom of entire nations, of wide-spread social changes, the rise and fall of principalities and powers.

European History. Twenty-five thousand years ago, at the close of the last Ice Age, or glacial epoch, primitive Man had already made his home in Europe. From the caves of France, Spain, Germany, and elsewhere; from wooden villages set on piles driven into lake- or river-bottoms; from southern Sweden and Switzer-land to the south of Italy and the Black Sea, the smoke of his camp-fires floated over the forests. Slowly and painfully he was rising from savagery to barbarism.

More advanced civilization began, about 2500 B.C., to come from Egypt and Asia by way of the islands of the Aegean Sea. In course of time this flowered into the splendours of Greek and Roman culture. With these two peoples there begins the recorded history of Europe, as opposed to our dim glimpses into its pre-historic past.

On the death of Theo-dosius the Great (A.D. 395) the Roman Empire was divided into two parts—the Western Empire with Rome as its capital, and the Eastern Empire (also called the Greek, or Byzan-tine, Empire), the capital of which was Constantinople (now Istanbul). Beyond the boundaries of the Roman world were numerous bar-baric peoples, divided into three main groups: (1) remnants of the Celtic stock in outlying parts of the British Isles; (2) Germans or Teutonic folk lying along the Rhine and Danube and in the Scandinavian pen-insula; and (3) the great mass of the Slavs, ances-tors of our modern Poles, Russians, Czechs, Yugo-slavs, and others, whose tribes even at that time lay eastward of the Teutons.

The German barbarians were divided into tribes called Goths, Burgundians, Vandals, Alamannians, Bavarians, Langobards (Lombards), Franks, Angles, Saxons, Frisians, etc. For nearly 200 years Visigoths and Ostrogoths had been established along the shores of the lower Danube and the Black Sea. This region was invaded by the Huns from Central Asia and its inhabitants pushed westward, causing the great Gothic invasion (A.D. 375).

Gaul was overrun chiefly by Visigoths, Bur-gundians, and Franks; Spain by Vandals, Suevi, and Visigoths; Africa by Vandals crossing from Spain. Italy suffered a number of invasions, especially those of the Visigoths, Ostrogoths, and Lombards; Britain, after being abandoned by its Roman garrison (A.D. 410), became a prey to Angles and Saxons sailing from the mouth of the

Drawing after Professor J. M. Tyler, New Stone Age

EUROPE'S PREHISTORIC LAKE-DWELLINGS

Thousands of years ago, during the New Stone and Bronze Ages, a broad-headed people came to western Europe and developed a new way of living. They constructed villages on piles over shallow lakes and marshes, connected with the land by wooden causeways. Similar lake-dwellings are still found in the Admiralty Islands in the Pacific Ocean.

Elbe. But the influence of Rome—language, law and government—has never been wholly effaced.

It was the task of Charlemagne (742–814), building on the foundations laid by the Frankish kings who preceded him, to consolidate the Germanic conquests into an empire which stretched from the River Ebro in Spain to beyond the Elbe, and from the North Sea to a little south of Rome. The decline of classical civilization was checked; something of the Roman tradition of unity, order and centralization was preserved in the face of advancing feudalism; and Christianity was spread through most of Western Europe. But Mahomedanism, established in Spain since 711, lingered until the Moors were conquered in 1492.

The division of the Frankish empire in the Partition of Verdun (843) became the starting-point of the kingdoms and nations of France and Germany. Under Otto I, German king from 936 to 973, the empire in the West was revived, in 962, as the "Holy Roman Empire." But it now included only Germany and Italy, and its power grew ever less until its extinction in 1806.

Remnant of Gothic Power in Spain

The Eastern Empire stood as a barrier against Asiatic conquest and Mahomedanism until it was overwhelmed by the Ottoman Turks (fall of Constantinople, 1453). Where Hungary now is dwelt the Asiatic Avars, whose place was taken in the 10th century by their kindred the modern Magyars. Nothing but the little kingdom of Asturias was left of the Gothic power in Spain; but from this seed grew the Christian realms

of Castile, Leon, and Aragon, which were consolidated in the 15th century into the kingdom of "their Catholic Majesties," the sovereigns of Spain until 1931, when King Alphonso XIII fled the land of his fathers.

The Viking Northmen, after raiding from their Scandinavian homes the coasts of all western Europe in the 9th century, settled in western France in 911; then as "Normans" they founded the kingdom of Naples and Sicily in Italy, and gave a new dynasty to England through William the Conqueror (1066). William's descendant on the female side, Henry II of Anjou, was king of England, lord of Ireland, and feudal holder of Normandy, Anjou, Brittany, and Aquitaine in France. Only gradually were the Capetian kings of France able to restore the unity of their kingdom and set it on that path which made it under Louis XI, 1461 to 1483, the first strong monarchical state of modern times.

Meanwhile the "States of the Church" were established in Italy as the temporal dominion of the Pope; Poland and Russia became settled Christian states; the heathen Prussians were Christianized and Germanized by the Order of Teutonic Knights; feudalism, Christianity, monasticism, and medieval art and learning spread everywhere, and the Crusades, the growth of town life, and the reviving commerce prepared the way for the Renaissance.

The expedition of Charles VIII of France, in 1494, to assert his claim to inherit the kingdom of Naples and Sicily, started a series of wars over Italy which embroiled France and Spain for half a century and enabled the Reformation started

ROME FALLS TO THE BARBARIC VISIGOTHS

Terror swept through Rome when the Visigoths (Western Goths) captured and sacked the capital of the tottering Roman Empire in A.D. 410. The Visigoths were a Teutonic people who came from the neighbourhood of the Baltic Sea and the River Vistula. They migrated southwards, and the Romans had allowed them to settle in a region approximately corresponding to modern Rumania. Under their leader Alaric they rebelled against Rome and in A.D. 400 invaded Western Europe by way of Northern Italy. After the fall of Rome Alaric's successor withdrew from Italy and established the kingdom of Toulouse, which embraced Spain as well as southern France.

EUROPE'S THIRTY YEARS' WAR AT AN END

On October 24, 1648, the Thirty Years' War, in which most of Europe had been involved, was terminated by a series of treaties which were signed either at Osnabrück or Münster in Germany. This picture by the Dutch artist Gerard Ter Borch (*c.* 1617–81) shows peace being concluded between Spain and the Netherlands at Münster. The Spanish ambassador is taking the oath to observe the treaty with his hand on a Bible upon which lies a crucifix.

by Luther (*q.v.*) to get such a hold that it could not be stamped out. The close of the conflict left the German Emperor Charles V ruler not only of united Spain and Germany, but also of Sardinia, Sicily and Naples, Milan, the Netherlands, the county of Burgundy (Franche Comté), and a great part of the New World. His brother, Ferdinand I, Archduke of Austria and emperor, and head of the German branch of the Hapsburgs after Charles, obtained by marriage Silesia, Bohemia, and that part of Hungary which had not fallen into the hands of the victorious Turks. The power of the Spanish Hapsburgs declined under Charles's son, Philip II, and his successors.

The close of the Thirty Years' War (1618–48) —the last of the wars of religion—left the Holy Roman Empire greatly weakened and practically confined to Germany and Austria. France became again the first power of Europe, having obtained much of the Burgundian lands (including Franche Comté), conquered by Louis XIV. Savoy, straddling the French Alps, was becoming an Italian power. Spain still held the Spanish Netherlands and a great part of Italy.

The Protestant Netherlands (Holland) and Switzerland had freed themselves by successful revolt from the Empire. Sweden, independent of Denmark since 1523, was one of the great powers, having conquered territories alike from Germany, Poland, and Russia. Denmark still ruled Norway. The duchy of Prussia, united to Brandenburg in 1618, was soon (1701) to give its name to a new German kingdom erected by the Hohenzollerns. During the 16th century Poland (in union with Lithuania since 1569) was one of the most powerful states of Europe, stretching from the Baltic almost to the Black Sea; but the 18th century saw its steady decline. Russia, under Peter the Great (1672–1725) and Catherine II (1729–96), became a formidable and disquieting power. Turkey, though reduced since its high-water mark of conquest in the 17th century, still retained the greater part of the former Eastern Empire. Venice held sway in the Adriatic and the Eastern Mediterranean; and Genoa held Corsica until it passed to France in 1768.

Soon after the outbreak of the French Revolution (1789) Poland ceased to exist, through partition by her neighbours. Prussia had risen to the rank of a great power following the wars of Frederick the Great. Sweden had lost the leadership of northern Europe. The Spanish Netherlands had passed to Austria in 1713; and branches of the French house of Bourbon ruled the parts of Italy that had been Spanish, as well as Spain herself.

Expansion of Britain Overseas

Britain meanwhile had built up a great overseas Empire in the New World and in the East, whose steady growth during the 19th century was to give her an influence quite out of proportion to her size. The Industrial Revolution, too, brought with it social changes as important in their way as those ushered in by the French Revolution of 1789 (*q.v.*). As the " Mother of Parliaments " Britain was in many ways a model to the world.

The wars of the French Revolution began a series of changes that ended in the extension of Napoleon's direct empire over Germany west of the

Rhine, the Netherlands, north-western Germany, and a great part of Italy and Dalmatia. In addition, Spain was ruled by his brother Joseph, Naples by his brother-in-law Murat, and the Grand Duchy of Warsaw and the Confederation of the Rhine by his nominees. After the fall of Napoleon at Waterloo the Congress of Vienna forced France to retire within her old limits, and in large part restored the old government. But Russia was allowed to annex Finland from Sweden and increase her Polish territories by absorbing the Grand Duchy of Warsaw. Prussia was enlarged at the expense of Saxony, and by annexations on the west bank of the Rhine. Austria was given northern Italy in exchange for Belgium, which was united with Holland until 1830. Norway was torn from Denmark and given to Sweden, with which it remained united until 1905.

Fantastic Brotherhood of Rulers

The states of Germany (now reduced from several hundred to 39, including Austria and Prussia) were organized into a loose union called the German Confederation, taking the place of the Holy Roman Empire which had now disappeared. A fantastic " Christian brotherhood " of sovereigns was formed by the Tsar Alexander I of Russia, called the "Holy Alliance." But the real power, which, under the lead of the Austrian statesman Metternich, through a series of European congresses, preserved peace and bolstered up absolute power for 30 years, was the " Grand Alliance " of states which had overthrown Napoleon.

The revolutions of 1830 and 1848, whose waves spread from France over a large part of Europe, showed that democracy and liberalism on the Continent were not yet dead. A series of wars and diplomatic incidents covering nearly a century reduced the Turkish power to a bare foothold in Europe and freed the Christian Balkan states.

In the second half of the 19th century the chief events were the freeing of Italy from Austrian rule and its union into a kingdom under the house of Savoy; the uniting of the German states by Bismarck into the German Empire under the hereditary rule of the king of Prussia; Germany's annexation of Alsace-Lorraine from France after the Franco-Prussian War of 1870–1; and the reorganization of Austria into the Austro-Hungarian monarchy.

Creation of the Triple Entente

France never ceased to resent her humiliation and the loss of Alsace-Lorraine in the Franco-Prussian War; and Bismarck, fearing French revenge, linked Austria and Italy with Germany in the defensive Triple Alliance. For more than two decades France was isolated diplomatically, but after Bismarck's dismissal from office in 1890 France succeeded in creating the Triple Entente —France, Russia, and Great Britain—as a counterbalance to the Triple Alliance. This action was based on the old theory of " balance of power "— that power in Europe should be so distributed that no one nation or group of nations should be able to dominate the others.

Both sets of powers steadily increased their military forces until Europe became an armed camp. Two peace conferences held at The Hague, in 1899 and 1907, failed to limit national armaments; and entangling alliances and the continual increase of great national armaments bred international fear, suspicion and unrest.

In 1912 and 1913 two Balkan wars gave rise to a clash of interest and ambition among the great powers of Europe, and resulted in territorial changes in the Balkans unfavourable to the Hapsburg empire. After 1913 this empire was especially desirous of crushing Serbia, which, doubled in size by the Balkan wars, was now looking enviously at

REVISING EUROPE'S MAP : THE VIENNA CONGRESS

After the abdication of Napoleon Bonaparte in 1814 statesmen of the European Powers met in Vienna to adjust frontiers and endeavour to lay the foundations of lasting peace in Europe. The Congress opened on September 20, 1814, and the final agreement was signed on June 9, 1815. Amongst the territory received by Britain were the islands of Malta and Ceylon. A result of the Congress was the union of the Austrian Netherlands (now Belgium) with Holland to form the Kingdom of the Netherlands, which lasted until 1830 when Belgium became independent. This lithograph by Dorndorf after the painting by the French artist J. B. Isabey (1767–1855) shows the Congress in session.

Bosnia and Herzegovina, where many Serbs lived. The assassination of Francis Ferdinand, Austrian crown prince, in the Bosnian capital of Sarajevo (June 28, 1914) was the result of Serbian propaganda. Austria's determination to crush the little Serbian state at length brought her system of alliances into operation and led to the First World War (1914–18).

Italy's desertion then of the Triple Alliance to adhere to the Entente (Britain, France and Russia) was balanced by the early successes of Germany and her allies, Austria, Bulgaria, and Turkey, against Serbia and Russia. There were campaigns in Italy, in Mesopotamia and Palestine, in Africa, in Eastern Europe. But the conflict was really decided on the Western front, where France and Belgium were the scene of four and a half years of terribly costly trench warfare; and at sea, where the British blockade was pitted against the Germans' unrestricted submarine campaign. The scale was finally turned against Germany with the entry into the war, in 1917, of the United States.

Peace was signed at Versailles in 1919. With the setting up of the League of Nations there were many who truly believed they had fought "a war to end war." A new and unfamiliar map of Europe emerged from the peace conferences. Poland was re-created as an independent

Imperial War Museum

SIGNING THE VERSAILLES TREATY

Terminating the First World War with Germany (1914–18) and establishing the League of Nations, the Treaty of Versailles was signed on June 28, 1919, in the Hall of Mirrors of the Palace of Versailles, not far from Paris. This picture, painted by Sir William Orpen (1878–1931), shows the German delegate, Dr. Johannes Bell (seated in foreground) appending his signature.

state. The Empire of Austria-Hungary fell in fragments: a part became the new republic of Czechoslovakia; a part joined with Montenegro and Serbia to form Yugoslavia; other areas went to Italy, Rumania, and the restored Poland. There remained only the republic of Austria and the kingdom of Hungary, reduced to about half its former size.

Birth of the Soviet Union

In Russia, beaten by Germany and forced in 1918 to sign the treaty of Brest-Litovsk, something had happened almost as significant as the war itself. There had been a revolution : the Tsar had been overthrown, and the "Bolsheviks," led by Lenin and Trotsky, had seized power. Russia was much reduced after the First World War: Poland in part, and Finland, Estonia, Lithuania, and Latvia wholly, were carved from its territories in the nationalist uprisings of peoples submerged for centuries in the Russian Empire. Together with the Ukraine, White Russia, the Caucasus and Central Asia, where the Bolsheviks had also seized power, Russia was transformed into the Union of Soviet Socialist Republics (U.S.S.R.) in 1923. Ravaged by war and by civil strife, the Russians began to build again on entirely new lines.

In Western Europe, France regained Alsace-Lorraine, Denmark recovered a part of the duchy of Slesvig lost to Germany in the war of 1865, and

Belgium received Eupen and Malmédy from Germany. In the Balkans, Bulgaria surrendered territory to Greece and Yugoslavia. Most of the changes were designed to resolve problems of minorities living under foreign rule.

At the same time advances were made in popular government. Many of the old monarchies—the Hapsburg, Hohenzollern, Romanov, and Ottoman dynasties—had been swept away, and the majority of Europeans now lived under republics. Twenty states, including Great Britain, Germany, Russia and Spain, joined Norway, Denmark and Finland in granting votes to women.

New instruments of international co-operation and the settlement of disputes were set up—the League of Nations and the Court of International Justice. The nations bound themselves to keep the peace by the Locarno treaties of 1925 and the Kellogg-Briand peace pact of 1928.

But there was no true peace. Poland fought with Russia, and Turkey with Greece. In 1922 most of Ireland broke with Great Britain to form the Irish Free State. High hopes placed in the League of Nations were dashed at the outset when the U.S.A. declined to become a member state. The nations returned to the making of alliances: France joined with Poland and the Little Entente (Czechoslovakia, Rumania, Yugoslavia) to block any attempt to mitigate the terms of the Versailles treaty. Impatient of Germany's half-hearted efforts to fulfil her obligations under the treaty, France occupied the Ruhr with armed forces.

Moreover, a Europe impoverished by the terrible waste of war now found many of its world markets lost to the U.S.A. and Japan. Policies of national self-sufficiency cut down trade, and high protective tariffs formed barriers to the free flow of goods. The world was gripped by economic depression; millions were thrown out of work. A great slump struck Europe in 1929.

Small wonder that there was unrest in many nations. As early as 1922 Benito Mussolini had made his Fascists masters in Italy. Eleven years later Adolf Hitler and his " Nazis " (National Socialists) ruthlessly seized absolute power in Germany, and before long these two dictators began deliberately to plan the conquest of the world. In 1935 Germany, in defiance of the terms of the peace treaty, began to rebuild its navy, to enlarge its army, and to develop a powerful air force. There ensued a race for rearmament, demands for new alliances and agreements: but Britain, France, and Russia were hesitant. In 1936 Italy opened an aggressive war against Abyssinia, resigning from the League of Nations.

Civil war broke out in 1936 in Spain, where a republic had been established in 1931. Germany and Italy sent troops to aid the anti-government forces under General Franco, profiting by the opportunity to test out their new weapons.

Coming of the Second World War

In 1938 Germany was strong enough to begin a series of demands against her neighbour states. In the spring she seized Austria. In the autumn she forced the cession of the Sudetenland province from Czechoslovakia with the acquiescence of Britain and France. Six months later the German army marched into the rest of Czechoslovakia, proclaimed a protectorate over Bohemia and Moravia, and set up a puppet state in Slovakia.

Meanwhile (Easter 1939) Italy had attacked Albania and annexed it to the Italian crown. Neither that unprovoked attack, nor the German seizure of Memel, in March 1939, roused the Western powers to action ; but it had become clear that an end must be made. War, long expected, came in September 1939. Hitler had now turned his attention to Poland, which resisted his demands, and was conquered in a few weeks. Britain and France declared war upon Germany.

In May 1939 Britain and France had opened belated negotiations for an anti-German alliance with the U.S.S.R., militarily very much an unknown quantity. To their dismay the Russians, pursuing their own immediate advantages, had come to an agreement with the Germans. Russia claimed a share of Poland, then seized the Baltic states and later, despite gallant resistance, wrested a large area from Finland. In the spring of 1940 Germany invaded Denmark and Norway, and launched the main attack against the Netherlands and France. The Allies were outfought by superior numbers and weapons ; the evacuation of Dunkirk (q.v.) followed. Italy entered the Second World War (q.v.) in June 1940, and France capitulated. With the fall of Yugoslavia and Greece the following spring the whole of Western Europe, save only neutral Spain and Portugal, Sweden and Switzerland, was in the

hands of the so-called " Rome–Berlin axis." Britain alone continued the fight, and though Hitler's bombers battered her towns and her factories the Germans never ventured on an invasion.

Hitler now felt strong enough to attack Russia; and in June 1941 he sent his armies in. Six months later, fulfilling his obligations to Japan, he declared war on the United States. The turning points of the war in Europe were the successful defence of Stalingrad by the Russians, in the autumn of 1942 ; the Allied invasion of Italy, September 1943, and Italy's surrender; and the Anglo–American assault on Europe, launched on the Normandy coast, in June 1944. While British and American bombers hammered the German cities and communications three great Allied armies converged from east, south and west, and in May 1945 Germany surrendered unconditionally. (With the surrender of Japan in August 1945 the long and grim world war ended.)

The war left world power concentrated in the hands of the Americans and the Russians. The U.S.S.R. was now the most formidable force in Europe, and, swallowing up the Baltic states and parts of Finland, Poland, Rumania, and East Prussia, began to work for the spread of her own brand of Communism. The whole of Eastern Europe turned Communist except for Greece and Turkey; Czechoslovakia was the last, standing out until the beginning of 1948.

It was clear now that European history could not be divorced from the fate of the whole world; and America threw her weight into the scales against Communism. Without help, a devastated Europe would be an easy prey to the Russian Communists. In June 1947, General Marshall, U.S. Secretary of State, called on the countries of Europe to unite for recovery, and the following year the U.S.A. voted enormous sums for aid to the stricken economies of the 16 participating nations. Under Russian pressure, the Communist-controlled states of Eastern Europe declined to take part in the scheme. This was known as the European Recovery Programme, or Marshall Plan (see Marshall).

Doubt of Russian intentions led to the signing in 1948 of a mutual aid pact by the governments of Great Britain, France, the Netherlands and Luxemburg. This Western Union partnership was strengthened in 1949 by the North Atlantic Treaty, whereby the United Kingdom, U.S.A., France, Belgium, the Netherlands, Luxemburg, Canada, Norway, Denmark, Italy, Iceland and Portugal undertook to help each other in the event of war and to co-operate in trading.

Further to deal with cultural, social, and economic problems of Western Europe a Council of Europe was formed the same year, this " parliament " being attended by representatives of the United Kingdom, Belgium, Denmark, France, the republic of Ireland, Italy, Luxemburg, the Netherlands, Norway, Sweden, Turkey and Greece.

How the failure of the Western and the Eastern Occupying Powers in defeated Germany to agree on administration led to the splitting of that country into two republics in 1949 is told in our article Berlin.

The task of the organization known as the United Nations (q.v.) was becoming more and more difficult. The many serious problems which it failed to solve increased the anxieties of a peace-hungry world.

Evaporation.

A small illustration of one of the biggest things in the world takes place when clothes dry on washing day. Evaporation makes the world fit to live in. It is the means by which water is drawn from the oceans and from minor sources of moisture—giving the air its necessary humidity, lessening the changes of temperature between day and night and between winter and summer, and creating the clouds that in their season give snow and rain to help to raise crops and swell watercourses.

The air at any given temperature has a certain definite capacity for holding water vapour, somewhat as a sponge holds water, and, like a sponge, the air takes water vapour from any exposed moist surface—rapidly if it is very dry, more slowly if moist. In desert regions rain may be seen to fall from the clouds though not a drop reaches the ground; this is because the hot dry air drinks it up, or evaporates it.

Desert plants protect themselves against the dry air by exposing as little as possible of their surface for evaporation. The cactus, for instance, presents only spines and thick leathery lobes within which it seals up all the moisture it can gather. For the same reason some species of eucalyptus trees turn their large leaves edgeways to the sun. In more humid climates plants spread out big evaporating surfaces. The leaves of a single tree may give off many gallons of water in the course of a single day, in the form of water vapour.

The capacity of the air for water vapour increases as the temperature rises, and the amount of water actually present in the air at a given temperature, divided by the amount of moisture the air is capable of holding at that temperature, is called the relative humidity.

A very dry atmosphere parches the skin and mucous membranes; but if the air is very moist, as on some sweltering summer days, it does not evaporate perspiration rapidly enough to prevent a hot, " sticky," uncomfortable feeling. One of the most important effects of evaporation is to lower temperature. You are cooler on a hot day if you perspire freely, because the evaporation of the perspiration cools your skin. You are cooler in a breeze than in still air because a breeze assists evaporation by continually bringing new air along. Where there is no ice available in summer and no refrigerator, perishable foods may be kept sound and fresh by wrapping the container in a wet cloth.

The rapid evaporation of highly volatile liquids produces intense cold, where that of water merely chills. The evaporation of ammonia is used in making ice; and the numbing cold caused by the rapid evaporation of ether has been utilized by surgeons to produce local anaesthesia (*q.v.*).

Evelyn, JOHN (1620–1706).

With the exception of his Diary, which is less famous and popular than that of his contemporary and friend Pepys, John Evelyn's works are largely forgotten; yet in a variety of little books and essays he shows himself at least as pleasant a character as Izaak Walton, whose interest in, and love of Nature, he shared. But whereas Walton was obviously a lover of the open spaces, Evelyn possessed a mind which took its greatest pleasure within the limits of a walled garden; he became, indeed, the most famous designer of gardens of his age.

John Evelyn was born at Wotton, Surrey, on October 31, 1620. Though loyal to the king and an ardent churchman, he did not take up arms in the Civil War but divided his time between Wotton, where he beautified the existing gardens and designed new ones, and the Continent, where he travelled widely, taking particular interest in the scenery. In 1652 he purchased Sayes Court, Deptford, where, again, he proved a brilliant horticulturist, his gardens there and at Wotton becoming famous.

Royal Society

JOHN EVELYN

Painted by Sir Godfrey Kneller (1646–1723) in 1679, this portrait of the diarist shows him holding a volume of his Sylva. In this book, John Evelyn drew attention to the importance of forestry in England.

Ugliness or destruction of any kind was anathema to Evelyn, and one of his most interesting words was his Fumifugium, a protest against the damage wrought by coal-smoke in London, and a plea for beautifying the suburbs with flower-beds. His best-known publication was his Sylva, a beautifully written discourse on forest trees. His Pomona concerns fruit-trees and their relation to cider. Among Evelyn's other works on Nature are his Kalendarium Hortense, and Terra, a first attempt in English at a scientific study of agriculture. Evelyn died at Wotton on February 27, 1706.

Everest, MOUNT.

No one has yet climbed to the summit of Mount Everest, the King of the Himalayas, although the British expedition of 1924 nearly did so, Mallory and Irvine being lost on a last heroic attempt in that year. British airmen flew over the summit in 1933, but land assaults then and in 1936 and 1938 were unlucky.

These expeditions are led by experienced and courageous climbers with a large party of native carriers. The highest point (about 28,000 feet) reached by anyone who has survived was attained by E. F. Norton in 1924 and F. S. Smythe in 1933. The people of Tibet, and of Nepal, where Everest is situated, regard it with awe.

Everest is some $5\frac{1}{2}$ miles, or 29,141 (officially 29,002) feet high, and was named in honour of Sir George Everest (1790–1866), the English official who first fixed its position and altitude. (*See* Himalaya Mountains*).

Evergreen.

A tree or plant which retains its foliage throughout the year and is never at any time bare of leaves—such as holly and laurel

—is an evergreen. Evergreens are in contrast with deciduous plants, which shed their leaves every year, generally at the coming of winter, and remain bare for some weeks or months. Evergreens shed their old leaves whilst new young ones are in evidence, and so are never without foliage.

Everyman. The most famous of all " morality " plays, Everyman, which is still frequently performed in England and elsewhere, was originally produced here about 1530. The story tells how Everyman is summoned by Death to go on a journey, and of his attempts to find a willing companion to go with him. Modernized, the play has been very widely produced, being made especially suitable for large-scale open-air spectacular productions. The best known of these is that of the famous German producer Max Reinhardt, which was performed for some years at the music festival at Salzburg. Of all the old " moralities," Everyman alone has captured the imagination and held the attention of the modern world.

LIFE *seen* UNFOLDING *in* EVOLUTION

How and why did so many different kinds of animal and vegetable life come into existence? Easier to ask than to reply. But on all sides we have instances of Man's own ability to change living forms.

Evolution. Probably one of the first questions that men ever asked themselves was the whence, the why and the wherefore of living things.

Sea lilies were so numerous in the Silurian period that fossil remains (like this) formed beds of limestone.

And it is a question not yet finally answered. Even in the remote past Man made much progress both in taming animals and cultivating plants for use or for pleasure as companions and ornaments. As a result, these things became much changed from the wild forms from which they had originated. It is not too much to suppose that our remote ancestors often wondered if Nature had not also performed many similar experiments in changing the forms and functions of plants and animals.

The earliest records of attempts to explain the changes of living things from one form into others were those of the ancient Greeks. Aristotle, the great philosopher of the 4th century B.C., believed that the higher forms of life were derived from the lower—and there was a general belief then that even higher forms (such as frogs) might arise from non-living matter.

One popular error regarding the modern doctrine is that Charles Darwin was the " father of evolution," meaning, in this sense, the founder of evolution. But while we properly think of him as the greatest teacher of this doctrine in modern times, it should be realized that there had been a number of very able exponents of evolution before the publication of Darwin's Origin of Species in 1859, of whom J. B. de Lamarck (1744–1829), the great French zoologist, was the most notable.

Another mistake is that Darwinism (Darwin's theory) and evolution in general are the same, which is far from true. For, as we shall see later, while thinking people have accepted the general principles of evolution they are divided as to how evolution has taken place. Darwinism is only one explanation, and it continues to undergo modifications in the light of newer research.

We should not expect to see evolution taking place as an everyday occurrence. Man has worked wonders in changing wild animals into domestic forms, and wild plants into the many garden varieties; but drastic changes like this have taken thousands of years, and evolution in general has taken many millions of years.

Throughout these millions of years life in all its many forms has been struggling upwards, higher and higher in degree and complexity, till we have now the many kinds of living things that inhabit the earth. A vast number of illustrations can be cited from the mass of evidence that science has gathered, to show why belief in the doctrine of evolution is justified. One of the most important is to be found in palaeontology.

No Backboned Animals Existed

Palaeontology—the science of the fossils found in the rocks of the earth—gives us two types of evidence. First, that the early rocks contain fossils of the lower forms of life in great variety and abundance, but none of the higher. There were no backboned animals (vertebrates) in the world at that time. They came millions of years later, the first being the primitive fishes. Later, through succeeding millions of years, amphibia (frogs and their kin) came, and then early reptiles and the early birds and mammals. The early mammals gave rise to the many forms of hairy animals we are now familiar with, by a process of evolution extending through, perhaps, ten million years.

All along the line of evolution science shows that many forms of life have come into the world and vanished. This is especially striking in the case of reptiles. Through millions of years they were evolving. More than 20 orders of them were present at one time, during the millions of years called the Age of Reptiles when, as the vast dinosaurs whose fossil remains we know, they ruled the earth. Then, with the changing climate which encouraged the evolution of mammals, the reptiles grew fewer, till now there remain but five different orders.

The study of fossils also shows, in many cases, the certain evolution of some types. This is especially clear in the case of the horse—in which each foot retains only the middle finger or toe, with its nail greatly enlarged to form the hoof. We begin with horse-like animals the size of foxes, which had all five fingers and toes on the feet.

From these it is possible to trace a dozen stages, changing gradually through several millions of years, till the modern horse is developed.

Of course, the simplest forms of life did not leave fossils, for they had no hard parts to fossilize. Again, even among animals with hard parts, it is the rare individual dying a natural death under very special conditions that has a chance to form a perfect fossil. And of the ones saved as fossils Man has found but a small proportion, for he can explore only a few specks, as it were, of the earth's crust. The horse, however, is sufficient to prove the general principle of evolution.

The study of the comparative anatomy of animals also supplies much evidence for evolution. Here are examples, from the thousands that might be given. From low fishes to the highest animals, all vertebrates show the same plan of the brain, with nerves from the brain supplying the same parts of the head in all. Take the limbs of mammals or hairy animals: they are all built on the same plan. The bat's wing, and a whale's front flippers, have the same chief bones as the arm and hand of Man. Yet how different in outward appearance! And so case after case might be cited from the animal and plant kingdoms.

From embryology (*q.v.*) or the development of animals and plants from egg cells, much evidence could be given. The principles are the same for all the common forms of life—for an insect as for a mammal. The highest forms of life tend to pass through the same stages in developing from the egg as they have in their evolution from lower forms.

Mammals in general have the same two sets of teeth as has Man. The whale-bone whale has these two sets of teeth—but both sets are developed and lost before the little whale is born, and are never used at all. Again, the "vermiform appendix" in Man's digestive tract is a remnant of an organ that is useful in many other mammals. There are many such rudiments in Man's body, perhaps a hundred, inherited from the past when they once were useful.

Discoveries and Miracles

The study of the physiology of different animals also shows many striking similarities. Take the higher animals, for instance. They all do the same things—breathe, sleep, and move about, use the same general class of foods, form the same kinds of wastes. The most striking illustrations of these similarities are shown among the common higher animals, where scientists have made many discoveries of very great importance in medicine and surgery. We have all heard of "vitamins"— mysterious factors of several kinds which are equally necessary to the health of Man and other higher forms of animal life. Most of our knowledge of these substances has been learned from experiments on other higher animals and by then applying the results to Man.

Domesticated animals and plants show how very greatly Man, by artificial selection or breeding, has changed many of our common forms of life. Among fowls, for instance, the variety is great, ranging between the big Brahmas, weighing 10 lb. or more, and the tiny bantams, weighing but 1 lb. Yet all the breeds are derived from the same wild fowl of India. Among vegetables, cabbage, kale, cauliflower and Brussels sprouts

American Museum of Natural History

EVOLUTION OF THE HORSE
Reconstructed from a skeleton, this small creature (lower) lived millions of years ago. As the skull (upper) shows it was an ancestor of the modern horse. Named by scientists Eohippus, meaning dawn horse (Greek eo, dawn, hippus, horse), instead of hoofs it had toes and heels.

have been derived by Man from the same wild plant, as is told and illustrated in page 639.

The explanation as to *how* evolution of living things has taken place is a much more difficult matter. For while biologists are all agreed that evolution has taken place they are far from agreeing as to the processes involved. We may best begin with Darwin's explanation, and then trace briefly the changes in scientific opinion since his time.

First, we have to consider the materials with which evolution has had to work. These are the differences among the individuals of any kind of animal or plant. It is familiar to all that no two individuals are ever exactly alike. We notice the differences most clearly among humans, because we examine people more critically than we do other animals. But the same principle holds for any kind of animal or plant.

More young animals are born than can grow and reach the adult stage. In many species of animals and plants, thousands of individuals come into the world from two parents. A toad lays 20,000 eggs each year. But as soon as they are laid the losses begin. Some of the eggs perish or are destroyed; later, some of the tadpoles are killed and eaten by other animals; later still, the little toads perish, till at last only two perhaps, under normal conditions, are left to take the place of the two parents. That is where "natural selection" comes in to weed out the less good, and to preserve the ones best fitted for existence as toads. Only the best of every batch survive in the long run; should more survive (owing to some temporary change in conditions) the population will obviously increase rapidly, and that is how " plagues " of creatures come about. Thus, the toad is kept perfectly suited to its own mode of life. If conditions change, toads adapting themselves most closely to the new conditions will survive, producing a race changed slightly from the old one; a new race, in fact, has evolved. Elsewhere, others of the original toads may have become adapted to other conditions, so that two new races will now have been evolved.

One of the great controversies of evolution has been about the causes of the differences among animals and plants of any species, and the way in which they affect the creatures concerned. According to Darwinism, the effective differences are usually small, and come about largely fortuitously (without known causes); thus, an individual has some chance difference which makes it better suited to its life than its fellows. If this is inherited, its descendants will be more likely to survive.

Let us now examine briefly two or three modern views. The Lamarckians believe in the " inheritance of acquired characters "; in other words, they maintain that the difference among the individuals of any kind of plant or animal arises because the parent passes on what it has acquired during its lifetime to its offspring. As applied to Man, an athlete would have children stronger physically than his fellows; an educated man, children with better intellect, and so on. Among the opponents of this theory are the followers of August Weismann (1834–1914), who point out that satisfactory proofs are not yet forthcoming. As a matter of experience, there is ample evidence against it. For instance, the feet of Chinese women are of normal size if they are allowed to grow, though Chinese women have bound their feet for hundreds of years.

Another really important theory is that of Hugo de Vries (1848–1935), who has proved that Nature has taken advantage of the " sports," or " mutations"—that is, specimens remarkably different from their fellows—which from time to time are born or spring up in any species of animal or plant. Such a mutation is seen in a person with two joints in the fingers instead of the usual three, or with six fingers and toes instead of the usual five. Many of these mutations have been observed in both animals and plants, and it may be that they become the chief materials for the origin of new species. Obviously, if such mutations are favourable to the owner, enabling it to survive when its fellows are destroyed, or if they at least produce an equally efficient race, new species may come about. If they are antagonistic, the creature may fail and disappear in many cases.

There are other theories as to the causes of organic evolution, but the ones here given illustrate some of the points in dispute. It must be repeated that, while there are differences of opinion as to the *method* of evolution, the *fact* of evolution is undisputed by all authorities.

Examination. In China certain tests of knowledge have been required of applicants for a Civil Service post since the 3rd century B.C., and to China probably belongs the honour of having invented examinations. In those days, as often in our times also, the knowledge which was tested had no connexion with the knowledge which would be needed by a successful candidate; the same fault can be found in the university examinations of the Middle Ages, which were mere discussions, with students arguing small points of logic in the presence of the examiners. It was not until the 18th century that examiners really began to ask questions. A century later examinations were made compulsory for entrance into the British Civil Service—over 2,000 years after the Chinese had invented them.

In modern times entry into any of the professions is made by examinations, and education has only too often degenerated into the mere cramming of facts into a student to enable him to pass them. But attempts have been made to substitute tests of intelligence for tests of acquired knowledge.

Efforts have even been made to abolish examinations altogether, and to accept in their stead a report on a pupil's abilities. Still, an examination does test a student's ability to express himself clearly on paper and to acquit himself well in unfamiliar surroundings and at a critical moment.

American Museum of Natural History; reconstruction by Professor W. B. Scott
EVOLUTION : A HORSE WITH CLAWS
Like the Eohippus pictured in the preceding page, the Moropus (above) was an early relative of the horse. Skeletons, found chiefly in western Nebraska in the United States, are in museums at New York and Pittsburgh. The Moropus stood about six feet high, and the feet were each equipped with a strong middle claw for digging food out of the ground.

loading it into railway wagons for manufacture into Portland cement.

Other types of excavator are not unlike the bucket-ladder dredger illustrated in page 1047: there is the same kind of "ladder," with an endless chain of buckets traversing it. These machines also are much used for digging trenches, but we illustrate another type, in which the ladder is suspended, almost horizontally, from a jib. This is employed for digging out the soil to make a reservoir, or for shaping banks (page 1248).

In the drag-line machine a bucket or scoop is hung from a jib by wire cables. The jib is projected over the ground to be dug, and then the bucket is dragged over the earth towards the machine by other cables wound up on a winch, scooping up the soil as it goes. Other

Excavators. While smaller digging-jobs for trenches, cuttings and so on are still done by manpower, and the navvy continues to do much of the excavation for building work, all bigger jobs of this kind are carried out by power shovels, drag-line excavators, and scrapers. The earliest of these power-shovels was the so-called steam-navvy, invented in an age when steam was the only portable source of mechanical power. Today oil engines are used for big shovels, and petrol engines for the lighter ones. Often the entire machine is mounted on caterpillar tracks (which spread the immense weight over a larger area than could be safely done with road wheels) and is self-moving, with a separate engine to propel it.

The typical power-shovel has a dipping boom, on a jib like that of a crane; at the lower end of the boom is the shovel-shaped bucket. In use the jib is lowered until the bucket engages the soil to be dug; then the boom is drawn in by cables from a winch in the engine cab, and the shovel cuts its way into the earth. Now the jib is lifted until the shovel is clear of the truck or lorry along-side, into which the earth is to be dumped; the machine is swung round on its pivot until the shovel is brought over the truck, and a trap door at the rear of the shovel is opened to allow the earth to fall out. The digging of trenches for pipes or cables is one of the every-day tasks of such excavators. Another use is seen in page 741, where a large power-shovel is digging out and scooping up limestone and

EXCAVATORS OF TWO KINDS

Mounted on caterpillar tracks, the ditch-digger (lower) has an endless chain of buckets suspended almost horizontally from a jib. A big steam shovel (top left), which removes material above ground, is equipped with a bucket which can scoop up several cubic yards of earth at a time. Steam, petrol, oil and electric engines are used to operate these ' mechanical navvies.'

MECHANICAL DIGGERS WITH MIGHTY POWER

Topical; Fox

Bucket-ladder excavators (1) are used to scoop out soil in such operations as the construction of a reservoir. At (2) is a very large electrically-driven excavator, which digs out raw material for making bricks at a British brickfield. The drag-line excavator (3) hauls its bucket along the ground; it is here seen, with the jib raised, after dumping its load. Bulldozers (4) here scrape off the surface soil and push it before them to level ground for an airfield. On the extreme right is an angle-dozer. They can also be used to remove small trees and undergrowth.

types of excavator for shallow digging, or for moving rather loose earth on or near the surface, are scrapers and graders. These push and thrust the earth in front of them as they go, by means of a wide steel blade set in front of the machine or beneath its body. If the scraper blade be set at an angle to the line of travel, it will not only scrape off and move the soil but will push it to one side of the track. In road making, similar machines are used to shape the surface and give it a suitable camber (*see* Roads). Sometimes a separate tractor is used to draw the actual scraper unit.

A bulldozer is a particularly heavy kind of thrusting and scraping machine, pushed by its own built-in road motor, or else by a powerful tractor behind it. The bulldozer will push over walls, root out trees or their stumps, or shift masses of rubble or other such material on the surface. In clearing wooded land for building or for cultivation, or in the levelling of ground for airfields, it has no equal. A similar machine known as the angle-dozer has the blade set at a slope to its path of travel, like the scraper we mentioned earlier, and thus pushes the load out of its way to one side as it goes. (*See* Dredger ; Roads).

Exeter. On a ridge overlooking the river Exe, this, the county-town of Devonshire, is about 12 miles from the sea. A great part of the walls which surrounded it in the olden days still remains, though the four gateways have been destroyed.

The city possesses a small but very beautiful cathedral with Norman towers, which was begun in 1112. In its library is a manuscript collection of Anglo-Saxon poems presented in the 11th

century by Bishop Leofric. There are many other old buildings, including the Guildhall, built in 1330, with a pillared façade added in 1593; and the remains of Rougemont Castle, which, although Norman, occupied the site of Roman and British strongholds.

Exeter is an important railway centre, and is connected with the sea by a ship canal. Agriculture, brewing, and lace and paper making are among its industries. In April 1942, during the Second World War (1939–45), the city was bombed by German aircraft ; the cathedral and buildings in the High Street were damaged, and the main building of the City hospital, the library and several churches destroyed. Excavations of the bombed area revealed the remains of two Roman houses. The population is 69,000.

EXETER'S LOVELY CATHEDRAL AND GUILDHALL
The county town of Devon, Exeter possesses a small but beautiful cathedral ; the lower photograph shows the west front and the 14th-15th century stone screen, ornamented with sculptured figures of Biblical characters. The cathedral was damaged by German bombs in April 1942. The pillared front of the Guildhall (top) was added to the original building in 1593.

Explosives. The gases that explosives release when they " let go " are among the most powerful forces under Man's control. The pressure developed by ordinary gunpowder, when fired in a space which it completely fills, is more than 4,000 times that of the atmosphere. When we realize that the " high explosives," such as guncotton, dynamite, nitroglycerin, mercury fulminate, and scores of others, are many times as powerful as gunpowder, we see what an amazing force has come into men's hands. Mercury fulminate is the most violent of all the explosives in practical use, for it develops under certain conditions a pressure of something like 200 tons per square inch. The strongest cannon-barrel would fly into pieces under such a pressure.

What causes that sudden release of gases which we call an explosion ? To understand this we must first realize that many solids and liquids are composed in whole or in part of substances which ordinarily are gases. Water, for instance, consists of the gases hydrogen and oxygen; mercury fulminate is composed of mercury, carbon, and the gases nitrogen and oxygen. Water is not explosive, while mercury fulminate is. This is because the hydrogen and oxygen which form the water are very " friendly " to each other—they are linked by a strong chemical attraction and cannot be easily separated. But mercury fulminate is an unstable compound, and its components do not get along well together—they are constantly looking for an excuse to split up. If struck or rubbed or pressed, they fly apart very suddenly.

Instead of the solid mercury fulminate, therefore, we now have two gases—nitrogen and carbon monoxide—and mercury vapour, which occupy vastly more space now they are separated than they did when combined. It is the sudden and violent moving of the gases and vapours into this new space that constitutes the explosion. These gases are like " unchained winds."

Sensitive to a Fly's Tread

Any substance which breaks up easily and suddenly, producing a large volume of gas, is an explosive. There are some, like nitrogen iodide, which are so sensitive that they will explode at the tread of a fly or the touch of a feather. There are others which require a hot flame to set them off.

Broadly speaking, explosions may be of two kinds—extremely rapid burning, as in the case of gunpowder; and detonating, as in the case of mercury fulminate or nitroglycerin. In the first case the flame starts in one spot and spreads quickly over the entire mass. In the case of detonation, however, a shock or jar causes all parts of the substance to " let go " at virtually the same time. Guncotton illustrates both kinds of explosion. If set off by a flame it will usually burn rapidly, creating a large quantity of gas, but without exhibiting extreme violence. If, however, a cap or primer or fuse made of some detonating substance like mercury fulminate be set off in contact with the guncotton, the latter will in turn be detonated. The ordinary dynamite stick can be set on fire with a match without great danger, but will explode with shattering force in response to a fulminate cap.

Since the first-mentioned form of explosion is merely extremely rapid burning, it follows that any inflammable substance can become more or less explosive if it can be made to burn rapidly enough. Since all ordinary fire or combustion is caused by the combination of the burning substance with the gas oxygen (*q.v.*), it follows that the more oxygen is present the faster will be the blaze. For example, coal-gas, hydrogen, and the vapours of petrol, alcohol, ether, turpentine, etc., are themselves non-explosive, but they become explosive if they are mixed in the right proportions with the oxygen of the air. The loud back-firing which occurs in a badly adjusted gas ring is caused when too large a supply of air is admitted to the gas pipe through the vent. This principle of explosive mixture of gases and vapours with air is used in the motor-car engine and in all gas engines. (*See* Gas Engine.)

Many serious accidents have arisen from so-called " dust explosions." When the air is filled with finely powdered charcoal, coal, flour, soap, wood, sugar, starch, or any other combustible substance, a flame or a spark may start a blaze which will travel through the dust cloud so rapidly that it creates a violent and destructive blast.

Oxygen in Concentrated Form

Explosives which are to be used for practical purposes cannot depend upon the air for their supply of oxygen. It must be provided in concentrated form so as to be available even when the explosive is excluded from contact with the air. In black gunpowder, which is a mixture of charcoal, saltpetre and sulphur, the saltpetre (potassium nitrate) provides oxygen (*see* Gunpowder). But in most explosives each molecule of the compound contains all the oxygen needed. Liquid oxygen itself can be used as an explosive. A porous cartridge of wood pulp, powdered aluminium, or other combustible material is soaked in liquid oxygen, and fired with a detonator before the oxygen evaporates. Instantaneous combustion produces terrific explosive force. A few detonating explosives, such as nitrogen iodide, have no oxygen; they act when the compound splits and the parts expand because of heat generated by the break.

Some compound of nitrogen is used in most explosives because this element is extremely " unsocial " and ready to break away from the others in the compounds (*see* Nitrogen). It is usually introduced through the action of nitric acid, as a rule mixed with sulphuric acid. With cotton, nitric acid forms guncotton and nitrocellulose; with glycerine, it forms nitroglycerin; with ammonia, it makes ammonium nitrate. With phenol (carbolic acid) it produces picric acid, the base of such explosives as lyddite and melinite. Nitration of toluene obtained from coal tar (or by catalysis from petroleum) yields trinitrotoluene (T.N.T.), one of the commonest military high explosives. Dynamite is nitroglycerin mixed with some absorbent substance to reduce danger of explosion from shock (*see* Dynamite). Amatol is a mixture of T.N.T. and ammonium nitrate ; ammonal contains powdered aluminium, T.N.T., charcoal, and ammonium nitrate.

High explosives are used as bursting charges in shells and bombs, but they are too violent to use as propelling charges in firearms. For this purpose slower-burning smokeless powders have been developed. Most of them are nitrocellulose formed

EXPLOSIVES MAKE WAY FOR A NEW RAILWAY BRIDGE

Many uses, apart from war, are found for explosives. They are used, for example, in the manufacture of fireworks and signal lights, in mines and quarries, in civil engineering to break up rock for removal, coal or other material, and for blowing up wrecks or derelict ships. Here a railway bridge has been demolished to make way for a new structure, the task taking a fraction of a second instead of the weeks needed to carry out the work with manpower alone.

into grains, flakes, or cylinders. Certain kinds, such as cordite and ballistite, contain a proportion of nitroglycerin.

These powders, while less violent than the high explosives, are much more powerful than black powder and have the additional military advantage of producing little or no smoke. At the beginning of the explosion they are comparatively slow burning, and start the bullet or shell smoothly on its way, gradually increasing the pressure and speed as the projectile nears the muzzle, and reaching the maximum power at the moment of discharge. The speed with which these powders burn is also controlled by the shape and size of the grains— large smooth grains burning more slowly than small rough ones, and giving therefore a more gradual expansion of the explosive gases.

This smooth and gradual increase in velocity is of the utmost importance in firing shells filled with high explosives, for a sudden and violent shock might explode such shells before they left the gun. High explosive shells are equipped with detonators, which set off the bursting charge when the shell strikes its mark; or with time fuses which cause the explosion a certain time after the shell has left the muzzle of the gun.

From Fireworks to Farming

Besides their destructive use in warfare and hunting, explosives are of immense value in scores of peaceful pursuits—in mining, quarrying, and engineering enterprises, in making fireworks, signal lights and rockets. They are used to project lifelines to ships in distress off storm-beaten shores or to the roofs of burning buildings; to cast oil upon rough seas or to break up ice-jams. When pile drivers are not available, their work can be done by exploding dynamite on an iron plate placed on top of the piles. Floating derelicts which endanger ships at sea are destroyed with explosives, and great fires are halted by blowing up buildings in the path of the flames. Farmers use explosives for breaking up boulders, blowing out stumps, felling trees, and loosening the soil for deep cultivation.

Most nations and states find it necessary to regulate carefully the sale of explosives, for in the hands of lawless persons they are powerful instruments of crime, such as the blowing open of safes and vaults by " cracksmen," or the making of bombs and " infernal machines " by political fanatics and other enemies of society.

Dreadful Atomic Disruption

The explosives we have described so far have obtained their mighty energy by *changing the state* of the substances of which they are composed— turning solids into gases. But Man in his search for ever more powerful blasting and disruptive agents has produced an " explosive " of dreadful potency—the atomic bomb. This works its havoc not merely by changing the state of the ingredients but by *breaking up the very atoms of matter* themselves, splitting off fragments from their nuclei and starting a chain of disintegration which takes place in a tiny instant of time and ends only when all the matter has been broken up. This explosion, for such we will call it for want of a better name, releases vast quantities of gaseous matter, as does an ordinary explosion, and also liberates quantities of radio-active emanations deadly to life. Again like an ordinary explosion, the atomic disruption causes a fiercely scorching flash. (*See* Atom).

Eye. The eye, whether of Man, cat, fish, or hawk, is specially adapted for use where its owner lives. In the daytime the pupil of the cat's eye looks like a narrow slit because the curtain has been drawn together in order to shut out excess light. The eye of the owl, when he hunts by night, has the curtain pulled back, to admit the maximum of light. The dragon-fly's eye has many thousands of facets, in order that he may see in any direction.

The fish, which lives in deep water, often at the bottom of the stream or lake, has eyes placed well towards the top of its head, looking upwards as well as sideways. Again, the hawk, who gets his food by darting upon his prey, must have eyes so made that he can rapidly change the focus and take a true picture at constantly changing distances.

The human eye is rather poor as an optical instrument compared with many other animal eyes.

The inside lining of the eyeball—extremely thin and delicate, yet very complex in structure—is called the retina ; on this surface a picture of what is "seen" is imprinted upside-down.

From the retina spring nerve fibres which are gathered together to form the optic nerve. This great sensory nerve leaves each eyeball at the back, and passes to the brain. The endings of its nerve fibres in the retina are stimulated by light, and through the fibres the stimulus passes along the optic nerve to arouse the sensation of sight in the brain. The nerve fibres are not themselves sensitive to the light; hence where they come together to form the optic nerve they form what is known as the "blind spot" of the eye, a fruitful cause of accident when an image which should evoke action of protection or escape falls upon it. One tenth of an inch from this spot is the yellow spot. This lies

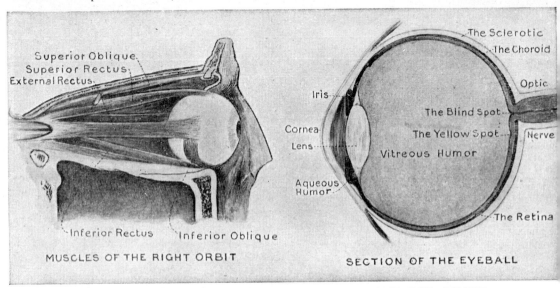

MUSCLES OF THE RIGHT ORBIT

SECTION OF THE EYEBALL

THE 'LIVING CAMERA' WITH WHICH WE VIEW THE WORLD

The way in which the eye may be turned by muscles towards any external object is shown by the illustration on the left. A pull upon the external rectus, for example, turns the right eye to the right. On the right is a section of an eye from front to back, showing how like a camera it is. The cornea is the protecting window in front ; the coloured iris is the diaphragm. Muscles attached to the lens pull its edges apart and flatten it, or relax and let it thicken, for focusing.

The eyeball resembles a sphere with a bulge on the front, where the light enters. Six muscles, four straight and two oblique, are fastened to the outside of this ball, so that it may be turned up or down, to the right or to the left, or slightly rotated, thus giving an extensive field of vision without having to turn the head.

The outside coat of this ball—known as the sclerotic coat, and seen as the "white" of the eye—is tough and strong. The bulge in front is transparent and is called the cornea; it is really the "window" of the eye. Just underneath this tough sclerotic coat lies the dark middle, or choroid, coat, which carries the blood-vessels that nourish the eyeball. The choroid bends away from the cornea in front to form a coloured curtain (black or brown or grey or blue, the iris ; and in the centre of this iris is an opening—the pupil. Circular and radiating muscles control the size of this opening, according as more or less light is needed—doing the same as the "iris diaphragm" of a camera lens.

exactly in the centre of the back part of the retina, and in a line with the central axis of the globe, and it is there that the sense of vision is most acute.

The interior of the hollow eyeball is occupied by the lenses. In front, between the cornea and the iris and pupil, is the *aqueous humour*, a clear, transparent liquid. Immediately behind the pupil is the crystalline lens, a solid which contracts and expands as one focuses on near-by or distant objects. Behind this and occupying the greater part of the eyeball is the *vitreous humour*, a jelly-like substance which is clear and "glass-like" in its transparency. The purpose of the humours is to keep the eyeball filled out at a constant tension.

"Vision" implies that the rays of light from an object enter the pupil, pass through the aqueous humour, crystalline lens and vitreous humour, and strike the retina at the back. These rays of light are so refracted, or bent, in passing through the lenses as to form an inverted or upside-down picture on the retina. The picture itself is not carried to

EYES TO SUIT MANY SPECIAL MODES OF SEEING

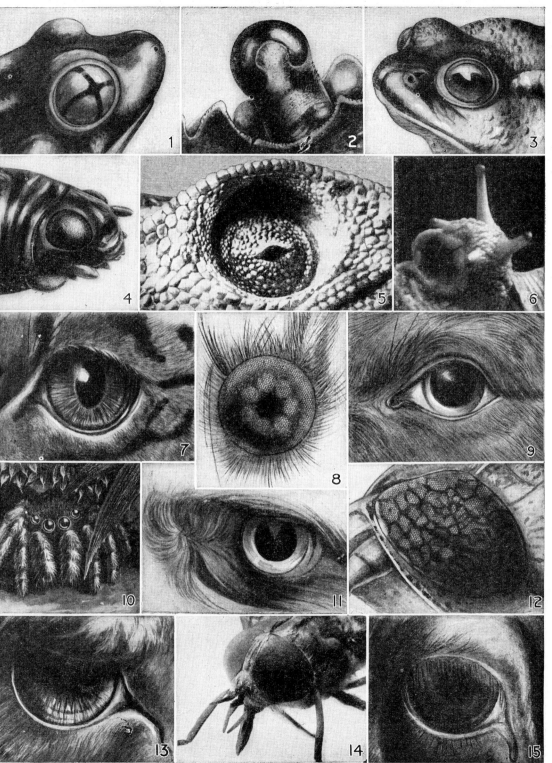

1) Eye of Frog, (2) Crab, (3) Toad, (4) Whirligig Beetle, (5) Chameleon, (6) Snail, (7) Cat, (8) Moth, (9) Dog, (10) Spider, (11) Eagle, (12) Grasshopper, (13) Sheep, (14) Fly, (15) Cow. Numbers 4, 8, 12, and 14 are compound eyes, each consisting of a number of closely packed small eyes. It will be noticed that the eyes of the Crab (2) and Snail (6) are on 'stalks.' The Chameleon's eyes (5) are entirely covered by eyelids except for a small hole.

the brain, but each part of the retina is stimulated strongly or weakly and by this or that colour, according to what part of the picture falls upon it. Therefore, each fibre carries a corresponding influence, or impulse.

These thousands of impulses correspond to the picture and are carried to the brain by the optic nerve. There the proper meaning is interpreted in consciousness, and it is the brain and not the eye that does the seeing. Nerve currents corresponding to the light refracted and reflected from an object cause the sensation of sight in the brain. The external eye is but a camera-like contrivance.

Often various parts of the human eye are abnormal. Sometimes the eyeball is too long or too short from back to front, and then the person is near-sighted or far-sighted, as the case may be. The cornea may not be a section of a true sphere; hence the picture is untrue, being indistinct in some directions and strikingly clear by contrast in others, a condition called astigmatism. Such conditions can be adjusted by lenses fitted by an oculist. A modern development is the so-called contact-lens, where the lens (almost invisible) is slipped over the eyeball itself and not worn in a spectacle frame.

Much harm is done to this invaluable and delicate optical instrument, the eye, by overwork, reading in a bad light, or wearing wrongly fitted glasses.

There are about four persons in every hundred whose eyes seem to be perfect except in distinguishing colours. According to one experimenter's figures, one person in every 55 cannot tell red from green, and one in 50 confuses brown and green. Pink and yellow look alike to some people, and blue and green to others. The cause of colour-blindness is thought to lie in the layer of the nerve fibres in the retina which is known as the " rods and cones."

A proper perception of colour is essential for some fields of employment. In the road, rail, sea and air services, strict tests for colour-blindness have to be passed by applicants.

There are about 85,000 blind persons in Great Britain ; in our story of the Education of the Blind (pages 470–73) you can read of the steps which are taken to help these unfortunates. Many of them are of pensionable age and draw State pensions; about 9,000 are in employment. Much blindness is now preventable, for a great many cases are due to infection of a baby at birth; modern germ-killing antiseptics are used to combat such conditions. Cataract (a condition in which the crystalline lens of the eye becomes clouded or opaque) has now but little menace, though its cause is unknown. Today, when the surgeon judges that the condition is " ripe," he removes the lens of the eye. The deficiency is made up by wearing special glasses.

Eyre, EDWARD JOHN (1815–1901). Born at Hornsea, Yorkshire, on August 5, 1815, Eyre emigrated to Australia in 1833, and became distinguished as an explorer there. His first travels in Australia were undertaken as an overlander—a man who drove herds of cattle to some far-away market on the coast. These journeys across the wilds of a great continent whetted Eyre's appetite for more.

After one or two minor journeys into the arid lands of Central Australia, Eyre set out in 1840 from Adelaide, South Australia, on his famous overland journey to the west coast of the continent. He had with him only one white companion and three natives, a few horses, and six sheep. From the first their chief difficulty was the scarcity of water, and after travelling for a week or two—the entire journey was done on foot—they were in serious straits.

" We were now 128 miles from the last water," wrote Eyre at one point. " We had been four whole days and nights without a drop for the horses, and almost without food, for, parched as they were, they could not feed upon the dry and withered grass we found."

On another occasion he was reduced to collecting with a sponge the dew which in the early morning sparkled on the bushes that grew on the dry plains. In an hour he had collected and squeezed out enough to fill a quart pot. With this he made his tea. One night two of the natives in the little party, fearing they were being led into the desert to die of thirst without any chance of escape, killed Eyre's white companion, and went off with all the food they could carry. Eyre and his remaining native companion struggled on, but it was over a year before the two reached Albany, Western Australia.

Appointed governor of Jamaica in 1861, Eyre in 1865 crushed a native rebellion with alleged severity, and was recalled and put on trial. Influential friends came to his assistance, and he was acquitted. He died on November 30, 1901.

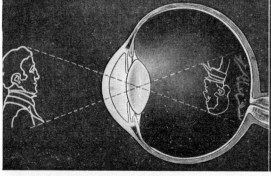
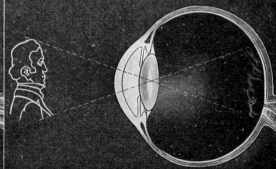

EYE : HOW THE LENS FOCUSES AN OBJECT

In a camera the lens must be moved forwards or backwards to bring near or distant objects into focus. The lens of the eye cannot be moved, but the same result is achieved by changing the curvature of the lens. In the illustration on the left the lens is in its normal (or relaxed) position and, if unaltered, would focus the image too far in front of the retina. The muscles attached to the lens contract and flatten it (right), thereby focusing the image upon the retina.

F

Fabre, JEAN HENRI (1823–1915). Born in Aveyron, France, on December 21, 1823, Fabre (pron. fah'-br) was from childhood greatly interested in insect life. When he was 19 he left the College of Rodez and took charge of a primary school at Carpentras, receiving a salary equivalent to £28 a year. His very first month's salary was spent in buying a book on insects.

Fabre married early, and soon had a large family to support with the small salary received as Professor of Natural Philosophy at the College of Ajaccio in Corsica, and later at the Lycée of Avignon in southern France. His was a long life of poverty, sacrifice, struggle and superb perseverance.

After 40 years of unceasing toil Fabre retired to a humble home at Sérignan, Vaucluse, where he could give himself without reserve to his favourite study. There he remained for the rest of his life, quite unconcerned about riches, caring nothing for worldly honours, sacrificing everything to his work, and gaining an astonishing knowledge of insects. Until nearly 80 years of age he was almost unknown to the world. Then the poet Mistral interested some scientists in him and rescued " the insects' Homer," as he came to be called, from poverty and obscurity. His greatest work, Souvenirs Entomologiques (Souvenirs of Insect Life) was praised by the French Academy, and five years before his death, which occurred on October 11, 1915, he was granted a pension.

This great naturalist, whom Darwin called " a savant who thinks like a philosopher and writes like a poet," wrote many books. He looked into the lives of insect " citizens " and revealed what he saw in stories curious, quaint, happy or tragic. Though many of his conclusions were erroneous, he is renowned as a painstaking observer. Among Fabre's principal works as translated into English are Social Life in the Insect World (1912) ; The Life of the Spider (1913); The Life of the Fly (1913); The Glow-worm and other Beetles (1915); The Life of the Grasshopper (1917); Our Humble Helpers (1918); The Wonders of Instinct (1918), and The Mason Wasps (1919).

JEAN HENRI FABRE
A schoolteacher at 19, Fabre spent his first salary on a book about insects. He continued his investigations of insect life right up to the time of his death at the age of 92.

Factors.

In the various subdivisions of arithmetic (*see* Addition; Division; Fractions; Multiplication; Subtraction) numbers are dealt with generally. When we come to factors we begin to deal with quantities of limited application. Thus, any two numbers may be multiplied and the answer obtained in whole numbers. But not every number can be divided by any other number without leaving a remainder. When, however, a number is divisible by another number, and the answer obtained is a whole number, the quotient (number resulting from the division) is called a factor. Only when a number is a factor of another—that is, a number which, multiplied by some other number, gives the second one—can it be divided exactly into it so as to give an answer in whole numbers. For example, $7 \times 2 = 14$, and $14 \times 5 = 70$. The numbers 7, 2, and 5 are the factors of 70; so any of them will divide into 70 exactly, and no other whole numbers (save 1 and 70) will without giving a remainder.

This rule explains why so many vulgar fractions cannot be converted into exact decimal fractions. The base of our number system is 10, which has only three factors, 1, 2 and 5. Adding additional o's beyond the decimal point, as we do in converting vulgar fractions into decimal ones, introduces these same factors again, making it impossible to obtain an exact division with any divisor containing any factor other than 1, 2 and 5. Such factors are called prime factors. (A prime number is one divisible only by itself and 1, such as 3, 5, 7, 11, 13, and so on).

To find the factors that make up a given number is important both as a test for the possibility of division and often as a substitute for it. Thus, suppose we are told to divide 231 by 21. Instead of using long division we find the factors of each number. Thus 7 and 3 are the factors of 21, and we find by trial (mental) division that both 3 and 7 go into 231 without leaving a remainder. We divide 231 therefore by 3 and 7 in turn, getting 77 and 11, then 3, 7 and 11 are our answers. Therefore $231 = 3 \times 77 = 3 \times 7 \times 11$, and, as none of these numbers is further divisible, the prime factors of 231 are 3, 7 and 11. We know the prime factors of 21 to be 3 and 7, therefore 231 divided by 21 becomes

$$\frac{231}{21} = \frac{3 \times 7 \times 11}{3 \times 7}$$

Cancelling out 3 and 7 from top and bottom we get

$$\frac{231}{21} = 11$$

Cancellation is the name given to the process of eliminating common factors.

Useful aids to quick recognition of factors are :

1. If a number ends in 0 or 5, it is divisible by 5.
2. If the sum of the digits is divisible by 3, the number is divisible by 3.
3. If the last digit is even the number is divisible by 2.

Under these rules we see that neither 231 nor 21 is divisible by 2 or 5. But $2+3+1$ (the sum of the digits of 231)=6, and 2+1=3, and each sum is divisible by 3. Dividing 231 by 3 gives 77, and dividing 21 by 3 gives 7, and from our multiplication table we get the final factor 11.

Again, suppose we want to divide 15 into 420. The rules tell us that 420 is divisible by 2 (because 0 is even), by 3 (because 4+2+0=6), and by 5 (because 420 ends in 0). Dividing $2 \times 3 \times 5$ (=30) into 420 gives 14, which factorizes into 7 and 2, both prime. That is, $420 = 2 \times 3 \times 5 \times 2 \times 7$. The number 15 has only 2 factors (except itself and 1), 3 and 5. Cancelling out the factors common to both (3 and 5) leaves $2 \times 2 \times 7$, or 28 as our answer.

Factorizing determines quickly any highest common factor—that is, the largest number which will divide evenly into two or more given numbers. To determine the highest common factor (often written H. C. F.) of 660, 1188 and 2520, we factorize each (using the hints just given) and so reduce each number to its prime factors, as:

$$660 = 2 \times 3 \times 5 \times 2 \times 11$$
$$1188 = 2 \times 3 \times 2 \times 3 \times 11 \times 3$$
$$2520 = 2 \times 3 \times 2 \times 5 \times 2 \times 3 \times 7$$

We at once see the factors common to all three to be 2, 3 and 2, and as $2 \times 3 \times 2 = 12$, this is the highest common factor we want.

Factorizing is useful also in finding the least common multiple—the smallest number, that is, which will contain two or more other numbers as factors. Suppose we want to find the least common multiple (often written L. C. M.) of 660, 840 and 1,008. Factors of $660 = 2 \times 2 \times 3 \times 5 \times 11$; $840 = 2 \times 2 \times 2 \times 3 \times 5 \times 7$; and $1,008 = 2 \times 2 \times 2 \times 2 \times 3 \times 3 \times 7$. Now the L.C.M. must contain each factor as many times as each number does. The factors therefore will be $2 \times 2 \times 2 \times 2 \times 3 \times 3 \times 5 \times 7 \times 11$, which, multiplied together, give 55,440, the L. C. M. wanted.

The ready use of factors is a valuable aid throughout arithmetic. In algebra the knowledge of factors is even more valuable, providing short cuts to intricate problems.

Fairs and Markets.

In most people's minds fairs are connected with roundabouts, boat swings and coconut shies. But in earlier days fairs were important trading centres. When a nobleman of the 13th century needed a new sword or lance, his lady a new gown of state, and his peasants a tool, where did they seek them?

Towns were far apart, and usually contained only a few small shops in which merchants displayed the wares made by their journeymen and apprentices in their own workrooms. So both nobles and peasants would usually wait to supply their different needs until the time of one of the large annual fairs, held in certain privileged cities, usually at the time of a Church festival. Then they hurried to the town, to gaze at the marvellous goods from far and near shown in the booths, and to buy such of them as they needed or fancied or could afford.

What a different aspect the town wore at such a time compared with ordinary days! The narrow

ST. GILES'S FAIR IN THE STREETS OF OXFORD

L.E.A.

In early times fairs were held primarily to promote trade and usually took place on a saint's day, as does St. Giles's Fair at Oxford. As can be seen here, enormous crowds attend it, mostly in search of amusement. The commercial side of fairs was gradually eclipsed by the 'fun of the fair,' and many of them, such as Donnybrook Fair in Dublin and all the London ones, became mere disorderly revels and for that reason were suppressed as nuisances.

Topical

FAIR : GOODS DISPLAYED BY BRITISH INDUSTRIES

To promote the sale of British manufactured goods, the Export Department of the Board of Trade organizes an annual trade fair. It is held in two divisions—light manufactures in London, at Olympia (above), and Earl's Court; and machinery and heavy industries at Birmingham. Buyers come from all over the world to visit the fair ; and on the left, at the top of a black-and-white column, is displayed a light designed for a lighthouse off the coast of Norway.

streets were now lined with wooden booths and stalls; or perhaps a special enclosure was set aside for the fair at the city's gates. Here were woollen cloths from Flanders, and costly spices from the East, with silks and velvets of wondrous hues. From Gascony in France came wine, from Norway tar, from Germany furs and amber. Here was the street of the goldsmiths, and those of armourers, weapon-makers, saddlers, and the like. On raised platforms, jugglers and tumblers performed feats of skill, while ballad singers sang their lays. Everywhere crippled or blind beggars reaped a harvest from the passers-by. The lord whose right it was to hold the fair levied fees and tolls upon the merchants, in return for which various privileges were granted them. Disputes were settled summarily by the Court of Piepowder (French, *pied poudreux*, meaning dusty foot—an allusion to the travelling pedlars). Quick justice was dealt out to all who broke their agreements or cheated their customers. For a week or two the fair continued. Then the merchants packed up their wares, and moved on.

The right to hold such a fair was one of the most highly prized privileges in the Middle Ages, one which could be obtained only by a charter from the king or some lord. Among the most famous fairs were those of St. Bartholomew at Smithfield in London, the Leipzig fair in Germany, and that of Troyes in France. From the weights used at the last we get our system of Troy weights. The medieval fair survives in some parts of the world

where commerce is still primitive, as in the interior of Asia. Its modern descendant is the trade fair.

The first trade fair held in Great Britain was in 1915, when the Board of Trade organized one on a small scale with the object of attracting some of the buyers who had previously attended the Leipzig Fair. Now the British Industries Fair, as it is called, is normally an annual event and has grown enormously. It is held in two divisions, that for light manufactures in London, and that for machinery and heavy industries at Birmingham.

To many towns which did not have a fair, and also to some which did, was granted the privilege of holding a market on a certain day of the week. Here were sold homespun linens and cloths, as well as farm produce brought by the peasants from near-by villages. Markets are still held in many country towns of England, in the main on the days and in the places fixed in the past.

Fairy-ring. Places in fields and on lawns where the grass grows suddenly very dark and strong and luxuriant—often in a complete ring, sometimes only in an irregular and broken one— are known as fairy-rings—fancifully ascribed to fairies dancing in a circle at night.

Fairy-rings are, in fact, the product of certain types of fungus, including the common mushroom. When one of these fungi is ripe, it sheds spores all round itself, in a more or less regular circle. In the place where the fungus has already grown, the

S. V. Waters

A FAIRY-RING—BUT MADE BY TOADSTOOLS

Though the making of fairy-rings is fancifully ascribed to fairies dancing in a circle at night, they are really caused by the growth of certain species of fungi (above). When one of these fungi is ripe, it sheds spores all round in a circle; but where the fungi have already grown the soil is impoverished, so only spores falling outside the circle produce new ones. Meanwhile the old fungi die within the ring, enriching the soil and causing grass to grow more vigorously

soil is impoverished and unsuitable for further growth; only those spores falling round the outside of this space, therefore, will grow to produce new fungi. These, again, spread their spores, and again only those towards the outside will flourish. Meanwhile the old fungi are dying down, within the new ring of spores, and with their death the soil is for a time enriched, and the grass grows more vigorously—especially where the old fungi have died most recently, that is, near the edge.

Falconry. One of the oldest of sports, falconry demands real co-operation between man and bird. This is difficult to achieve because the training of hawks requires great patience, and it cannot be considered successful until complete understanding and confidence between the falconer and his hawk are established. A falcon is not trained to bring the victim to its owner, but remains over it until picked up again by the falconer.

The hawk for training may be taken from the nest before it has learned to fly, when it is called an eyess or eyas, or it may be trapped full-grown and tamed. It is then called a haggard or blue hawk. A hood is used to cover the falcon's eyes in order to keep it quiet; and a brail, or strip of leather, is slipped over the wings to prevent fluttering. Jesses, or strips of light leather with bells attached, are fitted to the legs, the sound of the bells making the movements of the bird easier to follow. A leash is fastened to the jesses and to the falconer's wrist.

Two classes of birds are used—long-winged hawks, or true falcons, and short-winged hawks. The true falcons include the Icelandic gerfalcon, peregrine, hobby and merlin. The only short-winged hawks used to any extent are the goshawk and sparrow-hawk. Some falcons, such as the peregrine, kill their prey by stooping (swooping) from a great height, a blow of the talons killing or maiming the victim. Others, like the merlin, hunt down birds by sheer speed, following the prey's every turn.

The sport has a language all its own. The prey is called the quarry. Striking the quarry in mid-air and clinging to it is "baiting" when game is large, "trussing" when it is small. A "lure," often a stuffed bird or small animal, is used to tempt the hawk back. Fighting is "crabbing," and flying away with the quarry is "carrying."

After the Second World War (1939–45) experiments were carried out in the Royal Air Force with peregrine falcons to frighten flocks of birds from the neighbourhood of airfields, since birds sometimes caused accidents and damage by flying into aircraft.

FALCONRY : BIRDS AND EQUIPMENT

Some species of hawks and falcons used in falconry and parts of the equipment are shown here. (1) Goshawk, (2) Sparrow-hawk, (3) Iceland gerfalcon, (4) Italian hood, (5) Rufter hood, (6) Foot with jess and bell. Right, Peregrine falcon with Dutch hood, bell and jesses.

Falkland Islands.

Three hundred miles east of Magellan Strait, near the tip of South America, lie the Falkland Islands—low, rocky, treeless, swept by fierce winds and watered for three-fourths of the year by cold, drizzling rains.

Of the hundred or more islands in the group, only two are important—East Falkland and West Falkland, with areas of 2,580 square miles and 2,038 square miles respectively. On the eastern island, on the shores of a landlocked harbour, is the capital, Stanley (population, 1,200). From here are administered the affairs of the whaling colony of South Georgia, 900 miles away, and of the South Shetlands, South Orkneys, South Sandwich Islands and Graham Land, far to the south in the Antarctic Ocean. These are Dependencies of the Falklands.

Forbidding as they are in appearance, the Falkland Islands form a highly prosperous colony. There are large flocks of sheep and nearly 3,000,000 acres of pasturage. Whaling is an important industry. Steamers call regularly from England, and there is cable connexion with Montevideo, Uruguay.

At various times both Argentina and Chile have put forward claims to possession of the Falkland Islands, and in 1948 Argentina asserted her right to the ownership of the Falkland Islands and dependencies. This was vigorously repudiated by the British Government, and no further action was taken. Discovered in 1592, the islands were owned first by France, then by Spain, and were acquired by Great Britain in 1832. On December 8, 1914, during the First World War (1914–18), a squadron of German warships was overtaken and destroyed off the Falkland Islands by a British squadron. The estimated population of the Falkland Islands is 2,500.

Family AND Tribal Life.

Did the first human beings live together in groups as families, banded together for protection, or did they pursue individual paths as if afraid of other society? This question has occupied many great minds. A famous novelist wrote a story in which he pictured the earliest people living in small groups. At the head was a powerful male, and with him were his wives, his daughters and his younger sons. When these boys grew up they were driven away by the father. If they were sly or strong enough, they began to steal women from other groups and thus built up bands of their own. In this story early Man differed little from the animals which he hunted.

Other writers believe that at first there was no family at all. Children remained with their mothers until old enough to take care of themselves, then became independent members of the human herd. As Man began to fashion tools, the idea of property developed; children living with their mothers would take possession of her belongings when she died. They would come to know her sisters and associates, and with them would form a group, the members of which would consider themselves related. If a man from outside sought a mate in this group he would be accepted only as a visitor, and his children would remain with the mother. Since they would have no contacts with the father's family they would not think of them as relatives, and hence would not claim a share in their property. Thus, in time, a group would be established in which the children would inherit property through their mother and would consider all the members of her group as relatives. Anthropologists call such a group—descended from the same ancestor—a clan. Upholders of this theory believe that at one time the women were actually the heads or rulers of the clans. Such a society is called a matriarchy (Latin *mater*, mother; Greek *archē*, rule).

With the increase of population and wealth the man began to be more important, and mother-rule slowly changed to father-rule or patriarchy (Latin *pater*, father; Greek *archē*, rule). As protector of his group and of his flocks the man became a warrior, while household duties and the raising of crops fell to the woman. If the man had considerable property, he needed additional women to manage the camp; so he married more. The marriage of a man to more than one woman is known as polygamy, or polygyny; polygamy really means " much married "; polygyny means " many women." Sometimes warfare between the groups, or the loss of a band of hunters, would result in a shortage of men and lead to polygamy.

There are other theories concerning the development of the family and of society, but these examples serve to show that the form of family organization has not always been the same as it is with us today, when the word family, as it is generally used, covers father, mother and children.

Fan.

Although fans are seldom used in public now, there was a time when every lady not merely carried one but was continually fanning herself, and the art of using a fan was one of the first in which she had to be accomplished. In the East, especially, fans have been used from the earliest times, as we can see from Egyptian, Chinese, and Indian art, and the fans of China and Japan are world-famous. It is thought that the fan originated in China at least as early as 3000 B.C., and it has survived, unchanged in many respects.

The early fans were of fixed type, consisting of a mount, the blade part of the fan, attached to a handle; these are called screen fans. The fan usually seen now is of the folding type; it is of

FAN PAINTED BY AN ARTIST
During the 18th and 19th centuries the art of fan painting flourished in England and on the Continent ; this silk fan ornamented with medallions is the work of the French artist François Boucher (1703–70).

later date, and came in the first place from Japan, reaching Europe through Portuguese traders of the 16th century. The fan in Japan is more than a useful or ornamental article, for it has symbolic importance. During the 18th and 19th centuries especially the art of fan-painting flourished in England. Great artists devoted time to it, working on parchment, paper or silk; one or two made a speciality of it. Among these was Charles Conder (1868–1900), whose work, usually in the finest of pastel tints, brought him a wide reputation.

The use of the fan, from that made of palm leaves or feathers and handled by a slave in olden

part to which the blades are attached is called a runner or impellor. Small fans such as this are used for producing the air blast for a blacksmith's forge; larger ones supply air under pressure to furnaces. When dusty operations are carried out in factories and engineering works an exhaust system is installed to remove the dust-laden air, and centrifugal fans are used for this purpose, too.

Another use of the word fan is that ascribed to a devotee of sport, or cinema, when you get the term football or film "fan." The word may either refer to the fact that the fan encourages the footballer, fanning him to further efforts; or it may be abbreviated from the word fanatic, and thus refers to a person intensely interested in anything.

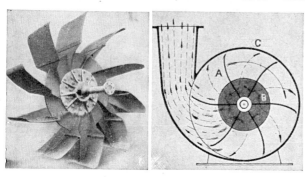

FAN FOR VENTILATING BUILDINGS
To remove dust-laden air from large buildings centrifugal ventilating fans are installed. The arrangement of the blades on this type of fan is shown on the left, and on the right is a sectional diagram : A, fan-wheel; B, air inlet; C, casing; arrows indicate the flow of the air.

Faraday, MICHAEL (1791–1867). Universally recognized as the founder of modern electrical science, Faraday's discovery of the induction of electric currents became the basis for the generation of all electric power by dynamos. Indeed, all the forms of electric power now in world use are ultimately due to Faraday. His discoveries made greater changes in the fabric of civilization than any other, with the possible exception of the petrol engine. The electro-magnetic unit of capacity, the farad, is named after him.

Michael Faraday was born at Newington Butts, London, on September 22, 1791, the son of a Yorkshire blacksmith who had settled in London. First he worked for a bookbinder, then at 22 he became laboratory assistant at the Royal Institution, London. As assistant to Sir Humphry Davy, he accompanied that great chemist on a tour of the Continent, 1813–15, and on his return resumed his work at the Royal Institution. At this time he was devoting himself entirely to chemical research, working chiefly on carbon compounds. Later he turned his attention to the liquefaction of gases, and to research on steel alloys.

times, to the most perfect example from Japan, has always been to keep the owner cool by agitating the surrounding air. Mechanical fans are used for moving air and other gases. These range from a tiny one, which you can carry in a handbag and work by compressing a spring, to the gigantic fan used at mines and other shafts and tunnels for extracting used air and circulating fresh air ; the fan in these cases may be twenty feet in diameter. The motor-car engine has a fan incorporated to force air through the radiator and cool the water; many electric motors have a fan attached for cooling the mechanism. Many of the fans thus mentioned are shaped rather like a ship's propeller, and move the air in a direction parallel with the spindle of the fan ; they increase its pressure very much.

When the air stream is to be raised to greater pressure a different type of fan is used, called the centrifugal fan. This is encased by a spirally shaped cover or housing. Air is drawn in at the centre, in a line parallel to the spindle, and is forced out at the circumference by centrifugal force (q.v.), being discharged through an opening in the casing. The rotating

MICHAEL FARADAY
Among the great pioneers of electrical science, Faraday was a brilliant experimenter. In 1835 he was awarded a Government pension and in 1858 was given a house at Hampton Court.

By 1812 Faraday had busied himself with the problem of electricity, and in that year he had made his first battery. In September 1821 he began his experiments on electro-magnetism, and on August 29, 1831, he arrived at his greatest discovery, the induction of electric currents, and on October 28 he made the first dynamo. In 1833 he proved the identity of electricity from different sources ; in the following year came the discovery of equivalents in electro-chemical decomposition ; in 1838 of electrostatic induction, followed by the announcement of the relation between electric and magnetic forces. His second great period of discovery began in 1845, when he returned with success to a problem that had long exercised his mind—the effect of a magnetic or electric field on transparent bodies.

FARADAY AT WORK IN HIS LABORATORY

Credit for the solid foundation of electrical science must be given to Faraday, and even today his pointers to the paths of investigation in electricity are still being followed, the results obtained being in accordance with his predictions. In 1903 the Faraday Society was founded in his honour to further the study of electro-chemistry, electro-metallurgy and other kindred subjects. This picture of Faraday in his laboratory is from a contemporary source.

Soon afterwards he announced the "magnetization of light," and the discovery of diamagnetism.

Faraday published his Experimental Researches in Electricity from 1841 to 1855; and his Experimental Researches in Chemistry and Physics appeared in 1859. All his researches were carried out at the laboratory of the Royal Institution. He had been made director in 1825 and Fullerian professor in 1833, but his unwillingness to undertake what he termed commercial work might have led to financial straits had he not been given a pension in 1835 and a house at Hampton Court, Middlesex. He died on August 25, 1867.

Fascism. (Pron. fash´-izm or fas´-izm.) In October 1922 great numbers of black-shirted young men converged on Rome from all parts of Italy. Though they were demanding fundamental changes in the political and economic structure of the State, there was no resistance from the Government. The Italian Prime Minister, Signor Facta, resigned and the leader of the movement, Benito Mussolini, who was then 39, took his place. So was accomplished the first stage in the Fascist Revolution.

The word Fascist is an echo of Ancient Rome. Fasces were the bundles of rods, with an axe in their midst, which were borne by the lictors (officers executing sentence on offenders) before the chief magistrates as symbols of their authority over life and limb. The term was revived by Mussolini for his anti-communist movement.

Italy at that time was in turmoil. Although she had emerged from the First World War (1914–18) on the winning side she was deeply disappointed with the terms of the Peace Treaty, for the new

territory and share of reparations that she received did not, in the opinion of most Italians, compensate her for the losses and sufferings she had undergone. For a short time the forces of discontent were headed by the Socialists, but when they proved incapable of restoring prosperity and security to Italy they were opposed by that body of young men who had gathered round Mussolini, a one-time Socialist editor.

To an Italy in which industry was crippled by strikes, in which poverty and unemployment were rampant, and with a government riddled with corruption and incompetence, Mussolini promised employment for all, competent government and land for the peasants. Great numbers of all classes rallied to his banner. The first organized Fascist unit was formed on March 23, 1919, and was composed very largely of ex-servicemen. During the next two years the Fascists—prominent figures in the black shirts which had been adopted as their distinguishing mark—were engaged in a furious struggle, fighting with the Socialists and Communists.

In May 1921 Mussolini and 32 other Fascists were elected to the Italian Parliament, and 18 months later, when that Parliament had earned still further the contempt of the majority of the people, Mussolini ordered the march on Rome. That was but the beginning of the Fascist Revolution. Although the methods of Mussolini and his henchmen were a negation of freedom, they succeeded, for a few years, in giving Italy a certain measure of prosperity. Parliament merely carried out Mussolini's orders, and later was abolished. All parties other than the

FASCISM'S SIGN

As a symbol the Fascists adopted the Roman fasces, which were bundles of rods with an axe in the middle.

Fascists were suppressed. All opinion, whether expressed in newspapers or on the platform, was rigidly controlled. Boys of six were compulsorily enrolled in a junior military organization in the service of the State—a service which ended only when the age of 55 was reached.

Freedom of the individual practically ceased to exist. Its place was taken by the conception of the Totalitarian State, in which everybody and everything was forced to submit to what was regarded as being in the interests of the State. Under Fascism the individual counted for nothing, except in so far as he was a unit in the life of the State. He had no rights opposed to the State's will. His freedom of action, his property, his life were privileges enjoyed solely through the power of the State, and the State might demand them from him again.

At the head of the Fascist state was the Dictator—*Il Duce* (the leader), Signor Mussolini. He was in supreme control; his every word was law and must be obeyed. The king of Italy was a figurehead. In later years there arose the Corporative State, in which all the country's industries and professions were grouped into 22 Corporations, whose affairs were directed by nominated representatives. These Corporations sent representatives to the Chamber of Corporations, which was the " parliament " of the Fascist State. The end of Fascism in Italy came during the Second World War (1939–45), when Mussolini resigned on July 25, 1943. Imprisoned by the provisional

government then set up by anti-Fascists, he was rescued by German paratroops and taken to Germany. On April 26, 1945, he was captured and shot by Italian patriots at Dongo, on Lake Como.

Mussolini once declared that " Fascism is not for export," but other dictators strove to follow his example. Thus Hitler led the Nazi movement in Germany; and the doctrine of Fascism made its influence felt in France, Hungary, Rumania, Belgium, Spain and Argentina.

Fates. Human destiny, according to the ancient Greeks and Romans, was controlled by Three Fates. The Greeks called them Moirai, the Romans, Parcae. Their individual names were Clotho, the spinner of the thread of life; Lachesis, who mixed good and evil fortune with it ; and Atropos, who cut the thread. In art they were represented thus: Clotho, with a distaff (short cleft stick on which was wound wool to be spun) or a roll (the book of fate); Lachesis, pointing with a staff to the globe; Atropos, with a pair of shears or scales.

Fats and Oils. One of the ways in which well-fed animals lay by food energy for future use is by manufacturing and storing in their bodies fats, including the liquid fats called oils. Plants also make fats and store them in their fruits and seeds for the future benefit of their offspring. All fats and oils are of similar living origin. Even the mineral oil petroleum (*q.v.*) has been trans-

E.N.A.

THE MARCH OF THE FASCISTS ON ROME

Mussolini's spectacular success in achieving almost overnight the position of Il Duce, Dictator of all Italy, had careful organization behind it. The people had already begun to listen in real earnest to the Fascist teaching, and this encouraged Mussolini to declare : ' Either the Government will be given to us or we shall seize it by marching on Rome.' His followers occupied the capital on October 30, 1922, and the Blackshirts are here seen entering the city.

formed from animal remains which had been buried ages ago beneath the surface of the earth.

In living creatures the energy stored up in fats and oils is held in the form of chemical structures which yield a high fuel value when burned in the body. Men use this fuel value in their own bodies when they eat fats or oils (*see* Food). They also use it when they burn oil in furnaces and engines.

Fats and oils have another chemical property, valuable to living creatures and also useful to Man in many of his manufacturing activities. To remain stored in living tissues, fats and oils must be insoluble in the watery liquids which surround them. Enzymes (*q.v.*) are required to break them up for digestion. Nature makes use of this water-proof property by putting oil into the skins of animals and the protective coverings of seeds and plants. Men make use of it in paints and many other ways. The physical and chemical structure of fats and oils makes a great proportion of them useful also as lubricants.

Animal Fats in Everyday Use

Butter, lard, tallow, neat's-foot oil, various fish oils, and whale oil are among the most widely used animal oils. Lard, the most important of the fats with the possible exception of butter, is the melted and purified fat of hogs. It is used in cooking, and in some countries is eaten with bread. Tallow is melted sheep-fat or cattle-fat; formerly used for candles, nearly all of it is now made into margarine. The highest grade of tallow is called oleo stock; it is put into presses which separate it into oleo oil and the solid oleostearin. Tallow and oleo oil are among the most important of the materials used in the soap (*q.v.*) industry.

Chief among vegetable oils are olive, cottonseed, linseed, maize, soya-bean, coconut, peanut, castor, palm-nut and poppy-seed oils. Most of them are obtained by pressing the seeds or fruit in special presses; most animal oils are "rendered," that is, extracted, by heating in steam or water.

Oils that have the property of rapidly taking up oxygen when exposed to air and of drying with a tough elastic surface are "drying oils." They are important in making paints and varnishes. Linseed oil is most commonly used for this purpose. China wood oil, or tung oil, which is used in varnishes, is superior in some ways to linseed oil; it is more water-resistant, and gives a higher gloss. This oil, an extract from the nuts of the tung tree, is mostly imported from China; but the tung tree is now grown in Florida.

"Non-drying" oils do not harden, but gradually decompose and become rancid when exposed to the air; olive oil is an example. Such oils are chiefly used in foods and in soap manufacture. The most important after olive oil is cottonseed oil, of which the United States furnishes 70 per cent of the world's production. Maize oil is another important food oil. It is obtained during the manufacture of glucose and maize starch, being pressed out of the tiny germ portion of the maize kernel. Soya-bean oil has in recent years become one of the most widely used non-drying oils. It dries more readily than most, and it is being developed into a partial substitute for linseed oil in paints and varnishes.

Coconut oil is used both in foods and in making soap. The oil is pressed from coconut "meat" (copra) produced in the Philippines, Ceylon, and elsewhere in the Far East. Ground-nut or peanut oil, used chiefly as a salad oil, came for the most part from China and Manchuria, but the British government has started a large enterprise for producing ground-nuts in parts of Africa. Olive oil, pressed from olives, is the best of all for salad oils and for soap-making, but little of it is used because of its high cost. The oil is imported mainly from France, Spain, and Italy. Palm oils come from African and South American palm nuts. They are used for food, for soap, and in the manufacture of tinplate and textiles. Castor oil, made from the castor bean, comes chiefly from India. It is valuable in making fine lubricants, soap, and sticky fly-paper, and is used in medicine.

When the oils are pressed from cotton, flax, and other seeds, the shells are left in the form of hard oily cakes called oil-cake, which is ground into meal and used both as feed for animals and as a fertilizer. Cottonseed meal, linseed meal, and castor-pomace are all rich in nitrogen and therefore exceedingly useful for both these purposes.

Chemically, oils and fats are mixtures of carbon-hydrogen-oxygen compounds, chief of which are olein, stearin and palmitin. These can be decomposed into glycerine and the fatty acids known respectively as oleic, stearic and palmitic acids. In soap-making, the oils and fats are boiled with alkaline solutions ; the fatty acids combine with the alkalis to form soap, and the glycerine is separated as a by-product. For practical purposes we apply the term "fats" to substances that are solid at ordinary temperatures ; and the name "oils" to those that are liquid at ordinary temperatures. All fats become fluid at comparatively low temperatures.

All the substances so far mentioned belong to the group of "fixed" fats and oils. Sharply distinguished from them in origin and character are the essential or volatile oils. The latter contain in highly concentrated form the odours of the plants from which they come, and therefore are largely used for perfumes, flavourings, and in medicine. Turpentine is one of the commonest of essential oils. Others are the oils of lemon, clove, peppermint, spearmint, eucalyptus, cedar, cinnamon, caraway, anise, and bitter almonds.

Faust. (Pron. foust). In the 16th century there sprang up, first in Germany and later in other countries in Europe, various tales of a magician, Dr. Johann Faust, who was in league with the devil and performed marvels with the aid of the evil one.

There seems to be little doubt that a personage of this name really existed, but the facts of his life have been lost amid the legends which have gathered about him. He was represented as an impostor who travelled from place to place in Germany, living by his wits, and claiming to be a physician, alchemist (able to change other metals into gold), astrologer and magician. The numerous stories popularly attached to his name were collected by an unknown compiler and published at Frankfort in 1587 as The History of Dr. Johann Faust. The book relates how he sought to acquire supernatural knowledge and power by a compact with Satan. This pact, signed with the blood of Faust, set forth that Mephistopheles, a devil, was to become his servant for a period of 24 years, at the end of which Faust agreed to give himself up to Satan.

Mephistopheles entertained his master with high living, long discussions on the relation of the devil towards God and the nature of heaven and hell, and with glimpses of the spirit world. At the end of the 24 years Faust was carried off by the devil.

The story gained wide popularity and was used as a theme by many writers. It became the subject of a great drama in verse, The Tragical History of Doctor Faustus, by Christopher Marlowe (1564–93), the father of English tragedy. Gradually the Faust legend degenerated into puppet-plays and Punch and Judy shows, until the German poet Goethe, at the opening of the 19th century, raised it to quite another level by telling the story in verse.

There had gradually crept into the legend the shadowy figure of a beautiful young German girl, Gretchen, with whom Faust fell in love. This element of the story grew in importance, until in the hands of Goethe it blossomed into the episode of Margaret, whose betrayal by Faust is one of the dominant notes in Goethe's poetic tragedy called Faust. Contrary to the early versions, Mephistopheles fails to absorb Faust completely in the pleasures he provides—one of the conditions of the

compact in Goethe's poem—and the result is the ultimate salvation of the magician. The French composers Gounod and Berlioz based musical works on this legend.

Fawkes, Guy, or Guido (1570–1606). For more than 300 years the Fifth of November has been celebrated in England by the burning of stuffed figures (guys) of this Gunpowder Plot conspirator. The old custom keeps alive the horror felt by England in 1605 when Guy Fawkes and his fellow conspirators, because of the harsh laws against Catholics, tried to blow up King James I and Parliament. They succeeded in storing several barrels of gunpowder in a cellar under the Houses of Parliament, but before Parliament opened, on November 5, the plot was discovered. Sentence of death was passed on all the conspirators, Fawkes being executed on January 31, 1606.

Fawkes was born at York on April 16, 1570, of a good Yorkshire family. His parents were Protestants, but his stepfather, if not a Catholic himself, was connected with many great Catholic families, and Guy early became a Catholic. He served for some years in the Spanish armies in Flanders. He was entrusted by the main conspirators in the plot with its actual execution, having been in charge of the preparations from December 1604 to May 1605.

Feathers. These are the characteristic covering of birds. Each feather arises from a nipple at the bottom of a pit in the skin that begins to form long before the embryo is hatched. Around this nipple there forms a cap of horny material

GUY FAWKES : LAST FIGHT OF HIS FELLOW CONSPIRATORS

Though Guy Fawkes was arrested on the night of November 4-5, 1605, some of the Gunpowder Plot conspirators fled to Warwickshire and endeavoured to rally the countryside to their cause. Their efforts were unsuccessful, and they took refuge at Hewell Grange. Pursuers were hot on their tracks, and on November 8 the sheriff found their hiding-place. The small band put up a last fight, as depicted in this painting by Ernest Crofts (1847–1911). The upper illustration, from an engraving in the National Portrait Gallery in London, shows Guy Fawkes and fellow plotters.

The vane may be nearly or quite absent from some feathers, or it may become solidified into scale-like feathers, as in penguins. These variations in structure are almost unlimited, and, together with varied colouring, make a feather one of the most beautiful things found in Nature. The colour of the feathers may be due to pigments supplied by cells in the bird's body, but brighter hues may result from diet or some other cause. The pigments are apparently waste products of the blood, and consist of black, red, yellow, and in some cases of a red or a green peculiar to certain families of birds.

Feldspar. A group of minerals composed of silicate of aluminium together with potassium, sodium and calcium. There are several varieties, known as soda-feldspar, lime-feldspar, potash-feldspar, etc., according to the mineral that is most abundant. Many igneous rocks (granite, gneiss, etc.) are made up of crystals of some kind of feldspar, associated with some other mineral or minerals.

The potash—and potash-soda—feldspars, within certain limits of temperature, melt without becoming fluid, and on cooling form a strong colourless or very light-coloured glass. For this reason they are

which presently becomes loosened and is pushed up by another cap forming beneath it. Thus a tube results, which is the shaft or quill of the feather, and in which the succession of caps may usually be seen. When the full size is reached the process ceases, the root end of the quill closes, and the feather is pushed .out of the skin at moulting time by new growth.

The plumage is preceded in the nestling by one or more coats of small immature feathers ("down"), which are successively shed and replaced until the final mature coat is obtained. The feathers eventually become worn and torn, and once, or in some cases twice, a year are moulted, and replaced by a new growth from the same sources. These moults may result in differences in colour and form according to the season in which they take place.

A feather consists of two parts, the quill, and its horizontally branching growths that form the vane in various shapes. Sometimes these branches are disconnected, or nearly so, as in downs and in ostrich plumes; but ordinarily they carry branchlets, or barbs, that hook together at their adjacent tips in a firm but elastic web, especially strong in the case of the large flight feathers of the wings and tail. Power to separate or close the feathers, thus keeping in or letting out the air compressed in flight, is a very important virtue in a bird's wing.

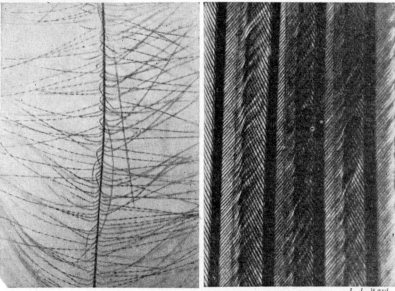

J. J. Ward

FEATHERS : SOME DETAILS OF CONSTRUCTION
A chaffinch's wing, closed and open, is shown in the two upper photographs. When closed the feathers overlap, taking up as little space as possible; when open the edges of each feather just touch those on either side. Below (highly magnified) are the soft filaments of an owl's wing; and (right) the interlacing of the barbs on a condor's wing.

extensively used in the manufacture of porcelains, serving as a flux to bind together the other materials, clay and flint. Feldspar is one of the principal ingredients in the glaze for chinaware and tiles, and of opalescent glass.

Felt. When a fabric is formed, without weaving, by matting together fibres of hair, wool or fur with the aid of moisture and heat by a process of rolling, beating and pressing, it is known as felt. According to the purpose for which felts are required the variation in weight, quality, hardness and thickness is great. It is used for many purposes, such as hats, underfelts for carpets, in engineering and motor-cars, insulation, packing, on pianoforte hammers and in shipbuilding. The inhabitants of the central and northern regions of Asia have used felt as clothing and a floor covering for many centuries. Roofing felts are impregnated with a waterproof solution, the basis of which is usually bitumen.

Fencing.

Quickness of eye, speed of thought, and suppleness of body form the essence of fencing. This sport includes the use of the epée, sabre, and other light weapons, besides the foil. The equipment for fencing with foils includes a tight-fitting padded white jacket, a mask, a button-tipped foil of flexible steel and a glove that comes well down on the wrist of the fencing arm.

The position that a right-handed fencer takes when on guard ready for a bout is with his feet well

FENCING WITH THE FOIL

Fencing positions shown here are : (1) Grip on foil, (2) Preliminary position, (3) On guard, (4) Lunge, (5) Parry of quarte, (6) Parry of sixte, (7) Parry of septime, (8) Parry of octave, (9) Riposte from parry of quarte.

apart, his right arm bent and pointing toward his opponent, the foil held slightly forward, and his left arm lifted so that the hand is about level with the top of his head. When he lunges he throws his right foot forward a few inches, bends his right knee and, straightening his foil arm, thrusts his weapon quickly at his adversary, at the same time lowering his left hand to a point within a few inches of his left thigh. A feint is a movement to mislead; a parry is the warding off of the opponent's foil ; a riposte is a quick lunge or thrust in return.

Fencing, as practised today, is a development of duelling which was carried out with deadly weapons and in no sense on friendly terms. The last duel in England, which resulted in the death of one of the opponents, was fought in 1843.

Fermanagh. (Pron. fer′-ma-na).

The main physical feature of this inland county of Northern Ireland is Lough Erne, which consists of two lakes—Upper and Lower. Upper Lough Erne narrows into two channels, which surround the island on which Enniskillen, the county town, is built. Agriculture is the principal industry; coal, iron and building stone are found. The area of the county is 653 square miles; the population is 54,600.

Fermentation.

When milk sours or bread rises, when fruit decays, when you digest food, when alcohol is produced in sugary substances and when that alcohol turns again to vinegar, we have in each instance an example of the process called fermentation.

Fermentation is always due directly or indirectly to living organisms, and consists of the breaking up of some substance into simpler forms. Common yeast, for example, which is a mass of tiny plants akin to bacteria, breaks up sugar into alcohol and carbon dioxide. This change is not caused directly by the yeast but by a substance called an enzyme (q.v.) produced in the living body of the yeast. Similarly, our own bodies produce enzymes which help to digest our food. In the case of sour milk, butter and cheese, the enzymes from certain types of bacteria produce the lactic and butyric acids that change the quality of the milk. Decay or putrefaction is similarly caused by a type of bacteria (q.v.) called saprophytes.

Ferns.

Most of the ferns (Filices) can be distinguished from other plants by their leaves or, as the latter are popularly called, fronds. These have a single midrib with, in most instances, leaflets branching off at both sides. Mostly these plants prefer damp places, but some kinds flourish on dry walls and rocks and in sandy hedgebanks exposed to full sun. A number are " epiphytes "—that is, they live upon the trunks or branches of trees.

Widely distributed over the world, some ferns are but a few inches high. Others, occurring in tropical countries, assume the stature of trees and are known as tree-ferns, with fronds 15 feet long.

The familiar bracken of Britain is known to botanists as the brake fern (Pteris aquilina). When it takes possession of a piece of ground no other plant can compete with it. But it has restful beauty in its favour; and it is often cut and dried for use as bedding for farm animals.

The life-story of ferns differs much from that of ordinary plants. Ferns do not grow from seed. They increase in bulk from year to year and thus occupy more space, but most kinds depend upon the dispersal of spores—which are contained in small cases, called sporangia, clustered thickly on the underside of each frond. The spore cases burst and their contents—tiny, dust-like grains—are scattered. These each send down a rootlet that

A GREEN ARRAY OF GRACEFUL FERNS

Variety of form and size is amazing among ferns, and many different species can be distinguished in this one small section of a greenhouse. Being lovers of shade, they thrive when grown in dense clumps. Some ferns are very hardy and need not be grown in a greenhouse, thriving on the north side of a wall or hedge. Gold and silver ferns are popular names given to several species to denote their appearance, which is due to the under surface of the leaves being coated with fine particles of white or yellow wax. Tree ferns are natives of both tropical and temperate regions, and in some cases they grow as tall as palms, with fronds up to 15 feet in length.

forms a flat green growth known as a prothallium. On the underside of this are "egg-cells" and also male organs. Spiral bodies, called cilia, from the male organs find their way (just one more of the great mysteries of life) to the egg-cells, fertilizing them and causing a union of cells from which a fern results.

Ferns live on from year to year, of course, though the fronds of native British ferns wither in late autumn, and droop to the ground and decay. New growth becomes visible in the spring, generally as brownish-green balls clustered together. As spring progresses to summer the balls gradually unroll and the full fronds are revealed.

Ferret. A bloodthirsty little animal, with a body about 14 inches long, plus a tail 5½ inches in length, sharp eyed and long furred, the ferret is most often heard of in connexion with rabbit-hunting and rat-killing. The trained ferret, often muzzled and on a long lead, will go into the rabbit burrow or rat run and drive the scared occupants into the open, where its owner is waiting to dispatch them.

This domesticated variety of the polecat has white or yellowish fur and pink eyes ; darker specimens occur, generally the result of crossing a ferret with the wild polecat. Though it has been used by Man for the destructon of vermin for many centuries, it is almost impossible to tame a ferret completely. It remains very uncertain in temper. The object in muzzling the animal and having it on a lead is to ensure its return from the burrow or run into which it is introduced. Without those precautions the ferret is likely to gorge itself on a victim and remain absent perhaps indefinitely.

H. Bastin
FERN FRONDS EXPANDING
Few natural objects are so beautiful as opening fern fronds (above), which are to be seen in woods and on shady banks during Spring. Ferns live on from year to year, though the fronds of native British species wither in late Autumn, fall to the ground and decay.

O. Reid
A FERRET, SMALL AND FIERCE
Only semi-domesticated, the ferret is a ferocious little beast and has no affection for its owner. Used chiefly to drive rabbits and rats from their holes, it is a delicate animal to rear, warmth and absolute cleanliness being essential.

Feudal System. If we could travel over western Europe as it was a thousand years ago, we should see woods and farms, small villages, a few walled towns, and now and then a well-protected monastery. Dominating the landscape were fortified castles. These arrangements came about through the break-up of the Roman Empire in the 5th century.

In the confusion of the barbarian invasions, the central government was helpless to defend the people. So, any landowner who was enterprising in repelling the invaders was regarded as the natural leader of his community. As a result, a new set of customs arose that determined the relations between the different classes ; this organization of society is known as feudalism, or the feudal system.

This system, which was set up in different parts of Western Europe, lasted until the end of the Middle Ages. First of all there was a king surrounded by a body of attendants. In theory he owned all the land, though the actual use of a large portion of it was enjoyed by some 400 or 500 great landholders, each possessing one or more castles, who received the land on condition that they helped the king with counsel and aided him in war by providing men.

The actual use of much of the land of these great landholders was enjoyed by other men, who were similarly owners of strong castles, on the same condition of military and other service. These in turn subdivided their lands, until at the bottom of the scale were men who had just enough land to enable the holder to live comfortably and to provide himself with a horse and weapons for fighting.

Each of these landholders was a little monarch within the limits of his land and they were known as nobles and lords. Their household servants and the peasants who worked their lands were called serfs or villeins, for the whole feudal system was based on a modified form of slavery. Those controlling a certain number of villages and serfs, and to whom other vassals (as they were called) owed military service, were styled barons, counts, or dukes.

The ceremony by which a man became a vassal usually took place before a number of other vassals. The man who was to receive the land knelt at the feet of his king or lord, and placing his hands within those of his overlord declared that he became his "man" to serve him in all such ways as a free man should serve his lord. This ceremony was called doing homage, from the Latin word *homo*, meaning man. Next the vassal rose and placed his hand on the Bible or the relics of some saint, and swore to keep the promise he had just made. This was the

FEUDALISM :   A   VASSAL   DOING   HOMAGE   TO   HIS   OVERLORD

Here is a vassal kneeling before his feudal overlord, with both his hands placed in those of his superior. He says : ' Sire, I become your man from this day forth, of life and limb, and will hold faith to you for the lands I claim to hold from you ; and I will serve you in all ways that a free man should.' The vassal then swears his oath of fealty, which binds him to keep this promise. Next, his overlord invests him with his fief (land), giving him a clod of earth or a twig.

oath of fealty. Then the overlord, as a sign that the vassal had become the holder of the land, handed over to him a clod of earth or a twig, or some other object. This was known as investiture.

The vassal was now said to hold a fief, which would pass to his eldest son on his death, and for which only occasional payments were made. Thus was formed a solemn contract binding on both parties. The king, for example, could not tax his vassals—except on certain rare and special occasions —unless they had first given their consent to the imposition. In England the vassals made use of this principle steadily to limit the power of the king.

The feudal system was gradually established between the 8th and 11th centuries. France was the land of its earliest and most complete development, but in some form or other it was found in all the countries of western Europe. It flourished more especially from the 11th to the end of the 13th century. After that period a transformation set in, through the increasing power of the kings, supported by the Church and the newly arising towns with their commerce and wealth, and the new weapon of gunpowder, which enabled the government to blow to pieces the castles of defiant robber barons. Down to the 20th century there remained survivals of feudalism in the laws and social usages of European countries.

Fielding, HENRY (1707–54). A very important figure in the early history of the English novel, Fielding was born at Sharpham Park, near Glastonbury, Somerset, on April 22, 1707, and was educated at Eton and at the University of Leiden in the Netherlands. Arriving in London when he was 20, he set about earning his living by his pen, writing a number of farces and light pieces, most of which,

though they filled his pocket for the moment, are now looked upon as little more than literary curiosities. In the meantime he had been studying law and was called to the Bar in 1740. Nine years later he was appointed, through the interest of an old schoolfellow, a justice of the peace for Westminster, and proved a conscientious magistrate.

The turning-point of his career came when he wrote Joseph Andrews. This was published in 1742, and was followed in 1743 by Jonathan Wild, although it seems probable that this grim portrayal of an 18th-century gangster may have been written first. In 1749 came Tom Jones, regarded by some critics as the greatest novel ever written. His last novel, Amelia (1751), is subdued compared with the boisterous high spirits of Tom Jones. In 1754 he went to Lisbon, and his delightful Journal of that voyage closed his literary career, for he died on October 8 of that same year.

Fifeshire. On the east coast of Scotland, between the Firths of Tay and Forth, the county of Fife has an area of 500 square miles. The surface is, as a whole, low-lying and fertile, 75 per cent of the land being under cultivation. The coastal towns and villages are mostly engaged in fishing, but there are mines, particularly coal-mines, in the Cowdenbeath district, linoleum factories at Kirkcaldy, and linen manufactures at Dunfermline. Cupar, or Cupar-Fife, is the county town.

St. Andrews is perhaps the most famous historic town in the county, with its ruined castle and cathedral, university and golf courses. Dunfermline, which includes the naval base of Rosyth, preserves the ruins of the abbey founded by King Malcolm Canmore in 1072. The estimated population of the county is 286,000.

Figs.

For centuries the fruit, fresh or dried, of the fig tree has made up a large part of the food of the natives of western Asia and southern Europe. And most other people eat figs whenever they can get them. But the story of figs concerns also a wasp. Every time you eat a Smyrna fig you owe thanks to the fig-wasp, for without this tiny insect no bigger than a gnat we would have none of those luscious fruits. The part these little wasps play in the life of the Smyrna fig is in aiding cross-pollination. The buds cannot develop unless they are fertilized by the pollen of the caprifig, a wild species that bears only sour and pithy fruit. This is due to a peculiarity in the structure of the Smyrna fig.

for the fruit did not ripen properly. Experts were sent to Asia Minor to study the tree in its native home, and there they discovered the important part the fig-wasp plays. So caprifig trees were planted, and little fig-wasps were carefully packed and brought across thousands of miles to the California groves. Now the figs of California rival those of Smyrna, and the drying of figs has grown to be commercially important.

There are varieties of fig which do not require cross-pollination, but their fruit is not so delicious and cannot be dried so easily and well as the Smyrna fig. The different species vary greatly, some being low trailing vines and others good-sized

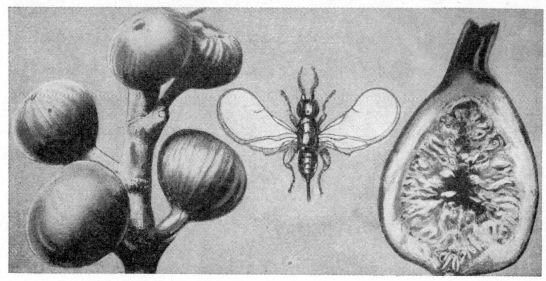

THE STORY OF THE WASP THAT HELPS TO MAKE FIGS

Have you ever noticed the round hole in the end of a Smyrna fig? Its existence enables Nature, with the aid of the tiny fig-wasp here shown (considerably enlarged), to perform one of her most unusual bits of magic. The Smyrna fig does not ripen unless it is provided with pollen from the wild caprifig. The little wasps grow to maturity in the wild fruit, then crawl out, becoming dusted with pollen. Later they creep through the hole into the Smyrna fig and deposit inside it the caprifig pollen that clings to their bodies. Thereupon the fig ripens into the delicious fruit we all love.

The pear-shaped figs, full of delicious pulp, are not the true fruit of the tree. They are rather the receptacles within which the little fig-flowers grow and ripen in great numbers, forming the true fruits which we commonly call the " seeds." This receptacle is closed save for a little hole at the very tip, so that cross-pollination cannot be accomplished in the usual way—by the wind or by insects of ordinary size.

The fig-wasps breed in the fruit of the wild fig. At the proper time bunches of these wild figs are hung in the tops of the cultivated trees, and when the little wasps push out to find a place to lay their eggs their bodies become covered with the pollen from the wild-fig flowers. As they enter the Smyrna fig, this pollen is brushed off on the flowers and fertilizes them. This process is called " caprification." One caprifig tree is sufficient to pollinate 100 cultivated trees.

Though figs had long been grown in the warmer parts of the United States there was no fig-growing industry there until a few years ago. Then Smyrna fig trees were brought to California for cultivation on a large scale. For years there were heavy financial losses and great disappointment,

trees. The fruits vary in colour from deep purple to yellow or nearly white. The Smyrna fig rarely grows more than 18 or 20 feet high. The India-rubber tree (*Ficus elastica*), from which most of the East India rubber comes, is a species of fig.

Figure of Speech.

When the English poet Wordsworth says of Milton," Thy soul was like a star and dwelt apart," we get a stronger impression of Milton's loftiness of spirit and his solitude than the plain words could possibly give us. This phrase is a figure of speech, in which there is an expressed comparison of one object to something of an entirely different order, and because of the use of the term *like* is called a simile (pron. sim′-i-lē).

When Shakespeare says in Julius Caesar—

There is a tide in the affairs of men,
Which, taken at the flood, leads on to fortune :

he does not expressly compare opportunity to a tide, but leaves the comparison to be inferred from his words. This figure of speech, in which a comparison between two unlike objects is not stated but only implied, or in which one is identified with the other, is called metaphor. It is a more daring and generally more powerful figure than simile. It is exposed, however, to the danger of what is called mixed metaphor, as in the case of the Irishman who said of his opponent that he "never opened his mouth but he put his foot in it." When the metaphor represents a lifeless object as a person, we call the figure of speech personification. Thus Shelley speaks of the moon as "that orbed maiden with white fire laden."

Sometimes, in order to arrest attention or to produce a vivid impression, the writer or speaker expresses more than the truth, or exaggerates, as when we say "a thousand apologies." This figure of speech is known as hyperbole (pron. hī-pêr'-bo-lē), from Greek *huperbole*, meaning overshooting. Other figures of speech owe their force to the use or arrangement of words in such a way that the sound aids the sense or produces greater emphasis. Thus, in alliteration the effect is produced by using words beginning with the same sound in close succession, as when we speak of "might and main," or "apt alliteration's artful aid." Often the effect of alliteration is very beautiful, as in Swinburne's "With lisp of leaves and ripple of rain." But often it is a mere trick, without beauty or force.

Fiji. (Pron. fē'-jē). A hundred years ago few of the white men in the Pacific could be induced to visit the beautiful Fiji Islands, for no spot on

earth had a more evil reputation. The dark-skinned natives, with their high mops of frizzled hair, seemed courteous and intelligent at first, but in reality they were treacherous cannibals. Yet today, there are few more law-abiding places in the South Seas than these same Fiji Islands.

The Fiji group, situated west of Samoa and 1,200 miles due north of New Zealand, is composed of about 250 islands, only 80 of which are inhabited. The largest, Viti Levu, has an area of 4,053 square miles the second in size is Vanua Levu, with an area of 2,130 square miles. The others are much smaller. On Vitu Levu, as on the other large islands of the

Sir Basil Thomson, K.C.B.; George Brown, Melanesians and Polynesians

FIJI ISLANDERS AT A DANCE AND PREPARING A FEAST

Dressed in curious skirts, these Fiji warriors (lower) stand ready to perform a 'meke' or war dance. Having worked themselves up into a state of great excitement, they squirm and prance around, brandishing their clubs and emitting blood-curdling war cries. Squatting before a hut made of palm leaves, three men (top) are preparing turtles in readiness for a feast. The natives of the Fiji Islands do not like hard work, which is done by coolies from China or India.

group, the coast hills rise rapidly to high peaks, mostly ancient volcanoes, often over 4,000 feet high.

The islands are fertile, chief products being sugar, copra (dried coconut kernels), bananas, maize, rice, rubber and tobacco, and rare woods. Gold and silver are mined on Viti Levu and Vanua Levu. Between December and April hurricanes occur which injure the crops and rip down the flimsy native dwellings, but the general climate is excellent for the tropics, with an abundant rainfall. Fiji is a British crown colony, with a Governor at Suva, the capital of the group.

The islands were discovered by the Dutch explorer Tasman in 1643, and were visited by Captain Cook in 1769. Great Britain took possession of the group in 1874 at the request of the ruling chiefs. During the Second World War (1939–45) Fijian units served in the south-west Pacific against the Japanese, and the islands were used by U.S. troops as a training ground in jungle warfare. There are a number of natives from the sub-continent of India on the islands, where they work as coolies. The population is about 246,000.

Finch. Distributed over most of the temperate zone, except Australasia, this large family of small birds is known as the *Fringillidae*. All have conical beaks and are, in the main, seed eaters. The plumage varies from the dull hues of northern sparrows to the vivid blues, scarlets, and yellows of the tropical finches. Vocal powers also vary, for the finch family includes, along with its non-singing members, such songsters as the canaries.

The goldfinch, *Carduelis elegans*, is one of the most beautiful of our British finches. About five inches long, the male bird has black, red, and white bands on his head, golden yellow and black on the wings. He and his more sombre mate are especially fond of thistle seed. His song is as cheery as his coat.

A curious finch is the crossbill, or grosbeak, for the curved mandibles of his sharp-pointed bill cross in a way that gives the impression of a deformity. This is really a special adaptation to the bird's feeding habits, enabling it to extract the seeds from the fir cones on which it feeds.

Another well-known member of the finch family which is resident in Britain is the bullfinch (*Pyrrhula europaea*). This handsome bird, with black head and red breast, is a visitor to our gardens, especially in

the spring when it is sometimes destructive to fruit buds. The greenfinch (*Ligurinus chloris*) is easy to know by its colour, and its long-drawn, single wheezing note. It is with us all the year.

The chaffinch, a common British bird, also stays all the year round. In the winter the females often form flocks while the males remain solitary. Hence the Latin name, *Fringilla coelebs* (coelebs meaning unmarried). The brambling, very like a chaffinch, but with a white rump, is a winter visitor. The siskin, another finch, is found in the pine woods of Scotland but is less common in England.

One of the most familiar members of the finch family is the linnet, seen and heard in many parts of England; the male has a rosy crown and breast. The smallest of our finches is the lesser redpoll, a close relative of the linnet but much less widely distributed.

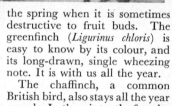

R. C. Hinkins; F. Vear

FINCHES : CHAFFINCH AND GOLDFINCH

One of the commonest British birds, the chaffinch (lower) has a loud cheery song ; the male has a slate-blue crown, a yellowish-green rump, two white bars on each wing, and a reddish-brown breast. The goldfinch (upper) is not so common ; it is the brilliant gold band across the black wings which gives the bird its name.

All the other finches fade into insignificance as regards numbers when compared with the house sparrow, *Passer domesticus*, the most common bird in Britain.

The ARTIST'S *Eager* QUEST *for* BEAUTY

What is the origin of the universal reaching out for beauty which is the source of what we call the Fine Arts? What are the ways in which it finds expression? Those are some of the questions answered here.

Fine Arts. The various arts are broadly divided into two classes, the useful arts and the fine arts. The former of these terms includes such branches of activity as industrial arts, manual arts, household arts, and others. The fine arts are considered to begin when there is a distinct reaching out for the expression of beauty in the thing created.

Sandro Botticelli (c. 1444-1510) painted this angel's head. This Florentine artist was a master of lineal design.

In accordance with this definition, the fine arts are generally considered to be three in number, namely architecture, sculpture and painting. To these some writers have attempted to add others, especially poetry and music, while dancing and acting have also been put forward. One idea of fine art may be gleaned from the following example. A famous artist says, " When I paint a wave I am that wave." True. And it is quite as true that when you look at his painting of the wave you are that wave. When he sweeps his brush up over the canvas, he feels himself doing just what the wave is doing; when you sweep your eye over the lines where his brush has led, you too become a sort of racing, conscious wave.

In answer to your question, " What is a wave? " the scientist will tell you that a wave is the result of certain causes and principles ; he will show you the materials that compose the wave; and, if your curiosity is still unsatisfied, he will separate those materials into their elements. He will show you the effects of conditions upon them, and he may continue, showing cause, and cause of cause, to the beginning of the world; or, in the other direction, he may deal with effect upon effect to the end of it. He always leads you into the relations of the wave to all others things, and always away from the wave itself.

The artist, on the other hand, fixes your attention on the wave, ignoring in his picture the fact that anything else exists. " The real work of art—its way leads nowhere and its frame ends the world." He bends all lines of attention to the thing in hand, fills the consciousness with it, excluding all other things, and uses it as a means of bringing you into the mood which he has experienced—a process known as visual experience.

Fine art may bring us into a condition of repose, by making captive, first, our sense of seeing and our imagination; and thence, through the unity and intensity of its interest, our whole consciousness.

But Art may also, too, rouse us to heights of far more active emotion; and indeed it is an essential of the fine arts that they do appeal, through our sense of beauty, to the emotions. This is not to say that everything which is included in the fine arts is necessarily of positive beauty; there are sculptures (for example, some of Jacob Epstein's and Henry Moore's) and paintings which rouse feelings of perplexity and yet no reasonable person would deny that they belonged to the fine arts. The vision of a great imaginative artist is invariably ahead of its (and his) time.

These works are far removed from those produced by the purely " representational " artists, whose work is at best an exact copy of Nature. At one time there was a general idea that true beauty could only be got by copying Nature, but few people nowadays would hold this tenet unconditionally.

In any case, it is clear that Nature does not always exist in perfect harmonies or perfect contrasts. Nature, indeed, appears to be preoccupied with organic patterns rather than with the forming of perfect pictures. If he would produce pictorial beauty, the artist must make many a change in the

British Museum

FINE ART OF JAPANESE COLOUR-PRINTING
Called The Hollow of the Deep Sea Wave off Kanagawa, this picture achieves the effect of a wave about to break. It is the work of a Japanese artist named Hokusai, who was born in Tokyo in 1760. His illustrations for books form a complete record of Japanese life, but his countrymen do not rate him as an artist of the first rank.

" landscape with figures amid which we dwell."
He must select, arrange, subdue, and accent the
elements of his work, so that they will produce the
mood or set forth the idea which he is endeavouring
to present.   This process of selection and arrangement is technically known as " composition." Let
us consider some of the requirements of good
composition and how it is obtained.

When, in looking over the fields, we send our
glance from the trees to the hills beyond them;
when we remove our eyes from a person to whom
we are speaking, to the walls just behind him; when,
in fact, we leave off looking at any one thing and
look at something either farther away or nearer than
that at which we were looking before, our eyes
change their focus for the occasion in somewhat
the way in which the focus of a camera is changed
to suit varying distances.

The eye, however, is the more subtle instrument
and is sensitive to variations of distance which
would make no appreciable difference to the
camera. It may, therefore, be said that each thing
we see in Nature is, when it is being seen, the centre
of a little picture all its own, and that it is the sum
of a number of these little pictures which gives us
our impression of " all outdoors."

Now, if the artist were to try to paint in one
picture the hills as he sees them when looking
directly at them, the trees as he sees them when

looking directly at them, the clouds as he sees
them when looking directly at them, he would have
a picture with as many separate interests as it
contained objects—a picture which would have
neither unity nor repose.   So the artist must select
some one thing for the main theme of his picture,
and this he must place before all other things which
may happen to occur in it.

A study of great paintings will show the various
ways in which artists accomplish this suppression
of the secondary things and emphasis of the important ones.   It will show that a figure may be made
prominent by the position it occupies on the canvas,
by its relations to other figures, by its having a
space of comparative quiet around it (notice the
effect of the haloes around the heads in the old
masters' paintings of the saints); by the focusing of
many important lines upon it or the introduction
of a contrast near it; by its being more minutely
drawn and finished than the rest of the picture;
and by the suppression of other figures or groups of
figures through partially hiding them from view,
turning them away from the spectator, causing
them to look or point toward the principal figure
or throwing them into a subdued tone.

Consistency of character, which has been
called harmony, consistency of attractions, which
has been called balance, and consistency of movement, which has been called rhythm, will keep all

QUIET POETRY OF A COROT LANDSCAPE

Not until he was more than 50 years of age did Jean
Baptiste Corot, the famous 19th century French artist,
produce his most typical work of the French countryside,
though he exhibited his first picture in 1827. This study,
Morning—Dance of the Nymphs, is in the Louvre at Paris.
Another of his landscapes is reproduced in page 914.   His
work is notable for extreme lightness and freshness, white
mixed with colours giving his foliage a translucent tinge.

National Gallery, London; photograph, W. F. Mansell

LAST PICTURE OF TURNER'S BEST PERIOD

Perhaps the greatest marine artist Britain has ever had, Turner's (1775–1851) technical gifts are well demonstrated in The Fighting Téméraire (above), which was painted in 1839 and is in the National Gallery, London. The veteran warship of the British Navy is being towed to her last berth before being broken up, and the genius of the artist manages to convey a feeling of deep melancholy. Turner concentrated attention on the suggestive effects of glowing colour.

elements of the work together in an integral whole. Here again the artist in forming his work must exercise his aesthetic judgement, varying from Nature's appearances if need be, to bring finer proportion into his work, more perfect unity, and deeper meaning.

Let us look at Corot's landscape Morning. It has come to be called "The Dance of the Nymphs." Is this because there is a group of tiny figures at the bottom—who in truth are scarcely dancing and who may hardly be called nymphs? Or is it because of the witchery of that great movement which takes us from the bottom up into the picture, across the top and down the other side, lastly circling round and round the bit of sky in the centre, leading us in an airy dance through the tree-tops?

For a contrasting mood see Turner's great picture, The Fighting Téméraire. What is there about this picture to show us that this old ship has valiantly fought England's battles, or to tell us that she is being towed away for breaking up? And yet Ruskin, Turner's greatest interpreter, says that, of all pictures not visibly involving human pain, this is the saddest. What has the artist done to make us feel the solemnity of this occasion? We see a sheet of still water under a great bending sunset sky. On the other side a tall ship is coming up, towed by a black tug. Long ripples are thrown to left and right, and smoke pours back from the

funnel of the tug. Shadows are gathering from all sides, and there are the buildings of a great city beyond in the gloom.

Study carefully the use of lines. Do they resemble those merry ones that circle round the canvas of Corot's Morning? Or are they the lines which we see in the solemn groves of pine or cypress, in the desert, and in the great cathedrals? Are they not like figures in a funeral march? Has the artist accepted Nature only as he found her?

In sculpture, as in the other arts, associational and psychological factors play a large part. The significance and meaning of form itself would seem to depend on the countless associations of Man's history. For example, rounded forms convey an idea of fruitfulness and maturity, possibly because the earth and most fruits are rounded. The greatest sculptors have depicted the precise plastic representation of certain universal shapes or ideas. Sculpture which represents objects of Nature or of the imagination in solid form in three dimensions, as distinguished from painting which uses but two dimensions, comprises two forms—sculpture in the round, and relief sculpture. In all ages the chief subject for sculptors has been the human figure, whether nude or draped.

The Greeks, who were the first people to give to the representation of the human form the illusion of flight, evolved an idealized type of beauty. The character of the subject was of paramount import-

Louvre, Paris

EARLY MASTERPIECE OF GREECE
Early Greek art created nothing more beautiful than this statue of Nike, the goddess of Victory, carved by a sculptor from the island of Rhodes in the third century B.C. It was found on the island of Samothrace, in the Aegean Sea.

ance, and not, as with us, chiefly a medium of aesthetic pleasure. The primary aim of a sculptor such as Pheidias, for example, was to make statues of gods and heroes. Greek artists attempted to transcend Nature, and this idealizing tendency is evident in the numerous examples of sculpture which have been preserved.

In his stone statues, Michelangelo represented only the human body, its suppleness and its force; he retained from reality the muscular play of great figures vibrant with effort or distorted by despair. He solved the most complicated problems of movement.

Almost every hard material has been used for sculpture. The ancient Egyptians worked in granite, basalt and diorite; Chinese carvings in jade are famous; cameos in antiquity and in modern times are wrought in onyx; and intaglios or incised sculptures are cut in chalcedony, sard, and amethyst.

The beauty of a picture or a piece of sculpture does not lie in pleasing the visual sense alone; it lies also in the completeness of the artist's vision, and in his ability to create a world. Perhaps it is impossible for the visual sense to be engaged at all without the mind receiving some deeper message through it. It is this fact which has caused critics to observe that art is a sort of language. But the message which that language has to deliver is not an intellectual one. It is not primarily for the rehearsing of facts that art exists. The message which a picture has to give comes to us in the form of an experience, a mood which the work awakens within us—not a story which the thing can tell us.

Expression, therefore, is the chief consideration which compels an artist always to turn away more or less from the copying of Nature; and the more deep and difficult the emotion he is trying to express, the finer will be a great artist's work. Yet, especially with contemporary art, there is always the difficulty that the artist may be expressing a feeling or an emotion far removed from popular experience.

Finger-prints. Fine curved lines or ridges cover the skin at the tips of the fingers and thumbs, and if a finger is pressed on an ink pad and then on a sheet of paper the pattern of these lines will be made on the paper, forming a finger-print. No two persons' finger-prints are exactly alike.

This fact is put to practical use by the police of many countries. When a criminal is caught, he is photographed and his finger-prints are taken so that he can be easily identified on any future occasion. Offenders are thus frequently detected by their finger-prints on door-knobs, window-panes, and furniture, at the scene of their crime.

Finger-prints for identifying persons who sign legal documents were first used by the Chinese; and in some early instances in the history of England thumb-prints have served as the signatures of persons who could not write. The system did not

FINGER-PRINTS UNCHANGED BY PASSING YEARS
From time to time the claim is made that the finger-prints of two persons have been found to be alike, but it has always been disproved. Here are three sets of finger-prints of the same person, taken respectively (from left to right) at the ages of 26, 44 and 83. It will be noticed that the loops and ridges have remained practically unchanged right into old age, when the skin is cracked and shrivelled. The individuality of finger-prints and their value in proving identity were known to the Chinese about 200 B.C., and a thumb impression was used by them instead of a signature.

come into use for the identification of criminals until Sir Francis Galton published in 1892 a detailed scientific study of finger-prints. The Metropolitan Police of London then began the formation of a collection of finger-prints, which enables an expert to identify one print from among many thousands in a few minutes.

The chance that two finger-prints are identical has been shown to be less than one in 64,000 million; and if we take the imprints of three or more fingers, all chance of error is eliminated.

Finland. A Republic of Northern Europe, this country is bordered on the east by Russia and on the west by the Gulf of Bothnia and by Sweden, and on the north by Norway.

The country consists of a plateau, hills seldom rising above 400 to 600 feet, and it is only in the extreme north that there are mountains reaching a height of over 2,000 feet. The Baltic coast of Finland is girded by steep cliffs fringed with many rocky islands, including the Aland group in the mouth of the Gulf of Bothnia. The area of Finland is about 117,975 square miles.

The winters are long and cold, rivers being frozen from December to May; but the summers, with the sun disappearing only for an hour or so, or not at all, are so warm that crops ripen in six or seven weeks. The hills are covered with birches, backed by pines and firs, and the rock-strewn meadows in summer are bright with wild flowers growing around barns and farmhouses.

Finland has been called the Land of a Thousand Lakes, and, indeed, 11 per cent of the surface consists of lakes. These are the result of glacial action in the Ice Age. The glaciers also left large marshy areas—hence the Finnish name for the country, Suomi, meaning swamp. But to the south and west lies rich clay soil, and here are the best farms and the chief cities. Forests occupy more than half the land and provide the country with its chief industries, saw-mill products and wood pulp.

The lakes, rivers and canals provide a vast network of waterways. Rafts of timber float down the rivers to the mills. Hydro-electric plants harness the rapids to furnish power, for Finland lacks coal. Copper, nickel, and low-grade iron ore are mined, and granite is quarried.

Only about six per cent of the land is under crops, but another five per cent is meadow. Wheat, rye, barley and potatoes are grown. Dairy products and fish are important exports in normal times. Small farms are the rule; most of them are on waterways and many of the farmers are fishermen as well.

The cities are small, but modern in appearance, with broad streets and many fine buildings. Helsinki (Helsingfors) is the capital and chief seaport, with a population of about 327,000. Here particularly a new school of architecture has given rise to stone buildings of an interesting character.

The Finns are related to the Turks and to the Magyars of Hungary, and speak a language quite different from their Slav and Scandinavian neighbours. There is a university at Helsinki, and two at Turku (Abo), one Swedish and the other Finnish. Technical education in Finland is excellent.

Until the 12th century Finland was a free country. It was then conquered by Sweden, who held it until 1809, when the Swedes withdrew from

Finnish Legation

FINLAND: VILLAGERS ROWING TO CHURCH

In a country like Finland, where so much of its area is occupied by lakes, the villages are scattered far apart in some districts. Consequently, as one church has to serve the needs of several villages, the people have to be carried somehow to their devotions, and, railways being few, they are generally taken by water. Here is a scene that is very common in these regions. The boats proceed from village to village to collect the peasant churchgoers. They are quite large, with a capacity sometimes of over 100 persons, and are the property of the villages that built them.

the country and it passed to Russia. In 1917 the Finns took advantage of the Russian Revolution to declare their independence. In 1939 Russia made demands, the granting of which would have destroyed effectively the independence of the country. These were therefore refused by the Finns, and Russia invaded Finland by land, sea, and air on November 30. Fighting continued until March 12, 1940, when a Treaty of Peace was signed.

When Germany attacked the Soviet Union in June 1941 (during the Second World War), the Finns joined the Germans. Russian forces again invaded Finland in June 1944, but an armistice was signed three months later; Finland then declared war upon Germany. Finland ceded to the Russians the Petsamo area in the extreme north, and the Porkkala headland, about 30 miles south-west of Helsinki. The Soviet Union also obtained military bases on the south and south-west coasts. The population of the Republic of Finland is about 3,930,000.

Fir. Although there are many different types of tree which we class as firs, they can easily be distinguished from the pines with which they are often confused. For in the pine the long, slender needles are grouped in sheaths by twos, threes, fours, or fives; whereas the short, flat needles of the fir-tree are single and grow in spiral rows round the branches. The needles of the fir are usually dark green above and light green below, and the cones grow erect on the branches (*see* illustration in page 890). Various firs are distributed all over the northern hemisphere, usually growing in high altitudes or cold climates and varying greatly in size and appearance. As a whole they are highly prized for their timber and resin or gums. The silver fir of Europe (*Abies pectinata*) grows in forests on the French slopes of the Pyrenees and elsewhere, at times attaining a height of 150 feet and a diameter of 6 feet. The silver fir of the North American Pacific coast (*Abies grandis*) towers to 200 feet.

Among the many smaller species is the fragrant balsam fir (*Abies balsamea*) of Canada and the northern United States. It yields the Canada balsam used in mounting microscopic specimens. None of these is native to Britain, but many are grown in parks.

Fire. It is hard to realize the awe with which early peoples regarded the "red monster," which they believed came down in magic ways from heaven (*see* Prometheus), and which many of them worshipped as a representative of their gods (*see* Zoroaster). The ancient Greek philosophers thought of fire, air, earth, and water as the four elements of which the whole universe was made.

It is supposed that the earliest primitive men obtained their fire accidentally, from trees set ablaze by lightning, or from erupting volcanoes, and that they kept it alive carefully in huts and caves. However that may be, Man from the earliest days seems never to have been without fire for warmth and cooking, and for protection from wild beasts. The time came when someone discovered how to create fire by rubbing dry sticks together, and they invented fire-drills to aid the process. When they began to chip flint to make axes they learned that fire may be kindled by sparks drawn from stone, a method which later developed into the flint-and-

H. Bastin

SILVER FIRS, NOT PINE TREES
Although none of the firs is grown successfully for timber in Great Britain, they are popular for ornamental purposes. Here is a group of silver firs. The name silver has been variously described as referring to the silvery undersides of the needles or to the pale bark.

OLD AND TEDIOUS WAYS OF MAKING FIRE

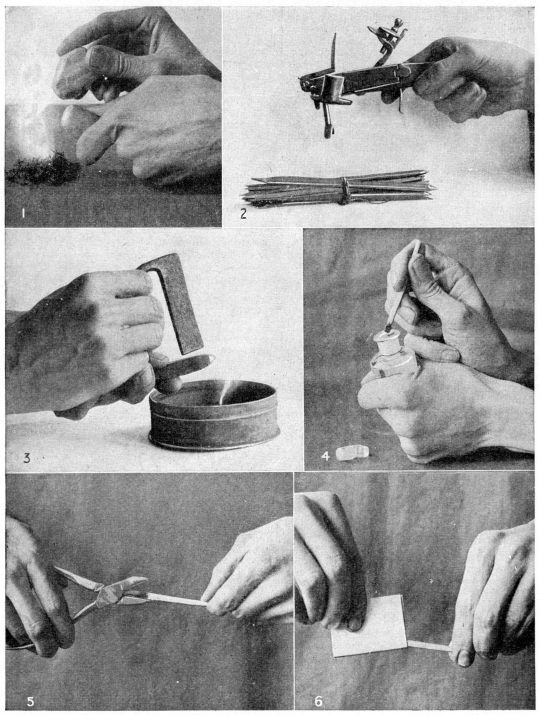

Among the oldest methods of making fire is that of striking stones (flints) together (1), the resultant sparks igniting dried moss or leaves placed below the stones. With one improvement—the use of steel instead of a second stone—this process served Man until some 100 years ago. In the fire pistol (2) the flint was struck against steel when the trigger was pulled. The ordinary flint and steel (3) were used without any mechanism. Then chemistry came to Man's aid with the first match (4). It was tipped with a substance that ignited when the match was dipped in acid. The old promethean match—named after Prometheus, the god of fire in Greek mythology, used the same principle, but the acid was contained in a tiny vial which was crushed with pliers (5). The first real match—the so-called lucifer or friction match—was invented in 1827 and was ignited by drawing the head through folded sandpaper (6). The modern safety match was not invented until about the middle of the 19th century.

steel device. Later, men found that fire could be made by focusing the sun's rays through a glass lens.

But they remained ignorant of its true character until the French chemist Antoine Lavoisier investigated, in 1783, the properties of oxygen (*q.v.*), and laid the foundation for modern chemistry. Before his death (he fell into disgrace when holding a position under the revolutionary government, was tried, and condemned in 1794 to be guillotined), Lavoisier had succeeded completely in disproving the old " phlogiston " theory, which held that when any object was heated or cooled this was due to a mysterious substance (phlogiston) which flowed into or out of the object in question. We know now that ordinary fire is due to the chemical process called oxidation, which means the combination of

FIRE-MAKER OF AUSTRALIA
One of the most primitive methods of making fire is being used by this Australian aboriginal. He twirls between his palms a stick, the end of which fits into a small hole in a block of wood. The heat generated by the rapid rotation of the stick eventually sets fire to tinder placed in the hole.

a substance with oxygen. That is why fires need air to burn properly, and why a flame will go out in a closed vessel after it has used up the oxygen.

When chemical combination is so rapid that it is accompanied by a flame it is called combustion. To start combustion, heat is required. The temperature at which any substance will catch fire is called the ignition point, which varies with the condition of the substance and the pressure of the air or the other gases involved. When the savage rubbed two sticks together he discovered, without knowing it, that the ignition point of wood is usually high; in other words, he had to use a good deal of muscle and create a good deal of heat before flames appeared. But the tip of a match has ordinarily a low ignition point, and the heat created

by scratching it once is enough to set up combustion. The ignition points of some vegetable and animal oils are low. They oxidize and generate heat if kept in a confined place. Many fires are caused by the spontaneous combustion of heaps of rags, paper, woollens, and other substances impregnated with oil. Coal, charcoal, and green hay, stored in large piles, sometimes generate heat enough to cause spontaneous combustion.

Thus we see how a fire is started. But what makes it keep on burning ? The answer in scientific language is this: A fire will be self-supporting only when the temperature created by the combustion of the burning substance is as high as, or higher than, its ignition point. Some very hard woods, like ebony, require a great deal of heat to burn them. If you put the end of a stick of ebony in a coal fire it will burn; but when you draw it out of the fire the smouldering ebony itself is lower in temperature than the ignition point of ebony, and so the flames go out.

This principle explains why you can blow out a match. Your breath carries away the heat until the temperature falls below the ignition point of the match-stick. The stream of water from a fireman's hose cools the burning walls of a building, with a similar result ; it also excludes air.

The heat of a fire depends upon the speed with which chemicals combine with oxygen. This speed in turn depends generally upon the quantity of oxygen present. If we take a bit of iron wire and put a match to it, it will not burn. But fasten the tip of a match to the end of the wire, strike it, and plunge it into a jar of pure oxygen. The wire will catch fire and burn, with sparks shooting off.

How Flame is Created

There are two kinds of fire, one with and one without flame. The presence of a flame is always due to the burning of a gas. When a coal fire flames, it is because gas is being forced out of the lumps of coal. By heating the coal in retorts in the absence of air, so that it will not catch fire, this same gas may be extracted and stored for future use. The coke, which is left after the gas is extracted from the coal, burns without flame; in this case the oxygen combines directly with the carbon in the coke, forming oxides of carbon.

It is the gas given off by the heated wax in a candle which produces the bright flame. To prove this, blow out a candle which has been burning for some time. A thin ribbon of smoke will arise. Pass a lighted match through this smoke an inch above the wick. A tiny flame will run down and light the candle again.

The brightest flames are not always the hottest; a luminous coal-gas flame is much cooler than the blue flames produced by the burners of a gas fire or gas cooker. When an inflammable gas is mixed with air in suitable proportions, it will burn so fast as to create an explosion. This is what takes place in a petrol engine. The carburetter provides the air mixture and the electric spark sets it on fire. The occasional small explosions after the burners of a gas-stove are turned off are due to the same fact; a little gas is left in the pipe, more and more air creeps in through the air-valve until the mixture becomes explosive, and the tiny flame remaining on the burner thereupon " fires back."

From ARQUEBUS *to Magazine* RIFLE

*Perhaps at your school you are taught to shoot. Then when next you hold a
rifle, remember that—despite its complexity and amazing accuracy—it is the
direct descendant of the guns whose story is told here.*

Firearms. The first hand-gun ever used
was a rough metal tube about three feet long,
closed at one end and fastened to a straight stick.

It was loaded through
the muzzle with crude
gunpowder and bits of
stone or metal, which
were rammed down to
the closed end. One man
held it firmly braced
under his arm. Another
applied a fuse, or match,
of smouldering tow to
a touch-hole, thereby
igniting the gunpowder.

The gun went off with
a tremendous roar, a
burst of flame and a
great cloud of smoke.
If the enemy were not

**This illustration of 1609 shows
a musketeer with the match
lighted; he carries the fork on
which to rest his weapon.**

more than 100 feet away,
a few might be slightly
wounded. But the gun
was just as likely to
burst and, in doing so, kill the men who operated it.

Now look at today's direct descendant of that
ancient hand-gun. It too has a metal tube, called
the barrel, fastened to a
wooden stock. It too is
loaded with powder and
with a piece of metal. The
principles are exactly the
same; but what a difference
in its performance! The
firer holds the wooden butt
tight to his shoulder, takes
aim through the sights, and
presses a small trigger.
Swifter than sound, the
bullet has reached a point
half a mile away, and with
sufficient force to kill a man.

Between the 15th century
hand-gun and the rifle of
the 20th century an almost
infinite variety of firearms,
developed out of men's keen
competition in warfare and
hunting, were evolved. Here
we can trace only briefly the
development of "small
arms"—muskets, rifles, shot-
guns, revolvers and pistols.

When the first hand-gun
was given a curved stock
with a wide butt to be placed
against the shoulder, it was
called a hackbut, or arquebus. This was soon improved
by fixing a hammer on the

gun to hold the taper or match, which was brought
down to the touch-hole by a trigger. Weapons
equipped with this device were called match-
locks. They were clumsy arms, useless in rainy or windy
weather, not quick to operate and less effective
than the long-bow and cross-bow at their best.

About 1540 the Spaniards developed a longer
match-lock, with a bore (interior diameter of the
barrel) a little larger than that of the standard
modern shot-gun. This was called a musket, a
term which came to be applied to all military hand-
guns up to the time of the rifle. The early muskets
were so heavy that they required a support, and
musketeers carried long forked rods which they
planted in the ground in order to support their
weapons while firing. Muskets were usually loaded
with a single round bullet of lead, which was forced
down against the powder with a ramrod.

Early in the 17th century the flint-lock was
invented, which made the burning fuse, or match,
unnecessary. The hammer, operated by a spring,
had a head like a vice, holding a piece of flint.
Around the touch-hole on the side of the barrel
was a priming pan with a hinged cover, which
had an up-thrust piece of steel. When the trigger
was pulled, the hammer fell and the flint struck the
steel on the hinged cover, opening it and sending a
shower of sparks to fire some
powder placed in the pan
beneath. This "priming"
powder flashed through
the touch-hole and set off
the charge in the barrel.

During the first half of
the 19th century the per-
cussion cap for igniting the
powder slowly replaced the
flint-lock. This system depended on the fact that certain explosives (*q.v.*), called
fulminates, were detonated
when struck a sharp blow.
In percussion-cap guns a
hollow nipple was set up-
right in the breech, and
on this was placed a small
copper cap containing the
fulminate. The cock or
hammer, when released by
the trigger, struck and exploded this cap, sending a
flame down into the powder.

The old musket had
a "smooth" bore, and the
spherical bullets had to be
of large diameter, in order
to produce the required
striking force; air resistance
slowed them down very
rapidly. Also, they were not

British Museum

FIREARMS OF CRUDE DESIGN
**When firing their hand cannons these 15th-century
soldiers aimed with the left hand and applied a
lighted taper or 'match' to a hole bored through
the metal cylinder, so firing powder in the barrel.**

FROM HAND CANNON TO THE BREECH-LOADER

HAND CANNON, 14th Century

ARQUEBUS (MATCHLOCK) and

REST, 16th Century

WHEEL-LOCK GUN, 16th Century

WHEEL-LOCK PISTOL, 16th Century

MUSKET, 17th Century

FLINTLOCK GUN, 17th Century

FLINTLOCK PISTOL, 18th Century

"BROWN BESS" (FLINTLOCK), Late 18th Century

SPRINGFIELD RIFLE (PERCUSSION CAP), 1863

COLT REVOLVER 1861 – 1865

PRUSSIAN NEEDLE-GUN (BREECH-LOADER), 1866 –1871

Five hundred years in the history of the development of firearms from the hand cannon to the breech-loader are depicted here. The hand cannon was merely an iron tube, loaded with gunpowder and bits of iron and fired by applying a taper or piece of red-hot metal to a touchhole. In the arquebus the stick-handle of the hand cannon was changed to a stock held against the shoulder. The barrel was lengthened and by pulling a trigger a burning match was applied to the powder. It was rested on a fork when aiming. The next six weapons, including the Brown Bess of Wellington's armies, used a flintlock for firing. The Springfield rifle introduced rifled barrel and percussion ignition, also used in revolvers. The Prussian needle gun proved the great superiority of breech over muzzle loading

1282

ccurate at any distance over 100 yards. To vercome these defects the principle of *rifling* was dopted. This consisted in cutting spiral grooves nside the barrel to grip the bullet as it passed hrough and so give it a spinning motion. The ifling put an end to erratic flight, and eventually ermitted the use of long cone-shaped bullets, thus iving the projectile greater weight without ncreasing air resistance. The spinning motion :eeps the point of the bullet forwards, preventing the ullet turning end over end.

Although the principle of rifling was discovered n the 16th century, no great use was made of it

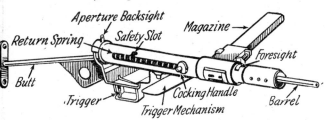

STEN GUN OF THE BRITISH ARMY
During the Second World War (1939–45) the Sten carbine (above) was introduced into the British Army. The calibre (inside diameter of the barrel) is 9 mm. (about ·35 inches), and the weapon, which is accurate up to about 50 yards, is well suited to close fighting.

or 100 years. Not until the idea was further developed in the long small-bore guns of the back-woodsmen of the North American colonies did the rifle become a truly effective weapon. The rifles were loaded at the muzzle with round bullets wrapped in a patch of greased linen or buckskin; it was a slow process to force the bullets home down the grooves, and the smooth-bore musket with its loosely ·fitting ball continued to be the chief military weapon for that reason. As for the cone-shaped bullet, the increased friction of its long sides made its use next to impossible in the muzzle-loader, until the invention of the Minié ball (named after its inventor and adopted about 1852 in Europe), which fitted loosely at loading and expanded to fit the rifle grooves when fired.

It was not until the breech-loading principle came into use that the rifle could rival the smooth-bore in speed of operation. In 1810 John H. Hall, an American, had invented a breech-loading flint-lock rifle, with a hinged chamber at the breech which tilted upward to receive the powder and ball, and then dropped down opposite the opening of the barrel. This device, however, allowed a great leakage of powder gases, as did the revolving-cylinder rifle invented in 1836 by Samuel Colt. This worked on the principle later used for "revolvers."

The first successful military breech-loader came with the use of cartridges, which contained in one paper package the powder and the bullet, and so could easily be inserted into the breech after tear-ing off a corner with the teeth to expose the powder to the fire from the per-cussion cap.

The Prussian needle-gun (the needle being a pointed piece of steel which struck the cartridge) was among the earliest military types of cartridge-firing breech-loaders, and with it the Prussian armies were able to overwhelm the Austrians in 1866. The adoption somewhat later of copper and brass cartridge shells stopped gas leakage at the breech, for the shell expanded on explosion, tightly sealing the breech opening.

The first metal cartridges were of the rim-fire type, that is, they were exploded by a blow of the firing pin on the outer rim, beneath which was the fulminate. These were soon displaced, in all except the smallest calibres, by the centre-fire cartridges of today, in which the cap occupies a small "pocket" in the base of the brass shell.

The breech mechanism of cartridge guns was early equipped with an ejector which cast out the empty shell when the breech was opened for reloading. It was a simple step to add a magazine in which several cartridges could be placed, with a device for bringing them successively into the proper position in the firing chamber, so that as fast as one was fired and ejected, another could be thrust into the breech. This gave us the various types of repeating rifles. The breech mechanism of such a weapon and the working of the magazine are shown in page 1284.

It remained for the arrival of smokeless powder to bring rifles to their present high state of efficiency. The increased propelling power of the new powder, however, caused the old soft-lead bullets to jump the rifling, and so brought about the invention of the hard metal jacket or skin for bullets. This jacket, composed of steel or of an alloy of copper and nickel, gives the bullet so secure a hold on the rifling that a much sharper twist can be given, imparting to the bullet a more rapid spin and greater muzzle velocity. This, in turn, makes possible the use of longer and narrower bullets, which can be driven to great distances at very high speeds.

The crowning achievement of rifle construction is the self-loading weapon, commonly called the automatic. In these guns the recoil, or else the gas generated by the explosion, is used to operate the mechanism, so that the cartridge is fired, ejected, and another put in its place by pulling the trigger. In the Second World War (1939–45) automatic firearms like the Thompson sub-machine-gun and the Sten carbine were used on a large scale.

The early pistol was simply a gun small enough to be fired with one hand. The pistol's develop-

FIREARMS : THOMPSON SUB-MACHINE GUN
Designed and manufactured in the United States, the Thompson sub-machine gun (above) was used chiefly by Commando and Airborne units of the British Army in the Second World War, though it was eventually largely replaced by the Sten. The magazine held 20 rounds.

MECHANISM OF A MILITARY MAGAZINE RIFLE

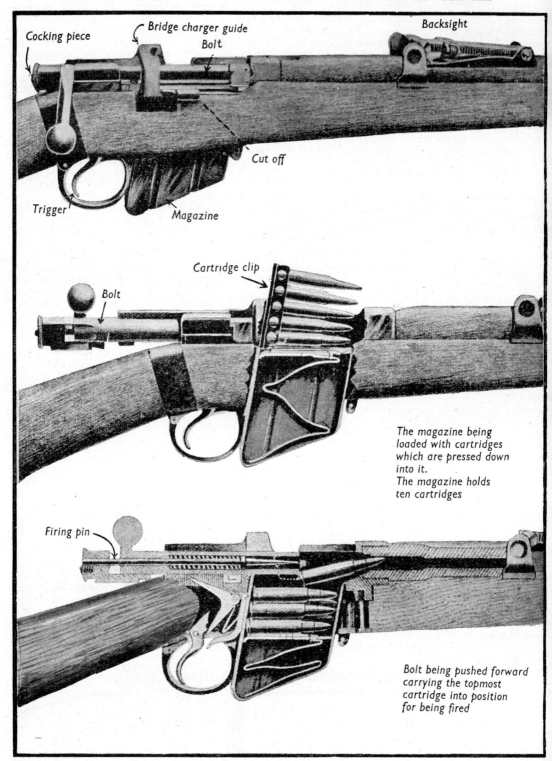

Cocking piece

Bridge charger guide

Bolt

Backsight

Cut off

Trigger

Magazine

Cartridge clip

Bolt

The magazine being loaded with cartridges which are pressed down into it.
The magazine holds ten cartridges

Firing pin

Bolt being pushed forward carrying the topmost cartridge into position for being fired

Nearly all modern armies are equipped with a rifle which has a bolt action and magazine loading. At the top details of the breech of such a rifle are shown. The cut-off, which fits over the top of the magazine, must be pulled out sideways before a cartridge from the magazine can be pushed into the breech. The middle picture shows how the cartridges are loaded, five at a time in a clip. The cartridges disengage from the clip as they are pressed into the magazine. In the bottom diagram the bolt is shown thrusting a round from the magazine into the breech.

ment followed step for step that of the musket. The first great departure in pistol-making came with the invention of the revolver, which had a revolving cylinder containing five or six charges of powder and ball which could be fired in rotation through the same barrel. The self-loading, or automatic, pistol has largely superseded the revolver. Capable of firing from eight to 10 shots with extreme speed, it is superior in mechanical principle to the revolver, for in the latter there is always imperfect alignment and gas-leakage at the junction of the barrel and the cylinder.

As early as 1580 fowling pieces seem to have been made for the purpose of shooting birds. Blunderbusses, with bell-mouthed barrels loaded with small shot or bits of metal and stone, were used as " scatter-guns " in battle or for defending stage-coaches from highwaymen. Out of these grew the modern shot-gun, whose development followed rather closely that of the musket and rifle.

Modern shot-guns have barrels ranging in size from 8-bore to 24-bore, a system of measurement which has come down from the days of the musket. The standard 12-bore gun, for instance, is one whose barrels are large enough to accommodate a round leaden ball of such a diameter that 12 of them would weigh a pound.

Shot-gun cartridges for breech-loaders, usually made with a brass base and paper sides, may be loaded with many different sizes of shot, from the tiny pepper-shot used on small birds to the heavy buckshot for deer and other large animals. Choke-boring, by which the barrel is made slightly narrower at the muzzle, causing the shot to fly in a closer group and thus be more effective at long range, is the chief device which has improved the shooting qualities of these guns since the days of the old fowling pieces. The standard double-barrelled shot-gun is nearly always made with one " choked " barrel, giving longer effective range.

How we BATTLE with OUTBREAKS of FIRE

To the peace-time hazards of conflagrations have been added those due to fire-raising as an act of war. Severely tested by aerial incendiary bombs, our fire-fighters conquered even this most fearsome menace.

Fire-Fighting. In 1189 the ward-motes of the City of London ordered " all persons who dwell in great houses within the ward (district) to have a ladder or two ready to succour their neighbours in case of fire; and to have in the summer time a barrel full of water for quenching fires." Under Edward I, watchmen were appointed who, between sunset and sunrise, were to give alarm in case of fire; and some attempt was made to provide organized fire-fighting. For example the city of Worcester in 1467 ordered " bucket carriers to be ready with their horses and buckets to bring water to every citizen when a fire occurred." In 1583 the City of London ordered houses to be pulled down with " engines," hooks and ladders so as to prevent the spread of a fire.

Houses in those days were built largely of wood, and many were roofed with thatch. Later, about 1770, the fire insurance companies kept up their own fire brigades, manned by volunteers, who were paid for attending fires on property insured by the particular company to which the fire-fighting brigade belonged. Insured houses bore a metal plate or other sign with the mark of the company; you may still see such ancient signs on old houses in our cities and towns. A great step was taken towards our modern fire brigades in 1833, when the London Fire Engine Establishment was formed, supported by the insurance brigades.

London is a good example of what happened, and we will continue briefly with its story. In 1865 the Metropolitan Board of Works set up the Metropolitan Fire Brigade—with seven large and 14 steam fire engines, 64 manual engines—pumps worked by teams of men—and two floating fire engines for use on the river. Twenty-four years later the London County Council took over the governing duties of the Metropolitan Board of Works; and in 1904 the brigade became the London Fire Brigade. So fire-fighting became the responsibility of the local governing body, and

FIRE-FIGHTING : HORSE-DRAWN STEAM PUMP
In 1861 the first horse-drawn engine was adopted by the Metropolitan (London) Fire Brigade. Later vehicles carried a steam boiler and steam-driven pumps, which could be operated within 10-15 minutes of lighting the fire under the boiler. Steam propulsion replaced horses in 1902, and a year or so later came the motor engines.

all outbreaks within its district boundaries were attended. Fires in adjoining districts were served by their own local brigades; in emergency, help was sent from beyond the district boundary.

Between 1845 and 1865 some of the larger cities in Britain were given powers to establish their own brigades, and during the years up to 1938 local

authorities were permitted—but not compelled—to establish their own fire-fighting services. In 1938, when it seemed likely that a European war might break out, the fire brigades were brought into the great Civil Defence organization; more pumps and other appliances were provided, and volunteers were enrolled into a new Auxiliary Fire Service, nation-wide in its extent. The brigades were grouped into area groups and district organizations, with a central control so that they could be mobilized quickly to cope with incendiary bombing.

The fierce bombing attacks by German aircraft during 1940 and 1941 showed up defects in the organization. In May 1941 an Act of Parliament transferred Britain's fire brigades to central (national) control; and they were reorganized into the National Fire Service. By 1942 there were 100,000 men and women serving in the National Fire Service. By the end of the war, in 1945, a total of 700 had been killed and ten times that number injured, in fighting fires set up by enemy action. The war over, a new Act in 1947 gave back the brigades to the control of local authorities; but instead of nearly 1700 separate local bodies there were now only 141 fire authorities.

Modern Fire-fighting Appliances

The steam fire engines which had been the main appliances for pumping water on to fires had by now given place to motor-pumps, ranging from a tiny one, on a carriage which one man could push and operate, to huge motor-drawn pumps of enormous power. Ladder appliances too had been enormously developed; and there were turntable ladders which enabled a hose to be taken up to a height of a hundred feet and directed from above on to the heart of a fire.

Other engines projected a jet of chemical foam on to a burning building; the foam smothered the fire by excluding air. New appliances had been developed to cope with petrol and other oil-fed conflagrations, against which a water jet was useless. Asbestos suits protected firemen in such tasks; the fear of attacks by poison-gas during the late war had made it necessary for firemen to work with gas-respirators " at the ready," but fortunately they never needed to use the gas-masks for the intended purpose. In ordinary duties, however, firemen have at times to contend with dense smoke, with chemical fumes, and even with deleterious gases released by fires at warehouses, factories and chemical works. So there are often occasions when respirators must be worn.

One of the most important parts of the fire-fighting organization is the warning system—by

Keystone; Topical

FIRE-FIGHTERS IN ACTION
S.anding at the top of ladders 100 feet above the street, these firemen (lower) are directing streams of water into the heart of a fire. The steel ladders, with extensions, are fitted to a turntable mounted on a motor vehicle (top).

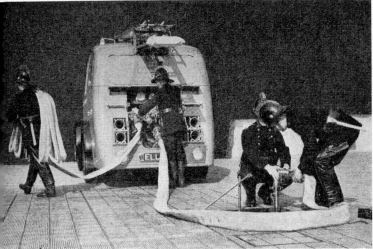

Associated Press

FIRE-ENGINE WITH DIESEL MOTOR-PUMP

Connecting up the hose to a water main, these firemen are part of the crew of a fire-engine which has the pump enclosed. Two hoses are attached to the pump, which is operated by a Diesel motor. The first hand-operated pump appeared in London about 1724, though one had been made at Nuremberg, Germany, in 1650.

telephone calls made through an exchange to the local fire station; and by summoning a brigade by the public fire-alarm posts erected at frequent intervals in our towns and cities. All this would be useless but for its counterpart in the internal organization of the fire stations and of the area controls. A fire alarm, whether from an alarm box or by way of the telephone exchange, causes a loud bell to ring at the fire station; the duty crew of firemen rush to their posts and man the pumps and ladder trucks. The doors open, and out dashes the team of fire-fighters.

At some of London's fire stations in the busy zones the traffic control lights in near-by streets are linked up with the warning system; by this means, whenever an alarm reaches the station, the traffic lights can

A FIRE-FLOAT OF THE LONDON FIRE BRIGADE

Named after Sir Eyre Massey Shaw, the commander of the Metropolitan Fire Brigade when it was first formed in 1865, the fire-float Massey Shaw (above) is 78 feet long and has a speed of 12 knots. Mounted amidships is a 'water gun,' which can deliver 1¼ tons of water a minute, drawn from the river by the pumps. The vessel was one of the historic armada of 'little ships' sent to Dunkirk beaches in May and June 1940 to assist in the evacuation of the British Army.

ONE-MAN FIRE-ENGINE ON A TRAILER

Topical

In 1937 Fire Brigades began to receive light motor-pumps (above) which were mounted on trailers and formed part of the emergency equipment for fighting fires started by air raids. They were capable of pumping 120 gallons of water a minute.

be set so as to give the fire engines the right-of-way in the direction in which they are bound. Farther along, as traffic policemen hear the engine bell, they control the streams of other vehicles so that the fire-fighters may have unimpeded passage. When a really big fire breaks out, the central control arranges for aid to be sent immediately from stations outside the local district.

London's riverside fire-fighters have their own floating pumps. One of these, the Massey Shaw, named after Sir Eyre Massey Shaw, first commander of the Metropolitan Fire Brigade, made the perilous journey to Dunkirk beaches to help in the evacuation of the British Expeditionary Force in 1940. During the Second World War period the river service was extended, and pumps were installed at London's bridges to enable river water to be used in fighting the fires set up by incendiary bombs.

Fireflies AND GLOWWORMS. These insects possess the most curious lighting system in the world. Man-made lamps generate heat as well as light, and the heat represents wasted energy. Fireflies and glowworms are ahead of Man in their ability to produce " cold light."

Fireflies—which are not flies at all, but members of the beetle order—have been objects of wonder in all ages. Flitting about on warm evenings, or creeping in the damp grass, these "living stars" produce a weirdly beautiful effect. Certain large and brilliant fireflies of tropical America, called "cucujos," are captured by the natives and kept in wire cages, where they are fed on sugar-cane. On festival nights they are sold to the young women of the region, who thread them together and place them in their hair or fasten them to their dresses, to glow there like flaming jewels. The ancient

Aztecs are said to have confined large numbers of the insects in fine-meshed baskets, which were used as lanterns on night journeys.

The glowworm, which is chiefly a native of Great Britain and northern Europe, is also a beetle. Its scientific name is *Lampyris noctiluca*. The female is wingless and crawls about on the ground at night devouring snails and other small creatures, and she gives a much brighter light than the winged male. The purposes of the light appear to be to attract a mate, and in order to make this simpler she has the habit of climbing a tall grass stem and hanging there, her " tail-lights " shining in the darkness. Among the true fireflies both sexes have wings.

There are several theories as to the cause of the light, one being that it is produced by luminous bacteria in much the same way as is the phosphorescence seen on dead fish. Another is that the fuel in the firefly's " lamp " is a substance named luciferin, which consumes oxygen and so generates light. To speed the process, luciferase, a catalyst (*q.v.*), is necessary. When luciferin is burned, it is not gone for ever; instead it is changed back to its former state, and the firefly is ready to produce another phosphorescent flash.

The European glowworms and the fireflies found in the United States are not more than half an inch long, but the " cucujo " of tropical America sometimes reaches two inches in length.

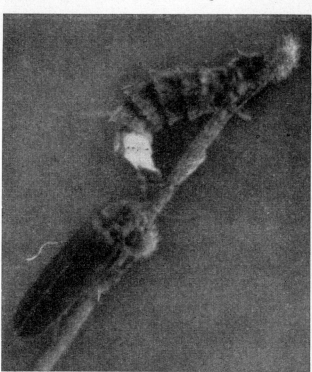

British Instructional Films, Ltd.

GLOWWORMS : MALE AND FEMALE

At the top of the twig is a female glowworm with a bright light showing at the end of her body. Below her is a male who has been attracted by the light. Glowworms are beetles and are found chiefly in Great Britain and northern Europe.

Fire Prevention.

In no circumstances is the old adage " prevention is better than cure " more applicable than in fire prevention. As you may read in our story of Fire, when some combustible material reaches its "ignition point" it may burst into flames. So our task is to see that it never reaches its ignition point in dangerous circumstances.

Out of doors, grass and dead bracken, leaves, and similar material become dry and easily ignited not only in the hot weather but after autumn winds have robbed them of their moisture. Heath fires are easily started by a dropped cigarette end or a match thrown down alight. If paper and such litter should be lying around, the fire will get a good hold, and the small local flame will raise the undergrowth to the ignition point; suddenly, even as we watch, a whole patch flares up, and the fire may soon become uncontrollable. Here is a good reason, apart from the question of tidiness, for not strewing parks and heaths and camping places with litter.

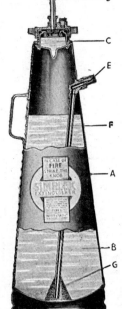

If a fire *has* to be made out of doors, choose a clearing free of undergrowth; rake an area of the ground free of burnable stuff all around the place where you are to kindle a fire. Before you leave the spot, rake out the fire; stamp out the glowing embers, and if possible strew earth on them. A heath fire can usually be quelled by using a beater vigorously at the start. The beater is made like a besom broom—a biggish bundle of twigs tied around the end of a stick. But using a beater to douse your own fire is a confession that you have not taken care to prevent damage. It is possible that a piece of broken bottle may act like a lens and focus the sun-rays rather like a burning glass, so igniting dry grass, etc. Here is another reason for tidying our heaths and woodlands.

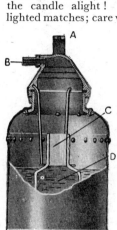

FIRE EXTINGUISHERS

At the left is a soda-acid extinguisher : (A) Steel bottle charged with (B), a solution of sodium bicarbonate ; (C) Glass bottle containing sulphuric acid, which is shattered by striking knob (D) ; (E) Jet connected by tube (F) to base of extinguisher ; (G) Strainer to prevent glass fragments from obstructing jet. On the right is a foam-generating extinguisher : (A) Handle ; (B) Nozzle ; (C) Glass container ; (D) Acid.

Mather & Platt, Ltd.

A word about picnic stoves is timely. Never use petrol stoves if possible. As you may read under Blowlamp, the paraffin stove is safer and little more bother to start. Don't let paraffin get on to the grass or undergrowth about your camping place. Always use a funnel to fill your stove or lamp. If you use a paraffin hurricane lamp inside a hut or other building, see that it is hung where its heat will not harm any timbers above. Stand the lamp securely on some support where it is unlikely to be knocked over. It is not wise to leave an oil lamp unwatched for long. The heat may cause the flame to grow much bigger and to crack the glass chimney even if it does no other harm. Clean all lamps periodically.

When using petrol or benzene to clean a garment, *never* do this anywhere near a naked flame, or near an electric fire. Carried by an air current, petrol-air vapour may travel 25 yards towards a naked light and become ignited, flashing back to the bowl in which is the petrol. If you must use petrol for cleaning, do it in the open air well away from any room where there is a flame.

Inside the house, do not stoke up a big fire in a stove or grate when the house is to be left for some hours. Putting a lot of paper on to a fire may cause burning fragments to be drawn up the chimney by the draught and to set light to soot higher up. Thatched roofs are often set on fire by burning paper flying up and out on to the straw. Cigarettes put on to an ash tray should not be left on the edge or rim; as the cigarette burns, the portion outside the rim comes to be heavier, and often falls down where it may cause a fire. Be careful with candles; always use a proper candlestick, and mind you do not drop off to sleep with the candle alight ! We have already mentioned lighted matches; care with them indoors is even more necessary than out of doors.

Memorise the position of the nearest available telephone, in case you ever have to give an alarm of fire; if you live in a town, keep in mind the nearest alarm post or the fire station itself. When the season for fireworks comes round, use them for their proper purpose, and never play tricks with them. If you use an electric smoothing iron, turn off the current when you are called away or when you finish ironing. The safest thing to do is—after turning off the switch—to *pull out the plug.* *Then* you have made a double check, and if someone else should carelessly turn the switch on again no harm will be done. An electric iron left unused with the current "on" will scorch its way right through a wooden table-top, and long before this may have set things afire near by. Never use a portable electric fire plugged into a two- or three-way adaptor which serves other appliances. Someone wishing to use the other appliance may inadvertently switch on the fire, which may not then be standing in a safe position. Finally, remember our opening admonition: Prevention is *much* better than Cure!

Fireworks.

China is believed to have been the birthplace of fireworks. There and in India they attained high perfection. When gunpowder was invented in Europe, probably early in the 14th century, fireworks also came into use. As early as 1540 they were manufactured in Italy, and firework displays of a primitive kind became fairly frequent on the Continent.

The brilliant colours of fireworks are due to certain bright-burning chemicals such as sodium, which gives a deep yellow colour; calcium, which gives red; strontium, crimson; barium, green;

BLAZE OF FIREWORKS OVER THE THAMES

P.A.-Reuter

During the Victory Celebrations of June 8, 1946, the night sky of London was lit up by fireworks and searchlights. This cascade illuminated the Thames; in the immediate foreground is Charing Cross railway bridge, with a temporary wartime bridge beyond. On the right are the Houses of Parliament, with the face of the clock in the tower lighted up. Notable firework displays, which included portraits and other pictorial effects, were given at the Crystal Palace at Sydenham, in south-east London, for many years until it was burnt down in 1936.

and copper, green and blue. Iron and steel filings are used to create showers of brilliant sparks.

In all fireworks there must be the ignition powder, which first catches fire; and the fuse, which leads the spark of fire from one point to another. This fuse is made of cotton wick which has been saturated in a paste of gunpowder and starch and dried. An explosive causing the final detonation is also included in many fireworks.

The stars in Roman candles are hollow balls, made of gunpowder mixed with light-giving materials, shaped with the aid of gum or shellac, and resting on layers of loose granulated gunpowder. These balls are then evenly distributed through the cardboard case, the spaces between the balls being filled with a closely packed mass of slow-burning material. Catherine-wheels are made by coiling long paper tubes, lightly filled with an explosive composition, about a round wooden frame which revolves freely on its axis.

For many years rockets, Roman candles, and Bengal or coloured lights were used as signals between vessels at sea, with an elaborate code by which vessels could " talk " to one another at night. Rockets especially are used as signals of distress at sea, and many lives have been saved by lifeboat crews answering the call of distress rockets. Rocket guns are used to shoot ropes to vessels wrecked close to the shore.

In war, fireworks are used as a means of recognition and communication. Illuminating flares suspended from parachutes were employed by aircraft during the Second World War (1939–45) to light up targets at night. Firework mixtures, burned in metal canisters, were used to lay smoke screens to conceal troop movements.

WHAT *to* DO *before the* DOCTOR COMES

Everybody should be familiar with the principles of first aid, and here is a useful article giving clear instructions for dealing in emergency with a number of common accidents and ailments.

First Aid. Two boys were out camping. While chopping wood for a fire the younger one cut his leg badly, and the blood gushed in spurts. The older boy as he ran towards his friend told him to lie down and raise the leg as high as possible. Quickly exposing the injured part, he folded his handkerchief into a small firm pad, placed it over the wound and secured it firmly in position with another handkerchief, thus stopping the bleeding. When they got to a doctor, the older boy was praised highly. By knowing just what to do he had probably saved his friend's life.

First aid treatment is not intended to take the place of that given by the doctor. But before he comes we can give much help. Thus it is important that bleeding should be stopped as quickly as possible; that an open wound be protected against infection; that a broken bone should not do further injury to the tissues, and that the patient be made as comfortable as can be contrived.

When a person is injured, leave him (or her) in the position in which you find him, until it is determined that his injury is not serious, when he should be carefully placed on his back, with a blanket or coat underneath. It is important that the patient should have plenty of air, and at the same time be kept warmly wrapped, as shock accompanies all injuries. Send someone to call a doctor or ambulance, and do not be hurried into moving the injured person unless that is absolutely necessary. Never give an unconscious person any fluid, such as tea, as it may enter the windpipe and choke him. But if the injured person is conscious give him sips of cold water to drink, or hot tea if he is cold and there is no serious bleeding. In addition to making the patient comfortable, cheer him to allay his fears and keep his spirits up. If it is necessary to move the patient before the arrival of doctor or ambulance, use a blanket or the patient's clothing for carrying purposes. A tactful message to the patient's family may avoid much distress and will certainly be appreciated.

If you have to remove part of the patient's clothing, do so carefully. In removing a coat, the sleeve on the uninjured side is taken off first; if necessary the stitches in the seam of the other sleeve can be cut and the coat lifted gently away.

One should have a knowledge of materials that may be safely used as dressings and have skill in applying bandages to hold these in place. " Dressing " is the name of the material applied directly over a wound, burn or scald. The materials most commonly used are gauze or lint. Do not use cotton wool directly over wounds, burns or scalds, as it sticks and is very hard to remove. In handling dressings, never finger the surface that is to be applied to the injury. The inside of a really clean handkerchief will serve as a useful improvised dressing.

Of the bandages used in first aid the triangular is the most useful (*see* Fig. 1); a large handkerchief folded diagonally will serve. The roller bandage is frequently used for minor cuts and injuries, but it is less easy to apply than the triangular. Bandages are used for any of the following purposes: to control bleeding; to hold dressings in position; to keep

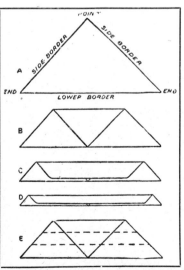

TRIANGULAR BANDAGE

Fig. 1. A, parts of the bandage named. B and C, triangle folded twice to make a broad fold bandage. D, narrow fold bandage made by folding once more, the folds being shown by broken lines at E.

FIRST AID FOR MINOR AND MAJOR INJURIES

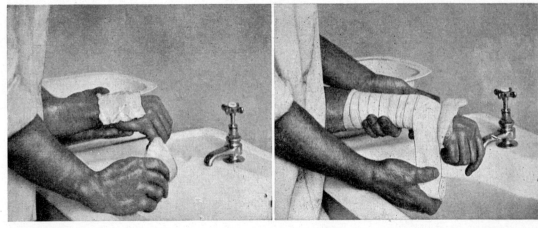

How to dress a surface wound. After cleansing the wound and the surrounding area with an antiseptic solution, and drying carefully, cover it with a layer of lint or gauze (left). Apply a roller bandage (right) tightly enough to keep the dressing in place without impeding the circulation. The arm should then be supported in a sling.

First-aid treatment of a fractured knee-cap (left): apply bandages immediately above and below the knee-cap; lay a splint at back of limb and secure with bandages round thigh, foot and ankle; re-apply knee bandages to include splint. Treat a black eye (right) with cold compresses, then cover with a pad of lint, a layer of cotton wool and a firm bandage.

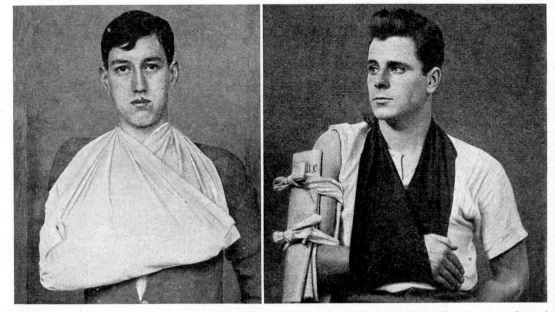

Greater arm sling (left) made with a triangular bandage: place one end over the sound shoulder, the point directed to the injured side; bring arm across the bandage, turn lower end over the arm and shoulder, and tie to first end; pin the point round the elbow. A splint can be improvised from folded newspapers (right).

IMPROVISED WAYS OF CARRYING A PATIENT

A patient who is conscious (left) can be carried on a four-handed seat (*see* inset, below), supporting himself with one arm (both should be used if possible) round one of the bearer's shoulders. The fore-and-aft method of conveyance (right) is used for a patient with an injured leg. The legs are tied together, and the front bearer cradles them in his arms.

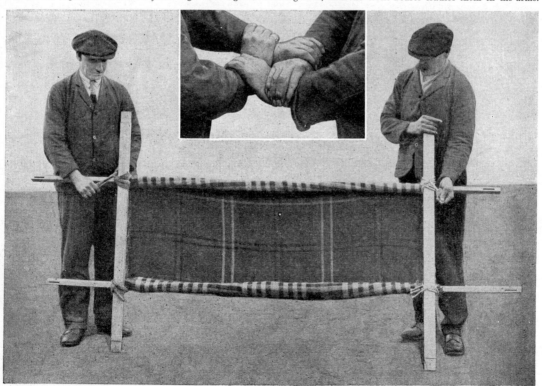

How to improvise a stretcher. Roll two poles about eight feet long into the sides of a rug or blanket until they are about two feet apart. Then tie the four corners of the rug to the poles, and fix cross-pieces of wood at either end to prevent the poles being drawn together by the patient's weight. Inset, how to make a four-handed seat.

EMERGENCY SLINGS

Fig. 2. Three ways of utilising parts of a jacket to support an injured upper limb.

splits firmly in place; as arm-slings. When there are no proper bandages available we must improvise, using a tie, scarf, braces, string, etc. Slings may be improvised with a jacket (see Fig. 2).

A bandage must protect the injured part, and usually hold it still; at the same time, it must not be in the way more than necessary, and, above all, it must not slip. The ends should be fastened with a reef knot. In almost all serious injuries to the arm a sling of some sort is necessary.

When a bone is broken, steady and support the injured part and secure it with bandages or improvised materials. Splints can be improvised with an umbrella, walking-stick, tightly rolled newspapers, etc. They should be padded with a thick scarf, cardigan, or anything else available. When in doubt treat as a fracture. In suspected fracture of the skull, ribs or breast bone, keep the patient flat on the back. *Do not* give stimulants to drink or use smelling salts.

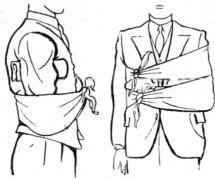

COLLAR BONE AND ARM

Fig. 3 (left). First aid for a broken collar bone (see text). Fig. 4 (right). How to secure a fractured arm to the trunk with two bandages.

A fractured jaw should be bandaged to the upper jaw, the bandage being tied on the crown of the head. For fractured collar bone or shoulder blade, place a rolled pad 2 in. thick, by 6 in. in length, in the armpit on the injured side, and bandage the forearm to the trunk, making sure the elbow is in line with the side of the trunk (see Fig. 3). For fractures of limbs, secure an upper limb to the trunk (Fig. 4), and a lower limb to the opposite limb (Fig. 5).

If the patient is unconscious, examine for serious injury, and stop any bleeding at once. If the face is bluish, indicating that breathing may have ceased, perform artificial respiration (Fig. 6), taking care that the air passages are not obstructed and that there is an abundance of fresh air. Clothing about the neck and chest should be loosened. The patient is then laid face downwards, with arms stretched out beyond his head, and the face turned to one side, so that nose and mouth are free. The operator kneels beside the prone figure, placing his hands in the spaces between the short lower ribs, the thumbs being parallel and close to each other. By pressing with the entire weight of the upper body, air is

FIRST AID FOR A FRACTURED LEG

Fig. 5. If no splints can be improvised, secure the injured limb to its fellow with broad-fold bandages round feet, ankles, legs and thighs. The feet and ankles should be bandaged first.

HOW TO APPLY ARTIFICIAL RESPIRATION

Fig. 6. Have the patient lying face downward, head to one side and arms extended. Kneel at one side, place hand on small of back as shown, swing slowly forward, keeping arms rigid and exerting pressure by weight of body only; then swing slowly back, relaxing pressure. Alternate these two movements rhythmically about 12 times a minute.

forced out of the lungs; then by relaxing the pressure the chest cavity is enlarged, and air rushes in. By pressing and relaxing alternately 12 to 15 times a minute, artificial breathing is accomplished. Continue artificial respiration until natural breathing is restored—if necessary, with relays of helpers. Keep patient warmly wrapped.

When the patient is unconscious and he has a flushed (red) face, lay him on his back. Raise the head (turn to one side) and shoulders, and support in that position. When the face is pale, keep the head low and on one side. If possible raise the feet.

Lose no time in handing the patient over to more skilled first aiders, or, better still, to a doctor.

First-aid material in the home is usually scattered about the house, in the Medicine Cupboard, on shelves, in drawers. Thus the material often becomes soiled and as a result much is wasted. See to it that the items are put in a suitable container and this kept where it can be got at quickly. There is not space here to give more than an outline of first aid methods. Everyone should take the first opportunity to acquire a fuller knowledge, by attending classes, which are held in most districts.

AN ALPHABET OF EMERGENCY HINTS

The following directions give details of First Aid treatment for everyday mishaps.

Abrasions. Caused by rubbing or scraping of the skin. Cleanse with a non-staining antiseptic and apply a dressing.

Apoplexy. Frequently called a stroke. Patient usually elderly. Face red and breathing stertorous (snoring). Lay patient on back with head and shoulders raised. Apply cold water cloths to top of head. *Do not* give stimulants.

Asphyxia. Condition in which breathing is absent, due to drowning, smothering, etc. Apply artificial respiration at once and send for doctor and ambulance. Keep patient warm.

Bites by animals. Wash wound to remove saliva. Apply antiseptic and dress wound, and take patient quickly to the doctor.

Bleeding. First stop the loss of blood. This is best done by applying direct pressure with a small dressing made into a firm pad. It may be necessary to apply a further pad on top of the other and bandage firmly. By laying the patient down the heart will not work so quickly, and by raising the bleeding part if possible much will be done to stop the escape of blood whilst dressings are being prepared. Obtain ambulance quickly.

Blisters. Do not break. Apply boracic powder. If large, or there are many, a doctor should be consulted.

Boils. Infection of a skin gland or around the root of hair. Do not squeeze. Apply dressings that have been wrung out of hot water to which common table salt, one teaspoonful to the pint of water, is added. Do not use poultices. Consult doctor early.

Bruises. Apply dressings wrung out of very cold water. They will keep down swelling and relieve pain.

Burns and Scalds. Quickly cover whole area with dressings and take to doctor or hospital quickly. If medical help not readily available, in addition to covering the affected area, saturate the covering and clothes, if over injury, with bicarbonate of soda solution (one dessertspoonful to pint of warm water) or use saline solution (one teaspoonful of salt to pint of warm water). Keep area moist. Give patient plenty of warm sweet weak tea. Keep him warm. Do not expose burnt area. Arrange for doctor or ambulance according to circumstances.

Burns caused by the sun. Apply calamine lotion. Epsom salts solution is excellent if burns very severe.

Concussion. Caused by a severe blow to the head. Patient usually dazed, if not unconscious. Keep him lying down. Apply dressings wrung out of cold water to head. Do not give any stimulants. Keep body and lower limbs warmly wrapped. Arrange for doctor and ambulance.

Choking. Slap the patient on back between shoulder blades. If choking persists, cause vomiting by passing protected fingers to back of mouth, turning head to one side when vomiting starts.

Cramp. Apply warmth—hot-water bottle—to the part. If frequent consult a doctor.

Dislocation. Bone out of joint and fixed. Support in position which gives most ease. Apply dressings wrung out of cold water. Take patient to doctor.

Epileptic Fits. The patient is completely unconscious, during which the whole body and limbs are twitching or there may be spasmodic movements of limbs. Quickly drag him away from objects against which he may strike himself. Cover with four folds of a handkerchief a pencil or similar hard object and place between patient's teeth. When patient comes round let him rest —sleep if practicable.

Faint. Lay patient flat on back; raise feet. Keep head to one side. Do not attempt to give anything by mouth whilst unconscious.

Foreign Body in Ear. If an insect, float it out with warm olive oil or warm water. If anything else do not attempt its removal in any way. Take patient to doctor.

Foreign Body in Eye. Advise patient not to rub eye. Pull down lower lid and, if seen, remove with the wetted corner of a clean handkerchief. Pull upper lid over the eyelash of the lower lid and release; the lower eyelash will brush the under side of the upper lid. Repeat several times. If not successful, put a drop of medicinal paraffin or castor oil on eyeball and take patient to doctor or hospital.

Foreign Body in Nose. Do not attempt removal. Instruct patient to breathe through the mouth, and take him at once to doctor.

Foreign Body in Stomach. Give nothing by mouth, but take patient to doctor. Smooth objects such as coins or buttons need not cause alarm.

Fractures or Broken Bones. Immobilise the injured parts. If fracture accompanied with a wound, arrest the bleeding, apply dressing, and then fix fracture. Handle gently. Arrange for ambulance.

Hysteria. Be firm with the patient. Do not fuss; leave alone. Persistent case needs doctor's attention.

Insect Bites and Stings. If a sting, remove this if still present. Weak ammonia or solution of baking soda will relieve pain. For a sting in the mouth, or for multiple stings, get a doctor's help.

Nose Bleeding. Sit patient in current of air, head thrown slightly back and hands raised above head. Undo tight clothing. Tell patient to breathe through mouth and to avoid blowing nose. Apply cold-water dressing over the nose and on the nape of neck.

Poisoning. Give an emetic (two tablespoonsful of salt in tumblerful of lukewarm water) in all cases when lips and mouth are not burned. When lips and mouth are burned, give copious draughts of cold water or milk. Speedily obtain doctor or ambulance, which ever is the quickest. Keep patient warm. Preserve any vomited matter for doctor's inspection.

Shock. Results from injury, although emotions such as fear, fright, bad news, are sometimes an important factor. Shock may be only slight, lasting for a short while; or it may be serious and even fatal. Some degree of shock follows most injuries. In all cases prompt treatment is necessary. Important points to remember in shock treatment are : 1. Warmth. Wrap body and limbs with blankets or clothing and apply covered hot-water bottles to sides and pit of stomach; such warmth *must not* extend to over-heating patient. 2. Keep the patient in a restful position, usually lying flat on back, with feet raised on pillows or other suitable support. Do not worry patient by asking unnecessary questions.

3. Give hot strong tea in sips unless serious bleeding is present or suspected, or patient has a severe head injury. 4. Obtain doctor or arrange for ambulance.

Sprains. Expose joint and apply firm bandage; wet bandage with cold water, and keep it wet. If out-of-doors, bandage a sprained ankle over the shoe.

Wounds. Cover with a clean dressing, such as the inside of an unused handkerchief, and bandage. When indoors cleanse wound, apply a non-staining antiseptic, dress wound, and bandage.

DENIZENS *of the* WORLD *of* WATER

Wonderfully fashioned each for its particular mode of life, fishes present an absorbingly interesting story. And in their pursuit and capture Man, aided by Science, exercises considerable ingenuity. (See Frontispiece to this volume).

Fish AND FISHERIES. The fishes form a class of the animal kingdom developed especially for life in the water, cold-blooded, gill-breathing, and with the limbs developed as fins. One major group comprises the cartilaginous fishes—having a partly cartilaginous skeleton—and with the gills fastened by the longer side, like leaves in a book, sometimes as many as five on a side. This group includes sharks, rays and skates. The outstanding features of this group are the skeleton, consisting of gristle without bone, and the peculiar skin. They have no overlapping scales; the skin is tough and mottled, and is naked, or covered with wart-like projections tipped with a hard bony pimple, or with bony scales resembling teeth.

Found in the waters round the southern shores of England and Eire, bass (above) are usually about a foot long.

The other great group, the bony fishes, includes most of the food and game fishes in fresh and salt water—cod, bass, perch, trout, pike, mackerel, and others. Minor groups contain the armoured fishes or ganoids, covered with enamel-like scales and sometimes further protected with spines and prickles; and the mud-fishes or lung-fishes, possessing both gills and lung-like organs, which enable them to live in the air under certain conditions.

The body of a fish is streamlined to perfection, allowing it to move through the water with as little resistance as possible. There is no neck, and the greatest width of the body is in front of the middle. A flattened tail is used to propel the fish through the water, the fins directing the course.

Most fish depend on speed to secure their food or to escape from their enemies. But there are some that hide on the bottom of the sea, or in crevices; and others, as already mentioned, that are protected by bony plates. Some of these fish are almost globular in shape. The body is generally covered with overlapping scales, growing attached to the skin. Some are covered with smooth skin, as the cat-fishes; and the ganoids, as stated, are armoured.

Movement of tail and fins is controlled by muscles. The backbone is loosely jointed, so that the fish may turn, twist and dart at ease. Most fishes possess an air-bladder, but its purpose is not clear; it has been regarded as a balance, weighting or lightening the body as required. In the lung-fishes the air-bladder is divided to form the lungs.

A heart pumps the red blood through the body, just as it does in the higher animals. The blood is purified in the gills by the oxygen in the water. Sometimes, when the water is foul, the fishes come to the top and try to gulp in the air, but their gills are not fitted to use the oxygen in the atmosphere. Fishes breathe the water by taking it in at the mouth, letting it flow over the gills and out through the opening behind the gill covers.

Along the sides of fishes there is a line called the lateral line, which is made up of peculiar scales, beneath which there are a great number of nerves. This is, in all probability, a sense organ, helping the fish to perceive disturbances in the water.

A fish has a face something like that of the higher animals. There are eyes, a nose, and a mouth. The eyes vary greatly in size and form. There are no proper eyelids, though certain fishes have outgrowths of the head-skin over the eyes which may be called lids. A fish can see but a little distance, although it sees over a very wide angle on either side above and below. In caves the fishes are blind; once they had eyes, but through long disuse those organs have lost their sight. The power of smell is situated in the nostril, but it is very feeble; this nostril is a closed sac and has nothing to do with breathing. There is hardly any sense of taste. The tongue is hard and gristly and fixed, and the fish eats very fast, chewing merely to cut or crush the food, and often swallowing it whole.

Fish hear, in our sense of the word, scarcely at all; the hearing apparatus is buried in the skull and has nothing to do with the ear-like flaps. They are, however, very sensitive to disturbances in the water, as the sense of touch is highly developed. If they come in contact with a suspicious object, fish dart quickly away. Some have sensitive feelers or barbels by which they explore the bottom or feel their way to food. These barbels are highly specialized, attached sometimes to the nostrils, sometimes to the jawbone, sometimes to the skin of the chin or snout, and sometimes over the eyes.

The nervous system of the fish is not highly developed, and so far as we can determine it feels very little pain. It often happens that a fish which has torn itself loose from the hook will be caught again soon after. The mouths of the various genera and species differ widely. Sometimes the mouth is a great horizontal gash almost from gill to gill, sometimes it is round and tiny, and sometimes it is developed into a long beak. The jaws also differ greatly. Sometimes the bones are joined with ligaments that may be stretched, especially among deep-sea fishes, so that the fish may swallow other fish larger than itself. Sometimes the jaws are tube-like, and it is a wonder that the fish can swallow anything. In sharks, rays and skates the mouth is on the underside of the body.

The mouth may have no teeth, or the teeth may be on the jaw-bone only, or on any bone in the mouth's circumference. Just inside the mouth are gill rakers, which strain the water, and at the opening of the gullet behind the gills are bones with additional short thick teeth.

Nature's Gift of Protective Colouring

The colour of the backs of most fish is usually protective, with mottled or barred colourings, usually grey or a sort of olive, with the belly white. To birds looking down on the water the back with its mottled stripes is the colour of the water with the shadows on it; to fishes below in search of prey the under part is the colour of the surface of the water, with the atmosphere above it. In the tropics, where red seaweeds and other aquatic growths of brilliant colourings abound, the fish are bright-coloured. In the greater depths of the ocean the fish are deep black or violet-black, sometimes with silvery phosphorescent lights.

Little interest is displayed by most fishes in their young. After the eggs, a jelly-like mass, are deposited they are left to hatch or be destroyed as chance wills. There are exceptions. The freshwater stickleback builds a nest of sticks cemented with a kind of gum from its body, and after the eggs are deposited stands guard until the fish are hatched. Bass and sunfish also guard their eggs, and so does the uncouth lump-sucker. Some species, among them the salmon, leave the sea and ascend to the headwaters of rivers to deposit their eggs ; others, as the common eel, living in fresh water, go to the sea to spawn.

Some fish hatch their young in an egg-sac; some of these baby fish are tiny at birth, others quite large. Some sharks and a few other fishes are born alive and well developed, and most young fish take care of themselves from the first. The destruction of eggs and young is very great, for almost every species is a prey of larger fish, so the vast numbers of eggs that are deposited by some fishes are necessary to preserve the existence of the species. A large cod produces about 10 million eggs every year.

In general the young fish differs from the adult only in size and proportions. The eyes and head are comparatively larger, the fins are lower, and the body more slender. Most fish live on indefinitely, until they fall victims to larger species. The exceptions to this rule are those, such as the salmon, which have a definite period of growth before spawning, and after spawning probably die.

Some fish are killed more readily than others. Fish usually die very quickly in the air or in foul water. The lung-fishes, however, live in a ball of half-dried mud during the dry season; and some of the Asiatic mud-fishes can maintain themselves for a long time out of water. Carp which have been frozen in the ice are said to revive in the spring.

Some fish eat both vegetable and animal matter, others eat only vegetable matter; and still others confine their diet to other fish. Many live on minute organisms strained from the water, the plankton of the oceans.

Altogether there are about 20,000 species of fish, all interesting, and many with remarkable characteristics and weird shapes and colourings. The tunny, a giant mackerel, grows nearly 20 feet long and weighs 1,000 lb. or more. Some sharks reach a length of 40 feet and weigh many hundredweight.

Some have curious weapons of offence and defence. There are the electric fishes, with power to inflict electric shocks on their prey or their enemies. The electric eel, which is the most powerful of these forms, inhabits the rivers of Brazil and other countries of South America; its shock is powerful enough to stun a man. Some fishes are provided with a poisonous slime or mucus which flows over the spines, so that a wound made by them is very painful. The spines of the common cat-fish have this property to some extent. In some fishes the spine is modified so as to form a poisoning instrument, and the poison is pressed through the tube as the spine is thrust in. The greater weaver of the African coast has poisonous spines on its gill covers.

The frog-fish of tropical seas have two fins resembling legs, with which they creep along the rocks like toads. The head is the largest part of the body, and the mouth is the largest part of the head. The jaw muscles are strong and the teeth sharp. This fish belongs to the anglers—fishes with barbels hanging down in front of their mouths, the use of the barbels being, presumably, to attract other fish within reach. Some of these barbels are bright-coloured, while others glow with a phosphorescent light. In the sword-fish and saw-fish the snout is prolonged into a flat blade, used for slashing up the food such as giant squids on which these creatures generally feed.

Fish that Climb and Fly

Then there are such curiosities as the climbing perch. When there has been a heavy rainfall and the water runs down the trees at the edge of a pool, these perch crawl up the tree sideways, sometimes to a height of seven feet. If the fish is thrown on the ground it runs rapidly along in the same sideways manner, as long as the mucus remains on its skin. The flying-fish are capable of lifting themselves from the water and soaring through the air, sometimes for several hundred feet, the large pectoral fins spreading as a parachute.

Fishes of the tropics are often brilliantly coloured. The parrot fishes of the Mediterranean coast and the Indian Ocean have vivid colourings of red, green and purple; and the butterfly-fishes are striking examples of black and yellow coloration. The goldfish of China and Japan are found only in domesticated specimens, the brilliant colouring being retained by artificial selection; the originals of the gold-fish are olive-coloured.

Fish are particularly interesting from the evolutionary point of view because they are regarded as the first vertebrate (backboned) creatures. At a very remote period certain animals began to develop a spinal cord. At first this was little more

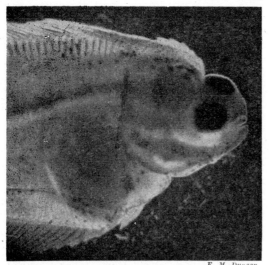

FISH : EYES THAT SHIFT

Though they are not so far round as they will be when the fish is full grown, the eyes of this young plaice are on the top of its head. When hatched flat fish have an eye on each side of the head, and are upright in the water.

than a bundle of nerve fibres down their backs. But in the course of time this cord in some of the water dwellers became covered with a jointed rubber-like sheath of cartilage which served as a protection, and rib-like arches grew out from this sheath. At the same time the skins developed many horny dots. These creatures were the ancestors of the fish. Sharks and rays are survivors of this primitive type. In another group the bony dots developed into armour-like plates, and this ganoid type survives in fishes like the sturgeon. These two families ruled the sea as late as the Coal Age.

Meanwhile, another branch developed air-breathing apparatus, and crawled out occasionally upon land, as in the case of the present-day climbing perch. From such creatures developed amphibians, reptiles, and birds. Under water the course of evolution developed the cartilage skeleton into bone, and changed the bone-like dots into silvery scales, thus creating the highest type of fish, such as the trout. The development continued until the period which geologists call the Pliocene, since which time the fish family has undergone practically no change. Fishes of the flat type may be said to have formed, in the course of their evolution, the permanent habit of travelling and resting entirely on their sides. In conjunction with this an amazing thing has happened. If they lay normally on their sides, one eye, of course, would be buried in the mud where it was useless, and the mouth would be set at an awkward angle for feeding. We may imagine, then, that for generations these fish tried, while still lying on their sides, to twist their heads round so that their buried eye would be where it could see, and the jaws would reach a more effective position for their work.

They finally succeeded in part, but their heads would only twist half as far as required, and the lower eye was still half buried. So gradually this eye left its place and travelled round the top of the head until it came out on the upper side, next to the eye which was already there. Thus, with two good eyes to watch for danger, both looking upwards, these fishes got along very well.

Such is the history of the modern flat fishes, from the huge halibut to the flounder and the small sole. But although this transformation of shape probably took thousands of years, the young flat fish today inherit the early habits of those remote forefathers who swam upright. When they are hatched from the eggs, these youngsters at first are upright in the water, like any normal fish, and have an eye on each side of their head. As they grow older, they come to lie on one side and their head begins to twist out of shape ; the under eye comes out on top, the mouth turns at an oblique angle, and this queer process of evolution is gone through again in the lifetime of each fish. This is the reason for the strange deformed shape of the flat-fish tribe.

This family is a large one, consisting of over 500 species. A few of these lie on their right sides, but the great majority prefer the left. The underside, which is not exposed to the light, is whitish, while the upper is usually dark, mud- or sand-coloured. However, this colour-scheme, which is designed to make the fish invisible to its foes, changes with the surroundings. For instance, if a flounder is put in an aquarium with a glass bottom through which light is allowed to shine, the underside will turn brown.

Almost all flat fish are valued highly as food. The European sole (*Solea vulgaris*) is considered by many to be the most delicious of all fish. The largest of the family is the lordly halibut (*Hippoglossus vulgaris*). Since the discovery that halibut liver oil was the richest known natural source of Vitamin A (also possessing a high Vitamin D content) halibut fishing became specialized, and special types of halibut ships were built on the Humber. But by far the most important fish commercially is the plaice (*Pleuronectes*). This species, recognizable by its red spots, is common around the British coasts; so is the flounder, which comes up many of our tidal rivers.

Fisheries the Wide World Over

Since the earliest days of history men have fished for their food in seas, lakes and rivers, and today the catch of the fisherman appears on the tables of every country in the world. Fresh fish are boiled, broiled, baked, fried, and even eaten raw, as in Japan, the Pacific Islands and certain parts of Russia. For future use fish are salted, dried, smoked, pickled or preserved in tins, and in these forms find their way to places far distant from the waters in which they live.

Trading in fish is of great antiquity. Ponds in which the ancient Egyptians kept rare foreign fish alive until they were ready for use have been found in Northern Africa. A thriving trade in highly prized lampreys and eels was carried on between Rome and distant portions of the empire, and fish are said to have been imported into Italy in those days from points as far distant as the Caspian Sea, between Europe and Asia. The Mediterranean Sea has always been famous for its fisheries, but in recent times the European centre of the fish industry has moved to the northern countries—Britain, France, Norway and Germany.

FISH AND FISHERIES

In the Western Hemisphere are the great fisheries of North America, extending from the state of Massachusetts to Labrador and along the Pacific coast. Shortly after explorers reached Newfoundland in 1497 and reported the cod fisheries there, the French sent their fishing fleets to those waters. Other nations soon followed, and the abundance of food fishes had a great influence on the colonization of North America. The countries where fishing is a principal industry are Great Britain, Japan, China, France, Canada, Russia, Norway, Germany, the Netherlands and the United States.

Cod fishing, as practised on the " Banks," is particularly perilous. Large fleets make their way to the seas off Newfoundland, where the depth is only a few hundred feet. Each ship has a number of small dories or flat-bottomed row-boats, manned usually by two members of the crew, who put off from the mother ship each morning. Sometimes in a sudden fog the dories cannot find their way back to the trawler, sometimes they are driven far out to sea by storms, and sometimes a wave swamps a boat overloaded with a big catch.

The fishing is done with hand-lines, with trawl-lines, and with nets. The trawl-lines consist of great lengths of rope, from which hang numbers of short lines carrying the hooks. These are baited and the whole contrivance is carried to the bottom by anchors. A small buoy with a line running down to the trawl marks the spot. Each dory may set out several such trawls, visiting them at intervals to lift them, clear them of fish, and rebait the hooks.

Icelandic waters and others within the Arctic Circle now vie with the Newfoundland banks as the richest cod fishing grounds in the world. Here the great fleets of modern ocean-going trawlers from Hull and Grimsby reap a rich harvest of cod, haddock, ling and halibut. Equipped with wireless, ice-storage accommodation, liver oil extractors, and powerfully engined, a big trawler can remain six weeks at sea before returning with her great cargo. The working of the trawl is shown below; it is a bag-shaped net, with the larger end kept open by " boards." The trawler steams over the fishing grounds and scoops up fish in its path. Then the trawl is hoisted up and the small end opened over the deck to empty out the catch.

The most important fish commercially, exceeding even the cod in world trade, is the herring. The leading herring fisheries today are in Norway, Sweden, France and Great Britain, and the industry is growing rapidly in Canada. These fish travel in great shoals closely packed together over areas many miles wide. They are caught mainly in drift nets. These are curtain-like nets in which the fish become entangled by the gills (see below). Such a net may also be used for cod. In herring fishing the vessel, after shooting long series of nets, is allowed to drift over the fishing area.

To reduce the time lost in locating herring shoals some trawlers are equipped with echo-sounders:

FISH : TWO KINDS OF NET USED IN DEEP WATER

On the left a gill-net is shown. The fish thrusts its head through a mesh too small to allow the body to follow ; the gills are caught in the mesh and the fish is trapped. These nets have floats on top and weights below to keep them hanging straight down. The trawl net, which is shown at the bottom, is pulled over the sea bed like a dredge, scooping up the fish in its path. In herring fishing a similar net is employed, and the fishing vessel is allowed to drift.

two electrical instruments are fitted to the plating in the bottom of the ship, one transmitting sound impulses and the other receiving their echo from the sea-bed or other solid objects. These echoes are in part interrupted as they pass through a shoal, thus informing the master of the trawler that the herring are there. Further, in experimental work, radar systems have been adapted from war-time uses to the location of fish shoals.

The herring industry of Britain is controlled by the Herring Industry Board, under the direction of the Ministry of Agriculture and Fisheries.

The most important freshwater fishery is that for salmon. The salmon of the Pacific coast of North America are caught when they are entering the rivers from the ocean to spawn. The fish move near the centre of the current, keeping close to the surface, and the fishing is done by nets or traps. In another method a large wheel is sunk in

the river just below the surface at a narrow place. It has paddles, on the rim of which are set wide-mouthed baskets which turn slowly in the current. It meets the fish as they swim upstream, lifts them and dumps them into a chute which leads to the shore. In Britain, salmon are netted in tidal estuaries, and caught in considerable numbers with rod and line. A valuable Mediterranean fishery is that for the tunny, which is dried and canned or eaten fresh. Anchovy, sardine, and brisling fisheries are also of commercial value. Besides fishes caught for food, many are taken for their oil and skin.

The artificial culture of fish for food (pisciculture) is a scientific pursuit of some importance. A female fish normally produces thousands of eggs which are never fertilized—or which, if they are, never reach the adult stage. It is the main object of fish culture to diminish this waste. The fish are kept in "hatcheries" only until they are ready to be

released in the rivers and lakes. The usual method of hatching is for the spawn to be artificially extracted from a number of female fish, and the milt from the male fish is then mixed with it and placed in water. After about 30 minutes the eggs are removed to hatching boxes. The eggs hatch out after anything from six weeks to two months. Freshwater fish such as carp are bred extensively in central Europe, and species of trout are raised in the hatcheries of Great Britain and the U.S.A. to stock rivers for anglers.

FISH : CATCHING SALMON IN ALASKAN WATERS

In the lower photograph men are taking salmon out of a trap on a river in Alaska. The fish swim upstream along an underwater fence, which directs them into a series of enclosures, their instinct to maintain an unchanged course upstream preventing them turning round and swimming back to sea. The motor-boat (top) is paying out a net, the other end of which is secured to a boat, which will circle back to the parent vessel, enclosing a shoal of fish.

CAMERA 'CATCH' OF FISH AND FISHERS

It is both difficult and dangerous to try to photograph a shark under water. But the American who took this picture, J. E. Williamson, the originator of undersea photography, was let down from a boat inside a compartment, so that he and his camera were safe. Some species of shark (littoral or shore-region) remain close to the coast; but the one seen here is of the pelagic or deep-sea kind, and is cruising far below the surface of the Atlantic Ocean.

AMERICAN FISH THAT 'FLOCK TOGETHER'

Elwin R. Sanborn

These handsomely marked fish are American bass. They live in fresh water, and their tender flesh is very good to eat. But the New York Aquarium, where they were photographed, is seemingly not hot enough for them, and so they flock together, heads all pointing in the same direction, in this extraordinary floating cluster. Bass of a quite different species frequent the southern shores of England and Ireland; this, the marine-bass or sea-perch, is popular among sea-anglers as a sporting fish. It is considered by some to have an attractive and delicate flavour.

BEAUTY AND UGLINESS IN THE WORLD OF WATER

W. S. Berridge; Schensky

The pretty little fish seen in the upper photograph are angel fish, one of the most popular sorts to have in a private aquarium. Those long, bony projections are used to protect their delicate fins from harm when they swim among rocks. These fish must not be confused with another angel fish, a relative of the sharks. Below, is a repulsively ugly creature, a male lump sucker, so called from the flat sucking disk on its underside, by means of which it clings to rocks. It frequents Northern waters, and is here guarding a pile of eggs seen in front of its mouth.

TRAWLING FOR FOOD-FISH IN THE NORTH SEA

Fox

The men who catch the fish you eat lead the hardest life of all mariners. For days and weeks at a time, North Sea trawlers remain cut off from the land. The 'trawl' is a huge bag-shaped net with an open mouth. It is sometimes 80 feet long, and is dragged through the water along the sea bed. The North Sea is shallow, and fish abound, especially on the Dogger Bank; they include halibut, soles, turbot, brill, plaice, cod, haddock, and others. North Sea waters are particularly rich in 'plankton,' the minute drifting organisms on which fish feed.

THE YARMOUTH DRIFTER FLEET IN PORT

Fox

Yarmouth, in Norfolk, is noted for its bloaters or cured herrings, but the several hundred tons of fish on the quay here consist of bigger game, for the port has a large share in the North Sea cod fisheries as well. The Yarmouth herring fleet employs thousands of people and consists of hundreds of vessels, some of which can be seen in this photograph. They are called drifters, because of the fine-meshed net which is suspended like a curtain in the water, with floats at the top and weights at the bottom. The vessel is allowed to drift over the fishing ground.

FISHERY WORKERS WHO DO NOT GO TO SEA

Every autumn thousands of girls come from Scotland to Yarmouth to deal with the enormous catch in the East Anglian herring season. Here some of the girls are splitting and cleaning the fish which will soon be salted, smoked and distributed all over Great Britain as kippers or bloaters. Normally other large quantities are sent abroad. Yarmouth also borrows a number of Scottish drifters for this season to reinforce its own fleet. Herrings, like sprats and pilchards, which belong to the same family, are an extremely nutritious food.

'SLUMP' AND 'BOOM' IN THE FISHING INDUSTRY

Fox

There are so many fish in the sea that the fishing industry, unless carefully controlled, cannot always make the supply fit the demand, and sometimes the markets are unable to dispose of heavy catches. The upper photograph shows thousands of barrels of herrings left over at Yarmouth. Record catches had made herrings too plentiful. Below, a fine trade was expected at St. Andrew's Dock, Hull, when this photograph was taken just before Easter, because plenty of fish would be wanted for the Good Friday, when many people do not eat meat.

SETTING THE NETS IN RIVER AND SEA

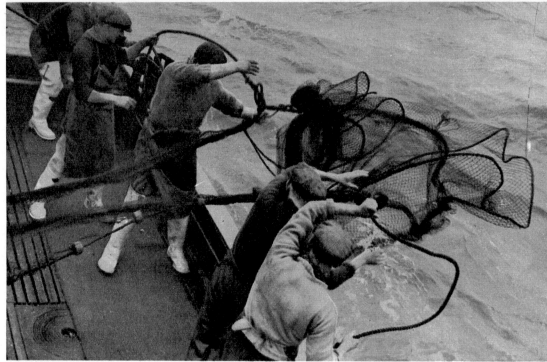

Fox

Here is a contrast in fishing methods, though both parties are using a curtain-like net suspended from floats. Long-net salmon fishing (upper) in the River Severn at Epney, Gloucestershire, is carried on today in much the same way as it has been for hundreds of years. How different is this riverside fishing from the busy scene on a herring-drifter in the North Sea. The net being 'shot' in the lower photograph may be as much as two miles in length, and one drifter has been known to catch as many as 100,000 herrings in three days, using nets of this type.

CATCHING FISH *with* ROD *and* LINE

The art of angling is one of the most ancient of human crafts, and it cannot be acquired without much practice. But that and patience bring their reward. Here some of the main points are explained.

Fishing. Whether you are angling with the traditional worm on a bent pin, or landing a giant tunny or sword-fish on board a motor yacht, you are taking part in perhaps the oldest sport in the world. In no country has fishing been so developed as a sport as in Britain; the literature of it goes back to Roman times, and in the English language there has been a stream of books since the Treatise of Fysshynge with an Angle (1496); prominent among them is Izaak Walton's Compleat Angler.

You will probably start your fishing in one of two ways: with a hand-line at the seaside; or with a length of bamboo and a line bearing a float and a single hook with a worm, in a stream or pond near your home. However you start, your first catch will be one of the great moments of your life. The usual form of freshwater angling is that known as bottom-fishing—although indeed you by no means always fish on the bottom.

For this is needed the ordinary tackle used in all parts of Britain—a simple rod, of three or four joints, 11 to 13 feet in length; a strong but not too coarse line; a length of strong gut, and a hook at the bottom. The gut should be soaked in water or glycerine before use: it is then straightened easily. After use the line should always be thoroughly dried (over the backs of chairs is an easy way) and then a reliable line grease should be rubbed into it with a piece of soft cloth.

Other accessories are the float, and some split shot—soft little lead shot which are split open so that you can squeeze them on to the gut. You first find the depth of the river, which you do by setting up rod and line and using a leaden plummet or weight attached to the hook. You then bring up the line, remove the weight, and attach to the line sufficient split shot to allow the top of the float to show above water whilst the hook is held just off the bottom of the stream or pond.

Baits for bottom fishing vary. You may use a worm, or maggots, or a paste made of soaked bread squeezed dry, or a cheese paste, or cubes of bread-crust. Besides your bait on the hook, a certain amount of "ground bait" is used which consists of bran, bread-crumbs, cheese parings, chopped worms, and some of the bait which you already have. The object of this ground bait is to attract the fish to your part of the stream. The method is to throw in a few handfuls of the bait on arrival. Sometimes it is advisable to throw in balls of ground bait the previous day, mixing them with clay so that the water washes the food out gradually.

The object of the float is to indicate when a fish is biting, and that is why a fisherman must have patience and an ever-watchful eye. Round and round the float goes in an eddy; or perhaps it swings steadily downstream. Then suddenly it bobs under and up again. Quickly you flick the butt of the rod downwards so that the tip goes up. This is called "striking," and until you are expert at it you will miss far more fish than you hook. You will in time learn that not every dip of the float is a bite; that some dips may be due to deep eddies pulling at your line, or to a floating weed; you will know whether the nibbles are from minnows or larger species of fish by the difference in the vibrations that pass up the line and down the rod to your hand.

There are two main ways of handling your tackle when bottom fishing. You can sit on the bank or on a camp stool, some feet back from the water's

Ogden Smith Ltd.

FISHING TACKLE

Some of the equipment used by anglers is shown here : 1, and 2. Types of float ; 3. Artificial fly ; 4. Artificial minnow, which spins in use; 5. Reel for coarse fishing.

Fox

YOUNG ANGLERS AT HAMPSTEAD

Freshwater anglers usually begin by fishing in a local pond or stream with a light bamboo rod and a line bearing a float and a single hook. These boys are at Hampstead Ponds, London, and probably hope to catch minnows or roach, using bread paste or maggots as bait.

edge, your rod supported on a rod rest, letting your float swim in the same spot; or you can cast up river and sit watching the float as it drifts down, then lifting it out and casting up stream again. The sun should not be behind you when you cast; you don't want the shadow of the line to be cast on the water, thus frightening the fish. In which of these two ways you handle your tackle depends on the state of the water, as well as on the fish you are after. When the water is cloudy (coloured) the float is kept in the same spot; you cast up river when the stream is clear. Coarse fish such as roach, dace, barbel, carp, chub, and others, feed near the bottom. With the game fish—salmon, trout and grayling—you are on the move the whole time; and, except for salmon, you will usually be fishing with a fly.

An artificial fly, a dainty affair of feathers and silk tied on a hook so as to look, when it is in or on the water, like a real fly, is cast with a rod that is finer, less stiff, and lighter than that used for other fishing. Casting is an art that takes some time to acquire. In place of the simple cane or greenheart rod for bottom fishing you have a split cane rod, so strong that it can be bent easily and will spring back to its original form.

Salmon flies are not made to represent any particular fly, but they certainly attract these big fish, which do not normally feed in fresh water. You can also catch salmon with a prawn bait (real or imitation), or by spinning (using bait which revolves in the current) with a real or imitation minnow or a gudgeon or small roach. Trout are caught by spinning, and so are pike, which are sometimes taken by trolling—that is, towing a bait behind a boat at a low speed. Pike and salmon, after being hooked and played, are landed with a steel hook called a gaff which is inserted in the gills; other fish are landed in a simple net.

Fox

TROUT-FISHING IN SCOTLAND

When the catch has been brought into shallow water, it is scooped up in a landing-net (above) and then released from the hook. Trout-fishermen use a split-cane rod, the bait consisting of artificial flies made of feathers and silk.

The fresh-water fisherman studies the weather. North and east winds are bad, because when these are blowing fish will not bite. A south wind is good, a westerly breeze is best of all.

Before fishing in any waters inquiries should be made of the local angling club, because fishing rights are nearly always privately owned, and a permit to fish may have to be obtained from the owner of the rights. Make sure of the local size limits. In most districts a rod licence (usually obtainable at a local fishing-tackle shop) is necessary. It should not be forgotten that there is a close season (when fishing is forbidden) for fresh-water fish. For coarse fish it is March 16–June 16; for salmon, November 1–January 31; for trout and char, October 1 to the last day of February.

Sea-anglers use a short, stout, heavy rod; the catch may weigh many pounds and tackle must be of the strongest. Among the finest sporting sea-fish are mullet, mackerel, tope (species of small shark), bass, halibut, codling, and bream of various types. Best of all in European seas is the tunny (a big relative of the mackerel). There is a good deal of tunny fishing, especially off Scarborough, on the Yorkshire coast, and these

FISHING : DEATH-BLOW FOR A PIKE

Large fish, such as pike, are landed with a steel hook or gaff, similar to the one on the bottom of the boat on the left. They are then killed by a sharp blow on the back of the head with an instrument called a 'priest,' as in the case of this fine specimen caught on the Norfolk Broads. Pike can inflict a nasty bite.

TENSE MOMENTS THAT THRILL THE ANGLER

G. Turnell; F. C. Ward; H G. Grainger; P. B. Abbey

Having brought the big bream over the ring of the net, the fisherman, with a steady upward movement, engulfs the fish in the landing net (lower left). The angler in the act of casting (lower right) is fishing for trout in the East Dart, Devonshire. On the river Waveney at Beccles, Suffolk, two boys (top left) are enjoying a day's sport; the one at the stern has hooked a fish. A fine salmon has been gaffed (top right) ready to land on the upper Wye in Wales.

fish run to well over 500 lb. They are caught from a boat and may take hours to land. They are so strong that the angler sits usually in a special swivel-chair, with harness to take the strain off his arms. The rod is only six to eight feet long, but the reel carries several hundred yards of line.

Fives. The game of fives is particularly popular in the English public schools. The origin of the name is doubtful; it may be derived from the five fingers of the hand, as the game is played with the gloved hands. There are various recognized forms of the game, the best-known being named after Eton, Rugby and Winchester. Eton fives is played in a court with three walls, the fourth end being

FIVES : THE ETON GAME
A buttress projecting from the wall and a step on the floor form additional obstacles in an Eton fives court. These pictures show a doubles game in progress, with the partners taking opposite corners. In the inset a player is about to volley the ball.

open. There is a step dividing the floor into two parts, while a curiously shaped buttress, called the pepper-box, projects from the left-hand wall. The buttress is a reminder of the first Eton fives court—the outside wall of the college chapel. The Rugby fives court is covered in, and has four plain walls. Winchester fives is similar, but a buttress on the left-hand wall forms an obstacle.

The object of the game is to volley the ball or hit it on the first bounce above a line or hedge on the front wall, in such a way as to prevent one's opponent (or either of one's opponents, if it is a doubles game) from hitting it back. The first player who fails to hit the ball above the ledge loses a point, or if he were the server yields the service to his opponent; a game consists of 15 points. To serve, one player throws the ball on to the wall; his adversary can refuse any service, but if he does not refuse it he must hit the ball on to the right-hand wall and thence it must rebound on to the front wall above

the ledge. Either hand can be used for striking the ball, special padded gloves being worn. The weight of the ball in Eton fives is 1¼ oz.

Flags. In ancient times standards of various sorts and materials were used by the Persians, Greeks and Romans, the brazen eagles of the Roman legions being the best-known instance. But it was not until the Middle Ages that cloth banners and flags came into use, partly as a result of the necessity of distinguishing different forces in the Crusades. The emblems on our flags arose in part from the colours and devices of heraldry.

Early flags often had a religious character. The banner of early England was the red cross of St. George on a white background, and the present Union Jack (its correct name is. Union flag) of Great Britain is formed by combining with this the diagonal white St. Andrew's cross on a blue background for Scotland, and the red diagonal St. Patrick's cross for Ireland. The white ensign, consisting of the red cross of St. George and the Union flag in the upper left-hand corner, is worn by ships of the Royal Navy and yachts of the Royal Yacht Squadron.

The story of the origin of the Stars and Stripes of the United States covers the early history of the country. At first the British North American colonies used the English flag, but in 1777 the Continental Congress or Parliament created the Stars and Stripes by passing this resolution: "That the flag of the 13 United States be 13 stripes, alternate red and white; that the union be 13 stars, white in a blue field, representing a new constellation." When a new state came into the union a star was added.

Flamingo. A flock of these great birds on the wing has been compared to "a gigantic, brilliantly rosy scarf, waving to and fro in mighty folds as it flies away." For though the flamingo is pale pinkish when at rest, the brighter colour of the undersides of the wings shows up in flight.

A full-grown bird is between five and six and a half feet in height. It has a humped body and long, thin legs. Its slender neck curves upwards like a big letter S, and ends in a small head with a great flat down-curving beak. When the bird is feeding on shell-fish or water-plants in shallow mud flats, the neck is twisted like a corkscrew until the head is upside down; then the top of the beak is pushed along like a scoop or shovel, gathering in the mud from which the food is filtered out.

Thousands of these birds gather in remote places during the nesting period. Each female builds a curious mound of mud like a miniature volcano, in the "crater" of which a single egg is laid. On this the mother sits with legs drawn up like a grotesque statue on a pedestal. The young at first are clothed in white down, and have a straight bill.

There are several species, mostly living in tropical and sub-tropical countries. The most beautiful is the scarlet flamingo, plentiful in the West Indies and along the Central American coast. The name derives from the Latin *flamma*, meaning flame.

LONG-LEGGED FLAMINGOES FEEDING IN A POOL

creature shows to some extent the influence of its feeding because these affect its bodily structure. In wading such as flamingoes, this is more than usually obvious. ....s bear the body high above the water ; the long slender neck enables food to be sought in the mud at the bottom of pools. The beak itself, too, is adapted for the rapid filtration of food-organisms from muddy water. The European flamingo is common in southern France and Spain in the nesting season.

FLAMINGOES GATHERED IN A CROWDED COLONY BESIDE A LAKE

During the breeding season flamingoes live in colonies beside pools or lakes, as shown here. The females are seated on their nests; the males keep watch near by; and the young birds wander about in the vicinity of their homes. Flamingoes are neighbourly birds, living together quite peacefully under very crowded conditions. The nests are made of scraped-up mud, with a shallow cup-like depression at the top in which the eggs are laid. An egg is visible in the third nest from the left, and in the second from the left is a young bird, just hatched. Flamingoes are fairly strong on the wing and can swim well. The name is from the Spanish flamenco, which in turn is derived from the Latin flamma, meaning flame, in reference to the bird's colour, which ranges from pale pink to scarlet. This picture is from a group in the American Museum of Natural History, New York. The birds in front are stuffed specimens, while the background consists of a painting, models and picture being blended to form a realistic scene.

Flanders. In the Middle Ages this name was given to a district extending westward from the River Scheldt to Calais in France. Most of this territory now lies in Belgium, where the old name is retained in the two provinces of West and East Flanders; most of whose inhabitants still speak Flemish, a language which closely resembles that of the Dutch. Part of the French Department of Nord is Flemish and is often referred to as French Flanders; and that portion of the Netherlands between the Scheldt estuary and the Belgian frontier is known as Zeeland Flanders.

So many battles have been fought in Flanders that it is known as the Cockpit of Europe. There was much fighting there in the First and Second World Wars. In the First World War (1914–18) there was a prolonged struggle at the Belgian town of Ypres and along the line of the River Yser; not until September 1918 when Belgian, French and British armies opened an offensive on a front extending from Ypres to Dixmude, were the Germans driven from the Flanders coast and forced to retreat in this sector.

In the Second World War (1939–45) the Allied campaign against the Germans in Flanders of May 1940, which ended in the retreat to Dunkirk, was described as the Battle of Flanders. The Germans were driven out of Flanders by the Allies in the autumn of 1944, when there was heavy fighting to clear the Scheldt estuary so that Antwerp could be used as an Allied supply base.

Flax. Cultivated both for its dark brown seed and its strong fibre, flax (*Linum usitatissimum*) is an annual plant of the family *Linaceae*, and grows to a height of about three feet. The seeds yield linseed oil, which is used for mixing paints, and in making printer's ink, patent leather, linoleum and oilcloth. The residue of the seed after the oil has been extracted is used for fattening cattle.

The fibre, which lies just beneath the outer skin of the stem is, after cotton, the most generally employed textile in the whole range of vegetable fibres. From it is produced linen, so widely used in making choice table-cloths and napkins, towels, handkerchiefs, laces and other articles.

If the flax seed only is to be used, the crop is harvested with a mower after the seeds are ripe and brown. If the fibre is to be used the plants are pulled up before they are quite mature, and the pulled flax is tied together in bundles and left upright in the field until it is dry, when the seeds are separated from it; or the separation is made just after pulling, with an iron comb called a rippler. Next the flax is retted, or soaked, by various methods, usually in tanks, pools or rivers, until through the action of bacteria the fibre is loosened from the decaying woody part of the stalk, after which it is spread out on the grass to bleach and dry. The pure fibre is then freed from the stem by two operations—first, by " breaking," in which the woody part of the stem is cracked by grooved rollers; and scraping mechanism, working in conjunction with these rollers, removes the bulk of the weedy centre of the stem from the fibre. Second, the remainder is separated from the fibre by scutching, in which the flax is beaten by machinery. Then the flax is heckled, or combed with an iron comb. The short coarse fibres furnish the " tow " that is used for various purposes.

Chief flax-growing countries are Russia, the Netherlands, Canada, Argentina, Egypt, the sub-continent of India, Belgium, Central Europe and the United States. It is grown to a limited extent in England, chiefly in Norfolk, but British cultivation on a large scale is confined to Northern Ireland.

During the Second World War (1939–45) the cultivation of flax for fibre became a vital industry. Fabric and cordage woven from flax was used in aircraft coverings, flying suits, parachute harness, machine-gun belts and other service needs. The British Government helped Northern Ireland farmers to pay for building flax-dams, to impound water in pools where the flax could be retted. The flax acreage was increased fourfold.

Flea. This troublesome little insect belongs to the order *Aphaniptera*. In recent years it has also been recognized as one of the most dangerous, for it carries the germ of bubonic plague and the virus of typhus fever from rats to Man. Old World typhus is spread by human body lice, but a local strain of this disease is transmitted by rat fleas

FLAX : SOAKING THE PLANTS IN WATER
After the flax plants have been pulled out of the ground, they are retted or soaked, usually in tanks or ponds (above). Here they remain from seven to 12 days, while the fibre is loosened from the decaying woody part of the stalk. When sufficiently retted the flax is spread out in the open to dry and bleach.

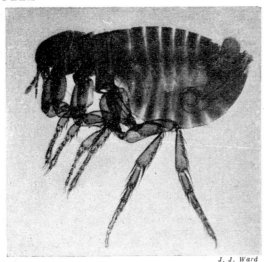

J. J. Ward

A FLEA HIGHLY MAGNIFIED

At the front of a flea's head are the piercing organs used for sucking blood—its principal food. Its legs are very powerful, the vertical leap of a common flea (above) being stated to be nearly eight inches.

in the United States. Fleas are tiny insects, with bodies thin and flattened from side to side (as a fish is flattened). This makes it easy for them to slip quickly about among the hairs of animals.

They have no wings, but they are wonderful jumpers by reason of their long hind legs. Their heads have a sharp sucking beak, with which they puncture the skin and suck the blood. The female flea scatters her eggs about in rugs and carpets and in places where animals sleep. The larvae or young look like little hairy worms; they have biting mouth parts, and live on animal tissues and rubbish. Fleas especially infest rats, dogs, cats, rabbits, pigeons, and poultry. There is also the kind (*Pulex irritans*) that prefers to live upon human beings. There are nearly 1,000 known species, all parasitic on mammals or birds.

Fleming, Sir Alexander (b. 1881). "It was a curious thing that this discovery ever happened. Every bacteriologist has had moulds drop on to a plate by mistake; and when this happens every bacteriologist throws them away, with suitable language. But in this case it happened that I did not throw the plate away at once, and so we got penicillin."

Thus simply did Professor Alexander Fleming describe his discovery of one of the most effective drugs known to medicine (*see* Penicillin). He had been aware of the existence of penicillin as far back as 1929, but it was not until 1943 that it began to be used practically, in the treatment of men wounded in the Second World War. The laboratory experiments of Professor Fleming combined with the work in the field of the Australian Professor Howard Florey must have saved many thousands of lives.

Professor Fleming, a Scotsman, was educated at Kilmarnock and trained as a doctor at St. Mary's Hospital, London. During the First World War (1914–18) he served as an officer in the Royal Army Medical Corps, returning to the hospital after the war as professor of bacteriology.

Honours were showered upon him after his discovery of penicillin. In 1943 he was made a Fellow of the Royal Society, in 1944 he was knighted, in 1945 he was awarded the Nobel prize for medicine. In 1946 the Albert gold medal of the Royal Society of Arts and the Honorary gold medal of the Royal College of Surgeons were bestowed upon him.

Flint. This mineral is a variety of quartz, consisting almost entirely of silica with a little lime, oxide of iron, water, and sometimes carbon; it varies in colour from almost black to light brown, red, yellow and greyish-white, and is sometimes mottled or spotted, but is commonly grey or smoky brown. Flint was largely used by prehistoric peoples to make axe-heads, arrow-heads, knives and other edged implements.

There has been much controversy as regards the earliest flint implements, for there is often little about them to indicate any definite purpose in the way in which the flaking and shaping was done. However, there must have been some point at which men did begin to "work" the flints, and those which are claimed as the products of the first period are termed eoliths or dawn-stones (Greek, *eos*, dawn ; *lithos*, stone). They are for the most part large and rough, and bear signs of much wear.

In the second period, the Palaeolithic, or Old Stone Age (Greek *palaios*, ancient) there is little doubt that the working was deliberate. Implements of this period vary considerably in size and type, from rough axe-heads to small scrapers and

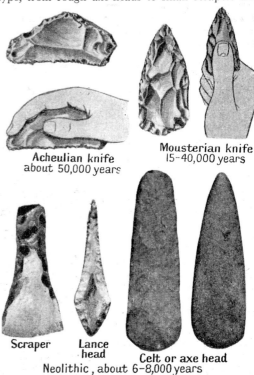

Acheulian knife about 50,000 years

Mousterian knife 15–40,000 years

Scraper

Lance head

Celt or axe head

Neolithic, about 6–8,000 years

FLINT IMPLEMENTS

Many thousands of years ago these and other types of stone implements were all that Man had for fighting his enemies and procuring food. How some of these flints were held and their uses are shown here. There are many parts of Britain in which such implements are to be found

FLINT-MINE WORKED BY MEN OF THE NEW STONE AGE

The earliest flint weapons and tools were made from stones found near the surface, but men of the later Stone Age discovered that by digging deeper they could obtain stones of better quality, and so flint-mining became an extensive industry. Where the flint lay not far below ground shallow pits were sufficient, but sometimes methods somewhat similar to those obtaining in coal-mining were employed on a small scale, and a shaft 30 feet deep was dug with galleries radiating from it. This illustration, from the London Museum, shows a Neolithic (New Stone Age) flint-mine.

early arrow-heads. The scrapers, characteristic of this period, were usually small tools, flat on one face, more or less rounded off on the other, with a thick, blunt edge used for scraping hides and similar work. Often, too, you may find the round, battered " hammer-stones " used for " making " the flint. In later palaeolithic work the edges of the tools are finely finished—smooth, sharp, or saw-like as required. The flakes from larger pieces were worked into little knives and small scrapers, or even teeth to be embedded in wood for making saws.

Fine as is the work of the palaeolithic period, it cannot compare with that of the Neolithic, or New Stone, age (Greek, *neos*, recent). The axe-heads and other implements are smoothed and sharpened to a keen edge, cut so as to fit the wooden hafts and generally worked in a manner which commands our admiration. There were also sling-stones, for use from a sling.

In many parts of Britain, especially where there are gravel deposits, or on chalk hills, you may find flint implements, or the waste fragments split off in making such implements. On these hills, too, the prehistoric flint-mines have been discovered.

Flint was long used for striking against steel to produce sparks to set fire to tinder or some other inflammable substance, which was used to start a fire. Natural flints were also fixed to the side of the lock of the old flint-lock muskets (*see* Fire-arms).

The so-called flints used in our modern automatic lighters are made of quite another substance—an alloy of iron and the " rare-earth " metal cerium (*q.v.*)

Flintshire. Situated to the west of the Dee estuary, with a detached portion lying to the east of Denbighshire, Flintshire is the smallest county in Wales. Its area is 256 square miles. The county contains the lower courses of the Dee and Clwyd. Dairy and sheep farming are important, and there are iron and steel works along the Dee estuary. Artificial silk, flannel and cement are manufactured. Mold is the county town; Rhyl and Prestatyn are seaside resorts. The population of the county is 113,000.

Flodden, BATTLE OF. Fought on September 9, 1513, at Flodden, a ridge of the Cheviots on the English side of the Scottish border, this famous battle was a victory for the English army under the Earl of Surrey over the forces of James IV, king of Scotland.

The English crossed the river Till, and took up a position between James's army and their line of retreat. The Scottish left wing attacked the English right and forced it back, but meanwhile the English routed the Scottish right and caused the centre and left to retreat. The Scottish losses were heavy, especially among the nobles, King James himself being killed.

Floods. Streams and rivers carry water from the lands back to the oceans; here, under the influence of the sun, water vapour is produced and gathered up into cloud to be carried to land again and fall as rain. This sequence is what scientists call the *hydrological cycle*. When the rivers receive more run-off from the land than they can carry for the time being, we get overflowing of the banks ; and floods, sometimes disastrous, are the result.

The current becomes more swift as the water rises; the banks may be breached by the torrent at places where the channel narrows, or where a bend imposes some obstacle. A comparatively " young " river, flowing through mountainous country, will have dug out for itself a deep channel and can cope with big increases in water flow. But an older river which traverses low-lying land (which will most likely be of a softer nature) will carve out a broader and shallower channel.

A river flowing through softer soil will carry along with it mud and silt; as the pace of the current slows down, this mud is deposited upon the river bed, and upon the low-lying land alongside if the waters overflow. In this way the river gradually raises the level of its bed until in time the channel may be higher than the adjoining countryside. This kind of bank, when it gives way to the impetuous flood, may spill its waters over a wide area. Another cause of flood is the increased depth and rate of flow in a tidal river when certain circumstances coincide—a period of higher tides coming at a time when the river is already swollen by rains or by the run-off from snow-laden land.

Rain falling upon the countryside is absorbed by the soil and by the vegetation; more is taken up by evaporation. Only the water not held or transformed by these two processes reaches the rivers. There is a certain level of the soil, according to the shape of the strata and their nature, at which the ground will hold water; the entire area drained by a river may be likened to a sponge, and if more rains falls over a period when the "sponge" has absorbed its maximum, most of this rain will run off into the ditches, brooks, streams and rivers.

Snow, when it thaws rapidly, sends up the water level very quickly and is a common cause of floods. If the ground remains frozen, while the snow melts, the burden imposed upon the waterways is greater still. In rainy seasons the air is moisture-laden for long periods, so that the amount of vapour which the atmosphere can take up by evaporation is diminished; a heavier fall than usual will quickly raise the river level.

From the earliest times men have settled in river valleys, where the very conditions which brought danger from flood produced fertile land, overlaid with the life-generating mud and silt. So Man long ages ago began to take steps to control the water. He built earthen mounds along the rivers of China, for example; and no better device was discovered. But in time the mighty rivers raised their beds so much that they broke out a new course unconstrained by man-made boundaries. Then the older bed became productive agricultural land.

Along some of the great American rivers, such as the Mississippi, which run through low-lying

Graphic Photo Union

FLOODS : THE RIVER WYE OVERFLOWS ITS BANKS AT HEREFORD

Snow, when it thaws rapidly, sends up the water level of rivers very quickly and is a common cause of floods. If, in addition, the ground remains frozen and cannot absorb moisture, then the burden imposed on the waterways becomes even greater. Severe floods occurred in England in 1947 when snow melted while the earth was still frozen ; the River Wye overflowed at Hereford, the water invading the city (above). Floods may also be caused by high tides.

FIGHTING FLOODS TO SAVE THE LAND

P.A.-Reuter; Graphic Photo Union

When the banks of a river have been breached by floods, mats made of tightly-bound bundles of willow branches (bottom) are sometimes sunk to fill the gap. Another method was tried in England in 1947, when obsolete fighting vehicles were placed across the gap (centre), the spaces between them being filled with sandbags. Top, a causeway of sandbags, supported by stakes, is being built across an opening in a river bank through which water is pouring.

country or traverse valleys with a gentle rise at either side, similar long embankments were built, known as "levees." Deepening and straightening the river channel are other methods of flood prevention. The cutting of canals to by-pass a twisting narrow portion of a river is another remedy. The general drainage of an area is improved by regular attention to ditches and the smaller streams, for these are the first feeders of the bigger waterways.

Low-lying regions such as the fenlands have their own special problems. Much land has been reclaimed from the sea in past times; if you visit some of the fenland churches you may often see a memorial to benefactors who gave sums of money for the building of dikes and the reclaiming of land. Before the water-logged region can be drained it must be barricaded off from the ocean by earthen mounds and embankments. Then follows the digging of drainage canals, or the deepening of other natural channels, and the pumping out of the water impounded by the banks. Such a region is prone to flooding from the sea afterwards, and constant care and observation are needed.

A method of flood control adopted abroad more often than in Britain is the making of large reser-

voirs, or the utilisation of suitable natural lakes, as "safety valves" to accommodate the surplus flow of rivers in flood. Dams (*q.v.*) and barrages allow the water in the reservoir to be let out gradually at suitable times. By emptying a reservoir in a low-water period before a season of expected floods, the reservoir is ready to absorb the surplus when it builds up later. Flood-control is usually combined with irrigation schemes: on the one hand the water is prevented from doing harm, and on the other it is sent where it will benefit agriculture. Many of the great dams built in recent times have a multiple purpose; they may be mainly intended for generating electric

power, but they are usually constructed as part of a general scheme for controlling river flow.

Erosion of the soil in regions drained by rivers is normally a rather slow natural process; but if the land be stripped of its trees and hedges, or if forested areas are denuded without compensatory planting of young trees, the soil dries up and is carried away by wind; then soil erosion becomes a swift menace. The amount of silt reaching the rivers is immensely increased, and the rivers flow more sluggishly and become shallower. In times past Man unwitting made the general situation worse by draining lakes, swamps and marshes to turn them into agricultural lands. This lessened the amount of ground water which could be held by a region, and took away a natural reserve of water which became available in time of drought. In America some such reclaimed regions have even had to be allowed to revert to their former water-covered state, to redress Nature's balance.

Florence, ITALY. Famous in literature and art, this Italian city lies upon both banks of the Arno, which before the Second World War (1939–45) was spanned by six bridges, of which the Ponte Vecchio, built in 1345, was world-famous. On all sides low hills covered with villas surround the city, which in the 14th century was the artistic and intellectual capital of the world.

From these hills about Florence the scene is one of striking beauty. In the heart of the city rises the dome of the 13th-century cathedral, and by its side is the exquisitely beautiful campanile, or bell-tower, designed by Giotto (*c.* 1266–1337). Near by is the baptistery, with the artist Ghiberti's (1378–1455) celebrated bronze doors.

Many buildings in the old part of the city were associated with famous people. In such

Graphic Photo Union

FLOODED STREETS AND COLLAPSING BRIDGE
Despite the use of various methods of flood control, exceptionally heavy rain or snowfalls will cause riverside towns to be inundated, as Windsor (lower), Berkshire, was in 1947. Sometimes a river in flood will undermine the foundations of a bridge causing the structure to subside, as in the case of this bridge at Shardlow, Derbyshire.

FLORENCE'S CATHEDRAL : FOURTH LARGEST CHURCH IN EUROPE

E.N.I.T.

Situated on both banks of the Arno in a valley among the Apennine foothills, Florence is dominated by the dome of the cathedral of Santa Maria del Fiore, founded in 1298. The campanile or bell-tower, designed by the Italian painter Giotto, was built between 1334 and 1387. At one time the city was the artistic and scientific centre of Italy, as well as the commercial capital. Most of its many art treasures survived the dangers of the Second World War (1939–45).

a house Dante (1265–1321) was born, and over there Petrarch (1304–74) wrote one of his many sonnets to Laura, his lady-love. Here Michelangelo (1475–1564) carved his famous statue of the youthful David, and Leonardo da Vinci (1452–1519) learned to paint. In the public square before the civic palace Savonarola (1452–98), the reformer-monk, was martyred amidst the jeers of the populace. Not far away was the home of the Amerigo Vespucci (1451–1512), who gave his name to the continents of North and South America. In Florence, Machiavelli (1469–1527) wrote his celebrated work The Prince. The list of famous places and famous names is almost endless. Florence was Italy's capital not only in arts, but also in science, literature and statecraft, in many skilled trades and in commerce.

No other Italian city except Rome attracts so many art lovers in normal times. Its two famous picture galleries, the Uffizi and the Pitti (both damaged during the Second World War, 1939–45), contain collections of immense value. Almost every church in Florence has famous frescoes on its walls; while the tombs of the city's great men are embellished with notable sculpture. Michelangelo's celebrated statues over the tombs of Giuliano and Lorenzo de' Medici, in the church of San Lorenzo, are among the world's masterpieces of art.

In the course of the Allied campaign in Italy against the Germans during the Second World War the Allies reached the southern bank of the River Arno opposite Florence in August 1944. The Germans destroyed all the bridges over the river, except the Ponte Vecchio, but they blew up all the old houses on the latter. The heart of the old city around the bridge was badly damaged by shell-fire.

The Germans removed many works of art, but these were all accounted for and returned to Florence by July 1945.

Silk, woollen and wooden goods are manufactured in Florence, and there are mosaic and jewelry industries. The population of the city is about 322,000.

Florida. In the extreme south-east of the United States, Florida State is bounded on the north by Georgia and Alabama, on the west and east by the Gulf of Mexico and the Atlantic Ocean respectively. It has an area of 58,560 square miles. The surface is flat, and in the south there are many miles of overgrown marshland known as the Everglades. Numerous lakes include Lake Okeechobee, with an area of 717 square miles. The climate varies from warm temperate in the north to sub-tropical in the south, and its mild winters have made Florida a notable resort.

Famous for oranges and grape-fruit, Florida also grows pineapples, bananas, coconuts, ground-nuts, cotton, tobacco, oats and sugar cane. Phosphate rocks, limestone and lime are important minerals. Cattle raising is carried on along the coast of the Gulf of Mexico. Tallahassee is the capital of the State.

On Easter Sunday (in Spanish, *Pascua florida*, or Feast of flowers) of the year 1513, the Spaniard Ponce de Leon sighted the land, which he named Florida in honour of the day. The territory was held in turn by Spain, France and Great Britain till 1819, when it became a part of the United States, being bought from Spain for the equivalent of £1,000,000. In 1842 there was war with the Seminole Indians of Florida, and a few hundred of the tribe escaped removal to reservations by hiding in the Everglades. There they have lived ever since, hunting and fishing, and cultivating small gardens. The population of the State is 1,897,000.

Flour AND FLOUR-MILLING. Wheat as it comes from the fields must be changed into flour before bread, our principal article of food, can be made from it. The process of grinding the grain into flour and separating the fine flour from the coarser portions is called milling.

In early times a stone was hollowed out and a smaller stone, with one end rounded, was used to pound the grain which was placed in the hollow. The flour was then mixed with water and baked on a hot stone (*see* Bread). A little later a hand-mill, called a quern, was used. This consisted of two disks of stone, one on top of the other, with a

Newtonian Illustrated Press Service

PRIMITIVE FLOUR MILL
Some people, like these Arab women of the Syrian desert, still grind grain by hand between millstones. The grain is poured through a hole in the middle of the upper stone, which is then rotated on the lower, producing coarse flour.

hole in the middle of the upper one through which the grain was fed. The upper stone was rotated on the lower by means of a handle. Next came large mills made on the same plan, with stones having grooved surfaces to give a cutting edge, and turned by oxen, water-power or the wind.

It was not until the latter half of the 19th century that roller mills, which now grind nearly all the world's flour, were introduced. Rollers made of chilled steel with grooved surfaces grind, or mill, the grain as they revolve against each other.

Before we can understand milling, we must know something of the size, form and composition of a grain of wheat. It is an oblong grain with a furrow down one side, and on the outside is a brownish husk consisting of layers of woody fibre; when milled this part of the husk gives us bran. Within the husk lies the white kernel, composed chiefly of gluten and starch, from which white flour is made. In one end of this kernel is the wheat-germ, which, if the grain were planted, would produce a

new plant. In milling, the bran and most of the wheat-germ must be removed from the starchy white kernel in order to obtain fine white flour. Modern mills are so arranged that one part of the process is done on one floor and another on the floor beneath, so that gravity chutes can be used to convey the grain from one machine to another.

When the grain first comes to the mill it may contain dirt, particles of straw, and other seeds. These must all be removed before the grinding begins. The removal is effected by sifting and shaking the grain and fanning it with strong currents of air. The wheat grains are scoured bright and clean in rapidly whirling cylinders. Then they are moistened with steam to toughen the husks so that when the grains are crushed the husks peel off whole and are easily separated. The grain is then dried in a drying room.

Let us follow this wheat through the mill. It descends from one floor to another, each time passing through a set of rollers called break rolls. The grain cannot be ground very fine at first, because the bran must be removed and the wheat-germ separated from the kernel of starch and gluten in the early stages. And so each break, or set of rollers, is adjusted to grind a little finer than the one before. The wheat-germ is tough and is rolled flat, and is quite easily removed by sifting.

At each break, part of the wheat is reduced to fine flour and part still remains in comparatively large granules. The fine flour is separated by passing it through very fine sieves of specially made silk. The middlings, or coarser flours of the kernels, are then separated from the tailings, that is, the bran and other rejected parts of the wheat, and passed on to another set of rollers to be further reduced. This process is repeated again and again, until all the wheat has been reduced to flour or to its by-products. The by-products, known as milling offals, are used to feed farm animals.

In milling most flours the bran and the germ are almost entirely removed, but in some they are retained, and ground up fine with the rest of the wheat, forming what is called wholemeal flour.

Henry Simon, Ltd.

MODERN ROLLER MILLS
Before the grain goes to the roller mills (above), all dirt, straw and seeds are removed by sifting and fanning. The grain cannot be ground very fine at first, so each set of rollers is adjusted to grind a little finer than the one before.

EARTH'S *Bright* GARMENT *of* BLOSSOM

The development of any flowering plant, growing from a seed and in due course producing quantities of seed of its own, is a tale of astonishingly intricate wonders. It is told with the aid of the microscope.

Flowers. The objects which we call flowers are, for the most part, the "attractive" organs of the higher plants, but the term is used generally in a very broad sense. In every ordinary flower each part has a special "function." Thus, the brightly coloured parts of the flower are usually the "petals," and it is their mission to attract insects, by their form or colour. Many flowers also attract by scent, which comes from glands in various parts of the flower. Not only have colour and fragrance been developed, but also the shapes of flowers have been modified until they favour certain types of pollen-bearing insects. The deep-throated flowers, such as the petunia, are fitted for the long tongues of moths and butterflies; the deep nectar of the nasturtium (*Tropaeolum*) which grows in South and Central America is easily accessible to the humming-bird; the lower lip of the sage flower seems made for the bee to alight upon. In fact, almost all flowers are shaped with reference to securing pollination and, thus, fertilization.

Since the use of the petals is mainly to attract the flower's helpers, we naturally find the most important parts of the flower set in the midst of the petals. These consist of, first, a *pistil*, comprising the basal part called the ovary, in which the seeds are developed and perfected; and the tip, or style, terminating in the stigma. The last is a sticky, spongy tissue which catches the pollen grains and holds them while they send down their tubes to the ovules in the ovary, carrying the material necessary for fertilization.

The second essential part is the *stamen*, which consists of a filament bearing the anther, which usually forms a double pocket in which the pollen grains grow. When the anther is ripe the pockets open, letting out the pollen dust to be carried by insect or wind to some waiting stigma of the same species—or to fall upon a stigma of the same flower. The pollen grains are so small that they look like dust, but each grain is of definite form and in some species is ornamented with knobs or recognizable markings.

The arrangement and number of pistils and stamens in different flowers show an amazing amount of variation. In many of the most familiar garden plants, every part of the reproduction system is found in each flower, the pistil rising from the centre, surrounded first by stamens, and then by a ring of petals. Some flowers, however, have just one or more pistils but no stamens, and they are termed pistillate; others have stamens and no pistils, and are called staminate. Sometimes both pistillate and staminate blossoms grow upon the same plant, and such plants are said to be monoecious, meaning that they bear both male and female reproductive elements. In other types each plant produces only one kind of flower, and plants of this sort are therefore termed dioecious.

To guard these parts from harm while the young flower is developing, many flowers have *sepals*, which are tougher and firmer than the petals and completely cover and protect the very young bud. Sometimes, as in the tulip and lilies, these sepals take on the colour of the petals as the flower opens; and in others the sepals alone are developed and are coloured brightly as the petals would be. In some species sepals are altogether absent. The sepals combine to form the calyx, and the petals taken together form the corolla.

In form and arrangement flowers have infinite variety. Some, such as the clovers, geranium and verbena, have such small blossoms that singly they could not very well attract insects, but, growing in clusters, they make quite a show. Such flower clusters are sometimes in the form of close spikes or spikelets; sometimes as racemes, with the blossoms distributed loosely upon an elongated axis; sometimes in the form of pyramidal clusters (like the lilac), called panicles, in which the arrangement of blossoms is regular.

The guelder rose, a common shrub, has its outer flowers in the disk very much larger than the others, but they are incomplete. The *Compositae* form a large

All the species of Narcissus have been widely cultivated in Britain, one of the favourites being this double variety.

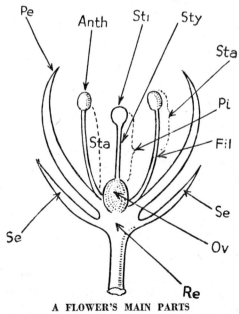

A FLOWER'S MAIN PARTS

Here is a key-diagram of the constituent parts of a flower. **Anth**, anther; **Fil**, filament; **Ov**, ovary; **Pe**, petals (corolla); **Pi**, pistil; **Re**, receptacle; **Se**, sepals (calyx); **Sta**, stamen; **Sti**, stigma; **sty**, style.

family of plants that has adopted a cooperative plan for its flowers. The tiny florets, as they are called, are set close together in a solid head, those at the centre being perfect flowers, while those set in the rim develop long petals of bright colours to attract the insects. The sunflower is a good example; the outside row of florets produces the petals which form the rays of the sunflower, while the inside flowers, which are called disk florets and have an abundance of nectar, develop the seeds. The dandelion, thistle, dahlia, chrysanthemum, marigold, daisy and a host of other common flowers are of this sort. Strictly speaking, therefore, we should talk, not about a daisy " flower," but about a daisy " flower-head." (*See also under* the headings Botany, Leaves, and Plant Life).

THE LIFE-STORY OF A FLOWERING PLANT

TO trace the life-story of a flowering plant, let us begin with the seed. Long before the first shoot appears above the surface of the ground the seed is at work. It begins by pushing out a root, which, delicate as it is, forces its way through the ground. Its tip is protected from injury by a sheath known as a root-cap.

This root gives out branches, which in their turn branch again and then again, until the soil round the seed is a network of delicate threads. The root fixes the plant to the ground, and supports the stem which presently springs up. It gathers the nourishment which the hungry and thirsty young plant needs to make it grow. Growing out from the roots of many plants are little root-hairs—thread-like structures so delicate as to require a powerful magnifying glass before they can be seen. Through their thin walls they absorb the rain water that has soaked into the ground, together with the chemical substances dissolved in it.

While the roots are burying themselves in the soil, another little shoot is pushing its way in the opposite direction. This is the stem, which is working upwards towards the light, and before very long the tip appears above the surface of the ground. Hidden away in this stem are the leaves and flowers, which, unborn as yet, will later expand under the welcome rays of the sun.

Two Classes of Flowering Plants

Flowering plants are divided by botanists into two classes. There are those, such as the sunflower and the scarlet runner, which have two cotyledons, or seed-lobes. These are called dicotyledons. Others, such as the lily, have only one seed-lobe, and are called monocotyledons. Both types have " pipes," or food channels, running through them, by means of which nourishment can pass up and down. These pipes are contained in bundles called vascular bundles, and one of the differences between dicotyledons and monocotyledons is that, while in the former these bundles are arranged in a circle in the stem, in the latter they are spread about anyhow.

Before very long a tiny bud pushes its way out of the stem, and, aided by the light and warmth of the sun, quickly expands into a leaf. The air which we breathe consists for the most part of oxygen and nitrogen, with a small amount of carbon dioxide, a gas which is harmful to animals if the air contains a large quantity of it. The leaves of plants take in carbon dioxide gas which is exhaled into the air by humans and animals, or is present in the atmosphere from other causes, and take away the carbon from it, to use as plant food. This starchy foodstuff is built up of carbon, hydrogen and oxygen. The oxygen which is left over is returned to the atmosphere. In this process, called *photosynthesis*, sunshine and the green colouring matter in the leaves, called *chlorophyll*, play the principal parts. Photosynthesis derives from two Greek words which simply mean " building up with the aid of light."

The chlorophyll enables green leaves to manufacture carbohydrates (*q.v.*). Sunlight, warmth, and moisture are essential for this. We must also remember that green leaves, in " breathing," give out carbon dioxide. In daylight, however, this exhaled gas is utilised almost immediately for photosynthesis; at night-time the carbon dioxide goes into the atmosphere. Thus a number of green plants kept in a closed room at night would add to the carbon dioxide content of the room.

How Pollination Takes Place

Returning now to the life-history of our plant, we find the first leaf followed at rapid intervals by others, as well as by lateral stems, and eventually by flower-buds. These develop and expand until they become full-grown, with the parts and organs we have already described. It remains to describe the way in which pollination takes place. In many flowers, where both stigmas and anthers are present, either the former or the latter ripen first. In other cases they ripen together, and so favour self-pollination. If the stigmas ripen first, the flower is said to be protogynous; if the anthers mature first, it is protandrous. In either case, sooner or later, if it is an insect-pollinated bloom, a bee or other insect will come along. If this is a bee, it will enter the flower in such a way that, brushing against the ripe anthers, it knocks off some of the pollen on to some part of its legs, back or underside. When it visits *another* flower, this pollen is in such a position as to come into contact with the surface of a stigma, and in this way cross-pollination is assured, the sticky stigmatic surface picking up the pollen off the bee. A great many flowers are so constructed that pollination from another individual of the same sort is favoured.

The pollen which has been picked up from the bee by the sticky surface of the stigma begins to grow, and sends out a little tube. This makes its way through the surface of the stigma and soon reaches the hollow style, growing on downwards until it reaches the ovary.

The ovary has a wall to protect it, but the pollen tube pushes its way through this wall, to reach an ovule. For inside the ovary are ridges, and on these ridges cluster the little green ovules. These are the forerunners of the seeds, but, unless they meet the pollen tube, they are doomed to die. When the pollen tube reaches an ovule, the male element passes in and fertilization takes place. Then the ovule begins to swell and grow, to produce, when the time comes, a new and similar plant.

From now onwards the petals fade and droop, and before long fall to the ground. We may say that the "flower" is dead; but we should be wrong —it is more alive than it has ever been. The change merely means that the beautiful colours have done their work, and so are no longer required. The calyx, however, may enlarge now to protect the growing embryo, and in many plants it forms part of the fruit.

In the botanical sense "fruit" means the enlarged and ripened ovary. We eat many such fruits, and also give the same name generally to many others which are not strictly fruits in the botanist's classification. For example, the ripe red pulp of the strawberry is formed by the enlargement of the stem of the flower ; the brown, dry pips are the real fruits, each formed from an ovary. Botanists call the strawberry a "false fruit."

The rest of our story of the life-cycle of a flower can best be told by the pictures from microscopical slides reproduced in the following pages, along with the full explanations printed with them.

As a guide to the identification of the various members of a flower, we have printed in page 1321 a simple diagram in which the parts are named. In the centre of this imaginary section cut down vertically through the flower we see the stigma (Sti), on its stalk or style (Sty). At the lower end of the style is the ovary (Ov) with, lower still, the receptacle (Re). Enclosing the flower at the base are the sepals (Se) ; above these are the petals (Pe). From the lower part of the flower cup spring the stamens (Sta), each composed of a filament (Fi) and bearing at its top the anther (Anth) or pollen sac. It is not difficult to cut a flower down or across so as to disclose its inner beauty of construction in this striking manner.

in this hidden box, the silent factory in which Life works out its wonders. It is inside the swelling at the end of the stalk. The following illustrations show you, enlarged under the microscope at various magnifications, the inside of this flower.

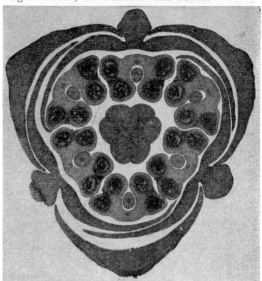

2. The inside of the flower-bud is like this, shown in cross section. Going into it from the outside, we pass three sepals, three petals, and six anthers, and then come to the central style, at the top of which are the stigmas, and at the bottom of which is the ovary.

You should look back now at the diagram in page 1321, showing a vertical slice down through a flower. The same organs are shown as in No. 2, and by a comparison of the two illustrations you can get a good idea of the structure. It will help still further if you cut a flower, or a well developed bud, across with a sharp knife or a razor blade— and make a section for yourself. You can also cut another flower vertically, to get the equivalent of our diagram in page 1321.

1. This is a Bermuda lily. On the outside are three coloured leaves—the sepals; inside these are three other leaves something like them—the petals. Sheltered within these protecting leaves are six slender rods—the stamens; they are something like pins with long double heads—the anthers. In the middle of these rods are three sticky little stigmas. They rise from the columnar style, which runs down into a hidden case, the ovary, the very home of life. We shall see the wonderful things that happen

3. Here is one of the petals; on the right is the petal as we see it under the microscope, showing the veins that point the way for the bee when it comes to find the nectar deep down in the flower.

4. Let us look still closer at these petal-tips; their framework is beautifully built.

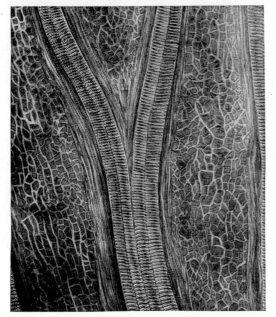

5. Adding to the power of our microscope again, so that we can see still farther into the petal, we find that these veins are wonderful things. Here, in the middle, is a forking vein made of four marvellous tubes built up like a spiral staircase. They carry food to the petals up from the root.

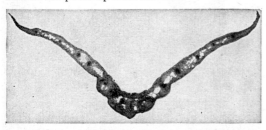

6. If we cut this slender petal in two and put the edge of it under a microscope, this is what we see in this thin edge like paper. The black patches scattered along the strip are the delicate veins.

7. Now look closely at the six anthers, six little factories we may call them, clustered round the style that swells above them till the three-fold stigma bursts out at the top. No. 9 (at top of page 1325) shows an anther seen under the microscope.

A low-power pocket lens is useful in this study. Better still is a watchmaker's eyeglass, of 3-inch focus; but you will have to acquire the knack of gripping it, as the watchmaker does, in your eye socket. A great advantage of this type of magnifying-glass is that it leaves both hands free for the purposes of manipulation or dissection.

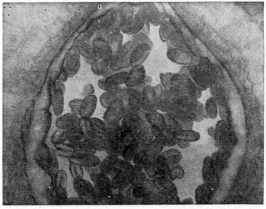

8. Inside these anthers are made the little grains of pollen we see lying in the anther here—the yellow powder that sticks to your finger if you touch it. In No. 12 (bottom of facing page) is a view of the pollen grains, highly magnified, to show their rough coat.

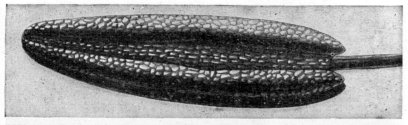

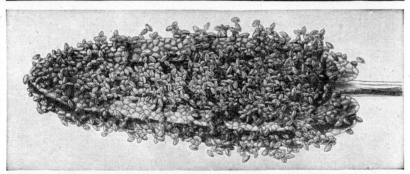

9. Let us look at the anther now under a microscope, while the walls of this "workshop" stand secure. For they are about to fall, pushed outward by the growing strength within them. Notice what a delicate structure it has.

10. Sheltered from all harm are the pollen grains, seen clearly in this cross-section of the anther, growing in power and building up the force that is soon to make itself known to us. Owing to the risk pollen grains run of being lost in their business of getting from one flower to another, Mother Nature sees to it that a great many more pollen grains are produced than are really needed.

11. Now the grains have burst their bonds, and the anther is yellow with pollen. Like a magician's wand it is, for a touch of this pollen brings a new flower into the world. All that is needed is a breath of wind or the passage of a travelling insect to transport the golden dust, and the miracle of fertilization is accomplished.

12. We see the pollen grains closely here, greatly magnified. Note their rough coats by which they will cling to the hairy body of the bee when it comes. Another thing that enables the pollen grains to travel with the wings of nectar-seeking insects is that in many cases they have a sticky substance over their whole surface, and this and their variously shaped grooves make them cling together, so that insects carry away large masses of the grains in going from flower to flower. This tends to make the process of fertilization more certain. Much pollen is stolen by bees, who feed it to their larvae.

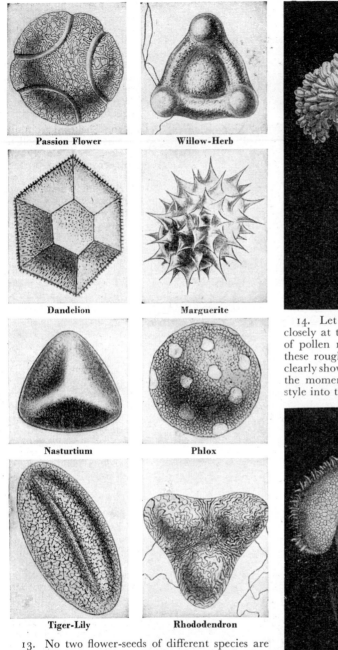

Passion Flower   Willow-Herb

Dandelion   Marguerite

Nasturtium   Phlox

Tiger-Lily   Rhododendron

14. Let us now examine the stigma, and look closely at the top of it. We see how easily a grain of pollen may lodge in this rough place held by these rough sticky points which the microscope so clearly shows. Here the grain lies and waits until the moment comes for it to descend through the style into the ovary on its errand of fertilization.

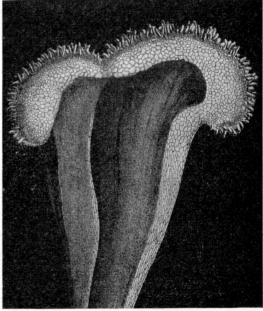

13. No two flower-seeds of different species are quite the same; nor are their pollen grains alike. These eight pollen grains have been photographed under the microscope. It is a mystery how and why, in the course of numberless generations, such differences have come about. Almost certainly such variations of form serve some purpose. We must remember that many flowers are self-pollinated, the pollen from the anthers dropping by its own weight on to the stigma below. In other flowers, which have organs of one sex only, it is the wind which carries pollen grains from the male flowers to the female ones on another plant.

15. And now we cut right through the stigma downwards until it looks like this. We see its delicate structure and, more important still, we observe a hollow passage down the style, through which a pollen grain will travel down to the seeds in the ovary. (Compare with No. 19 in facing page.)

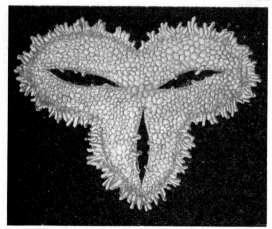

16. Here is the stigma seen from on top, after being sliced across. There are three of these narrow ways through which there comes to the heart of the flower the messenger of Life. Through each of the three heads of the stigma this hollow passage runs, until the three join in the style and run as one to the ovary below. Through these passageways, as we shall see, the pollen tubes will travel on their errand of creation.

18. And now appears the wonder of wonders. The pollen specks make their way down through the stigma till they reach the hollow space. They swell up and each one sends out a tube. This pollen tube shoots out and passes down the narrow space until it has reached the ovary, the place where the seeds will grow and develop from the ovules—but only if a pollen tube reaches them.

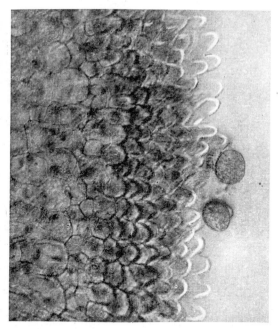

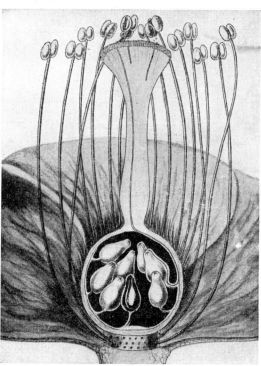

17. A bee alights on the flower, fresh from another flower, its body covered thick with pollen-dust. It must brush past the stigma on its way to the nectar, and it leaves on the stigma tiny grains of pollen from another flower. Here we see them as they lie on the surface of the stigma.

Although bees are the great pollen bearers, other kinds of insects also play their part in securing fertilization of flowers. Even moths and other creatures which fly during the dusk pollinate certain flowers.

19. This is the place where a flower is born. In this sheltered chamber are colonies of little green things called ovules, attached by tiny stems to the walls. Soon the pollen tube arrives, making its way through the wall of the ovary and pushing on until it touches a little green ovule. If the tube does not touch it the ovule must die, but at the touch of the pollen tube it bursts into activity, becomes a seed and, all things being favourable, will in the course of a season develop into an independent plant.

This is the climax to the life-cycle. All that has gone before was but a preparation for this fruition of the seed—the gay petals and sepals for attracting not Man but the insects; the tall or tiny stem and simple or complex leaves; the strange defensive weapons such as thorns or stinging hairs; the sweet fragrance in some flowers and the repulsive—to Man, at least—carrion-like odour of others. All contributed to the supreme function, reproduction of the species and the birth of a new generation !

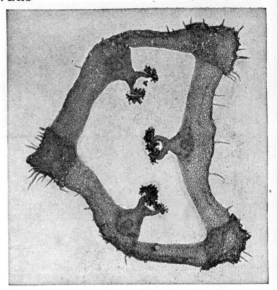

22. Compare this picture with No. 20, where we had cut through the ovary downwards; now we see it cut across. The little ovules are clustered on the walls of the three ridges.

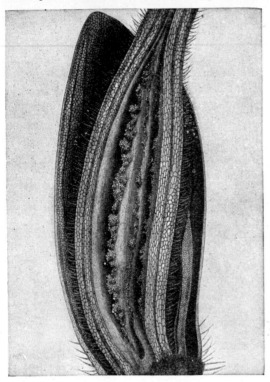

20. Now we will peep into the ovary itself, cutting through it downwards. It happens that we have taken the lady's slipper, a distant cousin of the lily, for this picture. The little white specks on the ridge in the heart of it are ovules. Well sheltered is this inner chamber where a flower is born, yet the gold dust the bee has brought from far away throws out its tubes and pushes down with its quickening touch until, from this hidden place, there comes out into the world the seed which can give birth to another flower.

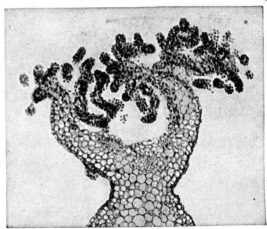

23. Now we turn the microscope on to one of the three ridges and see the ovules more closely. Each little group of specks makes up an ovule.

The ovule is, of course, a rudimentary seed; it needs the magic stimulus of fertilization to enable it to develop further.

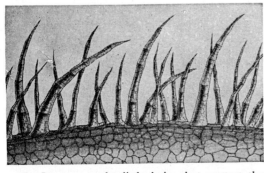

21. Let us note the little hairs that protect the outside walls of the ovary. Here we see a few of them greatly magnified, and we can realize how powerful they are to serve their great purpose.

24. The fertilized ovule grows into a seed like this. Even here, in this highly magnified photograph, the eye discerns almost nothing; yet this tiny thing, after the union with it of a pollen grain, has in it the power to reproduce a new plant of the same sort as that in which it grew.

Fly. The common house-fly, *Musca domestica*, was at one time thought to be just a harmless nuisance. Not until the 20th century was it discovered that these flies carry disease germs to food, and thereby cause millions of deaths a year. Far from being harmless, it proved to be one of Man's deadliest enemies. Look at a fly through a magnifying glass. You will see that its claws, padded feet, and body are covered with bristling hairs, and its tongue is coated with sticky liquid. Samples of the dust and dirt clinging there may, under a powerful microscope, reveal bacteria of such diseases as typhoid fever or dysentery. Flies get these germs mainly from infected human excrement. If they touch our food later, it too may become infected.

We cannot avoid this menace by just " swatting " flies. They can multiply faster than we can kill them. It has been calculated that between April and September one female fly could have many millions of descendants if all her female offspring lived and their descendants also lived. Of course, this does not happen; but plenty of flies will be produced every summer if only one female in a hundred escapes death long enough to lay eggs. The way to suppress flies is to prevent breeding.

Prolonged exposure to freezing weather kills flies, and in cold climates only a few females lying torpid in sheltered places survive the winter. Warm weather reawakens them and they seek moist spots such as manure heaps and other refuse in which to lay their eggs. The eggs look like tiny white grains of wheat, about 1/20th of an inch long. The female will lay 150 or more in several clusters; and within 24 hours the eggs hatch into white maggots. These feed and grow for about five days, then become pupae. Some five days later an adult fly emerges; and within two weeks more, each new female is ready to lay eggs. Flies can be suppressed by eliminating the places in which their eggs can hatch and the maggots can feed. Refuse heaps which cannot be removed should be sprayed or dusted frequently with a strong insecticide. Dustbins

should be kept covered. Earth-closets should be emptied regularly, and the contents buried deeply. And, of course, food of all kinds should be protected against the visits of flies.

The adult house-fly is about a quarter-inch long and about half an inch across the outspread wings; and a thousand adults weigh less than an ounce. Each foot on its three pairs of legs is equipped with claws and two hairy pads called pulvilli. These pads secrete a sticky liquid, which enables the fly to cling to almost any surface. Without any fuss or bother it can run upside down along a ceiling or on the under side of a glass skylight.

To help it in finding food and dodging danger it has five eyes. Two of these are huge compound structures and cover most of the head. Between these are three tiny simple eyes, set in a triangle. The sense of vision, however, is not sharp; the fly relies more upon its acute sense of smell. The mouth parts are adapted for sucking up liquid food. A long " tongue," which is really a proboscis like an elephant's trunk in miniature, has two pads or lobes

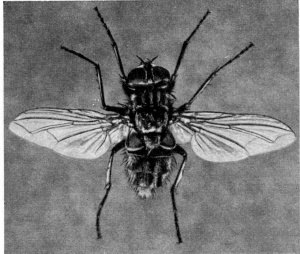

at the end which act as funnels for drawing in liquid. The fly can also reduce soluble foods such as sugar to liquid by spreading saliva on them. House-flies have no equipment for biting.

Most two-winged insects (*Diptera*) are properly called flies. In place of the second pair of wings possessed by bees, dragon-flies and many other insects, the true flies have club-shaped balancers (*halteres*). About 45,000 members of the order *Diptera* are known; they are divided into two groups, according to the nature of the antennæ.

Next to the house-fly and the blue-bottle or blow-fly (*Calliphora*), which lays its eggs in meat, the most widespread members of the tribe are probably mosquitoes. Some of these rank also among the deadly disease carriers. Another dangerous biter is the tsetse fly of central Africa. Much damage is done by fruit flies in tropical and semi-tropical countries, particularly Hawaii. Especially harmful is the Mediterranean fruit fly (*Ceratitis*

J. J. Ward; H. Bastin

HOUSE-FLY : SPREADER OF DISEASE

One of Man's most dangerous enemies, the common house-fly (top, magnified five diameters) spreads disease wherever it goes. Its long tongue, with a disk at the end for sucking up food, projects from the bottom of the head (lower left) ; on the feet (lower right) there are other disks by which the fly clings to the ceiling.

F. Jefferson

A PIED FLY-CATCHER
Perched beside the hole in a tree trunk in which is its nest, this pied cock fly-catcher displays its handsome black-and-white plumage ; the hen bird is not so bright, being grey-and-white. These birds feed on flies and other insects.

capitata). With the sharp end of her body the female punctures the skin of fruits and deposits from one to six eggs. When the maggots hatch they eat into the pulp and cause decay. Flesh flies lay their eggs and breed in stored meats; bot-flies torment cattle, sheep, and horses; horse-flies also bite men. There are bat flies, and sheep keds, which live as parasites and hence have lost their wings. (These are sometimes miscalled " ticks ".)

Useful members of the order are the hover flies, whose grubs eat the greenfly on garden and other plants; and drone flies, whose larvae live in foul water, eating decaying vegetable matter.

Fly-catcher. These birds, as their name implies, feed on flies, and on other insects such as grasshoppers, weevils, moths and caterpillars. Fly-catchers of the Old World belong to the family *Muscicapidae*. The male pied fly-catcher, *Muscicapa atricapilla*, is black-and-white, the female grey and white. It breeds in the north and west of England and in Wales. It nests in holes, and the eggs are of a pale greenish-blue. The spotted fly-catcher, *Muscicapa griseola*, which seldom arrives in England until late in May, is more common, especially in the south. Grey-and-brown, it nests in ivy and in cracks in walls. The greyish eggs have brown markings.

Flying-Bomb. In the early morning of June 13, 1944—a week after Allied armies had landed on the Normandy beaches for the reconquest of France from the Germans—strange hostile aircraft were seen approaching over the coast of Kent. They were the

first of the new German " V-weapons." This name comes from the enemy's own title of *Vergeltungswaffe*, or " reprisal weapons," and the flying-bomb was officially termed "V.1." A second missile, the rocket-bomb, was called the "V.2," and is described in a later volume under Rocket-Bomb.

The flying bomb was a small pilotless aeroplane, with a wing-span of 16 feet or a little more; at its nose it was armed with an explosive head like that of a torpedo. This " war-head " was exploded by an impact fuse which acted if and when the nose of the aircraft hit an obstacle; or by two mechanical fuses which acted if the aircraft glided into the ground. There was also a clock-fuse which detonated the explosive after, say, two hours if the other fuses had failed. The charge of explosive weighed three-quarters of a ton. There was little penetrative power, but the blast at near ground level was very powerful and destructive.

The flying-bombs could be carried singly by an ordinary bombing aircraft and launched in mid-air; but the chief method was to project them along a sloping concrete ramp by the thrust of a piston driven by compressed air. The ramps had to be orientated in the direction which the missile had to take. The launching speed was about 200 miles per hour; once successfully launched, the flying-bomb then flew on quite automatically until its complicated mechanism caused its engine to shut off and the aircraft to glide down to earth. Its flying speed was about 360 miles per hour, which made it a difficult target for the anti-aircraft guns of the time, and also " gave it the heels " of all but the fastest fighter aircraft then employed. It flew at a height of 800–2,500 feet.

The engine was one of the earliest practical examples of jet-propulsion applied to aircraft (*see* Jet-Propulsion); it was simple and efficient—necessary qualities in a machine which had to be mass-produced quickly and secretly. The propulsion unit consisted of a bell-mouthed tubular steel casing mounted above the rear of the fuselage. At the front, was the air intake; at the opposite end, where the casing projected over the rudder and fins, was the jet orifice. Behind the air intake there was a series of shutters

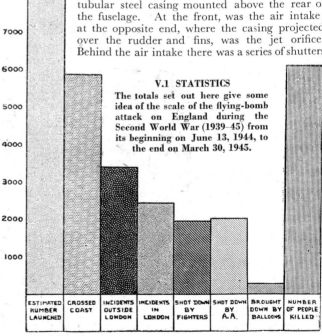

V.1 STATISTICS
The totals set out here give some idea of the scale of the flying-bomb attack on England during the Second World War (1939–45) from its beginning on June 13, 1944, to the end on March 30, 1945.

10000		
9000		
8000		
7000		
6000		
5000		
4000		
3000		
2000		
1000		

| ESTIMATED NUMBER LAUNCHED | CROSSED COAST | INCIDENTS OUTSIDE LONDON | INCIDENTS IN LONDON | SHOT DOWN BY FIGHTERS | SHOT DOWN BY A.A. | BROUGHT DOWN BY BALLOONS | NUMBER OF PEOPLE KILLED |

hinged together in pairs so that they would open if air pressure at the front was greater than gas pressure within the funnel-shaped mixing chamber behind. When gas pressure within grew greater, the shutters would close. There was a grid behind the shutters, shaped to produce what is called a venturi—a narrowing passage or series of passages in which the air gained velocity at the expense of pressure. In rows between the horizontal slats of the grid were the fuel jets; at the top were also jets through which air at very high pressure was forced to start the engine as it was launched.

The flying-bomb was run out of its concrete house and along the launching ramp; then it was shot forward by compressed air acting behind a piston on the ramp. As soon as the pressure of air "rammed" into the intake of the bell-mouth rose sufficiently high—remember that the aircraft left the ramp at about 200 miles per hour—the air shutters opened and air pressure piled up in the mixing chamber. At this point, fuel was automatically sprayed in, a sparking plug ignited the mixture of vaporized fuel and air, and a violent explosion took place in the combustion chamber, where the fuel turned into gas with an enormous increase in volume.

Owing to the greater pressure behind, the air intake shutters now closed, so that the reaction from the exploding gases thrust forward against a solid wall formed by the closed shutters. A fiery jet of hot gases spurted out with a roar from the jet orifice behind, and the force of the reaction urged the aircraft forward. There was no resistance, of course, to the rush of the burnt gases rearward. Most of the forward impulse came from the thrust against the closed shutters; the rest was due to the discharge through the rear orifice.

The fuel-air mixture was ignited about 50 times per second; the fuel jets shut after each such impulse. When the explosion had pushed out the greater part of the burnt gases, and the pressure within the engine thus fell to less than the air pressure at the front, outside, the air intake shutters opened anew, and more air was rammed in by the high speed with which the aircraft rushed along. Again the fuel jets sprayed in more oil, and now the heat inside the mixing chamber was sufficient to fire the mixture without using a sparking plug. The air shutters closed, and the cycle repeated itself. The engine made a noise like that of a very powerful motor-cycle, and worked roughly on the principle of the blow-lamp, except that it was intermitten and not continuous.

The flying-bomb was kept on a level by gyroscopic controls; it was maintained on its pre-set course by a repeater compass in the nose which caused the gyroscopes to correct any deviation from that course, which had been calculated beforehand to

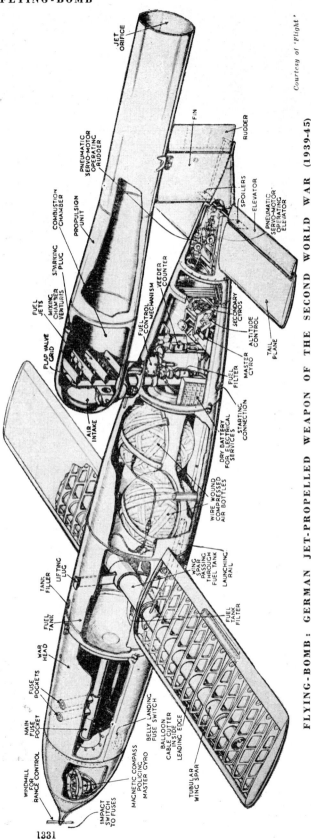

Courtesy of 'Flight'

FLYING-BOMB: GERMAN JET-PROPELLED WEAPON OF THE SECOND WORLD WAR (1939-45)

British Official

FLYING-BOMB TACKLED BY A SPITFIRE
One of the methods adopted by the Royal Air Force against flying-bombs in the Second World War (1939–45) was for the pilots of fighter aircraft to fly alongside and tip them over with their wings. Here a Spitfire is approaching a flying-bomb (left) and tipping it over (right), thus diverting it from an important target.

bring it to its target. The altitude of its flight was automatically controlled by an aneroid barometer. The duration of its flight, which governed the range at which it would begin to glide down to its target, was determined by an air-log. This last was worked by a free airscrew mounted in front of the nose; the screw was turned by the wind of the forward flight, and gradually rotated the air-log backwards until a point was reached at which the log set off detonators attached to the tail-plane. These detonators forced downwards two control tabs and made the aircraft dive. On reaching the ground the detonators earlier described came into action and fired the charge in the war-head.

Defensive measures against the flying-bomb comprised a balloon barrage in the routes taken by the missiles; a massed array of anti-aircraft guns ; and direct attack by fighter aircraft. Our fastest fighters chased and shot down the V.1s, or even crept alongside and tipped their wings to divert them away from a vulnerable target, cr to cause them to crash to the ground. Bombers made continual attacks on the launching sites on the Continent, and on the places where the flying-bombs were known to be built or assembled. From June 13 to September 4, 1944, more than 8,000 flying bombs were launched against England.

Flying Fish. A " fish out of water " is not always the helpless flopping creature which has given us this common expression for the awkward bungler. Indeed, few things are more beautiful than the sight, so frequent in warm seas,

of a company of silvery fish rising suddenly out of the waves under the steamer's bow and darting through the air like huge dragon-flies.

Flying fish do not vibrate their fins in flying as birds flap their wings. They gather speed under water and swoop up into the air. High-speed photographs show that sharp blows of the tail on the water's surface, with a sculling motion, give added power to the take-off. Then the air catches under the broad fins and the fish soar like glider planes. The smaller species of the Atlantic Ocean cover short distances only out of the water, but the larger species, found off California from Point Conception southward, often travel 200 yards. Their fins are eight or nine inches long, and the body may be 18 inches long. It is deep blue on the back and sides, and is silvery underneath. Some 65 species of flying fish are known. All flying fish use their power of flight to escape from their numerous enemies, chief among which are sharks and tunny fish. Most varieties are excellent food. The scientific name of the common flying fish is *Exocoetus volitans;* that of the larger California species, is *Cypselurus californicus.*

Foch, MARSHAL FERDINAND (1851–1929). Among the most famous of the Allied commanders of the First World War (1914–18), Foch (pron. fosh) was born at Tarbes in southern France on October 2, 1851. He became an artillery officer in 1874, studied military strategy, and was appointed director of the French Staff College in 1907. Soon

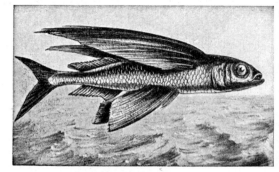

FLYING FISH IN THE AIR
When pursued by underwater enemies, flying fish are in the habit of leaping out of the water and making gliding flights, supported by their long pectoral fins, which resemble wings. The fins are not flapped like a bird's wings.

after the outbreak of the First World War Foch was given command of the 9th Army and played a large part in defeating the Germans in the Battle of the Marne in September 1914. In 1916 he reached the retiring age and gave up his command. In 1918 he had charge of a general Allied reserve on the Western Front, and as a result of the victorious German offensive of March 1918, he was appointed Commander-in-Chief of all the Allied forces on that front.

After checking the German attack he launched his decisive counter-offensive on the Marne on July 18, 1918, which ceased only with the German request for an armistice on October 28, 1918. Made a Marshal of France in August 1918, and later a British Field-Marshal, he was chief military adviser to the Allied delegates at the Peace Conference at Paris, and had much to do with the framing of the Treaty of Versailles between the Allies and Germany. He died on October 20, 1929.

Fog. Dew and fog are much alike, and both are forms of water. Dew is moisture which forms on vegetation. Fog is caused by the presence of tiny drops of water vapour in the atmosphere and a lowering of the temperature to a point at which the moisture in the air is deposited on dust or on other hygroscopic (moisture-attracting) particles in the air which form nuclei upon which vapour can condense into water drops.

Formerly it was thought that dust, and the particles of carbon which make up smoke, were the chief factors in fog formation. Today, however, the theory is that most of the nuclei are tiny particles of salt—from sea spray or from the sand of beaches; or are similar chemical substances passed out by domestic and factory chimneys. Over big towns the dust and smoke particles gives us " pea-soup " fogs when atmospheric conditions are favourable to the condensing of vapour into water drops. So we get the " white " fogs of coastal or country areas, and the " black " fogs which plague industrial regions.

There are several ways in which the temperature of a layer of air is lowered. Warm moist air blowing over a cold surface is cooled, condensing some of its water vapour. The fogs off the coast of New-foundland are due to the fact that air from warmer parts of the Atlantic Ocean blows over the icy Labrador current, becomes chilled, and so condenses its moisture. Wind or rising temperature clears away fogs. It is for this reason that fogs often disappear as the day advances.

The reasons for London's fogs are not hard to find. The prevailing winds are moisture-laden since they blow in from the Atlantic. In winter they meet cooler currents over the land, and mingle with the large amount of dust and chimney-smoke floating about over the city. The fog particles become coated with an oily substance and, therefore, evaporate less readily than over the ocean. The more smoke that rises from a city, the thicker and more frequent its fogs become.

Fogs cause severe hindrance to road and rail traffic and are a source of grave danger to shipping and to aircraft. Until the general use of radio-communication for ships the chief means by which one vessel could warn another of its nearness was by the siren, sounded at frequent intervals. Light-houses and lightships sound foghorns to warn ships of the presence of shoals and rocks. Today several devices based on radar (*q.v.*) aid the mariner to avoid collision. On the roads, mobile acetylene flare lamps, or others which burn petroleum, are brought out and installed at important points along busy arteries.

On our railways, despite the advance of science, we still employ the sound signal given by the explosion of a detonator as the main warning when light or semaphore signals are obscured by fog. Fog-men are called out when a bad fog threatens; the train service is thinned down and runs more slowly. At every important signal post a fog-man takes up his stand; when the semaphore moves to danger he sets a detonator on the running rails so that the approaching train explodes it and warns the driver. Mechanical appliances are used to some extent to apply the detonators to the rails.

The chief danger to aircraft in foggy weather is in approaching and landing at an airfield. Radar, and various systems of guiding in an aircraft by lights and by radio beams are used, but still leave considerable risk. In 1942, during the Second World War, the Petroleum Warfare Department of Britain devised " Fido " (a system of oil-burning flares), which enabled our bombers to continue operating in conditions which would otherwise have kept them grounded.

Folklore. The traditional tales, songs and dances which make up a country's folklore are very old. When the day's work was done, the older folk would tell the younger generation weird tales of gods and men, of ghosts and fairies and animals, which they themselves had heard their fathers tell. They sang stirring songs of battle and mournful ballads which had been handed down from a past so remote that no one can be sure when it began; and mothers crooned their babies to sleep with lullabies almost as old as the human race.

When the harvest had been gathered, or at other times of festival and ceremonial observance, groups of young men and maidens danced the strange old dances that others before them had known for untold centuries. Today many of those ancient tales, songs and dances still live.

Little did the ancient people think that scholars would one day search out and study their simple lore—which is now being done by students and societies in many lands. The first to make a serious study of folklore were the brothers Wilhelm (1786–1859) and Jakob (1785–1863) Grimm, two German scholars whose names are as familiar now to children as to men of learning. Among the tales which they collected from the peasants of Germany are the stories of Lucky Hans, Hansel and Gretel, Princess Snow-White and others. In a similar way we received our own Mother Goose rhymes; from France the stories of Puss in Boots, Little Red Riding Hood and Cinderella; from the North American Negro the stories of Brer Rabbit and Brer Fox, and from other lands and peoples tales which now belong to the children of all the world.

So, too, men have sought and written down the old songs of all nations—the songs of sowing and harvest, of winter and summer, nursery songs, love songs, marriage songs, funeral songs, war songs. The folksongs of Switzerland tell us of mountains and valleys; in their melodies we hear the shep-

FOLK-DANCERS OF HUNGARY AND DENMARK

P. Popper

Originating in religious custom and ceremony, folk-dancing has continued long after the religious significance has died out. Many European folk-dances commemorate more recent customs. Thus, the Hungarian Soldiers' dance (lower) dates from the 17th century when men, previously bemused with wine and dancing, were persuaded to join the army. It is danced by men only. The upper photograph shows a typical Danish folk-dance in progress.

herds' pipes and the yodel of the Alpine dwellers. The folksongs of Scandinavia suggest something of the surging of the ocean in their steady rhythm and through them creeps the murmur of the waves. Those of the British Isles reflect the different characteristics of the people of England, Scotland, Wales and Ireland.

Have you heard the old French song, On the Bridge of Avignon? This was sung by the girls and boys of France more than 400 years ago. It tells how the people of all classes passed over the same bridge in the same way—lords and ladies, clerks and soldiers, pipers and street urchins. So it gives us a picture of France in those early days. In the same way the song Jenny Jones gives us a good description of customs and costumes in early England— with its washing and folding and starching and ironing, and its sickness and death.

Folk-dances are closely connected with folk-songs, and often they even have the same tune. Many folk-dances tell stories just as the songs do. The Swedish weaving dance portrays the story of the flax harvest and the making of the linen. The rows of dancers advance and retreat, advance and retreat, imitating the beating of the flax to separate the fibre from the stem. They whirl and skip and clap their hands, pretending they are using an old spinning wheel ; then the couples go to and fro to represent the movement of the shuttle in weaving, and also imitate the over-and-under progress of the bobbin. Then the finished cloth is rolled up in pantomime, and the workers skip to their homes.

Nearly every nation has its own distinctive dances, such as the Scottish reel, the Irish jig, the Italian tarantella, the Spanish fandango and the Polish mazurka.

Foochow, CHINA. Thirty-four miles up the river Min from the China Sea is the ancient city of Foochow, or Minhow. In spite of some of the modern installations such as an electric-light plant, the city remains less Europeanized than most of the great port cities of China. This may result from the lack of direct import or export trade with foreign lands other than Formosa. Foochow is an old walled city, with wooded hills, tall pagodas, and a trade with other coast cities in local manufactures and agricultural products.

The river teems with traffic. Jostling for space are dilapidated houseboats and ornate junks, frail river craft, and smart new steam launches. Downstream from the interior come small boats laden with fruit, cotton and rice. Outgoing boats are stacked with tea, timber, paper, canned foods, bamboo, matches, spices, grain, and silk and cotton goods from the Foochow mills. Other exports are fine lacquers, dainty steatite or soapstone figures, carved ornaments, and artificial flowers.

The streets are narrow and dirty. Passage is difficult in some because of the crowded display of goods. The principal thoroughfare runs through the south gate, continuing to the river, where it meets the famous Bridge of Ten Thousand Ages. This ancient structure, more than eight centuries old, connects the river-bank with the busy little island of Tongchiu. The bridge is 1,350 feet long, built of enormous slabs of gray granite.

Foochow lies about midway between Amoy and Shanghai, opposite the northern end of the island of Formosa. It is the capital of Fukien province, which by geographic conditions is cut off from the rest of China. The city reached its greatest prosperity in the early 19th century, when the tea trade was at its height. In 1842, by the Treaty of Nanking, it became one of the ports where Europeans and Americans enjoyed freedom from Chinese taxation and jurisdiction ; but these privileges were renounced by Great Britain and the United States in 1943, and by other Powers later. In the city is Fukien Christian University.

During the 1937–45 conflict between China and Japan, Foochow was taken by the Japanese in April 1941, and reoccupied by the Chinese in the following September. The Japanese captured it again in October 1944, the Chinese finally regaining the city on May 18, 1945. The population of the city is estimated at 323,000.

E.N.A.

FOOCHOW : CHINESE PORT ON THE RIVER MIN

The capital of the province of Fukien, in China, Foochow stands on the river Min, which is spanned by the bridge of Ten Thousand Ages (above). Built of enormous granite slabs, this structure is supposed to be 800 years old and is 1,350 feet in length. Foochow is a busy port, its exports including tea, timber, bamboo, and silk and cotton goods from the local mills.

VITAL FUEL *for the* HUMAN MACHINE

No machines can go without fuel, and the human body—the most wonderful machine of all—is no exception. Here we read of what our fuel is (or should be) composed of, and how it makes our ' wheels go round.'

Food. Of Man's three elemental necessities— food, clothing, and shelter—the first which confronts him and the most vital to his existence is food. Plants and animals either adapt themselves to find food or perish as life about them changes. Primitive men, using their wits and strength, struggled for their meals in jungles and on plains; and out of this long fierce contest have come many of the inventions and institutions of our civilization.

Today we continue to struggle for food, but instead of seeking it directly, as did our ancestors with club and spear, we find work for which we are paid; and then, in the more favoured parts of the world, we may choose what we want from an amazing abundance and variety of good things to eat.

When primitive men were hungry they ate wild berries, nuts, fruits, seeds, and roots; they devoured the raw flesh of small animals and the shellfish, for it took them a long time to learn how to make weapons of stone and wood with which to kill or snare the large animals and the darting fish. In those early days, life was either " a feast or a famine "; they gorged after a lucky hunt, and they starved when frost nipped the fruits and the grains. Primitive folk of today live in the same way, consuming vast quantities of food when it is available, and going short for weeks at a time when it is not. However, the difficulties of the primitive food quest benefited early peoples, for they soon found that a group could work better than a single hunter, and thus they learned co-operation and leadership and tolerance. Primitive religions, too, were influenced by the food search. Our ancestors held mystic ceremonies to bring them good fortune in their fishing or hunting. After they began raising crops they worshipped the earth, the sun, the river, as powers to whom they owed fine harvests.

Hunting Gives Way to Cultivation

Domestication of animals brought about a great change both in food supply and in character. Primitive people guarded their flocks and herds from raiding beasts and envious neighbours. As herders they moved from place to place to find fresh pastures —a nomad life, but a far more responsible, happier existence than they had known as hunters, for they had learned to control and multiply food supplies. On up the scale of civilization they moved, by cultivating plants and by changing from hunters or herders to farmers. With herds and crops their food supply was better and steadier than ever before. As hunters, who lived from day to day on whatever they could find for food, they had had little need for the sense of ownership, but now, with herds and flocks, they wanted to hold the animals they guarded, the land they cleared, and the food and skins that they stored to tide them over the winter.

From this sense of property rights, authority and law developed. Conflict and war arose from it, and also the building of defences to protect territorial rights. In wars over fertile farming and grazing lands, some tribes made captives of their enemies, putting them to work on the soil ; and thus the practice of slavery began.

These farming peoples could live in closer settlements than ever before. Hunters require from five to ten square miles per person; from three to five herdsmen may get their food supply from a single square mile; but agricultural folk use far less land— the amount depends upon their farming methods, the fertility of the soil, the kind of crop which is cultivated, and the rainfall.

In the course of time, our ancestors made discoveries and inventions which are now such common features of everyday living that we sometimes do not realize their great significance. They learned how to cure meats and to make pottery bowls in which they stored dried grains and berries. Their diet was greatly improved by the discovery of fire and cooking. When a grower or a herder found himself with more food than he needed, he learned to barter it for other things, and so commerce developed.

Necessity of a Balanced Food Supply

The struggle for food means more than simply finding enough. People who have developed the healthiest bodies, the keenest minds, and the greatest civilizations have been able to get a balanced food supply that contains a sufficient amount of all the elements the body demands. In the Arctic regions, this balance is lacking. The primitive Eskimos live almost wholly on fat and proteins, and their bodies crave the carbohydrates we easily get in vegetables and sweets. On the other hand, in the Tropics, where nature furnishes an abundant supply of carbohydrates, the natives become indolent and will not exert themselves to get the proteins their bodies need.

In the wet monsoon regions rich crops of rice support life for vast populations. China can provide a wide variety of food, but as yet has not developed its great resources. Even today there is comparatively little poultry and cattle raising. The Chinese secure some protein from fish and beans, but lack the acids and the minerals of fruit, which they consider a great luxury. Rice is the great staple crop, and apart from the health aspects, this lack of variety in diet has two disadvantages: it is monotonous, and if the rice crop fails the people may starve.

Since people can best secure a balanced diet in the subtropics and in the southern part of the North Temperate zone, we should expect the first great civilizations to develop in those regions; and it is true that they did—in Egypt and Mesopotamia. Then nomadic peoples from the less fertile north, lured by irrigated fields and orchards, overran those lands and wrecked much of the culture.

In the East, China protected her civilization by throwing a great wall across 1,500 miles of hill and valley to stop the hungry hordes from the north. Likewise in the West, wave after wave of barbarians from the north swept into the fertile Mediterranean lands in search of a better, easier food supply. The Greeks and the Romans were part of this Indo-European flood, but they in turn were conquered by fresh tribes. The Celts of southern Gaul had an advanced agriculture, while that of their British brothers was more primitive. Most of the food plants we know had their origin in the alkaline soil of central Asia or in the Mediterranean basin, and the most prosperous communities have grown up on soils of this kind.

The fertile valleys of Greece supplied its population with the principal foodstuffs—wheat, fruit, and oil—until the 8th or 7th century B.C., when there were too many to be fed by crops from the narrow rocky land. Early wars were fought for land and food, and part of the population was sent to colonize Asia Minor, Italy, and Sicily. Increasing stores of grain had to be imported from Pontus, Thrace, Syria, Egypt, Libya, and Sicily. Sparta defeated Athens by destroying the navy that guarded Athenian commerce.

In Rome, constant warfare took farmers from their fields. Great landowners raised luxuries with slave labour, instead of cultivating food crops. Rome imported its wheat, and sent out expeditions to take new lands until most of Europe came under its sway. Colonies went forth to secure this agricultural domain. The cry for grain from Rome's hungry citizens brought "corn laws" to provide cheaper bread.

History abounds in wars over fertile lands. Caesar tells us of the Helvetians, who finding their mountain valley could not yield enough wheat, poured down into the rich Rhône valley. Many battles have been fought for India's rich acres, the Nile delta, the wheat lands of North Africa, and other rich areas. And, lest we should be tempted to think that this "land-grabbing" belongs only to past ages, we may remind ourselves that Adolf Hitler's avowed motive for his seizure of neighbouring lands during the years 1937 to 1945 was Germany's need for more agricultural lands to support her growing population, which was being forced from agricultural work into factories.

As the nations of the world have prospered and their populations have increased, they have looked for new territory to raise food to fill their growing needs and to provide homes for their colonists. Spain sent Columbus across an uncharted ocean to find another route to the eastern spice countries; then it attempted to spread a vast empire in the New World. England, too, made the northern section

of this new land a part of her far-flung empire. Since then, North America has been a haven for people from other overpopulated nations. It offered not only rich acres but also new food plants that have improved the world's diet—potatoes, sweet potatoes, tomatoes, maize, ground-nuts, cacao, new types of beans. Its spreading acres have multiplied the world's available food supply.

Science, of course, has increased the available food supply—directly by improved agricultural methods; and indirectly in a score of ways concerned with improved preservation, packing and transport. Thus the food-growing areas of the world support a constantly increasing population, unless Man with his destructive wars upsets the balance. This he can do by killing off hundreds of thousands, or even millions, of the persons who should till the soil; and also by physical devastation of the land. It is significant that great wars in our time have usually begun at a season when the harvests of the aggressor states have been safely garnered. And a

PLANTS THAT GIVE FOOD AND DRINK
Some of the plants which supply us with food and drink :
1. Wheat: ripe ear, flower spike, foliage. 2. Oats. 3. Barley: ripe ear, flower spike, leaves. 4. Maize: plant and ripe cob. 5. Rice: plant and ripe head. 6. Tea. 7. Hops. 8. Vanilla: flower and pod. 9. Sugar-cane. 10. Coffee : leaves and berries. 11. Cocoa (cacao) pods.

succession of poor harvests is sufficient to deter a would-be conqueror from invading the territory of his neighbours.

Every time you wink your eye, or move your arm, or take a breath, you are using the energy provided by food you ate some time in the past. Our foods supply the energy for the movement of our bodies. They also furnish the fuel that keeps our bodies warm. Our bodies are constantly losing heat, and they would soon become cold if we did not keep supplying them with fuel in the form of food. Foods help us to grow; they give us strong teeth, bones, and muscles; and they make blood. They build up our tissues as these wear out. They keep up the fuel supply that gives us energy and provide fuel reserves which we store up in the form of fat. They also keep our body engines regulated by supplying minerals and roughage and other materials needed to make them run smoothly.

Scientists have divided the nutrients contained in food into five classes: fats, proteins, carbohydrates, minerals, and vitamins. Fats, proteins, and carbohydrates are all fuel foods. Proteins and minerals are important in body building and repair work. Minerals and vitamins play an essential part in regulating the body. Another important body regulator is water.

Some People Need More Food Than Others

The more active we are, the more fuel our bodies use. Children use more food than do adults, in proportion to their sizes. Adults who work or play hard use more than inactive persons. Furthermore, the larger and heavier the body, the greater the amount of fuel used in moving it. The amount of heat contributed by the various foods is measured in *calories*, as weight is measured in pounds. A calorie is the amount of heat required to raise the temperature of a kilogram of water (about a quart) one degree Centigrade. While an eight-year-old child may require 1,500 calories of food each day, an older boy may need as many as 4,000 calories and his father perhaps only 3,500.

Foods vary in the amount of heat they give off in the body. Have you ever seen oil or lard burn? If you have, you will remember that they gave a very hot flame. Similarly the fats in our bodies, such as butter and oils, give many calories of heat. They are the greatest heat-producing foods. Butter, cream, lard, and the fat of meat are typical animal fats. Olive oil and cocoa butter are vegetable fats. When we eat more of the fats than we immediately need for energy, the excess is deposited as a layer of fat just under the skin, covering the bones and filling out the hollows between the muscles, and at various places about the organs within our bodies. That is why we can live for some time without food. We use our reserve fat for energy. Primitive peoples, whose food supply was often very irregular, could survive times of famine by using up the fat that they had stored in their bodies during the days when food was plentiful. Even today, when most of us have regular daily meals, we call upon our reserve fuel supplies when we are ill.

The fat we store up also helps to keep our organs in good working positions and forms a padding for nerve centres, thus keeping us from being irritable. To be thin is a great disadvantage, especially for young people. On the other hand, a considerable degree of overweight in middle-aged persons shortens the number of years they can expect to live. If we habitually maintain about the weight that is normal for us, we can be certain that we are taking in the proper number of calories.

The carbohydrates, which are chiefly the sugars and the starches, are also heat producers. Sugar, in particular, is a better fuel for muscular work than is fat. But the carbohydrates contain only about 1,820 calories to the pound; whereas the fats average 4,080 calories. In other words, the fuel value of the carbohydrates is less than half the fuel value of the fats. This class of foods, which includes cereals, bread, potatoes, and certain other vegetables, forms the bulk of our diet.

While the protein foods, such as eggs and lean meat, also supply fuel for the body, their most important service is in building and repairing its tissues.

Everyone is born with the possibility of growing to a certain height, and nearly everyone has the possibility of developing a healthy body. Whether we grow as strong and tall as our inheritance allows depends, for one thing, on whether we supply the right kind and amount of materials for building our bodies, since our bodies are made of the same substances as are our foods.

For growth and repair of tissues the body must have a constant supply of protein which, for example, is used largely in the building of the muscles. Though proteins are found in both animal and vegetable foods, they are of different kinds, and not all of them are equally nourishing. Meat contains the highest percentage of protein. Milk, eggs, fish, cheese, nuts, beans, peas, and cereal products are other foods that contain a large amount.

Minerals are widely distributed among our foods, and almost any mixed diet supplies a sufficient quantity. Two important minerals, however, may not be contained in sufficient quantity in our ordinary diet. One of these is lime (calcium). If we do not get enough lime, our bones will be small and weak and perhaps misshapen. Our teeth will be of poor quality, and our blood will lack an essential element. Milk is the one rich source of calcium. Since milk is used in the preparation of ice cream, soups, creamed vegetables, and other dishes, such foods help to supply our milk requirements. Egg yolk and cheese contain more calcium than do most foods; some vegetables contain small amounts. Meat is poor in calcium.

Iron Essential for Red Blood Cells

Iron is another mineral to keep in mind. If we get too little, our blood will not be able to do its work of carrying oxygen to all parts of the body. As a result, we may become anaemic and weak. Liver, egg yolk, syrup, whole wheat, beans, peas, prunes, and spinach are rich in iron. Lean meat, if the blood has not been washed out of it, is an excellent source of iron. Recent studies show that not all of the iron in foods is available for use in the body. Scientists tell us, for example, that only 25 per cent of the iron in spinach is usable, whereas 60 per cent of the iron in liver and 50 per cent of the iron in beef can be used. It has also been found that copper as well as iron is necessary for building the colouring matter, or *haemoglobin*, in our red blood cells.

Two other minerals, phosphorus and iodine, are lacking in some diets. If we get enough protein, we

Proteins: Body Builders. — Some valuable sources of animal proteins are milk, meat, fish, liver, chicken, cheese, and eggs. Among foods rich in vegetable proteins are beans, peas, whole-wheat bread, and whole-grain cereals. Animal proteins are the easier to digest.

Carbohydrates: Energy Makers.— Bread, potatoes, carrots, spinach, bananas, apples, oranges, prunes, tomatoes, cereal (with sugar and cream), baked beans, maize or Indian corn, figs, ice cream, jelly, syrup — all are good sources of carbohydrates, and many provide roughage.

Fats: Heat and Energy Makers.— Here are shown the main foods containing fats; ways in which they blend with other foods are also seen. Milk contains fat as well as protein. Butter, lard and many vegetable oils are among the commonest fats present in a normal diet.

Minerals: Bone, Teeth and Muscle Builders, Body Regulators.—These foods supply the minerals needed to make strong bodies and red blood. Milk is the best source of calcium and contains almost all the essential minerals. Many of the foods on this page provide vitamins.

need not worry about phosphorus, for most foods that contain protein also contain phosphorus. Like calcium, this mineral is used for bones and teeth. Iodine is needed by the thyroid gland, an important gland in the neck (*see* Gland). In most parts of Britain this mineral is plentiful in the water and in the soil, and the normal diet contains enough of it. But in other lands, especially in regions far from the sea, iodine is often lacking and must be supplied by including such foods as fish or iodized table salt in the diet.

Even when we are full grown, our diet must include all of the building materials, since each day small quantities of them are lost. The body is constantly breaking down and being repaired, and if the repair materials are not at hand, bones, muscles, teeth, and all other tissues gradually deteriorate, Children as well as adults need these repair materials.

Chief among the body regulators are the vitamins. which must be in the diet for proper nourishment. Even though we supply the fuel and the building materials, the body cannot use these satisfactorily without the vitamins. We do not know exactly how each vitamin does its work, but we do know what foods are rich in vitamins and what happens when we do not get enough of them. We know that vitamins help us to grow and protect us against such "deficiency" diseases as beri-beri, scurvy, and rickets. (*See* Vitamins).

Why the Diet Needs Roughage

Cellulose is needed in the diet to keep our digestive organs working satisfactorily. Cellulose is the "roughage," the coarse indigestible fibres, found in vegetables such as green beans and celery, in the bran of cereals, and in the skins and pulp of fruit. Green vegetables and fruit are the best foods to eat for roughage because they supply minerals as well.

Although many of our foods contain water, we need to drink at least six glasses of water a day to keep our bodies working smoothly. Water makes up nearly two-thirds of our weight. We use it in breathing, and also to throw off waste by perspiration and through the kidneys and bowels.

By supplying the right kinds of foods in the right proportion—that is, by a "balanced diet"—we give our bodies an opportunity to serve us well from childhood until we are old. When we fail in any respect, we may be sure that in the long run we shall suffer for it. The intervals at which food should be consumed are very largely dependent on habits, but it is of importance that physiological habits should be engendered from the earliest childhood onwards, in order that the digestive organs also may fall into rhythmical habits of activity, rest and recovery.

Finally, we must remember that the method of cooking food plays almost as important a part in getting proper nourishment as the selection of the food itself. Some important food constituents dissolve in water, and so may be lost unless care is taken to preserve them. This applies to most fresh vegetables, and for this reason they should be cooked in as little water as possible and the water in which they have been boiled should be served with them. Careless cooks often throw away the most nourishing parts of a dish. Greasy fried foods, rich gravies, and rich pastries, while they are energy-producing foods, should not be eaten in excess because they are difficult to digest. (*See* Cooking).

Food Preservation.

At some time in his early history Man, the hunter, found it convenient to dry or "cure" some of the flesh of animals killed in the chase. He was by no means as particular as his later descendants, and as long as the meat was eatable it cannot have mattered much about it being what we should call fresh or "good." The discovery that the sun dried and preserved meat probably came about accidentally; this crude process was used from very early times and is still common in all but the coldest regions. An example is the "biltong" of South Africa—strips of bullock's flesh dried in the sun. People living in the regions where there is a long and hard winter naturally came to use quite the opposite method of preserving their food—by freezing it. In Siberia today people dig out the frozen bodies of animals, preserved by Nature, and eat the flesh. As a result explorers came to hear about the carcases of ancient mammoths, buried nobody knows how many ages ago where they died, but with the flesh still clothing the bones.

These two methods of keeping meat eatable are basic ones on which we rely much today. They are "physical" methods, not utilising any chemical process for the purpose. Chemical methods *are* used in food preserving, but much less than formerly. Strict laws prescribe just which preservatives may be used, since some that were employed years ago were harmful to persons eating the foods so treated. Sulphur dioxide and benzoic acid are used to some extent in sausages and other forms of meat, and in jams, other fruit products, and beverages.

The laws mentioned above allow such preservatives as salt, vinegar, and sugar to be used. Bacon and hams are salted and then cured in the smoke from a fire to preserve them. Fish are salted or pickled in brine ; some kinds are also smoked. At many fishing villages in Britain you may see fish strung in a stick or a line and hung out to dry in the sun for the family needs. Pork, beef and mutton are pickled in brine. The pickling of onions or shallots in vinegar, after boiling with herbs and spices, is a commonplace. Vegetables such as beans or cabbage are salted down in barrels and so kept in good condition for use.

Scientific Methods of Dehydration

All the processes so far described alter the flavour of the foods for which they are used—all, that is, except refrigeration or cold storage as we understand it today. We must put up with the salty flavour of bacon or ham, though that is an attraction to most people. We must tolerate the dryness of sun-dried meats, for we cannot put back the juices and flavour which the sun took out of the flesh. But there is a modern process of drying, called dehydration, which takes out the moisture from meat and vegetables and does not rob them of their typical flavour.

Vegetables are cooked before being dried by artificial heat in the absence of air; fruits are often dried uncooked. Dehydrated vegetables can be restored to an appetising form by adding water and by heating them. Dehydration is now a scientific method of preserving; its products are eaten by soldiers and sailors; explorers take them with their other stores when venturing into regions where food supply is problematical.

FOOD PRESERVATION

Powdered milk and powdered eggs are invaluable forms of preserved food. The milk is first concentrated, with or without its cream content; it is then sprayed along with hot air into a chamber where it dries and falls as a powder to the floor. In the case of "evaporated" milk the greater amount of the water content is driven off by heat, the process being controlled so that the flavour is not impaired. Sweetened evaporated milk, and what we knew many years ago as "condensed" milk, contain sugar. Some of the products we have mentioned are canned or bottled to keep them free from contamination by germs (*q.v.*) in the atmosphere after the preliminary process has been completed. The heat needed for preserving—killing any bacteria or other germs present—serves for cooking or partially cooking such foods as soup, meat, fruit, or vegetables. (*See* Canning.)

Refrigeration and cold storage (*see* Freezing) enable meat and fruit to be brought in perfect condition from producing countries overseas. Food reserves are built up in our port warehouses by storing these comestibles in refrigerated chambers where the temperature is kept low enough to pre-

Fruits naturally contain acid, some more than others. A fruit not plentiful in acid will not " set " as well as a more acid fruit when being made into jam. That is one reason why apples, rich in acid, are mixed with blackberries to make jam, since the latter fruit is not so acid. Pectin prepared commercially from fruit residue, or from that of sugar beet, may be added to jam in the making, to set it. Chemically pectin is an *ester*—a product of the reaction of an alcohol with a concentrated acid.

The jam jar or bottle has to be sealed from the air by a special lid or by a sheet of waxed paper tightly fastened over the mouth; otherwise the jam may go mouldy. The reasons for excluding air are made plain in our story of Bacteria. Having killed harmful bacteria by "heat-treatment"—raising the foodstuff to a temperature at which most germs cannot live—it would be futile if we did not take steps to prevent access of such organisms thereafter.

In preserving fruits and vegetables by sterilization and by bottling, the food is placed in a wide-mouthed jar and juice or syrup added if necessary. Then the jars are placed in a sterilizing pan containing water, and the water raised to the boiling point. While steam is still rising freely from the mouth of the jar, the lid is applied and clamped or screwed, and the jar allowed to cool. Steam still in the jar condenses, and leaves an airless space at the top; atmospheric pressure outside holds the lid down tightly on to a rubber sealing ring, and so hermetically seals the jar until we need its contents. This is essentially the same method as that used in canning.

FOOD PRESERVATION : PASTEURISED MILK IN SEALED CONTAINERS
Pasteurisation does not alter the taste of milk but greatly reduces the number of bacteria present. In the process milk is subjected to a temperature between 145 and 150 degrees Fahrenheit for at least half an hour and then cooled rapidly to about 55 degrees. Here the pasteurised milk is seen being sealed in sterilised paper cartons.

Milk is heat-treated, in a great many of our commercial dairies and bottling establish-

vent germs living and growing. Fruits such as bananas are allowed to ripen gradually in Britain by controlling the temperature of the chambers in which they are stored on arrival. Most butcher shops have a refrigerated store room in which they keep meat until needed for sale. The thrifty cook puts the meat purchased at once into *her* refrigerator.

By boiling fruits with sugar we obtain the delicious jams and jellies which enable us to enjoy summer's gifts all through the wintry days. Boiling drives off most of the water contained in the fruit; it also binds the rest of the water into a syrup with the sugar and makes it unavailable for bacteria to feed on, or those organisms which cause fermentation. A substance known as *pectose* is naturally present in fleshy fruits, and is changed into *pectin* as the fruit ripens, by the action of an enzyme (*q.v.*). Boiling fruit along with water causes the pectin to form a jelly when sugar and an acid are present.

ments, to kill the germs of bovine tuberculosis which may be present. Pasteurising, named after Louis Pasteur (*q.v.*), was the forerunner of such germ-killing processes; the name applies strictly to a method in which the temperature is raised to about 145° F., which kills the tubercle bacteria along with others which cause milk to go sour. But unless milk is decanted into a sterilized jug or other container, and protected from the air, it may pick up new souring bacteria from the atmosphere.

Owing to the improvements in the manufacture of "dry ice" (solid carbon dioxide) it is possible to pack fresh fruits or vegetables taken from a refrigerator and to send them out under temporary refrigeration to the shops. A piece of dry ice will keep the temperature in the container low enough to ensure that strawberries (for example) reach the purchaser in prime condition even when they are out of season, (*See* Freezing.)

Foot. In the simplest forms of animal life we do not find special organs for locomotion. In one-celled animals, such as the amoeba, a bit of the living substance is pushed out and then the remainder of the body is pulled up to it. The movement of the worm is somewhat similar; one section of the body is thrust forward and then the other parts are brought up by a creeping or crawling motion. As we ascend the scale of animal life, we find definite organs developing to move the animal about. These organs, which we call feet and legs, occur most commonly in pairs of two, four or six.

Comparison of the foot in various animals shows many interesting adaptations. In the human foot we distinguish the ankle (*tarsus*), the instep (*metatarsus*), and the toes (*phalanges*). The heel rests upon the ground, making what is called a " plantigrade " foot. The bear also has such a foot. Other animals, like the cat and dog, walk on their toes, or digits. They are said to have a " digitigrade " foot, with the heel up in the air and the instep lifted away from the earth.

In deer, cattle, horses, and some other animals, the animal stands on the tip-end of a single toe; the heel, instep, and digits are then away from the earth and only the tip of one toe is in contact. Animals with the digitigrade foot are much swifter than those with the plantigrade type.

The horse has the most remarkable example of a modified foot. Not only are the heel and instep off the earth, but the bones of the instep have become reduced to one and the animal walks upon the tip of a single toe on each of its four feet. Fossils found in rocks show that the horse's foot has been derived from that of an original five-toed ancestor, by suppression and consolidation of parts. It is estimated that these changes in the formation of the horse's hoofs extend over a period of geological history of more than 40 million years. (*See* Evolution; Horse.)

The animals which have feet most nearly resembling those of Man are the monkeys and apes. But their feet are more like hands, for the great toe can be used like a thumb, and there are no arches in their feet, such as Man has developed.

The human foot is beautifully adapted to the work it has to do. Its many small parts, like those of a delicately balanced machine, are perfectly co-ordinated and adjusted to bear the weight

of the body and to carry us over the ground. It has 26 bones. Held in place by ligaments, tendons, and muscles, the bones form two main arches— one from the heel to toes, called the longitudinal arch; the other across the instep, called the transverse arch or mediotarsal arch. These give the foot strength, and support the body's weight. The longitudinal arch adds spring to the instep. It rests on thick muscle, which softens the jolting as the weight of the body is shifted from one foot to the other in walking or running.

The movement of the foot is largely controlled by the muscles of the lower leg, which are attached to it by tendons passing through the ankle. The ankle is above the heel, and has a joint which acts as a hinge between leg and foot. The toes are jointed, so that the foot bends easily and the motion of walking is, or should be, almost as smooth as the rolling of a wheel.

HUMAN FOOT AND ITS STRUCTURE

From heel to toes the foot is built rather like an arch. The calcaneus is the bone forming the rear pillar, the metatarsals constituting the front one. The astragalus is the ' keystone ' of the arch.

In walking one should point the feet straight ahead and shift the weight from heel to toes in such a way as to give one the feeling that the toes are gripping the ground at the end of each step. No machine deserves better care than the foot. It should be rested frequently and bathed daily. Stockings that are smooth, well fitted, and free of darns, help to prevent blisters, callouses, and corns. Shoes should be fitted with extreme care. A good shoe has a straight inner line, a flexible inner shank, a broad toe, and a broad, low heel. An ill-fitting shoe may cause bunions or even in time dislocate the bones. After buying well-made and well-fitting footwear it is foolish to risk having them spoilt or even made a danger by unskilled repair. Amateur cobbling may upset the balance of the foot, besides rendering the shoes uncomfortable.

The condition called " broken or fallen arch " is really a displacement of the bones of the arch. It is sometimes incorrectly called " flat-foot," which is a permanent deformity of the bones of the foot, originating in infancy or peculiar to certain racial types. The foot as a measure of length comes from the assumed length of the human foot, and is very old. The Greek foot was 12·45 inches long, the Roman 11·65 inches, and the French 12·8 inches.

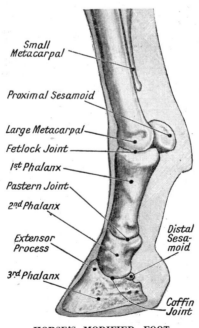

HORSE'S MODIFIED FOOT

In a horse's foot the bones are the same as those of a human finger or toe. Fossils show that the horse's foot has been derived from that of a five-toed ancestor.

FEET FOR LIFE ON LAND AND WATER

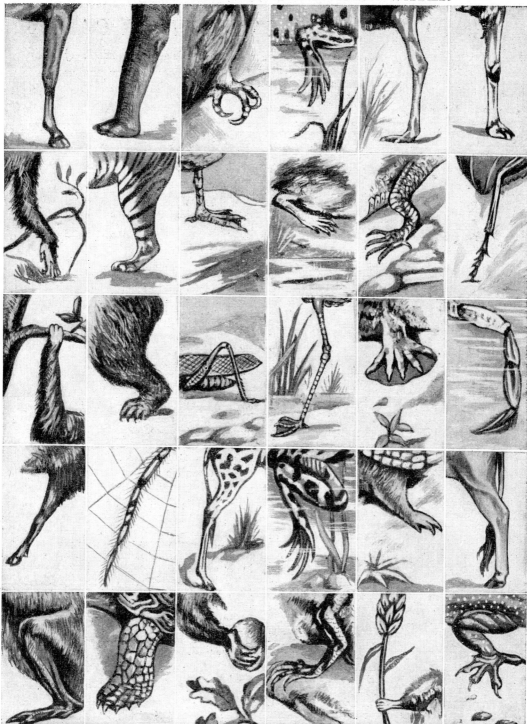

Here are diverse kinds of feet. From left to right, in the top row : Horse, Elephant, Eagle, Newt, Ostrich, Camel ; second row down : Chimpanzee, Tiger, Duck, Water Shrew, Lizard, Tiger Beetle ; third row : Sloth Bear, Locust, Flamingo, Duck-billed Platypus, Crab ; fourth row : Peccary, Garden Spider, Giraffe, Frog, Armadillo, Ox ; bottom row ; Kangaroo, Box Tortoise, Squirrel, Iguana, Harvest Mouse, Gecko. The animals which have feet most closely resembling those of Man are the apes and monkeys ; but their feet are really more like hands, having no arches, such as Man has developed. A camel's foot is like a spongy pad, which spreads out when put to the ground, allowing the animal to travel over loose sand without sinking in, owing to its weight being distributed over a wide area. An elephant's foot somewhat resembles a camel's, in expanding under pressure.

BRITAIN'S NATIONAL WINTER GAMES

Association and Rugby football are watched or played by hundreds of thousands of people in Great Britain every week during the winter months. Here the main points of the two codes are explained.

Football has long been the principal winter pastime in Britain. No one knows exactly how it was first introduced into the country. The ancient Romans and Greeks had their ball games, and it is probable that football had its origin in one of the games brought to this country by the Romans.

Association football or Soccer is played with a round ball (upper), Rugby players using the oval one (lower).

The earliest authentic references to the game occurred in the 12th century, but for a long time it was unpopular with the authorities, one of their objections being that it interfered with the practice of archery. In 1349, during the reign of Edward III, it was unlawful to play football, and it was banned in Scotland in 1458. It was not until the 17th century that it began to receive official recognition, and Charles II is said to have been the first king to arrange a game. From then onwards, except for a few years early last century, it increased in popularity.

We do not know very much about the game of football as it was played originally. There is evidence, however, that not so very long ago a game took place in which all the players wore boots with projecting nails. The pitch was some 200 yards long, and the goals consisted merely of two upright posts without a cross-bar. Even the 1860 rules of the Blackheath Rugby Club allowed the practice of hacking or kicking an opponent !

The Association game is controlled by the Football Association, which was formed in 1863. Rules were drawn up, referees appointed, and many improvements made. Gradually the game became less rough and more skilful until the present-day standard of excellence was reached.

North America, Eire, Australia and certain of the English public schools have their own particular kinds of football, but here we shall confine ourselves to a description of the two main codes as played in Britain—Association (Soccer) and Rugby (Rugger). The title Soccer is derived from an old Anglo-Saxon word meaning a ruffian or hooligan and was applied to players of Association football by supporters of Rugby who considered Soccer a rough, vulgar game. Rugby football took its name from Rugby School where it originated in 1823. The chief difference between the two is that in Rugby handling is permitted, whereas in Association it is almost entirely forbidden.

ASSOCIATION : Each team has 11 players, five forwards, three half-backs, two full-backs and a goalkeeper. The only member of the side who is allowed to touch the ball with his hands while it is in play is the goalkeeper, and his side is penalized if he carries it more than four steps, or handles it outside the penalty area. The ball is round, has a circumference of 27 to 28 inches, and must weigh not less than 14 nor more than 16 ounces. The duration of a game is two equal periods of 45 minutes, and after the interval the teams change ends. The object of the game, started by a centre-forward kicking off from the middle of the half-way line, is to score goals by kicking or heading the ball into the opponent's goal, the team scoring most goals winning the game.

The game is stopped, and a free kick awarded to the other side, if a player is guilty of tripping or otherwise fouling an opponent, or if he handles the ball while it is in play. If the ball is sent beyond the touch (side) lines, it is thrown in by one of the team opposing that of the player who last touched it. Should a member of a defending side cause the ball to go over his own goal-line, a corner (a kick taken from near the corner flag) is awarded to the other side by the referee—the sole controller of the game.

The technique has altered considerably in recent years, the individual art of dribbling—running with the ball in front of the toes—having been dropped in favour of teamwork and tactical passing.

What Constitutes being Off-side

One of the most difficult of the referee's many tasks is to decide whether a player is off-side. A player is off-side if he is nearer his opponents' goal-line than the ball at the moment the ball is played unless : (1) he is in his own half of the field of play ; (2) there are two opponents nearer to their own goal-line than he is ; (3) the ball last touched an opponent or was played by him ; (4) he receives the ball direct from a goal or corner kick, a throw-in, or after it has been dropped by the referee.

Twelve yards from the goal is the penalty spot from which a penalty kick is taken when the referee has adjudged a foul to have been committed within the penalty area. Players of the penalized side (except the goalkeeper) are not allowed to defend their goal, so that in most cases a penalty kick results in a goal.

Association football was played by amateurs only until 1885, when professionalism was sanctioned, and in 1888 the Football League came into being, with a membership of 12 clubs. There are now 88 clubs organized within the League into three Divisions, the Third Division having a Northern and Southern Section. Altogether about 400 clubs engage professional footballers, and there are approximately 40,000 amateur clubs scattered throughout great Britain.

In 1872 the first international match between countries of the United Kingdom was played in Scotland, with an English eleven opposing a home team. Normally annual matches are played between England, Ireland, Scotland and Wales, sometimes supplemented by contests with teams from abroad.

Every year when conditions permit the leading English, and some Welsh, teams compete for the Football Association Cup. This competition was started in 1871 and since 1923 the final has been played at Wembley Stadium, London.

The dimensions of the playing field are : length—minimum 100 yards, maximum 120 yards ; breadth minimum 50 yards, maximum 80 yards. The goals are eight yards wide and eight feet high. To mark the goal area lines are drawn from a point six yards from, and at right angles to, each goal-post for six yards, and then connected by a line drawn parallel to the goal-line. To mark the penalty area, lines are drawn 18 yards from each goal-post for a distance of 18 yards at right angles to the goal-line, and connected by a line parallel to it.

RUGBY. The ball used in this game is oval in shape, about 11 inches long, 24 to 25½ inches in circumference, and weighs between 13 and 15 ounces. The goal posts are 18½ feet apart, with a cross-bar 10 feet from the ground and the uprights extending at least a foot above it. A team consists of 15 players, usually made up of eight forwards, four three-quarter backs, two half-backs and one full back. Games between teams of seven are also played by some clubs at the end of the season.

Scoring is done by tries and goals. A try, scored when a player grounds

FOOTBALL : SOCCER PLAYERS
Incidents in a game of Association football : 1. Scoring a goal ; 2. Breasting the ball ; 3. Heading ; 4. Dribbling ; 5. Good save by the goalkeeper ; 6. Overhead clearance ; 7. Throwing in ; 8. A pass ; 9. Goalkeeper punching the ball away. On the left is a plan of the field.

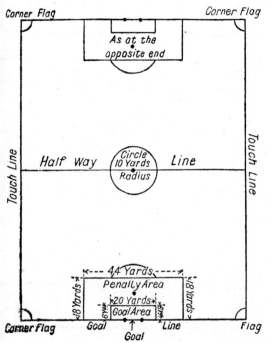

the ball behind his opponents' goal-line, counts three points. A converted try adds two more points to the score, a conversion being made when the ball is placed on the ground and kicked between the posts and over the cross-bar. A dropped goal counts four points and is made when a player in possession of the ball lets it fall from his hand or hands and kicks it at the first rebound over the bar and between the posts. A goal from a free kick or penalty kick counts three points.

Passing the ball forward is not allowed, but the use of both feet and hands is permitted. The game includes individual running with the ball and interpassing of the ball from one player to another. Tackling is allowed, a tackle occurring when the holder of the ball in the field of play is grasped by one or more players of the opposing team in such a way that there is a moment when he cannot pass the ball or play it with his feet. One of the main features of Rugby football is the scrummage. A loose scrum or scrummage is formed by one or more players from each team closing round the

FOOTBALL : THE RUGBY CODE

Unlike Soccer players (*see* preceding page) Rugby footballers are allowed to handle the ball. The field of play is shown below on the right. Above players are seen in action : 1. Passing on being tackled ; 2. Taking a pass ; 3. About to kick ; 4. Tackling ; 5. Scoring a try ; 6. Taking a place kick ; 7. Running with the ball ; 8. Making a mark ; 9. A tight scrum.

ball when it is on the ground and trying to force it out backwards with their feet. In a set or tight scrum the forwards close up in three rows (usually three in the front row, two in the second and three in the third) in readiness to allow the ball to be put on the ground between the two sets of forwards. As soon as the ball has been put in the scrum, the forwards endeavour to force it backwards out of the scrum with their feet.

Play is divided into two halves of not more than 40 minutes each, the teams changing ends after the interval. The game, which is played by amateurs only, is controlled by the Rugby Union, formed in 1871, and international matches are played between England, Scotland, Ireland, Wales and France in normal times. Teams from New Zealand, Australia and South Africa also occasionally visit Great Britain. Professional clubs in the north of England play a game called Rugby League Football, in which only thirteen players form the team. It also differs in other respects from the Rugby Union game.

The dimensions of a Rugby Union playing-field are 75 yards wide and 110 yards long. The field is further marked out by two lines drawn at a distance of 25 yards from either goal-line ; and two more lines 10 yards on either side of the halfway line.

Ford, HENRY (1863–1947). In 1893 a horseless buggy, as motor-cars were then called, chugged through the streets of Detroit, Michigan, in the United States. Crowds gathered whenever it appeared. Terrified horses ran away at its approach. That motor-car, driven and made by Henry Ford, was the first of many millions produced by the genius who was destined in later years to make more cars than any other man in the world.

Henry Ford was born on July 30, 1863, on a farm near Dearborn, Michigan. His mother died when he was 12. At 16 Ford secured a job in a machine shop in Detroit, also working four hours every night as a watchmaker's assistant. Later he was employed in an engine shop, and set up and repaired steam- engines used on farms. In 1884 he took charge of a 40-acre farm his father had given him, married, built his own house from timber felled by himself, and seemed to have settled down. But after two years of farming he went back to Detroit and worked as night engineer for the Detroit Edison Company.

There he began to experiment with a petrol motor vehicle. In 1899 he left his engineering post and helped to found the Detroit Automobile Company then about to build motor-cars. But the business men whose financial support he was

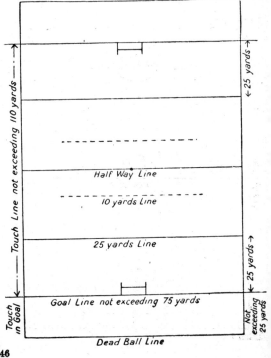

His son, Edsel Bryant Ford (1893–1943), was president of the company from 1918 to 1943. A grandson Henry (b. 1918) became president in 1945.

Foreign Exchange. If we go into a shop and offer £1 in payment for something we have bought, we have money ready where the seller of the goods is. But if a person in London wants to buy from a firm in Edinburgh something priced at £1, it will actually cost him more than a pound; he will have to pay in addition the expense of transferring the money from London to Edinburgh—postage plus 3d. registration fee, or postage plus 2d. poundage on a postal order, or postage plus 2d. stamp on a cheque. To make £1 available in Edin-

forced to seek refused to manufacture the type of car Ford insisted upon. He wanted to manufacture cars in quantities at a price within the reach of many; they wanted to make more expensive cars to order. He, therefore, resigned in 1902 and built two racing cars, one of which established, by an unbroken series of victories, a reputation which enabled him to found the Ford Motor Company early in 1903.

The original car, a twin cylinder of 8 h.p., was gradually developed until 1909, when Ford decided to concentrate on a one-design programme

HENRY FORD : GENIUS OF THE MOTOR-CAR

As the pioneer of the production of motor vehicles in large numbers at low cost, Ford built up one of the most amazing factory systems in the world. The English Ford works at Dagenham, Essex (lower) use the same mass-production methods as the vast plant at Dearborn, near Detroit, in the United States. Henry Ford made his first car in 1892, and in the upper photograph he is seen seated in that historic machine.

with the "model T." This model was continued until 1928, when a new one was introduced, to be followed by the small 9 h.p. and the large 8-cylinder designs. Throughout his career Ford kept his three original points in front of him: simplicity, lightness and low initial cost. He aimed to make every part that went into his cars. He acquired iron and coal mines, forests, mills and factories to produce and shape his steel and alloys, his fuel, wood, glass and leather. He built up railway and steamship lines, and an aeroplane freight service, in order to transport his products. The same methods he applied to the manufacture of farm tractors.

Mass production was Ford's main idea. Each man was given only one task, which he did over and over until it became automatic. Conveyors (q.v.) brought the job to the man, instead of the workman wasting time going to the job. Mechanization was brought to the farthest possible pitch, while in all Ford factories, both American and English, the latest and best tools were invariably used. Ford died on April 8, 1947.

burgh costs a person in London at least £1 0s. 4½d. This shows the difference between money *here* and money *elsewhere*. A person with £100 in London cannot use it to pay for goods in Edinburgh, Glasgow, Belfast, etc., until he has transferred some of his money *here* for a right to money *there*; usually some expense will be incurred to do this, so that £100 in London will not yield quite £100 in, say, Edinburgh.

Thanks to our excellent postal services and the network of post offices and banks, the cost of transferring money is nowadays quite small. In medieval times it was considerable, since a messenger would have to be sent with it; and even 150 years ago it was so expensive and hazardous that instead of sending gold from, say, London to Edinburgh, a merchant would contrive to transfer a debt. Thus, suppose A in London owed B in Edinburgh £100. He might try to locate another merchant (C) in London to whom D in Edinburgh owed £100, and then arrange that C should ask D to pay the money to B instead of to D. A would really buy C's right to £100 in Edinburgh and transfer that right to B. The arrangement was thus:

A (London) bought goods from B (Edinburgh)

A pays C ↓　　　　　　　　↑ D pays B

C (London) sells goods to D (Edinburgh)

Often C would draw what is called a bill of exchange on D. Thus:

> £100.　　　　　London,
> 　　　　　　　　June 15, 1800.
> 　On demand pay to B of Edinburgh for the credit of A of London the sum of One Hundred Pounds value received.
> To D.,
> 　Edinburgh.　　　　　　　C.

Nowadays a postal order, money order or cheque would generally take the place of such a bill of exchange; but fundamentally the arrangement is the same. If the post office in London (C) sells A a money order, it is really asking its agent, the post office in Edinburgh (D), to pay £100 to B. If A sends a cheque to B, he is really assuming that his bank in London (C) has already arranged that its branch in Edinburgh (D) will pay the amount to B. Most payments at a distance are made not by sending banknotes and coins, but by transferring from *here* to *there* rights possessed by people here to be paid money there.

This is true when payments have to be made abroad. Suppose, for example, you proposed to spend a fortnight's holiday in Switzerland, and that you had £60 in cash in England. That money represents a right to goods and services in the U.K.; but it does not entitle you to goods and services in Switzerland. The Swiss hotel proprietor could not pay his own bills or his employees' wages in English money. You have to change some of your English money into Swiss money, which denotes a right to goods and services in Switzerland. This you can easily do, so far as current foreign exchange regulations permit, through any bank with agents in that country, or through any foreign exchange dealer. For, say, £30 you would have got in 1948 about 520 Swiss francs, the *rate of exchange* in June 1948 being about 17·3 Swiss francs to the £.

Why the Rate of Exchange Varies

This rate reflects roughly what money will buy in the two countries. The possessor of £100 has, very broadly, the same purchasing power, the same ability to secure goods and services, in the United Kingdom as the possessor of 1730 Swiss francs would have in Switzerland. If prices doubled in England while remaining unchanged in Switzerland, the rate of exchange would tend to fall to less than 10 Swiss francs to the £; conversely, if most prices in Switzerland trebled while those in this country remained unchanged, the £ should become worth roughly 50 Swiss francs.

The rate of exchange is also really a price; for example, the price people in England will pay for Swiss francs and the price the Swiss are prepared to pay for £s. This price, like others, is affected by supply and demand. If an unusually large number of people wanted to go to Switzerland, there would be an increased demand for Swiss money; those who had it for sale would tend to charge more for it—that is, give fewer Swiss francs for £1. If on the other hand an unusually large number of Swiss bought goods from this country or decided to visit the United Kingdom, there would be an increased supply of Swiss francs. Banks in Berne, Basle, etc., would receive relatively more offers to buy sterling (£s) than to sell Swiss francs, and they would charge more for each £— that is, require more Swiss francs for it.

Exports from a country cause a demand abroad for that country's currency, and tend to make it dearer; conversely, imports by a country tend to decrease the value of its currency, since they increase the country's need to exchange its currency for that of other countries. Thus, in 1948, American dollars were in great demand because America exported so much more than she imported, and traders in various parts of the world had to pay American traders so much more than American traders had to pay their suppliers abroad.

We see, therefore, that underlying the rates at which the currencies of two countries exchange there are two important facts: (a) the general scale of prices in each country; and (b) the relative strength from time to time of the demand for and the supply of each currency. This last is largely the result of each country's balance of trade, that is, the difference between its imports and its exports.

"Hard" and "Soft" Currencies

The term "hard currency" has been used to denote a currency hard to come by, principally because the payments to be made to that country are so much greater than those that have to be made by it, largely in consequence of its exports exceeding its imports. In 1948 all the currencies of the American countries and of Sweden and Switzerland were hard currencies. The others were sometimes called "soft" currencies. The so-called Sterling Area included all those countries that had agreed to link their demand for hard currencies with that of the United Kingdom and with the £ sterling. These countries included, in addition to the U.K. and Eire, South Africa, Australia, New Zealand, and the British Colonies, the countries of Western Europe and the Mediterranean.

It greatly interferes with business of all kinds between nations if rates of exchange fluctuate widely. For example, an importer cannot judge what he will have to pay for his supplies; an exporter quoting a price in the foreign currency cannot know how much he will eventually receive in his own currency. Consequently, governments try to fix an official rate of exchange that seems most suited to prices and to trading conditions, and endeavour, once the rate has been fixed, to keep it steady. The Second World War (1939–45) shattered normal trading conditions and hence the pre-war basis of the foreign exchanges.

At the Bretton Woods (U.S.A.) Conference in 1944 it was agreed to establish an International Monetary Fund, whose principal task is to maintain stable currencies and rates of exchange. In September 1946 the countries that had co-operated were invited to state how much gold the standard of their currency would represent, so that a permanent ratio between their currency and other currencies could be calculated. Such a permanent ratio is called a *parity of exchange*. Thus, the parity between the U.S. and the U.K. in 1948 was $4·03 to the £; that between Switzerland and the United Kingdom was 17·35 Swiss francs to the £; that between Belgium and the U.K. was 176·63 Belgian francs to the £. In 1949 the U.K. found it necessary to devalue the £ from $4·03 to 2·80, countries in the sterling area (except Pakistan) following suit. Things were difficult because of devastation caused by the war; and the governments of most countries except the U.S.A. were obliged to control imports and exports and the foreign exchange transactions resulting from them, and to limit the amount of currency that could be brought into or taken out of their country.

Forel, AUGUST (1848–1931). Though probably best known for his works on the human mind and its diseases, in which he attained a worldwide reputation, the Swiss scientist August Forel made also a lifelong study of ants and bees. He felt that Man might well imitate on a higher plane the remarkable social systems of these insects.

Born on September 1, 1848, he studied medicine and in 1879 became director of a mental hospital near Zurich in Switzerland, where he remained nearly 20 years. From the age of five he observed the ways of ants and made brilliant discoveries concerning the sense of sight, smell and hearing in social insects. His collection of ants comprised over 6,000 species. Forel published several works on insects, of which the most important is his book—the result of the labours of 75 years—The Social World of the Ant. He died on July 27, 1931.

Our PRECIOUS HERITAGE *of* FOREST LANDS

Timber-clad regions are largely the result of Man's care and foresight. Even if a country is fortunate enough to possess virgin forest, it must be guarded from unwise treatment and handed on as a legacy to future generations.

Forests. The forest is one of Man's most useful servants. Forests protect the headwaters of rivers and help to prevent floods, because the roots of trees hold back soil which might be washed away to clog river beds, causing the streams to overflow. Forests also moderate the climate; but besides all these things they supply Man with wood and wood products, without which he could have made little progress in civilization.

In their relation to climate (*q.v.*) forests may be considered great natural reservoirs, which accumulate the rainfall in the thick covering of decaying humus beneath the trees; the foliage intercepts, and causes the deposition of, moisture in wind-borne clouds and mists sweeping over the tree tops. The denuding of former forested lands is one of the causes of soil erosion, which quickly turns a fertile region into an arid and barren one.

There are three main types of forests; one, typical of cold regions, composed chiefly of conifers or evergreen (needle leaf) trees; the second, in temperate zones, made up almost entirely of deciduous or hardwood (broad leaf) species; while the third consists of evergreen hardwood trees of the tropical rain-forests.

The wooded area of Russia, one of the largest forest regions in the world, covers most of the north and middle of the country. This area consists either of continuous forests or of plains with forests scattered over them. The trees in the northern section are coniferous; those found elsewhere are deciduous, although the two groups occur together in places. Birch, oak, pine, larch, cedar, ash, beech, silver fir, lime, and willow are among the trees that flourish.

Except for the "virgin" forests of unexplored and undeveloped regions, which have come about by Nature's own sowing, timber-clad areas are the result of Man's sowing, transplanting and careful nurture—often without prospect of reward in his own generation. He who plants hardwood trees thus "plants for posterity," since these timbers take many years to grow and mature before they are

Topical

FORESTS : A STURDY BRITISH OAK

For timber purposes trees grown closely in woods or forests are the most valuable as under such conditions there is a constant struggle upwards towards the light, and the trunks grow long and straight. Among British trees oak and Scots pine afford the most useful timber, the oak for its strength and hardness, the pine for its elasticity.

worth felling. Conifers, such as spruce, fir and pine, give a return in the same generation, because the young trees thinned out can be sold earlier.

Conifer timbers are much used in building construction, joinery work and for a thousand other industrial purposes. The two world wars of 1914–18 and 1939–45 robbed Britain's forests of most of their timber; foreign grown timber was shut out by the blockades, and the result was a great shortage of timber for building. Houses had to be designed to use steel sheeting and concrete wherever possible

instead of wood; and even so, not enough could be built for the needs of the people.

Another example of Man's dependence upon the products of his forests is given by the coal mines. Hundreds of thousands of pit props are needed to shore up the roofs and sides of tunnels dug into the coal-bearing seams. Here again the shortage of timber brought about a difficulty throughout and after the war periods. One way in which shortages are remedied is in using up every available scrap of timber in our forests.

Today the factory is taken to the forest; sawmills " convert " the timber on the spot; complex machines turn certain portions into plywood there, stripping off an endless sheet of wood from suitable logs. By glueing or cementing several plies together, with the grain crossing, an immensely strong sheet of wood is made. Much of this material would in older days have gone to waste; and only the trunks would have reached the saw-mill and the factory.

The natural seasoning of timber is a process which takes years to complete. While the better timber, such as is used for furniture, will probably still continue to be seasoned by natural methods, science has shown us how to speed up the process for workaday timber, and to do it in months instead of years. None the less, afforestation—or the planting of new timber trees to replace those felled—m st keep pace with the cutting of timber.

Forestry is a highly skilled branch of agriculture, and the great timber-growing countries have forestry services which look after the timber reserves and ensure that new areas are planted to maintain supplies. Felling is very strictly controlled

today, but we might say that in many lands this is a case of " locking the stable door after the pony has gone ! " It is computed that Europe today has left only about one-third of its former forest lands. This is not the worst, for while Scandinavia has still about half its earlier forest area, Southern Europe as a whole has lost a matter of eight to nine-tenths of its timber reserves.

In the United States of America, where there are about 450 million acres of commercial forest land, 70 million acres have been so exploited that they now produce almost nothing for industry. A further 175 million acres have been stripped of all trees worth taking to the sawmill, and what timber they do yield is fit only for pulping to make paper and for similar secondary purposes. Not so long ago there were 850 million acres of virgin forest in the country. Some of this depletion in America is due to forest fires which raged in years past. Here again science has stepped in, and outbreaks are taken in hand at once,

FORESTS : FIRE-FIGHTING
During periods of drought in England, forest fires sometimes do enormous damage, despite the precautions taken to prevent outbreaks. Men in observation posts (lower) keep constant watch and can summon help to beat out a fire (upper) before it grows to serious proportions.

warning being given by observers at key points and by patrols who fly regularly over the forest areas.

To check the unwise depletion of forests, a Forests and Forest Products Division was set up after the Second World War (1939-45) by the Food and Agriculture Organization of the United Nations as a permanent international agency to deal with the conservation and planned use of the world's timber.

We have mentioned that forests prevent soil erosion. In the United States of America a national " shelter-belt " began to be planted in 1935. This is a system of wind-breaks formed of trees planted— as triangular groves or in strips at right-angles to the prevailing winds—to check wind erosion and to conserve moisture in the soil.

How are forests grown? you may ask. Well, we begin, as in other forms of plant culture, with the sowing of seed in a nursery; when the young plants are advanced enough they are moved to plantations on suitable land. You may often have seen such plantations, with their regular rows of young trees; and we hope you have taken care not to damage them. Unfortunately, thoughtless or greedy people have been known to raid conifer plantations to obtain " Christmas trees " for the house. Apart from this being theft, it is a stupid destruction of future forest resources, since the saplings will take five to ten years to replace.

The closeness of the planting depends upon the species; one object is to prevent the growth of side branches which would take away the value and quality of the timber. Another object is to afford protection where the trees are much exposed to bleak winds. Trees which are planted closely run up straight and grow tall— qualities in demand for timber. The plantations are thinned out when necessary; diseased or defective trees are dealt with. By the time that the thinnings have been removed, the remaining trees are at the right distance from each other for their adult growth. Twenty, thirty or more years later they will be ready for the sawmill.

The world's most extensive forest belts are to be found in : Canada (British Columbia, Quebec and Ontario) ; the United States (Pacific coast states, just west of the Great Lakes, and Alaska); Europe (Finland, Sweden, Norway, Germany and Russia); and Asia (Siberia and the Caucasus). Other important forest regions, some of them producing special woods, are in the sub-continent of India, in Burma, West Africa, South and Central America, and Australia. From the forests of the tropics come the most beautiful and valuable woods— mahogany from Mexico, Honduras and West Africa; ebony from India ; teak from Burma, Siam and India ; redwood from the eucalyptus tree of Western Australia.

Great Britain has comparatively little forest and woodland and has lagged far behind other countries in her forestry organization. A Forestry Commission was established in 1919 to control those woodlands owned by the State, but its work was hampered by lack of co-operation from private owners. After the Second World War, in which Britain lost half of her standing timber, thousands of acres were acquired by the Government for planting, and the number of National Forest Parks set aside as reserves was increased. Afforestation on private

Fox

FOREST RANGER IN AUSTRALIA
An elaborate Government organization protects Australia's vast forests against fire. This photograph shows a forest ranger, equipped with a portable wireless set, receiving from an aeroplane reports of a fire's position and extent.

lands was encouraged by Government grants of money to private owners, and in 1945 the Forestry Commission was placed under the control of the Ministry of Agriculture and Fisheries.

In the year 1947–8 the Forestry Commission spent nearly £5,000,000 in its work of maintaining and replenishing our timber resources—almost double the sum spent in the previous year. The Forest Products Research Laboratory, a branch of the Government's scientific services, investigates the causes of disease and decay, and aids growers and manufacturers to get the best results in their endeavours. After the end of the war of 1939–45 young men released from the fighting services were encouraged to take up forestry as a career, and it is a very attractive one. Some of our universities grant degrees in Forestry; Oxford University has a Diploma Course in the subject.

Forget-Me-Not. Perennial plant of the family *Boraginaceae;* the true Forget-me-not is *Myosotis palustris,* but the name is now also given to all the members of the genus Myosotis. Natives of Great Britain, their height ranges from seven to 18 inches. *Myosotis palustris* is the well-known blue variety which, though found growing wild by the sides of streams, will thrive equally well as an edging to a flower bed in moist peaty

E. J. Bedford

TRUE FORGET-ME-NOT
Many plants of the same family are called forget-me-not, but the only one that correctly bears this name is *Myosotis palustris*, a common plant growing in moist places. The flowers are bright blue, with yellow centres.

soil. There are several cultivated species, but a rare natural variety is *Myosotis palustris alba*, which has white flowers.

Formosa. In 1590 some Portuguese traders were sailing off the coast of China when they sighted an island whose beauty struck them so forcibly that they cried out, " Ilha Formosa ! Ilha Formosa ! " (Beautiful Island). A few years later the word Formosa appeared on the charts of Dutch navigators, and at last became the accepted name of this semi-tropical island.

The beauty of the island contrasted strangely with the savagery of the native inhabitants. For these muscular, broad-chested people, with their huge hands and feet, large mouths, and broad flat noses, were cannibals and head-hunters, and until fairly recently any unfortunate mariner cast away on the coast in the terrible storms (typhoons) that sweep the China Sea, could expect no better fate than death.

On a map Formosa is a small oblong patch off the east coast of China. In reality it is 235 miles long and 90 miles wide, its area being nearly 14,000 square miles. Niitaka-Yama, called by Europeans Mount Morrison (14,000 feet), is the highest peak.

The island is rich in plant life. Wild flowers bloom all the year round, many of them beautiful varieties of lilies, orchids, azaleas, rhododendrons, and other flowers which are commonly known elsewhere only as hothouse plants. In the southern districts grow such tropical fruits as the pomegranate, bread-fruit, figs, guava, and oranges.

Tiger cats, deer, civet cats, wild boars, apes, armadillos and squirrels abound. In all parts are found venomous snakes. One of the most beautiful of the many birds is the blue magpie, with its black head and neck, vermilion bill and legs, and blue and white body. The most important domestic animal is the water buffalo, which long ago was brought in from China as a beast of burden.

Farming is the chief occupation, and the principal products are rice, tea, sugar, sweet potatoes, jute. In the eastern part are forests of camphor trees, which give the island a virtual monopoly of the world's supply of natural camphor. There are also great forests of hardwood timber as yet almost untouched. Gold, silver, copper, sulphur, and coal are mined in considerable quantities.

There is a network of excellent roads. Schools have been established for the Formosans and Chinese, and in 1928 the University of Formosa was founded. The chief town, Taipoi, has a population of 340,000.

Incorporated as part of China in 1683, Formosa became a Japanese possession after the war between China and Japan in 1895. During the Second World War it was a Japanese naval and military base. Formosa was returned to China in 1945, and in 1949 it became the last stronghold of the Chinese Nationalist forces. The population of the island is some 6,500,000.

Fortuna. The goddess of Fortune was worshipped in Italy as Fortuna, and in Greece as Tyche. In Italy there were two famous shrines of Fortuna—at Praeneste and at Antium. It seems probable that the Italian Fortuna was not so much a goddess of chance in general, as a deity

Dr. C. Hose

FORMOSAN WATCH-TOWER
At one time the natives of the island of Formosa were cannibals and head-hunters, using look-outs, like the one above, to watch for enemies. Now these points of vantage are occupied by hunters who scan the countryside for game.

to be invoked by men and women on particular occasions of crisis or danger. As time went on, the Italian Fortuna grew more and more like the Greek Tyche, and her help came to be invoked throughout the Roman Empire at every hour of the day and night, whenever her supposed powers were needed. On coins and in statues, Fortuna is represented with a cornucopia (horn of plenty), as the giver of prosperity; with a rudder, as the controller of destinies; with a wheel or a globe, to indicate the revolutions of chance, or the world as subject to chance; and sometimes with wings.

Fossils. These are the remains of animals and plants, buried ages ago and turned to stone by chemical processes in the rocks—the bones of monsters, the trunks of ancient trees, the moulded forms of huge insects, of queer fishes and shells, of birds with teeth, of real sea-serpents, and so on. Not all these things would be found in any one place, but all have been found in places very widely distributed over the earth.

This word "fossil" comes from a Latin word meaning "to dig," and by the study of fossils scientists have been able to piece together some of the most important pages in the history of the earth and life on it, both vegetable and animal. From fossil remains we have learned that the ancestors of the elephant once roamed over Britain, that tropical forests once covered Europe and the United States and that a luxuriant vegetation grew where now are the Polar regions with their snow and ice.

Fossils tell us that the great coal-seams and chalk-beds of the world were formed from the remains of living things; and that millions of years before the pyramids of Egypt were dreamed of tiny animals were making shells which became limestone from which, eventually, were built those pyramids.

Fitting together the scattered parts of the fossil story, science has traced animal life back to the earliest worms and shell-fish, and has shown how, one after another, there appeared the higher invertebrates, the cartilaginous

fishes like sharks, the amphibians (half-land, half-water animals like the frog), the reptiles, the birds and bony fishes, the mammals and, last in the scale, Man.

Fossil plants and fossil animals are found in many forms. In some cases a fossil is only the footprint of some prehistoric beast in the mud of bygone ages, which has been buried and preserved

under a fresh layer of sand or silt. In others it is the delicate imprint of a leaf, stem, root or seed on some soft material which later hardened into solid rock. Sometimes the body of an animal was buried and decayed, leaving a hollow mound which filled up with mineral matter and formed a cast of the animal's shape. Sometimes the bones and teeth have survived. In a few relatively recent cases even the flesh of the creature has been preserved,

Topical; British Museum, London

FOSSILS FROM BRITAIN AND NORTH AMERICA
Of British fossils those of extinct shell-fish called Ammonites (top) are the commonest. Some strata of Old Red Sandstone are packed with fossil fish (centre). At the bottom is an unusual complete example of a petrified snake from South Dakota in the United States.

as, for example, the mammoths embedded in the frozen mud cliffs of Siberia for thousands of years.

The science of fossils is called Palaeontology, and to understand fully its importance you should read the articles on Biology, Evolution and Geology. Many strange relationships have been made known, based upon the fossils of some of the animals which came into existence in the early days of the world's history; and the more such fossils are examined, the better idea we get of the steps by which animals and plants have evolved.

The strangest of all creatures to have been dug up out of the earth as fossils are the giant monsters of the Reptile Age—the dinosaurs, the ichthyosaurs, etc. Some of these primeval reptiles were nearly 100 feet long, and some were perhaps the largest animals that ever lived. The farther back we go the smaller is the proportion of brain space in the animal's skull. Among the latest fossil remains are those of early Man. (*See* Cave Dwellers).

One of the most widely distributed of the fossil families is the trilobites, ancient crab-like animals whose horny helmets and back-shields are found in ancient rock-formations in nearly all parts of the world. Once the prevailing form of marine animal, they died out in the Permian period, about 200 million years ago. The king crab of the present day is considered to be probably the descendant of the trilobite stock.

There is a very unusual type of fossil bed occurring near Los Angeles, California, U.S.A., consisting of asphalt deposits, which were once soft and sticky and, probably, covered with water. Animals coming to drink became stuck in the asphalt, much as sticky paper catches flies. Great numbers of prehistoric skeletons have been dug out of these dried-up pools.

The practical use for fossils consists in their indicating the age of the rocks and hence what minerals, oil or coal are likely to occur in them.

FOSSILS: TRACKS OF ANCIENT MONSTERS PRESERVED IN ROCK

In Jurassic times, about 130 million years ago, the climate of North America was moist and hot, and what is now prairie was swamp, with marsh-vegetation and fern-like trees. Through the forests and around the marshes roamed great reptiles, like the dinosaur (upper). Most of the footprints they left in the mud were washed out; but occasionally the mud hardened and then was overlain with mud of another kind which did not mix with the lower layer. As time went on (lower), the weight of the mud hardened the lower layers into rock and thus the footprints were preserved.

H. Barrett

FOX CUBS OUT OF THEIR ' EARTH '
Usually four or five fox cubs are born at a time, and they look very much like puppies, except that their ears are erect and the pupil of the eye is elliptical (oval), instead of circular. Foxes sometimes make their own burrows or ' earths,' but more often they adapt those of badgers or rabbits.

Fox. The boldness and cunning of the fox (*Vulpes vulpes*) have long been celebrated in innumerable folk-tales. The fox is closely related to the dog and jackal, but is distinguished by the sharp muzzle, erect ears, elliptical pupil of the eye and long bushy tail. There are several kinds, common in different parts of the world with the exception of South America and Australia. All females of the species are called vixens.

The Arctic fox, which ranges southward to Labrador and Newfoundland, has beautiful silky fur, bluish or brown in summer and pure white in winter. The silver fox holds first place among fur-bearers and its skin sells for a good price ; hence the introduction of silver fox farming as an industry. In this species the hair is jet-black save for the silvery white tips. The common fox, *Vulpes canis*, is reddish-brown in colour, with white beneath, but the hue varies locally, as in the so-called grey-hound fox of the English Lake District.

All foxes are predaceous animals, that is, living on other animals and birds. They sometimes make their homes in hollow stumps or holes in rocks, but often use another creature's burrow as an " earth." As a rule, they hide by day and hunt by night.

In the sport of fox-hunting (*see* page 1162) a pack of fox-hounds is used to start the fox from his hide-out in a spinney or a covert, and to chase him by scent until he is run down. The hunters follow over hill and dale across country, leaping hedges and fences, until the quarry is brought to bay and killed by the pack. The sport is justified by the aid it gives to the breeding of fine horses and by the training it affords to men and women who follow the hounds. Farmers and land owners are compensated for any damage done by the hunt to crops or fences ; or for poultry taken by Master Reynard on his nightly raids.

The fox-hound is a breed of dog derived probably from the bloodhound and the pointer, noted for its speed and its endurance, which enable it to follow a fox for hours on end. The fox terrier, today known mainly as a popular house dog and companion, got its name from its use for un-earthing a fox which had gone to ground while being hunted.

Fractions. This word comes from a Latin verb meaning to break. A fraction of any substance is really a part broken off from the whole ; so in arithmetic, when we talk about fractions, we are really finding out all about the size of these broken parts, how we can build them together or break them down into still smaller pieces.

If we fold a square sheet of paper (Fig. 1, A) so as to bring top and bottom edges together, the crease made by the folding will divide the paper into two equal parts or *halves*, as in B.

If we open the sheet, spread it out and fold the top and bottom ends to the middle crease, the paper will be divided by the three creases into four equal parts or *fourths*, (C).

By opening the paper again and now folding it crosswise so that one side lies upon the other, we shall divide it into *eighths* (D).

By opening the paper and folding each side to the vertical crease, we shall divide it into *sixteenths* (E).

These parts—halves, fourths, etc.—are called *fractions*. They are measures or ratios of quantity and do not depend upon measuring.

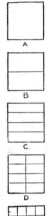

Fig. 1

Halves

1. How many halves in 1 ? (*See* Fig. 1, B.)
2. What is ½ of 3 ? ½ of 5 ? ½ of 7 ? ½ of 9 ? Draw lines 3 inches long, 5 inches long, etc. Halve each measure, and you have the answers.
3. Add:

2½	3½	4½	3½	6½	6
2½	3½	4½	4½	7½	5½

4. Subtract:

7	9	8	12	9½	18½
3½	4½	3½	4½	2½	7½

To solve $7 - 3\frac{1}{2}$, draw a line 7 inches long. Cut off 3½ inches. How much is left ?

Fourths

Cut out pieces of paper like those shown in Fig. 2 ; (a) 4 inches square ; (b) 2 inches by 4 inches ; (c) 2

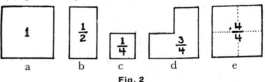

Fig. 2

inches by 2 inches ; (d) irregular form 4 inches by 4 inches on the long sides ; (e) 4 inches square, creased into fourths. Write the fraction name on each form.

1. Compare ½ with two of the ¼ forms put end to

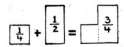

end; $\frac{3}{4}$ with three of the $\frac{1}{4}$ forms; 1 with $\frac{1}{4}$. What do you find? They are the same sizes.

2. Study the picture problems in Fig. 3. Place $\frac{1}{4}$ and $\frac{1}{2}$ together. Which fraction could be covered by their sum? Place $\frac{1}{4}$ and $\frac{3}{4}$ together. Which form does their sum equal? Place two of the $\frac{3}{4}$ forms together. What fraction must be added to 1 to equal their sum?

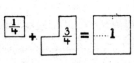

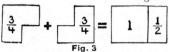

Fig. 3

3. In the same way, find other sums, as $\frac{1}{2}$ and $\frac{3}{4}$, $\frac{1}{4}$ and $\frac{1}{4}$, $\frac{1}{2}$ and $\frac{1}{2}$, $\frac{1}{2}$ and $\frac{1}{4}$ and $\frac{1}{4}$.

4. Add: $1\frac{1}{4}$ and $1\frac{1}{2}$ $3\frac{3}{4}$ and $2\frac{3}{4}$ $2\frac{1}{4}$ and $2\frac{1}{4}$ $1\frac{1}{2}$ and $2\frac{3}{4}$

5. Add:
$8\frac{1}{4}$ $4\frac{1}{4}$ $7\frac{1}{4}$ $3\frac{1}{4}$ $6\frac{3}{4}$ 5 $6\frac{1}{4}$
$6\frac{1}{2}$ $3\frac{3}{4}$ $2\frac{3}{4}$ $2\frac{1}{4}$ $5\frac{1}{4}$ $8\frac{1}{4}$ 9

6. Place $\frac{3}{4}$ on 1. Which other unit added to $\frac{3}{4}$ will cover the 1? Then $1 - \frac{3}{4} =$ what?

7. Place $\frac{1}{4}$ on 1. How much added to $\frac{1}{4}$ will equal 1? Then $1 - \frac{1}{4} =$ what?

8. Subtract:
$7\frac{1}{2}$ $13\frac{3}{4}$ 6 $8\frac{1}{4}$ $6\frac{3}{4}$ 10
$6\frac{1}{4}$ $4\frac{1}{4}$ $2\frac{1}{4}$ $2\frac{1}{4}$ $2\frac{1}{2}$ $3\frac{3}{4}$

Draw a line $7\frac{1}{2}$ inches long. Cut off $6\frac{1}{4}$ inches. How much is left? Measure.

Eighths

Cut pieces of paper like the shapes in Fig. 4. Let the 1 be 4 inches by 4 inches, the $\frac{1}{2}$, 2 inches by 4, etc. Make sums and differences as in the exercises with fourths.

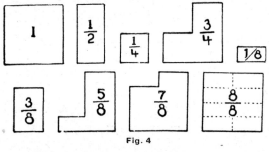

Fig. 4

1. Which fraction equals $\frac{4}{8}$? Which one equals $\frac{2}{8}$? Which equals $\frac{6}{8}$? Changing $\frac{4}{8}$ to $\frac{1}{2}$ or $\frac{6}{8}$ to $\frac{3}{4}$ is called *reducing to lowest terms*.

2. Add:
$4\frac{1}{8}$ $7\frac{1}{8}$ $2\frac{1}{8}$ $9\frac{1}{8}$ $6\frac{1}{8}$ $5\frac{3}{8}$ $7\frac{7}{8}$ $4\frac{1}{8}$
$2\frac{3}{8}$ $3\frac{1}{4}$ $5\frac{5}{8}$ $5\frac{1}{2}$ $3\frac{3}{8}$ $6\frac{1}{4}$ $3\frac{3}{8}$ 8

Verify the results by drawing lines $4\frac{1}{8}$ inches and $2\frac{3}{8}$ inches long, end to end, and measuring; and so with the remaining examples.

3. Add:
$2\frac{1}{4}$ 7 $6\frac{1}{8}$ $5\frac{1}{4}$ $4\frac{1}{4}$ $6\frac{1}{2}$ $7\frac{7}{8}$ $6\frac{1}{4}$
$3\frac{3}{8}$ $3\frac{3}{8}$ $2\frac{1}{8}$ $8\frac{1}{8}$ $2\frac{5}{8}$ $5\frac{1}{8}$ $4\frac{7}{8}$ $7\frac{7}{8}$

4. Subtract:
$11\frac{1}{4}$ $12\frac{5}{8}$ $12\frac{1}{2}$ $5\frac{5}{8}$ $9\frac{1}{4}$ $7\frac{7}{8}$ 13
$3\frac{3}{8}$ $5\frac{1}{8}$ $4\frac{1}{8}$ $3\frac{3}{8}$ $4\frac{1}{8}$ $3\frac{1}{8}$ $9\frac{1}{8}$

5. Which form equals $\frac{2}{3}$ of $\frac{3}{4}$? Find one that covers $\frac{2}{3}$ of $\frac{3}{4}$. Then $\frac{2}{3} \times \frac{3}{4} =$? (Read the sign $\times$ as "of.")

6. Add:
$3\frac{5}{8}$ $4\frac{1}{8}$ $5\frac{5}{8}$ $2\frac{5}{8}$ $9\frac{3}{4}$
$7\frac{1}{2}$ $2\frac{5}{8}$ $6\frac{1}{4}$ $3\frac{5}{8}$ $7\frac{7}{8}$

In solving these problems notice that:
$\frac{10}{8} = \frac{5}{4} = 1\frac{1}{4}$; $\frac{11}{8} = 1\frac{3}{8}$; $\frac{12}{8} = \frac{3}{2} = 1\frac{1}{2}$

Thirds

Cut forms of paper like those in Fig. 5. Let the $\frac{1}{3}$ be 3 inches square. Write the fraction names upon the forms.

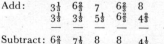

Add:
$3\frac{2}{3}$ $6\frac{2}{3}$ 7 $6\frac{2}{3}$ 8
$3\frac{1}{3}$ $3\frac{1}{3}$ $5\frac{1}{3}$ $6\frac{2}{3}$ $4\frac{2}{3}$

Subtract:
$6\frac{2}{3}$ $7\frac{1}{3}$ 8 8 $4\frac{1}{3}$
$2\frac{1}{3}$ 6 $2\frac{1}{3}$ $2\frac{2}{3}$ $2\frac{2}{3}$

To solve 8 minus $2\frac{1}{3}$ use the *additive method* (as in giving change). Think $\frac{2}{3}$ added to $2\frac{1}{3}$ makes 3, and 5 more makes 8. We added $5\frac{2}{3}$, so 8 minus $2\frac{1}{3}$ $= 5\frac{2}{3}$. To solve $4\frac{1}{3} - 2\frac{2}{3}$, think how much must be added to $2\frac{2}{3}$ to make $4\frac{1}{3}$. Thus $\frac{1}{3}$ more makes 3, 1 more makes 4, and $\frac{1}{3}$ more makes $4\frac{1}{3}$. We added $1\frac{2}{3}$, so $4\frac{1}{3} - 2\frac{2}{3} = 1\frac{2}{3}$.

Fig. 5

Sixths

Cut forms as in Fig. 6, making the $\frac{1}{6}$ either 3 inches or 6 inches square. Write the fraction names upon the forms.

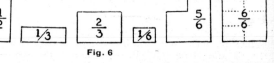

Fig. 6

1. Make sums by placing any two forms together. *Example:* $\frac{2}{3} + \frac{1}{6} = \frac{5}{6}$.

2. Observe the forms and answer: What fraction equals $\frac{2}{6}$? $\frac{3}{6}$? $\frac{4}{6}$?

3. Place $\frac{1}{3}$ on $\frac{2}{3}$ and tell what part of the $\frac{2}{3}$ is covered. What part of $\frac{2}{3}$ is $\frac{1}{3}$?

4. Lay the form $\frac{1}{6}$ on the form $\frac{1}{3}$; on $\frac{1}{2}$; on $\frac{2}{3}$; on $\frac{5}{6}$. How many sixths remain uncovered in each case? Change the remainder to lowest terms in each case.

5. Lay the form $\frac{1}{3}$ on the form $\frac{1}{2}$; $\frac{1}{2}$ on $\frac{2}{3}$; $\frac{2}{3}$ on $\frac{5}{6}$; $\frac{5}{6}$ on 1. How many sixths are left uncovered in each case?

6. Show $\frac{1}{3} + \frac{1}{2}$; $\frac{1}{6} + \frac{5}{6}$; $\frac{1}{2} + \frac{2}{3}$; $\frac{1}{2} + \frac{5}{6}$; $\frac{1}{3} + \frac{5}{6}$. Reduce $\frac{7}{6}$ (called an improper fraction) to a mixed number, that is, a whole number and a fraction: $1\frac{1}{6}$. Reduce $\frac{2}{6}$ and $\frac{9}{6}$ to lowest terms and then to mixed numbers.

7. Show $\frac{5}{6} - \frac{1}{3}$ by laying the form $\frac{1}{3}$ on the form $\frac{5}{6}$. Which form equals the uncovered part of the $\frac{5}{6}$?

8. Lay the form $\frac{1}{6}$ on the form $\frac{2}{3}$ to find out how many times $\frac{2}{3}$ contains $\frac{1}{6}$. Then $\frac{2}{3} \div \frac{1}{6} = 4$. $\frac{5}{6} \div \frac{1}{6} =$? $\frac{1}{2} \div \frac{1}{6} =$? $\frac{1}{3} \div \frac{1}{6} =$? Show.

Twelfths

1. Cut a form one-half as large as $\frac{1}{6}$. How many such units does 1 contain? Call it $\frac{1}{12}$. $\frac{1}{2}$ of $\frac{1}{6} = \frac{1}{12}$.

2. Measure the form $\frac{1}{2}$, using the form $\frac{1}{12}$ as a measure. $\frac{1}{2} =$ how many twelfths?

3. In the same way change $\frac{1}{3}$ to twelfths. Change $\frac{5}{6}$ to twelfths. Lay form $\frac{5}{6}$ on form $\frac{10}{12}$.

4. Make a form 3 times as large as $\frac{1}{12}$. Apply this $\frac{1}{12}$ to the 1. $\frac{3}{12} =$ what? $\frac{9}{12} = \frac{3}{?}$.

5. Change $\frac{1}{2}$, $\frac{1}{4}$, $\frac{1}{3}$, $\frac{1}{6}$, $\frac{5}{6}$, $\frac{3}{4}$, $\frac{2}{3}$ to twelfths.

6. Write $\frac{1}{12}$, $\frac{2}{12}$, $\frac{3}{12}$, $\frac{4}{12}$, etc., in order, to $\frac{12}{12}$, changing each fraction that can be so reduced, to its lowest terms.

Common Denominators

1. Add $\frac{1}{2}$ and $\frac{2}{5}$.

Solution: Evidently $\frac{1}{2}$ and $\frac{2}{5}$ cannot be added until they are reduced to a common denomination. The unit or 1 thought of here must divide into 2 parts to show halves and into 5 parts to show fifths. For convenience draw a form 5 inches long and 2 inches wide. Divide it into halves by a horizontal line and into fifths by vertical lines. Each small division of this form must be $\frac{1}{10}$. Why? So tenths is the denomination we seek. $\frac{1}{2} + \frac{3}{5}$ $= \frac{5}{10} + \frac{6}{10} = \frac{11}{10} = 1\frac{1}{10}$. 10 is the common denominator.

2. Add $\frac{5}{6}$ and $\frac{3}{4}$.

Solution: In the figure below (Fig. 7) we see that if we measure a 24-inch line with a 6-inch ruler, we say 6, 12,

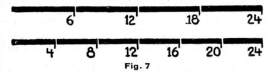

Fig. 7

18, 24; if we measure it with a 4-inch ruler, we say 4, 8, 12, 16, 20, 24. 12, 18, and 24 are *multiples* of 6; 8, 12, 16, 20, 24 are multiples of 4. We notice that 24 is found in both sets of multiples. It is therefore a *common multiple* of 4 and 6. But we notice that 12 is also a common multiple of 4 and 6 and since it is the smallest possible common multiple of 4 and 6, it is called the *least common multiple* of 4 and 6. 12 is the *least common denominator* desired and twelfths the *least common denominator* of fourths and sixths.

Hence $\frac{5}{6} + \frac{3}{4} = \frac{10}{12} + \frac{9}{12} = \frac{19}{12} = 1\frac{7}{12}$.
($\frac{5}{6} = \frac{10}{12}$; $\frac{5}{6} = \frac{10}{12}$. $\frac{3}{4} = \frac{9}{12}$.)

3. Subtract $\frac{4}{9}$ from $\frac{5}{6}$.

Solution: 9, 18, 27, 36, 45, 54, multiples of 9.
6, 12, 18, 24, 30, 36, 42, 48, 54, multiples of 6.
$6 \times 9 = 54$, a common multiple of 6 and 9.
But 18 and 36 are also common multiples of 6 and 9.
Hence 18 is the *least* common multiple wanted
($\frac{5}{6} = \frac{15}{18}$; $\frac{4}{9} = \frac{8}{18}$. $\frac{5}{6} = \frac{15}{18}$; $\frac{5}{6} = \frac{15}{18}$.) $\frac{5}{6} - \frac{4}{9} = \frac{15}{18} - \frac{8}{18} = \frac{7}{18}$.

4. Find the common denominator of $\frac{1}{8}$, $\frac{1}{12}$, $\frac{1}{16}$, $\frac{1}{3}$.
Hint: Notice that 8 will exactly divide 16 and 3 will exactly divide 12. What is the least number 12 and 16 will exactly divide?

Reducing a Mixed Number to an Improper Fraction.

Example: $8\frac{4}{5} = $ what?
Solution: (a) $1 = \frac{5}{5}$.
(b) $8 = 8 \times \frac{5}{5} = \frac{40}{5}$.
(c) $8\frac{4}{5} = 8 \times \frac{5}{5} + \frac{4}{5} = \frac{44}{5}$.

Reducing an Improper Fraction to a Mixed Number.

Example: $\frac{44}{5} = $ what?
Solution: $\frac{44}{5} = 44 \div 5 = 8\frac{4}{5}$.

Multiplication

1. $8 \times \frac{3}{5}$ (8 times 3 fifths) $= $ what?
Solution: $8 \times \frac{3}{5} = \frac{24}{5} = 4\frac{4}{5}$. (Multiply the numerator. Keep the denominator the same.)
2. Find $\frac{3}{4} \times \frac{2}{5}$ (three-fourths of two-fifths).
Solution: Divide a unit (1) into fifths by vertical lines, and fourths by horizontal lines (Fig. 8). Show $\frac{2}{5}$. Divide

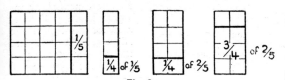

Fig. 8

into 4 equal parts. Show $\frac{1}{4}$ of $\frac{1}{5}$. How many parts each equal to $\frac{1}{4}$ of $\frac{1}{5}$ in a whole 1?

(a) $\frac{1}{4} \times \frac{1}{5} = \frac{1}{20}$ ($\frac{1}{4}$ of $\frac{1}{5}$).
(b) $\frac{1}{4} \times \frac{2}{5} = \frac{2}{20}$.
(c) $\frac{3}{4} \times \frac{2}{5} = \frac{6}{20} = \frac{3}{10}$.
(d) $\frac{3}{4} \times \frac{2}{5} = \frac{3}{10}$.

(Cancelling the common factor 2 in both numerator and denominator brings the result in its lowest terms.)

3. Find $\frac{2}{3} \times \frac{3}{4}$.
Solution: $\frac{2}{3} \times \frac{3}{4} = \frac{6}{12} = \frac{1}{2}$.
or: $\frac{2}{3} \times \frac{3}{4} = \frac{1}{2}$.

(By cancelling the common factors 3 and 2 we can save a step and obtain a result in its lowest terms.)

4. Find $2\frac{2}{3} \times 6\frac{1}{4}$ ($2\frac{2}{3}$ times $6\frac{1}{4}$).
Solution: $2\frac{2}{3} \times 6\frac{1}{4} = \frac{8}{3} \times \frac{25}{4} = \frac{50}{3} = 16\frac{2}{3}$

Division

1. Divide 5 by $\frac{1}{4}$.
Solution: (a) $1 \div \frac{1}{4} = 4$. ($4 \times \frac{1}{4} = 1$.)
(b) $5 \div \frac{1}{4} = 5 \times 4 = 20$. (In 5, $\frac{1}{4}$ is contained 5 times as often as in 1.)

2. Divide 5 by $\frac{3}{4}$.
Solution: (a) $5 \div \frac{1}{4} = 20$.
(b) $5 \div \frac{3}{4} = \frac{1}{3}$ of $20 = 6\frac{2}{3}$. ($\frac{3}{4}$ is contained in any number $\frac{1}{3}$ as often as $\frac{1}{4}$ is, because it is 3 times as large.)
or: (a) $5 \div 1 = 5$.
(b) $5 \div \frac{1}{4} = 4 \times 5$. ($\frac{1}{4}$ is contained in any number 4 times as often as 1 is.)
(c) $5 \div \frac{3}{4} = \frac{1}{3}$ of $4 \times 5 = \frac{20}{3} = 6\frac{2}{3}$.

3. $\frac{3}{4} \div \frac{1}{3} = $ what?
Solution: $\frac{3}{4} \div \frac{1}{3} = 3 \times \frac{3}{4} = \frac{9}{4} = 2\frac{1}{4}$.
($\frac{1}{3}$ is contained in any fraction or number 3 times as often as 1 is. 1 is contained in $\frac{3}{4}$, $\frac{3}{4}$ of a time, so $\frac{1}{3}$ is contained in $\frac{3}{4}$, $3 \times \frac{3}{4}$ times.)

4. $\frac{3}{4} \div \frac{2}{3} = $ what?
Solution: $\frac{3}{4} \div \frac{2}{3} = \frac{3}{4} \times \frac{3}{2} = \frac{9}{8} = 1\frac{1}{8}$ (because $\frac{2}{3}$ is contained $\frac{1}{2}$ as often as $\frac{1}{3}$.)

Thus we see that division of fractions is accomplished by inverting the divisor and multiplying.

Adding Mixed Numbers

In adding mixed numbers, expand the fractions to a common denominator, add them, then add the sum of the fractions to the sum of the integers.

Example: $12\frac{2}{3} + 21\frac{3}{4} + 8\frac{1}{2}$.

Form in Full		Short Form	
$12\frac{2}{3} = 12\frac{8}{12}$		$12\frac{2}{3}$	8
$21\frac{3}{4} = 21\frac{9}{12}$		$21\frac{3}{4}$	9
$8\frac{1}{2} = 8\frac{6}{12}$		$8\frac{1}{2}$	6
$41\frac{23}{12} = 41 + 1\frac{11}{12} = 42\frac{11}{12}$		$42\frac{11}{12}$	$\frac{23}{12} = 1\frac{11}{12}$

Subtracting Mixed Numbers

Example: $24\frac{1}{8} - 10\frac{3}{4}$.

$24\frac{1}{8}$
$10\frac{3}{4}$

$\frac{1}{4}$ (add $\frac{1}{4}$ to make the subtrahend 11).
13 (add 13 to make the subtrahend 24).
$\frac{1}{8}$ (add $\frac{1}{8}$ to make the subtrahend $24\frac{1}{8}$).

$13\frac{7}{12}$ total added.

Multiplying Mixed Numbers

To multiply a mixed number by an integer or an integer by a mixed number, add the product of the integer and fraction to the product of the two integers.

Example: $32 \times 2\frac{1}{5}$.

32
$2\frac{1}{5}$

$\frac{1}{5} \times 32 = \frac{32}{5} = 6\frac{2}{5}$
$2 \times 32 = 64$

$70\frac{2}{5}$

'The PLEASANT LAND of FRANCE'

In her cities some of the world's richest treasures of architecture, in her countryside a multitude of small but fruitful farms, the charm and the greatness of the land of France are mirrored in the character of her people.

France. Situated at the hub of Western Europe, France is the least isolated of the great nations of the continent, and inevitably throughout her long and stirring history she has played an important part in world affairs. In France the Latin cultures of the south meet the sterner spirit of the north, so that culturally as well as geographically she is the centre of European civilization.

To the north-west is Great Britain; to the east Belgium, Germany, and Switzerland; to the south-east Italy; to the south-west Spain. Across the Mediterranean lies Africa. The sea routes to the Balkans, the Near East, and the Suez Canal skirt her southern shores.

Bordering at once on the Mediterranean, the Atlantic, the English Channel, and the North Sea, France belongs equally to southern and northern Europe—to the old era and to the new. When Rome was the centre of the civilized world, Gaul (as France was then called) formed a notable part of her Empire, and the Romans gave her her speech; and when Venice and Genoa controlled the world's commerce, their roads to Western Europe led through France. The discovery of new worlds to west, south, and east shifted the centre of world power northwards from the Mediterranean to the great seaways; and when, later, Portugal, Spain, and Italy waned, France waxed in power.

It is only natural that, in a region so open to the world, we should find a varied racial mixture. Traces of several important prehistoric races abound; but at the dawn of recorded history most of France was inhabited by the Gauls, a people of Celtic blood. In the south-east, however, lived the Ligurians, of the same race as the ancient dwellers in northern Italy; and in the south-west the Iberians, probably survivors of a race who had inhabited western Europe before the Celts.

Phoenician merchants settled at a very early date on the Mediterranean coast; and about 600 B.C. Greek traders founded the colony of Massilia (modern Marseilles), and rapidly extended their commerce far into the interior. Then came the Roman conquerors and Gaul became Romanized.

The invasion of the Germanic tribes followed—Visigoths, Burgundians and Franks, the last-named giving the land their name and supplying a dominant influence never overthrown. Moors or Saracens from Spain settled for a time north of the Pyrenees and exercised a fleeting rule; and fair-haired Northmen from Scandinavia made their homes along the English Channel and became in time the Normans.

All these later settlers were more or less absorbed by the original Gallo-Roman population, but some of them through intermarriage effected great changes in the customs and physical appearance of the native inhabitants.

France presents to this day marked differences in the types of her people. In Normandy we find the tall, blue-eyed, light-haired descendants of the viking Northmen. In the southern provinces—Gascony, Languedoc, and Provence—the short, dark-haired pre-Celtic type prevails. In Brittany we have people of purest Celtic descent, still speaking a Celtic tongue closely akin to Welsh; while on the north slopes of the Pyrenees live descendants of the ancient Iberians, called the Basques.

Among the contrasting qualities that make up the French character, none is more typical than the hard-headed thrift of the peasant landowner. He is the backbone of the nation, and is so strongly attached to the soil of his forefathers that his kind has never followed the example of other Europeans in emigrating in numbers to foreign lands.

France is shaped roughly like a pentagon or five-sided figure. Its apex lies just beyond Calais on the North Sea; the Pyrenees mountains and the Mediterranean make up the base; the Atlantic and the English Channel form the western and north-western sides; and Belgium, Luxembourg, and part of Germany, and Switzerland and Italy form the north-eastern and eastern sides respectively. The greatest length north to south is about 600 miles; the greatest width about 570 miles. The island of Corsica, which lies more than 100 miles from the mainland coast in the Mediterranean, is an integral part of France, and for most purposes Algeria, in North Africa, is also treated as an equal part of the republic and not as a colony.

The western coast-line of France shows two pronounced land projections—the Norman, or Cotentin peninsula, which reaches out into the English Channel, with Cherbourg in its head; and

Extent.—North to south, about 600 miles; east to west, 400 to 570 miles. Coast-line: English Channel, 672 miles; Atlantic, 831 miles; Mediterranean, 369 miles. Area (including Corsica and Alsace-Lorraine), 212,659 square miles. Population (including Corsica) 41,800,000.

Physical Features.—Alps (Mont Blanc, 15,782 feet), Pyrenees, Jura, and Vosges Mountains, Rhône, Garonne, Loire, Seine, Somme, Meuse, and Moselle rivers; the Rhine now forms part of the eastern boundary. Climate, temperate; semi-tropical on the south coast.

Products.—Textiles (cotton, woollen, linen, silk), laces, clothing, objects of art and fashion; coal, machinery, iron and steel, porcelain, glass and chemicals; wines and cider; grains and potatoes, dairy produce.

Principal Cities.—Paris (capital, about 2,725,000 population); Marseilles, Lyons (more than 500,000); Bordeaux, Nice, Toulouse, Lille, Nantes (more than 200,000); Strasbourg, St. Etienne, Le Havre, Toulon, Rouen, Nancy, Reims, Roubaix, Clermont-Ferrand, Rennes, Dijon, Grenoble, Limoges, Nîmes, Le Mans (more than 100,000).

French Union.—In Asia, Federation of Indo-China (comprising the independent state of Viet-Nam, and the kingdoms of Cambodia and Laos). In Africa, Algeria (treated as a part of France proper, for most purposes), Tunis, Morocco, French Equatorial Africa, Madagascar, etc. In America, French Guiana, Martinique, Guadeloupe. Various islands in the Pacific (New Caledonia, Tahiti, Marquesas Islands, etc.).

FRANCE, FROM CHANNEL TO MEDITERRANEAN

With her shores washed by the North Sea, the English Channel, the Atlantic Ocean and the Mediterranean, France belongs equally to northern and southern Europe, and is the least isolated of the great countries of the continent. It is only natural that in a country so open to the world that we should find a varied racial mixture.

the rock-bound peninsula of Brittany, with the thriving maritime city of Brest near its westernmost point. In the angles between the Norman and the Breton peninsulas lie the Channel Islands, still owing allegiance to the English Crown.

The coasts of France are either dangerously rocky, or low and sandy, so that there are comparatively few good harbours, except those at the mouths of rivers. Of these river ports the most important are Le Havre and Rouen on the Seine, St. Nazaire and Nantes on the Loire, and Bordeaux on the Garonne. The Rhône, owing to the sediment carried down by its rapid current, and the low swampy character of the delta, offers no good anchorage.

The principal seaports not situated on rivers are Marseilles, the greatest in France; Cherbourg, guarded by a huge breakwater and an important naval station; Boulogne, Dunkirk and Calais, in the extreme north; and La Rochelle and La Pallice on the west coast. Brest in Brittany, and Toulon on the Mediterranean, are important naval stations.

It is mostly a smiling and fertile land that the French have inherited from their ancestors. A line drawn from Bayonne in the south-west to the wooded hills of Ardennes on the north-east border roughly divides the rolling plains of western France —less than 600 feet high—from the highlands of the east. In the midst of the highland section lies the confused mass of the Auvergne Mountains, with summits rising to 6,000 feet and numbering hundreds of extinct volcanoes; adjoining them to the south-east lies the chain of the Cévennes, extending some 200 miles, from the foot hills of the Pyrenees to beyond Lyons.

To the east, separating Alsace from the rest of France, are the forest-clad Vosges; along the border of Switzerland rise the more important Jura Mountains, while from Switzerland to the sea, along the whole Italian frontier, stand the mighty peaks of the Alps. The summit of Mont Blanc (15,782 feet), which lies seven miles inside the French boundary, is the second highest peak in Europe, surpassed only by Elburz peak in the Russian Caucasus.

In Brittany and Normandy are minor groups of hills and mountains, rugged, but of no great height. North of the river Loire, in what is called the Paris basin, the successive low elevations have a uniformly gentle slope towards the west, but towards the east they present abrupt faces; and in historical times this rendered difficult the military invasion of France from the east.

Rivers Great and Small

Four great river systems—the Rhône, the Garonne, the Loire and the Seine—each with numerous tributaries, drain the well-watered soil of France. The Rhône, which carries the greatest volume of water, rises in Switzerland, flows into Lake Geneva, then out again, and enters France through a gap between the Jura and the Alps. At Lyons it picks up the waters of its great tributary, the Saône, and then turns sharply to the south by the bluffs of the Cévennes Mountains. The Rhône valley from this point to the Mediterranean coast is one of the most picturesque parts of France.

The River Garonne in the south-west of the country gathers its waters almost equally from the Pyrenees and the western slope of the Cévennes. The Loire, the longest of the French rivers, rises in the Cévennes south-west of Lyons and crosses the breadth of central France, receiving numerous tributaries and pouring at last into the Atlantic south of the peninsula of Brittany.

In northern France the Seine, after collecting the waters of the Paris basin, winds sluggishly across the plain of Normandy and empties into the English Channel at Le Havre. Its chief tributary, the Marne, and the Aisne which flows into the Oise, another tributary, formed barriers sufficient to hold the German armies advancing on Paris in the First World War (1914–18).

There are several smaller rivers to be noted. The little River Somme, which runs parallel to the Seine 50 miles to the north, has been famous in history since the campaign which led to the battle of Crécy in 1346. The Meuse and the Moselle, rivers which rise in north-eastern France, have most of their course in Belgium and Germany respectively. The Rhine also may be reckoned as partly French, for it forms a part of the eastern boundary, separating Alsace from Germany.

All the streams mentioned are more or less navigable; and connected as they are by a great network of canals, they form a system of waterways extremely valuable to French industry and commerce. The Canal du Midi, which dates from the reign of Louis XIV and connects the Mediterranean with the River Garonne and so with the Atlantic, is one of the most famous of French canals. There are others that join the Rhône, the Loire, the Seine and the Rhine systems, so that heavy freight can be carried entirely by boat to or from every important industrial region. The Rove Canal links the Rhône with Marseilles and includes the famous four-and-a-half-mile tunnel under the Rove hills. This tunnel, 70 feet wide and 50 feet high, is large enough to accommodate the heaviest of the barges that carry raw material from the chief port of southern France to the inland factories.

The greatest industry of France is agriculture. About half of the inhabitants earn their living on farms. The winds from the Atlantic Ocean, unchecked by coastal mountain ranges, carry abundant moisture to practically the whole land, thus producing conditions favourable to a wide variety of crops. Only in the extreme south-west, where a stretch of sand-dunes borders the " Landes " (marshy tracts of unproductive land), is there barren soil.

Wheat is the main cereal crop, particularly in the broad Paris basin, and France ranks as a great wheat-growing country, though production fell after the Second World War. Oats rank next, and rye and barley are raised on the poorer soils of the coast and of the eastern mountain regions.

Sugar-beet, grown on the rich plains of the north, provides the raw material for hundreds of sugar factories and refineries. A coarse tobacco is grown in some scattered parts of France; its cultivation, manufacture and sale are a government monopoly and it supplies a half of the country's need.

Among vegetables, potatoes take the first rank, as is to be expected in the land where the scientist Parmentier popularized the growing of them by inducing King Louis XVI to wear the flower of the plant in his buttonhole.

Premier Wine Producing Country

More wine is produced in France than anywhere else, though the French export so much of their finest vintages that they themselves drink poorer wines from Algeria. The provinces of Champagne and Burgundy, the regions about Bordeaux, the valleys of the Loire and the Rhône, and the hills of Languedoc in the south, are famous the world over for the products of their vineyards. Brittany and Normandy are noted for their cider.

On the luxuriant meadows of the great French plain beef and dairy cattle are raised in great numbers, and there are many tasty varieties of French cheese; while the northern provinces rear those famous breeds of draught horses—the Breton, Norman, Percheron and Flemish. The slopes of the Pyrenees are noted for mules; pigs thrive everywhere; sheep and goats are raised in great numbers on the high pasture lands of the Cévennes, the Vosges and the Jura; and vast quantities of poultry and eggs are marketed in all regions. Live-stock production increased steadily from the beginning of the 20th century, but the effects of two World Wars were disastrous.

Since before the days of the French Revolution the land of France has been divided up among many small owners, and the laws of inheritance and the customs of the people tend to perpetuate these small holdings. The average size of a French farm is

E.N.A.

A YOUNG GIRL OF ALSACE

An enormous bow of broad black silk, such as this girl is wearing, is typical of the
peasant costume of Alsace, a part of the territory for which France and Germany
have long contested, and which during the Second World War (1939–45) was
restored to France. Girls in the districts south and west of Strasbourg wear a
similar but smaller head-dress. This girl has on the full Alsatian costume.

E.N.A.; Underwood

BY GORGE AND RIVER VALLEY IN FRANCE

France presents landscapes of great variety and beauty, ranging between the flat country of the north and the mountainous district of the south. Top left is a scene on the River Tarn, which is a tributary of the Garonne. Between La Malène and Le Rozier it runs through limestone gorges of impressive grandeur. Here in the Défilé des Etroits the cliffs are beautifully coloured. Below it are the great cliffs towering above the River Drac, which drains the southern slopes of the Dauphiné Alps. Viaducts, marvels of engineering achievement, are a feature of this great ravine. Above is a scene on the Dordogne, which in its 300-mile course from Puy de Dôme to the Garonne flows through some of the most beautiful scenery in France.

E.N.A.

PEASANT LASS OF NORMANDY

In Normandy and Brittany many of the peasants still preserve their native costumes
and do their daily work in them. This girl goes about her business, with her
pannier-laden donkey, in a costume that is at once picturesque and serviceable. The
carved wooden front of the house before which she stands is typical of Normandy.

To face page 1361

FRENCH PEASANT TYPES
Carrying her baby, well-swaddled in brightly embroidered clothes, is a woman from Brittany. On the right, below, are two men of the Basque country, who, with a primitive zither and a violin, provide music for folk-dances.

about 17 acres. It is this peasant ownership which tends to promote thrift, hard work and intensive cultivation, as well as that spirit of independence and attachment to the soil which characterize the French peasant.

France ranks high among fishing countries. The north coast provinces send large fleets each year to the cod fisheries of Newfoundland and Iceland, and to the herring grounds in the North Sea. On the west coast oysters and sardines are fished, and in the Mediterranean sardines, anchovies and tunny.

About 19 per cent of the soil of France is covered with forests, especially the more mountainous regions. The quarries of the highlands produce plenty of stone for constructional work, particularly granite. The typical French farmhouse is built of stone with a thatched roof; the barn is also of stone, and many land boundaries are low stone walls.

The greatest of France's mineral resources are her iron and coal deposits, on which are based her important manufacturing industries. After 1918, when Germany was forced to return Alsace-Lorraine, France became one of the greatest iron-mining countries in Europe, her chief mines being in Lorraine. Most of the French coal seams, which are

much less extensive than the iron deposits, are along the Belgian border. After the First World War the administration of Germany's rich coalfields in the Saar basin, just across the border from Lorraine, was committed for 15 years to the League of Nations. In 1935 the Saar was reunited with Germany after a plebiscite in which most of its people voted for this union ; but in 1947 the Saar voted for economic union with France. The principal centres of French steel and iron manufacture are Lille, Nancy, Le Creusot (famous for making big guns) and St. Étienne. The last two have their own coal deposits.

The textile industries of France are famous the world over. The city of Lyons on the Rhône is one of the great silk centres in Europe. Normandy, and particularly the city of Rouen, is noted for its cotton cloth. Woollens, which rank high among French exports, are mostly manufactured in the region from Lille to Reims. Linens are made in Lille, Roubaix and other northern towns. The laces of Normandy and Brittany fetch high prices.

France is distinguished also for her fine leather goods, the exquisite porcelains of Sèvres and Limoges, the cut glass of Baccarat, the clocks of Besançon, the dresses, hats and jewelry made chiefly in Paris and its environs, and other articles of art and fashion, such as perfumery and cosmetics.

All children are compelled to go to school in France. Many of the schools are run by the State, and many more by the Roman Catholic Church ; for, though there is no established church in France, the majority of the people are Catholics. Probably the most famous of the French universities is the

Crété

FRANCE

Sorbonne, in Paris, which was founded in the middle of the 13th century by Robert de Sorbonne.

The French are not perhaps such keen sportsmen as the British, but at some games—notably lawn-tennis—they have produced players of world champion class. Motor-racing has for many years been at a very high level in France, both as regards the design of the cars and the dash and skill of the drivers; for the French character, with its indefinable " swagger " (the French word for it is *panache*) is particularly suited to such sports.

More than in any other great nation, perhaps, the life of France centres in her capital. Paris is the real heart of the nation's commerce and industry, as of its social and political affairs. The system of French roads (the Routes Nationales),

built up and extended from the famous old Roman roads, focuses upon Paris. All the big railways, which since 1937 have been owned by the State, converge there, and so do the waterways. So strong is the intellectual and artistic influence of Paris that it has earned for the metropolis the title of " intellectual capital of the world."

France is a republic, its form of government being modelled on the parliamentary plan. The principles on which it is governed are mainly those laid down at the time of the French Revolution in 1789. The Third Republic, which had arisen during the Franco-German war of 1870, died on October 21, 1945, a few months after the end of the European conflict of 1939-45. The Fourth Republic succeeded it. Under a new constitution adopted in a referendum on October 13, 1946, a Council of the Republic and a National Assembly replaced the Senate and Chamber of Deputies of the Third Republic.

For administrative purposes France is divided into some 90 " departments," taking the place of the pre-Revolution provinces, the names of which are still sometimes used. In each of the departments a certain number of deputies are elected by popular vote of all citizens 21 years old or over. These, with representatives of some of the former French colonies, form the National Assembly which sits in Paris. The upper house of the Parliament, called the Council of the Republic, consists of about 320 members elected by communal and departmental bodies.

The Council and the National Assembly jointly elect the President, whose term is seven years. Although he is the nominal head of the government, the true executive head is the Premier or President of the Council of Ministers, who is selected by the President from the dominant political party, and who in turn chooses the other members of the ministry or cabinet.

The French Republic stands at the centre of the French Union in much the same way as Great Britain in the British Commonwealth and Empire. The French Union comprises Metropolitan France (including Corsica); the Government-General of Algeria; the so-called Overseas Departments (Martinique, Guadeloupe, Réunion Island in the Indian Ocean, and French Guiana) and Overseas Territories (the French Colonies in West and Central Africa, Madagascar, and a number of

French National Railways

FRANCE : SPLENDID CATHEDRAL AT AMIENS

Regarded as the finest example of Gothic ecclesiastical architecture in France, Amiens cathedral was built mainly in the 13th century. In the above photograph can be seen the wonderful stonework of the west front. Between the towers is a magnificent rose window, and in niches below it are statues of the kings of Judah. Amiens is an important centre for the spinning and weaving of textiles.

HISTORIC SPOTS IN PICTURESQUE FRANCE

1. One of the seven noted gates of the city of Nancy, the capital of the department of Meurthe-et-Moselle. 2. Mont St. Michel is a little village built on a steep rock in the Bay of St. Michel, south of the Channel Islands, and connected with the mainland by a raised causeway. On top of the rock stands a Benedictine Abbey, founded in 708. 3. In the department of Indre-et-Loire is the château of Chenonceaux, begun in 1515. 4. At Nîmes, capital of the department of Gard, are the ruins of a Roman amphitheatre capable of accommodating 20,000 spectators. 5. Over some of the medieval timbered houses of Strasbourg towers the spire of the Gothic cathedral.

TWO CHARMING BITS OF SOUTHERN FRANCE

The whole coast bordering the Mediterranean from Cannes to the Italian frontier is known as the French Riviera. It stretches for miles, with famous resorts, quaint villages, and vistas of great beauty. This view of Nice affords some idea of the charm of this part of France. The hill in the centre is the Chateau, the site of the original village. In normal times thousands of visitors go to the Riviera in the winter to enjoy the warm climate.

The Palace of the Popes in Avignon on the Rhône is one of the most historic structures in the south of France. Influenced by the French, Pope Clement V decided in 1309 to leave Rome and to live in France, and the fortress-palace, with its great square tower, was built between 1316 and 1370. Beside it is the 12th century Cathedral of Notre Dame des Doms. The popes were in Avignon for 70 years, and later the palace was a barracks and a prison.

islands, mostly in the Pacific); and, lastly, the French Associated States, being the protectorates of Morocco and Tunis and the Federation of Indo-China. The New Hebrides in the S.W. Pacific are governed jointly by France and Great Britain.

A peculiarity of the French empire as compared with the British is that, while the British have tended to give more and more self-government to their overseas possessions until at last, as Dominions, they become entirely independent, France has adopted the opposite method, and tends to regard her dependencies as a part of France itself. Thus Algeria and the Overseas Departments are represented in the French parliament in Paris by Deputies and Councillors.

Certain small districts and factories which France had in the sub-continent of India she handed over to the new Indian Government in 1947; and in 1949 the settlement of Chandernagore elected to break away and join the Indian Union. The mandate over Syria and the Lebanon entrusted to France after the First World War was ended in 1943, when those countries became independent.

Everywhere in France one finds evidence of the country's stirring history. Perhaps it is an old walled city such as Carcassonne, whose stone towers and battlements still stand much as they were in the far-off Middle Ages. Perhaps it is the marvellous triple-arched Roman aqueduct, flung across the river valley near Nîmes 18 centuries ago and still standing in its majestic simplicity. Or it may be the twin spires of William the Conqueror's famous Abbey church at Caen in Normandy, or the queer crooked streets of Rouen and the ancient houses that once looked down upon the procession which bore Joan of Arc to the stake in the year 1431.

Those who have seen the great Gothic churches which, like gigantic carved jewels, are to be found everywhere in northern France—at Amiens, at Chartres, Le Mans, Reims, Paris—will never forget their soaring grandeur. And those who have visited the famous châteaux of France will have read some of the most stirring pages of French history in letters of stone. The list is endless. Besides these great monuments of the past, France possesses, in the Palace of the Louvre in Paris and elsewhere, some of the rarest of museum and picture collections.

Everywhere the tourist and the student find inspiring associations and reminders of the great men and women who shaped France's destiny. Here St. Bernard's fiery eloquence launched the Second Crusade. There the dramatist Molière spent his childhood. Here Rodin worked on his statue of "The Thinker," and there Cézanne painted his glowing sun-drenched landscapes. In this village Pasteur showed doubting scientists how germ diseases could be warded off. In that house the chemist Lavoisier discovered oxygen. There Marie and Pierre Curie discovered radium.

It has been France's unhappy fortune to be a principal battlefield in the two most terrible wars in history. In both the First World War and the Second, British and French fought side by side; and it will be many, many years before any British soldier, or his children after him who visit the old battlefields, will forget the glory won by British arms on French ground at Arras and Cambrai, Dunkirk and Caen.

But, perhaps more than all else, it is the charm of the French people that remains indelibly in the visitor's mind. Courteous and hospitable, elegant and witty, they extend a welcome that has led many a weary traveller to make his home in France.

From OLD GAUL to the FOURTH REPUBLIC

French history is full of famous names—from Charlemagne to De Gaulle—and of such stirring events as Joan of Arc's campaign and the great Revolution. Something of this thrilling tale is related in this chapter.

France, HISTORY OF. At the time of the Roman conquest, France was occupied by a large number of independent tribes, who were of Mediterranean stock and spoke various dialects of a Celtic tongue. The Romans found the conquest of these tribes no easy matter, but Julius Caesar overcame them and established organized Roman government (58–51 B.C.). The Gauls, as the Romans called them, adopted the Roman dress, language, and customs. Christianity spread from Rome to Gaul, where it was widely accepted as early as the 4th century.

With the decline of the Roman Empire, German barbarian invaders entered Gaul. Chief among these were the Franks, who under Clovis (481–511) established Frankish rule over most of that land. His adoption of Christianity led to the conversion of all those who served him.

The Merovingian dynasty, of which Clovis was the founder, was thrust aside by a new family—the Carolingians—who gave new life to the declining Frankish state. The greatest ruler of this line was Charlemagne (768–814). He became the supporter of the Christian Church and was crowned Emperor of the Holy Roman Empire by the Pope in Rome on Christmas Day, 800.

Charlemagne's empire after his death fell into three parts, the western part becoming the kingdom of France. But the word kingdom meant little, for the spread of the feudal system (q.v.) distributed the power of government among local rulers, and left to the king little but nominal overlordship. Under the Capetian kings, of whom Hugh Capet was the first (987), this system reached its height.

Some progress was made under Philip Augustus (1197–1223), Louis IX (1226–1270), and Philip IV (1285–1314). But France was still in a disorganized state when the Hundred Years' War with England (1337–1453) impoverished her and led to conditions approaching anarchy in many parts of the country. (Since the Norman Conquest, of course, the kings of England had been lords also of a great part of France.) A French peasant girl, Joan of Arc (q.v.), turned the tide against the English, and by 1453 only Calais remained in English hands.

France slowly recovered, and her kings—notably Louis XI (1461–83)—were able gradually to unify the nation and to centralize government in their own hands. Louis XIV (1643–1715) marked the culmination of the power of the sovereign. His authority was envied by the sovereigns of Europe and his court was widely imitated (*see* Louis, Kings of France). Meanwhile, the Protestant ideas of the so-called Huguenots spread in France in the time of Francis I (1515–47), and civil wars over religion occupied the latter part of the 16th century. Persecution of the Protestants culminated with the Massacre of St. Bartholomew in 1572; partial toleration was granted by Henry IV (1589–1610) in the Edict of Nantes (1598).

The 18th century witnessed a long struggle between England and France for colonial empire. The Treaty of Paris (1763) marked the loss by France both of her great dominions in North

From the painting by H. Levy

CHARLEMAGNE'S CORONATION

In the fifth century of the Christian era the Franks possessed most of Gaul, as France was then called. Their greatest ruler was Charlemagne (742–814), who was crowned Emperor of the Holy Roman Empire in 800 (above).

America and of her ascendancy in India. This loss, together with inefficiency and abuses at home, brought much criticism upon the government. An educated middle class was growing up who were dissatisfied with the old regime, and demanded an influence in the government proportionate to their wealth and education.

The crisis came when the financial difficulties of the state, which had been increased by the help afforded to the British North American colonies in their struggle for independence, forced the government to summon the Estates-General in 1789. There followed the Revolution, a struggle against foes within and without in order to establish a new political and social system.

The Revolution's leaders were determined that nothing should remain of the old order, and Robespierre sent thousands to the guillotine. But no just and able government was found, and in 1799 Napoleon Bonaparte, a young general born in Corsica, seized power. (*See* French Revolution ; Napoleon).

As Emperor of the French (1804–15), Napoleon attempted to make French power supreme in Europe. The attempt failed, though for a time the whole of Western Europe, save only the impregnable island fortress of Great Britain, came under the Emperor's sway. By the Congress of Vienna (1814–15) France was reduced to its former limits, and surrendered some of its colonies to Britain. But the great principles of the Revolution—nationality, constitutional government, and equality before the law, summed up in the battle-cry of "liberty, equality, fraternity"—had laid the foundations, not only of a new France, but also of a new Europe. Perhaps the most permanent work of the Revolution was to divide the big estates between the peasants.

But France was slow in accustoming herself to the new order. The Bourbons, restored on the fall of Napoleon, had "learned nothing and forgotten nothing," and they were again overthrown by the Revolution of 1830, to make way for the Orleanist prince, Louis Philippe, as a constitutional monarch. But he too fell, in the Revolution of 1848; and after a second republic, the Second Empire began under Louis Napoleon Bonaparte (nephew of Napoleon), who had a troubled reign (1851–70) as Napoleon III.

The lightly-begun but disastrous war of 1870–71 with Germany (*see* Franco-Prussian War) ended the Second Empire, and cost France Alsace-Lorraine and her boundary on the Rhine. For several years the government of France was unsettled, but with the establishment of the Third Republic (1875) a new stability and political control became evident.

The republican system of government was severely tested by the First World War (1914–18). French losses in manpower and property were prodigious. More than one-fifth of the total population was mobilized, and losses in killed and wounded were over three million. More than 9,000 square miles of northern France were occupied by the rival armies. This region contained approxi-

FRANCE : NAPOLEON OVERTHROWS THE DIRECTORY

The Republican Government established in France in 1789 by the Revolution did not work very efficiently, and 10 years later the country was virtually controlled by only five men, who called themselves the Directory. They became very unpopular, and a young but very successful General, Napoleon Bonaparte, determined to overthrow them. He achieved his purpose, with the aid of the Army, on November 9, 1799. The above painting by the French artist François Boucher (1703-70), which is in the Louvre at Paris, shows the scene in the Council of Five Hundred (parliament) when Napoleon's soldiers dispersed the assembly and arrested two members of the Directory.

mately one-eighth of France's population, and a large proportion of the nation's industries and mines. Four years of trench warfare reduced the area to one vast scene of desolation.

Restoration of this area required the expenditure of millions of francs, but it was expected that whatever was spent would ultimately be recovered from Germany under the terms of the Treaty of Versailles (1919). Failure to secure large amounts in reparation payments brought the downfall of the cabinet of Aristide Briand in January 1922. Raymond Poincaré, who succeeded Briand, attempted to force payments by seizing the Ruhr Valley, Germany's greatest coal and manufacturing district. This was an unsuccessful venture.

France had regained Alsace and Lorraine, with their coal and steel; the coal of the Saar basin, too, was controlled by France until its return to Germany in 1934. But the huge reparations originally fixed were scaled down and finally, in 1932, almost cancelled. At the same time France ceased payments on its war debt to the United States.

Feeling its security menaced by the nations that demanded revision of the Treaty of Versailles, France vigorously supported the League of Nations, the Locarno Pact (1925), and the Briand-Kellogg Pact outlawing war (Pact of Paris, 1928). At the same time, however, France enlarged its army and navy, protected its borders facing Germany with a mighty steel and concrete line of fortresses—the Maginot Line—and formed alliances with Belgium, Poland, Czechoslovakia, Yugoslavia, Rumania, and Russia.

The cost of this defence programme and of reconstruction caused in the French budget a deficit which by 1926 reached alarming size. The treasury was empty, taxes were high, prices rose, and the value of the franc slumped in the foreign exchanges. A National Union cabinet, headed by Poincaré, balanced the budget by drastic economies, and late in 1926 stabilized the franc on a gold basis at approximately 125 francs to the pound sterling.

The French Chamber of Deputies, divided into many small parties, proved an unstable body for facing troubles at home and abroad. No party had a majority; to stay in power, a premier had to satisfy several parties. Premiers who succeeded in foreign affairs were defeated on domestic issues, and a crisis abroad often brought the fall of a cabinet engaged in domestic reform. Fascist groups, such as the Croix de Feu, began to demand a dictator who would end all party bickerings.

Fear of a Fascist revolution caused Communists, Socialists, and most Radical Socialists to unite for the first time in a Popular Front of left-wing parties. In the 1936 elections the Popular Front won a sweeping victory, and the Socialist Léon Blum became premier. Most important of Blum's economic reforms was the assumption by the government of control over the Bank of France, carrying with it control over government finances and over much of the industry of the country.

Abroad, at this time, relations between Germany, Austria, and Italy suggested troubles ahead for France. Hence the Blum ministry made vigorous efforts to get the other Powers to pledge themselves to neutrality in the Spanish civil war (1936–39), which had come about with a movement headed by General Franco (*q.v.*) to overthrow the Spanish Republican regime.

But while his foreign policy received a large measure of support, Blum's direction of home affairs was violently criticized, and in June 1937 he was forced to resign when the Senate refused to grant him the semi-dictatorial powers which he declared were made necessary by the country's critical financial situation. He was succeeded by Camille Chautemps, whose government lasted only until March 10, 1938, when the Socialists refused to support Chautemps's demand for special financial powers. Hitler, dictator of Germany, seized the opportunity provided by the French Cabinet crisis to occupy Austria. Blum returned for a short space, but resigned on April 8; two days later Edouard Daladier formed a Government.

Approach of the German Menace

Daladier strove to live up to the reputation of France's strong man. He ended a wave of strikes, devalued the franc yet again, and enacted a 48-hour week in factories engaged on vital national work. But international affairs overshadowed domestic matters. Step by step Hitler destroyed the territorial system in Central and Eastern Europe which France had so carefully built up. At Munich in September 1938 Daladier concurred in the dismemberment of Czechoslovakia, and was able to do nothing more than protest when in March 1939 the rest of that state was engulfed. There were influential people in French politics who would do little to balk Germany's plans for conquest and foray. Others, with the memory of France's dreadful losses in the war of 1914–18 before them, sought peace at almost any price.

Hitler backed up his supporters with a pretence of peaceful intentions towards France, and in December 1938 Herr von Ribbentrop and M. Bonnet (Daladier's Foreign Minister) signed a non-aggression pact in Paris. But still the French situation worsened both at home and abroad. Daladier was still at the helm when on September 3, 1939, France, none too willingly, followed Britain with a declaration of war against Germany.

From September to the following May neither France nor Germany seriously attacked the other; and when the German onslaught finally came in the summer of 1940, it was the miserable story of 1870 over again. The French army was big, but its equipment was old-fashioned; practically the whole of France's preparations for war had gone into fortifying the Maginot Line, and when the attack came the Germans broke through north of the Line's northernmost fort. The French and British forces were cut in two and forced to surrender or escape by sea. The Germans overran France without great difficulty, and Paul Reynaud, who had replaced Daladier as premier in March 1940, himself gave place to the aged Marshal Pétain, hero of the First World War, who in June sued for an armistice with the Germans.

France under Hitler's Yoke

The whole of northern and western France, including Paris, was occupied by the Germans, leaving an unoccupied area to the south-east. In Vichy, within this zone, Pétain set up a government which was virtually a dictatorship, and in late 1942 this zone was occupied also.

The French were at first dazed by the speed of events; but within a couple of years it was evident that there was considerable resistance going on "underground." At last, in 1942, Admiral Darlan, who had been one of Pétain's chief collaborators, crossed to Algiers and offered his help to the Anglo-American Allies who had landed there.

The French might have been completely crushed in 1940 had it not been for the action of one man, General Charles de Gaulle. As soon as he learned that there was to be an armistice he crossed to London and there broadcast an appeal for Frenchmen to leave France and continue the struggle from outside, along with Britain. Thus was born the movement called at first the Free French, later the Fighting French.

Some of the French colonies rallied to the cause of the Free French; and with the Allied landings in the French North African territories in November 1942 the tide began to turn. General de Gaulle set up a Committee of National Liberation in Algiers, which was virtually an exiled government.

British and American forces landed in France in the great invasion of the continent, June 1944. Free French forces were with them, and it was a French division under General Leclerc that re-took Paris the following August. On August 31 the Committee of Liberation left Algiers for France, and General de Gaulle became head of a provisional government.

But the Third Republic could not be restored in its old form. After two plebiscites the constitution of a Fourth Republic was approved in October, 1946, and Vincent Auriol was elected president in January, 1947. The constituent assemblies of 1945 and 1946 had nationalized the mines, gas, electricity, insurance and the big credit banks, and reconstruction of the country's economy had begun. General de Gaulle retired from office, while one political leader after another strove to establish financial stability. France had been liberated from the invader, but she had still to find her feet. The dramatic events of 1939-1945 had left scars which would take many years to efface.

SPLENDOURS OF FRENCH PAINTING

Now in the National Gallery, London, this superb portrait of the French statesman Cardinal Richelieu in the grand manner is strangely enough almost a replica of another painting by the same artist in the Louvre, Paris. Philippe de Champaigne (1602–74) though one of the earlier French portrait painters, was none the less a brilliant artist, especially when he had a great man as his subject. Also in the National Gallery is another most interesting portrait by Champaigne, showing three views of Richelieu's head.

THE GRANDEUR OF CLAUDE LORRAIN'S ART REVEALED IN A CLASSICAL COMPOSITION

In many ways the inventor of the classical school in painting, and also the first great master who was essentially a landscape painter, Claude Lorrain (1600–82), like Philippe de Champaigne, was painting during the most notable period of French figures (which he seldom did himself), with classical and pseudo-classical buildings and ruins, with ships, and with exquisite studies in landscape. Yet they command attention by their unity and completeness as works of art. This picture,

EARLY MASTERPIECES BY POUSSIN AND LE NAIN

he artists of the two pictures seen here came before the awn of the great period of French painting. Nicholas oussin (1594–1665) painter of the upper picture was the roducer of many fine early landscapes. Le Nain—the name is used to describe the work of three brothers, Antoine, Louis and Mathieu—bringing something quite new to French art, depicted the life of the lower classes. 'The Card Players' (lower) is one of their finest works.

FAMED BEAUTIES IMMORTALIZED ON CANVAS

Two famous beauties are depicted here. At the top, done with all the easy grace of François Boucher's (1703–70) brush, is Madame de Pompadour (in the National Gallery, Edinburgh); below is Jacques Louis David's (1748–1825) study of Madame Récamier (in the Louvre). The lace and fripperies of the Golden Age of Louis XIV (1638–1715) have given way to the classical severity of the Empire manner, which came in with Napoleon I (1769–1821).

SIMPLE CHARM OF CHARDIN'S RESTFUL ART

It is perhaps characteristic of the encouragement given by the State to all genuine artists in France that Jean Siméon Chardin (1699–1779), who was doing such quiet, homely studies as this during the rich and florid age of Louis XIV, should have received full recognition from the greatest in the land. In any other country he might well have worked almost unknown, This lovely painting ' La Mère Laborieuse,' is in the Louvre, Paris ; but there are some fine examples of Chardin's work in Britain, especially at the National Gallery, London. He was a splendid colourist, and, learning from the Dutch, knew well how to make the most of light and shade in his interiors.

PEASANTS AND COUNTRYSIDE BY BARBIZON MASTERS

Jean François Millet (1814–75) was the real founder of the Barbizon School. Glorifying the French peasants in a series of pictures, of which The Angelus (upper, in the Louvre, Paris) is perhaps the best-known, he drew round him a group of similar painters who, however, specialized more in the countryside itself than in the inhabitants. Of these a typical artist was Théodore Rousseau (1812–67), whose Sunset at Fontainebleau (lower, in the Louvre), though influenced by Corot (see example of this artist's work in page 914) has a truth to Nature which is distinctly pleasing. Tremendous prices were paid towards the end of the 19th century for pictures such as this.

IMPRESSIONISM AND AFTER: MONET AND CEZANNE

Claude Monet (1840–1926) was the actual originator of Impressionism, perhaps the most important movement in pictorial art since the Renaissance. He was mainly interested in the effects of light, and in their correct reproduction in paint, as is well shown in his Break-up of the Ice (upper). Paul Cézanne (1839–1906), on the other hand, a leading figure in the Post-Impressionist movement—so called only because it followed Impressionism—was more concerned with the constructional aspect of Nature. In this quiet beautifully-modelled river scene (lower) can be seen how simply Cézanne could convey the solidity and mass of natural objects.

RENOIR FINDS BEAUTY IN UMBRELLAS

Pierre Renoir (1841–1919) is one of the Impressionists whose work is often difficult to understand and to appreciate, but such a lovely painting as this appeals to nearly everybody. Entitled Les Parapluies (the umbrellas), it shows a Parisian crowd caught in a rainstorm. All his women and children have a delightful vitality which contrasted strongly with the stiff, severe and dull academic pictures of his day. Renoir's work, which includes many landscapes, is also distinguished by brilliant colouring. This painting hangs in the National Gallery, London.

A GALAXY *of* GREAT FRENCH PAINTERS

For centuries France has led Europe in the arts, succeeding Italy in the 17th century in the brilliance of her painters, whose achievements well deserve to be set beside the masterpieces of her men of letters.

France, ART OF. The art of France—or, at least, the pictorial art, with which we are here principally concerned—begins with the glories of the illuminated manu-

National Gallery

Delacroix (1798–1863) has been called the founder of Modern Art. Above is his portrait of Baron Schwiter.

scripts. As in England, these went through a number of periods and schools, of which the culmination was that of the 15th century, marked by the superb manuscripts done for the Duke of Berry. Early paintings which survive include the famous Parement de Narbonne, executed on silk about 1375 ; the works of Jean Malouel, with their pronounced Sienese influence; and other works, also showing Italian influence, which resulted from the establishment of the Popes at Avignon during the 14th century.

It is, however, to the last of the schools of illumination that we turn for our first really great French pictorial artist, Jean Fouquet (*c.* 1415–85). Combining both Italian and Flemish influences, Fouquet was not only an absolute master of miniature painting and illumination, but also a painter of the first rank, both of portraits and altar-pieces.

During Fouquet's lifetime, too, were done the Pietà of Villeneuve-les-Avignon, which is now in the Louvre at Paris ; the lovely Annunciation of Aix-en-Provence; and the glorious triptych of Moulins cathedral—none of them attributable to any known artist. Mention may be made also of the works of Nicolas Froment and Enguerrand Quarton. It is, however, in the 16th century that we find the first great names in French painting.

Jean Clouet (died *c.* 1541), his son François Clouet (died 1572), and other members of their school, did many excellent portraits, distinct enough from all other contemporary art to make them the founders of a predominantly French school. Corneille de Lyon (1505–74) was another painter whose rather more life-like portraits are executed in much the same manner. A great advance is seen in the works of Ambrose Dubois (1543–1614), who, like the majority of these earlier French painters, was of Flemish extraction. Through him Italian masters exercised a tremendous influence in France. Simon Vouet (1590–1649) similarly worked from Italian principles, as did Sébastien Bourdon (1616–71), whose small pictures of scenes of everyday life were full of charm.

While the French Academic school were still working on Italian lines—for the Academy had been founded in 1648—a new, more national art was springing up. It was due in part to the work

of the three brothers Le Nain, whose individual efforts cannot therefore always be distinguished. They were Antoine (*c.* 1588–1648), Louis (1599–1648), and Mathieu (1607–77), and they principally depicted the lives of the French working classes. A far greater figure than any so far encountered was Nicolas Poussin (1594–1665), who, living for many years at Rome and influenced by Titian and Raphael, brought about a complete revolution in French art. He illustrated the myths of classical antiquity and scenes from the Bible, and painted some of the world's finest landscapes. In figure-painting, too, he stands high above all his French contemporaries.

With the policy of Louis XIV, art had begun already to come under the direct patronage of the State, and many fine portraits, such as that of Richelieu, were done by Philippe de Champaigne (1602–74) and others of the same school. Charles Le Brun (1619–90), Louis's court painter, was in 1660 put by Colbert in charge of the royal tapestry works of Gobelins, and from that date art in France, officially recognized, encouraged and supported by the State, has been one of the country's major export industries.

Portrait painting under Rigaud (1659–1743) became frigid and stilted. An excess of " good taste " led to lifeless representation and over-emphasis of detail. The impressive style of the 17th century portraitists, such as Mignard (1610–95), was about to give way to the fantasies of Antoine Watteau (*see* below).

The next great figure is Claude Gelée (1600–81), known usually as Claude, or as Claude Lorrain (*see* Lorrain, Claude). Claude worked in Rome, which accounts chiefly for the antique decoration, the classical ruins and the titles of many of his finest pictures. But the figures in his works were hardly ever done by Claude himself, and it is as the first great landscape master that he stands supreme. In painting the effects of light, and especially the warmer lights of evening, Claude has never been surpassed, except, possibly, by Turner.

These last-named French painters, together with innumerable lesser men, were contemporaries, flourishing for the most part in the earlier half of the reign of Louis XIV. In the later part of the reign and on into that of Louis XV come many fine painters, such as François Desportes (1661–1743) and J. B. Oudry (1686–1755), and the great master, Antoine Watteau (1684–1721). Watteau lived in Paris, so that here at last we have an artist whose work is truly French. He was influenced by Rubens and by the great Venetians. And though fame came slowly, he is known now as one of the greatest of all decorative artists as well as a superb draughtsman; his influence on all subsequent European painting is immense.

Contemporary with Watteau are other great painters, such as Lancret (1660–1743), who, though older, was his pupil and who emphasized the frivolous side of Watteau's manner; and Chardin (1699–1779), one of the world's greatest painters of still life and interiors, all of which showed strong Dutch influence, and a fine portraitist in pastel. He it was who taught Fragonard (1732–1806), another painter in the Watteau tradition, with whom is associated Boucher (1703–70), known for his portraits of Madame de Pompadour and equally lovely nudes. Many of these artists, it should be noted, were also fine etchers.

With the death of Fragonard comes the end of the exquisitely decorative period of French art known as Rococo, when not only painting, but all the other arts, from book-illustration to ceramics and furniture, had flourished exceedingly, influencing the whole of western Europe. You have only to think of Gobelin tapestries, Sèvres porcelain, and furniture which bears the name of André-Charles Boule (1642–1732), to see this. But with the French Revolution, or shortly after it, came the Industrial Revolution, and few artists indeed could survive the double storm. Among them, however, was one great painter, Louis David (1748–1825), who was equally important under the Republic and under Napoleon, for whom as court painter he did much of his finest work. David painted portraits, such as the wonderfully observed Madame Récamier, and he was also the chief founder of the Directoire and, later, the Empire styles, which had tremendous influence in England and were a direct reaction to the aristocratic art of the

Tate Gallery, London

LANDSCAPE BY BONNARD

Amongst the more important of modern French artists, Pierre Bonnard (1867–1947) displayed a masterly technique in his interiors, still lifes, and landscapes, which are chiefly urban in character, such as The Window, above. Bonnard was an exponent of a modified form of Impressionism.

18th century. Other painters of this time were the miniaturist Isabey (1767–1855), Prud'hon (1758–1823), Gros (1771–1835), and finally Greuze (1725–1805), whose small and sentimental paintings enjoyed popularity throughout the 19th century.

The first name of the next period is that of Eugène Delacroix (1798–1863). He was a great admirer of the English painter Constable, the chief manifestation of this being the brilliance and purity of his colour. A fine draughtsman, he painted some superb portraits, and for his originality in breaking away from tradition he has been called the founder of Modern Art. Parallel with him worked Ingres (1780–1867), whose pictures are remarkable for their fine draughtsmanship, the smooth quality of the paint and the delicacy of the brush-work; and indeed it was Ingres's proud

boast that he carried on the old tradition of his master, David, rather than indulging in novelties as did his rival. At the same time, too, the master of the Barbizon school were beginning to work among the fields and woods of Fontainebleau. The chief of these were Diaz (1808–76), Théodore Rousseau (1812–67), Courbet (1819–77), Daubigny (1817–78), and—in a sense slightly apart from the others—Corot and J. F. Millet. The Barbizon landscape painters enjoyed a tremendous vogue during the 19th century. Corot (1796–1875) alone has suffered no eclipse. His French landscapes may no longer command attention ; but his earlier work, his landscapes of Rome, and his fine portraits are the more appreciated. Millet (1814–75), with his famous series of pictures which glorified for the first time the French peasantry, worked chiefly at Barbizon, where he painted his famous Angelus, and The Reapers.

Very different in their aims were Puvis de Chavannes (1824–98), greatest of modern mural decorators, Daumier (1808–79), a caricaturist and realist of immense power and great originality, and Courbet (1819–77), who began the reactionary movement against the insipidity of the classicist descended from Ingres and David. As these men reached the height of their fame the great French Impressionists, derided by critics and public alike, were already at work. For by the middle of the 19th century art in France had at last become freed from officialdom, chiefly through the efforts of Delacroix, both a painter and teacher. Thus, when Napoleon III inaugurated the Salon des Refusés, in 1868, for those whose works were not accepted by the Salon, artistic freedom was complete.

The Impressionists are described under Impressionism, where some account of their successors, the post-Impressionists, is also given. Here it remains to do little more than name them. First, as the originator of the Impressionist manner, was Claude Monet (1840–1926). His leading followers were Edouard Manet (1832–83), who painted landscapes, portraits, and interior scenes, and whose Déjeuner sur l'herbe was one of the most discussed pictures of its time; Renoir (1841–1919), a painter of portraits and scenes of everyday life; Degas (1834–1917), painter of ballet and horses; and the satirist, Toulouse-Lautrec (1864–1901).

Others whose work was based on Impressionism were Seurat (1859–91) and Camille Pissarro (1830–1903). Their successors, known as the post-Impressionists, were Gauguin (1848–1903), Cézanne (1839–1906), and Van Gogh (1853–90), who was a Dutchman by birth. Picasso (b. 1881), founder of Cubism and by far the most important influence on 20th century painting, is a superb draughtsman, a tireless experimenter, the leader of the now ceaseless efforts to find a pure art, an unrepresentational art for art's sake. His contemporaries include Braque (b. 1881), who during the years before the First World War (1914–18) worked with him; and Matisse (b. 1869), whose chief preoccupation is the creation of a fine colour-pattern. With him was Derain (b. 1880), famous as a painter of still-life, and as a designer of theatrical settings.

The work of Vlaminck (b. 1876), like that of Bonnard (1867–1947) and Vuillard (1868–1940) and of Utrillo (b. 1883), shows Impressionist influence. More recent exponents are Dufy and Jean Lurçat, the first representing a severe formalism and the second a modish decorative quality in painting. Rouault, another important painter, was a daring experimenter in form and colour. The tragic tone and absence of satire or moral implications put him in a class by himself, though he has been compared to the Flemish Jerome Bosch.

Many of the best abstract painters, together with the Surrealists and representatives of other kindred movements, cannot be discussed here in the space available; nor can France's fine modern sculptors, such as Maillol (a successor of Rodin), and her architects, such as Le Corbusier. (*See also* Impressionism; Surrealism; and articles on the individual painters).

In general it must always be remembered that art in France, more than in any other country in the world, tends to become an industry; and the outstanding painters, no matter what their creed, are sooner or later enlisted to apply their own art for the uses of the general public.

The SPEECH and WRITINGS of the FRENCH

The French tongue is a superb instrument for the expression of thought, in which it is possible to state subtleties that are lost in other speech. This language and what has been written in it are examined here.

France, LANGUAGE AND LITERATURE OF. Latin is the parent language of French, as it is of all the Romance Languages (*q.v.*). Traces of this parentage are clearly to be seen in the great numbers of words that have come directly from Latin. Such words as *père* (father) from the Latin *pater*, and *mère* (mother) from the Latin *mater* clearly show this origin. French words, in the main, are simply Latin words which have been modified by natural development.

Of the various dialects of Latin which sprang up over Europe during the early centuries of the Christian era, French was the first to be recognized as a separate language. By the 9th century the dialect spoken in the north and centre of what is now France, and that spoken in the south, had undergone such marked differences that they were known by distinct names. The tongue (*langue*) of the south was called the *langue d'oc*, and that of the north the *langue d'oïl*, from the fact that yes in the south was *oc* and in the north *oïl*.

Out of the northern tongue has developed the French language of today, a language which yields to none in clearness and richness. Not that in French it is necessary to express all thought bluntly and crudely. On the contrary, the language lends itself to the greatest precision in thought and phrase. And for all fine variations of meaning, for delicate differences, French is the perfect tongue, because even in vague, cloudy matters, French must be clear. The very word *nuance*, by which the French indicate a subtle distinction, is used by us in default of an exact English equivalent.

This love for preciseness and clearness in literature is sharpened by the French social instinct. More than any other people, the French put the emphasis on society; less than any other do they interest themselves in the individual. For this reason they have a social literature, that is, a literature which concerns itself with matters of general social interest, rather than with the personal problems of the individual. Their writers remain within the circle of common experience, and less often explore the uncommon, the mystic, the fantastic.

In depth French literature compares favourably with any other. But it has a depth of intelligence rather than of emotion, its fine distinctions are of thought rather than of feeling, its beauties are more often of form than of content, its triumphs are analytical and concrete rather than poetical or visionary. In view of such qualities as these in the French mind, it is, therefore, not surprising that French literature has gathered more laurels in prose than in poetry, whose very fabric is reverie, the intangible, the inscrutable. The French ardour for beauty of form has rendered their style of verse somewhat severe and rigid, though most graceful, elegant, and polished.

But when reading French prose, we discover how French clearness, French elegance and French insight truly come into their own. In a world bitter with prejudice and disturbed with fantastic visions, the Frenchman seems able to see with clear eyes, to perceive with a cool heart. Such have been the distinctions of French literature through a long history, that any brief account of it runs the risk of becoming little more than a mustering of world-famous names.

But before we come to the earliest of these names, those of the chroniclers Villehardouin, Joinville, and Froissart (*c.* 1338–1404), there is a vast mass of folk-epics in verse, of lyric poetry, of mystery and miracle plays, and of chronicles. As in all other literatures, verse preceded prose. The songs of the troubadors offer a typical example of the age of chivalry, and it is not until the 14th century that we find any considerable body of prose composition. This took the form of history, or chronicles, represented at their best by Froissart, the famous contemporary of Petrarch in Italy and Chaucer in England, who enriched and invigorated the French tongue, as Petrarch did Italian and Chaucer did English. Soon after Froissart came Villon (c. 1431–c. 1485), the vagabond poet, whose hauntingly sweet and powerful lyrics reveal him as the greatest figure in French literature up to the time of the great men of the 16th century. These—Rabelais, the jovial humorist and satirist; Montaigne, first of the essayists; Calvin, the luminous theologian; Ronsard, the elegant and original poet—these were the men who moulded the French tongue into much the form it has today, expanding its resources, and making it the pliable, powerful vehicle of one of the world's greatest literatures.

The French translation of the Bible, made in the 16th century, was a factor of weight in shaping the modern French language, in the same way that the development of English, German, and other European tongues was vitally influenced by their own popular versions of the Scriptures.

During the closing years of the 16th and the opening years of the 17th century, while Shake-speare was liberating English poetry from its rigid formalism and artificiality, Malherbe, poet and critic, was framing a concise form and cramping tradition for French poetry. In the 17th century came also the first of the *salons*, or fashionable literary gatherings of Paris, and the establishment of the French Academy, two powerful factors in the cultivation of taste and a sense of literary form.

One of the supreme ages in French literature was the long reign (1643 to 1715) of Louis XIV. During this period flourished the three dramatic giants Corneille, Racine, and Molière; the preacher Bossuet; that strange mixture of cleric and mystical philosopher Fénelon; the saint and savant Pascal; the poet and critic Boileau; the inimitable letter-writer Madame de Sévigné; the wits La Rochefoucauld and La Bruyère ; and many others.

Then came the satiric Voltaire—sharply rational, gay, capricious, witty, chatty, vindictive, generous, who attacked superstitions and social abuses in scores of volumes, which have been termed " a chaos of clear ideas." His influence lay over all France until the advent of the Swiss Jean-Jacques Rousseau.

Bibliothèque Nationale, Paris

AN ILLUSTRATION FROM FROISSART'S CHRONICLES

Events in England, Scotland, Ireland, France and Spain between 1325 and 1400 were recorded by Jean Froissart in his famous Chronicles. A period of chaos in France followed the defeat of the French by the English at the battle of Poitiers in 1356, and in 1358 the peasants in Normandy rose in rebellion. The rising was suppressed with great severity, and this illustration from the Chronicles shows peasants being slaughtered by French knights.

MOLIÈRE AT BREAKFAST WITH LOUIS XIV

There is a story that when the great dramatist Molière (1622-73) held a position in the household of Louis XIV, the members of the Court refused to sit at breakfast with him because he was an actor and, therefore, in their opinion, not a gentleman. The king, who appreciated Molière's genius, invited him to share his own meal. When the courtiers entered the room they were astonished to see the actor at the table with the king, because usually nobody was permitted to be with Louis at breakfast. This illustration is from a painting by Jean Léon Gérôme (1824-1904).

A vagabond and lackey, Rousseau voiced the ideas which found their logical development in the French Revolution and overthrew the existing social order; half-starved, cooped up in a garret, he launched advanced notions of hygiene and education.

The 18th century died in the horror of the French Revolution. Diderot, joint editor of the great French Encyclopédie, and Buffon, the philosophic naturalist, did not live to witness the Revolution. Bernardin de Saint-Pierre survived to produce his once popular romance, Paul and Virginia.

The Revolution destroyed a world of formalism and feudalism, and raised the curtain on the modern age. The old classical rules of writing, such as the strict observance of the unities of time, place, and action, were smashed, along with political laws. Writers made new forms, used words in new and vivid ways. This was known as romanticism.

The acute and cynical Stendhal (Henri Beyle, 1783-1842), when reproached for his romanticism, declared he held a lottery ticket for the year 1935. His fame did not delay so long, however. Stendhal may be regarded as the creator of the modern novel of psychological analysis, and his style was intended to attain the exactitude and detachment of an official document.

Balzac and Hugo, Mérimée and Dumas and George Sand, were the true leaders of the romantic movement. The vast stage of living beings of Balzac dwell in a world expressly made for them by Balzac. Hugo found no theme too dramatic, no tale too powerful, for his gifted pen. Mérimée introduced the use of local colour, painting an exotic background, as in Carmen. George Sand lost herself in a morass of sentimentality; and Dumas (1802-70), the elder, poured forth a flood of lively tales.

The poet Alfred de Musset wrote fervid and impassioned lyrics, and Charles Baudelaire made great poetry of dark themes; Hugo said he gave the world a new shiver. Théophile Gautier wrote poems, novels, and dramas of flawless excellence.

With Gustave Flaubert (1821-80) the new page of realism was turned in French literature. Flaubert presented life in its true colours. He worked upon his prose like a sculptor of gems. His insight into character made the novel of incident seem trivial. Even more self-consciously realistic, or naturalistic, were the Goncourt brothers, who took notes on scenes in hospitals to get at the facts.

Dumas, the younger (1824-95), a more careful workman than his famous father, wrote dramas rebuking a wayward world. He was far exceeded, however, by Émile Zola (1840-1902), whose own energetic temperament infused power into his tales of degradation.

More typical of the French genius was Ernest Renan, gentle sceptic, brilliant historian, and stylist, as were also Hippolyte Taine, Émile Faguet and Ferdinand Brunetière, all critics of widely recognized distinction.

Anatole France (1844-1924), who recommended irony and pity as the best reply to modern life, has been likened to the great essayist, Montaigne, as having most delicately distilled a penetrating, smiling, disbelieving quality in the French spirit.

Guy de Maupassant (1850–93), genius of the short story, perfected condensation, cold analysis, and the bare, powerful style. Lover of the Orient and of the exotic, master of poetic prose, was Pierre Loti (1850–1923), whose slight plots served as frames to long, delightful travel sketches. Paul Bourget (1852–1935), in his long list of novels, opposed naturalism but borrowed its method, weighting his tale, however, with a heavy moral or sociological thesis.

Determined to present the spirit of France, Maurice Barrès (1862–1923) turned abruptly from the pure egoism of his earlier works, such as Le Culte du Moi, to an almost fanatical belief that " every living being is born of a race, a soil, an atmosphere, and genius manifests itself only in proportion as it is linked with its land and its dead." Barrès was profoundly affected by German philosophy; and so likewise was Henri Bergson (1859–1941), a philosopher noted for his forceful charming prose. Bergson held that the true nature of things is revealed to us more by intuition than by reasoning. This idea, essentially un-French, has influenced 20th-century French writers so widely as to give Bergson literary importance.

An unusual understanding and appreciation of German character appeared in the ten-volume Jean-Christophe, by Romain Rolland (1866–1944), whose freedom from national prejudices won him much harsh criticism. Rolland's masterpiece was as well known outside France as were the plays of his contemporary, Edmond Rostand (1868–1918), whose Cyrano de Bergerac and Chantecler delighted audiences in many lands.

Symbolism, which makes its appearance from time to time down the centuries in all literatures, was rediscovered in France and elsewhere towards the end of the 19th century, particularly by the poets. Leader of the symbolists was Henri de Régnier (1864–1936), until he made an abrupt return to classical Greek traditions.

Quite the opposite was Francis Jammes (1868–1938). Simplicity, love of Nature and of animals, and a deep understanding of the character of the French peasant and provincial, brought his verses great popularity. His Catholicism was less austere, his poetic fire less brilliant, than that of Paul Claudel (born 1868), dramatist and poet.

Thoroughly pagan and thoroughly modern was the poetry of the Comtesse de Noailles (1876–1933). She wrote of the rapture of love, the terror of death, of her search for beauty. A similarly pagan trend pervaded the novels in classical style of Pierre Louÿs (1870–1925).

ANATOLE FRANCE
Author of many works of fiction, satire and criticism, Anatole France (1844–1924) occupied a position of unrivalled influence in French literature during his lifetime.

Of all modern writers, Marcel Proust (1871–1922) most deeply influenced world literature. His thoughts trailed out in a filigree of elaborate sentences, and he was the first and most convincing of novelists to recognize that a man is not the same from moment to moment. His series À la Recherche du Temps Perdu constitutes a whole world, a whole literature, enshrining the past with mastery of technique.

MARCEL PROUST
The literature of many countries has been influenced by the works of Marcel Proust (1871–1922).

As distinguished as Proust, though less famous, was Paul Valéry (1871–1945), who succeeded to the place of Anatole France in the Académie Française. Because of his horror of facility, Valéry's slowly and carefully written volumes make but a thin package. In his work one feels that intelligence, like a keen steel blade, typical of French writing. His deep study of the human spirit, not as a social unit but as a lonely thing, is as fine, in a totally different way, as the slow brooding of Proust. Valéry was induced to publish his works by André Gide (born 1869), himself a deft writer, whose L'Immoraliste and Symphonie Pastorale are fine studies of the Puritan conscience.

One of the best-known of French books of the First World War (1914–18) was Le Feu (Under Fire) by Henri Barbusse (1874–1935), who did not surpass his war success. Jean Giraudoux, with Lecture pour une Ombre, and Henri de Montherlant (born 1896), with Le Songe, produced meritorious books on the First World War.

Georges Duhamel (born 1884) opposed war in a number of effective short stories. The taint of decay left in Europe by the war and political upheavals was implied in the books of Paul Morand (born 1888), who had a considerable success with Ouvert la Nuit, as did André Maurois (born 1885), a keen observer of English life and character, with his popular Les Silences du Colonel Bramble, and with Ariel, the life of Shelley. Jean Richard Bloch's (born 1884) Et Cie, displayed a talent with the flavour of Balzac. He also wrote one of the best recent French plays, Le dernier Empereur. A vast realist novel in more than 20 volumes, Les Hommes de Bonne Volonté, brought fame to Jules Romains (born 1885). François Mauriac (born 1885), tortured by a sense of the evil nature of love, wrote bleak, powerful tales.

Jean Cocteau, (b. 1891), after experimenting with the freakish literary style known as Dadaism, revealed his power in Thomas l'Imposteur, 1923, and Les Enfants Terribles.

An important aspect of French literature during the inter-war years (1919–39) was the subconscious tendency of prose writers and poets to give expression to the discoveries of psycho-analysis. One of the chief exponents of Surrealism was André Breton (born 1896), who edited La Révolution Surréaliste, 1924, a publication that influenced contemporary painting and poetry.

Georges Bernanos (1888–1948) also turned to political subjects during the 1930s, as in Les Grandes Cimetières sous la Lune, a survey of international problems and the French attitude to them in 1938. Much of the political literature relating so the turmoil of Europe at this time failed to survive the Second World War (1939–45). The leading figure of the 1940s was Jean-Paul Sartre, whose Existentionalist philosophy, which was primarily concerned with the nature and experience of the individual, was expressed in drama rather than literature. Jacques Maritain (born 1882) was the leader of a more academic group. The Rights of Man and Natural Law, 1944, re-stated the need for Christian ethics to be applied to a society which was in danger of destroying civilization.

Francis I, KING OF FRANCE (1494–1547).

The son of Charles, Count of Angoulême, Francis I was married at an early age to Claudia, daughter of his cousin King Louis XII of France, and the death of that monarch without a son brought Francis to the throne in 1515.

In his reign the Renaissance (revival of art and learning), which had begun in Italy, flowered in France. He fostered literature and art, invited painters and scholars to his kingdom, founded libraries, opened schools, and built several of the finest palaces in France.

Not content with building up his kingdom within, Francis sought also to extend its boundaries by engaging in a series of wars with Charles V, king of Spain and Germany. His immediate object was to win Milan; the more distant aim was to reassert France's claims to supremacy throughout the Italian peninsula. These wars filled the greater part of Francis's reign, and left France exhausted. He won a great victory at Marignano in 1515, but failed at the Field of the Cloth of Gold in 1520 to secure the support of Henry VIII of England; in 1525 Francis was defeated at Pavia, taken prisoner, and forced to pay a huge ransom (1526). In 1529 he won certain concessions from Charles, whose sister he married in 1530. The struggle was resumed in 1536, but had reached no definite conclusion at his death on March 31, 1547.

Francis Joseph, EMPEROR OF AUSTRIA AND KING OF HUNGARY (1830–1916).

Born on August 18, 1830, Francis Joseph ascended the Hapsburg throne in 1848, when his uncle, the weak-minded emperor Ferdinand, was forced to abdicate by the insurrections that swept his dominions.

After the painting by Horowitz

FRANCIS JOSEPH I

Ruler of a dual monarchy including peoples of diverse race and culture, Francis Joseph held his empire together during one of the longest reigns in the world's history.

Austrian prestige suffered seriously in 1859 owing to the loss of Lombardy in a war with France and Piedmont, and in 1866 by the further loss of the leadership of the German states through defeat by Prussia.

The emperor in 1867 proclaimed a constitution by which the empire of Austria and the kingdom of Hungary became two equal and almost independent powers, united only by the person of their common sovereign and by a common administration of military, financial, and foreign affairs (the Dual Monarchy). Francis Joseph retained a large measure of personal control, but he never openly repudiated constitutional government.

To his mastery of the many languages and dialects of his realm, as well as to his tact, generosity, and attractive manners, he owed a large measure of popularity. Personal misfortune again and again assailed him. He lost his only son by suicide, and his wife by assassination; and popular sympathy inclined the more to him.

Meanwhile, Austria had entered into close alliance with the German Empire, and together an ambitious policy was pursued in the Balkans and the Near East. The assassinations of the Austrian heir-apparent, Francis Ferdinand, and his wife at Serajevo, Bosnia, on June 28, 1914, afforded a dramatic opportunity to strike the decisive blow which, in the opinion of the German and Austrian emperors, would settle Balkan affairs once for all. But it was with great reluctance that Francis Joseph agreed to the harsh and ruthless terms of the ultimatum submitted to Serbia, and subsequently, to the declaration of war. Francis Joseph died in 1916, and it was left to his grand-nephew and successor Charles Francis, who abdicated in 1918, to see the break-up of the Hapsburg empire.

Francis of Assisi, SAINT (c. 1182–1226).

The founder of the great order of the Franciscans, Friars Minor, Minorites, or Grey Friars, and one of the most beautiful characters in all history, Saint Francis was born at Assisi (pron. *a-sē'-zē*), in central Italy, of a well-to-do family named Bernardone. A great change took place in Francis's life in his early twenties, after confinement as a prisoner of war and a serious illness. The old round of worldly pleasure and display no longer appealed to him; he sold his property in order to give to the Church, and began to tend the poor.

This conduct angered his father, and he disinherited his son. Then Francis, wearing an old cloak, occupied himself with repairing tumble-down churches and chapels round Assisi. At last, throwing aside even his stick, wallet and shoes, like the apostles of old, he lived in absolute poverty, tending the lepers, preaching in the streets and public squares, and often treated as a madman.

Soon this saintly man began to attract followers. In grey habits, barefoot, and without money, they went forth two by two to spread the gospel of service and divine poverty through central Italy. When he had a dozen followers, Francis received Pope Innocent III's sanction to continue his work. Later, as they grew very numerous, the Pope began to give them many privileges.

The humble founder, fearing lest his order should become ambitious and powerful, drew up a rigid rule showing how " in poverty and humility serving God " they should remain absolutely possessionless, and should confidently seek alms and minister to the poor and sick. When a girl of 18 named Clare left her home to become a follower of Francis, he instituted a separate order for women known as the Franciscan Nuns, or Poor Clares.

The Little Flowers of St. Francis

For the rest of his life " little brother Francis," as he called himself, continued his labours. He made long missionary journeys, even seeking martyrdom in the lands of the Mahomedans. He gathered new followers, had visions, and performed miracles.

A legend has come down to us of his preaching to the birds, telling them how thankful they should be to God, their creator. He was a poet, too, and his lyric lines are very touching and beautiful. The Little Flowers of St. Francis have been the delight during seven centuries of all who have read them. In these sketches of the life of the earliest Franciscan friars the unworldly simplicity, the

ST. FRANCIS PREACHING TO THE BIRDS
In a fresco in the church of St. Francis at Assisi, Italy, reproduced above, the Italian artist Giotto (c. 1266–1337) has immortalised the famous legend of St. Francis, founder of the Franciscan Order of Friars, preaching to the birds.

gaiety, the exquisitely poetical imagination of Saint Francis shine forth with the happiest light.

At his death, on October 3, 1226, it is said that on his body were found the Stigmata—the marks of the five wounds of Christ, in the hands, feet, and side. Two years later he was canonized as a saint. He is lovingly remembered as the most blameless and gentle of all saints, the most Christlike figure of the Middle Ages.

Franco, FRANCISCO, GENERAL (born 1892). As a junior member of a revolutionary movement this Spanish soldier had no political expectations, but the death or failure of other rebel leaders thrust him to the fore, and within a few years he had made himself Dictator of Spain.

Franco was born at Ferrol in the province of Galicia, Spain, on December 4, 1892, and entered the Spanish army. He saw service in Spanish Morocco ; was promoted Colonel in 1926 ; and when King Alfonso XIII lost his throne in 1931 was sent to the Balearic Islands by the Republican Government, later being transferred to Morocco. In July 1936 Franco took part in the military revolt against the Republican Government that led to the Spanish Civil War.

He assumed the leadership of the insurgents on the death of General Sanjurjo and proclaimed himself head of the State (*el Caudillo*) and Commander-in-Chief on October 1, 1936. The civil war was waged with terrible bitterness by both sides, and when it terminated in 1939, the victorious Franco made little effort to gain the support of the vanquished section of the people.

The Cortes (parliament) was replaced by a Grand Council of Franco's adherents and Spain was transformed into a Fascist State. In 1942 Franco announced the reinstitution of the Cortes; but the postponement of free elections announced for 1945, the continued persecution of political opponents, and the publication of documents revealing Franco's dealings with Germany and Italy during the Second World War caused Great Britain, France and the United States to condemn his regime. In December 1946 the United Nations General Assembly called on all members to withdraw their representatives from Spain as long as Franco remained in power. On March 31, 1947, Franco announced that Spain was to become a monarchy again on his death.

Franco-Prussian War (1870–71). The cry " On to Berlin ! " echoed and re-echoed through the streets of Paris in the exciting days at the beginning of the Franco-Prussian War in July 1870. For four years, after Prussia had defeated Austria and won the leadership of the German states in 1866, the chiefs of the Second French Empire had longed to humiliate this upstart country or to obtain "compensation" for its rise in power.

For four years the Prussian rulers, too, had wanted war with France. Bismarck, the Iron Chancellor, was convinced that such a conflict was necessary before the unification of the German states could be completed, and he rejoiced when France declared war on July 15, 1870. The occasion of the war was the offer by the Spaniards of their vacant throne to a German Hohenzollern prince, distantly related to the Prussian King, William I. The offer was refused for political reasons. Then came the blundering demand of France on the Prussian king that he should guarantee that his relative should never accept it; and Bismarck so altered the telegram to the French ambassador replying to this request that the French considered they had been insulted and demanded that war be declared on Germany.

"Everybody is ready," declared the French minister of war, "to the last button on the last gaiter." But when the French troops began to mobilize, it was found that hardly anything was ready. There were horses without harness, cannon without ammunition, new pattern guns without men who knew how to use them. Prussia, on the other hand, had been completely prepared by General von Moltke. The plan for the invasion of France had been formed long before. France, moreover, stood alone without a single ally, while the other German states rushed to the aid of Prussia.

In an astonishingly short time after war was declared, German troops invaded France in Alsace and Lorraine. The French troops met them as best they could, and, though they fought bravely, they were defeated in one battle after another between August 6 and September 2. One of their armies was shut up in the strongly fortified city of Metz, while the other on September 1 was fighting before Sedan. This battle resulted in the surrender of the largest army then known to have been taken in the field. On September 2 the French army of nearly 82,000 men, with the Emperor Napoleon III himself, surrendered as prisoners of war at Sedan.

Such a terrible disaster to France astonished the whole world. The early defeats of August had been announced by the government as victories, but the deception could no longer be kept up. When Napoleon's message—" The army has been defeated and is captive; I myself am a prisoner "—arrived in Paris, the mob began to cry " Down with the Empire! Long live the Republic! " The Empress Eugénie fled; a republic was proclaimed by Léon Gambetta on September 4, and a Government of National Defence was organized. After Sedan the Germans hastened on to Paris, and on September 19, 1870, began the famous siege of that city.

Early in the siege Léon Gambetta, now Minister of the Interior, escaped from the city in a balloon, and worked desperately to raise new armies. But there was no possibility that they could break through the circle of iron around the doomed city. The sufferings of the Parisians during the siege were terrible. Only when starvation was upon it did the city surrender (January 28, 1871). A government recognized by Germany was formed, with the aged statesman Adolphe Thiers at its head, February 16, 1871, and peace was made with Germany (Peace of Frankfort, May 10, 1871). The victors demanded harsh terms. The greater part of Alsace and Lorraine was to be given them. An indemnity of £200,000,000 was to be paid, and until it was paid a German army was to remain in France. France

NAPOLEON III SURRENDERS
On September 2, 1870, the army of Napoleon III was defeated and surrounded by the Germans at the battle of Sedan, and the French Emperor with 82,000 of his troops was taken prisoner. Above, Napoleon III is surrendering his sword to the King of Prussia, who became Emperor William I of Germany with the formation of the new German Empire.

was humiliated by the German troops marching in triumph through Paris, and by the proclamation at Versailles of the new German Empire.

Even now the troubles of Paris were not ended. Extremists among the working men set up the " Commune " on March 18, 1871 ; this revolt lasted until May 28 and the Germans stood aside until the troops of Adolphe Thiers had crushed the Commune in the " Bloody Week " of May 21–28.

Frankfort. There are two cities named Frankfort or Frankfurt, in Germany. One is Frankfort-on-Oder in the province of Brandenburg, 50 miles east of Berlin; the other, Frankfort-on-Main, in the province of Hesse-Nassau. The latter town is the subject of this article and until the Second World War (1939–45) was a great commercial centre of the Rhine basin, with a history dating from the time of Charlemagne (742–814).

Situated on both banks of the River Main, Frankfort—Frankfurt, the ford of the Franks, in German—was an important inland shipping centre, a road and railway junction and the headquarters of the huge chemical and dye trust, I.G. Farbenindustrie. (This corporation was broken up by the Allies in 1946, because of the part it played in Germany's munitions industry.) Motor-car, electrical and engineering factories, shoe-making and furniture plants were also established in the city. It became, too, a centre of the publishing trade.

Owing to its industrial importance, Frankfort was heavily bombed by the Allied air forces during the Second World War. Columns of the United States 3rd Army fought their way into the suburbs

FRANKFORT-ON-MAIN BEFORE THE BOMBING
Owing to its importance as a great German industrial centre Frankfort-on-Main was heavily bombed by Allied aircraft during the Second World War (1939–45), scarcely a house remaining intact. On the right can be seen the tower of the Rathaus, or Town Hall, which was destroyed; on the extreme left is St. Leonard's church, dating from 1219, which still stands.

Electricity). Learned societies and universities welcomed him, and he soon won equal distinction as a diplomat. His chief triumph was in getting the Stamp Act repealed. An eminent English statesman once said that, had the king and Parliament accepted Franklin's just contention that the American colonies were self-governing, owing allegiance only to the Sovereign, the Revolutionary War might never have been fought.

Franklin, after more than a decade of working in vain for agreement between the Mother Country and the colonies, returned

on March 26, 1945, but the city was not cleared of German forces until March 29. The ancient town hall, the market place, the birthplace of the poet Goethe and the museum next door, and the main shopping centre were destroyed. The opera house and the Cathedral were heavily damaged, and scarcely a house remained intact. The city became the headquarters of the United States zone of occupation in Germany, and in 1947 the centre of administration of the joint Anglo-United States zone. Frankfort had a population of 556,000 in 1935.

Franklin, BENJAMIN (1706–90). The son of an English immigrant, a tallow chandler, Benjamin Franklin was born at Boston, Massachusetts, on January 17, 1706. He was apprenticed to his elder brother, a printer, but at 17 ran away to Philadelphia.

At 23 he owned a printing office and was publishing the Pennsylvania Gazette. For the next 20 years he was the foremost journalist in the British North American colonies. Poor Richard's Almanac, issued annually for a quarter of a century, made him known from city mansion to the remotest frontier cabin. While making fame and fortune as a printer, publisher, and writer, he was studying foreign languages and literatures, experimenting in science, and taking a conspicuous part in local affairs. Although his early plans for a union of the colonies failed, as Deputy Postmaster-General under the Crown for 20 years he linked them together by means of the postal service.

After 1747 Franklin spent over a quarter of a century more or less continuously abroad as the Agent of the State of Pennsylvania. His investigation of problems connected with electricity had already made him the best-known American in Europe (*see*

to help Congress to draft the Declaration of Independence in 1776. He then negotiated the alliance between the North American colonies and France, later becoming their representative in Paris.

When Franklin returned to America in 1785, he took part in framing the new constitution of

BENJAMIN FRANKLIN : AMERICAN SAGE
Among the prominent leaders of men and thought in the 18th century Benjamin Franklin's scientific successes added prestige to his diplomatic career as agent for Pennsylvania and as ambassador of the North American colonies in Paris.

the United States. No life of Franklin is comparable to his own autobiography. As literature it is a classic, and as a human document it is unsurpassed. He died in Philadelphia on April 17, 1790.

Franklin, SIR JOHN (1786–1847). One of the pioneers of Arctic exploration, Franklin was born on April 16, 1786, at Spilsby, Lincolnshire. After serving in the Navy—he was present as a midshipman at the battle of Copenhagen in 1801—he made three expeditions to the Arctic, in which he surveyed many thousands of miles of North American coast-line, as well as the Mackenzie river basin.

Then on May 19, 1845, he sailed from the Thames in search of the North-west Passage, the sea route to Asia around the North American continent. His ships were sighted in Baffin Bay, and then disappeared. No fewer than 39 successive expeditions went in search of him, but for 14 years nothing further was heard of Franklin and his gallant men. Lady Franklin never gave up hope, and in April 1859 an expedition dispatched by her discovered, at Port Victory, a cairn in which was a record of Sir John's expedition down to April 25, 1848, with proof that he had in fact discovered the North-west Passage, and that he had died on June 11, 1847.

Frazer, SIR JAMES GEORGE (1854–1941). Among the most famous anthropologists of his time, this great scholar was born in Glasgow on January 1, 1854, and after attending Glasgow University continued his studies at Trinity College, Cambridge. He became a barrister, but he was soon attracted to the study of anthropology (natural history of the human species) and folklore, with which his name has ever since been associated.

His most famous work, The Golden Bough, was originally published in two volumes in 1890, but has since been expanded to 12 volumes and a Supplement. The original purpose of the work was to investigate a curious custom mentioned by Virgil, connected with the worship of Diana at the Lake of Nemi, where grew the Golden Bough which gives the book its name. In the course of his investigations Frazer was drawn to seek for similar customs and possible explanations among many other peoples, so that the work contains an amazing amount of information about primitive races in all parts of the world. By reason of both its matter and its style, The Golden Bough has been described as one of the great products of the human mind, and its influence upon thought has been immense. The book discusses and explains many customs and superstitions besides that with which it principally deals, and one result of reading the work is to make the reader acutely aware of the extent to which his thoughts and beliefs are inherited from his primitive ancestors.

The Golden Bough is only one of several great works written by Sir James Frazer. In Totemism and Exogamy (1910) he devoted four large volumes to the old custom of marrying outside one's own family, which is widely found among savage races. In Folklore in the Old Testament (1918) he described many primitive customs found among the Hebrew people, and by citing instances of similar customs among other peoples showed that they were part of the heritage of the human race, and not peculiar to the Jews.

Professor of social anthropology at Liverpool University (1907–19), he was knighted in 1914 and received the Order of Merit in 1925. Sir James Frazer died on May 7, 1941.

THE LEGEND OF THE GOLDEN BOUGH

ABOUT 16 miles from Rome in the Alban Hills, occupying what was once the crater of a volcano, is Lake Nemi. It is about three and a half miles in diameter, and from its sides hills, rocky in part, rise precipitously to a height of over 300 feet. The whole scene—the lake, the steep hills, and the trees—is remarkable for its beauty, and suggests peace and tranquillity. Near by is the village of Aricia.

In ancient times the lake was associated with the worship of the goddess Diana, and there were a grove and a temple upon its banks that were sacred to her. She was worshipped here with harvest festivals as the deity who gave fruitfulness, and with a torchlight procession as being the goddess of light. She was often identified with the moon, and the Lake of Nemi was sometimes called the Mirror of Diana, doubtless because the moon was often reflected in its waters.

The priest or guardian of Diana's shrine was a gladiator or a fugitive slave, and on moonlit nights he might have been seen creeping stealthily among the trees. He walked in terror of his life, for, by a curious rule, if any other slave could take a twig from a mistletoe bough, known as the Golden Bough, growing on an oak in the grove and slay the guardian of the shrine (or king of the wood, as

he was also called), he would become king in his place. Macaulay has graphically described the scene in his poem on The Battle of the Lake Regillus :

> From the still grassy lake that sleeps
>   Beneath Aricia's trees—
> Those trees in whose dim shadow
>   The ghastly priest doth reign,
> The priest who slew the slayer,
>   And shall himself be slain.

The origin of this curious priesthood was for long a puzzle to scholars, but Sir James Frazer in his The Golden Bough has pointed out similar customs in other parts of the world which throw considerable light upon the problem. For example, in many lands, especially in Africa, kings reign only for a definite period, or until their powers begin to fail, and are then put to death. The reason for this is that the king is worshipped as a god, and is thought to be the source of rain and of good harvests, so that his people fear infirmities in him lest he prove unable to supply them with food. They prefer, therefore, to put him to death while his powers are unimpaired. So the king of the wood at Nemi may have been regarded as the incarnation of the spirit of the forest, and this curious rule of succession was instituted in order

Tate Gallery, London; Mansell

WHERE GREW THE GOLDEN BOUGH OF FRAZER'S MASTERPIECE

At Lake Nemi, not far from Rome, grew the Golden Bough, supposed to have been a mistletoe branch, which in ancient times was guarded by a priest with his very life. This strange custom inspired poets, like Virgil (70–19 B.C.), to write about it ; scholars, such as Sir James Frazer, to investigate its origin ; and the British artist Turner (1775–1851) to depict the scene (above). A symbolic figure in the left foreground is seen holding up the Golden Bough.

to make sure that the person who held the post should always be virile, symbolizing fruitfulness.

Then again, oak trees were highly regarded by the early Latins and by kindred people, such as our own ancestors, the Celts. This may be due to the fact that oak trees are more often struck by lightning than other trees, and lightning has always been feared as an instrument of divine wrath. And it may be that a mistletoe bough somewhere took root upon a tree struck by lightning. What would be more natural for simple and credulous people to believe than that it was planted there by the lightning, and that the plant itself was therefore divine ? Certainly mistletoe was highly revered by the Druids, who cut slips from it ceremonially with golden knives each year; and in Scandinavian mythology the hero Balder was impervious to all else, and could be wounded by mistletoe alone. Even in our own day it retains some slight fragment of its ancient fame, for few would dream of celebrating Christmas without having sprigs of mistletoe among the decorations in the home.

Frederick. EMPERORS OF THE HOLY ROMAN EMPIRE. During the Middle Ages three rulers of the Holy Roman Empire bore the name of Frederick.

FREDERICK I (c. 1124–90), of the German family of Hohenstaufen, ruled from 1152, and was in many respects the ideal emperor of the Middle Ages. His red beard led the Italians to nickname him Barbarossa (*barba*, beard ; *rossa*, red.) His

ambition was to restore the Roman Empire to the place it had occupied under Charlemagne (742–814) and Otto the Great (912–973). But times had changed. Frederick had the strong city republics to contend with in Italy, and furthermore the Pope was playing a larger part in European affairs than was formerly the case. In his attempt to govern the Italian towns, Frederick was eventually defeated by the Lombard League formed by the cities of northern Italy. These cities were henceforth practically independent. Frederick was likewise unsuccessful in his contest with Pope Alexander III, and was forced to sign the Treaty of Venice with him in 1177.

FREDERICK I

At Reichenhall in Bavaria, Germany, is this figure of Frederick I, who was nicknamed Barbarossa.

In Germany, however, Frederick was more successful than in Italy, and his long reign marks one of the most brilliant epochs in the history of medieval Germany. He established control over the turbulent and troublesome German nobles. Land was cleared of forests, agriculture was improved, and the country advanced in wealth and in culture.

Towards the end of his reign Frederick joined the Third Crusade but before he reached the Holy Land he was drowned in a little stream in Asia Minor, on June 10, 1190.

FREDERICK II (1194–1250), the grandson of Frederick Barbarossa, was born on December 26, 1194, and on the death of his mother in 1198 he inherited the kingdom of Sicily under the regency of Pope Innocent III. He was crowned German king in 1215, and Emperor of the Holy Roman Empire in 1220. He wrote sonnets and was the author of a treatise on falconry, had a knowledge of six languages, of mathematics, philosophy, architecture and other sciences, founded the University of Naples in 1224, and furthered the progress of the medical school at Salerno.

His court in Sicily, where he spent most of his life, was the most splendid in Europe, and a centre of intellectual activity. But he neglected Germany in order to defend himself against the Pope in Italy. The nobles and the towns north of the Alps came to exercise powers which rightly belonged to the emperor, and Germany grew more and more into a country of city states and feudal principalities. Frederick died in Sicily on December 13, 1250.

FREDERICK III (1415–93) was a Hapsburg prince and ascended the throne of Germany in 1440. His reign has been called the longest and dullest of all the reigns in German history. He was listless and incapable as a ruler. All he could do was to watch the power and prestige of the Holy Roman Empire decline, while he studied botany and astronomy. The last of the Holy Roman Emperors to be crowned in Rome, Frederick died on August 19, 1493.

Frederick the Great, KING OF PRUSSIA (1712–86).

The future king of Prussia had a hard time when a boy. His father, rough old Frederick William I, planned an education for his heir that was military, practical, and matter-of-fact. But the lad was fond of music, literature—especially French—and art. He hated military exercises ; he detested tobacco, heavy eating and drinking, and hunting, all of which appeared to his father as manly and royal pleasures. The king forbade the prince's tutors to teach him Latin because it " had no practical use "; but Frederick studied the classics when his father's back was turned.

As Frederick became older the thought that this youth would one day be king, and would probably wreck the Prussian state by his incompetence, enraged the tyrannical, hardworking Frederick William, who thought only of Prussia's greatness. He became more and more severe with his son, even caning him and boxing his ears in public.

When Frederick was 18 he decided to run away, but he was caught before he crossed the border. He was kept in solitary confinement for a time, and from the window of his cell he was forced to watch the execution of his most intimate friend

who had accompanied him in his flight. For a time the enraged king even thought of executing his son as a military deserter. After this, Frederick changed. He became self-contained, crafty and cynical, but outwardly submissive. He spent several years in learning the dry details of administration. Gradually he bore greater responsibilities.

When he came to the throne in 1740, at the age of 28, Frederick had a keen mind, a will of iron, and an ambition that was soon to set the world on fire. He ruled for 46 years, of which the first 23 were devoted chiefly to unscrupulous warfare, and the second to peace and recovery.

This man, who as a youth had hated the life of a soldier, plunged all Europe into war immediately after he came to the throne. He seized the rich Austrian province of Silesia and so began

Alinari

FREDERICK III WITH HIS BRIDE
Three days after his marriage to Leonora, daughter of the King of Portugal, in March 1452, Frederick III was crowned in Rome. In the foreground of this painting by the Italian artist Pinturicchio (1454–1513) Frederick is shown greeting his bride. Frederick was not a capable ruler and under him the power of the Holy Roman Empire declined.

a European conflict. It was in this struggle that his military genius won him the title the Great. During his reign he nearly doubled the size of his kingdom, for he not only compelled Maria Theresa, the Empress of Austria, to cede Silesia to him, but also seized part of Poland in 1772.

In peace he vastly increased his country's resources by draining marshes, clearing forests, encouraging industries, opening schools. He re-organized the army, replenished the public treasury, and remodelled the legal code.

Frederick raised Prussia to the rank of one of the first powers in Europe, and by his military successes and his crafty diplomacy gave it the stamp of his own character. Strangely enough, this greatest of the Hohenzollerns spoke and wrote French almost exclusively. He died child-less on August 17, 1786, and was succeeded by his nephew Frederick William II.

Free Churches. In the stormy days of the Reformation in the 16th century, there were many religious people who were dissatisfied with the close connexion of Church and State that ensued upon the breaking of the ancient ties with the Roman Catholic Church. In England in particular there were many who objected to an officially recognized Church, because they feared that the State would interfere with the individual's liberty of conscience and of worship. In Queen Elizabeth's time there were religious groups who broke away from the national Church and formed themselves into sects determined to worship God in their own way. Some of the earliest of these were the Brownists, so called from the name of one of their leaders, Robert Brown (c. 1550–1633). Each Brownist community or congregation was independent of all other Churches or congrega-tions; hence the religious communities established on these lines have been called Independents, or, to use the modern term, Congregationalists.

Another of the Free Churches—free in the sense that they are self-governing and do not acknowledge the authority of the king or Parliament in religious matters—are the Baptists, who also date from soon after the outbreak of the Reformation. The distinctive practice of the Baptists is adult baptism by total immersion, as opposed to the infant baptism practised by most other Christian bodies; they claim scriptural authority for their practice in that Christ was an adult when He was baptized.

Presbyterians also arose in the 16th century, when the doctrine and government of their Church were decided by such great reformers as John Knox in Scotland and John Calvin in Geneva. They are called Presbyterians because their churches are governed by officials called elders, the Greek word for which is *presbyteres*.

The largest of the Free Churches is the Methodist, which dates from the 18th century, when John Wesley, and his brother Charles, by their fervid preaching and untiring labours, revolutionized the religious life of the country. Until a few years ago there were three principal Methodist Churches in Britain, but in 1932 they were all united into the " Methodist Church."

Amongst the other Free Churches may be mentioned the Society of Friends, better known as Quakers, who have no paid ministers and are remarkable for their whole-hearted opposition to war and the use of force generally; the Christian Scientists, whose teachings are largely based on the writings of an American lady, Mrs. Mary Baker Eddy (1821–1910); the Plymouth Brethren, whose first congregation was founded at Plymouth in 1830; and the Unitarians, who do not believe in the divinity of Christ, but regard Him as a prophet superhumanly endowed. An organization akin to the Free Churches is the Salvation Army.

Free Churchmen are often called Noncon-formists because in 1662 their spiritual ancestors refused to conform to the Act of Uniformity, which required the assent of all ministers to the contents of the Book of Common Prayer.

There are several million Free Churchmen in England, and in Wales they constitute the majority of the people. In Scotland the greater part are Presbyterians, though in the strict sense they are not Free Churchmen, for in the northern kingdom Presbyterianism is established by law.

The Free Churches are famed for their missionary zeal, and they maintain many hundreds of mission-aries. David Livingstone, the African explorer-missionary, and William Carey, the Northampton-shire shoemaker who went to India as a missionary in 1793, were both Nonconformists.

Freemasonry. No one knows how or where the secret society known as the Free and Accepted Masons really began, and there are various traditions about it. Many of its ceremonies and practices are not unlike the ceremonies and ritual of the Eleusinian, Samothracian, Dionysian, and other ancient mysteries, and also resemble the most ancient religious ceremonies known, parti-cularly the initiatory rites and ceremonial proved to have prevailed among Indian races, the Druids, and others. It is said to have arisen from guilds of masons or stone-workers, which sprang into being in the Middle Ages; in order that travelling members might be recognized by their brother craftsmen they made use of secret signs and pass-words. Other stories, with little warrant, carry the origin of the order back to the building of the temple at Jerusalem in the days of Solomon.

Scotland possesses the earliest record of the presence of masons organized in lodges or groups. Edinburgh Lodge No. 1 has record books dating from 1599, but these do not record the beginning of the lodge. The famous Kilwinning Lodge is also claimed to have been in existence at that date as a governing body, but its recorded history dates only from 1642. Modern freemasonry, with the three symbolic degrees (apprentice, fellow-craft, and master-mason) dates from the early 18th century. The organization of the Grand Lodge of England was effected in 1717, by the union of four lodges then meeting in London. The Grand Lodge of Ireland was formed in 1729, and the Grand Lodge of Scotland in 1736.

The many Masonic rites are now largely com-bined into the English, Scottish, French, American and Swedish rites. These observances variously combine admission to the various degrees and other ceremonies. In all, the emphasis is on the member's duty to his family, his country, and his God, and to aid his fellow members. A set of passwords,

Larkin Bros.

FREEMASONS HALL, LONDON

In Great Queen Street, Kingsway, London, is the headquarters of the Grand Lodge of England. The temple was opened in July 1933 as a memorial to English Freemasons killed in the First World War (1914-18).

kept strictly secret, and a peculiar grip of the hand enable the initiated to recognize one another.

Freemasonry is noted for its benevolent activities. In England there are three well-known institutions—the Royal Masonic Institution for Girls, founded in 1788, which has a senior school at Rickmansworth, Herts, with a junior school and convalescent home at Weybridge, Surrey ; the Royal Masonic Institution for Boys, at Bushey, Herts, founded in 1798; and the Royal Masonic Benevolent Institution for Aged Freemasons and the Widows of Freemasons at Croydon, Surrey. In 1932 a hospital for freemasons was opened at Ravenscourt Park, London. The British headquarters of freemasonry is in Great Queen Street, Kingsway, London.

Freezing and Refrigeration.

If a jar of water is placed in a refrigerator, with a thermometer standing in it, the temperature will slowly drop until it reaches 32° F. (or 0° C., if a Centigrade thermometer is used). The water will then begin to freeze and ice will form on the surface, but the temperature will remain unchanged until the whole of the water has turned into ice. Thus we can say that the freezing point of water is 32° F., or 0° C. Further, if we measure the time taken for all the water to freeze, we shall find that it takes approximately eighty times as long as the water took to drop from 1° C. to 0° C. All the time the water is freezing, heat is being taken from it, although the temperature does not fall. This heat is known as the latent heat of freezing. On the other hand, if we remove the ice from the refrigerator and allow it to melt, the temperature will again stay fixed at the freezing-point until all the ice has melted. In this case the ice absorbs heat from the surrounding objects to enable it to melt.

Freezing is the general name given to the process of turning a liquid into its solid form by cooling it down. All matter exists either as a solid, a liquid

or a gas, and a great number of substances can exist in one or the other state. For instance, the liquid mercury can be cooled down by immersing it in a very cold substance, such as liquid air, until it freezes to a solid metal. The solid mercury is then very similar in its physical properties to any other metal. On the other hand, liquid mercury can be heated up and turned into a gas, mercury vapour. We are all familiar with the bluish light of the mercury vapour lamps in some of our streets. In these the light is caused by discharging electricity through mercury gas.

All pure substances have a definite freezing and melting point, which are at the same temperature. Thus we can think of a molten metal as " freezing " when it solidifies. There are many substances, however, such as butter, wax and tar, which are really mixtures of pure substances, and they have no definite melting point, but gradually soften as they are heated, first behaving like a very thick liquid, and then flowing freely. Glass behaves like this, too, but there is evidence to prove that the " solid " glass is really an extremely viscous liquid which has been cooled to far below its melting point without crystallising. Other mixtures of pure substances freeze in steps, one component of the mixture solidifying at a higher temperature than the others. Some types of solder behave like this, and the plumber uses such a solder for making his wiped joints on lead pipes.

To solidify a gas it must usually be turned into the liquid form first, and then cooled down even further. The gas carbon dioxide is an exception to this, and can be directly solidified merely by letting it expand from a high-pressure cylinder into the air, where it forms flakes of " dry ice." This dry ice, whose freezing point is at −79° C., is widely used for keeping ice-cream and perishable goods cold when a refrigerator is not available. It is a white solid which is marketed in blocks, and in use it merely evaporates into the air as it absorbs heat. Some gases solidify very near the " absolute zero," the limiting low temperature to which any substance can be cooled. Theoretical reasoning goes to show that this lower limit lies at about −273° C. At this temperature the atoms which go to make up any substance stop their natural vibrations, and it loses all its physical properties. The absolute zero of temperature is a " critical " standard, like the velocity of light (186,000 miles per second) and so can never be ultimately attained. However, scientists working at the Low Temperature Laboratories at Cambridge have managed to get down to −272·9956° C. by a method of liquefying helium gas in a strong magnetic field.

The properties of a substance can change very rapidly when it is cooled down to these very low temperatures. One of the most remarkable things that can happen is that the electrical resistance of a metal may drop to practically zero. It then becomes a " super-conductor," and an electric current induced in it may go on flowing for many hours after it first started. Another thing that happens at low temperatures is that photographic plates lose their sensitivity to light.

Most substances contract when they freeze, but we all know from experience that water is an exception to this rule. Water jugs and pipes often burst in winter-time if left exposed to the cold weather, and we can gather from the damage often done that an enormous pressure must have been developed by the action of the water in freezing. A cubic inch of water becomes 1·09 cubic inches of ice, on freezing, which explains why ice floats. As little ice crystals form in the water of a pond they float to the top and unite as a solid surface of ice.

Just as water confined in a small space exerts great pressure, so will the effect of compressing ice be to lower its melting point. When we make a snowball the powdery snow is pressed together so that it momentarily melts, and then freezes again into a more solid piece of ice when the pressure is released. The melting of ice by pressure explains why a skater can travel so easily over its surface. There is an instantaneous melting of the ice under the skate, and the water film so formed acts as an almost perfect lubricant. If the ice were very cold (well below its freezing-point), the skater would find it impossible to travel, since his weight could not exert enough pressure to melt the ice. By a similar principle an explanation can be given of why glaciers are able to flow round corners.

The freezing point of a substance can be altered in other ways than by exerting pressure on it. By dissolving salt, or any other soluble substance, in water, the freezing point is lowered. A saturated salt solution has a freezing point of −22° C. This explains the principle on which the old ice-cream making machines worked. Ice and salt were mixed in the outer portion of a double container, the inner part holding the ice-cream mixture. Now the pure ice and the salt solution surrounding it have different melting points, and in order that they shall remain in equilibrium with one another the ice has to melt. In melting, it must get its latent heat of freezing from somewhere, and so it takes it from itself. The temperature drops as a consequence, and refrigerating action takes place. The melting of ice when salt is mixed with it is also made use of in icy weather, when salt is sprinkled on pavements to stop them from becoming slippery.

How a Refrigerator Works

The type of refrigerator described above (the ice-cream making machine) is of very limited use, as it needs ice to begin with, and in any case soon uses this up. What is needed is some kind of cold-producing machine which will work continually. Now it is a well-known fact that, whereas by mixing ice and hot water, one gets warm water, it is not possible to accomplish the reverse process of separating the cold from the hot. This fact is expressed by scientists as the Second Law of Thermodynamics, which states that heat cannot be transferred from one body to another at a higher temperature without some work being done. This is the reason why all refrigerators must be supplied with some kind of energy (electrical, mechanical or heat energy) to make them work.

Many refrigerators make use of the fact that certain gases can be liquefied at ordinary temperatures merely by compressing them. The compressed gas gets hot in the process, and it is allowed to cool by being passed through cooling pipes, or through a radiator. The liquid and compressed gas are then allowed to expand through a constricting valve into a low-pressure region, where the gas cools rapidly and partly liquefies again. The cold gas and the evaporating liquid both withdraw heat from the refrigerating chamber, around which the low-pressure pipes are wound. Finally the low-pressure gas is again pumped round the cycle by means of the compressor. In the diagram is shown the arrangement of a refrigerator which employs sulphur dioxide as the working substance. This gas is used widely for domestic refrigerators, whereas larger machines often employ ammonia or carbon dioxide. A thermostat is fitted to most refrigerators, in order that the machine shall switch off when a low enough temperature is reached, and switch on again when it rises.

By an ingenious arrangement it is also possible to produce cold with a continuous process which does not need a compressor or any moving parts. The absorption refrigerator uses heat energy in the form of an electric element or gas flame to supply its power. This heats up a strong solution of ammonia in water which is contained in a boiler, and the ammonia gas boils off. It is passed down cooling tubes and in this way it is condensed to liquid ammonia,

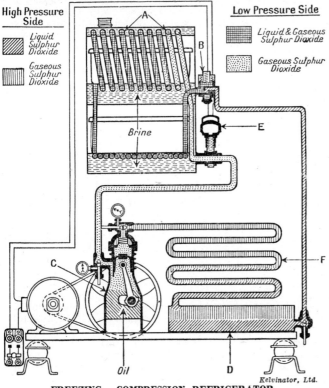

High Pressure Side

Liquid Sulphur Dioxide

Gaseous Sulphur Dioxide

Low Pressure Side

Liquid & Gaseous Sulphur Dioxide

Gaseous Sulphur Dioxide

A
B
Brine
E
C
F
Oil
D

Kelvinator, Ltd.

FREEZING : COMPRESSION REFRIGERATOR
The arrangement of a refrigerator which uses sulphur dioxide can be seen above : A. Evaporating coil surrounding cooling chambers ; B. Expansion valve which regulates the flow of refrigerant ; C. Compressor ; D. Liquid sulphur dioxide receiver ; E. Thermostat ; F. Radiator.

which is allowed to drip down the refrigerating chamber tubes. Here it is helped to evaporate by a stream of hydrogen gas which is passed over it. The temperature drops rapidly on evaporation, just as one's skin will get cold if it is wet and air is blown over it. The ammonia gas leaves the refrigerating tubes and is finally absorbed in water once more, to begin the cycle again. Although the principle on which this type of refrigerator works is quite simple, the piping arrangements are complicated, because of the necessity for providing a stream of hydrogen in the evaporating tubes, whilst also making the machine a continually-operated one.

Refrigeration is an absolute necessity in our modern system of supplying and distributing food to large town populations. By keeping perishable foodstuffs at a sufficiently low temperature, the harmful bacteria are prevented from multiplying, and food can thus be kept in perfect condition for long periods. All our imported meat is transported by means of refrigerator ships, whose holds are kept at a low temperature throughout the voyage ; and of course fish must similarly be kept cold.

A great deal of research work has been done to find out the right temperature at which to keep various foodstuffs so that they do not go bad, but yet retain the full flavour and food value of the original product. For instance, the domestic refrigerator only freezes water in a special compartment, the main body of the refrigerator being kept at a few degrees *above* freezing point. Recently, too, quick-freezing methods have enabled us to enjoy fresh vegetables, retaining their correct flavour, many months after they were picked. (*See* Heat.)

The STORY of the FRENCH REVOLUTION

This great social and political upheaval, which took place towards the end of the 18th century, ended the old regime in France and brought about great change throughout the world. Its inner history is told here.

French Revolution. Liberty, Equality, Fraternity : these words are the motto of the French Republic, and were the ideal of the French Revolution. Of the three, Equality—the abolition of privileges enjoyed only by aristocrats and the clergy—was to the Frenchman of 1789 the most important. For it he was ready to sacrifice political liberty, as he did later, when he accepted the despotic rule of Napoleon. For it Fraternity, or brotherhood with all men, was allowed to remain an unfulfilled dream. But Equality before the law was achieved then and has been retained ever since.

The Frenchman had a reason for his passionate devotion to equality. Before 1789 inequalities met him at every turn, and hampered all progress. The nobles and clergy, the privileged orders, were almost exempt from taxation, and the chief burden fell upon the peasants, artisans, merchants, and professional men. Even among these, taxes were not equal, some provinces being exempt from certain taxes. Then, too, the collection in certain cases was done by contractors, or tax farmers, and the tax-gatherer collected whatever he could. And woe to the man who seemed prosperous! As a result, the peasant lived in a hovel and concealed his resources; when he had meat to eat, he ate it in secret.

There were social and economic inequalities as well as political ones. The peasants were regarded as the serfs of the aristocratic landowners, to whom they were legally bound to render payments and unpaid service. Rabbits might destroy the peasant's garden, and pigeons eat his grain, but he must not kill them, for they were protected for the lord's sport. His fences were broken down and his crops trampled in the chase, but he could claim no damages. On top of the dues to king and nobles came the dues to the Church. These and other obligations were often more irritating than burdensome; they seemed senseless and unreasonable to an age that was coming to rebel, through the writings of the French philosopher Voltaire (1694–1778) and others, against the intolerance of the Church.

At last the day of reckoning came. The funds in the national treasury had been exhausted by the costly wars of Louis XIV, and by the extravagances of Louis and his successors. The £50,000,000 that France spent to help the rebellious British colonies in North America tipped the scales against the reigning monarch. Turgot and Necker, as ministers of finance, had tried to save the State from bankruptcy by cutting down the expenses of the court. But the court, led by the sprightly, frivolous and extravagant queen, Marie Antoinette, would not listen to the word economy. Loans were tried, but in the end the foreign bankers refused to lend more money. Public opinion was deeply stirred by the Parlement of Paris, a judicial body which defied the king and refused to levy new taxation.

In 1788 Louis XVI, as a last resort, called a meeting of the States-General. This body represented the three estates—clergy, nobles and commons—of the French kingdom. It had no legislative functions, and could only make its influence felt by petitioning against grievances. First summoned in 1302 by Philip IV, it had not met since 1614, when Louis XIII dismissed it for criticizing the national finances. The representatives of the three estates came to Versailles, near Paris, early in May 1789, all demanding reforms.

First Meeting of the National Assembly

With the meeting of the States-General on May 5, 1789, the Revolution began. The representatives of the Third Estate (middle class) led the way. Some of the nobles and many of the clergy joined with them. They changed the name of the gathering from States-General, which represented classes, to National Assembly, which represented the people of France. When the king shut them out from their usual place of meeting, they adjourned to a neighbouring tennis court, where they took the famous Oath of the Tennis Court (June 20, 1789), pledging themselves not to separate until they had given France a constitution or established form of Government. When the king sent a messenger to remove them, the fiery Mirabeau cried out:

Couderc, Musée de Versailles

COMTE DE MIRABEAU

When the States-General met on May 5, 1789, Mirabeau became the leader of the Third Estate, which represented the middle classes. He wished to retain the king as head of the State, but to limit his powers through a Parliament. He failed to gain the support of the Court, and the monarchy was overthrown the year following his death on April 2, 1791.

" Go and tell your master we are here by the will of the people, and that we will be removed only at the point of the bayonet."

The people of Paris, 14 miles away, were alarmed by rumours of the gathering of troops about Versailles. A Paris mob stormed and captured the old state prison in Paris, the Bastille, on July 14. When the king in Versailles was informed of what had taken place, he exclaimed: " Why, this is a revolt! " " No, sire," was the reply, " it is a revolution." The incident was trivial, but its significance was beyond words. To the present time, July 14, the date of the fall of the Bastille, is celebrated as the birthday of French liberty.

Next, a revolutionary committee of middle-class citizens governed Paris. A national guard was organized and placed under the command of General Lafayette. The provinces followed the lead of Paris and formed revolutionary governments.

A report of the peasant outbreaks made a wonderful impression on the Assembly. Some liberal nobles in that body set the example of renouncing their feudal rights. Amid the wildest enthusiasm, men weeping and embracing each other, one noble after another gave up some exclusive privilege, until finally a decree was

passed which aimed at abolishing the entire feudal system. That wild night of August 4, 1789, saw the beginning of Equality, though remnants of feudal dues kept the peasants uneasy until 1793.

But what had become of the constitution which the Assembly had promised to France? Work on it progressed piecemeal, and it was completed in 1791. Nobility was abolished. France was made a limited monarchy, with a single-chamber Parliament. The immortal part of the document was the Declaration of the Rights of Man. It included these points:

1. All men were born free with equal rights.
2. All citizens have the right to take part in electing representatives to make the laws.
3. Every person shall be free to speak, write or print his opinions provided he does not abuse this privilege.
4. The amount of taxes which a person is called upon to pay shall be based on the amount of wealth that he possesses.

The Declaration of the Rights of Man came to be regarded as the charter of democracy (government by the people). The equality of all men in the eyes of the law is its essence. Property was still inviolable, for the chief supporters of the new order held property or desired to hold it.

If the king had possessed the courage and the vision to put himself at the head of the movement, France might have remained a monarchy. At first he did promise to obey the constitution of 1791, which placed a narrow limit on his power. But then he listened to evil counsellors. Many nobles had fled before the storm. These *émigrés*, as they were called, later headed by his own brothers, were in Germany, Austria and Switzerland, appealing to the princes of Europe to stop the Revolution in France, and threatening a reign of bloodshed when they returned to that country.

Boze, Musée Carnavalet, Paris

JEAN PAUL MARAT

His sincere hatred of tyranny and desire to see free society established made Marat a true friend of the people. His bloodthirsty nature caused him to be feared and hated even by his fellow revolutionaries, and he was assassinated in his bath by Charlotte Corday on July 13, 1793.

Louvre, Paris

FRENCH REVOLUTION: THE FALL OF THE BASTILLE

On July 14, 1789, the huge prison-fortress of the Bastille in Paris was captured by the people, its fall heralding the end of the old regime in France. The frenzied Paris mob, to whom the grim structure was a symbol of autocratic rule, stormed the lightly-guarded prison quite easily and razed it to the ground. Here is depicted the confused scene in the courtyard, as represented in a drawing by F. L. Prieur. The site of the Bastille is now marked by a bronze column.

The people of France, apparently with good reason, mistrusted the king and still more Marie Antoinette. In October 1789 a disorderly mob of women and men had brought the rulers—and the Assembly with them—from Versailles to Paris, that they might be more closely watched. The suspicions against the king and queen were changed into certainties for most of the people in June 1791, when the king and queen with their children sought to escape abroad. They were captured at Varennes, on the edge of the Argonne, just before they reached the border of France. From that day the monarchy was doomed.

These events hastened the division of the revolutionists into two parties: the constitutional royalists, who supported the king, and the democratic republicans, who desired a republic. In September 1791 the king ratified the constitution, and the new Legislative Assembly was strongly in favour of the king remaining as head of the State, but as the weakness of the government became more apparent, popular support shifted to the side of the republicans.

On August 10, 1792, a mob invaded the Tuileries (the royal palace), killed the guards, and forced the royal family to seek refuge in the hall of the Legislative Assembly. On September 21, 1792, a decree was passed that "royalty is abolished in France," and a republic was proclaimed. Four months later Louis XVI was sent to the guillotine, the newly-introduced beheading machine.

The overthrow of the monarchy was not entirely due to the weakness of the king. Affairs generally in France seemed to be going from bad to worse. The clergy and many devout Catholics had withdrawn their support from the Revolution because of its laws against the Church. First of all, Church property had been taken by the State; this was a financial measure and generally approved. Then the Civil Constitution of the Clergy was drawn up, according to which all clergy from bishops to parish priests were to be elected, and all must take an oath to support the government. Of all the clergy only four bishops took the oath.

By a blunder the Assembly had thus divided the patriots. Others, especially merchants and tradesmen, were irritated by the paper money with which the country was flooded, and which soon became worthless. Royalist uprisings were occurring in some provinces, as in the Vendée. Austria and Prussia had formed an alliance and declared war on France. England was drawn into the war when the French revolutionary armies occupied the Austrian Netherlands (Belgium).

To guide the Revolution through this crisis a strong government was needed, and for this reason the people of France sacrificed liberty. A Convention was summoned to draw up a new constitution, and for three years (1792–95) a committee of this assembly, known as the Committee of Public Safety, ruled France with an iron hand. The power of this committee did not come from the Convention, but from the members of a fanatically republican group known as the Jacobins.

The most influential men of this group were Danton, Marat, and Robespierre, until Marat was assassinated by Charlotte Corday. Through agents and spies the committee spread its net over the whole of the country. By terror it maintained its power and position, and so this period of the Revolution is known as the Reign of Terror.

By means of it, the royalist uprisings were sternly suppressed. Hundreds, even thousands, were sent to the guillotine. Marie Antoinette, aristocrats and tradesmen, atheists like Hébert, finally even Danton himself (because he urged moderation), were executed, usually with no trial or only a mockery of one. Old institutions were changed. The worship of the Goddess of Reason supplanted religious services in the Paris churches. The calendar was reorganized, 1792 becoming the Year I, the first year of the French Republic, and the names of the months being altered.

But the Terror accomplished its purpose. The Prussian-Austrian invaders had been turned back at Valmy (September 20, 1792). Then the French armies carried the war into the lands of their enemies. Belgium, Nice and Savoy were added to the domain of France.

At length, however, the enemies of the Revolution at home and abroad seemed to be suppressed. Only Great Britain and Austria continued the war. The people were tired of the Terror, and when Robespierre showed no signs of stopping the bloodshed, the rest of the Convention took matters into their own hands. Robespierre himself was arrested and sent to the guillotine (July 27, 1794).

More moderate men now governed France. A young artillery officer, Napoleon Bonaparte, protected the new government, which was called the Directory and had five members. He was practically unknown at that time, but before long his history became the history of France. The Directory proved unable to meet the problems within disorganized France, and the victories which France won under it were due to Bonaparte. At length, on November 9, 1799, he overthrew the Directory and in effect transformed the Republic into a military monarchy.

Few events in history have so powerfully influenced the life of modern peoples as did the French Revolution, and on the whole that influence has been a permanent one for good.

Freud, SIGMUND (1856–1939). The creator of psycho-analysis, Freud (pron. froid) was born at Freiburg in Moravia, then part of Austria, and was educated at Vienna; here he lived until he fled to England in 1938, when Hitler annexed Austria. He qualified as a doctor in 1882, and proceeded to concentrate upon the study and cure of mental illnesses. His book on hysteria, published in 1895, is said to mark the beginning of the science of

psycho-analysis (investigation of mental life). His studies led him to assert that many forms of hysteria could be explained by the existence of an unconscious mind which influenced conscious behaviour. The desires of this unconscious mind, or suppressed *ego*, may be sometimes traced in dreams, to the interpretation of which Freud also devoted much attention.

From the first the revolutionary nature of Freud's theories, and the undue stress that they seemed to lay on sex impulses, aroused much antagonism. But there is no doubt that Freud, by applying his own methods, did achieve some wonderful cures with patients suffering from mental ailments, and the future alone will show whether these methods can be more widely applied for the benefit of mankind. He died in London on September 23, 1939.

Friction. We all know from experience what happens if we neglect to oil the bearings of our cycle at regular intervals. The machine runs stiffly. This is because most machinery is designed to run in bearings which are coated with a thin film of oil in order to reduce friction. Ball bearings and roller bearings like those illustrated in page 386 are used because *rolling friction* is less than *sliding friction*; an ordinary " plain " bearing—merely a shaft turning in a hole which fits it closely—gives more of a sliding action. But lubrication has to be done wisely; many a clock has stopped because some well-meaning person has applied too much oil; or has oiled parts which did not need lubrication.

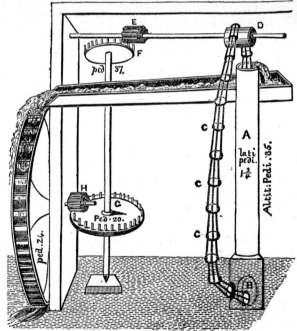

FRICTION MADE THIS MACHINE IMPOSSIBLE
Numerous inventors have sought to make machines which, once started, would run for ever. Above is a design for a perpetual pump, from a book by Robert Fludd (1618). Water flowing on to the wheel (left) turned it, and, through the crown wheels C and F and the pinions H and E, rotated the drum D, causing the bucket-and-chain pump (A, B, C) to raise more water to the sloping trough, whence it flowed on to the big water wheel. At least that was the inventor's intention.

In such case the oil gathers and harbours dust and grit, which act like a file on the surfaces.

A clock pendulum might go on swinging for ever if it were not for friction, which gradually brings it to a halt when the original momentum—given by some outside force—becomes exhausted. Friction was the plague and torment of the numberless inventors who sought "perpetual motion" during past ages. The idea was something like this: You constructed a water wheel with buckets which a stream of water caused to turn; you arranged that the wheel operated some kind of pump or other device for lifting water to a tank overhead; the water raised by the machine then gushed out on to the buckets of the wheel and pumped up more water—and so on. Stupid as this scheme appears to us today, there were thousands of " inventions " just as foolish and impracticable. And the officials of government Patent Offices find today that people still submit schemes which cannot possibly work because they ignore the laws of Mechanics !

E.N.A.

A MALE FRIGATE BIRD COURTING

One of the most curious characteristics of the male frigate bird is an air sac on the throat, which can be inflated to a great size (above), then looking like a red balloon, and having a great attraction for the females. When deflated it is invisible under the plumage of the neck. The frigate bird is noted for its effortless soaring flight.

The amount of work we can *get out* of a machine depends on the amount of energy *put into* it. We may, for example, wind up a 10-pound weight on a cord coiled around a drum; if we raise the weight 2 feet, we have an available energy of 10 × 2 foot-pounds stored up. If we now allow the weight to descend freely we shall not get back all the stored energy, for some will be wasted in friction between the cord and the drum, and between the pivots of the drum and the bearings in which they run. Again, if we change the direction of the cord by interposing a pulley, we lose more energy by friction.

The amount of frictional resistance depends on the smoothness or roughness of the surfaces in contact, and upon the kind of material. Tiny particles at the surface grip one another and hinder movement; even the smoothest metal surface looks rough if we examine it through a powerful lens. Engineers use a factor called the *co-efficient of friction* to denote the ratio $\frac{F}{W}$ between the force (F) required to move one body over another, and the load or weight (W) representing the total pressure between the two bodies. For iron sliding on iron, the co-efficient is only about half that for an oak block sliding over an oak board. We are at once reminded of the difference in behaviour of a sledge or toboggan with plain wooden runners, and one in which the runners are shod with iron or steel tires.

Friction represents a waste of work, but what becomes of the energy thus uselessly spent? It is dissipated in the form of heat. Primitive peoples use a " fire-stick " to obtain flame; a thin stick twirled by the hands, or by a bow, and the end is rested in a hollow in a block of wood. The friction generates heat, and soon there is a flame.

So far we have spoken about friction between solid materials; but water or oil flowing in a pipe sets up friction between the liquid and the walls of the pipe. So pipes are made smooth inside to lessen friction; where the pipes make a turn, the bends are rounded to avoid further frictional losses. Gases, too, cause friction in pipes and ducts; and the large ducts and trunks through which ventilating air is taken into public buildings are similarly made with gradual bends. In every machine with moving parts some power is lost by the friction of these parts with the air through which they move.

Though friction is a hindrance in many ways, it is a help in others. Brakes (*q.v.*) and clutches depend on friction for their working, and much machinery would be uncontrollable without its aid.

Frigate Bird. Related to the gannet and the pelican, the frigate bird is noted for the way in which it soars in the air for hours, apparently without moving its wings.

The larger (*Fregata aquila*) of the two species occurs in the tropics of both hemispheres, mainly north of the Equator. The other species, *F. minor*, is found in the Central Pacific and Indian oceans.

Frigate birds have long, stout, hooked bills; the tail is extremely long and deeply forked; and the bones are so formed as to make this bird lighter than any other bird of equal wing span. When spread, the long narrow wings measure 10 feet from tip to tip. But frigate birds have very small legs and are almost helpless on land.

Perhaps the most striking characteristic is the air sac of the male, which lies along the throat and, when fully distended, obscures the breast; it then looks like a red balloon. When deflated the sac is invisible beneath the plumage of the neck. This sac is distended during courtship to attract the attention of the female. The feathers are deep brown; the female birds, however, have light under-feathers.

Frigate birds nest mainly in colonies on tropical islands, building in trees, low bushes or on the ground. The nest contains a single white egg. The birds feed on fish, which they either catch themselves or steal from other birds.

Frobisher, SIR MARTIN (c. 1535–94). Knighted on his own ship, the Triumph, by Queen Elizabeth after the defeat of the Spanish Armada in 1588, Sir Martin Frobisher was one of the great English seamen of Elizabethan days. Born in York-shire, he made a voyage to West Africa in 1564 and later visited the Levant and North Africa. In 1575 he set out in the tiny vessels Gabriel and Michael to seek the North-West Passage, r e a c h i n g Greenland, and finally anchoring in Frobisher Bay in Baffin Land, at the entrance to the Davis Straits. This spot is the beginning of the long-sought North-West Passage—the " short cut " to Asia around North America—that was to baffle explorers for nearly four centuries until Amundsen (q.v.) navigated it in 1905.

In 1577 and in 1578 Frobisher made similar voyages, enduring all the hardship of Arctic explor-a t i o n in small, ill-provisioned ships. Then from 1586 till 1594 this gallant sailor was busy fighting the Spaniards off the coasts of Spain and in the Channel. But in the brilliant attack on Brest, which was then held by the Spaniards, he was mortally wounded; he died at Plymouth on November 22, 1594.

Froebel, F R I E D R I C H WILHELM (1782–1852). T h e great German educational re-former Froebel (pron. frê-bel) was over 50 years old before he found his real life-work, the kinder-garten, and yet the various occu-pations of his youth and manhood were, in a sense, a necessary preparation for it. An unhappy boyhood turned his thoughts early to the mental misery suffered by lonely, neglected children.

Born on April 21, 1782, in his early 20s Froebel was engaged as a teacher at a school at Frankfort, Germany, which was conducted on the principles of Pestalozzi, the famous Swiss educational re-former. He spent several years studying with Pestalozzi and also at several German universities.

In 1816 he established his first school. It was not until 1837, however, that he founded the sort of school that has had so wide an influence on educa-tion all over the world. That was the kindergarten (children's garden in English; from the German

words *kinder*, children; *garten*, garden), a school for children between the ages of four and six. The great idea which he developed in his books and in his schools was that children must not be taught by rule, but according to their natural instincts and activities. Play was the basis of his teaching.

But Froebel did not live to see his idea fully accepted. The Prussian government abolished kindergartens in 1851, because the authorities considered them socialistic. Froebel died on June 21, 1852, considering his life a failure. But, as is often the case with men of new ideas, his teaching lived on in many lands all over the world.

Bodleian Library, Oxford
MARTIN FROBISHER
Like most of the Elizabethan seamen, Frobisher was something of a pirate, too. He was knighted after the defeat of the Spanish Armada in 1588.

Frog. Like toads and newts, frogs belong to the class of backboned animals known as *Am-phibia*, which means that they are able to live both in water and on land. They all have a moist, clammy skin without scales; all lay their eggs in water, in jelly-like masses ; and all pass through a tadpole stage.

Here the life history of the British common f r o g (*Rana temporaria*) is described as an ex-ample of frogs in general.

First, we must look for the eggs in water a foot or less in depth, at the edges of ponds and small lakes. Here, in the spring, both males and females gather for the annual egg-laying. They can be located by their low croaks. Usually in the night or early morn-ing the female lays her yearly batch of eggs, enclosed in a single mass of jelly which is attached to a pond plant of some kind.

A small frog may lay 2,000 to 3,000 eggs, a large one 6,000 to 8,000. Each egg is perfectly spherical in shape, black above, light below, and about one-six-teenth of an inch in diameter, and is surrounded by jelly. When first laid, the whole mass is the size of a teacup, but it swells up with water and increases in size several times before the eggs hatch.

From each egg is born a tad-pole. A few days later the tadpole has grown gills for breathing, a tail for swimming, and horny plates for jaws, with which it nips off bits of pond vegetation. So it lives and grows till in eight weeks or so it is a full-grown tadpole, more than an inch long. Then it begins to develop lungs, while the gills and tail gradually disappear, and the four limbs make their appearance. Many other changes take place in the creature, inside and out, during his wonderful change into a frog.

For the rest of his life the frog lives chiefly among vegetation in marshy places, but always near the water. He absorbs water through his skin, to keep his body moist. When the autumn frosts come he buries himself in muddy places to hibernate (sleep through the winter).

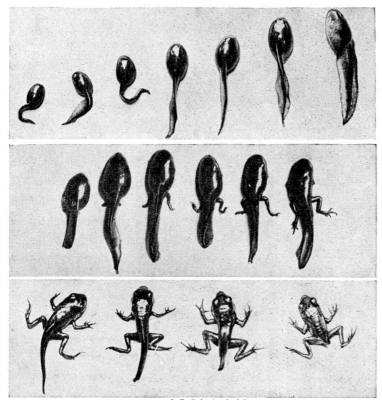

J. T. Roberts; S. Johnson

FROG FROM TADPOLE

Stages in development from tadpole to frog are shown here. First the head of the tadpole swells considerably (top); then the legs appear (centre); the tail is still attached but soon disappears (bottom). On the right, below, is an adult frog.

When summer comes round again he feeds and grows still more, and sleeps again the next winter. He comes out in the spring, but is not really full-grown till five years old or more.

From the beginning of his life to its end the frog is a wonderfully fascinating creature, and likewise a very useful one; for he captures and gets rid of thousands of mosquitoes and other insects of many kinds that pester Man and animals.

Frogs can be distinguished from toads by their outward characteristics. While frogs have damp, slimy skins, toads are dry and look as if they were covered with warts. The hind legs of the frog, being adapted for swimming, are very long in proportion to its body, while the toad, which spends most of its time on dry land, has comparatively short hind legs. Their reactions when disturbed are also different. A frog will almost certainly rise on all four legs and, after one look, hop away; while a toad will immediately crouch down to the ground and remain quite still, in an endeavour to make itself as inconspicuous as possible.

Froissart, JEAN (*c.* 1338–*c.* 1410). The son of an heraldic painter, Froissart (pron. frwah'-sar) gloried in the stirring life of his age, in its gorgeous colouring and heroic deeds. He sang of it in verse, and he wrote a history, his famous Chronicles, which gives us our most vivid account

of the superstitious, romantic, war-torn world of that time.

Froissart's Chronicles—four volumes—trace the history of the main events in England, Scotland, France, and Flanders between the years 1326 and 1400, and form one of the greatest of medieval historical works. The first book takes the English point of view, having been written under English patronage. But on the whole Froissart gives a fair version of events as he saw them, or as the witnesses available described them to him. Modern research has corrected errors of dates, statistics and topography, but though in his own day he received little praise, Froissart shows a great advance on most of his predecessors. His work is chiefly prized for its lively narrative of the best side of the age of chivalry, and for its accounts of Crécy, Poitiers, and other battles of the Hundred Years' War between France and England (1338–1453).

Froissart was born at Valenciennes, France, and to collect the stories he tells us, he travelled

to many lands. He became secretary to Philippa of Hainault, queen of Edward III of England, in 1361, and in her service visited the court of King David II of Scotland. In 1366 he followed Edward the Black Prince to Gascony, and visited several courts of North Italy. When Philippa died in 1369, Froissart found other patrons in Duke Wenceslas of Brabant and Gui de Blois, overlord of Chimay, to whom he became chaplain. In 1385 he travelled with a knight named Espaing de Lyon, whose stories gave him much picturesque matter for his

British Museum, London

FROISSART : A SCENE FROM HIS CHRONICLES
The history of main events in England, Scotland and France between the years 1326 and 1400 are traced in Froissart's Chronicles, and the above illustration is taken from a manuscript of the work in the British Museum, London. It shows John Ball, a revolutionary priest (mounted), addressing Wat Tyler and his followers in 1381. (See also page 1380.)

formed instead of dew. If the air in a room is dry, frost will not form on the window-panes, no matter how cold it is; but boil a kettle of water in the room or bring a number of people in to fill the air with moisture-laden breath, and at once frost patterns will form on the glass, provided the temperature remains low. Still air is also essential.

Sometimes the air is too dry or too windy for hoar frost; but the temperature falls below 32° F. This is what is known as black frost. Plants freeze in the night-time and turn black when the sun melts the sap in the morning. Glazed frost occurs when rain falls through cold air close to the earth, forming clear ice on the ground.

Frosts are matters of particular concern to

Chronicles, to the brilliant court of Gaston Phoebus of Foix at Orthez. Leaving Gaston, he went to Valenciennes to start the fourth book of his Chronicles. Having spent some time gathering further information, he found a new patron in Count Robert of Namur, to whom he dedicated his famous work. From 1400, when he ceased writing his Chronicles, until his death, probably in 1404, his life is obscure.

As an example of the way Froissart described events in England we give his account of the stern measures taken by Richard II in dealing with the Peasants' Revolt of 1381.

" The King entered into Kent, and came to a village called Ospringe, and called the mayor and all the men of the town before him; and when they were all come into a fair place, the King made to be showed them by one of his council how they had erred. And because that the King knew well that this business was begun by some of them, and not by all, wherefore it were better that some did bear the blame than all, he commanded that they should show who were culpable.

" In like manner as the King did at Ospringe he did in other places in Kent and in all other places of his realm where any rebellion had been ; and there were hanged and beheaded more than fifteen hundred."

Frost. Best known is the white frost, that covers vegetation with white feathery crystals. This is a hoar frost and may consist partly of frozen dew. When the air is ready to form dew, that is, when it is calm and saturated with moisture or water vapour, and the temperature falls below freezing-point, then frost or crystallized water is

G. A. Clarke

FROST PATTERNS
Moisture running down a window and freezing sometimes forms the most beautiful patterns, such as these feathers of frost. If the air in a room is dry, frost will not form on the window-panes, no matter how cold it may be.

THE APPLE AND ITS CLOSE RELATIVES

Fred Bond

At the top are the blossom and fruit of the apple. Then come its close relatives, the pear (centre) and the quince (bottom). All belong to the same family (*Rosaceae*) as the rose, their blossoms resembling those of the wild rose.

x

THREE MEMBERS OF THE PEACH FAMILY

Here are the blossoms and fruit of the plum (top), the peach (centre), and the apricot (bottom). Like many similar fruits that grow in a temperate climate, they belong to the rose family, and all have stones as seeds.

SMALL FRUITS OF TREE, BUSH AND VINE

Fred Bond

he cherry (top) belongs to the peach family and the order of roses. The grape (centre) and red currants (bottom) are among the few temperate-climate fruits which are not related to the roses.

BERRY FRUITS OF THE GREAT ROSE TRIBE

Fred Bo

Something of the amazing variety of the rose family is shown here by the red raspberry (top), the blackberry (centre) and the strawberry (bottom). Although the fruits, stems and leaves differ greatly, the relationship can be seen in the flowers.

To face page 14

farmers, because early autumn frosts may kill crops before harvests, and late spring frosts often kill planted crops and fruit buds or seriously retard their growth. Often it is not the actual cold that kills, but the sudden expansion when the sun warms the vegetation in the morning. That is why fruit farmers put a light cloth canopy over their trees to prevent the early morning sun reaching them. At night, too, a canopy over plants prevents radiation of their heat into the air, and reflects back the heat from the soil. A fire which produces an abundance of smoke to warm the air is useful. One way in which this is done in a large fruit plantation in America is shown in the illustration in page 1403.

It is a matter of common knowledge that crops on hill-sides often escape frost, while crops in the valley are destroyed. This is not caused, however, by cold air flowing down hill into the valley, as is commonly supposed. All the air cools and becomes denser and heavier after nightfall. The air in the valley, since it is already as low as it can get, remains in position and becomes colder and colder. The air on the hill-sides falls a little because of its weight, and then settles on top of the air in the valley, as though over the surface of a lake, and warmer air from above takes its place. Thus the temperature on the hill-sides is kept higher during the night than that in the valley.

FRUIT and METHODS of its CULTIVATION

By means of scientific selection, skilful culture and hygienic ways of gathering, grading and packing, the average household can now enjoy fruit of a variety and quality unknown to primitive Man—the first fruit-eater.

Fruit AND FRUIT GROWING. Although primitive Man undoubtedly ate wild fruits of all sorts, he did not enjoy the wonderful variety of choice flavours and splendid colours that we have today, for these are largely the outcome of human skill and industry exercised over a period of many years.

Highly-developed fruits with tempting flavours, seedless, thin-skinned, and over-sized fruit, and fruit stalks, without spines or thorns—these are some of the marvellous changes due to Man's experiments in fruit growing. Such results have been obtained in some cases by cross-fertilization between two species, so that the

Grown in nearly all countries with a temperate climate, apples are divided into dessert and cooking varieties.

desirable qualities of both are combined in one hybrid; but in general they have come about only after many years' work by experts.

However, the seeds of hybrids and other choice varieties obtained by careful selection and cultivation will not usually run true to type. Trees and shrubs grown from such seeds tend to go back to the form and habits of their wild ancestors. To overcome this difficulty, the process of grafting is used, by which a bud or twig of the choice variety of tree or shrub is made to grow on the roots or stem of a common or even a wild member of the same family. The bud or twig, called the scion, is inserted in a cleft cut in the stock plant, and the joint is then dressed and bandaged to protect it from the air. If this plant surgery is properly performed, the two will grow as one tree, which will bear fruit of the same quality as the scion's parent.

Great changes in the fruit industry have come about by improvements in packing, and by refrigeration and rapid means of transport. Formerly apples were practically the only fresh fruit enjoyed

in winter. Perishable fruit could be eaten fresh only in season and in the locality where it was grown. Now fruits of all kinds are regularly shipped from one country to another, and many kinds are kept in cold-storage warehouses for winter use. Apples, lemons, bananas, and oranges are normally obtainable throughout the year in Britain, while pears, grapes, and peaches, which a half-century ago were enjoyed only for a few weeks, are now on the market for many months.

There are many tropical fruits which are little known—such fruits as the papaw of the tropics, a fruit resembling a small cantaloup melon, the tamarind, which has long brown-shelled pods containing a brown acid pulp, used in preparing cooling drinks and in the making of sweet preserves; the loquat, a Chinese or Japanese fruit resembling a yellow plum ; the guava, represented by the two varieties, red and white, one shaped like an apple and the other like a pear, the pleasantly acid pulp of which is made into guava jelly; mangosteen, a reddish-brown fruit about the size of an apple and having white juicy pulp of a most delicious flavour; custard-apple, the small heart-shaped pulpy fruit of a tree which is a native of Brazil; and the star apple, a West Indian fruit like an apple in size and appearance, with a star-shaped centre formed by the seed cells.

In the chief fruit-growing countries thousands of workers are employed in the large orchards in picking, sorting or grading, packing, and marketing the fruit. The fruit, picked just at the right time, which is before it is quite ripe, is carefully handled, wrapped, and closely packed to prevent bruising, which might cause the fruit to rot before reaching the distant market.

The United States is the leading fruit-growing country, both for quantity and variety of fruits grown. Apples are her most important crop and the most widely distributed; oranges rank second. Vast quantities of apples also come to us from Canada, Australia, New Zealand, and Tasmania, while the Canary Islands and the West Indies normally supply us with bananas.

The fruit-grower chooses well-drained land for the orchard site, with good subsoil to the depth reached by the tree roots. The young trees, grown

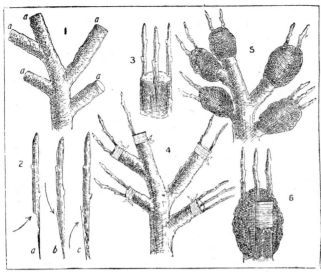

that would uselessly encumber the tree. Even old neglected orchards may be restored to bearing fruit by proper pruning of the roots as well as of the branches, and by careful cultivation.

Frost coming after the trees have begun to bud can do enormous damage to the orchard. When warning of an untimely frost is given out on the wireless, the fruit-growers of any region act promptly to protect their precious trees. Special fires are lit (*see* illustration in facing page) to form a blanket of smoke overhead to prevent the loss of heat through evaporation during the night; curtains of vapour may be formed over the orchard by spraying water high into the air ; and still another method is the installation of a system of hot-water pipes running all up and down the rows of trees to keep the temperature well above freezing-point. (*See* Frost).

FRUIT TREES : GRAFTING

Cultivated apples are obtained by grafting shoots, or scions, from a choice variety of tree on to stocks—young but common members of the same family. A field of stocks is shown on the right. The diagram above illustrates one method of grafting : 1. Tree prepared at (a) ; 2. Scions—(a) correctly, (b) and (c) badly, prepared ; 3. How scions are inserted ; 4. Scions bound in position ; 5. Final binding with grafting wax ; 6. Section showing raffia binding of the graft under the wax.

in a nursery, are set out in regular spaced rows in the orchard when they are one or two years old. The orchard is cultivated to keep out weeds: sometimes crops such as clover or alfalfa are grown and then dug into the ground to add nourishment to the soil, while sheep and pigs may be kept in an orchard to manure the ground.

Another important operation in orchard and vineyard is that of spraying to prevent injury to the tree or its fruit from insect or fungoid pests. Some sprays kill the insects by closing their breathing apparatus, while others, used against insects that chew or bite the leaves, poison them. These are usually arsenic solutions of one sort or another. Dusts or powders are also used, sometimes even being distributed on large orchards from aeroplanes. In general, power spraying machines are now used in large orchards, and hand sprayers in gardens and small orchards. The fungicides may also be either dusted or sprayed upon infected plants ; they destroy the delicate tissues of the fungus without injury to the tree.

Pruning is also very necessary to good fruit production. By a proper cutting back of wood growth, fruit-bearing wood may be given increased vigour and the tree opened up so that the sunshine will reach the fruit. Pruning away dead branches prevents injury to the tree through spread of the decay, removes a natural harbour for insects and other enemies of trees, and gets rid of weight

Fresh fruits, like green vegetables, contain much water, and are not therefore substantial foods. Their great value lies in their aid to the digestion of other foods and in the desirable mineral salts, fruity acids and vitamins which they contain. Dried, preserved, and tinned fruits occupy an important place in our diet. (*See* Canning Industry).

Fruits in the botanical sense are the parts of the plant which contain the seeds. To the botanist, the seed-carrying portions of all plants are fruit. Here are the three main fruit classifications: (1)

fleshy fruits, such as berries, oranges, melons, tomatoes, and apples, with seeds in the flesh; (2) stone or drupaceous fruits, which contain stones, such as plums, peaches, and cherries; (3) dry fruits, including nuts and grains, legumes, such as beans and peas, and capsules, pods, or similar containers, such as the seed-vessels of flowers.

In the fleshy fruits, the whole seed envelope, or pericarp, is juicy. In the drupes, the part of the fruit round the seed (the endocarp) becomes hard or stony, forming the peach or plum or cherry stone, while the outer portion (the exocarp) is fleshy. Dry fruits may be divided into splitting fruits, like peas, beans, and poppy capsules, which burst and scatter the seeds, and non-splitting fruits, like acorns, grains, and nuts.

Fry, ELIZABETH (1780–1845). Today what Elizabeth Fry did is done as a matter of course, what she advocated has been wholly adopted. But for her personality and persistence, the problems of prison reform and relief of the destitute might have been left untouched for many years to come

Fox

EXAMINING FRUIT FOR DISEASE
Although a diseased apple or any other fruit cannot be cured, it is possible to prevent the trouble occurring again. Above is the laboratory at Covent Garden Market, London, to which fruiterers can bring any abnormal fruit. Experts examine the fruit, report on the cause of the sickness, and suggest a treatment.

throughout Europe. The daughter of a Quaker banker, John Gurney, she was born on May 20, 1780, near Norwich, Norfolk. At the age of 20 she married Joseph Fry, a London merchant, and also

FRUIT : FROST PRECAUTIONS IN CALIFORNIA
Even in warm climates where oranges grow, the nights are sometimes cold and frost is liable to do much damage if precautions are not taken against it. In some instances special stoves (above) are used to provide a blanket of smoke overhead, which will prevent loss of heat through evaporation during the night and so ward off frost.

From the painting by George Barratt

ELIZABETH FRY PAYS A VISIT TO NEWGATE PRISON

In the 19th century many improvements were made in Great Britain in the administration of prisons and in the care of the destitute, among the most ardent advocates of these reforms being Elizabeth Fry. In the above painting she is seen reading to prisoners in Newgate Prison, London, which she first visited in 1813. Elizabeth Fry, a minister of the Society of Friends (Quakers), also did much to bring about improved conditions in hospitals and asylums.

a Quaker. Already she had begun what was to be her life-work, visiting the sick and relieving distress; and she had gained her first impression of prison conditions when, as a child of 13, she visited the Norwich house of correction.

In 1813 she paid her first visit to Newgate prison in London. She was warned that it was hardly safe to go, that the prisoners were vicious and dangerous.

The misery and filth she saw made her wonder not that the inmates were so savage, but that they were not insane as well. At once she embarked on schemes of practical and spiritual relief. She supplied clothes and other necessities, and in 1817 formed the Association for the Improvement of Female Prisoners, which was devoted to the establishment of what we now look upon as the first principles of prison discipline—classification of criminals, separation of the sexes, female supervision for female prisoners, and provision for religious and other instruction and for useful employment. Largely through her efforts these principles were widely adopted abroad as well as in Britain. Her reforming activities included the hospitals and the nursing system, as well as the administration of lunatic asylums. She died at Ramsgate on October 12, 1845.

Fuchsia. Named after the German botanist Leonhard Fuchs (1501–66), Fuchsias were introduced into Britain in 1788. They are natives of South and Central America and New Zealand, and members of the *Onagraceae* family. Their colours are all shades and mixtures of white, cream, pink, purple, crimson and violet. They grow freely in the open in Devon and Cornwall, and in some parts of Ireland, sometimes attaining a height of from 10 to 12 feet. A hardy and beautiful outdoor variety is *F. Riccartoni*.

FUCHSIA : TWO VARIETIES
Natives of South and Central America and New Zealand, fuchsias grow freely in the open in south-west England. On the left are seen single blooms and, on the right, the double type.

Fuel. Somewhat as our bodies depend on food for life and strength, so does the civilization of the world today depend on fuel. It gives us all our steam power and most of our electric power. It drives our motor-cars and aeroplanes. Virtually every ounce of metal we use is extracted from the Earth's minerals with the aid of fuels. Look around you and try to find a manufactured article that is not in one way or another a product of fire. There are a few —a hand-carved piece of wood or ivory, for example —but they are not important. Cloth, leather, glass, paper, rubber, celluloid, cement, brick, paint, ink, glue—all require the use of fuel during the course of their production.

The similarity of the common fuels to food is much closer than we might realize at first. Both contain carbon compounds. When we " burn " the carbon from our food inside our bodies with the aid of the oxygen we take into our lungs from the air, we get the heat energy that supplies power to our muscles and nerves. In the same way, the ordinary fuels we burn in our furnaces, power plants, engines, and chemical processes release their stored-up energy by oxidation of their carbon ingredients.

Primitive Man burned wood to heat his cave, to cook his food, and to frighten off wild animals. At his simple hearth he learned to fashion crude tools and weapons. And he found he could use animal and vegetable oils and fats for light and sometimes for heat. The first step toward the development of a better fuel probably was the discovery, made in prehistoric times, that charcoal gave more intense heat than wood. A statement by the philosopher Theophrastus suggests that the

CHARCOAL BURNING
Although metal kilns are being used on an increasing scale for making charcoal, the old method is still followed in places. Large conical heaps of logs are built, covered with turf or clay, and then fired from the centre.

Greeks employed coal for smelting metal in the 4th century before Christ, but coal was not used extensively until modern times. Manufactured gas came into use early in the 19th century, and fuels made from petroleum a half-century later.

Fuels may be divided into solids, liquids, and gases. Of the solid fuels, coal is by far the most important. It furnishes about two-thirds of the power and heat used by civilized peoples, and more than half of the heat energy used, even if fuels employed by primitive peoples are taken into account. (*See* Coal).

Coke, which is left after the extraction of coal-gas and coal-tar products from coal, is much used in homes and factories because it gives intense heat without smoke. Peat burns slowly, is smoky, and has a low heat value, but it is cheap and is invaluable to the inhabitants of regions where no other fuel is available. Wood has greatly declined in importance as a fuel. In heat value it is inferior to coal, and it is much more expensive than coal in the centres of population that lie far away from woods and forests. Coke has replaced charcoal for smelting ore. Other solid fuels are paraffin-wax, and tallow, usually burned in candles.

The principal liquid fuels are products of petroleum—petrol, paraffin, and partly refined crude oil or residue called fuel oil (*see* Petroleum). Fuel oils are sometimes used for heating homes and other buildings, and are widely used to drive oil engines and in steamships. Fuel oils are easy to store and handle; they can be piped into the oil tanks of ships with little labour, and they have twice the fuel value of coal in proportion to space occupied. Animal and vegetable oils once were the only fuels used in lamps for lighting; today paraffin has replaced them in all but primitive communities.

The most important gas fuels are natural gas from petroleum wells, manufactured coal-gas, and water gas (*see* Gas Manufacture). Gas is widely used for cooking and heating in our homes, and for heating in

W. F. Taylor

FUEL : CUTTING PEAT
In many districts of Ireland and in some parts of Wales and Cornwall the chief domestic fuel is not coal but peat. Here men are cutting blocks of peat, which later will be stacked to dry. Peat burns slowly, but gives out little heat.

many industrial processes. Gas fuels have high convenience value, since they can be turned on or off instantly and give no ash or smoke. Acetylene is another important fuel gas. It is used in oxy-acetylene welding and in acetylene lamps, such as are used for the lighting system of buoys.

Steam engines and steam turbines use fuels indirectly to generate power. The fuel is burned in a boiler to make steam, and the steam drives the engine. The internal combustion engine eliminates the boiler by burning fuel in the engine itself, and using pressure from the hot gas to drive the engine. This type of engine has been particularly valuable for transportation.

Internal combustion engines have created many fuel problems, however, because they need a fuel which generates power almost explosively. The Diesel engine accomplishes this with cheap fuel oil by using high compression. Petrol is the favourite fuel, in all countries which can obtain a cheap supply.

Wherever petrol is expensive, constant efforts are being made to use cheaper fuels. Charcoal and coke have been tried with some success in Europe, in China, and elsewhere. A current of steam or moist air, passing through a glowing hot mass of charcoal or coke, generates gas which burns like petrol in the engine. The principal objection

Topical

FUEL FROM NATURE'S GAS
In the Canadian province of Alberta natural gas is a valuable source of power. The gas is tapped by pipes and when it reaches the surface is separated from the accompanying naphtha. A separator is shown here covered with frost, for the gas comes to the surface at a temperature of 22 degrees below zero.

FUEL : A BENZOLE PLANT
Coal is a basic fuel, from which others are obtained. Above is part of a plant which distils coal gas, coal tar and certain by-products from soft coal. The gases are treated in these towers to extract benzole (a motor fuel) and other products.

to charcoal or coke is the bulkiness of the fuel and of the gas-generating apparatus required.

Alcohol has many desirable properties as a fuel for internal combustion engines and for heating. It gives intense heat or power in proportion to bulk, and creates no ash or smoke. But it is not as powerful as petrol, and countries which use it to lower the cost of motor fuel do so by mixing alcohol with petrol. Such mixtures have been tried in the United States, but they have no advantages over low-cost petrol. Their use has been urged in America rather as a means of conserving petroleum, and of giving farmers a new market for grain and other produce suitable for making alcohol.

The development of nations has been greatly affected by the possession or lack of fuel. Great Britain, for example, owed the rise of her industrial power largely to her abundant coal deposits. Much of the prosperity of the United States is traceable likewise to natural wealth of coal and oil. South American countries, on the other hand, have been handicapped by difficulties in obtaining adequate fuel supplies. An interesting incident in the history of fuel was the rise of the rich whaling industry of New England in the 18th and early 19th centuries—an industry dependent largely on the use of spermaceti and whale oil for making candles and for burning in lamps. With the advent of paraffin, the industry virtually disappeared.

What will the world do when its natural supplies of fuels have been exhausted? It is doubtful if even our remote descendants will have any cause to worry. Alcohol, if necessity arises, can always be manufactured in virtually unlimited quantities; and scientists know already how to produce many synthetic fuels which would be available now if the supply of cheaper natural fuels were cut off.

The not very distant future may see atomic energy used to augment, if not to replace, the present sources of power and heat.

The thermal or heating value of fuels is measured in calories or in British Thermal Units. (*See* Heat).

Fulton, ROBERT (1765-1815). An artist and a steamboat pioneer, Fulton was born in Pennsylvania, in the United States, on November 14, 1765. He showed talent as a painter and came to England where he studied under Benjamin West (1738-1820). Abandoning art for engineering, in 1794 he invented improvements for canal systems, and in 1796 went to Paris where he began experiments in fitting ships with steam engines. He also carried out tests with a submarine in the harbour at Brest, in Brittany, but received no encouragement from the French naval authorities.

Fulton built his first successful steamboat in 1803, and in 1807 constructed a larger vessel, the Clermont. This had an engine built by the famous Boulton and Watt, of Birmingham, England. It made its maiden voyage on August 17, 1807, on the Hudson river at New York, whither he had returned the previous year. In 1815 Fulton built the first steam warship for the United States navy. Though he was not the inventor of marine engines, Fulton was the first to apply steam successfully to navigation as a commercial undertaking. He died in New York on February 24, 1815.

Fungi. (Pron. fung′-gī). A large group of very simple plants, distinguished by the fact that they do not contain the green colouring matter (chlorophyll) possessed by higher plants, is known as fungi. This group includes all moulds, mildews, rusts, smuts, bacteria, truffles, puff-balls, toadstools, and mushrooms. Since they lack chlorophyll with which to manufacture their food out of raw materials, the fungi are compelled to live upon the food produced by other plants and animals. When they get their food from living creatures, fungi are called parasites; when they live on dead animal or vegetable matter, they are called saprophytes. Parasitic fungi do a vast amount of harm in the world, causing diseases in men, animals, and plants. But the saprophytes do a great deal of good as scavengers.

Fungi range in size from the tiniest moulds to huge toadstools. Many varieties such as the lichens

ROBERT FULTON'S STEAMBOAT: THE CLERMONT

In some respects Robert Fulton, the American engineer, was far ahead of his time, carrying out experiments in fitting ships with steam engines in 1796. His first successful steamboat was built in 1803, and in 1807 a larger vessel, the Clermont (above) was constructed. It had an engine of 24 h.p. fitted in a hull 100 feet long, and made its maiden voyage on the Hudson river in the United States. In 1815 Fulton built the first steam warship for the U.S. navy.

S. V. Waters; A. S. Martin; V. L. Breeze

FUNGI THAT GROW ON GROUND AND TREE

Typical examples of the varied fungi are shown here. At the top, left, is the candle-snuff or stag's horn, a black-and-white species of unusual form. Next to it is the oyster fungus, which grows on decaying trees and somewhat resembles a mass of oysters. On the left, below, is the shaggy cap, which lives on rotting vegetable matter. Right, the earth-star, whose outer skin breaks open at the top, the segments folding back to give it its curious shape.

are eaten by wild animals. Some, like mushrooms and truffles, are highly prized delicacies for human food. Certain others are used for making dyes and drugs; e.g. the mould *Penicillium notatum*, from which was prepared the antibacterial drug penicillin (q.v.). Yeasts are among the most useful of all fungi.

Fungi are divided into the following main groups : *Phycomycetes*, such as black mould, downy mildews ; *Ascomycetes*, such as mildews, truffles, cup-fungi, yeasts ; *Basidiomycetes*, for example, rusts, smuts, mushrooms, toadstools, and puff-balls ; and *Fungi Imperfecti*, which are probably modified forms of Ascomycetes.

Furnace. This word conjures up in our minds a picture of an immensely hot chamber, with leaping flames. The name comes from a Latin word meaning " oven," which is understandable when we remember that old-fashioned baking ovens were brick chambers having flues and a door. A fire of wood was built on the floor and fed until the oven got very hot. After the fire had burned itself out, the embers were swept out and the bread was put in to bake. You may still see such ovens in old houses. But " furnace " today means one of two sorts of appliance: the fire-box or combustion

SOME OF THE FAMILIAR EDIBLE AND DEADLY FUNGI

Painting by Marshall Smith

The artist has assembled here 12 of the most important members of the fungi group, including one deadly species. They may be identified by reference to the key plate overleaf.

ASSEMBLY OF EDIBLE AND DEADLY FUNGI

KEY TO PRECEDING COLOUR PLATE

SUCH an assembly is possible only in a printed page, for we may be sure that nowhere in the world can we find growing in one spot all the fungi shown on the preceding plate.

But this coming together at the magic summons of the painter's brush is a great convenience for purposes of comparison. We can identify the various species through the small key-picture at the left.

From top to bottom we see the Shaggy Pholiota, *Pholiota squarrosa* (1), Puff Ball, *Lycoperdon bovista* (2), Dog Mushroom, *Cortinarius caninus* (3), Coral Clavaria, *Clavaria coralloides* (4), Red Clavaria, *Clavaria rufescens* (5), Violet Clavaria, *Clavaria amethystina* (6), Meadow Mushroom, *Agaricus campestris* (7), Parchment Lactarius, *Lactarius pergamenus* (8), Deadly Amanita or Fly Mushroom, *Amanita muscaria* (9), Common Morel, *Morchella esculenta* (10), Magpie Mushroom, *Coprinus picaceus* (11), and Yellow Chanterelle, *Cantharellus cibarius* (12).

With the exception of the Amanita, all these are edible, though the Coral Clavaria and the Parchment Lactarius are sometimes slightly poisonous when immature or stale. The best rule to follow with mushrooms, however, is never to attempt to select edible varieties from pictures or verbal descriptions alone. Always get the advice of real experts and ask them to point out to you the actual growing specimens that are safe.

Many so-called tests for distinguishing poisonous species have found their way into popular tradition and popular literature. None of them is a safe guide, as many people have tragically discovered.

chamber of a steam boiler; and a closed chamber in which minerals are smelted for their metal, or in which metals are melted and otherwise treated.

The furnace of a boiler is described in our story of Boilers. The blast furnace (*q.v.*) is that towering structure of brick, concrete and steel in which iron ore is smelted to make pig-iron. In steel making the open-hearth type of furnace is used (*see* Iron and Steel). This is a shallow bath made of refractory materials—which will withstand immense heat—and is warmed by causing flaming gases to sweep over the roofed-in chamber of which the hearth forms the floor. The metal is not in contact with the burning fuel, and the heat " reverberates " from the roof and sides of the furnace, so that this type is often called a reverberatory furnace.

Then there are the different forms of electrically heated furnace, for smelting ores (*see* Aluminium),

melting metals, making such materials as calcium carbide for acetylene generation, or producing the artificial abrasive known as carborundum. In the electric arc furnace the electricity flashes from the tips of carbon electrodes down to the steel or other metal in the base of the furnace, and generates heat of an almost incredible temperature, 30 times as hot as boiling water.

The second main type of electric furnace produces heat without flame—by electro-magnetic induction. (This is explained in the story of Electricity.) A coil of insulated copper rod runs around the furnace body, and a high-frequency current of electricity is passed through the coil. This current " induces " a secondary current in the steel which is to be melted within the furnace; the current generates heat *in* the steel itself, with the result that heat loss is small, and it is quickly melted.

HOW *we* GOT *our* FINE FURNITURE

*A*rchitects as well as designers have played a most important part in giving us furniture pleasing to the eye as well as serving our comfort and convenience. An interesting story is briefly told.

Furniture. At one time the making of furniture distinguished for beauty and grace, as well as merely for utility, was a handicraft which bore the stamp of the individual, whether he was a great designer or a mere copyist. To-day, the invention of modern machinery has made it a factory process, in which fine individual workmanship is too often lacking. However, in normal times it is possible to obtain fine pieces in the most modern manner, designed by artists or, more often, architects, and executed as single pieces never to be repeated.

Ornate Jacobean furniture followed the simpler Tudor pieces early in the 17th century. This chair is of Jacobean workmanship.

In ancient times and throughout the Middle Ages houses were very scantily furnished. Chairs were reserved for the lord of the house and favoured guests; otherwise stools and benches, chests for clothing, beds, and tables—which were often just boards laid across trestles—formed the greater part of the furniture. The Egyptians, Greeks, Romans, and other ancient nations had elaborate pieces of furniture made of ivory, bronze, silver, and gold, but these were rare and belonged only to the great.

The early Egyptians were adept in woodworking, and pictures on their tombs and some pieces that have been preserved indicate that they had wooden furniture, sometimes carved and gilded and covered with splendid textiles. Fine specimens were found in Tutankhamen's (reigned 1358–53 B.C.) tomb, and there is in the British Museum a wooden throne of an Egyptian queen who lived 3,000 or more years ago.

The period of the Renaissance (15th century) marked an important development in furniture making. Florence, Milan, Rome, and Venice became centres of cabinet-making, and the idea of furnishing the home as a place of comfort and beauty was for the first time given serious consideration. But all the time, in England and elsewhere, craftsmen were making fine tables and chests especially, using only local woods and developing along traditional lines their own national style. English chests, inlaid with scenes done in several woods, sometimes dyed various colours; huge, sturdy refectory tables, used especially in monasteries; chests for churches and large houses; sturdy oaken chairs with turned legs; all these and other minor pieces, besides such large things as bedsteads, were produced by craftsmen, and showed the development of styles from the useful Tudor to the more ornate Jacobean. It was after Charles II came to the throne in 1660, however, that the first great period of English furniture-making began. This came about with the increasing use of walnut for whole articles, usually as veneer but sometimes as solid wood.

The Age of Walnut, as the beginning of the 18th century came to be called, did indeed produce much superb furniture, especially chairs, small tables and the lighter types of bureau and bookcase. It showed a good deal of Dutch influence. In the middle of the century walnut was succeeded, with a complete change of designs, by mahogany.

Thomas Chippendale (died 1779), the first and greatest of British furniture artists, devoted his life to producing chairs, tables, and other articles that were strong as well as handsome. At first he used mahogany only, and became celebrated for his chairs with a wide seat narrowing towards the back, and a perforated, decorative, convex back. He enriched his designs with caning, and used no inlay.

Chippendale's work revolutionized the whole trade in England, his patterns being copied in all parts of the country. About the same time Robert Adam and his three brothers were doing almost

SPECIMENS OF FURNITURE OF MANY PERIODS—

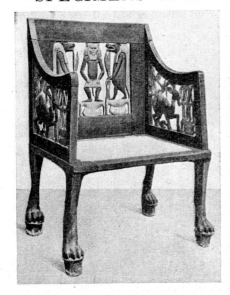

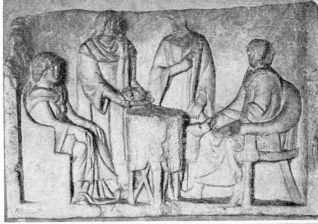

In this and the facing page the photographs show the development of household furniture from early Egyptian times to the 18th century. Immediately above is an early Egyptian chair with an open-work back carved in the form of the god Bes. On the right above is a bas-relief showing a Roman and his wife taking a meal, seated in armchairs at a small table ; beneath it is a 13th-century English oak chest.

British Museum; Musée S. Germain (Archives Photographiques); and Victoria & Albert Museum

On the left is a Tudor four-poster bed, dating from the end of the 16th century. It is of carved walnut and the posts of the canopy at the foot are separate from the bed frame. Immediately above is an English oak chair of the 17th century.

Victoria & Albert Museum

—FROM ANCIENT EGYPT TO GEORGIAN ENGLAND

The three photographs at the top of the page show : left, a pedestal secretaire in marquetry, period Louis XV ; centre, a Sheraton sideboard of mahogany, inlaid with satin wood ; and, right, a Hepplewhite walnut armchair of the late 18th century

Victoria & Albert Museum and Gill & Reigate, Ltd.

Above in the centre is shown a room decorated and furnished in the Georgian style with panelled walls ; note the ornamented ceiling and pediments over door and chimneypiece. The furniture is Chippendale. On the left is a 17th-century walnut bureau.

Courtesy of Country Life (above) and Gill & Reigate, Ltd.

equally important work in making the house and its decorations and furnishings an artistic whole. Though they were architects by profession, these men designed furniture of all types to fit the beautiful houses they created: their chief influences, however, came from abroad, notably from Italy and France. Their work influenced George Hepplewhite (died 1786), whose best designs combine lightness with usefulness and simplicity.

Thomas Sheraton (1751–1806) went further than any of his predecessors or contemporaries in the direction of delicacy, harmony, balance, and lightness. Some of his later work, however, is marred by extravagance and fantastic forms, and a great deal is too flimsy for any but drawing-room use. From time to time, too, the use of gilt and marquetry, and metal and marble, by the great French designers—such as André-Charles Boulle (1642–1732)—had much influence on the designers of English furniture, especially noticeable at the end of the 18th century and start of the 19th.

About 1815 the steam lathe was first applied to the making of furniture, and in 1825 the circular saw was invented. Furniture, which formerly had been very plain, was now covered with elaborate, meaningless scroll-work and mouldings, easily produced by the new machinery. Since 1859 most furniture has been made by machines, which cut, polish, and even assemble the articles. Some of the polishing of furniture is still done by hand, but there is very little individual workmanship.

Since the latter half of the 19th century, largely inspired by the work of the English artist, William Morris (1834–96), there has been a growing demand for a revival of the individually produced pieces of original design.

The woods used in making furniture are varied, and change as often as do the designs: from oak, beech, and holly we passed to walnut, thence to mahogany and satinwood, and now again oak, maple, ash, and sycamore are popular, with birch and many rare imported woods for inlay and veneer work.

Metal, both in pressed sheet and tubular form, enamelled or chromium-plated, is used mostly for office, kitchen and bathroom furniture.

Furs. The skins of fur-bearing animals are bound up with the history of nearly all civilized peoples. Wherever winters were cold, one of the first concerns of primitive Man was to provide himself with coverings made from the warm thick coats of animals, for garments roughly fashioned from skins and furs were worn long before he had learned to spin and weave wool.

For furs he hunted and toiled, and when he had obtained more than he needed for himself, he bartered them to his fellows for food and weapons. Thus furs became an early medium of trade and exchange; and as the people of more temperate regions came to covet them for ornament as well as warmth, the fur trade became one of the chief of primitive industries.

To get the rarer and more beautiful skins, men have dared the dangers of the jungles, of the tropics and the trackless wastes of Arctic snows. In their never-ending demands for furs men mercilessly hunted some of the most prized species, until such animals as the beaver, the fur-seal, and the sea-otter were threatened with extinction. In all ages the most costly furs have been the badge of wealth or dignity. In the Middle Ages the snowy white ermine with its black-tipped tails could be worn in England only by members of the royal family, but today it is used for official robes, ladies' cloaks and capes.

The colonization of North America is inseparably linked with the fur trade, the Hudson's Bay Company being the chief agency. The first settlements were mere trading-posts, to which the Indians brought the furs of trapped animals, and bartered them for guns and other articles. Other pioneers followed the fur-traders, settled at or near the trading-posts, and thus formed the nucleus of many of the cities and thriving towns of the present day. Winnipeg was one of these so founded.

The increasing demand for furs caused prices to rise very considerably at one time, and one of the results of this was the beginning of the industry of fur farming. The most notable example of this new industry is the breeding of the silver fox in many northern countries, and even in Britain. Other varieties of foxes, mink, racoons and skunks are bred on farms that imitate as nearly as possible the natural homes of these animals. The musk-rat, imported for breeding purposes into Europe from North America, has caused untold damage to vegetation, fruit trees, river and canal banks. Escaping from farms, these animals have bred in enormous numbers and musk-rat farming is now forbidden.

Another result of the increasing demand has been the dyeing and counterfeiting of inferior skins to resemble the better varieties. The furs of domestic cats and wild rabbits masquerade under a variety of names, but may be sold only with an indication of their true origin. White rabbit fur is prepared to imitate ermine and chinchilla. Clipped and dyed musk-rat pelts are sold as Hudson Bay seal, sable, and otter. Otters furnish the most durable of all furs; then in the following order come beaver, seal, racoon, skunk, Persian lamb or astrakhan, and fox.

The following are some of the principal furs, with the sources from which they are normally obtained :

Badger.. ..	North America, Europe, Asia
Beaver.. ..	Throughout North Temperate Zone
Caracul ..	Russia, China, North America
Chinchilla ..	Peru, Bolivia, Chile
Ermine ..	Stoats in their white winter coat from North America, Siberia
Fox, blue ..	Alaska, Canada, Siberia
Fox, cross, grey, red	North America
Fox, silver ..	North America, Siberia
Kolinsky ..	Weasels from Siberia, China, Japan
Lynx	North America, Europe, Asia
Marmot ..	North America, Asia
Marten ..	Europe, Northern Asia
Mink	North America, Russia, China, Japan
Musk-rat ..	North America
Opossum ..	Australia, United States
Racoon ..	North America
Sable	Siberia, China, Japan
Seal	Bering Sea
Skunk	North America
Squirrel ..	Siberia, Canada
Wolf	North America, Russia, Asia

Gaels AND GAELIC. Early occupiers of Britain were people of Celtic origin named Gaels, who fought the Roman legions for possession of the island. Their descendants live on in the Highlands of Scotland, where the Gaelic language may still be heard. Similar languages are spoken in Wales and in Ireland, and to these the name of Gaelic is also sometimes applied.

Gaelic is a difficult language to learn, owing to its pronunciaticn, so that few people learn it, hence its literature, which is rich in songs and folktales, is not very much read. Yet even a slight knowledge of the language is valuable to any traveller in Scotland, for most of the place-names are derived from Gaelic. Words like *ben* (or *beinn*) or *cairn* for mountain and *cnoc* for hill, *strath* for a wide valley and *glen* for a narrow one, *dun* (or *dum*) for a fort, *kil* meaning cell, and usually found associated with a saint's name, *aber* meaning the confluence (or flowing together) and *inver* the mouth of a river, are found in place-names all over Scotland.

Gainsborough, THOMAS (1727–1788). A founder of the English school of painting, Thomas Gainsborough was born at Sudbury, in Suffolk, and was baptized on May 14, 1727; his father was a prosperous wool merchant and manufacturer, and Thomas was the youngest of nine children. It was his mother, a cultured woman of considerable artistic ability, who encouraged the boy. One of his earliest efforts was a rapid sketch of a man whom he saw examining his father's orchard; when the orchard was found to have been robbed, young Tom's sketch was successfully used in identifying the thief. The incident delighted his father, who decided to send the boy to London to study art.

Arrived there in 1741, Gainsborough studied engraving and set up as a portrait painter in Hatton Garden, also painting landscapes for dealers. But he failed to make a sound living, and in 1745 returned to Sudbury. He married, in 1746, Margaret Burr, a lovely young lady whose private income enabled the young couple to set up house on their own in Brook Street, Ipswich. At this time Gainsborough painted many small portrait groups. These are as

National Gallery of Eire

A GAINSBOROUGH PORTRAIT

Appointed painter to King George III in 1774, Gainsborough excelled in full-length portraits of the noted men and women of the day, his work being unlike that of any other artist. His slightly superficial later style is revealed in this painting of the Duchess of Cumberland.

delightfully simple and pastoral as his later work was brilliant and true to the life of the city. He moved to Bath in 1760, and there he attracted many sitters among the rich. His fame quickly spread to London, and he was made one of the original members of the Royal Academy at its founding in 1768.

Gainsborough, who was always abrupt, rude, and tactless in manner, quarrelled with Sir Joshua Reynolds (1723–92) in 1772 and for four years refused to exhibit at the Academy. But shortly after his arrival in London, in 1774, he was appointed painter to the king, and his prosperity was assured. His sitters included George III, whom he painted eight times; the great statesman, Pitt, of whom he made seven portraits; and the actor, Garrick, of whom he made five; and, in fact, all the noted men and women of the day sat to him. Gainsborough quarrelled once more with the Academy in 1783 and he never exhibited there again. He died at his own home in London on August 2, 1788.

The great majority of his works are very easily recognized. His great full-length portraits of English ladies, for example, are quite unlike the works of any other painter. Pale silvery blues, greys, and greens in the foreground and on the sitter's clothes attract the eye, while the brown and deeper greens and blues of the background often make the portrait into a real picture as well. In his landscapes his command of colour and understanding of Nature are seen to the full.

It was as a country lad that Gainsborough first began to paint, depicting the trees and streams and landscapes of his native Suffolk; and it was as a landscape painter that he always liked to think of himself. Yet his portraits brought him fame and fortune, and it is still as a portrait painter that we inevitably consider him in a study of English art. (*See* illus., page 1187).

Galahad. Among the knights of King Arthur's Round Table Galahad was blessed with great faith and purity which enabled him to find the Holy Grail, the cup said to have been used by Christ at the Last Supper. This sacred vessel, so the legend runs, had been brought to Britain by Joseph of Arimathea, but when the land fell into wickedness it was hidden away; and the search for it became the quest of King Arthur's knights.

One day, when the knights were talking of the Holy Grail, the torches in the great hall went out. Across the darkness streamed a band of silver light. Against that, faintly as through a mist, they saw a flush of rose. Only Sir Galahad saw the sacred cup clearly—"all crimson and glowing like a ruby," and heard a voice which said, "Galahad, follow me."

All the knights of Arthur's court swore a vow to live a holy life for a year and a day, while they searched for the lost Grail. Only four returned. Sir Bors and Sir Lancelot had seen the Grail in blessed visions. Sir Perceval had seen it because he was Galahad's friend, and next to him the purest in heart. After long wandering he had found Galahad in prayer in a hermit's cell.

"Oh, my friend," said Galahad, "the Holy Grail shines always before me, blood-red, and glowing like a star, guiding me to Heaven. It gives me victory over every sin and shame and wrong in the world. Come with me." The Knights went out into a storm, and over a hill top. Galahad ran before, across a bridge which spanned a black marsh, to the sea, and was seen no more. As Perceval knelt, weeping and praying, there came the beam of silver light, and on it the glowing Grail. In the morning he found Galahad's body, beautiful, thin and worn as a saint's, and buried it by the sea.

The story of Sir Galahad is treated in Malory's Morte d'Arthur and in other medieval romances. It is also the theme of Tennyson's Sir Galahad, and of The Holy Grail in his Idylls of the King.

Galapagos Islands.
Some 600 miles off the coast of the South American Republic of Ecuador, the Galapagos (pron. ga-lah'-pa-gos) Islands lift their lava peaks out of the Pacific Ocean. Nine islands and about fifty islets and reefs are scattered over an area about 200 miles in diameter, directly astride the Equator. But the tropical heat is moderated by the moist south-east trade winds and by the cool Antarctic Current that reaches its northernmost range in this vicinity.

Many of the islands have both English and Spanish names. The largest is Albemarle (Isabela), about 75 miles long. Here at the southern end a volcanic cone rises nearly 5,000 feet, the highest point in the group. The other chief islands in order of size are Indefatigable (Santa Cruz), Narborough (Fernandina), Chatham (San Cristobal), James (San Salvador), Charles (Santa Maria), Bindloe (Marchena), Hood (Española), and Abingdon (Pinta). About 100 miles north-west of the main group are the islets of Wenman and Culpepper.

From the shore, the land rises in a series of volcanic craters. The windward coasts, drenched by mists, are tangles of mangrove swamps. On the dry leeward coast, at the north and west of each island, grey lava cliffs rise straight out of the sea, or beaches of white sand recede to desert growth of cactus, thorn trees, and barbed grass. On the uplands, often swathed in clouds, rain falls in the winter, filling rocky pools but flowing springs are rare.

The islands are remarkable for their animals. When Charles Darwin, the first of several scientists to visit Galapagos, came here in 1835 he found that half the birds and plants were different from species in other parts of the world. About a third of the shore fish and nearly all the reptiles also differed. These variations helped to suggest to Darwin the theory of evolution set forth in his Origin of Species.

As Man has made few attempts to settle in the Galapagos, the animals show little fear. Giant land iguanas, three feet or more in length, bask under cactus like prehistoric "dragons." Sea iguanas swarm over the coastal rocks, which are frequented also by herds of sea lions and seals. Among the birds peculiar to the islands are species of pelican, penguin, flightless cormorant, heron, dove, finch, mocking-bird, hawk, and albatross.

An occasional giant tortoise recalls the days when these monsters were so abundant that Spanish explorers named the islands after them, from the Spanish word galapago, tortoise. Some weighed 200 pounds or more and were strong enough to carry a man. In the days of sailing ships they were a source of fresh meat. Sailors caught them by the hundred, and dumped them into the hold, where the tortoises lived without food or water until needed. Early in the 20th century, Ecuadorans slaughtered enormous numbers for oil. On some of the larger islands roam wild dogs, cats, goats, donkeys, and even some cattle—descendants of animals left there by passing vessels.

The Galapagos were discovered in 1535 by the Spanish bishop of Panama, but no attempt was made to settle on them. Late in the 17th century, the islands became hideouts for buccaneers and sea rovers. Here too came Alexander Selkirk (Robinson Crusoe) in 1709 after his rescue from the Juan Fernandez islands. Buried treasure has been found.

After being unclaimed by any nation for nearly 300 years, the Galapagos were annexed by Ecuador in 1832. In 1892 Ecuador officially named the islands Archipiélago de Colón. Chatham is now the centre of government. Its only town, Progreso, is built in the hills, and its few hundred people grow coffee, fruit, and sugar cane. Wreck Bay, on Chatham, is the chief port of the islands. Area, 2,868 square miles ; population, about 1,500.

Galileo
(1564–1642). The first astronomer to use the telescope for examining the sun, moon and stars, the discoverer of the pendulum's laws, and the founder of modern physics, was Galileo (pron. gal-i-lā'-ō) Galilei (usually known as Galileo). He was born in Pisa, Italy, on February 15, 1564, and died January 8, 1642.

When Galileo was a youth of 19 he saw a lamp in the cathedral at Pisa swinging regularly. He realized—what no one had realized before—that a pendulum swinging to and fro could be used to measure time, and so laid the foundation for the invention of the modern clock (see Pendulum). He dropped objects from the Leaning Tower of Pisa, and proved that falling bodies, however heavy or light, fall at the same rate (see Gravitation). He held the professorship of mathematics in the universities of Pisa and Padua; in 1610 he left Padua for Florence, where he lived henceforth.

GALILEO EXPLAINING THE USE OF THE TELESCOPE

Founder of the science of mechanics and the first astronomer to use a telescope, Galileo laid the foundations of
modern physics and astronomy. Right up to the end of his
long life, even after he became blind, he continued to work
on new theories, and made valuable contributions to the
science of physics. His published papers filled 20 volumes
when they appeared 250 years after his death. Galileo
is depicted here entertaining visitors to his laboratory.

Galileo made his first telescope with a piece of
organ pipe, placing a lens at either end. It
magnified only three times, but later he made a
telescope that magnified 30 times. With this he
saw the mountains on the moon's surface; found
that the Milky Way was a mass of very faint stars;
discovered the four largest satellites of the planet
Jupiter and the peculiar appearance of Saturn,
later shown to be due to a series of "rings."

What he saw through his telescopes also convinced him of the truth of Copernicus's view that
the earth rotates on its axis and revolves round the
sun. Galileo's ardent support of this theory was the
cause of difficulties with the Church. In 1616 he
was given a formal warning, but nevertheless he
again aroused the anger of the Church authorities
by publishing a book entitled Dialogue of the Two
Great Systems of the Universe. For this publication he was summoned before the Inquisition in
October 1632. No one knows what happened
during his examination, but we do know that he
formally admitted that his views were wrong, and
he was compelled to live apart from everyone for
the rest of his life. He then published what is
perhaps his most valuable book, Dialogue of the
New Sciences, which is a summary of his lifelong
studies on the principles of mechanics.

Galileo was the first to have any concrete idea
of force as a mechanical agent, and in this also he
did much to clear the ground for Newton, who
was born in 1642, the year that Galileo died.

Galsworthy, JOHN (1867–1933). An English novelist and dramatist, Galsworthy wrote
about people of the upper-middle class, and he
also showed much pity for the oppressed.

Galsworthy was born on August 14, 1867, at
Coombe, in Surrey. He went to Harrow and then
to Oxford, and passed his Bar examinations with
no particular intention of practising. Having
ample means, he travelled a good deal.

John Galsworthy's great year came in 1906,
when the first of the Forsyte novels, The Man of
Property, appeared, and his play The Silver Box
was produced. The novel launched him on his
career as a social historian; the play placed him
at once among the first dramatists of his time.
From this year onward Galsworthy continued
his double career of novelist and playwright.
He had founded in The Man of Property that
background of a rich, upper-middle-class England
which was to serve for a long series of novels later
known as the Forsyte Saga. The most important
of the successive Forsyte novels, as they followed
The Man of Property after a long interval, were In
Chancery (1920), To Let (1921), The White
Monkey (1924), The Silver Spoon (1926), Swan
Song (1928), Maid in Waiting (1931), Flowering
Wilderness (1932), and, published after his death,
Over the River (1933). He also wrote short stories,
essays, some poems, and further novels.

Of his plays, The Silver Box was followed in
1909 by Strife, which exposed the uselessness of

strikes. The most impressive of his social dramas, Justice, revealing the horrors of the existing prison system, was produced in 1910, and resulted in some immediate reform of the evils he portrayed. After the First World War (1914–18) Galsworthy returned to the theatre with renewed powers. The Skin Game was produced in 1920, Loyalties in 1922, and Escape in 1926. The first dealt with the conflict between that settled class of the author's origin and the new rich; the second with the eternal struggle between Jew and Gentile; and the third with the reactions of a normal world towards a hunted convict.

Galsworthy refused a knighthood in 1918, but was awarded the Order of Merit in 1929. He received the Nobel prize for literature in 1932, and died on January 31, 1933. He played a large part in the campaign for the humane slaughtering of animals. In his private life he was shy, but he was accessible to all cases of distress, and was sympathetic to all young authors.

Galvani, LUIGI (1737–98). An important Italian physiologist, Galvani was born at Bologna on September 9, 1737. He became a professor of anatomy in 1762 at Bologna university, where, in 1790, in the course of some experiments on "animal electricity," he hung a dead frog over an iron balcony railing by a copper hook through the frog's back. The creature's body was at once convulsed by lively twitchings. Galvani's conclusion was that the frog was a kind of naturally charged Leyden jar (*q.v.*), with negative electricity on the exterior surface of the muscles which discharged through the iron railings, and positive electricity along the nerves of the interior which discharged through the copper hook.

Galvani published his experiments and deductions, which aroused great interest and much controversy. His work On the Force of Electricity in Muscular Movement was published in 1791. He died on December 4, 1798. His collected works were published between 1841 and 1842.

The voltaic pile, cell, and battery are sometimes called "galvanic" in his honour and the current they generate was long known as "galvanism." Galvani is also remembered in the "galvanometer" (*see* Electricity), the instrument that measures electric current, and in "galvanized" iron, which is iron coated with zinc to prevent it from rusting. This coating was formerly applied by "galvanic," or electrolytic, methods, though it is now more commonly given by dipping the iron in a bath of molten zinc.

Galway. In the province of Connacht or Connaught, Galway is one of the most wild and beautiful of all the counties of Eire, and has an area of 2,293 square miles. The eastern part of

Clive Edis

JOHN GALSWORTHY

The life of the upper middle class during the first 30 years of the 20th century formed the theme of Galsworthy's novels. He was awarded the Nobel prize for literature in 1932.

the county is flat and fertile, but the western region on the Atlantic seaboard contains several mountainous districts, including Connemara, wherein the noted Connemara marble is quarried, with the famous Twelve Pins, varying from 2,000 to 3,000 feet in height; and Lough Corrib, the largest lake in Eire, which is noted for its trout. Agriculture and fishing are the main industries.

About 30 miles off the coast, in Galway Bay, are the Aran Islands—Innishmore, Innishmaan, and Innishere—the home of hardy fisherfolk who speak the Erse language, and who cling to ancient Gaelic customs. They spin their own wool and make their own hide shoes or pampooties, such as were worn over 1,000 years ago; and they still make most of their own boats (or currachs) of tarred canvas similar to those which have been used for centuries.

The county town, Galway, is an ancient city, which stands on the river Corrib, where it flows into Galway Bay. Galway city flourished in the 12th century, and traded with Spain and other countries of Europe. In recent years the city has developed considerably since it became a port of call for some of the Transatlantic liners, as it has a good harbour. As the capital of Connacht province Galway city has a university college, founded as Queen's College in 1845 and part of Eire University.

In Connemara is Clifden, where the British aviators Alcock and Brown landed after the first non-stop Atlantic flight in 1919. The population of the county is 166,000.

Gandhi, MOHANDAS KARAMCHAND (1869–1948). One of the most influential figures in modern times in India was Gandhi (pron. gun'-dē), who came to be known affectionately among his millions of followers as the Mahatma (great soul).

Gandhi was born on October 2, 1869, at Porbandar, the capital of a small state in Kathiawar, in Western India. His father was Kaba Gandhi, who, though belonging to the despised Bania (money-lending) section of Hindus, was the prime minister or Dewan of the state of Porbandar. Mohandas was married at the age of 13. He gained his education first at Rajkot, and later in London, reading law and being called to the Bar at the Inner Temple. He had a great admiration for Western ideas, and while in England was influenced by his studies, especially of Ruskin and Tolstoy. Although a Hindu he had a deep appreciation of other faiths, and it was this tolerance which led him to work for the interests of others, especially the untouchables, or outcasts, of his country.

He returned to India and practised law in the Bombay high court, and eventually in 1893 set up in practice in Durban, South Africa. The next year he founded the Natal Indian Congress, and agitated for Indian rights within the South African colonies. He gave up his legal practice in 1909 to become secretary of the Transvaal British Indian Association. During the First World War (1914–18) he went to England, and organized an ambulance corps from among Indian students, later returning to India.

He had always favoured passive resistance, and, by 1919, when he had won many followers by championing the cause of the oppressed in India, and by his desire to secure self-government for India, he had become concerned in many serious disturbances. Unfortunately his own genuine desire and insistence on non-violence, coupled with non-cooperation, led to many unforeseen instances of violence by the people, and the authorities somewhat reluctantly imprisoned Gandhi in March 1922. After his release he became president of the Indian National Congress Party in 1924.

From this time his influence among the Indian masses was tremendous, and he created an awareness of nationhood. By his own people he was treated as a saint; even his critics respected his courage and determination. He had an intense dislike for mechanisation in industry, and to combat this encouraged the use of the hand-loom, and sponsored the revival of many other native crafts.

He started a campaign of " civil disobedience " in March 1930, defying the salt laws, and for this was interned in May for six months; after this (March 6, 1931), he signed a pact with the Viceroy to end such disturbances, and took part in the Round Table Conference on Indian affairs in London the same year. Again in the following January he was imprisoned for further disturbances; during this term he intended fasting for 21 days in September unless the Poona pact (giving separate legislature seats to the untouchables) was suspended or withdrawn. He broke his fast only when political leaders of the two parties effected a compromise which Gandhi had approved. On several later occasions he resorted to fasting to bend others to his will, as well as encouraging civil disobedience.

When the Second World War (1939–45) broke out, though he appeared to sympathise with the war against aggression, his main thought was for a free India. By August 1942, however, largely owing to his own aversion to force, he rebelled and instituted a mass obstruction campaign against the war effort. Because of this he was interned until he had to be released for health reasons in May 1944. His wife died in February during the internment period.

Gandhi's encounters with authority never once broke his spirit ; they served only to strengthen his determination to free India from British rule, and to give to the caste of untouch-

MOHANDAS GANDHI
Leader of the peoples of India in their struggle to free their country from British rule, Gandhi was assassinated in January 1948, shortly after this goal was reached.

ables political equality with the higher castes. Though his ideals were so high, he always remained something of an enigma to all his associates, yet it was with sincere regret and profound sorrow that millions of Indians (both Moslem and Hindu) as well as Europeans learned of his death at the hand of an assassin on January 30, 1948, just when Britain had voluntarily handed back the rule of India to her own peoples.

Ganges. (Pron. gan'-jēz). Rising in eastern Pakistan, in an ice-cave beneath the Himalayan snows above Gangotri, the Ganges, the sacred river of the Hindus, begins its life as the Bhagirathi; at the point where this is joined by the Alaknanda at Devaprayag, a famous place of pilgrimage, the river is called the Ganges. Thence it breaks through the last mountain barrier at Sukhi just above ancient Hardwar. A shallow stream before it receives the waters of its many tributaries, the river keeps to a south-easterly course through the land of the Jats, to Cawnpore.

Half-way on its journey through the most densely populated region of the world, the Ganges is joined by a sister stream, the Jumna, which also rises in the Himalayas, west of the Ganges. The land between the two rivers is irrigated by two canal systems fed from the Ganges. The canal system was begun in 1842 as a result of a terrible famine which raged in 1837–38, the Ganges Canal being opened in 1854. Allahabad is the true Prayag or holy of holies where devout Hindus wash away their sins. Here the river becomes deep enough to bear small native craft, and it is navigable throughout the remainder of its 1,557-mile journey to the sea.

In a great circle the stream sweeps past Benares. The banks are crowded with temples, whose ghats (steps) swarm with pilgrims of every rank, come to wash away their sins in Mother Gunga (or Ganga). *(See illus. page 412.)*

Swollen by new tributaries, the Ganges flows past village and city until it meets the mighty Brahmaputra, whose silt assists in the unceasing building-up of its extensive delta, which lies between the rivers Hooghly, on the west, and Meghna on the east. This delta begins more than 200 miles from the Bay of Bengal, the river flowing southward through swamps to the sea. Chief of its channels is the Hooghly ; it bears majestic ocean liners 80 miles to busy Calcutta, but constant dredging is needed to keep it free of silt. The northern part of the delta is fertile country ; but the southern area nearer the sea is swampy, and is known after the Sundarbans, named after the tree called the sundri which is found growing there in the shifting unhealthy mudbanks.

Hindus worship the Ganges as the ancient Egyptians deified the Nile, because it gives life to the millions that swarm upon the 391,100 square miles of its fertile basin. When the tropical summer rains beat down, all the tributaries of the Ganges roll in a flood down to the holy river. The muddy waters creep across the broad flood-plain, mile upon mile, deepening to 60 feet in places. The river, its numerous tributaries and its canal system form the largest irrigation scheme in India. When the rains have spent their force, the deluge recedes, leaving a new layer of rich soil on millions of tiny farms. If a farmer should lose one crop through flood, the second will inevitably be so abundant that it makes up for the earlier failure. Rice, sugar, wheat, cotton, jute, spices, and other crops spring from the soft warm loam, feeding almost as many people as live in both North and South America, and producing a rich surplus which is exported to all parts of the world.

Gannet, or SOLAN GOOSE. Vaguely like a gull, but bigger in length, and far stronger, with stream-lined body, big, broad-webbed feet, and a long, dagger-like beak, the gannet is about three feet in length. The European variety (*Sula bassana*) nests in enormous numbers in a few sites, such as the island of Grassholm off the coast of Pembroke, and the Bass Rock in the Firth of Forth, and Lundy Island off the North Devon coast. Such places, during the breeding season, are so covered with the birds that they gleam white for a distance of many miles. Immature gannets, of which there

GANNETS AT THEIR NESTING SITE

In early spring gannets assemble at their nesting sites, one of which is on the little island of Grassholm, off the coast of Pembroke, Wales (above). The nest of grass and seaweed is constructed on the bare rock, and the female sits so closely on her one egg that she will often allow herself to be touched rather than leave it.

is one to each nest, are brownish in colour, and, when covered with their first woolly down, look very strange indeed. The gannets of Grassholm were the subject of a very fine Nature film.

Garibaldi, GIUSEPPE (1807–82). It was his fourth attempt which brought Giuseppe Garibaldi, the ardent Italian patriot, his signal success and enduring fame. Twice he joined in vain attempts to free Italy from Austrian rule, first in 1834 and again in 1848—and each time he was forced to flee from the country. In 1834 he escaped to South America with a sentence of death hanging over him, and there he stayed for 14 years, taking part in the civil wars of Brazil and Uruguay. Returning to Italy, he took part in the unsuccessful Revolution of 1848, and commanded the forces of the short-lived Roman Republic. When this collapsed, Garibaldi escaped to New York.

His third opportunity came in 1859, when the kingdom of Sardinia-Piedmont, with French aid, went to war with Austria. Garibaldi's Alpine infantry were victorious in the north, but further advance was checked by the peace made in June 1859 with the Austrians at Villafranca by the faint-hearted French emperor, Napoleon III.

Secretly encouraged by Cavour, the great prime minister of Piedmont, Garibaldi and his army set forth in 1860 for Sicily, which was part of the kingdom of Naples. Within a few short weeks after landing, Garibaldi had driven all the Neapolitan forces out of the island with little loss of life to his own men.

He had come into possession of money, arms, boats, stores of all kinds, had increased his army to some 25,000 men, and was the idol of all Sicily.

When Garibaldi crossed from Sicily to the mainland, in August 1860, his march from Reggio to Naples resembled a triumphant procession. He handed the kingdom of Sicily and Naples over to Victor Emmanuel, the king of Sardinia, whom he acknowledged as king of Italy.

Garibaldi himself, although he was the hero of Italy, was the most difficult problem that the new government of united Italy had to face. He never forgave Cavour for the surrender of Nice—where Garibaldi, a fisherman's son, was born on July 4, 1807—to France as the price of Napoleon III's aid to Italy. Only with difficulty was he restrained from attacking Rome, although he knew that such an attack would bring against the struggling

After a painting by Arthur Dixon

GIUSEPPE GARIBALDI

Italian patriot and soldier, Garibaldi devoted his life to freeing Italy from Austrian domination and to forming a united nation out of the petty States into which the country was then divided. When he died in 1882 his objects had been achieved.

kingdom of Italy the combined forces of France and Austria—one a friend, the other an enemy.

Twice the government was forced to send troops after Garibaldi and take him prisoner, in 1862 and 1867. When, finally, Italian troops entered Rome in 1870, Garibaldi had no part in it, for he was helping France in her struggle against Germany.

When the Franco-Prussian war was over, he retired again to his island home of Caprera, where he spent the rest of his life receiving admiring visitors and attempting to stir up the people to establish a republic in Italy. He was easily influenced by unscrupulous agitators who sought the overthrow of the united monarchy he had helped to establish. Fortunately the plots did not succeed, and Garibaldi today is regarded as the hero of Italian unity. He died on June 2, 1882.

Gas. The air we breathe, which is composed mainly of nitrogen and oxygen, is the most familiar example of a gas. Many gases are invisible, tasteless, and without smell, and can be detected only by their effects.

Gases have small densities as compared with liquids and solids, which is another way of saying that they are light in weight for the space they occupy. Water is 800 times denser than air, and air in turn is more than 14 times heavier than the gas hydrogen.

Gases are indefinitely elastic ; that is, they have no definite surface boundaries, but tend to expand indefinitely and occupy any space within which they may be confined. The molecules of which they are composed are supposed to be much farther apart than those of liquids or solids. These molecules are in ceaseless rapid motion, bounding and rebounding from each other like rubber balls. When they strike the walls of the vessel which contains them, they produce a constant stream of tiny blows on all parts of it, thus exerting a pressure which we utilize to drive our motor-cars and to send bullets and shells flying from guns. This explanation of the action of gases is called the " kinetic theory " of gases.

Gases are greatly affected by changes in temperature and pressure. Robert Boyle (1627-91) and Jacques Alex Caesar Charles (1746-1822) studied the effects of compressing and heating gases, and found that all gases expand or contract to the same extent when heated or compressed to the same degree. They deduced two laws, known as Boyle's Law and Charles's Law, which enable us to calculate easily the amount by which a given volume of any gas will contract or expand when compressed or heated to a known pressure and temperature. Briefly, doubling the pressure halves the volume, and a rise of temperature of 1° C. increases the volume by 1/273 part. Gaseous pressures are often measured in " atmospheres." Gases at ordinary pressure are at one " atmosphere "; if you double the pressure they are at two " atmospheres," etc.

When heavy gases are mixed with lighter ones, they at first tend to float on one another in layers, but they gradually mix by " diffusion " until the mixture of gases is homogeneous. If two *different* gases are separated by a porous partition, they will still " diffuse " through the partition and mix, but the rates at which they pass through the partition will be different. Thomas Graham (1805-69) discovered that the rates of diffusion of any two gases are inversely proportional to the square roots of their densities. The different rates at which gases diffuse provide us with a method for separating isotopes (*see* Isotope). A kind of gaseous diffusion has been used to separate uranium isotopes for the preparation of atomic bombs.

How Gases are Liquefied

Gases can be converted into liquids by cooling and compressing them, but for every gas there is a temperature known as the " critical " temperature, to which the gas must be cooled before it can be liquefied by applying pressure. Hydrogen has to be cooled to minus 234·5° C. before it can be liquefied by compression, and, at this very low temperature, it becomes liquid when compressed to 13·4 atmospheres (its critical pressure). Gases like hydrogen, oxygen, and nitrogen, which have critical temperatures below ordinary temperatures, and which cannot, therefore, be liquefied by pressure alone, are called " permanent " gases. These gases are stored and sold in heavy metal cylinders, which contain the gas in a highly compressed form, but still as a gas, not as a liquid.

Gases which have critical temperatures above ordinary temperatures can be liquefied by pressure and stored as liquids. Sulphur dioxide (a gas produced when sulphur burns, and which causes the sharp smell sometimes given off by a coke fire) has a critical temperature (157° C.) well above ordinary temperatures, and can be stored as a liquid in glass siphons. "Vapours," and gases that are highly compressed, or near the critical temperature, do not obey exactly the simple laws of Boyle and Charles. Vapours is the name given to gases formed by evaporation of substances normally solid or liquid, such as water, alcohol, and petrol.

Human beings and land animals cannot breathe and live without a supply of the gas oxygen. Breathing gases like pure nitrogen or carbon dioxide causes suffocation merely by exclusion of oxygen ; such gases do not actually damage the breathing passages and lungs, and are not really poisonous. The truly poisonous gases, like carbon monoxide, chlorine, and mustard gas, actually interfere with the action of the blood, or damage the tissues, so that a gassed soldier, even if not killed, often never completely recovers. Mustard " gas " is actually a liquid which gives off a poisonous vapour ; land over which liquid mustard gas has been scattered continues to be dangerous for a long time. Contamination of boots and clothing by the liquid may produce dreadful blistering of the skin. There are other poison gases, such as Lewisite (a compound containing arsenic), which also produce blistering. These blister-producing gases are known as " vesicants."

Gases enter into or are produced by many natural changes, and are of great value to Man. He has to have air to breathe, and he uses gases like coal gas to provide him with light and heat. The atmosphere contains small percentages of the rare gases helium, neon, argon, krypton, and xenon, and these can be collected during the preparation of liquid air and used for various purposes such as the production of neon lights and gas-filled electric light bulbs. Carbon dioxide (a gas produced when fuel is burnt), or during the brewing of beer, or when chalk is heated to make lime, etc.), when cooled and compressed, solidifies to a very cold white solid known as " dry ice," and used to cool and preserve food and things like ice cream. Nitrous oxide (N_2O) is used when the dentist " gives you gas," and is called " laughing gas," because the patient often laughs for no special reason. Acetylene (C_2H_2), formed when water acts on calcium carbide (CaC_2), is used in acetylene lamps, for oxy-acetylene metal cutting and welding, and to produce many important substances such as synthetic rubber.

Gases dissolve in liquids ; ammonia (NH_3) and carbon dioxide readily dissolve in water, which also dissolves air to a certain extent, thereby providing fishes with the oxygen they need.

Natural Gas for Light and Power

In some parts of the world inflammable gas can be obtained from the earth's crust. Such gas is known as " natural " gas, and is often associated with deposits of crude natural petroleum, from which the gas separates as " casing-head gas " at the well-head. The gas is often found confined under pressure above the crude petroleum ; and when the containing rock is pierced in boring for the petroleum, there may be an enormously violent " gusher " of a mixture of gas, oil, sand, and sometimes brine (salt solution), which may wreck the boring equipment and cover a large area of the surrounding country with an oily mass. Nowadays, special precautions are taken to avoid this unnecessary damage to the plant and loss of valuable oil.

At Baku, on the Caspian Sea, an escape of natural gas has been burning from the earliest historical times, and is known as the " holy fire."

Sometimes natural gas is found alone, without petroleum ; such an occurrence at Heathfield, in Sussex, was used for some years to supply light for the railway station. A large occurrence of natural gas was discovered in 1939 in south-west France. The gas comes from the earth at a pressure of about 150 atmospheres, and about 30 million cubic feet will eventually be used each day.

Natural gas is usually composed mainly of methane (CH_4, an inflammable gas known to coal miners as " fire-damp "), with some ethane (C_2H_6), carbon dioxide (CO_2), etc.; it is an important source of the rare gas helium, which, though not so light as hydrogen, is used for filling airships because is is non-inflammable.

Natural gas is used as fuel, and has been made the starting point for the manufacture of many synthesised substances such as petrol and plastics.

Gas Engine. Everyone knows that coal gas will explode ; but by itself it will only burn quietly, and we must mix air with it if we wish to make an explosion. The first successful gas engine was produced by a Frenchman, J. J. E. Lenoir, who took out a patent in 1860. Two British inventors, R. Street (1794) and S. Brown (1823) had attempted the task before Lenoir. Lenoir's machine worked on somewhat the same principle as a steam engine, being double-acting, with a power stroke both on the outward movement of the piston and on the return movement. When the flywheel was pulled round to start the engine, a mixture of coal gas and air was drawn into the cylinder; at about half the way down the cylinder the mixture of fuel thus sucked in was exploded by an electric spark made by an induction coil and two Bunsen batteries.

The explosion pushed out the piston to its full extent and turned the flywheel by means of a crank; the burnt gases were let out by an exhaust valve. Next, on the return of the piston, fuel mixture was sucked in at the opposite end, and a second explosion was produced. Thus the piston was forced to and fro. Pierre Hugon patented a similar engine in 1865, after many years of work; he used a flame to ignite the mixture in the cylinder, and the jet was carried to and fro by a kind of slide valve. Both these engines had a water-cooling arrangement, with water flowing through jackets around the cylinder—a method afterwards generally adopted.

In 1866 two German engineers, E. Langen and N. A. Otto, patented a gas engine on a different principle. This had the cylinder vertical, whereas those of both Lenoir and Hugon had been horizontal. Langen and Otto used the pressure of the atmosphere to help in driving the piston on the down strokes. The piston was a heavy one, and at the top of its rod was a " rack "—a toothed rod—which at the end of the outward stroke engaged with a cog on the flywheel shaft and drove the wheel as the piston dropped down into the cylinder under atmospheric pressure and the effect of its own weight. (In rising, forced up by the exploding gas underneath, the piston had caused a partial vacuum beneath it.)

This engine had a " free " piston, an arrangement like the free wheel on your bicycle; the flywheel continued to run under the impulse given to it by the fall of the piston. When the wheel began to slow down, a governor connected the piston to the wheel cog, so that the piston rose and a new charge of fuel was drawn in, to be exploded as before. It sounds a strange contrivance, and at the time it was called a " noisy rattletrap," but it used less than half the amount of gas consumed by its rivals. Ignition was by means of a gas jet and a slide valve.

Ten years after he had joined with Langen in patenting the engine just described, N. A. Otto produced a much improved high-speed engine, working on a four-stroke " cycle " of operations which became famous as the " Otto cycle." But a Frenchman, Beau de Rochas, in 1862 had suggested this method of driving a gas engine.

The first stroke of the piston sucked in gas and air ; when the piston returned (driven by the flywheel), it compressed this fuel mixture ; now the piston was forced out (power stroke) by the explosion of the mixture; and on the fourth stroke, as the piston returned again, the burnt gases were expelled to the atmosphere (exhaust stroke). Ignition was by a flame. Note that the fuel mixture was compressed ; this allowed a smaller proportion of gas to be used. Also that only one stroke in four was a power or explosion stroke. This system became the standard one for many years, in all sorts of engines using a gaseous mixture as the driving fuel.

Later a two-stroke cycle, or sequence of operations, was introduced as well; but the four-stroke engine holds its own nevertheless—in aircraft, motor-cars, and stationary engines, using gas, petrol or some heavy oil. A two-stroke cycle was patented by Sir Dugald Clerk in 1881. A good many years later it came into use for petrol engines for motor-cycles, and was employed from the start for large gas engines.

Until the electric motor came into general use, with power supplies available in most towns, gas engines were the only small independent source of motive power. Today the gas engine is built in very large units, to yield up to 10,000 horse power, and a form of the two-stroke cycle is mostly used.

We must mention one strange form of gas engine which has no piston or wheels, and in which a column of water acts as the piston. This is the Humphrey gas-explosion pump. Five were built in

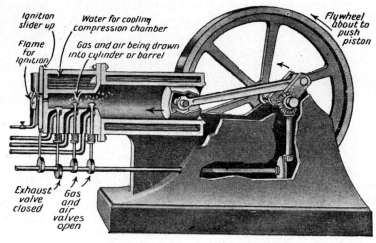

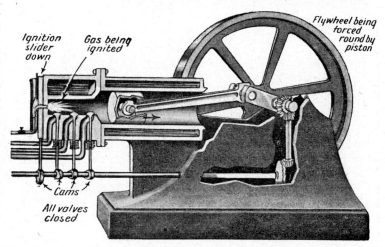

A GAS ENGINE AND HOW IT WORKS

In a gas engine power is derived from an explosion that takes place in the cylinder behind the piston, which is thereby driven forward. In the upper picture the flywheel has drawn the piston to the end of the cylinder. By gear wheels and cams on a shaft two valves have been opened, admitting gas and air into the cylinder. The flywheel then drives the piston forward, compressing this mixture of gas and air. Next, the flywheel begins to draw the piston back again, at the same time moving an ignition slider and admitting flame to fire the mixture. The explosion drives back the piston, as shown in the lower picture, working the crank and giving the flywheel a fresh impulse to continue rotating. When the piston once more comes forward it opens an exhaust valve and expels the burnt gases. Then the flywheel draws it backward once more and the whole operation is repeated.

1913 at the Chingford reservoir of the Metropolitan Water Board, to pump water from the River Lea.

In order to explain this engine we must ask you to imagine a U-tube open at both ends, and partly filled with water. If you attach a piece of rubber tube to one end of the U, and blow into it gently, the column of water will fall in the one arm and rise proportionately in the other. Moreover, the column will oscillate backwards and forwards. Once we have started the oscillations, a comparatively small outside impulse at each oscillation will keep them going.

The Humphrey pump was built in the shape of a U with a long bottom limb and shorter uprights. The bottom part, called a play pipe, was of cast iron 6 feet across and about 60 feet long. At the " en-

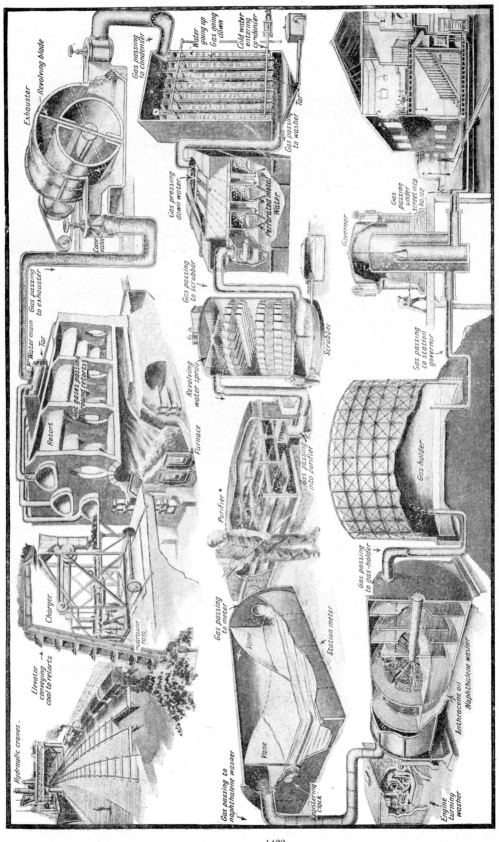

HOW COAL GIVES US GAS FOR MANY DOMESTIC USES

The manufacture of gas is a great nationalised industry, and here we can see how gas is produced from coal and is eventually distributed to consumers through mains laid under the streets. The various by-products formed in the making of gas were once a nuisance, as it was difficult to dispose of them, but science has found many uses for them, and now they are as valuable as the gas itself, yielding scents, dyes, coke, road-making material, chemicals, oil and explosives.

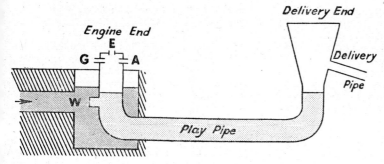

GAS ENGINE WITH A WATER PISTON

Used to pump water, this Humphrey gas-explosion pump consists of a cast-iron U-tube, one end of which is provided with gas, air and exhaust valves (G, A, E), and also a water inlet valve (W). The play pipe is filled with water up to a certain level; in the 'engine' end, which is not filled with water, gas and air are exploded, driving water along the play pipe to the delivery end and sucking more water into the pump through the inlet valve.

gine" end (formed by one upright limb of the U) the pipe widened to 7 feet in diameter for a length of 10 feet; there were gas, air and exhaust valves near the closed top. Lower down this limb was a valve to allow water to be sucked in. At the further end of the U, the tube was taken higher, with a discharge pipe some way below the open top. This part of the U-tube widened out to a funnel-shape.

A mixture of gas and air was ignited in the "engine end," after the play pipe had been filled with water up to a level which left the engine end

still empty; the explosion of the gas drove the water forward so that it rose in the funnel-shaped end of the U, and some was delivered from the discharge pipe. Owing to its momentum, the mass of water kept on moving along the play pipe some time after the gas had spent its power; then a water valve opened and let water enter from the river, and the lowered pressure inside the play pipe caused it to be sucked in freely. After this the water column ebbed back again, and pushed out the burnt gases from the exhaust valve, the water-entry valve being closed at this time. (*See* the simplified diagram and explanation at left).

The water which was in the play pipe now moved forward again in its first direction, sucking in river water; gas and air valves were opened. As the water in the play pipe swung back for the second time it compressed the gas and air mixture in the engine end of the U; this mixture was now ignited, and so the sequence went on. There were four "strokes," as in the Otto cycle—explosion, exhaust, suction and compression. The four larger Chingford pumps were able to pump 40 million gallons each per day, raising the water to a height of 30 feet.

LIGHT and HEAT by TURNING a TAP

Although electric lighting and heating are displacing the use of coal-gas for domestic purposes, there are still millions of gas-users, and gas has very important industrial uses. This article explains the origin and uses of 'town's gas.'

Gas Manufacture. About 1792 William Murdock, a Scottish engineer and colleague of James Watt, began the experiments which resulted in the use of coal-gas for lighting purposes. He heated coal in a kettle, and, by means of an iron tube, carried the resulting yellowish gas to a tank. When he had collected enough gas he fitted over the end of the tube a silver thimble in which he had bored a small hole. Lighting the gas that escaped through the hole in the thimble, he found he had a good light to read by. He had a gas storage tank, a gas-pipe, and a gas-jet.

You can make gas just as William Murdock did. Fill a clay pipe with coal dust, cover the top with clay, then set the bowl of the pipe over a flame to get very hot. In a few minutes a yellowish smoke will issue from the stem. Apply a match to it, and it will burn, but not very clearly, for it is full of impurities. In gas plants these are removed.

By 1802 Murdock had succeeded in producing gas in sufficiently large quantities for lighting the Soho (Birmingham) foundry of Boulton & Watt, and five years later his system was used for the lighting of streets in London. Today coal-gas is used to light some of our houses and streets, to cook our meals, warm our rooms, and to furnish fuel and power for industry.

In the manufacture of town's gas, fire-clay retorts set in great brick ovens are filled with coal. The re-

torts are tightly closed, and the coal is roasted, producing coke (*see* Coke) and gas. This coal-gas is a mixture of various substances, chiefly hydrogen, carbon monoxide, marsh-gas (methane) and other hydrocarbons which burn readily. Nitrogen and carbon dioxide, which are non-combustible, are also present, and the gas also contains many impurities, such as ammonia, tar, sulphur compounds, etc.

To rid it of these, the gas is passed through water, where it loses some of its tar and ammonia; it is then condensed, and passed through the scrubber and washer to remove more tar and ammonia. Formerly the tar was not used, but today it is an extremely valuable by-product (*see* Coal-Tar). Finally the gas passes through layers of lime or oxide of iron to remove the sulphur, after which it goes into huge storage-tanks until it is used. Some of these tanks are great iron cylinders, closed at the top and open at the bottom, resting in cisterns of water—the "gasometers" that make so familiar a part of every urban landscape. They rise as gas is pumped in, and fall as the pressure of the iron cylinder forces the gas out through our taps. "Dry" gasholders are now often used; in these the iron cylinder contains a piston which rises and falls, a gas-tight joint being maintained by means of a tar-seal, which is kept filled with tar by a pump.

The old-fashioned flat-tip burner was for many years the only method of using gas for lighting, but two discoveries completely changed lighting methods and provided a much better light with the use of less gas. One of these was the Bunsen burner (*q.v.*), which mixes the gas with the air and thus produces complete combustion and much greater heat, with an almost colourless flame. The other was the incandescent mantle, discovered in 1886 by Dr. Carl Auer von Welsbach of Vienna. In this the light comes from a " mantle " heated white-hot by a mixture of gas and air as in the Bunsen burner.

The materials for these mantles come from opposite sides of the earth. Natives of India grow the China grass, whose fibre (ramie fibre) is needed for weaving the mantles, while in far-off Brazil rare earths are mined containing the chemical elements thorium and cerium, with which the mantles are saturated (*see* Chemistry). After the vegetable fibre of the China grass has been burned away, a mineral " skeleton " of the fabric is left, which glows with a bright white light. Artificial silk is now often used instead of China grass fibre.

But, with the development of electric lighting, the use of gas for illumination became less important than its use as fuel. The gas-cooker has largely replaced the coal-range in the homes of town-dwellers, its chief advantages being the ease with which the heat can be turned on and off, and its general cleanliness.

Gas is distributed from the manufacturing plant through " main " pipes. From these, service pipes lead to the individual consumers, where meters measure the amount used. The pressure in the service pipes is a little above atmospheric pressure—from about 1 to 2 oz. per square inch.

Crown copyright

GAS : LECTURE ON ITS USES IN 1804
Among the pioneers of gas-lighting was Frederick Albert Winsor, who was born in Brunswick, Germany, in 1763. In 1804 he gave a series of lectures on the domestic uses of gas at the Lyceum Theatre, London, as depicted in this exhibit in the Science Museum, London.

" Water gas," a mixture containing chiefly hydrogen and carbon monoxide, is made by passing steam over red-hot coke or coal. The gas thus produced burns with a very hot blue flame, but it is extremely poisonous because of the high percentage of carbon monoxide it contains. To fit it for use as an illuminating gas, it is " carburetted," that is mixed with gases which burn with a luminous flame, such as ethylene and acetylene. Many gas companies make carburetted water gas, and mix it with their coal gas. Another gas, highly useful in industrial processes, is " producer " gas. The best quality is made by passing air over white-hot coke, although coal and even peat may be used. Blast-furnace gas, generated in the operation of blast-furnaces, is another fuel of this type. Acetylene (*q.v.*) is a widely used gas where there are no central gas-works, and " Calorgas," a mixture of hydrocarbons compressed in cylinders, is also used.

Gas Turbine. When the first attempts were made to turn wheels by means of an electric current some inventors produced electric " motors " which were patterned on the steam engine, with a piston-like member going to and fro, and turning a flywheel by means of a crank. The piston was attracted by an electro-magnet at each stroke. Of course there was a waste of power in changing the direction of the piston at each stroke; the laws of mechanics tell us that force has to be applied to check a movement, or to make a moving member change its direction. Later some brilliant minds conceived the plan of making electro-magnets pull around a wheel directly, without the intervention of any levers, cranks or connecting rods. So we got the electric motor of today, which may whizz round at 2,000 revolutions per minute in comparatively slow types, or may turn at 10,000 revs. per minute in a vacuum cleaner.

Steam engineers eventually produced various steam turbines, and many of the old type of engine went out of use—reciprocating engines they are called, if they work by a to-and-fro movement of the driving mechanism. A gas turbine, in which the explosion of a gaseous mixture should drive a wheel directly without any reciprocating parts, was the dream of inventors for a century; but it was not until the middle years of the Second World War (1939-45) that successful practical machines were produced. Then gas turbines came into use for driving aircraft by means of airscrews, and gas turbines formed part of the machinery of jet-propulsion engines which drove aircraft directly by jets—without airscrews. In this last kind of machine the turbine drove the compressor which fed the supply of air to the combustion chamber, where it mixed with fuel and was burnt to produce the driving jets.

Air Commodore Frank Whittle, of the Royal Air Force—he was knighted in 1948—played the leading part in producing the gas turbine which was used in jet-propelled aircraft engines;

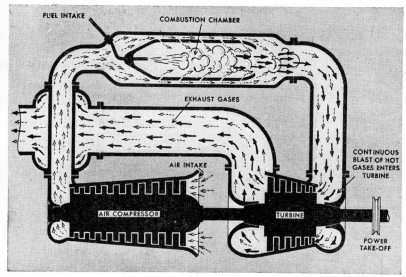

FUEL INTAKE
COMBUSTION CHAMBER
EXHAUST GASES
AIR INTAKE
CONTINUOUS BLAST OF HOT GASES ENTERS TURBINE
AIR COMPRESSOR
TURBINE
POWER TAKE-OFF

GAS ENGINE ON THE TURBINE PRINCIPLE

In its operation a gas turbine resembles the steam type, except that it has an air compressor attached to the turbine shaft, which feeds a blast of air to the combustion chamber. There the fuel is injected and catches fire, producing what amounts to a continuous explosion. The blast passes through the turbine, turning its rotors ; then the exhaust gases pass out of the engine, sweeping round the intake pipe to preheat the incoming air.

The air for the gas turbine is drawn in by a compressor, a vaned wheel which acts like a pump; it has several " stages," in separate casings. At each stage the degree of compression is increased, in steps. Then the air goes to a combustion chamber, where some form of oil fuel is injected and ignited. The fuel takes fire and expands enormously (*see* Gas), and a continuous blast of hot gases thus goes down to enter the turbine, driving the turbine shaft around. The power is taken off at the turbine shaft, and belts or gear wheels connect this shaft to any machinery which is to be driven.

On looking at the simplified diagram printed at the left, you will see that the air compressor and the turbine are fixed to the same shaft; consequently, when the turbine turns, it causes the compressor to turn also. After the turbine has been started up, it runs automatically, the turbine supplying some of its power to drive the compressor; the rest of the power output is available for outside work.

When a gas turbine is used as part of a jet engine, no power is taken from the turbine shaft, of course that the compressor has to be driven, as

without such a turbine the system would not be practicable, since an enormous quantity of air under pressure is consumed in such engines. In 1948 he was awarded the sum of £100,000 as a reward for his invention. In other European countries also the stimulus of war led to successful turbines being produced for driving combat aircraft. Enormous sums of money needed for research and experiment in these machines were provided from national funds; ordinary commercial concerns could not have financed these ventures.

In 1945 Britain's first industrial gas turbine was completed—an experimental one of 500 horsepower, designed and built by the firm of C. A. Parsons & Co., a name famous in the history of steam turbines. A picture of this engine is seen on the right. The working of a gas turbine is shown in our diagram (above). To save repetition, you should read the story of steam turbines in our article entitled Turbine, later in this work. The turbine is a kind of bladed wheel, the blades being forced to move by a powerful jet of water, steam or gas directed on and between them. Since the blades are fixed to a shaft, they take the shaft round with them.

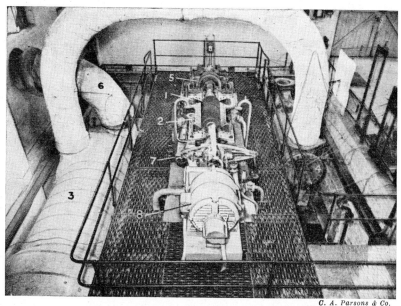

C. A. Parsons & Co.

BRITAIN'S FIRST INDUSTRIAL GAS TURBINE

Installed at Newcastle, Northumberland, in 1945, as an experimental plant, this turbine is of 500 h.p. 1. Air inlet. 2. Air compressor. 3. Heat exchanger, in which heat from the exhaust gases is recovered. 4. Combustion chamber. 5. Turbine. 6. Outlet for spent gases. 7. Brake. 8. Motor for starting the turbine.

before. The jet of hot gases which our diagram shows passing to the exhaust outlet is, in the jet-propulsion (*q.v.*) engine, the power jet by whose reaction the aircraft or motor-car is driven.

Gaulle. CHARLES ANDRÉ JOSEPH MARIE DE (b. 1890). " The war is not lost, the country is not dead, hope is not extinct. *Vive la France !* " To how many French hearts, in that June of 1940, must these words have brought an unlooked-for gleam of hope ! Seeing the downfall of their armies, the withdrawal of their British allies, many Frenchmen must have felt that the Second World War was already over. And then, on June 23, the voice of Brigadier - General de Gaulle called to them over the radio from Broadcasting House, London, to rally and stand firm.

To most Frenchmen General de Gaulle's name was unknown. Some perhaps knew that this regular officer had been called in by the Premier, M. Reynaud, on June 6, 1940, to become Under Secretary for National Defence in the cabinet.

Arriving in London on the day after Marshal Pétain had sued for peace, De Gaulle formed the Free French National Committee to maintain the independence of France. Volunteers, defying the severest penalties, came across the Channel to join him ; he himself was condemned to death in his absence by Pétain's Government—for " treason." A few of the French colonies declared for him. The Free French movement was born.

In September 1941 General de Gaulle set up a representative French national committee—in effect, a French government " in exile." An attempt to obtain the adherence of the West African territory of Dakar ended in failure, but in 1941 Syria was gained for the Allied cause after a short, bitter campaign. But it was after the Allied landings in French North Africa in November 1942 that the Free French movement (which in the previous July had been re-named " Fighting France ") began to grow strong. In June 1943 a Committee of National Liberation was set up in Algiers, General de Gaulle sharing its presidency with General Giraud, who had escaped from a German prison camp. In November General Giraud's resignation left De Gaulle sole head of the committee which was to take over the government of France on the country's liberation. On June 2, 1944, the committee was officially declared to be the provisional government of France. Landing in Normandy on June 14 of that year, General de Gaulle was wildly acclaimed ; and on the liberation of Paris, August 23, 1944, he went there and formed a new government which was recognized by the Allied powers. At

E. R. Yerbury & Son

GENERAL DE GAULLE

Head of the Free French Government and leader of the Free French forces during the Second World War (1939-45), De Gaulle in 1947 placed himself at the head of a political party called the Rally of the French People.

a thanksgiving service at Notre Dame cathedral, snipers fired at him, but he was unhurt.

In January 1946 after long-drawn bickering between the French political parties, General de Gaulle left public life and retired to his country house at Colombey. In April, 1947, seeing his country the victim of bitter internal dissension, he placed himself at the head of a Rassemblement (Rally) of the French people, which gained a sensational number of seats at the Municipal elections on a policy opposed to Communism.

Charles de Gaulle was born at Lille on November 22, 1890, the son of a professor. Trained at the French military school at St. Cyr, he fought in the First World War as an infantry officer, being three times wounded and finally made prisoner-of-war at Verdun in 1916. In May-June 1940 the tanks of the French 4th Division under his command drove back the Germans at Laon and at Abbeville.

De Gaulle became so famous later for his leadership of French patriots that his earlier achievements as a pioneer in armoured warfare and a talented commander of an armoured corps are in danger of being overlooked. In 1934 he published his book, Towards a Professional Army, in which he set out his ideas of how tanks and other armoured fighting vehicles should be used. He found few to listen to the revolutionary ideas of an obscure colonel, and has been called " a military prophet without honour in his own country." But the Germans were quick to appraise the value of De Gaulle's novel ideas, and the German commander Guderian later acknowledged his debt to De Gaulle, many of whose notions the Germans put into practice, with disastrous results for France.

Gelatine. In the raw state, this hard, yellowish, semi-transparent substance is obtained chiefly from animal tissues, especially bones, horns, and hoofs. When bones are soaked in weak acid, certain parts dissolve and leave behind the bone cartilage ; and when this is boiled it dissolves and forms gelatine. Vegetable jelly, similar in many ways to gelatine, is manufactured from a seaweed known as Irish moss.

In its crude condition, gelatine is cut into slices, dried, and sold as a glue. Gelatine is purified in various ways ; after treatment with suphurous acid it is used for making the tough, whitish, semi-transparent substance called " isinglass," valuable in refining liquors and stiffening food.

The best isinglass and edible gelatine are obtained from the air-bladders of fish. Formerly obtained solely from the sturgeon of Russia, they are now procured also from the cod and certain other fish.

Gelatine is one of the ingredients of printing-press rollers. It is used as a coating for pills, and as a capsule to contain unpleasant-tasting medicine in convenient doses; and is employed in dyeing and tanning, in making paper, waterproofing material, India inks, artificial leather, and artificial silks. It also forms the base in which are embedded the sensitive chemicals used in coating photographic plates, films, and papers.

Gems. Precious stones are ranked according to colour, lustre, hardness, durability, and rarity. The precious gems are diamonds, rubies, emeralds, and sapphires; the semi-precious include topaz, spinel, opal, amethyst, moonstone, aquamarine, chrysoberyl, tourmaline, zircon, peridot, garnet, and others. Fashion as well as other considerations may affect the value of any of these ornaments.

The sparkling diamond, the " king of gems," which is pure crystallized carbon, is the hardest of the precious stones (*see* Diamond). Rubies and sapphires rank next for hardness. The best rubies—which are usually a pure carmine red—come from Burma, Siam, and Ceylon. Pink, purple, and violet rubies are also found; those most valued are of the tint called " pigeon's blood." Large rubies are very rare. One of the most famous is set in the front of our Royal crown, used by King George VI when he was crowned in 1937. It is said to have been given by Don Pedro of Spain to the Black Prince, who wore it in battle, as did Henry V at Agincourt and Richard III at Bosworth field. It is 2 in. long and $1\frac{1}{2}$ in. broad. The so-called rubies found in South Africa, Australia, and the western United States are a variety of garnet.

The pretty, bright blue sapphires are valued for quality rather than size. Flawless emeralds are rare. Some specimens are of great size, one found in the Ural Mountains weighing $6\frac{3}{4}$ lb.

Gem cutting and engraving—the lapidary's art—has been practised from very remote times. Great numbers of precious and semi-precious stones have been found in Mesopotamia cut into cylindrical form and bearing engraved figures. When rolled over the soft clay of writing-tablets, these cylinders left the design in relief to serve as a personal seal. This art had been developed to a high degree of perfection by the ancient Sumerians at least as early as 3000 B.C. Seals engraved with the sacred beetle, called scarabs, were in use in Egypt in the same period.

Certain gem-stones can be made in the chemist's laboratory, and some of the synthetic rubies and sapphires thus formed can be told from the real stones only by experts. Chemists know what minerals compose these stones; the problem is to combine them artificially so as to reproduce in a few hours that process of Nature which took, perhaps, hundreds or even thousands of years. Generally the mineral substances used are fused by the terrific heat of the electric arc.

Some of the natural stones, such as rubies and sapphires, have long been used by watchmakers and instrument makers for the tiny bearings of wheel pivots, for the pallets of the escapements, and suchlike parts where extreme hardness is desirable. This demand encouraged the manufacture of synthetic stones, which could be formed in shapes and sizes more convenient and regular

than those found in the natural crystals. Another use for precious stones of the sort mentioned is for the tiny dies through which fine wire is drawn to thin it down to the minute diameter needed.

The making of imitation gems, as distinguished from synthetic stones, is an ancient art. The usual basis is a hard, brilliant glass, called paste or strass, with a high percentage of oxide of lead. False diamonds are cut from the pure paste, while colour is added for imitation sapphires, amethysts, etc. These mock gems are never as hard or brilliant as real ones. " Doublets " are made by mounting a thin front layer of real stone on a paste back. The colour of genuine gems is often improved by staining, or by treating them with heat or radium.

Genetics. From the Greek word " to become," this is the science which deals with heredity, with the origin of the characteristics of an individual animal or of an individual plant. " Like begets like " : this is a fundamental law. The individual will have most things in common with the species, and this relationship between parent and offspring is of the essence of the matter. A cow has a calf and not a piglet ; the bitch produces a puppy and not a kitten.

A child takes after its parents, so variations must in some way be transmitted from parent to offspring or evolution would be a false concept; and this variation must take place through some elasticity in the behaviour of the germ cells. Considering the higher animals, these cells are specially set apart for reproduction, and are the only direct connexion between successive generations.

At least something of this very intricate subject is understood. On the whole, " acquired " characteristics are not transmitted. The man who has lost an arm in the war does not sire a one-armed child; not does the blacksmith pass on his powerful muscles. On the other hand, the alcoholic person or the man who suffers from epileptic fits will pass on not the love of alcohol or, necessarily, the fits, but the unstable nervous system which could predispose his offspring to a similar pattern of behaviour. Such are known as heritable characters.

Inherited characteristics are always clear-cut. It is rather like jumbling together coloured beads, not like mixing coffee and milk. Thus, union between the hot-tempered and the mild-tempered does not produce the medium-tempered; the offspring are sharply one or other—not a blend of both. Moreover, heritable characteristics of colouring or of temperament can leap-frog down the generations, appearing here and missing there. Atavism (from the Latin word meaning " great-grandfather's grandfather ") is the term used to describe this phenomenon of " throw-back."

Today much interest is taken in human stock and pedigree, not for reasons of social grandeur, but from a wise anxiety to know the blood which runs in one's veins, so that decisions about health, climate, occupation, and affairs, may be made in the light of probability, if not of absolute knowledge.

Haemophilia—a failure of the blood to clot—and night-blindness spring to the mind as being two physical conditions travelling down " on the back of the genes "; insanity and genius are two mental extremes likewise due to gene combinations (*see* Heredity). Nor must one forget to mention here the all-important " environment," with its essential power to modify and eventually to effect change of function and structure, though here one must probably talk in terms of hundreds or even thousands of years.

Geneva, SWITZERLAND. This town nestles at the base of the Alps at the lower end of Lake Geneva (*Lac Léman*), the largest in Switzerland. It is built on both sides of the river Rhône, and the two districts are connected by bridges. There is a small island near the harbour which is called Jean-Jacques Rousseau, after the revolutionary writer who was born in Geneva. One of the features of this town are the broad promenades by the lake, and streets of handsome white stone houses and when, at sunset, the snow-clad peak of Mont Blanc, 40 miles to the south-east, becomes visible in delicate rose and white and lavender, the spectacle is one of particular beauty.

Lying nearly in the centre of Europe, and one of the gateways to Switzerland, Geneva has long been a favoured resort for travellers. Its beauty, its ancient traditions of culture, have induced many citizens of other lands to make it their permanent home.

The city was the home of the League of Nations, and the headquarters of many international organizations, including the International Red Cross.

Long before the formation of the League of Nations, Geneva was a centre for international meetings. The International Red Cross was established here in 1863–64, and in 1871–72 the dispute, over the ship Alabama, between the United States and Great Britain arising out of the American Civil War, was arbitrated in this town.

During the Reformation, Geneva was known as the " Rome of Protestantism." John Calvin had his headquarters here from 1536 until his death. Calvin practically ruled the city, and gathered about him many other Protestant reformers; he preached from the pulpit of St. Peter's Cathedral, a fine Gothic structure rebuilt in the 12th century (*see* Calvin, John). In 1559 Calvin founded an academy, which became part of the University of Geneva in 1873. Voltaire lived for years at near-by Ferney; and when Napoleon rose to power his bitter enemy, Madame de Staël, established her famous *salon* in a château on the north side of the lake, at Coppet. Her château still attracts many visitors. The city has beautiful university buildings, and magnificent palaces house the international organizations. The old walls, pulled down in 1848, are recalled by the Promenade des Bastions which leads out of the Place Neuve, the finest square in Geneva.

Genevese use the French language and have French customs, for Geneva is almost completely surrounded by France, only a narrow strip connecting it with the rest of Switzerland. Its principal manufactures are watches, scientific instruments, jewelry, machinery, and chocolate.

In the days of the Roman Empire Geneva was already a city. At the close of the Middle Ages the citizens freed themselves from the feudal control both of their bishop and of the neighbouring house of Savoy, and established a republic.

The most celebrated event in the city's history was the repulse of a surprise attack on Geneva in 1602 by the house of Savoy. In memory of the event the Genevese still hold a festival every year. Napoleon annexed Geneva to France in 1798, but on regaining its freedom in 1815 the city joined the Swiss confederation. The population of Geneva is 124,430.

Dorien Leigh

GENEVA BESIDE THE STILL WATERS OF ITS LAKE

Formerly the home of the League of Nations and the headquarters of many international organizations, the lovely Swiss city of Geneva has been noted for centuries as a refuge for the persecuted and a seat of international activity. The city here is seen from the suburb of Cologny, looking towards the point at which the river Rhône flows out of Lake Geneva. Beyond the left-hand corner of the lake can be seen the tower of the 12th century cathedral.

E.N.I.T.

GENOA: ITALY'S GREAT WESTERN SEAPORT

Rising from the Gulf of Genoa in white relief against the lower hills of the Ligurian Alps, Genoa is a magnificent sight. Since the Middle Ages the city has been a thriving port, because it is one of Italy's few outlets on the west coast and is the gateway to the northern plains which are the heart of the nation's agriculture and industry. During the Second World War (1939-45) as an important supply base it was bombarded from the sea and air by Allied forces.

The waters of Lake Geneva are of a beautiful deep-blue colour, and remarkably transparent. At the opposite end of the lake near Montreux, and a favourite excursion from Geneva, is the Castle of Chillon, made famous by Byron's poem, The Prisoner of Chillon.

Genoa, ITALY. Since early historical times Genoa " the Superb," rising from the Gulf of Genoa in beautiful relief against the sharp slopes of the Apennines, has been one of the most important seaports on the Mediterranean and a gateway to northern Italy. From its great harbour hundreds of noted sea captains have set sail on romantic adventures of conquest and commerce in distant lands, making it a fitting birthplace for its most famous son, Christopher Columbus.

Genoa is by far the largest port in Italy, and handles one-fifth of the nation's tonnage. It is linked to Switzerland by the Simplon and St. Gotthard tunnels. It was because of its good communications and its harbour that during the Second World War (1939-45) it was severely damaged by Allied air and naval forces.

The docks and warehouses of the harbour receive the cargoes of coal, wheat, maize, cotton, mineral oil, phosphates, iron and steel, timber, and chilled meats which Italy imports in normal times. The exports include silks, olive oil, wine, soap, marble, and paper. The city is the hub of Italy's air lines, and the junction point for rail transportation to the north.

After being held by the Lombards and the Franks, Genoa became an independent city upon the break-up of Charlemagne's empire.

The aristocratic and the democratic factions were in constant turmoil up to the 16th century, when the autocratic rule of the doges (chief magistrates, from the Latin *dux*, leader) began. Self-government continued until the days of Napoleon, after whose fall the city passed to Sardinia-Piedmont, and became a part of the kingdom of Italy in 1861. The population of Genoa is about 630,000.

Gentian. (Pron. jen'shun). Herbaceous plants of the order *Gentianaceae*, the gentians are hardy and are found in many parts of the world,

GENTIAN : THE MARSH VARIETY

One of the loveliest of the gentians is the marsh species (above), which grows in moist places on heaths and moors in the south of England. The blossoms are usually a brilliant blue, with darker spots deep within the funnel-shaped corolla.

in warm, cold and wet regions. The best known is the genus *Gentiana* which grows so well in the Alps as to cover some slopes with sheets of their blue flowers ; this plant is also easily adaptable for cultivation in rockeries. Almost all gentians are blue or purple, but a few rare species are white, yellow, or red, the last being found in the Andes. In Britain, two small, purplish species are found

growing wild on the chalk and limestone hills, but perhaps the finest, although less common, is *G. pneumonanthe*, the marsh gentian. Parts of the plant are employed in the preparation of tonics, *Gentiana lutea* being the species of chief medicinal value.

It is said that this plant was named after Gentius, king of ancient Illyria, in the Balkans, who discovered that the root could be used as a medicine.

LANDS & PEOPLES *of the* WIDE WORLD

*H*iding under the dull name of '*geography*' are all kinds of thrilling stories and colourful pictures of distant lands, their cities and races—and interesting explanations, too, of the '*whys*' and '*wherefores*' of the world as it is.

Geography. In the hot and very damp island of Borneo are the savage Dyaks, who live in houses set on piles along the rivers, hunting game with spear and blow-pipe, and planting crops of rice and vegetables. Up in Arctic Labrador the sturdy, squat Eskimos dwell amid snow and ice, getting their food and clothing from the animals of sea and land. The patient Chinese, bent with toil, works day and night in his little terraced rice-field, up to his knees in water, using his bare feet to pack the mud round the young rice plants and to pluck up the harmful weeds.

Along the Nile the Egyptian fellah laboriously lifts the water of the river by a *shadoof*—a pole with bucket and counter-weight—which raises the water into channels and so irrigates his field. On the vast prairies of North America, farmers drive great gang-ploughs drawn by six, eight, or ten horses or by mechanical tractors, producing enormous crops of grain to feed the hungry world. On the immense treeless steppes of Central Asia, where there are no mild ocean breezes to temper the cold of winter and the extreme heat of summer, the Mongols pasture their flocks and herds.

In the sweltering, fever-ridden jungles of the Amazon, naked savages, too low in civilization to have learned to plant crops, live on the fruits and nuts of the trees, the fish of the rivers, and the animals they slay; while only a short distance to the west, still near the Equator, the mountain shepherds of Bolivia dwell on the lofty heights of the Andes, where it is so cold that only the hardiest crops will grow, and men would perish but for the food and clothing they get from their flocks of llamas.

Civilization Controlled by Geographical Conditions

Why do the peoples of the world differ so widely in the way they live, in dress, appearance, customs, intelligence? The fascinating science of geography tells you, for it is the study of the earth as the home of Man. It shows how land and ocean, rivers and mountains, plains and valleys, temperature and wind and rainfall, in large measure control the ways in which men live, and the degree of civilization they attain.

Here and there men have come together and formed cities, giving each an individuality of its own and crowded with interest. London, Paris, Istanbul, Peking, Cairo, Cape Town, New York, Quebec, Bombay, Sydney, Buenos Aires—every name is a flash of romance and mystery. Why did these great cities spring up at just those spots ? Geography tells you. It shows how some towns, like Sydney, New

York, and Southampton, owe their existence chiefly to their excellent harbours; how others, such as Ontario, grew up where the abundance of water-power was favourable to the growth of manufactures. In Europe and America, great communities of this last kind are being formed even as you read these words. Rivers are being dammed to tap the bounteous energy from Man-made waterfalls. Towns have come to greatness because they stand at strategic points on great trade routes, while others, like Sheffield and Pittsburg, have been made by the proximity of great iron and coal deposits.

Classified Subdivisions of Geography

And so one might go on, merely suggesting some of the myriad interesting things the study of geography has to tell us about the earth as the home of Man. But this, while the most absorbing and important of the aspects of geography, is only a part of the story. As its name shows, geography (from the Greek words meaning " earth " and " descriptive writing ") is a description of the earth. Its vast subject-matter naturally falls into several main divisions, which are variously classified. The simplest division is into mathematical geography, physical geography, and bio-geography or the geography of living things.

Mathematical geography treats of the form, size, and movements of the earth from the standpoint of mathematics. In considering the movements of the earth and their place in the solar system it is closely connected with astronomy. And since mathematical geography has also to do with the measurement of the earth and the various methods of representing its surface on maps, it is related to surveying and map-making.

Physical geography, which is practically identical with physiography—which comes from two Greek words meaning literally a description of natural phenomena—treats of the physical features of the earth—land, sea, and atmosphere. Geology, oceanology, climatology, and meteorology all contribute to this department.

Then comes the great department which treats of the living things that dwell on the earth, their distribution and life conditions, culminating in the geography of Man. Man is the animal that has learned to adapt himself to geographical conditions and also in some measure to modify these conditions. By great engineering works he alters the earth's surface to his advantage. He irrigates the land, tunnels through mountains, reclaims land from the sea, and even divides continents by canals.

All other branches of geographical study rank lower than this crowning department and focus on it. Hence human geography, as it is sometimes called, is further divided into various subdivisions, such as political geography, which deals chiefly with the distribution of the human race, and economic or commercial geography, which treats of the manufacture and distribution of the world's products.

The progress of geographical knowledge has depended largely on the progress of discovery. The Phoenicians were the first people who communicated to other nations a knowledge of distant lands. Their voyages, before the time of Homer, through the Euxine (Black Sea), the Mediterranean, and even into the Atlantic, form the first link of the great chain of discovery which, centuries later, was extended by Columbus to the shores of America, and by Da Gama to India. Travellers like the Greek historian Herodotus did much for the advancement of geography, as did also the exploring and surveying expeditions of Alexander the Great. At the same time Pytheas, the Greek navigator, was following the path of discovery in the north, possibly as far as Iceland, and in 276 B.C. Eratosthenes first used parallels of longitude and latitude and made real maps.

By this time the old idea of the earth as a flat circular shield surrounded by a rim of water had given place to the belief in a spherical earth, revolving, with the surrounding atmosphere, on one axis. The practical genius of the Romans led them to make a study of the resources of the countries they conquered, which did much for geography. Their greatest work was a survey of the whole empire, including a description and measurement of each province, which was made under Caesar Augustus. In the 2nd century of our era Ptolemy, the Greek astronomer, wrote a work on geography occupying eight volumes, and this remained the great authority for many centuries.

The travels of the Venetian, Marco Polo, in the 14th century opened new fields of inquiry, and the close of the next century was marked by the epoch-making discovery of the American continent. Within 30 years the whole coast of America, from Greenland to Cape Horn, had been explored; the Pacific Ocean had been navigated by Magellan, and his ship had sailed round the world; the coasts of Eastern Africa, Arabia, Persia, and India had been visited, and numerous islands in the Indian Ocean discovered. The attempts to find a north-west passage to India increased the knowledge of the Arctic regions. In the 17th century the Dutch made known to the world the Australian islands (which the Portuguese had discovered a few years before). Captain Cook in his three voyages completed our knowledge of most of the Pacific lands.

At the beginning of the 19th century explorers were familiar with the outline of the continents and most of the islands, but four-fifths of the land area was still practically unknown. There was only the scantiest knowledge of Central and Eastern Asia, and of the interior of the Americas. Africa was still truly the "Dark Continent." Most of the Polar lands were undiscovered, and the existence of the Antarctic continent was doubted.

By the close of the century most of these immense gaps in geographical knowledge had been closed by the labours of such heroic explorers as Lewis and Clark, Fremont, Pike, and Selkirk in North America; Parry, Franklin, the two Rosses, McClure, Kane, Nansen, Peary, and a score of others in the Polar regions; Livingstone, Mungo Park, Stanley, Burton, Speke, and Schweinfurth in Africa; Younghusband and Sven Hedin in Asia. But it was not until our own century that the veil was torn from the two chief objects of exploration—the North Pole, reached by Peary in 1909; and the

The Legacy of Rome, Clarendon Press

ANCIENT GEOGRAPHER'S MAP OF BRITAIN
Ptolemy (died A.D. 180) worked at Alexandria, Egypt, on the journeys of Roman officials and merchants and delineated the whole of the then-known world. The distorted shape which he gave Britain (above), with Scotland projecting eastwards, suggests that he may have had separate pre-existing maps of these two regions, and joined them incorrectly.

South Pole, reached by Amundsen in December 1911, by Scott a month later. (*See* Polar Exploration).

The work of geographers is still going on today. There are vast tracts, notably in Northern Asia, Africa, South America, Arabia, and Northern Canada, of which we have only scanty knowledge. There is also much to be done in the study of the ocean and the atmosphere. Aerial photography has been a great aid in exploring difficult and mapping inaccessible regions, such as the densely forested areas of South and Central America and the icy mountains of Alaska.

Geographical societies and associations have performed an important part. The first of these was founded in Paris in 1821. The Royal Geographical Society of Great Britain was founded in 1830, and the American Geographical Society in 1852. Both issue valuable publications.

READING *the* STORY *of the* ROCKS

Have you ever considered the difference between granite and clay, or wondered why the countryside changes its appearance from valley to high hills as you journey through it? Geology answers such questions.

Geology. Everything which throws light on the history of the earth falls within the field of geology. The history of the atmosphere and of the ocean are really parts of geology, since they are intimately bound up with the story of the earth. The rocks of the earth furnish the larger part of the data for unravelling the history of the earth, but they are not the only sources of information.

Fossil palms, like this Eocene feather-palm from Bournemouth, Hampshire, show that the south of England once enjoyed a tropical climate.

The history of the earth has been largely worked out through the study of the changes which are now taking place on its surface. Rain falls on the land, and some of it gathers into streams, and the streams flow into the sea. In the flow of the water and by the action of the atmosphere, the substance of the land is worn away, carried to the sea, and deposited there in the form of gravel, sand, mud, etc. The sand and mud when bound together become sandstone and shale, two of the commonest sorts of rocks found on the land.

The Making of Rocks Continues

This process of destruction and building is now going on by natural means all over the world. In the sand and the mud, as they are deposited in the sea, shells and other parts of various animals and plants are embedded. The shale and sandstone of the land also contain shells and other traces preserved as fossils (*see* Fossils). Hence it is inferred that the sandstone and shale, as well as certain other sorts of rock found on the land, were originally deposited as beds of sand and mud in the sea, and that they have since been elevated to form dry land.

The activities of other surface agencies are studied similarly. The work now being done by volcanoes and earthquakes, by rain and rivers, underground water, waves and currents, the atmosphere, glaciers, changes of temperature, the force of gravity, organic agencies, and all other forces and activities operative on the surface of the earth, has shown geologists how the rocks were formed in ages long past. It is by the explanation of the recorded results of the past, in the light of the processes now taking place, that the science of geology has grown up.

Geology really begins with the origin and earliest ages of the earth's history, which are as yet speculative. The rocks of the earth are, geologically speaking, of three great classes : (1) igneous rocks, those which represent solidified lava, or are otherwise of volcanic origin; (2) sedimentary rocks, as limestone, shale, sandstone, conglomerate, etc., most of which are made up of fragments of older rocks, or of animal and vegetable remains, usually deposited in the sea, in lakes or river beds; and (3) metamorphic rocks, which have usually been so far altered by various means that they are now very unlike the materials from which they were first made. In the metamorphism of rocks, pressure is the most important agent. Chemical change, under the influence of moisture, is probably second in importance; and heat third. The sedimentary series are the rocks containing the vast majority of fossils.

The time since rocks have been laid down is divided into four eras, and most of these are divided into several periods, as shown in the following table:

ERAS	PERIODS
CAINOZOIC	Quaternary (Pleistocene and Recent)
	Pliocene
	Miocene ⎫
	Oligocene ⎬ Tertiary
	Eocene ⎭
MESOZOIC	Upper Cretaceous
	Lower Cretaceous
	Jurassic
	Triassic
PALAEOZOIC	Permian
	Carboniferous
	Devonian
	Silurian (=Upper Silurian)
	Ordovician (=Lower Silurian)
	Cambrian
PRE-CAMBRIAN	Torridonian
	Lewisian

The Pre-Cambrian era, which in America is classified quite differently—usually as Archaean or Proterozoic—contains in Britain rocks of two main types, the Lewisian being crystalline, the Torridonian, sedimentary.

Traces of fossils have been found in the later Pre-Cambrian rocks, some in the shape of tracks left by worms creeping through or over the mud, but few are definite enough to show what these earliest recorded creatures looked like.

The next era, the Palaeozoic (or Primary) era, contains systems of rocks, known as the Cambrian, Ordovician, Silurian, Devonian, Carboniferous, and Permian, deposited in that order.

How Sedimentary Rocks Were Formed

These systems of rocks are mainly of sedimentary origin, and the materials of which they are composed were derived from the land areas existing when these systems were being laid down. Most of the materials of the systems were washed down from the land to the rivers or the sea, and there deposited. The several systems of Palaeozoic rocks are distinguished from one another by their fossils, each group showing development in successive eras.

In the Cambrian period there were many algae and especially reef-building algae. Among animals, trilobites were most common. Shell-bearing molluscs appeared, and the Cambrian rocks contain the

19
18
17
16
15
14
14
13
12
11
10
9
8
7
6
5
4
2

 the old, old story of the earth was written, so to speak,
he successive layers of rock laid down age after age, and
 geologists have been able to read it because the wrinkling
of the layers, or ' pages,' into mountains and their wearing
n by wind and weather have brought them to light, is
n here. The crack through the upper layers (almost in
centre of the picture) is what is known as a fault ; such a
k, if it develops suddenly, causes earthquakes in moun-
ous regions. When reading the story in stone start at the
nning, which is at the bottom, where the first layers were
ed. The oldest formation (1), consisting of gneiss,

granite and schist, is called Archean. Next (2) come the
Torridonian and Laurentian rocks of the Pre-Cambrian times.
The dark green vertical formation (3) is trap rock formed by
molten stone that has welled up from below. The others in
order are Cambrian (4) ; Ordovician (5) ; Silurian (6) ;
Devonian (7) ; Carboniferous (8) ; Permian (9) ; Triassic (10) ;
Liassic (11), and Oolitic (12), both belonging to the Jurassic
period ; Lower Cretaceous (13) ; Cretaceous (14) ; Eocene
(15), when mammals began to appear ; Oligocene (16) ;
Miocene (17) ; Pliocene (18), when Man first appeared ; and
Pleistocene (19), the period also known as the Glacial or Ice Age

THREE PERIODS OF GEOLOGICAL TIME

Director, Geological Survey

In the Geological Museum, London, are these representations of geological formations. At the top, a scene in the north-west Highlands of Scotland shows, in descending order on the right, white Cambrian quartzite, Pre-Cambrian Torridonian sandstone and Lewisian gneiss. In the central view, of Edinburgh from the Braid Hills, are hillocks of hard volcanic rock with hollows carved out of softer sandstone and shale; the rounded contours are due to the hills being worn down by an ice-sheet. Bottom, is the Avon Gorge at Bristol, cut by the river in carboniferous limestone.

first well-known marine fauna. In the succeeding Ordovician period trilobites and graptolites were abundant while molluscs spread and corals and lampreys appeared. Land plants are first known in Silurian rocks, and in the Silurian period the ancient reef-corals spread, but the true graptolites died out: air-breathing land animals (scorpions) first appeared. True fishes appeared in Devonian times and amphibians then arose. There were also spiders and goniatites. Land plants began to be numerous.

Origin of the Great Coalfields

The Carboniferous period saw the chief deposits of coal-forming materials: these were the remains of countless forests of plants that grew on low-lying swamps. None of these plants is now alive, though some modern plants—*e.g.* tree ferns—resemble them. There were also giant club-mosses and " horsetails." The climate was probably not tropical and the air humid, as has been supposed, but was probably temperate and the air much as at the present day. Amphibians and ancient sharks spread. There was also an early race of insects and an abundance of " sea-lilies " (crinoids).

In Permian times there was a maximum extension of land over our area, and earth-folding ("Hercynian movement") and mountain-building, with the great ice age in the Southern hemisphere. Trilobites and ancient reef-corals died out, mammal-like reptiles appeared and reptiles spread. Many of the Carboniferous plants became extinct.

The several systems of Palaeozoic rocks have somewhat different distribution, and, since the area of the deposits of any period corresponds approximately with the submerged area of that period, the distribution of the several systems helps us to understand the relations of land and water during the several periods. In this way it is known that the relations of sea and land were different at different times. It would appear either that the continent repeatedly rose and sank, causing areas which were at one time submerged to become land (and vice versa); or that the sea-level itself rose and fell. If the sea-level rose, it would overspread the low lands; if it were lowered, it would cause areas which had been submerged to become land.

How far the many changes in geography during the Palaeozoic era were the result of land oscillations and how far of oscillations of sea-level, has not been fully determined. It would appear that the deep-sea bottom has at no time been land, and that the areas which were alternately above and below sea-level were low when they were land, and covered only by shallow water when they were submerged. Moreover, all these generalizations apply to the conditions during later periods as well.

The Mesozoic (formerly called Secondary) era was, as the term indicates, the era when life intermediate between the ancient and the present existed. This era is divided into several periods, as indicated in page 1432. During the Triassic period, which is not well represented in Britain, reptiles were the dominant type of animal life. They were not only numerous, but the individuals attained great size. The earliest known remains of mammals date from this period. Marine life abounded, but departed notably from the types which had prevailed in the Palaeozoic era. Vegetation was abundant, including " horsetails," ferns, Ginkgo, Cycads and Conifers.

The Jurassic period followed, and the life of this period was somewhat different from that of the preceding, though the same general types abounded. Reptiles were the most distinctive type, and vast and wonderful dinosaurs, even larger than in the preceding period, roamed the earth. The oldest remains of toothed birds are Jurassic.

The Jurassic period was followed by the Cretaceous period, during which our chalk hills were laid down at the bottom of the sea. In the early part of the first period chalk was not being deposited, but in the latter part chalk deposits were in process of formation in many parts of the earth. The chalk deposits are made up, for the most part, of the shells of minute marine animals (*see* Chalk). During the Upper Cretaceous period many modern types of plants and fishes made their appearance. Among trees, the plane, sycamore, oak, walnut, willow and palm abounded.

Mammals, the earliest remains of which are found in the rocks of the Triassic system, became the dominant land creatures early in the Cainozoic era, for the huge reptiles characteristic of the Mesozoic era had long disappeared. Reptiles still existed, but they were relatively small. As the Cainozoic era progressed, the forms of life approached more and more closely to those of the present time, and by the end of the Pliocene the life was nearly the same as nowadays.

The Pleistocene period was a remarkable one on account of the great climatic changes which occurred at this time. Coincident with these climatic changes was the spread of a large ice-sheet, affecting especially the north-western part of Europe.

What is the Age of the Earth?

The duration of the earth's history is a matter which has received much attention (*see* Earth). Various conjectures as to the number of years occupied in bringing the earth to its present condition have been made. They range from 25 million years to 15 hundred million since the time of the formation of the oldest rocks now accessible. It is probable that the Devonian period began about 500 million years ago, and lasted 40 million years; the estimated lengths of the periods (in millions of years) are: Ordovician 60, Silurian 25, Devonian 40, Carboniferous 75, Permian 40, Triassic 25, Jurassic 25, Cretaceous 60, Oligocene and Eocene 35, Pliocene and Miocene 24, Pleistocene 1.

The climatic changes which the earth has undergone have been great, but their causes are not well understood. There is little basis for the belief, formerly widespread, that the climate has on the whole been growing cooler. Cold periods seem to have alternated with warmer ones. There was local glaciation in the Palaeozoic era, and extensive glaciation at the close of the Palaeozoic. There was glaciation in the early Cainozoic era, and very extensive glaciation later in that era; and there is some indication of cold periods at other times. There is also ample evidence that the lands of high latitudes have enjoyed genial, not to say tropical, climates during some later periods of the earth's history. Volcanic activity, too, seems to have been greater at some periods than at others.

Much that is useful to mankind comes out of the earth. Fuel for warmth and power; stone, clay, and cement for our houses; metals for making the machines that serve the modern industrial world—all these materials are products of the earth.

These various useful commodities are not placed within the earth like plums in a pudding without order. Each deposit is where it is for some good geological reason. The study of the origin, distribution, and laws of occurrence of such deposits is all part of the science of geology.

Since geology is largely the application of other sciences to earth problems, the geologist must have at least an elementary knowledge of chemistry, physics, and mathematics. His work is largely the study of minerals, rocks, and ores, and their relations to one another, and particularly the relations of groups of rocks or rock formations to one another, and the relations of mineral deposits to the various rock masses in which they are found. Since a large part of his business is the making of maps, he must understand practical surveying and drafting.

There are four kinds of activities in which most geologists find employment. These are:

1. Work at colleges, universities and technical schools.

2. Work on state and national geological surveys, and in other research organizations.

3. Work on staffs of mining companies.

4. Work on staffs of oil and gas companies.

Our universities maintain departments of geology which give instruction in mineralogy, petrology (the science of rocks), economic geology, palaeontology (the study of fossils), and engineering geology, besides other branches.

In Britain, all official geological research is in the hands of the Geological Survey. Britain has been mapped from a geological point of view by this organization, the staff of which may be called in by outside agencies needing the advice of a skilled geologist. All over the Empire, too, there are official geologists, and when expeditions are sent to different parts of the world a trained geologist is included.

Nearly all mining organizations employ geologists. Most mining companies have accurate geological maps of their properties, and it is part of the geologist's work to keep these up to date as mining progresses. Moreover, the geologist is himself able to guide operations in opening up new country, for he can tell where deposits of any sort are most likely to be found. Similarly, large oil companies also maintain geological staffs. By mapping the rocks above the oil-bearing beds, it is possible to locate the oil, and thus to discover the places that are most likely to be productive. (*See* Petroleum).

The SCIENCE of SURFACES and SOLIDS

Though geometry may not appear a very attractive subject it is one of the most useful branches of mathematics. It will become surprisingly interesting, too, if you approach it in the right way.

Geometry. Many young persons are inclined to think that this branch of mathematics is one of the dullest; others simply revel in its theorems and examples. Why is this ? Perhaps it is because geometry makes us think out problems, and many of us are too lazy-minded to do this willingly. But we *should* think out things for ourselves, especially when we are young; this exercise of the mind trains it to work properly and independently, and when adult life and work begin, we are better equipped for life's journey.

If you do not believe that geometry can be interesting—even exciting—pay attention to your lessons, and then look at some book such as Lancelot Hogben's Mathematics for the Million. Hogben gives a chapter entitled Euclid Without Tears, or What you can do with Geometry. It tells you, in an entertaining manner, how ancient peoples and their heirs of today have used this science in practical forms, from the building of the Pyramids of Egypt, and the reckoning of time, to the mapping of lands and the navigation of the oceans.

Geometry had its origin in earth measurements in the early days of the Egyptian and Babylonian civilizations. The word geometry (from Greek *ge*, earth, and *metron*, measure) denotes this early function. The lands of Egypt, swept by the floods of the Nile, had often to be re-surveyed and re-measured to establish the vanished boundaries; and in 2000 B.C. the " rope-stretchers " or surveyors of Egypt had their own crude way of erecting a perpendicular, measuring distances, and calculating areas. In building the pyramids they applied well-defined mathematical principles, later incorporated into geometry as we now know it.

It was left to the reasoning mind of the Greek to make all this mathematical knowledge, dealing with the measurement of space, an exact science. One branch, *plane geometry*, deals with circles, angles, squares, etc., that is, with two-dimensional measurements; and another, *solid geometry* with cubes, spheres, and other three-dimensional bodies.

Thales (640 B.C.–about 550 B.C.) is credited with originating the geometry of lines and angles, and developing demonstrations of things which others took for granted. Pythagoras (about 582 B.C.–about 500 B.C.), and all the members of the great Pythagorean school studied mathematics in secret. Pythagoras proved that *the square on the hypotenuse of a right-angled triangle is equal to the sum of the squares on the other two sides*, and this is known as the Pythagorean theorem. It is one of the most important mathematical truths discovered. The work of Euclid (about 300 B.C.) has been the standard down to our own day for pure plane and solid geometry.

The student who approaches the study of geometry must be thoroughly familiar with the measuring of lines—that is, from point to point —by practice with a rule, a compass, or squared paper ruled to inches and fractions of an inch; or with centimetres and millimetres. When he applies this to measuring a room, it is with the object of applying another fundamental idea of geometry, that of ratio. When we say a room is ten yards long, we mean that it is ten times as long as the standard unit, in this case a yard, so that the ratio of the yardstick to the length of the room is as 1 to 10. Every measurement is the determination of a ratio and is often expressed as a fraction.

From these simple exercises we may proceed to some of the simpler geometrical constructions that arise out of the relation of lines to one another, and to the definition of the basic terms used in geometry.

If a straight line, as OX in any of the drawings of Fig. 1, rotates in a plane about a fixed point, as O, in the direction indicated by the arrow-heads (anti-clockwise) until it reaches the position OT, it is said to turn through the angle XOT. Thus, an angle is the amount of turning made by a line rotating about a fixed point in a plane (flat surface). As the rotation continues, the size of the angle increases. These terms are used :

Vertex.—The fixed point O is called the vertex of the angle.

Initial and Terminal Sides.—The line OX is called the initial side of the angle. The line OT is called the terminal side.

Symbol for Angle.—The symbol for " angle " is $\angle$; for " angles " it is $\angle$s. Thus, Angle XOT is written $\angle XOT$.

Kinds of Angles.—If a line rotates about a fixed point in a plane so as to make one-fourth of a complete turn (that is, one-fourth of 360 degrees), the angle formed is called a right angle (rt. $\angle$) and of course equals 90 degrees. (*See* Fig. 2a).

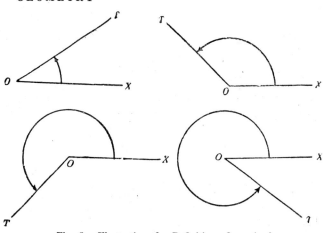

Fig. 1.—Illustrating the Definition of an Angle

common methods by which one may denote angles : (1) Designate the angle formed by two lines OX and OT, as the angle XOT or the angle TOX. Here the first and last letters denote points on the lines forming the angle, and the middle letter denotes the point of intersection (the vertex). In reading " angle XOT " we regard OX as the initial side and OT as the terminal

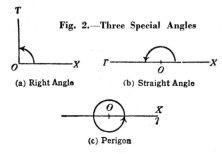

Fig. 2.—Three Special Angles

(a) Right Angle   (b) Straight Angle

(c) Perigon

If the line makes one-half of a complete turn, *i.e.*, 180°, the angle formed is called a straight angle (st. $\angle$). (*See* Fig. 2b). If the line makes a complete turn, the angle formed is called a *perigon*. (*See* Fig. 2c).

Angles are further classified upon the basis of their relation to the right angle, the straight angle, and the perigon. An angle less than a right angle is called an acute angle (Fig. 3). An angle which is greater than a right angle and is less than a straight angle is called an obtuse angle (Fig. 4). An angle greater than

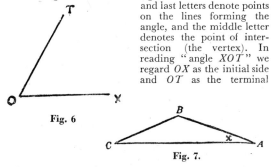

Fig. 3.—Acute Angle

Fig. 4.—Obtuse Angle

Fig. 5.—Reflex Angle

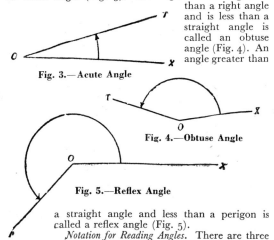

a straight angle and less than a perigon is called a reflex angle (Fig. 5).

Notation for Reading Angles. There are three

Fig. 6

Fig. 7.

side. (2) Denote the angle by a small letter placed as x in Fig. 7. In writing equations this method is the most convenient. (3) Denote the angle by the letter which is written at the point of intersection of the two sides of the angle, as " angle A." This last method is used only when there is no doubt as to what angle is meant. It is the method employed by land surveyors.

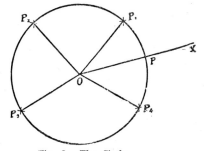

Fig. 8.—The Circle

If a line OX be taken as the initial side of an angle (*see* Fig. 8), and the line be rotated one complete turn (a perigon), any point, as P, on the line OX will trace a curved line which we call a circle. Thus *a circle is a closed curve, all points of which lie in the same plane and are equally distant from a fixed point.*

Centre and Circumference.—The fixed point O is the centre of the circle. The length of the curve (circle) is called the circumference (distance round) of the circle.

Radius and Diameter.—A line drawn from the centre of a circle to any point on the circle is a radius. Thus,

OP, OP_1, OP_2, OP_3, and OP_4 are radii (plural of radius) of the circle. A line connecting two points on the circle and passing through the centre of the circle is called a diameter.

From the definition of radius given above, it is clear that in a given circle or in equal circles, one radius has the same length as any other. Thus we obtain the following important geometric relation : *Radii of the same circle or of equal circles are equal.*

Ratios and Measurements.—The circumference of a circle has a certain ratio to the diameter (twice the radius) which is denoted by the Greek letter *pi* (π). The value of π is 3·14159265, usually taken as 3·1416, and this ratio is known as a mathematical constant. The circumference of a circle, therefore, is expressed by the formula $2\pi r$, and the area by πr^2, in which r is the length of the radius.

Arc; to Subtend; Central Angle.—An arc is a part of a circle. If two radii are drawn from the centre of the circle to two different points on the circle, they cut off an arc on the circle. The symbol for arc is $\frown$. Thus, $\frown AB$ is read " the arc AB." The angle formed at the centre of the circle is said to subtend the arc. The angle at the centre is called a central angle.

Quadrant and Semicircle.—An arc equal to one-fourth of a circle is called a quadrant. An arc equal to one-half of a circle is called a semicircle (Fig. 9).

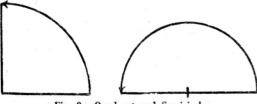

Fig. 9.—Quadrant and Semicircle

How We Measure Angles.—In many instances, the process of measuring angles is as important as that of measuring distances. An angle is measured when we find how many times it contains another angle selected as a unit of measure.

The protractor is an instrument devised for measuring and constructing angles. It commonly consists of a semicircle divided into 180 equal parts. Each of these equal parts is called a degree of a circle, which, as we have seen, contains 360 degrees.

If straight lines are drawn from each of these points of division on the semicircle to the centre O, 180 equal angles are formed, each of which is an angle of one degree ($1°$). Thus, the unit of angular measure is the degree. A degree is divided into 60 equal parts, each of which is called a minute ($1'$), and each minute is divided into 60 equal parts, each of which is called a second ($1''$). (Before clocks were invented, Man told the time by sundials; the dial itself was divided up into spaces of so many degrees and minutes to give the hour-angles.)

How to Use the Protractor.—To measure a given angle x place the protractor so that the centre of the instrument (point O in Fig. 10) falls upon the vertex and makes the straight edge of the protractor coincide with (fall upon) the initial side of the given angle x. Now,

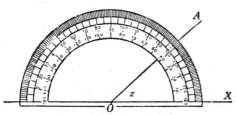

Fig. 10.—Measuring Angles with a Protractor

observe where the terminal side OA of the given angle intersects (crosses) the rim of the protractor. Read the number of degrees in the angle from the scale on the protractor, and you get the size of the angle XOA.

The protractor is also useful in constructing angles of a required size. For example, to construct an angle of $42°$ draw a straight line OX (Fig. 10) and place the straight edge of the protractor on the line OX so that the centre rests at O. Count $42°$ from the point on OX where the curved edge touches OX and mark the point A. Connect A and O, and the angle thus formed will contain $42°$.

One of the important phases of geometry work is that of constructing perpendiculars, angles, parallel lines, and so on.

For example, let us consider the following problem:

At a given point on a given line to erect a perpendicular to that line by using ruler and compasses.

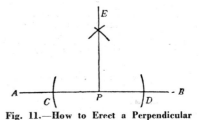

Fig. 11.—How to Erect a Perpendicular

Construction.—Let AB be the given line and P the given point (Fig. 11). With P as centre and with a convenient radius draw arcs intersecting AB at C and D.

With C and D as centres and with a radius greater than $\frac{1}{2}$ CD draw two arcs. These will intersect at some point E. Join EP. Then EP is the required perpendicular.

Another well-known construction problem is this:

At a given point on a given line to construct by means of a ruler and compasses an angle equal to a given angle.

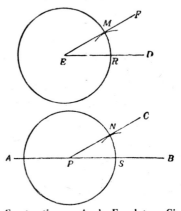

Fig. 12.—Constructing an Angle Equal to a Given Angle

Construction of an Angle.—Let DEF in Fig. 12 (top diagram) be the given angle and let P be the given point on the given line AB (lower diagram).

With E as a centre and ER as a radius, draw a circle. With P as a centre and with the same radius (ER) draw another circle. With R as centre and RM as radius cut an arc through M. With S as a centre and the same radius RM cut an arc at N.

The $\angle BPC$ is the required angle.

Definitions.—If two lines form right angles with each other, they are said to be perpendicular to each other.

The symbol for perpendicular is $\perp$. The meaning of parallel lines is shown in Fig. 13. *AB* and *CD* in that figure have had the same amount of angular rotation from the initial line *EF*. Thus, they have the same direction and are said to be parallel. The symbol for parallel is ∥. Thus *AB* ∥ *CD* is read "*AB* is parallel to *CD*."

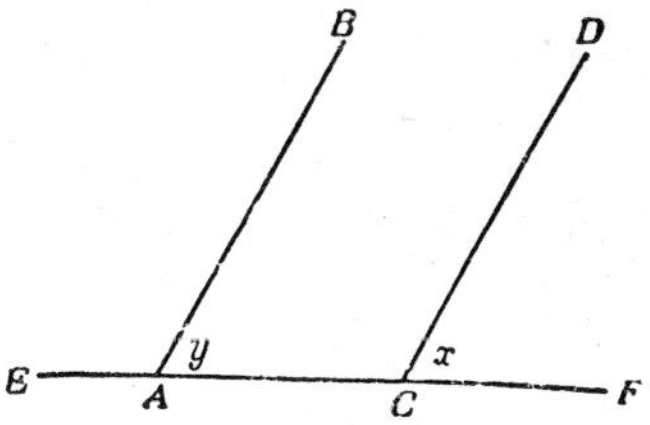

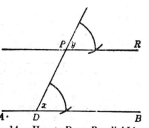

Fig. 13.—Parallel Lines

The angles *x* and *y* in Fig. 13 are called corresponding angles, and the line *EF* a transversal. It is clear that the lines are parallel only when the corresponding angles are equal and that the corresponding angles are equal, only when the lines are parallel.

Another important construction problem is that of drawing a line parallel to a given line.

Construction: Choose a point *P* outside the given line *AB* (Fig. 14). Draw a line through *P* so as to form a convenient angle *x* with *AB*. Call the point of intersection *D*. At *P*, using *DP* as initial line, construct an angle *y* equal to angle *x* (use method shown in Fig. 12). Then *PR* and *AB* are parallel because they have had the same amount of rotation from the initial line *PD*.

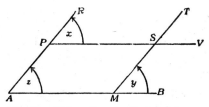

Fig. 14.—How to Draw Parallel Lines

If one pair of parallel lines cross (intersect) another pair, the four-sided figure thus formed is called a parallelogram; that is, a *parallelogram is a quadrilateral whose opposite sides are parallel.*

If we remember the method used for constructing one line parallel to another, it will be easy to construct a parallelogram.

Construction: Draw a working line *AB* (Fig. 15). Draw *AR* making a convenient angle with *AB*. Through

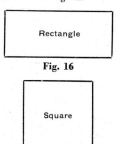

Fig. 15.—How to Construct a Parallelogram

any point, as *P*, on *AR* draw a line *PV* parallel to *AB*. Through any point as *M* on *AB* draw a line *MT* parallel to *AR*. The figure *AMSP* is a parallelogram, for its opposite sides are parallel.

If one of the interior angles of a parallelogram is a right angle, the figure is a rectangle (Fig. 16). Thus, *a rectangle is a parallelogram in which one interior angle is a right angle.* If all sides of a rectangle are equal, the figure is a square (Fig. 17).

Rectangle

Fig. 16

Square

Fig. 17

If we determine the amount of area enclosed within a polygon, or figure with many sides or angles, as in the triangle *ABC* in Fig. 18, we are measuring the area of the triangle. As in measuring length, the process is one of comparison. We compare the area of the given polygon with some

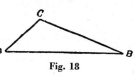

Fig. 18

standardized unit of area, and determine how many units are contained in the polygon, *i.e.*, we determine the ratio between the polygon's area and a standard unit of area.

The unit of area is a square, each of whose sides is a standard unit of length. Such a unit involves length and width. Thus, we may measure area and express the result in square feet, square inches, square metres, etc.

The drawings in Fig. 19 represent geometric solids. A solid is commonly thought of as an

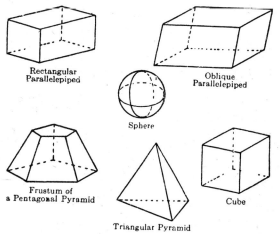

Rectangular Parallelepiped

Oblique Parallelepiped

Sphere

Frustum of a Pentagonal Pyramid

Triangular Pyramid

Cube

Fig. 19.—A Group of Familiar Solids

object that occupies a portion of space. It is separated from the surrounding space by its surface. In geometry we study only the form of the solid and its size. We are not interested in colour, weight, etc. A solid differs from the figures we have been studying in that it does not lie altogether in a plane, but involves a third dimension. A frustum is that part of a cone left after the top has been cut off by a plane parallel to the base.

Cube.—The cube has six faces all of which are squares. Two faces intersect in an edge.

Rectangular Parallelepiped.—The faces of a rectangular parallelepiped are all rectangles.

Oblique Parallelepiped.—The faces of an oblique parallelepiped are all parallelograms.

Measurement of Volume: Unit of Volume —When we determine the amount of space enclosed within the surface of a solid, we are measuring the volume of the solid. To do this, we compare the solid with a cube each of whose edges equals a unit of length. The volume is expressed numerically by the number of times the unit cube goes into the solid. The unit cube is called the unit of volume.

We must keep clearly in mind the definitions of certain geometrical terms.

Theorem.—In our geometry work we are concerned mostly with the proving of certain geometric relations;

for example, we may prove that "The sum of the interior angles of a triangle is two right angles." Such a statement of a geometric relation is called a theorem. Thus a theorem is something to be proved.

Problem.—A problem in geometry is something to be done. Thus " To draw a perpendicular to a given point in a line " is a problem.

Proposition.—A proposition in geometry may be either a theorem or a problem.

Corollary.—A truth which may grow out of, or depend upon, the truth of a proposition is called a corollary.

In geometry we should know the following :

Angle pairs formed by two lines cut by a transversal

When two lines such as *AB* and *CD* are cut by a transversal *EF*, as in Fig. 20—

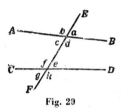

Fig. 20

the angles *c*, *d*, *e*, *f*, are called interior angles; and the angles *a*, *b*, *g*, *h*, are called exterior angles;

the angles $\begin{Bmatrix} a \text{ and } e \\ b \text{ and } f \\ d \text{ and } h \\ c \text{ and } g \end{Bmatrix}$ are called corresponding angles

the angles $\begin{Bmatrix} d \text{ and } e \\ c \text{ and } f \end{Bmatrix}$ are called interior angles on the *same side* of the transversal;

the angles $\begin{Bmatrix} d \text{ and } f \\ c \text{ and } e \end{Bmatrix}$ are called alternate-interior angles on *opposite* sides of the transversal;

the angles $\begin{Bmatrix} b \text{ and } h \\ a \text{ and } g \end{Bmatrix}$ are called alternate-exterior angles on *opposite* sides of the transversal.

The student of geometry should be careful to remember that when the lines cut by the transversal are parallel—

(a) corresponding angles are equal;
(b) alternate-interior angles are equal;
(c) alternate-exterior angles are equal;
(d) interior angles on the same side of the transversal are supplementary (together, equal to two right angles).

In geometry we have various methods of proving propositions. There is no one particular or invariable method of proof. The student of geometry should therefore become familiar with these methods. We shall explain each, and illustrate some of them by examples.

The demonstration of a theorem consists of three parts: the part that is given (the hypothesis), the part that is to be proved (the conclusion), and the proof. And in proving a theorem one should give a reason for each step taken.

The briefest general directions for proving a proposition are:

(1) Be sure to read the proposition carefully.

(2) If the proposition is a theorem or exercise, draw a careful general figure, *i.e.* if the theorem concerns a triangle draw a triangle all of whose sides are unequal (scalene), and not one all of whose sides are equal (equilateral), or one two of whose sides are equal (isosceles).

(3) Write down clearly the hypothesis (the given part) and the conclusion (what is to be proved), and do this in terms of the letters in your figure.

(4) Try to work out the proof by falling back on any-

thing you have previously learned that may apply, or draw some construction line or lines that may suggest the proof.

(5) Follow the outline given below for the form of your proof.

This makes it necessary to base each statement on (1) the hypothesis, (2) an axiom, (3) a definition, or (4) some other theorem which has previously been proved by geometrical methods.

The following proof will serve as an illustration : The theorem is: *The sum of the interior angles of a triangle is 180°* (Fig. 21).

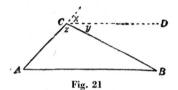

Fig. 21

Hypothesis: Let *ABC* be any given triangle.
Conclusion: Then $\angle A + \angle B + \angle C = 180°$.
Proof:

STATEMENTS	REASONS
Draw $CD \parallel AB$. Then $\angle x = \angle A$.	Because corresponding angles formed by two parallel lines cut by a transversal are equal.
And $\angle y = \angle B$	Because alternate-interior angles formed by parallel lines cut by a transversal are equal.
But $\angle x + \angle y + \angle z = 180°$.	Because the sum of all the angles about a point in a plane on one side of a straight line is 180°.
$\therefore \angle A + \angle B + \angle C = 180°$.	By substituting $\angle A$ for $\angle x$, $\angle B$ for $\angle y$, and $\angle C$ for $\angle z$.

At the end of such a demonstration we generally write Q.E.D. (*Quod erat demonstrandum,* " which was to be demonstrated "); or, if it is a problem, Q.E.F. (*Quod erat faciendum,* " which was to be done ").

METHOD OF PROOF BY SUPERPOSITION. The method of proof by superposition is the method used to show that certain figures have the same shape and same size, that is, are equal in all respects (congruent figures). The symbol for congruent is $\equiv$. It is the method always used to prove two triangles identical when two sides and the included angle of one are equal respectively to two sides and the included angle of the other. The proof is as follows (Fig. 22) :

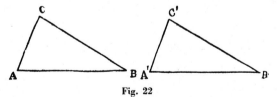

Fig. 22

Hypothesis: If in the $\triangle ABC$ and $\triangle A'B'C'$, $AC = A'C'$, $AB = A'B'$ and $\angle A = \angle A'$.
Conclusion: Then $\triangle ABC \equiv \triangle A'B'C'$.
Proof:

Imagine the triangle *ABC* placed upon the triangle *A'B'C'* so that angle *A* shall fit exactly upon its equal angle, *A'*, *AB* falling upon *A'B'* and *AC* upon *A'C'*.

Then since *AB* is given equal to *A'B'*, *B* will fall upon *B'*, and since *AC* is given equal to *A'C'*, *C* will fall upon *C'*.

Then *BC* will fall along and coincide with *B'C'*, otherwise there would be two different straight lines connecting the two points B and C, and this is impossible because only one straight line can be drawn between two points.

Hence the two triangles are congruent, *i.e.* they coincide and are therefore equal in all respects.

Since ABC and $A'B'C'$ are any two triangles having two sides and the included angle of one equal to the corresponding parts of the other, the theorem is true.

METHOD OF PROOF BY CONGRUENT TRIANGLES. In order to prove that certain lines or angles are equal, it is often expedient to show that the lines or angles are corresponding (homologous) parts of congruent triangles and are therefore equal.

For example, let us suppose we want to show that the base angles of an isosceles triangle are equal. To do this we would bisect the vertex angle of the isosceles triangle and then prove the two triangles thus formed congruent. The base angles of the original isosceles triangle would then be corresponding parts of the two little congruent triangles and therefore would be equal.

INDIRECT METHOD. The indirect method, or *reductio ad absurdum* (reducing to an absurdity), is one that is sometimes employed in geometry. The following proof will illustrate:

Theorem: If each of two lines is parallel to a third line, they are parallel to each other (Fig. 23).

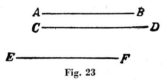

Fig. 23

Given: AB and CD each parallel to EF, to prove $AB \parallel CD$.

Proof:

STATEMENTS	REASONS
Suppose AB is not parallel to CD and that they meet at some point P. Then, through P there would be two lines parallel to EF which is impossible.	Because through a point outside a given line only one line can be drawn parallel to the given line.
Therefore AB and CD lying in the same plane do not meet. Hence they are parallel.	Because, when two lines lie in the same plane and do not meet, they are parallel.

METHOD OF ANALYSIS. The analytic method is a very powerful and useful one in geometry, especially in construction work.

Let us take the following problem as an illustration: From a point outside a circle to draw a

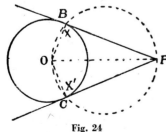

Fig. 24

tangent to the circle. A tangent is a straight line meeting a circle but not intersecting it when produced.

Given: a circle whose centre is O and a point P outside the circle (Fig. 24).

Required: to draw a line from P tangent to the circle.

Analysis: Imagine the two possible tangents PB, PC drawn. Join OP. Draw OB and OC. Then if PB and PC are tangents to the circle, $\angle x$ and $\angle x'$ must be right angles, because a tangent to a circle is $\perp$ to a radius drawn to the point of contact. This suggests the construction, for we know that if a second circle is drawn on OP as a diameter, $\angle x$ and $\angle x'$ will be right angles, because all angles inscribed in a semicircle are right angles. (An angle is said to be " inscribed " when it is made between two lines arising from the ends of the diameter. Thus $\angle OBP$ and $\angle OCP$ are inscribed angles. It can be proved, although the proof is not given here, that such an angle in a semicircle is always a right angle.)

Construction: Start with given circle and point P outside. Join OP. Then on OP as a diameter construct a circle, intersecting given circle at the points B and C. Join PB and PC and they are the required tangents.

Proof:

STATEMENTS	REASONS
Draw radii OB and OC. Then $\angle x$ and $\angle x'$ are each right angles.	Because any angle inscribed in a semicircle is a right angle.
Then BP and PC are tangents to the circle.	Because a line drawn perpendicular to a radius at its outer extremity is tangent to the circle.

CONVERSE. The " converse " of a proposition is another proposition in which the data given in the first is to be proved in the second, and what is to be proved in the first is given in the second.

For example, " An equiangular triangle is equilateral " is the converse of " an equilateral triangle is equiangular."

METHOD OF PROOF BY ELIMINATION. The method of proving a proposition by eliminating all of the possibilities except one is sometimes used in geometry (*see* Fig. 25). For example, let us take the theorem, *In any triangle where two sides are unequal, the angles opposite these sides are unequal in the same order.* ($<$ means " is less than," $>$ means " is greater than ").

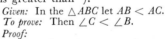

Fig. 25

Given: In the $\triangle ABC$ let $AB < AC$.
To prove: Then $\angle C < \angle B$.
Proof:

STATEMENTS	REASONS
There are three possibilities:	
(1) $\angle C = \angle B$.	
(2) $\angle C > \angle B$	
(3) $\angle C < \angle B$	
$\angle C$ cannot equal $\angle B$.	Because if it were, AB would equal AC and this is not true.
$\angle C$ is not greater than $\angle B$.	Because if it were, then $AB > AC$ and this is not true.
Therefore $\angle C < \angle B$.	By eliminating the other two possibilities.

DIRECT OR SYNTHETIC METHOD. The direct or synthetic method is the one commonly employed by textbook writers for setting down their proofs. It is logically ordered, and more elegant than the analytic method. An example has been given in Fig. 21, where the theorem *The sum of the interior angles of a triangle is equal to two right angles* is proved. This method is the minutely reasoned method, and is the one which we use to write out the final proof in complete form. It is the Euclidean method. The reader should endeavour to master all of the methods given here and consult the ordinary school text-books for illustrative material.

More advanced branches of geometry than the plane and solid are *analytical geometry*, a combination of algebra and geometry which can be studied after one has mastered elementary algebra and geometry; and *projective geometry*, which treats not so much the figures as their projections. The subject, however, is extremely interesting and helpful, and throws much light on the elementary field.

NON-EUCLIDEAN GEOMETRY. The geometry we have so far discussed is based on the axioms and postulates of Euclid. For many years mathematicians here and there have sought to erect a system which ignored or even contradicted these axioms and postulates. Einstein's Relativity (*q.v.*) theory presupposes a different view of space from that of Euclid, for example. The subject is too complex for any but advanced students.

George, SAINT. Everyone knows the story of how St. George overcame the dragon, but no one knows for certain whether there was really a St. George. Certainly in ancient days there was a George who was venerated as a saint at

ST. GEORGE AND THE DRAGON
The legendary encounter between the dragon and St. George, the patron saint of England, is depicted here by the Italian artist Raphael (1483-1520).

Lydda in Palestine; but his life is unknown, except for unproved statements that he held a high military command in the Roman army, and visited England on an expedition. We do not even know why he came to be adopted by England as her patron saint.

Probably the only historical fact concerning the patron saint of England is that he was George of Cappadocia, who was martyred in the year 303 during the Emperor Diocletian's persecution. According to the Golden Legend—the collection of lives of the saints compiled during the 13th century by Jacobus de Voragine, archbishop of Genoa—St. George, having slain the dragon, put off his knightly habit, gave all he had to the poor, went forth to preach Christianity, and was martyred.

St. George first became recognized as England's patron saint under the Norman kings. In 1346 Edward III founded the Order of the Garter, in the insignia of which the George, representing St. George and the dragon, is suspended from the collar. Some years later Edward IV built the magnificent St. George's Chapel at Windsor, in Berkshire, where, in the reign of Henry V, the supposed heart of the saint was deposited as a precious relic. St. George is also patron saint of Portugal and of Aragon. His feast-day is April 23.

The Six GEORGES *of* GREAT BRITAIN

An historic name among English kings is George, though the first four of its bearers were little English in their manners and little honoured then or since. But George V and George VI have won intense loyalty.

George. KINGS OF GREAT BRITAIN. It was the marriage of Elizabeth, daughter of James I of England, to Frederick, Count Palatine of the Rhine (*see* Thirty Years' War), that eventually brought to the British throne the Hanoverian or Guelf (Guelph) line of rulers, six of whom have borne the name of George.

GEORGE I, a grandchild of this marriage, and son of Ernest Augustus, was born on March 28, 1660, at Hanover; in 1698 he succeeded his father as elector of Hanover. He came to the British throne as the nearest Protestant heir on the death of Queen Anne. He ruled Great Britain, in addition to his German state, from 1714 to his death, June 11, 1727, dividing his time between the two countries. He was a silent awkward man, 54 years of age when he came to the English throne, and spoke only German. Because of this and of his paramount interest in his German lands, he left almost

everything to his English ministers, in whom he had implicit confidence. He gradually ceased even to attend Cabinet meetings. Sir Robert Walpole, the head of the Cabinet and the first real Prime Minister, became in effect the actual ruler of Great Britain so long as he was supported by Parliament. A rising of adherents of the Jacobite (exiled Stuart) line was easily put down in 1715.

GEORGE II, son of George I by his marriage with Sophia Dorothea, daughter of the duke of Brunswick, ruled from 1727 to 1760. Like his father, he was more interested in Hanover than in England. Born November 10, 1683, he was a vain, pompous man, fond of show but extremely economical. One of his favourite diversions, it is said, was counting his money like the king in the nursery rhyme. Although George II spoke broken English, he, too, left affairs of State to ministers—Walpole and, later, to the elder William Pitt, under whom the

National Portrait Gallery

TWO GEORGES, MORE GERMAN THAN ENGLISH
Of the Hanoverian kings of England, George I (left) and George II (right) unintentionally did most to assist the development of the British Constitution, because, as they could not speak English properly, there had to be a king's deputy in Parliament. Thus the appointment of Prime Minister was created.

drew the idea of restoring the king of England to his old position of sovereign power.

But this could have been done only by a strong king, and George III had but average ability. He had, however, more than average obstinacy, and he refused to give up his course until he had lost for England her 13 American colonies and (in the words of Lecky, the historian) had "inflicted more profound and enduring injuries upon his country than any other modern English king."

George III did not dare to attempt to rule without Parliament, as the Stuarts had done, but he sought to corrupt it—by gifts of offices, titles, contracts, and even money—and so built up a party known as "the king's friends." With the triumph of the American colonists over English forces at

country gained brilliant victories in the French and Indian War. (*See* Chatham, William Pitt, Earl of). The Jacobite rising (to restore the Stuarts) of 1745 was a much more serious affair than the rebellion of 1715, but it too proved unsuccessful. George's queen, Caroline of Anspach, was a woman of remarkable ability, and proved a tower of strength to him. George died on October 25, 1760.

GEORGE III, who was born on June 4, 1738, and reigned from 1760 to 1820, was the grandson of George II. His father, Frederick, Prince of Wales, who had been on the worst possible terms with George II, had died in 1751. George III was the first of the Hanoverian rulers who was born and educated in Britain. From his teacher, the Earl of Bute, and also from his mother, Augusta, a princess of Saxe-Coburg, George III

From painting by Sir William Beechey

GEORGE III AND HIS SON
First of the Georges to be born and educated in England, George III (above) became insane in 1811 and his son, who succeeded him as George IV in 1820, acted as Prince Regent (took the king's place). George IV is seen riding on the promenade at Brighton (lower).

Yorktown and the fall of Lord North, the king's figure-head minister, George's reactionary rule was ended. From time to time he was subject to attacks of insanity, and in 1811 his reason permanently broke down. During his later years his popularity increased. He died on January 29, 1820.

GEORGE IV (1762–1830), the son of George III, was born on August 12, 1762. For the nine years preceding his accession in 1820, he had been Prince Regent (acting as king), owing to his father's insanity. As a youth he was handsome and cultured, but his

KING GEORGE V

In 1922 King George V made his first broadcast, and he is here seen at the microphone at Sandringham House, Norfolk, whence he sent a Christmas message to his people throughout the world on December 25, 1935. During his reign the Crown became, as it had never been before, the connecting link between the Dominions and Great Britain.

The Times

profligacy and extravagance brought him into bad odour. Setting up his own establishment in 1781, he broke with his father, consorting with Fox and the Whigs, and making merry with the most reckless gamesters of the town. His extravagance embraced, besides jewellers' and tailors' bills and gaming debts, expensive schemes for building the Pavilion at Brighton, where he spent much of his time, and for clearing London streets so that he might ride at ease to Regent's Park. His treatment of his young queen was abominable, and when he attempted to divorce her, a wave of indignation swept over the land. The government, both in Great Britain and Hanover, was in the hands of his ministers. His brother, William IV, succeeded him in 1830, the only child of George IV (a daughter) having died some time previously. William IV was succeeded by his niece Victoria, daughter of his younger brother, the Duke of Kent. (*See* Victoria).

GEORGE V (1865–1936), the grandson of Queen Victoria and son of Edward VII, was born on June 3, 1865. As a young man he was trained for the sea, and had risen to be a commander in the British Navy when the death of his elder brother opened to him, at the age of 27, the eventual succession to the throne.

As king he ever maintained the wise policies of constitutional rule followed by his father and grandmother. Like his father, he had gained personal knowledge of the outlying posts of the Empire by a tour of the Dominions and colonies before he became king. During the First World War (1914–18) he crossed over to France several times, and was the first British king since 1743 to join his armies in the field. In 1917 he announced that henceforth his family would be known as the house of Windsor.

For nearly 20 years after the conclusion of peace George continued to rule his great Empire, and during this period the Crown became, as it had never

been before, the connecting link between the Mother Country and the self-governing Dominions. In May, 1935, the Silver Jubilee of his reign was celebrated. In 1928–29 the king had a serious illness, but he recovered. A second illness, however, proved fatal, and he died at Sandringham on January 20, 1936. He was the first English king to speak to his people, including those of the Empire, through the broadcasting microphone.

In 1893 George married Mary, the only daughter of the duke of Teck, and she survived her husband. Five of their children reached maturity: Edward, Prince of Wales, who became king as Edward VIII; the Duke of York, who succeeded his brother as George VI; the Dukes of Gloucester and Kent, and Mary, the Princess Royal, Countess of Harewood.

GEORGE VI (born 1895), King of Great Britain, Northern Ireland and the British Dominions overseas ; until 1947 Emperor of India, the last British monarch to bear that title. Upon the abdication of his elder brother Edward VIII (*q.v.*), the Duke of York ascended the throne on December 11, 1936, taking the name of George VI. He was crowned in Westminster Abbey on May 12, of the next year. The second son of King George V and Queen Mary, Albert Frederick Arthur George was born at York Cottage, Sandringham, on December 14, 1895. From his earliest boyhood his education was carefully planned. Trained like his father for the Navy, he went to school at Osborne in 1909. He spent two years there and two at Dartmouth. At the age of 17 he went to sea in H.M.S. Cumberland, visiting the West Indies and Canada, which Dominion he was the first of the king's sons to visit.

Karsh, of Ottawa

KING GEORGE VI

Trained like his father King George V for the Navy, King George VI was present at the battle of Jutland (May 31–June 1, 1916) during the First World War. He ascended the throne in December 1936 after the abdication of his brother Edward VIII, and was crowned in the following May.

During the First World War he served in H.M.S. Collingwood, and was with his ship when she was heavily engaged at the battle of Jutland (May 31–June 1, 1916), being mentioned in dispatches. In 1918 Prince Albert (as he was then called) was transferred to the Naval Air Service, taking his pilot's certificate in 1919.

He then went up to Cambridge for a course of study in history and economics. During this time he also acquired an interest in several branches of mechanics.

He has always been an enthusiast for sport ; he hunted and played polo, had inherited some of his father's skill in shooting, and played lawn tennis sufficiently well to enter for the men's doubles at the Wimbledon championship meeting in 1926.

Duke of York's Holiday Camp

Prince Albert was created Duke of York in 1920, and soon showed interest in social welfare by becoming president of the Industrial Welfare Society. In 1921 he founded the annual Duke of York's holiday camp for boys, first at New Romney, and later at Southwold. There boys from factories, mines, and schools live together in comradeship.

In April 1923 the Duke married Lady Elizabeth Bowes-Lyon (born 1900), youngest daughter of the Earl and Countess of Strathmore (*see* Elizabeth, Queen Consort). She was of the Scottish blood royal, an ancestor having married the daughter of the Scottish king Robert II in 1376. Their first daughter, Princess Elizabeth Alexandra Mary, later heir presumptive to the British throne, was born on April 21, 1926, and Princess Margaret Rose was born on August 21, 1930. (*See* articles on Elizabeth and Margaret).

In 1927 the Duke and Duchess undertook a Dominion tour which included the West Indies, all parts of Australia, New Zealand, and Tasmania. The culminating event of their tour was the opening of the Commonwealth Parliament House at Canberra in May 9.

In 1939, after succeeding to the throne, George VI and his Queen visited Canada and the United States of America. He became, thereby, the first British monarch to set foot on American territory. During the Second World War (1939–45), the King inspected his forces at Africa and Malta in 1943, and in June 1944, soon after the Allied landings in Normandy, he visited his armies on the beach-head. Throughout the grim conflict of the Second World War the King and Queen remained with their people—much of the time in Buckingham Palace, though this royal residence, like the rest of London, underwent its ordeal of air-bombing by the German Air Force. No one could have done more than Their Majesties to hearten and inspire the peoples of Britain and the Commonwealth, not least by their well-timed messages broadcast in days of anxiety and strain.

In the early months of 1947, the King and Queen, accompanied by the two princesses, made an extensive tour of South Africa, where they were given a great welcome. On April 26, 1948, the King and Queen celebrated their silver wedding anniversary by attending a service of thanksgiving at St. Paul's Cathedral, London.

The proposed Australian tour for 1949 was cancelled because the King had to undergo an operation for an affliction of the arteries of the leg, and for some time had to give up his public duties. Later it was announced that the tour would take place in 1952.

Georgia, U.S.A. The largest State east of the Mississippi river, Georgia is bounded on the North by the states of Tennessee, North Carolina and South Carolina ; by the Atlantic and South Carolina on the East ; on the South by Florida ; and on the West by Alabama. It has an area of 58,876 square miles. There is a mountainous region in the North and North-West, interspersed with wide fertile valleys. The most important river is the Savannah; several lesser streams are navigable.

The most important industry is cotton-growing, other crops including ground nuts, tobacco, maize, peaches, rice, sweet potatoes and sugar-cane. The pine forests provide timber, resin and turpentine. Georgia is the largest producer of china clay in the United States, and there are also vast deposits of fuller's earth (used in cleansing preparations). Other minerals are granite, marble, manganese, talc, gold, silver and mica. The capital of the State is Atlanta, having a population of 302,300.

The Spanish explorer De Soto visited Georgia in 1540, but the first European settlement was not founded until 1733, when British colonists formed a colony on the site of the city of Savannah. The Colony was called Georgia in honour of King George II of Great Britain, and was one of the 13 original states to declare their independence of Great Britain in 1776. In the American Civil War (1861–65) Georgia sided with the southern States, leaving the Union, to which it was readmitted in 1870. The population is about 3,123,700.

Georgia, U.S.S.R. A former kingdom of Transcaucasia with a history of more than 2,000 years as a State, the Soviet Socialist Republic of Georgia lies on the Asiatic side of the Caucasus Mountains. It is bounded on the North by these mountains, on the South by Armenia, on the East by Azerbaijan, and on the West by the Black Sea; area about 27,000 square miles.

Many of the inhabitants are engaged in agriculture, producing wheat and other cereals, cotton, citrus fruits and wine. Silk and cattle are other products. The forests are rich in valuable timber, especially box. Georgia possesses immense deposits of manganese, other minerals being coal and oil. Iron and steel works, and hydro-electric power stations have been constructed in the republic. There are 970 miles of railway, the main line connecting the Black Sea ports of Poti and Batum with Baku, on the Caspian. The ancient city of Tbilisi (Tiflis), the capital of Georgia and Transcaucasia, has a population of 519,200.

The kingdom of Georgia lost its independence in 1801 when it was annexed by Russia. After the Bolshevik revolution of 1917 the country became an independent republic, but in 1922 it formed, together with Armenia and Azerbaijan, the Trans-caucasian Soviet Federal Socialist Republic, which lasted until 1936, when Georgia became an independent republic of the Soviet Union. The population is about 3,542,300.

Geranium. The red, white or pink " geranium " plants, whose spicy fragrance scents summer gardens and window-sills, are not ger-

E. J. Bedford

GERANIUM AND ITS CULTIVATED NAMESAKE
Wild specimens of geranium are the herb robert and the blue meadow crane's
bill (left), both of the order *Geraniaceae*. Garden geraniums (right) belong
to a different family and are really pelargoniums.

The house plants known as geraniums—the pelargoniums—belong to the same family, *Geraniaceae*, but differ greatly from the true geranium in appearance. They are frequently grown in greenhouses and conservatories for indoor decoration, and are also extensively used for bedding purposes. In colour their flowers range from a pure white to a bright scarlet, and between these there are many beautiful shades of pink and cerise. The foliage, too, is often variegated with yellow or white.

German, Sir Edward (1862–1936). First performed at the Lyceum Theatre, London, in 1892, German's music to Henry VIII contains three dances which are, perhaps, his best-known works. This popular English composer first made his reputation with the incidental music to Shakespeare's play Richard III in 1889, the year after he became musical director of the Globe Theatre, London.

aniums at all; they are really pelargoniums. The true wild geraniums of our countryside are called crane's bills, on account of the shape of the seed pods. They usually have hairy, compound leaves and pinkish or purplish flowers, and like shady places. The finest is the blue *G. pratense*—meadow crane's bill—common by roadsides in many places; and another common species is herb robert (*G. robertianum*), a plant with dainty little light purple flowers streaked with red, found in damp, shady woods and on old walls. It has a strong, unpleasant smell. The hemlock stork's bill of the related genus *Erodium* is common in dry and sandy places.

He was born on February 17, 1862, at Whitchurch, Shropshire, and studied at the Royal Academy of Music, London. Though a competent violinist, he devoted the main part of his career to composition. After writing incidental music to several Shakespearean plays, he turned to light opera, the most famous being Merrie England (1902), A Princess of Kensington (1903), and Tom Jones (1907). German's music was influenced by the composer Sir Arthur Sullivan (1842–1900), whose opera, The Emerald Isle, he completed in 1901 after Sullivan's death. German was knighted in 1928. His music is still very popular.

The GERMAN LAND and Its PEOPLE

*A land of great natural charm and beauty, the birthplace of great writers,
artists and musicians, of philosophers and scientists, Germany has
also produced unscrupulous leaders who started two World Wars.*

Germany. As a political unit, Germany, under varying names, was the most powerful state in Central Europe after the collapse of the Roman Empire until modern times. By reason of its geographical position it provided a link between Eastern and Western Europe. Throughout the Middle Ages, the Renaissance, and later times its borders were constantly changing. Under the German Republic of 1919 its frontiers marched with those of the Netherlands, Belgium, Luxembourg, and France in the West; of Switzerland, Austria, and Czechoslovakia in the South; of Poland and Lithuania in the East; and of Denmark in the North.

As a result of defeat at the end of the First World War (1914–18) the German Empire built by Bismarck after the Franco-Prussian War, 1870–71, had collapsed, and Germany had lost her place among the dominant European Powers. Under Hitler's dictatorship her frontiers expanded to include Austria in a Greater Reich. At the end of the Second World War, in 1945, Germany lost great tracts of her former territory, including East

Prussia and Silesia, as well as portions of Pomerania and Brandenburg. These changes in extent can be traced in the maps in the following pages.

The North of the country tends to be flat; a range of hills and mountains in the centre runs from West of the Rhine to the Sudeten range between the Elbe and Oder. In the South stretches the Black Forest and ridges of the Alps. The Rhine, greatest of German rivers, flows from Switzerland to the sea. It is navigable as far as Basle, and is connected by canals with both the Danube and the Rhône, so that commerce from its shores can pass easily to the North Sea, the Mediterranean, and the Black Sea. Along the Rhine are innumerable heights crowned with ruined castles. The middle Rhine and the valley of the Moselle, its chief tributary from the West, produce some of the finest wines in the world. A wealth of legend, folksong, and romantic tales is associated with this river.

In the following survey of the German land much about its commerce and industry has had to be put in the past tense. After Adolf Hitler came to power in 1933 the Nazi government turned over hundreds of thousands of former agricultural workers to various armament industries and to the building up of a vast reserve of commodities which Germany would have to manufacture for herself when she later engaged in her bid for the domination of Europe. " Guns before butter " was the slogan coined by the authorities. As Germany swallowed up neighbouring lands during the years from 1938 onwards, she used them very largely as providers of agricultural produce and diverted more and more of her own people from the fields to work in factories. Thus it is that our story is very much that of Germany *as she was* before the Nazis came to power.

Northern Germany forms a part of the great lowland that extends from the vast expanse of Russia to the English Channel. Across it numerous large rivers flow northward— the Ems, Weser, Elbe, Oder, and Vistula—all with large seaports at or near their mouths and navigable either entirely across, or far into, the heart of Germany.

The German plain is narrowed in the west by the Thuringian hills and the Harz Mountains. Like all the mountains of Germany proper, these are old worn-down ranges and are forest-covered. In places, also, low hills parallel the sandy shores of the Baltic. Forests of beech, spruce, and pine, and numerous marshy lakes are found in the east, and there are moors near the western coast.

The sandy soil and harsh climate of the northern plain are unfavourable to agriculture, but science and patient labour produced (until the Second World War) on the great estates of Prussia and Pomerania bountiful crops of rye, barley, oats, sugar-beet, and potatoes—potatoes by the millions of bushels, for these are a staple food of the German people. Indeed, in one small German town (Offenburg, in the Black Forest) a statue was erected to Sir Francis Drake, as the man who first introduced this important tuber to Europe. Horses, cattle, sheep, and pigs are also raised extensively; while the turf cut from the Lüneburg moorlands supplements the coal and lignite from other regions.

In this northern half—the essentially Prussian part of Germany—lies Berlin, formerly one of the most modern of Europen capitals, at the centre of the nation's transport and commercial system.

Facing the North Sea are the maritime cities of Bremen and Hamburg. The former naval harbour of Kiel also stands at the Baltic end of the great canal (over 60 miles long) which cuts across the neck of Jutland. Excepting Kiel, all these German maritime cities are river-mouth ports. Shipbuilding and fisheries were among the most important industries in these regions.

This northern plain, owing to its lack of protecting mountain barriers, lies open to easy invasion. Hordes of barbarian Goths, Slavs, and Tartars swept across it in far-off ages. It was the battleground for the armies of Sweden, Spain, and France in the devastating Thirty Years' War, for the conquering hosts of Napoleon, and the advance and retreat of Austrian and Prussian swarms and, more recently, for the invading Allied armies which broke the power of Hitler's Reich in 1944-45.

Westward of the mountain-rimmed countries of Bohemia and Moravia lie the ancient homelands of German culture—Bavaria and the regions still sometimes known as Swabia and Franconia.

Seven hundred odd years ago, while the original Prussians beyond the Vistula were still pagan Slavs, Franconia and Swabia were great and flourishing duchies, the bases of leading branches of the German folk, from which sprang illustrious lines of emperors. As separate states they have long since disappeared from the map, but Baden, Württemberg, and Hesse occupy today parts of their former territory.

How welcome is the change from the north to the more picturesque land of the south of the Rhineland ! Instead of monotonous level plain, there is fertile valley, wooded upland, and occasional rounded mountains; and everywhere the eye is charmed by ruined castles and quaint old cities rich in historic and artistic memories. To the agricultural products of the north are added here wheat, flax, and tobacco. In Bavaria grow the hops used in the German beer, and in the Rhineland are wonderful vineyards. And everywhere we see churches and shrines, for South Germany and the Rhineland were as Catholic as the north was Protestant.

Across the frontier from France, in the elbow of the Rhine, lies the former grand duchy of Baden —famous alike for its picturesque Black Forest and for Heidelberg, the seat of a great university and with a fine ruined castle. The former kingdom of Württemberg, with its castle-crowned hills, is filled with memories of old Swabian days.

These wooded highlands of the south raise the total of Germany's forest area to one-fourth of the whole land. Beech, oak, pine, spruce, and birch are among the most important growths. In some parts of Bavaria the wood industries were almost the sole resources of the people. On the Rhine

---

Extent.—Area of German Republic (1939 census) was 181,630 square miles. Population about 69½ million.

Area of the Greater Reich (after the absorption of Austria and the Sudetenland region of Czechoslovakia in 1938), 226,000 square miles. Population about 80,000,000. In 1939 Germany took Memel from Lithuania ; and after the conquest of Poland she annexed Polish territory with an area of 72,400 square miles and a population of 21,000,000. The former Free City of Danzig was also seized. In 1940 Eupen and Malmédy were taken from Belgium and incorporated into Germany ; Alsace-Lorraine was annexed from France. In 1949 Germany was split into two republics—West German and East German. (*See* article on Berlin).

Rivers.—Danube, Rhine (Moselle, Neckar, Main, Ruhr, tributaries), Ems, Weser, Elbe (Saale, tributary), Oder and Vistula.

Mountains.—Bavarian Alps, Bohemian Forest, Erzgebirge (Ore Mountains), Sudetes, Black Forest, Thuringian Forest, Taunus, and Harz Mountains.

Zones of Occupation After the Second World War.— British Zone : W. Berlin, Schleswig-Holstein, Westphalia, Hamburg, Lower Saxony. American : W. Berlin, Bavaria, Württemberg-Baden, Bremen, Hesse. French : W. Berlin, Rhineland, Baden, Württemberg-Hohenzollern, Saar. Russian : E. Berlin, Brandenburg, Mecklenburg, Saxony-Anhalt, Saxony, northern part of East Prussia. (*See* map p. 1453).

Chief Cities.—Bonn (capital of West German Federal Republic), Berlin (eastern part cap. of East German Democratic Republic), Hamburg, Munich, Cologne, Leipzig, Essen, Dresden, Breslau, Bremen, Frankfurt, Dortmund, Düsseldorf, Hanover, Bochum, Nuremberg, Duisburg-Hamborn, Stuttgart, Wuppertal, Chemnitz, Gelsenkirchen, Magdeburg, Mannheim.

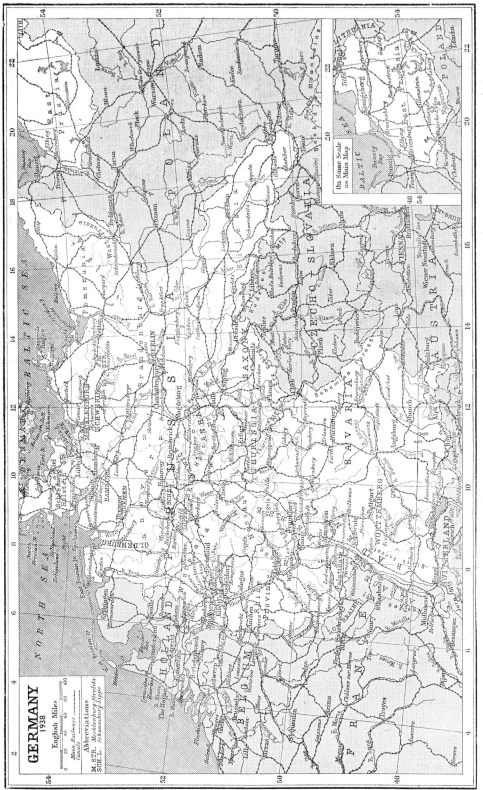

GERMANY: FRONTIERS BEFORE THE ANNEXATION OF AUSTRIA AND OTHER ACQUISITIONS

Until 1871 there was no united Germany. The map showed east of the Rhine only a number of separate States, ruled by independent kings and princes and inhabited by German-speaking people. After the defeat of France in the Franco-Prussian War (1870–71) all these States were united under the King of Prussia to form the German Empire. Following her defeat in the First World War (1914–18) Germany was shorn of Alsace-Lorraine and some of her territory in the east; but just before the Second World War (1939–45) Austria was annexed and Czecho-slovakia was dismembered, Bohemia and Moravia becoming German protectorates.

great timber rafts were frequently met with floating downstream to Mainz and other furniture-making and wood-using cities.

In Bavaria (q.v.) the traveller finds the loveliest scenery. Here only does Germany touch the Alps, for the Austro-Bavarian boundary runs along the ridge of the Northern Tirolese or Bavarian Alps, and in the distance are the peaks of the Vorarlberg. The Zugspitze (9,738 feet), 57 miles south of Munich, is the highest peak in Germany.

Bavaria's cities, too, were once her pride. In 1945 many of them lay in ruins. The art-loving capital of Munich, situated beside the Isar, on a lofty plain some 25 miles north of the foothills of the Alps, had a charm lacking in Berlin; while as for Augsburg, Nuremberg, Regensburg (Ratisbon), and Passau, each had an interest all its own. And where could Wagnerian opera be heard so well as at Bayreuth, or religious drama seen to better advantage than at Oberammergau ?

Between these two older Germanies of the north and of the south lies the " black " industrial region of central Germany—the Rhine-Westphalian region lying on both sides of that river north of Cologne, the Saxon districts northward of Bohemia, and Silesia. German industries comprised almost every kind of production. Industrial development was favoured by the wealth of coal of the Ruhr basin, Upper Silesia, the Saar, and Central Germany.

The Ruhr coal-field fed the fires of innumerable blast-furnaces, including the vast Krupp ironworks at Essen. Solingen was renowned for its knives and cutlery, Iserlohn for needles. Near by is the cotton manufacturing city of Wuppertal, " the German Manchester." On the left bank of the Rhine are Krefeld, the chief seat of the German silk and ribbon manufacture, and Düsseldorf, the banking centre of the district.

The industrial district of Saxony was based on the Saxon coal-field. From Chemnitz and Zwickau came German stockings, knitted underwear, and other goods made from imported cotton. Fine wools grown in Saxony and Silesia made these regions great centres also for woollen textiles.

OLD BAVARIAN COSTUMES
Traditional customs and clothes still linger in parts of Southern Germany, which is less highly industrialised than the North. These peasant girls in festival finery are from Nördlingen in Bavaria.

The clay deposits at Meissen, near the Saxon capital, Dresden, rendered possible the famous " Dresden ware."

Most of this industrial strength was developed after 1870, and the coming into being of the German Empire in 1871. Germany then rapidly extended her already widespread system of railways and canals, while with government co-operation, giant industries were built up—often with an eye to their wartime value. Under National Socialism the control of every aspect of industrial life was made more rigid. Germany became a totalitarian state, in which the economy of the country was regulated to suit the warlike plans of the Nazi leaders. This side of the story is told in later pages.

GERMANY'S PLACE *in the* HISTORY BOOK

Not until within living memory did Germany become a united country, with a common boundary and a single government. Here is chronicled her development—and the tragic end to her dreams of world domination.

Germany, HISTORY OF. As far back as we have any record, Germans have inhabited this land, but their ancestors probably came from the grass-lands of southern Russia. Romans and wandering German tribes fought one another as early as 113 B.C. While Julius Caesar was governor of Roman Gaul, which extended to the Rhine, he drove back two German tribes who had settled west of that river (55 B.C.).

In the year A.D. 9 a Roman army was entrapped and destroyed by a German chieftain named Arminius (Hermann) in the Teutoburg Forest in north-western Germany. About a century afterwards the Rhine and Danube were definitely established as the boundary of the empire. Tacitus (A.D. 98) described the Germans as a rough barbarian people, tall of stature, with fair com-

plexions and blue eyes. They lived in rude villages in their gloomy forests, wore garments of skins, and spent their time chiefly in war and the chase.

Two hundred years later the Germans—now formed into great groups or nations called Goths, Franks, Frisians, Saxons, Vandals, and the like—began to press into the weakened Roman Empire. By the time that the period of the migrations had ended, the Roman Empire had fallen in the west. Most of the barbarian conquests were absorbed into the kingdom of the Franks, which reached its height under Charlemagne (q.v.). The break-up of the Frankish Empire in the Partition of Verdun (A.D. 843) marks the real beginning of both France and Germany as separate states.

Between the two countries lay a middle strip called Lorraine, which at this time extended west-

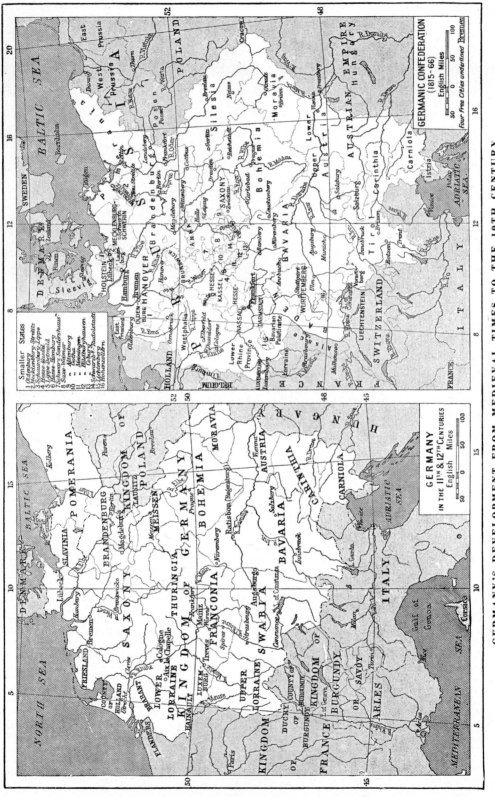

GERMANY'S DEVELOPMENT FROM MEDIEVAL TIMES TO THE 19TH CENTURY

For several hundred years after the division of the Emperor Charlemagne's empire, between his grandsons in 843, Germany was divided into a number of great duchies, each the home of a separate branch of the German people. The chief of these duchies are shown in the map on the left. After the fall of Napoleon Bonaparte the Congress of Vienna (1814-15) grouped the German states into a German Confederation (right), but in 1848 a movement arose for a united Germany. The Prussian Chancellor Bismarck created the first German Empire; he began in 1866 with the defeat of Austria, the annexation of several states, and the formation of a North German Federation.

ward from the Rhine to the river Scheldt, and from the Vosges Mountains to the North Sea. On the east Charlemagne's effective empire had extended only to the Elbe and its tributary the Saale, beyond which line dwelt Slavic tribes. The eastward extension of German rule to the Vistula and Memel rivers was the work of another ten centuries.

The conversion of the Germans to Christianity was achieved by Irish monks and then by the Englishman, St. Boniface (*q.v.*), the "Apostle to the Germans." The Saxons of North Germany remained pagan until the time of Charlemagne.

German Rulers in the Middle Ages

For several hundred years after 843 Germany was divided into a number of great "stem duchies," each the home of a separate stem or branch of the German people. The chief of these duchies were Bavaria, Swabia, Franconia (on the middle Rhine and its tributary the Main) and Saxony (from the Ems to the Elbe, north of Franconia). The Franconian duke was the first to become German king after the ending of Charlemagne's line (911). Then for five generations the Saxon dukes wore the crown. The greatest of this line was Otto I, the Great (912–73), who revived Charlemagne's empire. Following the Saxon kings the Franconian (or Salian) house again ruled. In its time the empire was convulsed by a great "Investiture Conflict" between Church and State, led by the Emperor Henry IV (1050–1106) and Pope Gregory VII (Hildebrand), and their successors. After the Salian emperors came the Hohenstaufens, so called from their ancestral castle in Swabia. Frederick I, called Barbarossa or "Red Beard" (*c.* 1124–90), and his grandson, Frederick II (1194–1250), were the most important of the Hohenstaufen emperors.

Feudalism and the attempt to rule Italy along with Germany broke up the stem duchies into a thousand or more fragments. Everywhere arose robber barons, who ruled from their hill-top castles by *Faustrecht* ("fist law"). Italy, as was said by Rudolph of Hapsburg (1218–91), the first of his house to become emperor, was "the den of the lion," with many tracks leading in and none coming out. So Germany remained an elective monarchy (in which the ruler was chosen by princes and others called electors), weakened by its connexion with Italy; while France, England and Spain were building up strong kingdoms based on the principle of hereditary (father to son, and so on) rule.

But the strength that ebbed from the German kingship flowed in the hereditary princely states. The Golden Bull (1356) of Charles IV fixed the right to elect the emperor in the Seven Electors—the archbishops of Mainz, Cologne and Treves, the Margrave of Brandenburg, the Elector of Saxony, the Count Palatine of the Rhine and the King of Bohemia. By confirming the powers of these and other states and "free cities," Charles IV is said to have "legalized anarchy and called it a constitution."

Even Charles V (1500–58), who in addition to Germany ruled the Netherlands, Spain, Austria, Naples and Sicily, and large parts of the New World, was unable to crush the Reformation begun by Luther, and one of the chief reasons was the support given to this great religious uprising by the rulers of important German states. The terrible Peasants' War of 1525, in which the people of Swabia and Franconia sought to free themselves from the bonds of serfdom, only riveted their chains more firmly. The great religious struggle called the Thirty Years' War (1618–48) raged all over Germany and weakened the central power still further.

For many years the head of each of the several hundred German states was practically an absolute ruler, and the Hapsburg emperor was a mere figure-head, without power save in Austria and his other hereditary lands. Then Frederick the Great increased his kingdom of Prussia at the expense of Austria and Poland, and he made of his possessions a strong well-ordered state. He thus prepared the way for a closer union of Germany.

The wars waged by Revolutionary France and Napoleon I helped in this unification, though again Germany was left trampled and bloody in the wake of battle. The crushing defeat of the Prussians at Jena (October 14, 1806) compelled a reorganization of Prussia, by which serfs were set free and a beginning made of the Prussian military system based on the principle of universal service. The mockery of the title "Holy Roman Emperor" was also ended when Francis II resigned it and became simply Emperor of Austria (1806).

After the fall of Napoleon the Congress of Vienna (1814–15) grouped the German states—now reduced from several hundreds to 39, including Austria—into a formless German Confederation. Its head was a diet or assembly composed of delegates appointed by the sovereigns, which met at Frankfort-on-the-Main.

When the wars of democratic revolution again burst over Europe in 1848, the Liberals of Germany rose in rebellion and demanded democratic government and a strong and united Germany. But when the German Imperial crown—with Austria left out —was offered by them to King Frederick William IV of Prussia, he contemptuously refused it.

Rise of the German Empire

The actual creation of the new German Empire was the work of Bismarck, who believed that only on the field of battle could that issue be settled. By skilful manoeuvring he brought about war with Austria in 1866. She was defeated at Sadowa (Königgratz) and forced to submit to a reorganization of Germany which excluded her. The states of Hanover, Hesse-Cassel, Nassau, and the free city of Frankfort, which had supported Austria, were ruthlessly annexed by Prussia. The other German states north of the river Main then united with Prussia in a North German Confederation (1866–70). South Germany remained aloof for the time.

Four years later Bismarck tricked France into declaring war; she was crushingly defeated, forced to pay an indemnity of £200,000,000, and to cede Alsace-Lorraine to Germany. The enthusiasm aroused brought the South German states into the Prussian organization. It was completed by the proclamation at Versailles (January 18, 1871) of the German Empire, with the King of Prussia as Emperor (Kaiser). There was a popularly-elected Reichstag, or legislative chamber, but the real power lay with the Prussian chancellor. At the head of the administration, he was responsible only to the Emperor. Under the leadership of Bismarck as chancellor, in the reigns of William I (1871–88) and Frederick III (March–June, 1888), the new

MODERN GERMANY'S FIRST EMPEROR ENTERS BERLIN

Following the defeat of France in the Franco-Prussian War (1870-71), the king of Prussia was proclaimed Emperor (kaiser) of the German Empire as William I in January 1871. He is here depicted receiving the victor's crown of laurels from a lady during the victory celebrations in Berlin. In the background is the gaily decorated Brandenburg Gate. France had to pay an indemnity of £200,000,000 to Germany and to give her the valuable territory of Alsace-Lorraine.

empire grew rapidly in vigour, industrial prosperity and power. The beginning was made of a colonial empire which ultimately included about 1,000,000 square miles in Africa (Togoland, Cameroons, German S.W. Africa, German E. Africa) and 100,000 square miles in China and the Pacific.

Two years after the accession of the Emperor William II (1859-1941), Bismarck was abruptly dismissed by the impetuous young Kaiser, whose many aggressive demands for " a place in the sun " led up to the First World War of 1914–18, which ended the empire and lost it all its colonies. (The story is told under the heading World Wars.)

The Peace Treaty of 1919 condemned Germany to pay huge indemnities, surrender her navy, limit her army to 100,000 men, lose Alsace-Lorraine, her Polish territories, part of Schleswig, and all her colonies, while her territory on the west bank of the Rhine was to be occupied by the Allies for 15 years. Just before the signing of the Armistice (Nov. 11, 1918) the Kaiser fled to Holland, the rulers of the states abdicated or were deposed, and republican governments took their place. A revolt of the extreme Socialists in January 1919 was suppressed by the moderate Socialist provisional government.

At the beginning of this story we quoted what Tacitus had said about the war-loving Germans of his day, 19 centuries ago. All through the intervening centuries the Teutonic peoples showed themselves ready to fight battles for causes chosen by their leaders. In no other European land was the army so honoured or the fighting services held in such esteem. After the war of 1914–18 Germany was permitted to keep only a tiny standing army, and hundreds of thousands of former officers found themselves out of a job and with little to which they could turn for occupation. Higher officers wielded great political influence, as they had always done. They gave support to the new government because it suited their temporary purposes. But they worked and plotted to keep in being a nucleus of skilled officers who should form the kernel of a new and mighty army with which Germany should wipe out the disgrace of her late defeat.

A constitution came into effect in 1919 providing for a Republic under a President and a responsible Cabinet, and the popularly elected Parliament (Reichstag) was strengthened. But the new regime failed to solve the difficulties with which it was faced. Unemployment was rife, risings broke out, the exchange value of the mark fell, reparation payments were not maintained, and French troops occupied the Ruhr (1923). Improvement attended the formation in 1923 of a ministry of the Centre Party, in which Gustav Stresemann as Foreign Minister initiated a policy of co-operation with the Allies. This ministry restored the currency by introducing the Reichsmark, accepted new reparations plans, signed the Locarno peace pact (1925), and joined the League of Nations (1926). Various plans were made by Germany's former opponents in an endeavour to render easier the payment of reparations for the late war.

Another economic crisis, however, arose in 1929. Ministries fell, and the Nazi movement, that of the " Nationalsozialistische Deutsche Arbeiterpartei " (National Socialist German Workers Party), grew in power under Adolf Hitler (q.v.). This party gradually won more seats in Parliament until it became strong enough to crush its opponents.

The first President (Friedrich Ebert) died in 1925, and was succeeded by the veteran Field-Marshal Paul von Hindenburg. On his death in August 1934 Adolf Hitler, who had been Chancellor since January 1933, combined the offices of President and Chancellor, adopted the title of *Fuehrer* (or Leader), and became a virtual dictator.

Hitler's goal was the totalitarian State, that is, a nation entirely without factions, in which all branches of activity were dominated by the State. The Reichstag, the federal state governments, independent courts, and the powers of the provincial authorities were abolished or severely curbed.

As the leader of a united nation, Hitler proposed to make it strong for war, so that Germany could once more hold up her head as an equal among the States of Europe. He had set out his theories of world politics in the book Mein Kampf, which title means My Struggle. It is a strange conglomeration of ideas borrowed mainly from earlier writers, coupled with audacious claims for the lands of Germany's neighbours and with Hitler's own peculiar political axioms. Hostility for France was fiercely proclaimed; the rich grain lands of south Russia were to be conquered; all German-speaking peoples were to be brought into a great German state; the treaty of Versailles was to be undone.

Then, besides all this, there was a lot of borrowed rubbish about the superiority of the so-called Aryan or Nordic race. The Jews, according to Hitler, had been responsible for all Germany's recent troubles; they had organized the war of 1914–18 so as to destroy the "Bastion of Aryanism" in Germany. Bolshevism and Marxism, with which Hitler coupled all forms of Socialism, were manifestations of the designs of world-Jewry. Hitler had been called upon, he said, to save Germany from these perils.

The Nazi programme offered the people not so much betterment of their own lot as participation in the national glory by joining one of the numerous military or semi-military bodies within the Nazi party such as the Brownshirts or the Blackshirts. Unemployment was abolished by a planned economy, chiefly devoted to enormous armament works and war-like preparations.

Jews, denied all participation in the new "all-Aryan" state, were cut out of the nation's economic life as well. Anti-Nazis and dissenting party leaders alike were slaughtered in the Nazi "blood purge" of June 30, 1934. Labour unions were merged into the Nazi "Labour Front"; youth movements were taken over by the "Hitler Youth." Universities, Churches, and farm organizations were brought into line, or co-ordinated, although the Church bitterly resented State interference. Press, stage and wireless were placed under the strict censorship of a propaganda minister, Joseph Goebbels. New People's Courts, with judges appointed by Hitler, tried the many crimes construed as high treason and sent political prisoners to concentration camps. Execution by the headsman's axe was reintroduced. Scientifically cruel methods of torture were used to extract information from accused persons, exceeding in grim horror anything which had been known in medieval times. In 1936 a new legal code subordinated citizens' rights to the aims of the nation, established severe punishments for many "crimes against the state."

Germany withdrew from the League of Nations in 1934. Her war power was renewed, in violation of the Versailles Treaty. Factories turned out guns and ammunition and military 'planes; shipyards launched new warships. Compulsory two-year military service was introduced. The demilitarized Rhine provinces were occupied and fortified. In 1936, with Mussolini, Hitler sent troops and air formations to Spain to fight with Franco's Nationalists against the Republicans. On March 13, 1938, Austria was overrun and declared a German state.

Meantime, there had arisen a dispute over the German minorities in the Sudeten territories of Czechoslovakia. This crisis came to a head in September 1938, when war with the Western Powers was only averted by the transfer at the Munich Four Power Conference (Britain, France, Italy, Germany), of these territories to Germany. This settlement was enforced upon Czechoslovakia.

In December 1938 the shooting of a German official in Paris by a Jew led to a terrible "pogrom" of the Jews, whose synagogues were burned and their homes and shops pillaged. Huge fines were imposed on them and the ghetto system of the Middle Ages was reintroduced. In March 1939 Hitler invaded Czechoslovakia. Bohemia and Moravia became a vassal Protectorate of the Reich; Slovakia was allowed nominal independence.

By the cession of the Sudetenland Czechoslovakia had lost her fine fortress line defending her from Germany. Her military alliances with France and Russia had collapsed, too. Now Germany felt secure enough for wider aggression.

Six months later, on September 1, 1939, Germany—who had demanded Danzig and a plebiscite

International Graphic Press

HITLER ENTERING PRAGUE IN 1939

In 1938 Czechoslovakia surrendered to Germany her German-populated district of Sudetenland ; but this concession failed to satisfy the German leader Adolf Hitler, and in March 1939 the whole country was occupied by German troops. Hitler is here seen entering Prague, the capital.

in the Polish "corridor," a strip of land giving Poland access to the sea across Pomerania—went to war with Poland, attacking by land and air. British and French ultimatums to Germany were followed by declarations of a state of war by those nations. The broad outline of the ensuing conflict is given under the heading World Wars.

Poland was overrun and beaten in four weeks ; Russian troops marched in from the east ten days before the final surrender, and Poland was divided between Germany and the U.S.S.R. There followed six months of little military action, with the opponents facing each other across their frontiers. In April 1940 Germany invaded Norway and entered Denmark. Norway resisted, and British and French troops landed to help her—only to fight a losing battle until they were evacuated on June 9.

Meanwhile, on May 10, German troops invaded Belgium, and the Netherlands. The French front facing the Ardennes was thinly held by inferior troops, and it broke near Sedan. German armoured columns drove down to the Channel coast and split the northern French and the British armies from the Belgian forces. The Dutch army capitulated on May 15, after the destruction of a large area of Rotterdam by German aerial bombing the day previous. The Belgian army capitulated on the night of May 27–28, heavily out-numbered by the enemy and doomed otherwise to complete destruction. The British army under Lord Gort fought its way down to Dunkirk, when, along with many French soldiers, it was transported to England (May 28–June 3).

France never recovered from the first great defeat on the Meuse. Though successive lines of defence were manned along the great rivers, the Germans outflanked or penetrated these barriers. On June 17 Marshal Pétain asked Germany for armistice terms. Paris had been declared an " open " town on the 13th, and was entered by the Germans on June 14. Italy had declared war upon Britain and France as from June 11. On June 20 the French government asked Italy in turn for an armistice. Armistices were in fact concluded with Germany on June 22 and with Italy on the 24th.

Aerial Attack on Britain Begins

On July 10 there began the aerial Battle of Britain, the story of which is told under Britain. The object was to beat down our air defences, and to open the way for invasion across the Channel. Heavy bombing of Britain by night and day continued until the demands of his invasion of Russia (begun on June 22, 1941) caused Hitler to switch most of his bombers to Russian targets. Before this, however, Germany had joined with Italy to crush Greece (April 6, 1941), and at the same time to conquer Yugoslavia. A British army landed to aid these nations, but the humiliating story of the Norwegian campaign was repeated, and the outnumbered British forces were withdrawn on April 22.

These British forces had been brought over from North Africa, where an army under Lord Wavell had repulsed an Italian force attempting to seize the Suez Canal region. Weakened by this transfer to the Greek theatre of war, the armies defending Egypt had to give ground. Germany sent over a finely equipped and trained Afrika Korps to aid the

Italians; under General (later Field-Marshal) Rommel, this force fought a hammer-and-tongs fight with the British Eighth Army—the tide of battle surging to and fro along the Libyan coast.

In November 1942 Anglo-American forces invaded North Africa in a campaign which was to drive out the Germans from Africa by the following May. In the previous June Rommel's army had reached to within 70 miles of Alexandria, but was stopped at El Alamein by the British Eighth Army. This army (under Montgomery) opened an offensive on October 23–4, 1942, which turned the tables on Rommel and steadily forced back the Germans and Italians—out of Egypt, out of Libya, and into Tunisia. Here, along with the Anglo-American armies, Montgomery's men broke the resistance of the German-Italians. By May 12, 1943, all organized opposition had ceased. French forces in North Africa had joined up with the Allies in bringing about this spectacular defeat of the Germans.

German Failure to Defeat Russia

Now we must turn to the German campaign in Russia. The greed for more territory (what the Germans called *Lebensraum*—living space) seems to have dictated this invasion, which was foreshadowed in Mein Kampf. But there was also the innate and age-long hostility between Germany and Russia. Hitler seems to have thought that if he did not settle accounts with Russia, she would turn upon him when he was engaged with his postponed but none the less inevitable struggle with the British Commonwealth. At first the German armies, in their momentum, struck deeply into Russia. But they were held up near Moscow, and they never succeeded in breaking the defences of the former capital, Leningrad. Russian armies retreated, but generally kept their integrity. When surrounded, they often fought their way out.

Germany had to wage bitter winter campaigns, since she failed to capture the Russian capital. A German force seized Rostov, key to the oil-bearing region of the Caucasus, but the winter of 1941–42 stopped major operations, and Rostov was recaptured. In the spring the Germans renewed their drive to the Caucasus. They overran the Crimea, and in August 1942 they stood before the great city of Stalingrad, on the Volga. Winter again brought a respite to the Russian armies.

Breaking out from Stalingrad in January 1943, they encircled and captured a score of German divisions with many high army commanders. By the beginning of February Germany had here suffered an irretrievable defeat from which her far-flung strategy never recovered. The Caucasus drive had to be halted. Now Russian armies began an offensive along the entire battle front. With some pauses and set-backs, this westward drive continued for nearly two years until southern Russia had been cleared and the Germans defeated in Rumania, Hungary, Poland and Austria.

Yugoslavia was freed by partisan forces under Marshal Tito. In May 1945 the German armies defending Berlin were encircled; after two weeks of street battles the German capital fell, on May 2. By this time Allied armies striking from the west had joined forces with Russians along the River Elbe (April 25). Now we must return to the Mediterranean theatre of war.

The Caucasus thrust had been intended to carry the Nazi armies into Asia Minor, and, given favourable action by Syria and Iran, to allow a join-up with German-Italian armies in Egypt, which was expected to have been conquered by the time the German spear-head from the east had pierced through Palestine. Rommel's defeat at El Alamein, and the disaster at Stalingrad, ended this scheme.

After Montgomery and the Americans had driven the Afrika Korps out of Africa, the Allied armies conquered Sicily and landed in the " foot " of Italy. Here there followed a skilfully fought series of delaying actions by the German commanders—holding on as long as they could before withdrawing to another strong river line. Meanwhile, preparations were being made by both sides for the Allies' invasion of France. This began on the beaches of Normandy, June 6, 1944. Two days earlier, Allied armies had entered Rome. Not until the end of July were the German defences around the Normandy beach-heads broken through. The battle of Normandy ended on August 22 with a decisive defeat for Germany. Then ensued a swift Nazi retreat to and across the Seine. The German garrison of Paris surrendered on August 24. In the meantime U.S. and French forces had landed in southern France and had advanced north.

There followed the advance to the Rhine and its crossing (March 1945), and the penetration of German territory by converging columns of Anglo-American-French forces. On May 4 the Germans in Denmark, the Netherlands and all northern Germany surrendered. Three days later the rest of the German forces in the west surrendered at Reims. Squeezed between the Russian armies on the east and those of Britain, America and France on the west, no other course was open to them. On April 29 the German forces in northern Italy and southern Austria had given in. So ended, miserably, the Nazi dream of world domination. Hitler killed himself on April 30, 1945, in his concrete refuge in Berlin.

Under the military government jointly of Britain, the United States, Russia and France, Germany was now divided into four zones of military Occupation (see map below). Chief purposes of this Occupation were to prepare for the reconstruction of German political life and for Germany's eventual co-operation in world affairs.

But Britain, U.S. and France on the one hand and Russia on the other, failed to agree on many vital issues. Open rupture came, in 1948, with the closing by Russia of the land and water approaches from the west to Berlin.

Withdrawal of the western allies from the former capital was unthinkable, so the British and U.S. authorities put into operation an air service which ensured that all essentials reached the city, until the blockade was raised in September 1949. In the same year Germany was split into two—an eastern republic and a western republic. (See Berlin).

Subject to over-all approval by the Allied High Commission, the western republic (capital at Bonn) enjoyed a certain measure of self-government, its elected parliament having Dr. Adenauer, leader of the Christian Democratic Party, as its Chancellor.

GERMANY 1947
SHOWING ZONES OF OCCUPATION
English Miles
0   50   100   150   200

GERMANY DIVIDED INTO ALLIED ZONES OF OCCUPATION

Following upon the unconditional surrender of German armed forces on May 7, 1945, Germany was divided into British, United States, French and Russian zones of occupation, each power being responsible for its own area. Greater Berlin was also occupied by forces of each of the four Powers and placed under the control of an inter-allied governing body. In December 1946 the British and United States zones in western Germany were united for administration.

A GLANCE at GERMAN PAINTING

Comparatively few Germans have made a name as artists, perhaps because the Teutonic genius is more critical than creative. The most important of those who have achieved distinction in this field, however, are noticed here.

Germany: PAINTERS AND PAINTING. The art of Germany, although producing few famous figures, has long been marked by strong national characteristics, and some of these are traceable in the Middle Ages when the first German painter of note flourished. This was one William of Cologne, the painter of a number of religious works, altar-pieces, etc.; and contemporary with him there arose in the 14th century a school in Bohemia, which was much influenced by Italian painters, and was therefore less national than the Cologne school. Of the latter school the triptych by Stephan Lochner (d. 1451) is the finest work. In the southern Rhineland the names of Conrad Witz (c. 1440–c. 1447) and Martin Schongauer (1445–91) are outstanding. In general, all these artists showed strong Flemish influence, but, meanwhile, Albrecht Dürer (1471–1528) had begun to work.

Dürer was pre-eminently an engraver (*see* Dürer, Albrecht; Engraving), and it is in his engravings that he chiefly shows his German characteristics, namely, a certain brutality, almost coarseness. As a portraitist he holds a high place, but in general his paintings are less important.

Dürer, a man of almost universal accomplishment, left few followers, and only a number of unimportant imitators. More in touch with the direct line of German painting are his own master, Michael Wohlgemuth (1434–1519), a good painter of the Nuremberg school, and Matthias Grünewald, who was active during the end of the 15th and first part of the 16th centuries. He was the painter of some fine religious pictures. Another rather isolated figure is that of Lucas Cranach (1472–1553), one of the best-known of all German painters, who is represented in our own National Gallery. Cranach was more notable as a technician than as a creative artist, yet there is something very pleasing in his little " nudes " drawn and painted with consummate skill, though lacking feeling. Cranach had several sons, of whom Lucas the Younger imitated his father.

Hans Holbein the Elder (c. 1462–1524), though influenced from Italy, did some very fine religious paintings; his son, Hans Holbein the Younger (c. 1497–1543), is far more famous. These two men came from Augsburg. Holbein (as the son is usually called, for short) was less purely German in his art than Dürer, and for that reason his works have far

MASTERPIECE OF CRANACH THE ELDER

One of the few German painters to achieve fame outside his own country, Lucas Cranach the Elder (1472-1553) put an enormous amount of detail into his work, which is pervaded by a slightly grim atmosphere. The title of the above painting is A Rest During the Flight into Egypt. Cranach's second son, who assisted and imitated his father, is known as Cranach the Younger.

HENRY VIII BY HOLBEIN

Brought to England by Sir Thomas More in 1528, Holbein entered the service of Henry VIII in 1536, painting several fine portraits of the king. In the above picture Henry's daughter Mary (later Queen Mary) is also depicted, with Will Somers, the Court jester, in the background.

the admirable Sunny Interior. Yet in his later years he did no work of the same type, confining himself to a representational naturalism; in 1884 he was president of the German Academy. Max Klinger (1857-1920) considered in Germany to be one of the most individual artists, was chiefly a searcher after new symbols. Max Liebermann (1847-1936), in many ways the most important German painter for hundreds of years, was at first a follower of Menzel's naturalism. Later, influenced by the Barbizon school and by Millet, he did for the German peasantry what that painter had done for the French. He founded the " Berlin Secession," and brought Impressionism, which he then (1900) followed, to Germany; yet he was also president of the German Academy, 1920-32. He originated a new German school of deliberately opposite ideals, which came to be known as "Expressionism," and in which the old violence and brutality of truly German art again became visible. Its later followers included Kandinsky, and the Swiss Paul Klee (1879-1940), who is now regarded as one of the leading and most important representatives of the Surrealist movement. Klee worked for many years in Germany, and in 1912 founded with Kandinsky and Marc the movement known as Blaue Reiter. He became an Abstractionist in 1914; love of poetry and music are reflected in his work, which is notable for delicate fantasy and fine draughtsmanship.

Lovis Corinth (1858-1925), whose work formed a transition between Impressionism and Expressionism, was, with Max Slevogt, and Oscar Kokoschka, (born 1886), classed as decadent under Hitler. During the Nazi period (1933-45) all artists save those content to glorify the totalitarian state had to make way for third-rate exponents.

less coarseness. Whether as a painter of religious pictures, as a portraitist, or as an engraver he is a great master; in our National Gallery is his superb Duchess of Milan. Holbein is of especial interest to us, not only because of his long sojourn in England, when the glorious series of portrait drawings now at Windsor was made, but also because he had at the same time a great influence on our painting and especially on our miniature painting. Holbein did several fine portraits of Henry VIII. Of the masters of the Augsburg school he is the one who best assimilated the lessons of Italian art. He defines the forms with a free touch and models them with light shadows. What he reveals—faces, hands, flowers—is put forward by this painter with a supreme degree of clarity.

Italian influence was established early in the 17th century. The Thirty Years' War (1618-48) paralysed German art, but the Italo-Teutonic alliance maintained its " art-for-art's-sake " attitude.

Anton Raphael Mengs (1728-79) was the founder of German classicism, working largely in Rome. His classical compositions are of less merit than his portraits, especially those in pastel. Of German origin, too, was Angelica Kauffman, (1741-1807), who painted classical allegories, though she is usually ranked with the English School. But in general, German art remained academic producing few figures of importance.

Three men stand out in the 19th century; the first of these, Adolf Menzel (1815-1905), was a fine engraver, and the illustrator of many books, but is notable chiefly for some paintings which he did about 1842, and in which he appears as the forerunner, in many ways, of Impressionism. He painted a series of pictures of the Life of Frederick the Great, but is seen at his best in his paintings of daily life. About 1845, under the influence of Constable, he painted

W F Mansell

KOKOSCHKA'S STUDY OF STILL-LIFE

Influenced by the French artist Cézanne (1839-1906) and the Dutch painter Van Gogh (1853-90), German art at the beginning of the 20th century lost some of its former ponderousness, as exemplified in this simple arrangement of a vase of flowers set before an open window by Oskar Kokoschka (born 1886).

The LANGUAGE of GOETHE & SCHILLER

*German language and literature are somewhat similar in history and content
to those of England. Here we may read of the great instrument into which
Germany's writers welded the somewhat unwieldy German tongue.*

Germany: PROSE AND POETRY. At the first appearance of the Germans, or Teutons, in world history, about the beginning of the Christian era, they form three distinct groups with corresponding tongues—the East Germanic or Gothic, the North Germanic or Scandinavian, and the West Germanic, from which originated primitive German, English, Dutch, etc. This primitive German continued to split up into dialects as the tribes settled permanently in various districts; but the chief dialects were the High German of the mountainous region of central and southern Germany, and the Low German of the lowland country in the north. High German prevailed over the dialect of the plains, and it is High German which is the official and literary language of the Germany of today.

German is a simple and direct language. The old Gothic characters, in which some German books are still printed, may offer a difficulty at first, but it is soon mastered The beginner is usually struck by the great length of many German words. But many of these are compounds, and when split up into their several parts they prove easy to understand and have a remarkable power of expression. Thus, " Volksschullehrerseminar " looks almost hopeless with its 23 letters, until we divide it thus : " Volks-schul-lehrer-seminar." Then we discover, by translating bit by bit, that it means " public-school-teachers' college."

Then there is the practice, so common in German syntax, of reserving the verb or part of the verb for the end of the sentence. This prevents us from jumping at the meaning and in this respect is a blessing in disguise.

The German barbarians of the 1st century had a rough poetry. But not until the 4th century do we find a book written in a Teutonic tongue. This book was a translation of the Bible made by Ulfilas, the native missionary to the Goths. Ulfilas was obliged first to invent the Gothic alphabet by combining Greek, Latin and Runic letters. The tongue of those ancient Goths, as we here find it, possessed much of the beauty and roughness which characterize the German language today.

The Nibelungenlied and other Epics

But, though Ulfilas began the conversion of the Germans to the Christian religion, their poets continued for centuries to sing of the old gods, of Brunhild and Gudrun, and the flying Valkyries, as well as of mighty historic figures such as Attila (Etzel) the Hun. The Nibelungenlied of the 13th century is the most famous of these dreams of gods and heroes, and has been the source of much modern German literature.

A lighter note, however, was heard alongside these resounding epics, the music of the " minnesongs," or love lyrics of knighthood. These dwindled finally in the wholly mechanical " mastersongs," composed by rule. Yet the same period (15th and 16th centuries) in which these stiff and dreary mastersongs were being manufactured was the very heyday of the delightful German " folksongs "—simple, abiding music, by poets whose names are unknown.

About this time also German prose began to develop, and German drama, too, chiefly in the hands of the clergy. Church plays grew into great and solemn spectacles, of which the celebrated Passion Play of Oberammergau is an impressive survival. And when the Reformation overtook the Church, religion found even more beautiful expression in the fine hymns of Martin Luther. But it was Luther's translation of the Bible which had the most important effect. This did for the German language what the works of Dante, Petrarch and Boccaccio did for Italian, or what the Authorized Version of the Bible did for English. It fixed a standard language from a confusion of dialects. Modern German dates largely from Luther's works. The influence of Luther's Bible and the invention of printing made it desirable that books should appeal to as wide a public as possible.

As the years went on, religious disputes became angrier; the Thirty Years' War (1618–48) broke out, and the light of literature vanished in its horrors. National feeling decayed, and a weak and war-worn generation mimicked French thought and customs in almost every field.

Literary Giants of the 18th Century

Therefore it was not until the time of Frederick the Great (1740–86) that German literature flourished again. This king of Prussia honoured French authors, notably Voltaire, far more than he did the rising generation of German writers. But Frederick raised Germany from the dust, and gave to German genius a sense of pride and independence which permitted it to break with French and English models and create beauty out of its own substance.

In this century glow the names of Klopstock, Lessing, Wieland, Goethe, Schiller, Richter, the brothers Grimm, Fouqué, von Kleist, Heine, and many more. Under the influence of English and French philosophers, such as Locke and Voltaire, whose views Frederick broadly championed, the Germans were led into new paths of thought.

To Klopstock goes the honour of moulding a new poetic language. In 1748 he published the first cantos of Der Messias, a religious epic inspired by Milton. Lessing, the first of the great German classic authors, is the master of style, the foremost German critic, who preached the harmony of content and form, and banished the long pages of description and allegory. Wieland, epic poet and novelist, paved the way for free expression of emotion, and ushered in a new and neater wit.

Then came the influence of Rousseau, the Swiss who set France on her way to the Revolution. Aided largely by the work of Herder, this influence produced in Germany what is termed the " storm and stress " movement. People began to talk of the perfect freedom of the individual, and to rebel at tradition and authority. Politically, the movement came to nothing in Germany, but in literature the effect of this influence was enormous.

Writers rejected the classical laws of composition under the impression that they were proceeding in the manner of Shakespeare ! Goethe played a considerable part in the movement, and likewise the poet Schiller, his shining contemporary.

But presently came the sobering effect of the philosopher, Immanuel Kant (1724–1804) with his stern doctrine of duty, followed by Goethe's swing back toward classicism. Perhaps the laughing irony of the novels of Jean Paul Richter (1763–1825) also had something to do with sweeping away the final vestiges of the Sturm und Drang or "storm and stress" movement.

However, something very similar to the "storm and stress" again developed during the Romantic period which followed. This was partly due to the philosophy of Immanuel von Fichte (1796–1879), who denied Kant's theories, and of Friedrich von Schelling (1775–1854), who offered the imagination for as good a guide in life as the intellect. The Romantics were individualists, obscure and capricious; but, on the other hand, they freed the wings of poetry and unveiled the beauties of folklore. And, above all, from them came Heinrich Heine (1797–1856) the greatest lyric poet after Goethe.

During that period there were great names— Wagner (1813–83), the dramatist-musician ; Schopenhauer (1788–1860), the brilliant philosopher; Theodor Storm (1817–88), famous for his dainty little idyll Immensee (Bee-Lake); Nietzsche (1844–1900), the apostle of the superman; Sudermann (1857–1928) and Hauptmann (1862–1946), the dramatists of modern realism.

In the 19th century German scholarship reached great heights, and some of the books of learning of the time are more important than many novels and plays and poems that were written. Thus the great historian Leopold von Ranke (1795–1886) raised the study of history to a new level by insisting upon the investigation of original documents. The Latin scholar Theodor Mommsen (1817–1903) was a storehouse of knowledge about ancient Rome. Ulrich von Wilamowitz-Möllendorff (1848–1931) contributed greatly to our knowledge of Greek life and literature. So also in archaeology and anthropology and philosophy, and in all the sciences, the Germans of the 19th century, by their surpassing thoroughness and industry, made great advances.

The beginning of the 20th century, with its trend towards social criticism, marked the entry of women writers into German literature. Gabriele Reuter, Clara Viebig, and Ellen Key were prominent. German writers of this period absorbed literary ideas in vogue in France, Russia and Scandinavia, and under this stimulus created the naturalistic novel.

Many of the books that met with success in Germany after the First World War (1914–18) reflected the nation's later experiences. Thus All Quiet on the Western Front, which Eric Maria Remarque (b. 1898) published in 1929, echoed the disillusionment of the generation that had gone through the war; and something of the same feeling is seen in the writings of Ernst Toller (1893–1939), of Fritz von Unruh (b. 1885), and of Stefan Zweig (1881–1942). Other German writers turned to the past. Lion Feuchtwanger (b. 1884) is best known for his historical novel, Jew Süss (1924); and Emil Ludwig (b. 1881) has written many biographies of famous men, such as Goethe, Bismarck, William II, Abraham Lincoln, and Napoleon, while to Arnold Zweig (b. 1887) we owe clever studies of many great authors. An outstanding name in modern European poetry is that of Rainer Maria Rilke (1875–1926).

We must not overlook Erich Kästner, whose book Emil and the Detectives is known to many English-speaking children.

On account of their Jewish origin, or " Left " or liberal political views, many of these contemporary German authors were exiled under the Hitler regime. The Nazi period was sterile. Hitler and his followers tried to produce a literature that should glorify the totalitarian state. Leading German writers such as Thomas Mann (b. 1875), Leonhard Frank and Franz Werfel (1890–1945) were driven into exile. All literature which had a humanist, liberal bias was suppressed, and many writers and poets were sent to concentration camps.

Between the First and Second World Wars a generation had grown up which was fed upon the destructive doctrine of National Socialism, and literature had scarcely any place in Nazi Germany. The Second World War left the country in ruins; civilized conditions which are necessary if art is to endure had collapsed not only in Germany, but throughout a great part of Europe. It was henceforth not so much a question of the survival of literature, but of the life of the community itself.

E.N.A.; New York Times Photos

FRANZ WERFEL AND ERNST TOLLER

As with many other German writers the First World War (1914–18) and the subsequent political strife gave the writings of Franz Werfel (left) a revolutionary tendency. The tragic death of Ernst Toller (right) in 1939 robbed drama and literature of one of the most courageous thinkers.

Man's DEADLIEST FOE—the MICROBE

Here we learn about the tiny organisms that cause many of our bodily ills, and of the ceaseless battle waged against them by the blood, aided often by the weapons of medical science.

Germs IN DISEASE. Most diseases, we now know, are due to the presence in the body of exceedingly tiny vegetable or animal organisms which produce poisons that attack the system. These poisons interfere with the functions of the body, cripple or destroy its various organs, bring about decay and often death. This is believed to apply to nearly all diseases in men, beasts, and even trees and other plants, although the germs of some diseases have not yet been discovered.

The world about us—soil, air and water, plants and animals—is filled with millions of invisible living beings called *micro-organisms*, from the Greek *mikros* meaning "small." These may be of the vegetable type, called *bacteria*, or the animal type called *protozoa*; there are still smaller bodies, called *viruses*, which act in many ways like the microscopic plants and animals. All three are often considered together as "germs." Not all germs are harmful to Man; indeed, many are his most active servants in the cultivation of crops and the destruction of putrefying matter. But others start a work of destruction as soon as they enter the human body in the air breathed into the lungs, with the food we eat, or through the pores or cuts in the skin. These are the disease germs. Their normal habitat is not in the human system, and it is only when an individual's normal powers of resistance to disease are weakened that such germs become harmful.

The development of powerful compound microscopes in the 17th and 18th centuries had shown the existence of many micro-organisms, but it was not until the middle of the 19th century that their activity in producing disease was established. At that time scientists observed that a particular form of bacillus (rod-shaped bacterium) was always found in the blood of cattle and sheep afflicted with anthrax, a violent disorder that killed thousands of the animals every year and even attacked human beings. But this observation was merely a beginning. To prove that these bacilli were the real cause of anthrax, they had first to be isolated, that is, separated from all other substances found in the blood of the diseased sheep or cattle.

This was done in 1863, by Robert Koch (1843-1910), a noted German bacteriologist. The anthrax bacilli next had to be grown in what is called a "pure culture"—that is, allowed to multiply under artificial surroundings without losing their poisonous strength. It was not until 1876 that Koch accomplished this and arranged the final conclusive

test. A quantity of the liquid containing the anthrax bacilli was injected into the blood of a few healthy sheep. Within a few days all had contracted anthrax and had died. Koch also discovered the bacillus of tuberculosis, and isolated the comma bacillus, the germ of cholera.

The anthrax experiment started a long chain of successful discoveries and tests which are continuing to this day. Scientists have isolated, one by one, the bacteria of blood-poisoning, erysipelas, cholera, typhoid fever, bubonic plague, pneumonia, meningitis, diphtheria, tetanus (lockjaw), tuberculosis, leprosy, whooping-cough, and a score of other diseases. So much for disease germs belonging to the *plant* group of organism. Among the ailments which have been traced to *animal* organisms (protozoa) are malaria, amoebic dysentery, kala-azar, and African sleeping sickness. Some diseases, such as chicken pox, small pox, yellow fever, infantile paralysis and perhaps measles, influenza and the common cold, are caused by viruses.

Certain diseases like beri-beri and pellagra appear to be due to a faulty diet which lacks an essential vitamin; other ailments are traced to the failure of organs to function properly, but even in such instances the possibility of germ influence has been suspected.

Disease germs do their deadly work by forming poisons or "toxins" in the system. The symptoms of a disease depend upon the nature of these poisons and the sites in the body occupied by the germs which generate them. Some germs remain in the blood stream, which carries their poisons to all parts of the system. Others seek out special organs like the lungs, the stomach, the liver, the intestines; and the effects of their poisons are felt most powerfully in these organs. Certain toxins, like those of hydrophobia, attack principally the nerves, spinal cord, or brain.

Probably the greatest benefit resulting from the discovery of the germ theory was the fact that it solved most of the mystery of how diseases spread. By studying the habits of germs, scientists discovered how they grow, how they travel from place to place, and how they enter the human body. Few disease germs can live long outside the body, though some may live for a time in water, or multiply in milk and food. The meat of diseased animals may carry bacteria.

Germs on the skin may be introduced into the blood and tissues by a cut or a scratch, and may thus cause disease. Abscesses, erysipelas, tetanus

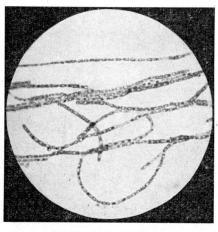

GERMS OF ANTHRAX

One of the most deadly diseases that attack animals is anthrax; here are anthrax bacilli, very highly magnified. The black spots on the bacilli are the spores by which they breed.

and blood-poisoning are caused in this manner. But, for the most part, bacterial diseases are transmitted by contact with persons suffering from the disease, or contact with "carriers"; carriers are persons not themselves ill, but who harbour (often in the throat) germs capable of causing disease in others.

Perhaps the most amazing of all these discoveries was that many deadly germs enter the body through the bites of insects. Malaria and yellow fever, for instance, are transmitted by certain types of mosquitoes (*see* Mosquito). Sleeping sickness is carried from person to person by the tsetse fly. The bubonic plague is transferred to human beings by fleas which have bitten diseased rats. Typhus fever, a scourge which often followed great wars, is carried by the common body-louse.

Not every disease germ which enters the human body actually causes trouble; otherwise we should be ill most of the time, for we take in germs with nearly every breath and every mouthful of food and drink. In the blood and tissues of all healthy persons there is a tendency to resist and destroy unwelcome visitors. Many persons, in fact, seem to be naturally immune to some maladies; the germs can secure no foothold in them. It is when the body is allowed to weaken through bad habits, overwork, improper food, insufficient exercise, etc., that microbes find themselves able to launch their deadly work.

Few germs are able to penetrate the human skin. The favourite breeding places of the *streptococci*, to which group the pus germs belong, are the teeth and the mucous membrane of the nose, mouth and throat. And these streptococci not only produce a great many disorders themselves, but they are a sort of advance agent, paving the way for other disease germs. Breathed in from the air, they find lodging perhaps in the folds of the tonsils, and if the tonsils have been weakened by mouth-breathing, by dust-laden air, or by exposure to extreme heat or cold, the germs may thrive and start forming pus, which soon gets into the blood stream and infects the whole body. Or it may be that the teeth, through improper care, become refuges for germs. Certain forms of heart trouble and rheumatism have been thought to be caused by bacteria entering the blood through the tissues about diseased teeth.

Many of the diseases caused by viruses are both dangerous and highly contagious. They can be fought by the same sorts of treatment used for other germ diseases. There seems to be a helpful virus, called *bacteriophage* (bacterium-eater), which attacks and destroys bacteria themselves. Medical science is now trying to use such bacteriophages in the process of combating diseases.

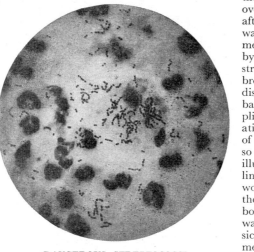

DANGEROUS STREPTOCOCCI
Producers of a great many disorders, including pneumonia, streptococci consist of rounded bodies occurring in chains (above). The favourite breeding places of these germs are the teeth, nose, mouth and throat, where they act as advance agents of disease.

There are three main ways of fighting the diseases caused by germs : (1) by the general destruction of the germs; (2) by preventing them from entering the human body; (3) by overcoming their evil effects, after they have made their way in. The first of these methods is usually carried on by public sanitation, which strives to do away with the breeding places of germs by disposing of sewage and garbage, by keeping water supplies free from contamination, by regular inspection of milk and other foods, and so on. The second way is illustrated by personal cleanliness, using antiseptics in wounds, the proper care of the mouth, nose and throat; boiling suspected drinking water, and by fumigating sick-rooms, etc. The last method includes the whole field of curative medicine and surgery, with particular emphasis on vaccine and serum treatments, and the use of specific drugs. (*See also* under Hygiene).

Geyser. (Pron. gē′-zer). Hot springs which erupt every now and then are called geysers. They occur in certain regions of the earth which were formerly volcanic and which have retained considerable heat near the surface.

A typical geyser consists of a crater with a funnel-shaped opening into the earth. From this opening, at fairly regular intervals, a column of hot water and steam is thrown out like a fountain, sometimes not more than a few feet, and sometimes to a height of 250 feet. It is possible to boil an egg in the waters of some geysers, and in some the native folk cook their potatoes. Until about 1870 Iceland was considered the principal seat of geysers, but we now know that Yellowstone Park, in Wyoming, in the United States, contains more geysers than all the rest of the world. New Zealand also has many.

The theory of the action of geysers put forward by the German chemist Bunsen, of Heidelberg, who went to Iceland in 1847 and made an elaborate study of the Great Geyser in that island, is still accepted in the main. The water in the outlet pipe of the geyser becomes heated until the lower portion reaches a temperature above boiling point. Eventually this " flashes " into steam, causing some of the water nearer the surface to be forced out violently. After this the water cools for a time, then it gradually becomes hotter, and the process begins again.

Mineral deposits are often found around geysers. These are due to the cooling of the water and to evaporation, but chiefly to the presence of minute plants (*algae*) which extract silica and other minerals from the water. The beautiful colours of the deposits are also due to the presence of these plants. Some geysers throw up mud instead of water. The name geyser is also applied to domestic appliances for heating water rapidly by gas or electricity.

Ghent (Pron. gent), BELGIUM. Sometimes called the City of Flowers from the extensive flower nurseries on its outskirts, Ghent is a picturesque city, with a network of canals spanned by more than 200 bridges, situated at the junction of the rivers Lys and Scheldt, about 31 miles north-west of Brussels. It is the third city of Belgium and in its streets past and present rub shoulders, for it is a thriving modern town that still retains much of its old charm.

Ghent is famous for its cathedral of St. Bavon; there are also some old guild-houses and monasteries, and a nunnery founded in the 13th century. The cathedral, which also dates from the 13th century, is not remarkable for its architecture, but it possesses numerous features of interest, including the famous altarpiece, The Adoration of the Lamb, painted by the Flemish artist Van Eyck (1366–1426). In the centre of the city still stands the belfry in which used to hang the bell Roland that called the citizens to arms at the approach of danger.

Perhaps the most picturesque building in Ghent is the imposing medieval castle of the Counts of Flanders, which is almost surrounded by water and is one of the finest examples of a medieval fortress in Europe. Founded in the 9th century, it was re-built by Count Philip of Alsace in 1180. Here was born John of Ghent (1340–99), or as we in Britain describe him, John of Gaunt, son of the English King Edward III, and uncle of Richard II.

Connected with the North Sea by a ship canal, Ghent exports agricultural and manufactured products in addition to flowers, large quantities of orchids, azaleas and other greenhouse plants being grown for overseas markets. Though not so notable for its manufactures as in the Middle Ages, when it was a centre of the cloth trade, the city has many important industries, chief among them being cotton-spinning, cotton-printing, flax-spinning, tanning, and sugar-refining. Other products are tobacco, paper and machinery.

During the Second World War (1939–45) the city was bombed by the Germans in May 1940, and occupied by them on May 24. Railway yards and factories were the targets for Allied aircraft May–July 1944, and there was some fighting in and about Ghent September 5–10, 1944, before the Germans were driven out by British troops. The estimated population is 161,400.

Ghiberti, LORENZO (1378–1455). Amongst the most eminent sculptors of the Italian Renaissance was Ghiberti (pron. gē-bêr´-te), who was born at Florence in 1378. His stepfather, Bartolucchio di Michele, taught him how to draw, and how to do ornamental metal work, in particular the art of working in gold. Ghiberti also learned painting. He had executed a fine fresco at Rimini, about 1401, when a competition was held at Florence to choose the sculptor for a pair of large doors in bas-relief worthy to rank with those earlier executed by Andrea Pisano about 1330, illustrating the life of St. John and the eight cardinal virtues, at the Baptistery of St. John.

From among the many entrants, seven were chosen to make a trial design on a given subject—the sacrifice of Isaac; they were Ghiberti, Brunelleschi, Simone da Colle, Niccolò Spinelli d'Arezzo, Jacopo della Quercia, Francesco di Valdambrino and Niccolò Lamberti. Only two designs have been preserved, those of Brunelleschi and Ghiberti, Ghiberti's being in the National Museum at Florence. These were the designs which reached the final selection. It was difficult to choose between them ; Brunelleschi was so impressed by his rival's work that he asked the 34 judges that the task of designing the gates might be left solely to Ghiberti.

These doors or gates are on the north of the Baptistery, and comprise 20 panels giving scenes in the life of Christ; the work, begun in 1403, was completed in 1424 with the assistance of Bartolucchio, and was cast in bronze.

The following year Ghiberti was asked to undertake a second pair of doors for the same building, this time on the west side. It is on these that Ghiberti's real fame rests, for his work on them, comprising 10 panels of Old Testament subjects, framed with small details of exquisite design, was so magnificent that it far surpassed, in beauty and skill in casting, his own earlier work. They are known as the Paradise Gates, for their sculptured beauty is without parallel.

The study of the laws of perspective was rather new at the time they were modelled, and these doors are remarkable for the skilful execution of various scenes on different planes. The borders of the panels consist of wonderful tiny statuettes and busts (two of the latter are of Ghiberti himself and his stepfather, who helped him on these doors also); there

GHENT'S FORTRESS OF LE RABOT

One of the finest of the many medieval buildings in the interesting old Belgian city of Ghent is the fortress of Le Rabot, which was constructed in the 15th century and somewhat altered in 1872. Ghent is the capital of the province of East Flanders and among its industries are cotton and flax spinning, tanning and sugar-refining.

O.B.L.U.T.

is, too, a decorative frieze of birds and fruits. This set of doors was finished in 1452. Ghiberti died in Florence on December 1, 1455.

Giants. Men have always been strangely ready to believe in things which they have not seen, and in earlier days a belief in the existence of giants seems to have been widely entertained. Legends like that of the one-eyed Cyclops are common in Europe and Asia, and are retained in the nursery stories like Jack and the Beanstalk. Goliath of the Bible was reputed to be a giant, eight feet nine inches tall.

Scientists and archaeologists are agreed that there never were real giants on the earth, but some individuals have grown to a great size, and have been called giants. One of the largest of which there is record was the Russian, Machnow, who appeared at the London Hippodrome in 1905. He was nine feet three inches tall.

In the museum of the Royal College of Surgeons there was a skeleton of a man who died in 1783, aged 22, and was eight feet two inches in height. The disease called acromegaly, which produces a form of giantism and to which many giants have succumbed, is characterized by excessive lengthening of the bones of the hands, feet and head.

Giant's Causeway. One of the most remarkable of the natural wonders of Britain is the Giant's Causeway. Situated on the northern coast of County Antrim, Northern Ireland, amid magnificent cliff scenery, the Causeway is a promontory formed of about 40,000 reddish basalt columns, most of them pentagonal (five-sided) or hexagonal (having six sides). The geological explanation is that these were formed by lava thrown up by volcanoes long ago, the shape being due to the contraction and cracking of the rock while it was cooling. In the Little Causeway is the Wishing Well, a drink from which entitles the visitor to three wishes in the so-called Wishing Chair in the Middle Causeway. It is the Grand Causeway, however, that contains the finest rock formations. There are also great terrace-like cliffs near by. Inevitably a host of legends have sprung up concerning the

W. Lawrence

GIANT'S CAUSEWAY IN COUNTY ANTRIM

According to legend the Giant's Causeway (above), in Northern Ireland, was built to enable the Irish giant Finn MacCool to cross to the isle of Staffa in the Hebrides. Geologically, the Causeway is the result of the strange crystallization of molten basalt, many millions of years ago. Most of the columns have five or six sides.

origin of this romantic spot. One of them says that Finn MacCool, a Celtic giant, built the Causeway to enable him to cross to the Hebrides.

Gibbon, EDWARD (1737–94). Author of one of the great books of the world, The Decline and Fall of the Roman Empire, and a fine historian, Gibbon was born at Putney, London, on April 27, 1737. He was educated at Westminster School, London, and at Magdalen College, Oxford. In 1753 he went to Lausanne in Switzerland, where he continued his studies. Setting out on a tour of Europe in 1763, he passed part of his time in Italy, and while he was in Rome the idea of The Decline and Fall came to him.

The task of writing this work proved a tremendous undertaking; it was four years before the first volume was published, and a further 12 years elapsed before the appearance of the final volume. This history falls into two parts, the first of which is extremely detailed, and the second is a sketch covering 800 years, which falls short in knowledge and accuracy. Nevertheless, the book won for Gibbon world-wide fame. He died in London on January 16, 1794.

National Portrait Gallery

EDWARD GIBBON

After a period spent in travelling in Europe and writing on literary topics, Gibbon began his life-work in 1772, though the first volume of The Decline and Fall of the Roman Empire was not published until 1776.

Gibbon. The smallest of the Man-like apes is the gibbon. It is rarely more than 3 feet in height, and its fore limbs are very long, the fingers touching the ground when it stands up. It runs upright on its hind legs, the fore limbs being used almost exclusively as arms. With them the gibbon swings itself from tree to tree in the jungle, while even on a branch 50 feet above the ground it runs surely on its hind feet alone. Its habit of standing, walking, and running in an upright position has affected the whole structure of the gibbon's body, so that it shows a marked difference from that of the monkeys which move about on all fours, and approximates more nearly to Man's. And, above all, this habit has resulted in the gibbon losing its tail, since this is no longer needed to hang on by.

It inhabits the great jungles and forests of Malaya and the neighbouring countries, there being several species, of which the siamang (*Hylobates syndactylus*) is the largest. Gibbons vary in colour from black to grey; their food consists chiefly of fruit, young shoots, insects and small birds. The animal has comparatively little importance other than as a scientific curiosity which may, perhaps, give us some idea of the primitive form from which earliest Man was descended.

Gibbons, GRINLING (1648–1720). Although he was born at Rotterdam, the Netherlands, of Dutch parentage, on April 4, 1648, Gibbons is always regarded as an English wood carver.

One day in the year 1671 John Evelyn, the diarist, was walking across a field near his home, Sayes Court, at Deptford, then outside London.

On his walk he passed by a house and looking in through the window saw there Grinling Gibbons, poor and unknown, carving wood at a table. His beautiful work attracted Evelyn's attention, and he went in to speak to the carver. Evelyn at once saw the quality of the work, and it was he, later on, who brought Gibbons to public notice and secured him royal recognition. Working for the king, Charles II, and for Sir Christopher Wren, the architect of St. Paul's Cathedral, London, Gibbons did much statuary, but it is as the greatest of all English carvers in wood that he is now remembered.

Much of Gibbons's carving fortunately remains. Notable pieces are the choir stalls of St. Paul's Cathedral; a ceiling at Petworth, in Sussex, perhaps his finest work ; and carvings in some of Wren's churches and in great houses all over the country. He was specially fond of depicting natural objects, such as flowers, fruit and birds, spending hours over the slightest detail; yet when he gave his attention to subjects such as lace he amazed everyone with his ingenuity. Besides the work mentioned, there are fine pieces by him in the Victoria and Albert Museum, London, especially a superb lace cravat intricately carved in lime wood. His statues, which are not of such a high standard, included two of his royal patron—at Chelsea and the Royal Exchange, London—and one of James II, in Whitehall. Gibbons died on August 3, 1720.

Gibraltar. The towering rock at the most southerly point of Spain is Gibraltar, the British colony, fortress and naval base. Its position is one of immense military importance, because it guards the entrance to the Mediterranean and the short sea route through the Suez Canal to Australia and the Far East. The Rock is 1,408 feet high and is connected to the mainland by an isthmus one and a half miles long and a mile wide. It has an area of nearly two square miles. The Strait of Gibraltar, 12 miles wide, separates this British possession from Ceuta in North Africa.

For more than 200 years Gibraltar has been a Crown Colony of Great Britain, and the fortifications are so strong that the rock is considered impregnable. The eastern side is so steep as to be secure from assault. Its western side is bounded by the Bay of Gibraltar, where is situated the town, and at the northern end of the colony is an open

Topical

GIBRALTAR, A BRITISH MEDITERRANEAN STRONGHOLD
At the southern extremity of Spain is the British fortress and town of Gibraltar. This aerial view, taken from the south, shows the harbour on the left, the almost sheer cliffs on the eastern side, and Spain in the far distance. The rock itself is honeycombed with underground passages, storage chambers, barracks and gun emplacements.

space, part of which, lying between the British and Spanish frontiers, is neutral ground, and as such is uninhabited.

Gibraltar and the opposing height on the African coast were called by the Greeks the Pillars of Hercules, and were once thought to mark the western limits of the world. The promontory takes its name from three Moorish words Jebel-al-Tarik, meaning the Hill of Tarik, Tarik being the name of the Moorish chief who led his troops across the strait in A.D. 711 and built a fort on the rock. In 1704 Gibraltar was captured from the Spaniards by the British, becoming a British possession by the Treaty of Utrecht in 1713. The fortress has endured many sieges, the longest being that of 1779-83, when the garrison held out against a force of French and Spaniards.

During the Second World War (1939-45) new batteries were mounted, and further tunnels and chambers were blasted out of the rock, considerably extending the existing works. Hospitals, barracks, offices and vast store rooms were built u n d e r g r o u n d to make the fortress invulnerable to attacks from the air. In September 1940 Gibraltar was bombed by Vichy French (pro-German) aircraft, and the next month Italian midget submarines made an unsuccessful attack on the harbour. The estimated population of the Colony is 19,200.

Gilbert and Sullivan. The remark-

able series of popular light operas, in the production of which Sir W. S. Gilbert was associated with Sir Arthur Sullivan as music composer and Richard D'Oyly Carte as theatrical manager, started in 1875 at the Royalty Theatre, London. William Schwenk Gilbert (1836–1911), English humorist, was the son of a novelist, and was born in London on November 18, 1836. He began his career as a Civil Servant, and later was called to the bar. In 1861 he started to contribute articles and drawings to Fun, in which his Bab Ballads, collected in 1869 and 1873, appeared. Then followed several burlesques and three fairy plays, The Palace of Truth, 1870, The Wicked World, 1873, and Broken Hearts, 1875; a classical romance, Pygmalion and Galatea, 1871; and two comedies, Tom Cobb, 1875, and Engaged, 1877. Gilbert also wrote several serious plays and short stories. Knighted in 1907, he met a tragic death by drowning at Harrow, Middlesex, on May 29, 1911.

Sir Arthur Seymour Sullivan (1842–1900), English composer, was the son of an army bandmaster, and was born in London on May 13, 1842. As a child he was a proficient performer on wind instruments. At the age of 12 he entered the choir of the Chapel Royal, London, and from 1856 to 1861 he studied at the Royal Academy of Music in London, and at Leipzig, Germany. He experienced

no difficulties in getting his early works performed and he sprang into immediate popularity with his music to The Tempest in 1862. His settings of Shakespeare's songs increased his popularity. In 1864 his ballet, L'Ile Enchantée, was performed at Covent Garden, London, where he was in the same year appointed organist.

Sullivan first made his name as a composer of comic opera with his music to Box and Cox, produced in 1867. After this he turned to serious subjects, his first oratorio, The Prodigal Son, being heard in 1869. In 1871 he returned to the stage with Thespis, the first light opera in which he had the collaboration of W. S. Gilbert.

Sullivan extended his reputation in many directions, his other compositions ranging from the part song, Oh Hush thee, My Baby, to a setting of the hymn, Onward, Christian Soldiers, and included a festival Te Deum, 1872; The Light of the World oratorio, 1873; and the music for The Merry Wives of Windsor, 1875. He was appointed in 1876 first director of the National

GILBERT AND SULLIVAN
Famous in the annals of British entertainment was the partnership of Sir William Gilbert (left) and Sir Arthur Sullivan (right). They collaborated in composing comic operas, Gilbert writing the words and Sullivan the music.

Russell; Elliott & Fry

Training School, later the Royal College of Music, and, knighted in 1883, acted as conductor of the Philharmonic Society, 1885–87. The oratorio, The Golden Legend, 1886, based on Longfellow's poem, achieved an unexpected success in this same period, of which, however, the best-known production is the song, The Lost Chord, 1878, which was written while Sullivan watched through the night at the bedside of his dying brother.

In 1891 Sullivan turned to grand opera, a field hitherto never successfully explored by an Englishman. At tremendous expense his opera, Ivanhoe, was produced by D'Oyly Carte, but it proved a failure. Sullivan's remaining compositions include songs, one symphony, incidental music to Macbeth, Henry VIII and the Merchant of Venice, and also some church music.

For 20 years Gilbert and Sullivan worked together in harmony, producing a series of light operas which never seem to lose their charm, despite their repeated revival.

Trial by Jury was produced at The Royalty in 1875; The Sorcerer followed at the Opéra Comique, London, in 1877; H.M.S. Pinafore in 1878; Pirates of Penzance in 1880; and Patience in 1881. At the Savoy Iolanthe appeared in 1882; Princess Ida in 1884; The Mikado in 1885; Ruddigore, 1887; The Yeomen of the Guard, 1888; The Gondoliers, 1889; Utopia Limited, 1893; and The Grand Duke, 1896.

The audiences of their own day possibly appreciated the satire of Gilbert's words better than those of later times, on whom much of the humour is necessarily lost and to whom Sullivan's music is probably the greater attraction. Nevertheless, words and music have never been more perfectly welded to form one delightful whole. Of the operas themselves perhaps The Mikado has proved the most popular, but Patience is the most brilliantly written, and The Yeoman of the Guard the most poetical.

Sullivan was seized by illness when writing his opera The Emerald Isle, and died on November 22, 1900, before it was complete. Sir Edward German finished this opera in 1901.

Ginger. The history of this herb goes back to a remote period in India. The Greeks and Romans imported it, and during the Middle Ages it was next in value among the spices to pepper, a pound costing as much as a sheep. It is an important commercial crop in the sub-continent of India, in China, West Africa, the West Indies, and in Central America. Jamaica ginger is the finest and most valuable.

Ginger spice is made from the powdered rootstocks (rhizomes) of a perennial reed-like plant, *Zingiber officinale*, similar in appearance to the iris. Ginger is marketed in two forms, preserved or green ginger, and dried or cured ginger. Preserved ginger is kept in a sugar syrup or honey. For dried ginger the root is dug up after the leaves of the plant have withered. When the skin is left on it is known as black ginger; when it has been removed before drying, it is white ginger. The essence of ginger used in flavouring is a tincture of ginger and alcohol.

Another important member of the ginger family is turmeric, whose powdered roots are used as a yellow dyestuff, as a condiment (especially in curry powder), and in medicine.

Gingko. (Pron. gingk'-gō *or* jingk-gō). Usually called the maidenhair tree, the curious leaves of this tree (*Ginkgo biloba*) resemble fronds of a maidenhair fern. A native of China and Japan, it is the sole survivor of a group once widely distributed over the world. It is a graceful tree, with numerous slender branches, which form a cone-shaped head. There are specimens in Kew Gardens, Surrey; these are mainly the tall, slender male trees; the females, which in Japan bear small cones, are broader and less tall.

Giotto (*c.* 1266–1337). Known as the Father of the Italian Renaissance, this painter was born about 1266 at Colle, near Florence. The son of a landed proprietor, Giotto (pron. jot'-to) was apprenticed to the wool trade and on his way to work used to call in at the studio occupied by the artist Cimabue (1240–1302). Eventually Cimabue, attracted by some of his drawings, made him his apprentice. Soon Giotto began to adorn church walls with frescoes of saints and Biblical characters, but it was the mosaics and paintings that he executed in Rome at a later date that established his reputation. One of his last works was the design for the beautiful campanile or bell-tower of the cathedral at Florence.

Giotto's life was one of tireless labour. In the 38 masterly paintings of the Life of Christ and the Virgin, of the Last Judgement, and other Biblical scenes, which he executed for the Arena Chapel in Padua, Giotto reached the supreme height of his genius. These and others of his works reveal the artistry of the greatest painter Italy produced before the Renaissance and one who, it has been justly said, revived the art of painting and gave it an impetus which endured for the best part of a century. Giotto, whose full name was Giotto di Bondone, died on January 8, 1337, at Florence, where he was working on the campanile. (*See illustrations in pages 1319 and 1384*).

Giraffe. The tallest of all living mammals is the giraffe, its head being from 16 to 18 feet above the ground. This height, however, is not due to the size of its body, which is smaller than that of the average horse, but to its exceedingly long and slender legs, and its extraordinarily long neck. When it drinks, the giraffe has to straddle its legs far apart to reach the water.

You may ask, Why did Nature produce such a freak? As usual science has an answer ready. The giraffe dwells in dry country where grass is scarce; its food consists of leaves. But the trees in such regions are almost bare of branches for quite a distance from the ground; therefore the giraffe has developed a long neck and long legs to enable it to browse on the tops of such trees. The tongue is in keeping with this purpose, for it often

GIRAFFES : QUEER ANIMALS FROM AFRICA
Unlike those of most other horned animals, the short horns of the giraffe are always covered with skin. Besides these two true horns, a central one lower down and less developed may occur. The giraffe is well adapted for feeding on vegetation that would be out of reach of most animals, having long legs, a very lengthy neck, and a long upper lip with which to grasp foliage.

THE GIRAFFE'S NECK IS NOT A BIT TOO LONG!

...ng as is the neck of the giraffe, it is none the less too short to enable the beast to drink without straddling the fore legs in a ...st ungainly manner. This is an outstanding example of the development of bodily structure in connexion with an animal's feeding habits, since the long neck allows the giraffe to grasp lea**ves** and twigs growing high up on trees.

THE LONG AND LANKY GIRAFFE

NO one would blame you for laughing at a giraffe, for there can be scarcely any other animal whose general appearance is quite so ludicrous. And it is no wonder that the ancients called it camelopard, for it does indeed look like a camel that has somehow tried to get into a leopard's skin. Just as the leopard uses its black spots on a yellow ground for concealment in the jungle, so the giraffe profits by the colour and design of its hide. For the pale network breaks up the darker brown patches and, by much the same system as the camouflage-painting of ships, makes the giraffe far less conspicuous than it would be if it were wholly of one colour. The tremendously long legs of the giraffe also look rather strange, because they join the body in a way which allows them to be bent with greater freedom than those of other beasts. With them the giraffe can run at a surprising speed over the dry African soil.

measures a foot and a half in length. Moreover, the giraffe's height enables it to see over trees and scrub, and so keep a watch on its enemies.

Having produced such a strange creature Nature has camouflaged it for protection by giving it a spotted skin of brown and yellow. As the giraffe stands among the mimosa trees (its favourite feeding place), its skin harmonizes with the play of light and shadow through the leaves, so that it is exceedingly difficult to detect.

In one species both males and females possess horns, but usually they are confined to the males. They consist of bony horn-like projections covered with skin, each crowned with a tuft of bristles. In front of and between these projections is a round bony elevation like an undeveloped third horn.

The movements of the giraffe are as curious as its structure. It cannot trot, but it runs at a heavy gallop, getting over the ground at great speed. The flesh is excellent and is in great demand for food, and the skin is used for leather.

In their native state giraffes are usually found in small herds. They chew their cud while standing erect, and hunters have occasionally seen a giraffe leaning against a tree fast asleep.

The giraffe is entirely without a voice, but the senses of sight and hearing are acutely developed, and it is very intelligent. Although it is good-natured and gentle, it will fight in self-defence, using both head and legs as weapons. In defence of her young a female giraffe has been known to kill a lion with kicks from her powerful hind legs.

Giraffes were known to the ancient Egyptians and Greeks, and many were exhibited in the old Roman games. They were thought to be a mixture of a camel and leopard, and were called camelopards—a name which remains in the scientific name, *Giraffa camelopardalis*.

The range of these animals formerly extended over the African continent from the Indian Ocean to the Atlantic, but they are now found only in the plains of eastern and central Africa between the Sahara desert and the Zambezi river.

Girl Guides.

When Lord Baden Powell organized the first Boy Scout troops in England in 1908, he little thought that he was preparing the way for a world-wide programme of scouting, in which girls, as well as boys, would take part. At the first Rally of the Boy Scouts, at the Crystal Palace, London, in 1909, a small group of girls faced the Chief Scout and insisted that they wanted to be Scouts, so that they could also enjoy the Scout programme of work and play.

Since that day, Guiding has gone forward steadily not only throughout the British Commonwealth but in nearly every foreign country as well. The present world membership is approximately two and a quarter million. The Guide Badge is a trefoil, the leaves representing the three promises that a Guide makes at her enrolment: To do my duty to God and the King (where there is no King the word country is substituted); to help other people at all times; to obey the Guide Law. Provided she is willing to make these promises, and to do her best to keep them, every girl is welcomed as a Guide, whatever may happen to be her nationality, religion, or circumstances.

The Guide Movement is divided into three main branches, to suit the interests of girls in different age groups. First come the Brownies, aged 7½–11. There are about 18 to 24 Brownies in each pack ; their leaders or Guiders are called Brown Owls and Tawny Owls. The Brownie programme includes tests in bandaging, ball throwing, knitting, skipping and many other things. Story-telling, acting and games are all included in the weekly Pack meetings.

The Guide Company for girls between 11–16 is divided into Patrols of six or eight, which are to a large extent self-contained units inside the company for games, competitions and hikes. When they have passed the Tenderfoot test, girls can be enrolled as Guides, and start working for their second and first class badges, and for some of the many proficiency badges. Hiking, camping, and other outdoor activities are an important part of the Guide programme.

Rangers are aged from 16–21, and girls of this age welcome the opportunity given to them through Rangering of developing their most varied interests from homecraft to astronomy, from drama

GUIDES LEARNING AN ACTION SONG
Under the direction of two officers (wearing dark uniforms) these Girl Guides are learning an action song ; in the centre of the circle is a pile of sticks representing a camp fire. Guides are organized in patrols of six or eight and, on joining, members have to pass a Tenderfoot test before being enrolled as Guides.

GIRLS EQUIPPING THEMSELVES FOR SERVICE

The Girl Guide Movement is divided into three main branches. First come the Brownies for girls between the ages of seven and a half and 11. At top left, Brownies are learning to signal with flags. Rangers, who are aged from 16 to 21, can engage in many activities, such as homecraft and child welfare. Some learn cooking (top right), while others engage in gardening (centre). Guides, aged 11-16, enjoy camping (bottom) and other outdoor pastimes.

ON LAND, IN THE AIR AND UPON THE SEA

The Girl Guides Association

Girls who prefer the sea to the land can become Sea Rangers (top). They are taught how to handle small boats and simple navigation. The Air Ranger section attracts girls who are interested in flying and gliding (bottom, left). Brownies are taught how to cross roads in safety and the correct signals to make to oncoming traffic. They are also trained to escort younger children (bottom right). The Girl Guide movement, formed in 1909, is now world-wide.

to child welfare. Many activities are carried on jointly with Scouts and other Youth organizations, and camps of a more adventurous type than are possible with Guides are a special feature of most Ranger Companies. As Sea Rangers, girls can gain practice in seamanship, sailing, rowing and other nautical matters; and the Air Ranger Section in the same way caters for girls with a special interest in gliding and flying.

Brownies, Guides and Rangers are always on the lookout for ways in which they can be of service to other people' and live up to their motto : Be Prepared. Guides may be called upon at any time to do jobs like collecting salvage and jam jars, gathering hips or helping at forestry camps.

During the Second World War (1939–45) Guides had a fine opportunity to show the results of their training to the general public, and they responded magnificently to this challenge. Everywhere Guides were to the fore in helping at day nurseries, at evacuation centres, as messengers and first-aid orderlies. The number of Guides in the enemy-occupied countries increased enormously, and many thrilling stories have been told of their courage and ingenuity in carrying on as Guides.

Directly the war was over International camps and the interchange of visits and correspondence between Guides of all nations started again, and everywhere Guides found that they met, not as strangers, but with the mutual bond of Guiding.

The Princess Royal is President of the movement, and Lady Baden Powell is the Chief Guide. Headquarters of the Girl Guides are at 17–19, Buckingham Palace Road, London, S.W.1.

Glacier. Of all the sculptor's tools at work carving and polishing the face of our earth, perhaps the strangest and most awe-inspiring is the glacier, a great river or sea of ice, pouring invisibly down a mountainside, carrying huge boulders, breaking off hillsides, building up walls and mounds of stone more grandly than ever an Egyptian king built up the pyramids. But they work slowly, imperceptibly, over the long years. They look as still and motionless as the rocks they move. How do they work? What starts them on their age-long tasks?

In many of the world's high mountains, the heat of summer is not sufficient to melt all the snow which falls in winter. And wherever this occurs year after year, the amount which accumulates in the upper ends of mountain valleys comes to be very great. These areas where the snow lasts from year to year are known as snow-fields. In the sunny days of summer the surface snow of a snow-field melts, and the water, sinking into the snow, freezes beneath the surface, just as it does in the last snow banks of spring, and helps to change the snow to ice. The weight of the snow above also compacts the snow below. By the melting and refreezing of the water, and by pressure, the larger part of the snow of a snow-field is changed into ice. Just below the snow the ice is not very compact, but farther down there is a solid mass of ice. A snow-field is, therefore, really an ice-field covered with snow.

When the snow and ice become sufficiently deep, the ice begins to creep down the slope. Ice which has this slow creeping movement down a mountain valley from a snow-field above is a valley glacier. There are many valley glaciers in the Alps and other high mountains of Europe, as well as in other parts of the world. There is also another great type of glacier. When the snow and ice accumulate in quantity on a plain or a plateau, it moves out from the centre in all directions. This sort of a glacier is an ice cap. If it is very large, it is a called a continental glacier. About four-fifths of all the surface of Greenland is covered with such an ice cap, and the area of accumulated ice around the South Pole, in Antarctica, is still larger. Glaciers move usually at the rate of a few inches or a few feet a day. There may be glaciers which advance as much as 100 feet a day, but few of them move more than three or four feet. During the movement the ice is cracked, especially where the ground over which it passes is rough.

New Zealand Government

A GLACIER IN THE SOUTHERN ALPS, NEW ZEALAND
Great crevasses and sharp pinnacles of ice cover the surface of the Franz Josef glacier in the Southern Alps, South Island, New Zealand. Such crevasses are often formed when a glacier rounds a curve as this one does. Glaciers move usually at the rate of a few inches or a few feet a day, gathering up great masses of earth and stones.

Thus arise the big cracks or crevasses which make travel across glaciers difficult and dangerous.

As the ice moves it gathers up great masses of earth and stones. This debris, carried either on top of the glacier or frozen within or underneath it, eventually forms belts or ridges, known as moraines, which are sometimes 25 to 100 feet high. A rounded, elongated moraine whose longer axis points in the direction of ice movement is called a drumlin. The unassorted, jumbled mixture forming the moraines and drumlins is known as glacial till or boulder clay, while the general term glacial drift includes all material which may be deposited by glaciers, regardless of its form or nature.

A huge ice cap which formerly covered the north-western part of Europe produced great topographical changes by eroding the surface of the land and by depositing drift. This change by glacial action is called glaciation. (*See* Ice Age.)

Gladiator.
" Hail, Caesar, those about to die salute thee! " This was the cry with which the gladiators, or professional fighters of the Roman amphitheatre, saluted the Emperor as they marched past his seat in their procession through the arena before engaging in mortal combat with one another, or with wild beasts, for public entertainment.

For the most part they were prisoners of war, slaves, or criminals, though some were men of good family or large means who loved fighting for its own sake, or young men who had lost their money. When a gladiator was disabled or disarmed, the spectators, by turning their thumbs up (or against the breast) or down, determined the fate of the beaten gladiator. There is doubt about the meaning of these gestures. According to some authorities " thumbs down " meant death; according to others, it was a signal for the conqueror to throw his sword down—in other words, the conquered gladiator was to be spared his life.

There were several different classes of gladiators. Of these, the *bestiarius* fought with wild beasts. The *retiarius* was armed with a trident and a net (*rete*), in the meshes of which he endeavoured to entangle his opponent. The *mirmillo* had a helmet adorned with the figure of a fish, and usually had as his opponent the *Thrax*, who wore a Thracian equipment, a round shield and a short sword. The *andabata* fought on horseback and wore a helmet which entirely covered his face. The *laquearius* tried to lasso his opponent.

The custom of giving gladiatorial shows seems to have been borrowed from the Etruscans, and is doubtless a survival of the practice of sacrificing slaves and prisoners on the tombs of illustrious chieftains. The first gladiatorial combat in Roman history took place in 264 B.C., and the fashion rapidly spread. Julius Caesar staged a show at which some 300 couples fought; and the Emperor Titus (A.D. 40–81) gave an exhibition of gladiators, wild beasts and sea fights which lasted 100 days, in which 10,000 men and all kinds of animals fought.

Such contests were finally stopped in A.D. 404 —it is said, through the courage of Telemachus, an Asiatic monk, who, rushing into the arena, strove to part two gladiators, just as the victor was about to put an end to his adversary. The spectators promptly stoned him to death, but his bravery had its effect, for the Emperor Honorius is said to have suppressed such exhibitions.

Gladstone, WILLIAM EWART (1809–98).
For over 60 years Gladstone sat in the House of Commons. For more than half that time he was the acknowledged leader of the Liberal Party. Four times he was Prime Minister (1868–74; 1880–

WILLIAM EWART GLADSTONE
Four times Prime Minister of Great Britain, the Right Honourable William Ewart Gladstone possessed extraordinary influence over his contemporaries. This photograph shows the great Liberal leader in 1886.

85; from February to July, 1886; and 1892–94), and his name became associated with a great number of political and social reforms.

Gladstone's father was a successful merchant in Liverpool, who also owned extensive coffee and sugar plantations in the West Indies. His youngest son, William Ewart, was born at Liverpool on December 29, 1809. When Gladstone was 11 years old he was sent to Eton, and from Eton he went to Christ Church, Oxford, where he took his degree in 1831. Deference to his father's wishes led him to give up his own inclination to become a Church of England clergyman, and to enter political life. To the end of his days he retained his interest in theology and in the classics, and in the midst of a busy political career one of his chief diversions was reading Homer in Greek. He also translated Horace's Odes.

Gladstone entered the House of Commons in 1833, at the age of 24. Less than 10 years later he became President of the Board of Trade, with a seat in the Cabinet. He first abandoned the Tories in 1846, but it was not until 13 years later that he definitely joined the Liberal Party, of which a few years later he became leader.

One of the spectacular feats which first brought Gladstone fame was the defeat he administered in 1852 to Disraeli, then Chancellor of the Exchequer, in a debate over the Budget. With eloquence and great mastery of detail he tore Disraeli's financial scheme to ribbons. The rivalry between Gladstone and Disraeli, who presently became the official leader of the Conservative Party, lasted until Disraeli's death in 1881.

In his first period as Prime Minister (1868–74), Gladstone secured the passage of a law which for the first time gave state aid to public elementary schools. He opened the Universities of Oxford and Cambridge to men of all religions. He introduced secret voting by ballot at elections, in place of the old public method of voting.

Although most of the Irish were Catholics, the Anglican or Protestant Episcopal Church was the Established Church of Ireland, until Gladstone passed the Irish Disestablishment Act (1869). He also passed the first Irish Land Act (1870), which removed some of the most serious economic burdens from which the Irish peasants were suffering.

When Gladstone became convinced that the majority of the Irish wanted the Irish Parliament restored, he introduced the first Irish Home Rule Bill. This bill (1886) was defeated in the House of Commons by the desertion of a large group of his followers, who thenceforth were called Liberal Unionists; and Gladstone was forced to retire as Prime Minister. When a change in the elections again brought him to that position, he introduced his second Home Rule Bill (1893); this passed the House of Commons, but was rejected by the House of Lords.

Gladstone's political work was now practically finished. In a short time the Grand Old Man, as he was called, now in his 85th year, retired from public life on account of approaching blindness due to cataract. His remaining years were spent at his home at Hawarden Castle in Wales, which had passed into his hands by his marriage, in 1839, to Catherine, sister and heiress of Sir Stephen Glynne, the Squire of Hawarden. Several times he had been offered a peerage, but he refused the honour, preferring to remain a commoner. He died on May 19, 1898, and was buried in Westminster Abbey, London.

Glamorganshire.

The second largest county of Wales, Glamorganshire is in the extreme south of the Principality, lying along the Bristol Channel. It has an area of 813 square miles. The chief rivers are the Taff, Tawe, Ogwr, Rhondda and Rhymney, all flowing south. The north is mountainous, the highest point rising to nearly 2,000 feet. There is some beautiful scenery, especially in the vale of Neath and the Gower peninsula in the west.

During the 19th century the development of the rich coal-fields made it one of the most important industrial districts of the country. The chief coal-mining area is in the valleys that run down to the sea from the hills in the north of the county, which are a continuation of those in Breconshire. The county has also large iron, steel, tin-plating and copper-smelting works.

Most of the southern portion of the county consists of beautiful fertile valleys where the chief industry is agriculture. On the coast of the Bristol Channel Glamorganshire has several seaside resorts, the best-known of which is Porthcawl. The county

town is Cardiff (q.v.). Merthyr Tydfil and Dowlais are the chief centres of the iron and steel industries, while Swansea (q.v.) and Aberavon are centres for tinplate manufacture and copper-smelting. The Rhondda valley, now a coal-mining area, was once one of the most picturesque beauty spots in all Wales. The population of the county is about 1,225,000.

Gland.

Every day the human body produces several quarts of liquid. Whenever you cry, a liquid called tears flows out between the eyelids. When you are warm a liquid called sweat comes out on the skin. All the time there is the liquid called saliva appearing in the mouth. Where do these liquids come from ?

The answer is that they are manufactured by organs of the body called " glands." Each gland takes water and other substances out of the blood and from these manufactures its own kind of liquid, which is called a secretion. Tears are secreted by the lachrymal glands. The saliva is the secretion of the salivary glands, situated under the tongue and jaw. A tube (duct) leads from each salivary gland into the mouth.

In the wall of the stomach are many small glands which discharge their secretion through short ducts into the stomach. These are called gastric glands, and the secretion is called gastric juice.

Situated near the stomach and discharging its secretion into the intestine just below the stomach, is the liver, the largest gland in the body. Its juice or secretion is called " bile." There is a pouch, called the gall-bladder, for storing bile. The tube which connects the gall-bladder with the intestine is the bile duct. Another large gland, the pancreas or sweetbread, makes a secretion called pancreatic juice, which flows through a duct into the intestine.

The saliva, gastric juice, pancreatic juice, and bile are all secretions which are useful in the digestion of food. They contain substances, called ferments, or enzymes (q.v.), which change complex foods into simpler substances. The saliva, by means of an enzyme called " ptyalin," splits starch molecules into sugar molecules.

All the glands mentioned so far, and some others, have ducts by which their secretion is carried either to the outside of the body or into the alimentary canal. But there are in the body certain ductless or " endocrine " (internally secreting) glands. The secretions they produce find their way directly into the blood stream and are carried all over the body. These secretions are called " hormones," from the Greek word hormao, meaning " to impel." Hormones act like little chemical messengers in our bodies, and are of great importance.

The thyroid gland, located in the neck, secretes the hormone thyroxin, an iodine-containing substance known to have a wonderful influence on the utilization of food by the body. If a baby has too little thyroxin, it does not grow properly but may become a peculiar idiotic dwarf known as a cretin. In adults the lack of thyroid secretion leads to myxoedema, a disease characterized by mental and physical sluggishness. Most forms of goitre are caused by too little thyroxin in the body. The thyroid glands of animals and the hormone thyroxin are used in the treatment of cretinism, myxoedema, and goitre. Thyroxin stimulates the muscular and mental activity, glandular action, and heart-beat.

The suprarenal glands are two small structures each fitting snugly on top of a kidney. They produce a hormone called epinephrin or adrenalin which is continuously being given off in very small amounts into the blood. During stress of certain emotions, such as fear or anger, the glands pour much larger amounts of this hormone into the blood.

The pituitary gland, which is made up of several lobes or parts, lies in a groove at the base of the brain. These lobes form hormones which play different rôles in the animal organism. Too little secretion from one of the lobes may cause a child to become a tiny dwarf or a miniature man. Too much of this secretion, on the other hand, may cause the baby to grow into a symmetrical "giant".

The parathyroid glands are four tiny bodies, looking very much like wheat grains, found alongside the thyroid. An extract prepared from these glands has a profound influence on calcium, or lime, metabolism and controls the calcium of the body. The hormones produced by these glands influence the growth of bones in our bodies. Removal of the parathyroid glands results in tetany, a condition characterized by convulsions, fits, loss of weight and, almost always, death.

In general, the ductless glands are essential to the body. Removal of the pituitary, suprarenals, or parathyroids causes death in a few days.

In 1921 Dr. F. G. Banting, Dr. C. H. Best and associates of the University of Toronto succeeded in isolating insulin. This is a hormone secreted by the "isles of Langerhans," patches of secreting cells in the pancreas. Insulin regulates the supply and use of sugar in the blood. Lack of it causes a fatal disease, diabetes mellitus. The disease can now be controlled by the physician giving daily doses of insulin, which is obtained from the pancreas of animals slaughtered for food. The name insulin comes from the Latin word *insula*, for islet.

Glasgow, SCOTLAND.

Smoke from the chimneys of scores of factories; a deafening clatter from thousands of hammers pounding on steel;

miles of shipyards lining each side of the river Clyde with forests of masts, acres of hulls, and skeletons of many vessels; and, alongside the nine miles of quays and docks, steamers old and new flying the flags of every nation—this is Glasgow, Scotland's industrial and maritime metropolis, which is not only one of the greatest manufacturing cities, but also among the chief shipbuilding centres of Britain.

" Glasgow made the Clyde and the Clyde made Glasgow " is one of the true sayings of this city, which is on the west coast of Scotland in the great industrial valley of the Clyde. Glasgow—which, next to London, is the largest city in Great Britain—has a fine artificial harbour, and in the great shipbuilding yards at

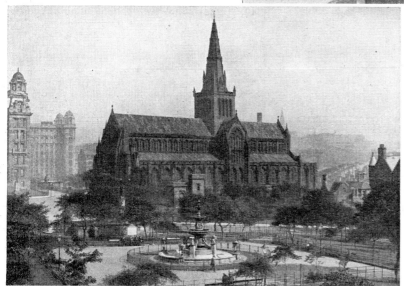

D. McLeish

GLASGOW'S CATHEDRAL AND GEORGE SQUARE
Dedicated to St. Mungo, Glasgow's Cathedral (lower) was completed in the 15th century and is a perfect example of Gothic architecture. Looking upon George Square (upper) are the municipal buildings, in front of which is the memorial to the fallen of the First World War. A statue of Sir Walter Scott surmounts the column, and in the foreground is an equestrian monument of Queen Victoria.

Clydebank, six miles from the city, many famous vessels have been built, including the Queen Mary and Queen Elizabeth.

With its excellent connexions by road, rail, and water, this commercial capital of Scotland—built in the midst of great iron- and coal-fields—makes good use of its opportunities. Besides shipbuilding, and the making of all kinds of machinery, the city has important cotton mills, textile factories, calico-printing and dyeing works, and distilleries. Its chief exports are cotton, linen, and woollen goods, machinery, coal, chemicals, paper, and whisky. Glasgow airport, at Renfrew, about six miles from the city, was the first civil aerodome in Scotland.

One of the few ancient buildings is the cathedral, built between 1197 and 1446. It is well situated on a hill to the north-east of the city, and is, next to Jedburgh Abbey, the finest example of Gothic architecture in Scotland. The Glasgow Art Gallery and

Museum in Kelvingrove Park is a magnificent pile in red sandstone and, after the National Gallery in London, it has the finest collection of pictures in the British Isles. The University, founded in 1450, is the second oldest of the four Scottish Universities. In George Square are the municipal buildings, the Scott Monument, and statues of famous people.

Glasgow's oldest open spaces are the Green in the east of the city, Kelvingrove in the west, and Queen's Park in the south. The city's water supply is obtained from Loch Katrine 30 miles away.

Glasgow appears to have been a place of some note in A.D. 397. It became the seat of a bishopric in 1115, and by the 17th century had developed into a thriving business centre. In 1686 a trade in the first red herrings was begun with France. Cotton weaving was established in 1780, and the first passenger steamer was launched on the Clyde in 1812. The population of the city is 1,075,000.

The MAGIC ART *of the* GLASS-MAKER

For centuries windows had to be small, because large panes of glass could not be made. Today glass is manufactured by a continuous process in very wide strips, as is explained in this article.

Glass. No one knows just where or when men first found out how to make glass. The elder Pliny told a story of some Phoenicians accidentally discovering the secret when they used blocks of natron, a crude form of soda, to make a fireplace on a sandy beach in Palestine, where a storm had driven their ship. The natron was part of a cargo destined for Syria. Next morning, so the story goes, they found lumps of fused glass in the embers—made by the fusion of beach sand and the natron. But glass had been known much earlier, and the Egyptians and other ancient peoples had learned to manufacture vases, cups, and beads of glass at least 4,000 years ago. Glass beads found in excavations of the Third Dynasty of Ur (2450 B.C.) suggest that the manufacture of glass may have begun in Mesopotamia, or even farther north.

In the British Museum, London, are these specimens of white Venetian glass. Venice was famous for glass in the 13th century.

Glass today is made from practically the same materials as those used centuries ago. Glass consists of 60–70 per cent (or more) of silica (sand), 10–15 per cent (or less) of soda, up to 15 per cent of potash, with minute quantities of other ingredients. The best English crystal glass contains no soda. In modern glass factories the mixture is melted either in special fire-clay crucibles for the finer grades, or in large tanks built of fire-clay slabs. These tanks are rarely more than three feet deep, but are often of great extent, holding 200 tons or more. The walls of the surrounding furnace are built of nearly pure silica, for even fire-clay cannot withstand the terrific heat (1300°-1500°C.) necessary to melt glass.

Just before the mixture of finely-ground sand, soda, lime, or other ingredients is put into the crucibles or the tank, a mass of broken glass called cullet is added to speed the fusion. As the melting proceeds, the mixture foams and bubbles until it becomes almost as liquid as water. Impurities are then skimmed off the surface, the mixture is allowed to cool until it is sticky, and is ready for drawing, moulding or blowing.

For ages glass was drawn by hand and blown by mouth. Now most flat glass, and bottles, are made by machine. In one modern system molten glass passes from the furnace to a refining chamber, in which it is gradually settled or refined. Next an iron " bait," about three inches wide and six feet long, is backed into the molten glass by machinery. Plastic glass, sticking to the bait, is drawn or pulled up two or three feet, moved out, and sent over a bending roll in the form of a wide, flat sheet. The thickness depends on the temperature of the glass and the speed with which it is drawn from the chamber.

From the bending roll the glass passes through an annealing oven—a tunnel 200 feet or more long, in which the glass is heated to just below the melting point and is then cooled by degrees. This hardens it. It is now cleaned in dilute acids and cut into large sheets.

This is a great advance on the earlier processes, mentioned below. But an even more remarkable method produces glass continuously, as follows. A slotted block of some " refractory " material—which resists great heat—is lowered into the drawing tank containing molten glass, and the glass flows up through the slot. Water-cooled tubes at the sides of the slot cool the glass sufficiently to impart the stiffness needed for resisting the upward pull that follows. The glass is drawn through pairs of asbestos-covered rollers, set in a shaft about 15 feet high. Each pair of rollers is in a separate compartment, and the heat of each compartment is **lower** as the glass ascends, so that by the time **the glass**

A LOVELY MASTERPIECE OF GLASS WORK

espite the development of machines to make glass the art of glass-blowing is not entirely dead, and hand-blown methods are sed for artistic pieces too delicate or too complicated for machines. This beautiful rhododendron is one of more than 700 life-size models of flowers and plants in the Harvard Museum in the United States.

INTRICATE GLASS MODELS OF SEA LIFE

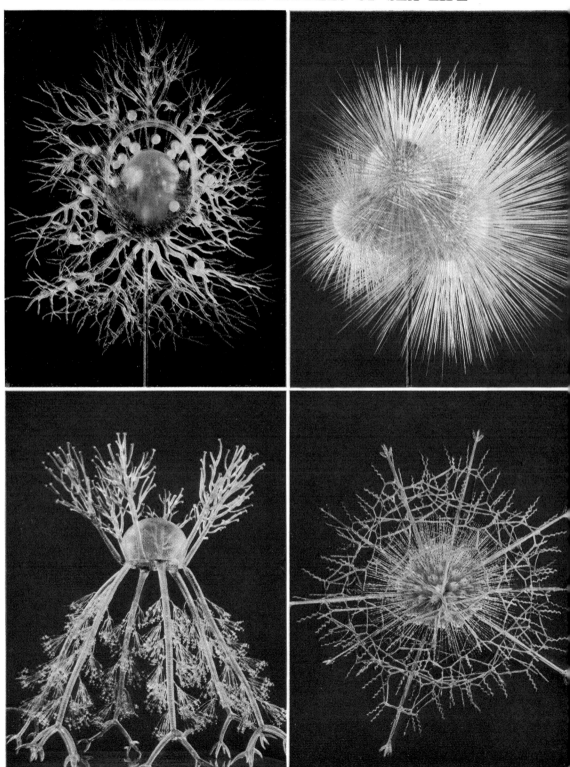

Life Magazine

The painstaking and delicate skill of the glass-blower can be appreciated in these superb models of radiolaria—minute one-celled creatures which float near the surface in warm seas. They are exhibited in the American Museum of Natural History in New York. Glass-blowing is employed for fine hand-made ware.

reaches the top of the shaft it has been annealed. At the top, the bait is broken from the glass, but rollers force the long continuous sheet up through a slit in a wooden platform until it projects to the height desired, when the sheet is cut off.

To make sheet glass by the cylinder process another method is used. Molten glass is poured into a series of pots, from which it is drawn up by a pipe. Compressed air is machine-blown through the hollow globe of glass, which adheres to the pipe and also to the glass still in the pot. So the globe stretches out to a long cylinder as the pipe rises and more air is blown in. When the cylinder is perhaps 50 feet long and 30 inches in diameter it is broken from tube and pot and lowered by a machine on to a cradle for further manipulation.

On the cradle the cylinder is cut into sections, which are split lengthwise by red-hot wires; next these pieces go to flattening ovens, where heat softens the glass and it is ironed flat by wooden rollers. After this it goes to the annealing oven, is cleaned with dilute acid, and is cut to stock sizes.

Plate glass is melted in pots set at the sides of a long regenerative furnace. When the molten mass is ready, a crane takes the pot to an iron table about 12 feet wide and 20 feet long, and the glass is poured out. Adjustable strips at the sides of the table regulate the thickness of the glass; iron rollers press the molten mass into sheets. After this the glass goes through an even longer annealing tunnel than the one previously described; the material is thicker, and must be cooled more slowly. In the continuous process of making plate glass, there is a threefold tank for melting the mix and refining it. From the refining chamber

the glass spouts out on to a moving table and under a roller, so that it emerges as a flat and continuous sheet of the required width and thickness. It travels on to a long annealing oven and is then cut into plates.

Plate glass is ground with sand and water, after being attached to the surface of a circular table. Polishing with iron oxide and water follows.

Window glass used to be made by spinning a bulb formed by the use of a blowing tube. As the bulb on the end of the rod was rotated it spread out into a flattened plate big enough for window panes. At the point where the rod was attached there was left a rounded knob which you can still see in old windows—but this effect is often imitated today.

The bulb already mentioned is formed by dipping the end of a blowing tube into a pot of molten glass,

GLASSWARE OF GRACEFUL APPEARANCE
Examples of 18th century English drinking glasses are shown at bottom, left. The one in the centre dates from about 1740 ; that with the opaque white spiral stem (left) from 1750-60 ; the plain stem (right) from 1730. The 14th century Persian glass beaker is decorated with paintings of birds. Phoenician glass (top, right) consists mainly of vessels, like the phials, vase and jug found in Syria, and on the islands of Cyprus and Rhodes.

some of which sticks to the end. By blowing through the tube the blob of glass is opened out into a hollow bulb. If the bulb be blown out and drawn simultaneously to lengthen it, it can be put into a mould, the mould closed, and then more blowing will force the plastic mass to take up the shape of the inside of the mould, so making a bottle, a jar, or some similar article. Bottle-making machines do this automatically, turning out an enormous number of finished bottles every day. The glass casings of electric lamps, radio valves and similar articles are made by machinery; even the process of sealing the filament supports into the casing is done automatically.

Cheap table glass is moulded to give an appearance resembling that of cut glass; the clear-cut facets of the latter are produced by grinding. It is a slow process which necessarily makes good glass-ware expensive as compared with imitations. The blanks for making cut-glass articles are made by the use of moulds. The patterns are then marked out with chalk, and the edges and facets ground with abrasive wheels, or with steel disks charged with some grinding powder. Polishing follows.

We naturally think of glass as a fragile, brittle material—and ordinary glass is just like this. But ways have been found of tempering and strengthening glass by heat treatment so that it will withstand temperature changes, and will bend without breaking, besides putting up with quite hard blows. This is one of the marvels of present-day science and manufacture. Glass is somewhat of a curiosity from the point of view of the chemist and physicist, who regard it as being in a state of solid solution, having been cooled to a temperature lower than that of its crystallizing point. Chemically glass is a fused mixture of various silicates and is not a compound (*see* Chemistry). There is even a soluble form of glass—silicate of soda, known as " water-glass." It dissolves in water, is used for water-proofing brickwork and for preserving eggs, and is mixed with asbestos to make hard and durable building board for lining roofs.

Reinforced Glass for Special Purposes

Plate glass is rolled while plastic to give it pleasing patterns and to take away its transparent quality, so that we can use it for partition glazing. Wired glass has enmeshed in it a strong wire netting which prevents the glass from breaking away if it should be fractured; wired glass is used for panes in fire-resisting doors, and for skylights, roof glazing, etc. Unsplinterable glass, as used for motor vehicles, aircraft and ships, consists of a sandwich of two sheets of glass cemented together with a thin sheet of some plastic material between.

Bullet-proof glass is a multiple sandwich of thick glass in layers with transparent strips of nitrocellulose. All these are *laminated* glasses, deriving their properties from being built up in layers. The flexible glass mentioned earlier, which withstands bending, is a solid material made by tempering the sheets so that the outer surfaces contract and subject the inner parts to tension. Such glass will bend to about 20 degrees; when it does break, it crumbles into small fragments without sharp edges.

Cooking vessels of glass which we can use in the oven, or on top of a gas-ring, are commonplace today. They are made of a mixture of borax and some form of silica. Still more durable articles can be made of fused quartz, but are expensive. Optical glass, for lenses, telescope mirrors and similar objects in which the material must be clear, uniform and able to be optically worked, are made from special mixtures of glass-making materials. Important here are the relative indexes of refraction (*see* Light) of the different forms. Compounds of barium, boron, magnesium and phosphorus are added to the more ordinary ingredients because of the change these chemicals make in the effect of the glass on light rays which pass through it.

Crown glass, which contains soda, has a very brilliant surface; flint glass or crystal glass contained lead, and got its name because the silica in the mixture was obtained from ground-up flints. The name flint glass is now applied loosely to almost any clear, colourless glass.

Glass can be spun into fine fibres, and is woven into mats to be used for insulating buildings against heat and cold. Glass wool, made in a similar way, is also employed for this purpose.

Glider. Inventors of flying machines pursued two main lines of experiment: there were those who sought to produce a machine which should flap wings like a bird; and there were others who tried to copy the soaring flights of birds as they " planed " up or down on air currents. The flapping-wing school of experimenter achieved no success, for the laws of Nature were against him. The would-be soarer came eventually to fly, since he utilised the supporting power of varying air streams in the atmosphere.

You might think that this method of travel was very uncertain, depending as it does on air currents of different velocity and direction, at higher and lower levels of the sky, and influenced by the presence or remoteness of mountains and hills—to say nothing of the effect of weather changes. But today the pilot of a modern " glider," or engineless aeroplane, can fly from point to point with a good deal of certainty, and can attain an altitude of 15,000 feet or more, all by taking advantage of suitable air streams. A point-to-point flight of about 150 miles is not unusual.

Long before a light and powerful engine had been devised to give power to an aircraft (in the time of the Wright brothers), the glider experimenters were busy. Otto Lilienthal, in Germany, made many glider flights between 1891 and 1896, when he was killed in the last of his ventures. José Weiss, in England, then took up the research, constructing many models and by the year 1909 beginning to make man-carrying gliders. Another who bore on the torch of experiment after the death of Otto Lilienthal was Octave Chanute, in America. Chanute was 64 years old when he made his first glider flight, in 1896; in all he flew in gliders more than 2,000 times. The Wright brothers built gliders and, achieving a good deal of success with their own particular design of machine, they turned then to making a powered aircraft. (You can read more details in our story of the Aeroplane.)

The glider is essentially an aeroplane in shape and form; though today men are experimenting with rotors to replace the wings. Lilienthal and Weiss and their contemporaries built light craft

SILENT AIRCRAFT THAT SOAR LIKE BIRDS

Planet News: Graphic Photo Union

Here are pictures of gliders in sport and in war. Top left, the wire launching rope is being fixed to a small glider: the other end goes to a winch. Top right, an advanced type of glider for soaring flight. At centre **left, we see two Horsa** military gliders about to land after having cast off the tug ropes which had linked them with the towing aircraft. The bottom photograph shows three similar military gliders, each with its towing aircraft. At centre right, airborne troops are entering a glider which will be towed to the spot where the men must land.

just able to support a man; they carried the glider to some lofty perch and then launched themselves into the air, aided by a slope of the ground which enabled the glider to become airborne without rising. A favourable air current would give support, and the aircraft might travel some yards or some hundreds before it finally came down—usually with a crash which damaged the framework and not infrequently hurt the pilot. Until, by hundreds of experiments, the basic principles had been established, gliding was a dangerous business, and even today the outcome of a flight is not predictable.

Glider clubs became popular in Germany in the 1920's and 1930's; the use of powered aircraft was forbidden by treaty, and the young men took up the building and flying of gliders. In Britain and other countries, too, gliding became a favourite sport. Lessons learnt from gliding were of profit not only to the enthusiasts but also to aircraft designers. One of the leading Continental record-holders, Robert Kronfeld, came to Britain in 1934 after Dollfuss, the Austrian chancellor, had been killed by the Nazis. He took British nationality in 1939, and did much to teach gliding. In 1935 he had made a double glide over the English Channel (in both directions).

On the outbreak of the Second World War he received an appointment under the Air Ministry and became a squadron-leader in the Royal Air Force. While making an experimental flight in a tail-less glider at Alton, Hampshire, in 1948, he was killed. These experiments were in connexion with the design of " flying-wing " aircraft (see Aeroplane)—a revolutionary new departure in design, from which much is expected in the future. The glider in which Kronfeld was killed was being towed by a normal aeroplane to launch it on its way; after being released it got into difficulties and capsized. During the Second World War (1939–45) towing behind powerful aircraft was a method of taking gliders to their destination, laden with troops, weapons, or supplies. Such gliders were aeroplanes in all respects save one— they had no power plant of their own. They were used by most combatant nations for invading enemy territory from the air, or for getting supplies to troops parachuted down beforehand to seize a suitable landing ground. When over the landing place the gliders were cast off from the tug, and the glider pilots took them down as best they could, often against enemy fire on to indifferent ground where many crashed. Some of the most successful military operations of the war would have been impossible but for the use of towed gliders. Britain and her allies owed some triumphs as well as some grievous set-backs to glider-borne operations.

The Glider Pilot Regiment was formed in February 1942. It consists of volunteers who are selected from the army, and provides

pilots and co-pilots for the gliders of an airborne force ; for administrative purposes it forms part of the Army Air Corps. Members of the regiment are trained not only to fly gliders but also as assault infantry ; after the gliders have landed and discharged their troops the pilots act as section-leaders. Each glider carries a section, and the sections are organized into squadrons. Glider pilots are trained by R.A.F. instructors.

Gliding as a sport is deservedly popular. As a means of research before big-scale experiments are carried out on powered aircraft, the flying of gliders is invaluable. Another development is the fitting of small-power engines in gliders, to act as auxiliary driving force. Kronfeld, for instance, flew such a machine, fitted with 5 horse power motor-cycle engine, from Croydon to Paris in 1935; his fuel cost him six shillings! By strict definition powered aircraft are *not* gliders.

Gloucestershire.

One of the western counties of England, situated about the estuary of the Severn, Gloucestershire falls into three natural divisions of valley, woodland, and hill.

The Cotswold Hills, in which rises the river Thames, stretch across the western part of the county from south to north, and reach a height of 1,135 feet in Cleeve Hill. The vales of Berkeley and Gloucester, excellent meadow lands, extend through the centre, the former being noted for its cheese. The woodland area is represented by the beautiful hilly Forest of Dean, whose area is about 35 square miles, and part of which is a coal-field.

In addition to the Thames and the Severn, which traverse the county from the north, the more important rivers are the Upper and Lower Avon, the Wye, on the Monmouth border, the Frome, and

J. Dixon-Scott

GLOUCESTER'S MAGNIFICENT CATHEDRAL
Occupying the site of an abbey established in 681, the oldest part of Gloucester Cathedral dates from the 11th century. Later additions include the tower, which was built in 1450. Gloucester, the county town of Gloucestershire, is one of the most historic of English cities and was a fortified place in Anglo-Saxon times.

Colne. Cattle and sheep rearing and agriculture are important industries ; several small towns, especially Stroud, are noted for cloth. The area of the county is 1,243 square miles.

Gloucester is the county town, but Bristol, part of which is in Somersetshire, is by far the largest city, and also the principal port. A navigable canal joins Gloucester to Bristol.

The city of Gloucester (population 52,900) has engineering and railway works, flour mills, and other industries. It has a fine cathedral, mainly Norman, which was originally the church of a Benedictine monastery founded in the 11th century. Other towns in the county are Cirencester (the Roman *Corinium*), Cheltenham (*q.v.*), and Tewkesbury, where a battle was fought during the Wars of the Roses (1471). The population of the county is 786,000.

Gloves. Kid, silk, lisle, and cashmere gloves for dress and leisure wear; buck-skin and dog-skin for riding, driving, and heavy uses; rubber gloves for surgery, electrical work, and housework; cheap cloth gloves for any rough task—there are gloves for every use and every occasion. But the two main classes are leather and fabric gloves.

Leather gloves are made of skins of deer, sheep, lamb, goats, and kids, but the name of the glove does not always tell the animal from which it came. While French kid is considered the finest glove material, more " kid," " doe-skin," and " buck-skin " gloves are made of lamb-skin than of kid-skin or deer-skin. " Chamois " gloves, too, are made from the inner layer of split sheep-skin or lamb-skin, tanned with fish oil to make the material washable. The so-called English dog-skin or Cape gloves are made from the skins of sheep obtained from the Cape of Good Hope.

Mocha gloves are made from Arabian sheep-skins, first shipped, it is said, from the port of Mocha which also gives its name to Mocha coffee. The mocha finish produces a leather much like suede or undressed kid in appearance, but stronger; it is produced by " buffing " or " friezing " the smooth surface from the hair side, whereas suede is finished on the flesh side. The finest grades of wool usually grow on skins which are much inferior to those which produce heavy, wiry wool. The best skins for gloves used to come from Russia; other varying grades come from Spain and eastern Europe.

The dried skins are soaked and softened in lime-water for two or three weeks, cleaned of hair and flesh, cured by the process necessary for the particular kind of glove desired, dyed, and given the required finish.

The prepared skins are next divided into tranks or slips, and each trank is cut by machine-operated dies into a glove blank ready for sewing, the scraps being used in making the strips for the inner sides of the fingers. Machines for sewing gloves, now universal, were not invented until 1875.

Fabric gloves may be made of silk, lisle, cotton, or of cashmere or other wool yarn. They may be knitted without seams, or stamped out of a fabric knitted with a special stitch which does not ravel when cut. They are cut and sewn somewhat as are leather gloves, but in larger sizes, being shrunk to the proper size after cutting. Knitted gloves and mittens are made in a number of hosiery mills.

In spite of the introduction of machinery, leather glove-making continues to be a hightly skilled occupation. French gloves have long had a high reputation, and the finest French gloves have come for centuries from Grenoble, Paris, Niort, and Vendôme. Copenhagen and Brussels are other continental glove-making centres. English glove centres are Worcester, and Yeovil in Somerset.

Glucose. If you have a " sweet tooth," and like raisins, you may have noticed little yellowish-white granular fragments on the outside of these dried grapes. This substance is glucose—also called grape-sugar or dextrose. It is present in all ripe fruits, and grapes contain up to about 30 per cent of it. Glucose is a sugar in the chemical sense—a mono-saccharide. (*See* Sugar).

Glucose is a white crystalline substance, easily soluble in water. It is manufactured from starch by many plants; and the honey produced by bees (from the nectar they collect from flowers) is composed of glucose and another sugar named fruit-sugar or laevulose. When honey sets it is because the contained glucose has crystallised and has left the laevulose still liquid. Commercially, glucose is manufactured by boiling starch with dilute mineral acids, and then separating the glucose. It is used in the brewing, confectionery and jam trades.

Glucose is easily asimilated by the digestive organs. After entering the blood it is changed into glycogen by the liver, and is stored as a reserve food material. Doctors sometimes tell patients to take glucose instead of ordinary sugar. Glucose is also taken, under doctors' orders, when extra nourishment is needed.

Glue. Strictly speaking, glue is an adhesive made from the bones, skins, and sinews of animals; but the name is often applied to adhesives made by altering the starch obtained from such plants as maize, arrowroot, cassava, and potatoes into a sticky gum. True animal glue is impure gelatine (*q.v.*).

The manufacture of bone glue starts with crushing the bones, and extracting the fat by boiling in naphtha or some other solvent. Pressure-steaming then dissolves out the glue. The solution is clarified, bleached, thickened by evaporation, and allowed to set. Then it is sliced and dried.

What is known as hide glue is made from clippings of skins and other meat-cannery waste. These are steeped in lime and then boiled. Fish glue is made from fish skins and bladders, and other fish offal. Waterproof glues are made from casein or from blood albumin. Elastic glue, used in making printers' rollers and for other purposes, contains glycerine. The sizing which paper-hangers put on plastering before pasting on wall paper is a thin solution of glue and water. The uses of glue are innumerable; it is still important in all joinery and cabinet-making, and few adhesives are so reliable and strong. Although glue has been made and used for a very long time, improved ways of extracting and drying it are still being invented and patented.

Glycerine. To keep a cosmetic moist and soft indefinitely, a manufacturer often uses glycerine. A druggist may use it to prepare drugs which do not dissolve well in alcohol or water. It can be used as an anti-freeze for motor-car engines, in preparing tobacco, and as a liquid in hydraulic apparatus. It is used in the manufacture of " Cellophane " and many plastics, and enormous quantities are employed to make nitroglycerin and dynamite.

Glycerine is valuable because it dissolves many substances, resists evaporation, and acts as a lubricant; also it tastes sweet and is harmless in drug and food preparations. It is easily obtained and comparatively cheap; all vegetable and animal fats consist largely of glycerine with fatty acids. The acids can be split off with an alkali, making soap and leaving glycerine. (*See* Fats and Oils ; Soap).

For extra supplies in wartime, or in countries that run short of fats and oils, glycerine can be made by fermenting sugar with special yeasts in certain salts. Propylene gas from petroleum can be made into glycerine by treatment with chlorine and an alkali.

Chemists classify glycerine as a trihydric alcohol and call it glycerol. The name is from the Greek word *glukeros*, meaning sweet. Certain compounds with phosphoric acid, the glycerophosphatides, provide special fats such as lecithin, which are present in eggs and nerve tissue. Glycerine weighs one-fourth more than water; it boils at 554° F., and solidifies at about 40° F. Related, sweet-tasting dihydric alcohols are called glycols. Ethylene glycol, $C_2H_4(OH)_2$, is used as an anti-freeze and to cool aero engines, because of its high boiling point, 387° F.

Goat. Few domestic animals are of greater service to Man than the goat. It gives nutritious meat and wholesome milk ; fine leather is made from its hide, and an exceptionally strong durable cloth from its hair; it is extremely hardy, and, most important of all, can grow fat on coarse vegetation on which other animals would not thrive. Part of the goat's unpopularity doubtless comes from the strong odour and surly temper of the males, and from the rather strong taste of the flesh and milk.

Goats, which belong to the genus *Capra*, are closely allied to sheep, but can usually be easily distinguished by the lighter build and longer, straighter

hair. Wild goats are found in Europe, northern Africa, and Asia ; the ibex is the most interesting species. The Rocky Mountain goat of North America is classified between the antelopes and the goats.

Domesticated goats (*Capra hircus*), which are thought to be descended from the wild goat of Persia, have been bred in many parts of the world from the earliest times. The Angora goat, named after Angora (Ankara), in Turkey, has a history that may be traced back to Old Testament times and came originally from much further East. This type has long spiral horns, and an abundance of long white silky hair, from which a strong cloth is made, called mohair.

Milch goats are found in all European and Asiatic countries, the Toggenburg and Saanen breeds of Switzerland being the best. From the Kashmir goat's beautifully soft silky undercoat are made the famous Kashmir shawls.

The hides of young kids are used extensively for gloves and shoes, though much of the so-called kid leather is an imitation. The skin of the Angora, with the hair intact, is often used for rugs. Goatskins are also used in the manufacture of shoes, portfolios, morocco for book bindings, and other articles.

Goethe, JOHANN WOLFGANG VON (1749–1832). The greatest work of this German poet was Faust, a dramatic poem in two parts. From early youth, when Goethe (pron. gê'-te) learned the story of Dr. Faustus from a puppet play, until he penned the last scene shortly before his death, there was scarcely a period of his life in which Faust was entirely out of his mind; scarcely a period that did not add something to the great work that was growing under the poet's hand. Faust desires all knowledge, to live Life to the full. Unsatisfied by the results of his studies, he turns to magic. He conjures up the demon Mephistopheles, and makes an agreement with him.

In Goethe's Faust Mephistopheles must gratify Faust's every wish; if he can satisfy Faust, Faust's

GOATS : SOME OF THE POPULAR DOMESTICATED BREEDS

The true wild goat is a native of Persia, and it is from this species that the domesticated goat is descended. Above are some of the best-known breeds. Reading from left to right, they are : Toggenburg, Nubian, Anglo-Nubian, Irish (long-haired), and a young Anglo-Nubian. Amongst the animals goats are placed between sheep and antelopes.

soul is to belong to Mephistopheles. Faust learns that pleasures are not happiness. His wishes become purer, and reach their highest point in a grand project that is to benefit others. The moral height he has reached calls the powers of Heaven to his aid, and they wrest his soul from the demon.

Goethe's other great work was his novel Wilhelm Meister. This, too, Goethe wrote at various times, changing the plan as he went on. But through it all Wilhelm Meister is seeing life and learning in the school of experience. Life is the best teacher, Goethe thought. He wanted the fullness of life himself, and tried to show others how to live fully.

He was born at Frankfort-on-Main, Germany, on August 28, 1749, and his boyhood was spent in that city. He was taught at home by his father. From Frankfort he went to the University of Leipzig, and from there to the University of Strasbourg. At Strasbourg he met the critic Herder, who directed his attention to Shakespeare and to folk poetry (the ballads and songs that seem to have no author, and live only in the recitation and singing of the common people). His first drama of note, Götz von Berlichingen, the story of a lawless baron, shows the influence of Shakespeare.

Goethe won the friendship of the Duke of Saxe-Weimar, a ruling prince of Germany, who made him a Councillor of State at Weimar. Goethe took his official duties seriously. He gave particular attention to developing the agriculture, forestry, and mining of the duchy. Later he was, for 22 years, the director of the duke's court theatre. In 1786–88 Goethe travelled in Italy, drawn there by his interest in Greek and Roman art.

Goethe's friendship with Schiller, the best-loved of German poets, was helpful to both. It gave Goethe new inspiration, and a surer guidance to Schiller's rather too impetuous genius. The death of Schiller in 1805 was deeply mourned by Goethe. Goethe died at Weimar on March 22, 1832.

Goethe's chief works, in addition to miscellaneous writings and songs and odes, were: Götz von Berlichingen (1773); Werthers Leiden (Sorrows of Werther) (1774); Iphigenie auf Tauris (1787); Egmont (1788); Torquato Tasso (1790); Reineke Fuchs (Reynard the Fox) (1793); Wilhelm Meisters Lehrjahre (Wilhelm Meister's Apprenticeship) (1796); Hermann und Dorothea (1797); Aus meinem Leben: Dichtung und Wahrheit (autobiography); Faust, complete (1832).

The WORLD'S Most Precious METAL

*F*rom the earliest days gold has been accounted the most precious substance and used as the basis of commerce. Here we are told how and where it is produced, and some of its manifold uses.

Gold. Although gold is widely distributed over the earth, it occurs mostly in such small quantities that it can by no means always be profitably extracted. It is even found in minute quantities in sea water. Gold is a mineral element; its atomic number is 79 and its atomic weight 197·2. It is a heavy metal, having a specific gravity of 19·32; its melting point is 1,061° C. When pure, its colour is a bright yellow with a faint reddish tinge, making it the most attractive ornamental metal of all. Despite the fact that gold has been mined from remote antiquity, the quantities have generally been so small, and have required such expenditure of time and labour, that it remained the most precious of metals until the discovery of a few even rarer metals in recent times.

Most of the gold mined in the earlier days was produced in the Spanish Peninsula, Greece, Asia Minor, India, and the Ural Mountains of Russia. After the discovery of the New World great supplies were obtained from Central and South America, but the production from then to the discovery of the California goldfields was less than the present annual production of about 25 million ounces.

An enormous jump in gold production resulted from the discovery of the California deposits (1848) and other great fields, the most important of which are, with dates of discovery: Australia (1851); British Columbia (1858); New Zealand (1858); British India (1884); Witwatersrand, South Africa (1886); Alaska (1897).

The greatest gold-producing region today is the Witwatersrand district of South Africa, centred round Johannesburg. Canada ranks next in production, followed by the United States and Russia. The Mysore mines in India are other big producers.

Gold is found both " native " and in combination with the element tellurium. It occurs, generally with quartz, iron pyrites and other minerals, in veins which cut across the rocks. Sometimes a single vein, such as the Mother Lode of California, may run for many miles, but only parts of it are rich enough to be mined. These parts are called ore-shoots. Many such veins are associated with intrusions of granite, and their filling is believed to have been due to watery fluids left after the granite crystallized. The great Witwatersrand deposits occur in an ancient pebble-bed or conglomerate. Geologists do not agree about the source of the gold here, some believing that it was derived from still older quartz veins, while others think it was introduced where it is now found in hot solutions. On the Rand, mining has reached a depth of 8,000 feet—over 1½ miles—below the surface. In Canada gold is recovered as a by-product from massive sulphide ores mined for their copper, zinc or nickel contents. Gold is also found in beds of sand and gravel deposited by rivers, when it is known as alluvial gold.

There are two principal methods employed in mining gold: (1) placer mining for alluvial deposits, and (2) lode or quartz mining, where the gold is in solid rock. Placer mining was known in ancient times. Gold washing, as early as 4000 B.C., is shown in Egyptian rock carvings.

In placer mining, Nature has already done the greater part of the work. In the process of wearing down hill-sides by erosion, gold, being one of the heaviest of minerals (19·27 times as heavy as water), naturally goes to the bottom of streams. There it accumulates, mainly as a fine powder (gold dust) though occasionally in large nuggets;

one of the largest ever found, the Welcome Stranger nugget, discovered in Australia, weighed 2520 ounces—the weight of a medium-sized man.

The prospector searching for alluvial deposits washes the sand in a pan or shovel with a little water, swirling it round so that the light material is thrown off. If gold is present, the characteristic yellow colour will then appear in the concentrate.

Great beds of sand and gravel are dug up by means of floating dredgers (see Dredger), or are washed out with very powerful jets of water from " monitors " which resemble large fire hoses. The sand and gravel then pass over sluices, where the same principle that has operated in Nature is used to separate the gold, the light materials being washed away while the heavy minerals, including the gold, are caught on riffles or ridges at the bottom. To the concentrates is added mercury, which readily unites with the gold. The resulting amalgam is separated by heat—that is, the mercury is vaporized and the gold is left free, to be melted into bullion.

Placer mining is becoming less important, because gold obtainable in this way is growing scarcer and less worth extracting, and most of the world's gold today is obtained by lode mining. The gold-bearing ores are taken out of the veins or reefs, crushed in stamping-mills, and passed over copper plates covered with mercury, to catch as much of the free gold as possible. The ores still contain a large proportion of gold, however, so further treatment is necessary. This usually takes the form of the cyanide process, in which a solution of cyanide of potassium is poured over the concentrated ore, dissolving the gold. From this solution the gold is precipitated on zinc

HOW GOLD IS DUG OUT OF THE EARTH OR DREDGED FROM RIVERS

Two of the principal methods of obtaining gold—mining and dredging—are shown here. Trucks loaded with ore (lower) are standing at the entrance to a gold mine in the Transvaal, South Africa. The rock is crushed in stamping-mills before it is passed over copper plates covered with mercury to catch as much free gold as possible. In the upper photograph a floating dredger is scooping up gold-bearing gravel from the bed of a river in California, United States.

shavings, or by electrolysis. In the great Rand mines, little more than 55 to 65 per cent of the gold was extracted before the introduction of the cyanide treatment in 1890. Now about 94 per cent is saved.

When first extracted from its ores, gold nearly always contains some silver, copper, or other metal, which must be separated. This separation, or refining, is done at refineries or at the mint, by electrolysis or by treatment with chemicals. Since pure gold is too soft for ordinary use, it is nearly always alloyed with copper or silver, or both. (The gold coins of Great Britain, no longer in circulation, were alloyed with copper.) These metals change the colour, copper making the alloy redder than pure gold, and silver whiter. The proportion of gold contained in an alloy is expressed in two ways: in *carats*, that is, the proportion on a scale of 24; or in *fineness*, on a scale of 1,000. Pure gold is 1,000 parts or 24 carats fine. Gold with 18 parts pure gold and 6 parts alloy is 18-carat

PREPARING GOLD FOR USE IN INDUSTRY
One method of making gold wire is shown in the lower photograph. The wheels draw the wire through a succession of apertures, each of which makes it a little thinner. To reduce gold to the thin strips used by jewellers and others, a bar of the metal is passed through a rolling-machine (upper), pressure being increased until it is the required thickness.

jewelry, is produced by applying thin sheets of gold to a plate of alloy, and rolling them together until the gold and the alloy are firmly welded.

Gold resists chemical action to a greater degree than any other common metal. One of the few liquids which will dissolve it is a mixture of nitric and hydrochloric acids, which early experimenters called *aqua regia* (royal water) because of this power. The resulting chloride of gold, in combination with certain other chlorides, is used in photography and in medicine. In combination with tin chloride, gold chloride produces a fine purple pigment, called purple of Cassius, which gives a rich pink, rose, or red colour to glass, pottery, and enamel.

The name " white gold " is often given to platinum, but is also used for alloys of gold with palladium or nickel, in which the yellow colour has been taken out by the alloying metal.

gold, or 750 parts fine. The standard British qualities are now 22c. (once used for coinage), 18c., 14c., and 9c.; 14c. is mainly used for fountain-pen nibs. The 14c. standard was introduced in 1932 to take the place of two (15c. and 12c.) which had almost dropped out of use.

" Hall marks," official marks stamped on gold and silver articles by the assay offices to denote the quality, or proportion of pure metal contained, may be expressed in decimals as well as in carats. Thus 9c. gold is marked 0.375, the decimal equivalent. This quality is the lowest which is hallmarked. Eighteen-carat gold is the best for good jewelry, being harder than 22c.,

In malleability, gold stands first among the metals, since it is capable of being beaten to a thickness of 1/250,000 of an inch as a sheet, or drawn into very fine wire.

Gold lace is made up of thin gold wires flattened into ribbons and wound over silk thread. Rolled gold, which is often used for watch-cases and

Goldfish. Swimming in its suit of burnished gold or its bright-red jacket with black or silver trimmings, the goldfish knows nothing of its humble ancestor, a dull-coloured species of carp, *Carassius auratus*. The wonderful variations of colour and form which we find so attractive were produced by the skill and infinite patience of Chinese and Japanese breeders.

The original goldfish must, it is thought, have been yellow " sports " appearing among ordinary dull-coloured fish. For centuries breeding was carefully controlled, until the golden colour was firmly fixed, and innumerable forms, from the beautiful to the grotesque, were produced.

Some of the most valuable goldfish are not golden at all. For example, the fantail is occasionally a brilliant and showy black, while others are virtually white. One of the prettiest varieties is the fringe-tail, whose enormous shimmering tail produces effects that a dancer might envy, as the little fish moves in the sunlight. Probably the ugliest

GOLDFISH WITH HUGE BULGING EYES

A freak breed of goldfish, called the telescope fish, is characterised by enormous eyes. The first specimens were bred in Japan, where the species is highly prized. The variations of colour and form in carp have been produced by the skill and patience of Chinese and Japanese breeders.

him a member of the society known as "The Club." (*See* Johnson, Samuel).

Goldsmith's writings brought him some means, but as a result of his love of gay clothes and fine dinners, his habit of gambling, and the ill-advised generosity which led him to help anybody who sought his aid, he was always in debt. In his 47th year he fell ill of a fatal fever, which was aggravated by his own attempts to cure himself and his constant worry over his money troubles. He died on April 4, 1774, and was buried in the Temple.

"Let not his frailties be remembered," said Dr. Johnson; "he was a very great man." This verdict has been accepted by the literary world. Of all Goldsmith's works The Vicar of Wakefield (1766) is the favourite. Dr. Primrose, the simple and true-hearted clergyman, and the blundering Moses, so like Goldsmith himself, are among the characters that are never forgotten, while the simple, wholesome village life pictured in this novel never loses its power to charm. Much of the same charm is shown in The Deserted Village (1770). His comedy She Stoops to Conquer (1773) is often played.

kind is the one most prized in the Orient. This is the telescope fish, so called because of its large and bulging eyes, which the Japanese are continually trying to make larger and more bulging by means of selective breeding.

Goldsmith, OLIVER (1728–74). There are few more eccentric or more lovable characters among literary men than Goldsmith. He was born either at Pallas, Co. Longford, Ireland, or at Elphin, Roscommon. Oliver was a most unpromising lad at school. At Trinity College, Dublin, his escapades brought him into disfavour with the authorities, and here he fell into the habit of squandering what little money he had and getting into debt; but he was able to obtain his degree when he was 21.

At the earnest desire of his family Goldsmith now spent two years studying theology, but when he presented himself in scarlet clothes as a candidate for Holy Orders he was rejected. He made an attempt at law, but failed in this also. Then he went to Edinburgh to study medicine. After remaining there a year and a half, he set out on a year's tramp through Europe. Earning money by playing the flute, he wandered through Flanders, France, Switzerland and Italy. He came back, if his own account may be believed, with a medical degree, though how he obtained it is not known. It proved of little service to him, however, for he met with no success in practice as a physician.

Failing in various other occupations, Goldsmith turned to literature. In his little garret at the top of Breakneck Stairs, off Ludgate Hill, London, he wrote essays, reviews, and histories. Among these writings was a series of observations on English civilization, professedly by a Chinese traveller, afterwards published (1762) as Letters of a Citizen of the World. These attracted the attention of Dr. Johnson, who befriended Goldsmith and made

Gold Standard. Prior to the First World War (1914–18) each of the countries of Europe and America and some countries elsewhere had a standard coin consisting of a certain amount of gold. Thus, the British sovereign or £ contained 113 1/123 grains of pure gold; the French napoleon (20 franc piece) contained 5 25/131 grams of pure gold. By considering the ratio between these two amounts of gold it was possible to work out a theoretical relationship between £s and francs, that is, a "mint par" of exchange : £1 = 25·2215 francs. Similarly, in American dollars £1 equalled $4·86⅔. Gold thus provided an international currency—related to a "gold standard"—by means of which the money of one country could easily be expressed in terms of that of another, and gold could be sent in settlement of debts.

Normally the amount that a country had to pay to other countries for imported goods, etc., approximately equalled the total that it had to receive for exports, etc., so most payments between traders in different countries could be settled by the transfer of debts through banks, and no gold had actually to be sent. But if, as sometimes happened, a country had at a particular date to pay to other countries very much more than it had at that time to receive from other countries, the cost of settling by transferring debts through banks might become more expensive than the cost of sending gold. When that was so gold would be shipped, principally by banks. Actually much gold was shipped from time to time from the Continent to London, New York, etc., and vice versa. Moreover, prior to the 1914 war, ordinary people could, if they wished, make payments abroad by sending gold. Golden sovereigns and half-sovereigns were then in use in Britain, not £1 and 10s. banknotes.

The outbreak of the First World War changed all that. Gold coins were withdrawn from circulation, and paper money was issued in their stead. Britain's stock of gold was concentrated in the Bank of England, to be used to pay for imports that could not be secured from the U.S.A., etc., on credit. Similar changes were made in other countries. As the war proceeded, the total nominal value of the paper money issued by governments far exceeded the former value of the gold they held. Each paper £, franc, etc., came to represent a much smaller amount of gold than formerly, and the old relationship between the currencies and gold was completely destroyed. Thus, on December 31, 1920, instead of the £ being equal to 25·2215 francs, it was worth 59·60 francs; instead of being worth $4·86⅔, £1 was worth only $3·5425. Some currencies on the Continent had become quite worthless.

Various conferences were held to consider if it might be possible to return to the gold standard; and in 1925 the attempt was made. The old rate, £1 = $4·86⅔, was restored; a new rate for the franc, £1 = 124·21 francs, was established. But the experiment did not work. The pre-1914 conditions of world trade had gone, and could not be revived. It was no longer possible to settle international indebtedness without continually transferring large amounts of gold to the U.S.A.;

indeed, gradually that country accumulated roughly four-fifths of the world's stock of gold. Eventually, in 1931, the government of the United Kingdom abandoned the attempt to operate the international gold standard. Strict control of payments to and from overseas was introduced, and the transfer of gold was again centralized in the Bank of England and controlled by the government. Other governments acted similarly. When the Second World War broke out in 1939 only the U.S.A. remained on the gold standard, that is, was willing to exchange dollars for gold, or gold for dollars, at a fixed rate and in unlimited quantity.

In 1944 at a protracted conference of the United Nations held at Bretton Woods, near New York, it was decided to make yet another attempt to link currencies to gold. The individual governments were invited in 1946 to state what were the gold equivalents to their standard currency. Some, including the British government, did so. An International Monetary Fund was set up to assist nations to maintain these new standards. There was, however, no immediate prospect of a return to the international gold standard, as it operated before 1914 and from 1925 to 1931. Most countries carefully control all overseas payments and transfers of gold. (*See* Foreign Exchange ; Money).

The ROYAL and ANCIENT GAME of GOLF

This game has increased in popularity year by year, and many of its terms have passed into general speech and writing in a figurative sense. Here is a description of golf and an outline of its history.

Golf. The national game of Scotland, golf is one of the few games in which both old and young may excel, for champions in this difficult but fascinating game have been as young as 18 and as old as 60.

More than any other game, perhaps, golf calls for the spirit of courtesy and fairness. A player stands quietly aside while his opponent makes his strokes. He assists in every way to give his opponent an equal chance with himself, and should a player lose a ball, the other searches for it as diligently as if it were his own. The golfer must wait until the player or players immediately ahead are out of range, or alternatively warn them with the cry of " fore." Golf also puts a player on his honour, for he alone keeps his score. These forms of self-discipline, combined with the skill required to excel and the excellent physical exercise obtained, usually in attractive scenery and surroundings, fully entitle golf to its high place in the list of games.

A full-size golf " links " consists of 18 " holes " of varying lengths, from about 100 yards to 500 yards and more, the distance being measured from the starting point, or " tee." This is a level plot of ground about 12 feet square, from which the players " drive off " into the " fairway," which is the name given to the broad avenue of turf leading to the hole itself. For 200 yards, perhaps, this fairway is smooth and undulating, with no obstructions, though woods and tall grass may flank it on both sides. Then a " hazard "—an obstruction either natural or artificial, such as a brook or a ditch or a mound of earth fronted by a sand-pit called a " bunker "—may cut across the fairway

and form a trap for the unwary player. If the golfer hits his ball into one of these traps, he generally has considerable difficulty in striking it out. But if he plays skilfully he remains outside the traps, and is able to approach the " green," which lies at the end of the hole, without wasting any strokes and adding to his score.

The " green " is a plot of ground of no regulation size or shape, but usually about 30 or more feet in length, breadth, or diameter. Here the grass is cut close, and in the centre is a hole 4¼ inches in diameter, lined with metal and marked by a flag on a " pin " or metal rod about three feet high. When the golfer is some distance from the putting green, this flag indicates the correct direction for his stroke. As soon as the player succeeds in putting his ball in the hole, and his opponent has done the same, they both move on to the next tee to play for the second green. They continue to play in the same manner until they have made the full round of 18 holes. Some golf courses consist of only 9 holes, and in that case the usual practice is to make two rounds.

The object of the game is to send the ball into each of the holes successively in the fewest possible number of strokes. In match play, each hole is counted separately. The winner is the one who has the most holes to his credit when the course has been completed. In medal play, the golfer who completes a certain number of rounds in the lowest total number of strokes is the winner, whether or not he wins the most holes.

The golfer may play alone, or he may play with one, two, or three others. In a " foursome " it is common practice to choose partners and to compete in match play, each partner striking the ball alternately. Whenever a player and his opponent complete a hole in the same number of strokes, the hole is halved and counts to neither. A player is said to be " dormy two " if he is two holes up and only two remain to be played. Should the next hole be halved, he has won the match by " 2 and 1 "—that is, two up and one to play.

The term " bogey " indicates the standard number of strokes which should be taken by a good player at any given hole. One under bogey is called a " birdie "; two under bogey, an " eagle." If, on the putting green, one ball comes to lie directly between another and the hole, and more than six inches away from the other ball, the position is called a " stymie."

A golfer normally plays off a handicap allotted to him by his club. Should a player (in a medal competition) take 88 strokes for the 18 holes, and his handicap is 8, his score would read 88−8= 80. But should his handicap be " plus " 2, the score would read 88+2=90.

The ball, about 1¾ inches in diameter, is made of many strands of rubber wound round a core which is now also of rubber, but which in the early days of organized golf was of gutta-percha (such a ball was known as a " gutty "). The white (or, for use in snow, red) casing is variously patterned to lessen wind resistance and in order to give greater carrying power.

Most players use at least six different clubs, each adapted for a particular kind of stroke. The clubs have a slender shaft about 3 feet long, now mostly made of steel tubing, and a strong wooden or iron head with which to hit the ball. When driving off, the player may place the ball upon a little elevation of sand called a tee, or on a wooden peg. This device gives him a chance to get the most effective stroke. In driving off, the golfer usually uses a wooden-headed club called a driver. Two hundred yards is a good drive, but many players are capable of driving over 250 yards.

The other clubs—such as the " cleek," the " mid-iron," the " mashie," and the " niblick "— are variously designed for pro-

THE DRIVER

THE SPOON

THE DRIVING-IRON

THE MID-IRON

THE MASHIE

THE NIBLICK

THE PUTTER

CHIEF GOLF CLUBS
Though most golfers carry more than seven clubs, those shown here are, perhaps, the most useful. The top two have wooden heads, the rest metal.

pelling the ball low and far, or raising it in the air to clear an obstacle. On the green the player uses a short straight-faced club called a " putter." The players' clubs are usually kept in a bag which may be carried by a man or boy called a " caddie."

The history of golf runs far back into the early centuries. The Romans, soon after the beginning of the Christian era, played a game with a mallet and a leather-covered ball stuffed with feathers, called *paganica*; the French in early times had a game akin to golf called *jeu de mail*; and the Dutch played a stick-and-ball game on the ice called *het kolven*. In all of these games the object of the player was to send the ball so that it would strike a mark. While the Dutch and the French were still hitting at marks, the Scots refined the game by making holes in the ground to receive the ball. James I (1566–1625) introduced the game into England, where it did not become really popular until the 19th century.

The most famous golf course in the world is St. Andrews, in the county of Fifeshire, Scotland, the headquarters of the Royal and Ancient Golf Club, whose rules form the international code of golf. This club, founded in 1754, is the ruling body in Britain.

The annual " Open " golf championship is unusual in that both amateurs and professionals are allowed to compete. The Open is held on various courses, such as St. Andrews, Sandwich, Hoylake, or Carnoustie, as is the Amateur Championship. There are numerous other championships, such as the English Amateur, the Ladies' Open, girls' and boys' championships, and so on. The professionals and amateurs of Great Britain and the United States meet in contests known respectively as the Ryder Cup and Walker Cup. Both these are normally held in alternate years.

Goose. Through Mother Goose this bird belongs to the nursery; the fable of the " goose that laid the golden egg " takes it into the schoolroom, where later it figures as the heroic and noisy bird that saved the city of Rome, and as furnishing Tiny Tim's Christmas dinner in Dickens's famous Christmas Carol. Sportsmen prize the wild goose, while the domestic goose is of great

SOME OF THE STROKES THAT MAKE GOOD GOLF

The correct stance (position of the feet and body) and the right way to execute some of the varied strokes that make golf such a fascinating game are shown above. Every detail of these shots should be practised with the utmost care, and any player who hopes to excel must learn to make them when he first begins to play. Once acquired, bad golfing habits can only be overcome with the greatest difficulty. The national game of Scotland, golf was introduced into England by James I (1566–1625). The governing body is the Royal and Ancient Golf Club of St. Andrews in Fifeshire, Scotland.

use to housewives, not only for its flesh and eggs, but for its feathers, which are used as stuffing for pillows and feather-beds. Goose fat is often used in place of lard for cooking, and from the livers is made the *pâté de foie gras* for which Strasbourg in France is famous.

There are about 40 species of geese, all belonging to the same family as the ducks and swans. The male, called the gander, resembles the female in plumage. All wild geese breed in cool and temperate regions, some even in the Arctic Circle, and migrate south for the winter.

Of British wild geese, the grey lag (*Anser anser*) breeds in the far north of Britain. It ranges over nearly the whole of Europe and northern Asia, and from it the domestic goose is descended. Other species, which visit us chiefly in autumn or winter, are the Brent goose (*Branta bernicla*) which has a black head and neck, and the barnacle goose (*B. leucopsis*), so called because of an ancient legend connecting it with barnacles (*q.v.*). Both are more marine in habit than the other species.

The Canadian goose (*B. canadensis*) is the most familiar of American wild geese. A grain-feeding bird, its flesh is most palatable.

Geese have been domesticated from a very remote period, for they are shown on the monuments of ancient Egypt. The long wing-feathers of the goose were used to feather arrows, and goose quills were in great demand before steel pens were invented.

Gooseberry. This useful fruit, though it grows wild in the north temperate regions, has been little cultivated except in England. Here cultivation began in the 16th century, with the result that our markets have gooseberries almost as large as plums and sweet enough to eat just as they are picked from the bush, while those of other countries, like our own wild ones, are small, hard, and proverbially sour.

Our own gooseberries are yellow, green, or deep purplish when ripe, and, besides being good to eat raw, make lovely jam, pies, and other sweets. The bushes are prickly, and the flowers small

Chas. Jones

GOOSEBERRIES
Everywhere the cultivation of the gooseberry has been neglected with the exception of England, where the fruit is far superior to that of other countries.

and bell-shaped, showing their relationship to the currants. Gooseberries are so called perhaps because geese are said to like eating them. Their scientific name is *Ribes grossularia*, and they are members of the family *Saxifragaceae*.

Gordon, GENERAL CHARLES GEORGE (1833–85). " Chinese " Gordon, as he was commonly called, was the son of a British general, and was born at Woolwich on January 28, 1833. He was educated at the Royal Military Academy at Woolwich, and began his career in the British Army in 1852 with a lieutenant's commission in the Royal

O. G. Pike; E.N.A.

WILD GEESE IN GREAT BRITAIN
At one time the grey lag goose (upper) used to breed regularly as far south as Norfolk, but now it is only found much farther north. A skein (term applied to geese in flight) of wild geese is seen in the lower photograph. All geese breed in cool regions, some actually within the Arctic Circle, and all migrate south for the winter.

Engineers. He served in the Crimean War in 1855, and afterwards in Asia. At the age of 30 he was allowed to assist the Chinese Government in suppressing the Taiping rebels, who sought to drive out the Manchu rulers. In 1864, within 18 months of Gordon taking command of the Chinese army, the 10-year-old rebellion which had cost millions of lives was suppressed.

The next nine years of Gordon's life were spent in constructing forts in England and serving on various international commissions. Then, in 1873, his services were lent to the Khedive of Egypt for the organization of the Sudan, of which he was governor-general from 1877 to 1880. In 1884 he was sent back to the Sudan by the British Government. His task was to bring out of the region the Egyptian garrisons endangered by the revolt of the Mahdi or Prophet, a religious leader whose aim was to make the Sudan independent of Egyptian rule. But, in disregard of his orders, General Gordon tried to retain possession of the country, and was besieged by the fanatical followers of the Mahdi in the city of Khartum. For 10 months the city held out; when it fell (January 26, 1885), two days before a British relief expedition reached it, the garrison, including Gordon, was massacred.

So fell a soldier of true heroic type, a Puritan mystic in the midst of 19th century materialism; a man who lived by the faith that can move mountains, doing whatsoever he did for the glory of God, in the full conviction that he was an instrument in the hands of God, fearing nothing and doubting nothing; one who, left to himself, had repeatedly accomplished the apparently impossible, chiefly through his extraordinary power of influencing others. When the public services had not demanded his time and energies, he had devoted them not to his own advancement but to tending the poor and sick and to the redemption of waifs and strays.

General Gordon's family placed a cenotaph to his memory in St. Paul's Cathedral, London; his character and work are fitly commemorated in the Gordon Boys' School for destitute lads, and in the Gordon Memorial College in Khartum.

Gorilla.

The largest and most Man-like of all the apes is the gorilla, a native of the dense forests of western Equatorial Africa. Gorillas stand and walk erect more frequently than the other apes, which led some early explorers to mistake them for savage men. Their bodies are covered with black and brown hair, and they have flat noses and very prominent ridges over the eyes. They feed upon berries, sugar-cane, and other vegetables, and live in pairs, with their offspring, or in small troops.

Until late years very few civilized persons had seen live gorillas, as they are shy and difficult to capture, and seldom live long when taken from their native forests. An old male gorilla, which was killed in 1919, stood five feet 11 inches in height, measured 58 inches round the chest and seven feet from tip to tip of his extended arms. His weight was not stated, but gorillas weighing more

By permission of Frost & Reed, Ltd.

GORDON'S DEATH AT KHARTUM

In 1884 the Egyptian garrisons in the Sudan were endangered by a native rebellion, and General Gordon was sent there to organize their withdrawal. He was himself besieged in Khartum, which was captured by the Sudanese on January 26, 1885, the whole garrison being massacred. The above picture (from the painting by G. W. Joy) shows Gordon bravely facing his assailants.

than 400 lb. are on record. In recent times gorillas have been kept in the London Zoological Gardens. (See Ape and illustration in page 183).

Goths.

First of the northern barbarians whose successive assaults brought low the might of Rome were the Visigoths, or West Goths. There were stories told by their old men of a time when their people had dwelt far to the north, on the shores and islands of what is now Sweden. Then had come long, slow wanderings through the vast forests of western Russia, until they reached the shores of the Black Sea. In a hundred years of contact with the Romans they learned many things, especially the Christian religion, which was spread among them by Ulfilas, a convert of their own race.

For a time, the Goths ruled a great kingdom north of the river Danube and the Black Sea. Then the Huns swept into Europe from Asia, in A.D. 374, conquering the Ostrogoths or East Goths, and forcing the Visigoths to seek refuge across the Danube within the boundaries of the Roman Empire. In the battle of Adrianople, in A.D. 378, the Visigoths defeated a Roman army and slew the Emperor Valens. For a time they lived peacefully on Roman territory; then, on the death of the

Emperor Theodosius in A.D. 395, they rose in rebellion under their ambitious young king, Alaric, and overran a large part of the Eastern Roman Empire. Rome itself fell into the hands of the Goths in A.D. 410.

Alaric's successors led their people out of Italy, and set up a powerful kingdom in southern Gaul (France) and Spain. In the year A.D. 507 the Visigoths in Gaul were defeated by the Franks and were forced beyond the Pyrenees into Spain. For 200 years their kingdom in Spain flourished. It did not come to an end until A.D. 711, when the Moors crossed over from Africa and destroyed it.

The Ostrogoths for a time formed part of the vast horde which followed the king of the Huns, Attila, settling south of Vienna. Their national hero was Theodoric the Great, who became king in A.D. 473. In 489 he invaded Italy and after several years of warfare Theodoric captured and slew Odoacer, a Teutonic chief who had deposed the last of the Roman emperors, and founded a powerful kingdom, which included all Italy together with lands north and east of the Adriatic Sea. The reign of Theodoric was one of the ablest and best in this period.

After Theodoric's death, in 526, the generals of the Eastern Empire reconquered Italy (see Justinian I). Defeated in their last battle (near Mount Vesuvius, in A.D. 552), the Ostrogothic nation left Italy, to mingle and merge in other barbarian hordes north of the Alps, and so they disappeared from history.

How AFFAIRS of STATE are MANAGED

Governments and their doings occupy so large a space in our newspapers and have such an influence on our lives that it is essential to know something of their history and their problems. That knowledge this article gives us.

Government. When a policeman steps into the road and lifts his hand, immediately all the traffic behind him stops. The drivers do not argue; they merely obey. If we tried to act as the policeman does, we should be promptly told to get out of the way.

Why this difference? In the eyes of the law the policeman and ourselves are on exactly the same footing. If a constable misbehaves himself he can be locked up like anybody else. The reason why the policeman has authority is because he represents the Government.

Let us stop for a moment and try to understand the meaning of the word Government, for it will explain a great deal. It comes from a Latin word *gubernare*, meaning to steer a ship; so it is very appropriate that this word should have been taken to apply to a nation, which may be likened to a ship voyaging through the world, sometimes sailing along smoothly, at other times in troubled waters. Government means all the authority, rules, laws, and customs whereby each individual in the nation, and the nation as a whole, is directed, ordered, and ruled. In Great Britain we are in theory governed by the King, acting through his advisers and the Houses of Parliament; but in practice the Cabinet of chief Ministers directs the affairs of the country.

In course of time, as men became more civilized and ceased to rely on brute force, they began to organize themselves into tribes or groups. Out of these communities grew the nations and states as we have them today. Their members chose an exceptionally gifted man of their number to be their chief, or king. He, in turn, chose other men also gifted to carry out his orders and to help him to make laws. The principle underlying this chieftainship or kingship was obedience by the subjects.

Some of the nations are governed by an emperor, some by a king, and most by a parliament in addition. France, the United States, and most other countries have no king. They are ruled by a president and a parliament. The president differs from a king in that he holds office only for a few years and is an elected administrator; whereas a king rules by hereditary right, until he dies or abdicates. Several European countries are governed by dictators with supreme and unlimited power. An example in the recent past was Germany, ruled by Adolf Hitler. The people had no voice in the making of the laws or in their government. An example of a dictatorship of a beneficent kind is that of Antonio Salazar, in present-day Portugal. He is the prime minister, but actually has supreme powers.

In most countries the people themselves, by their votes, elect men and women to represent and speak for them in Parliament; and as it is the latter that makes the laws, the nation, in one sense, governs itself. It is only through governments that nations express themselves.

Our own system took hundreds of years to reach its present perfection. In the time of the Norman kings there was no Parliament. The king was supreme—that is, he could do much as he liked, which was bad for the country, as he often acted cruelly. Before the reign of William the Conqueror there was a Great Council of the Anglo-Saxons called the Witan, or Assembly of the Wise, and forming it were the bishops and superior clergy and the nobles whose duty it was to advise the monarch.

Under the Normans was established the feudal system, by which all land was held under what was known as military tenure. That is to say, the man holding a certain area of land did not pay rent for it, but handed over a small sum of money to the king; the balance was made up by providing so many men to fight for the king when called upon. This plan

Britain's Parliament meets in the Palace of Westminster (above), London, which was badly damaged by German bombs in May 1941.

made the sovereign the owner of all the land, and gave him the right to demand what service he wished from his subjects. All the Norman and Plantagenet kings ruled like this until the misgovernment of John so exasperated his subjects that the leading barons made him grant Magna Carta (*q.v.*), the great charter of liberties, in 1215.

In the reign of his successor, Henry III, 1216–72, was founded what later became our present House of Commons, the assembly of elected men and women who make the laws by which we are governed, assisted by the House of Lords ; for, as will be seen, it takes both Houses to make a Bill into an Act of Parliament.

The first Parliament was called by Simon de Montfort (*q.v.*), Earl of Leicester, in 1265. He summoned certain men from the cities and boroughs, as well as the earls and barons and bishops who already acted as an assembly. Thus, for the first time, the ordinary people were given a voice in deciding the nation's affairs.

In the reign of Edward III, 1327–77, Parliament took a great step forward. The barons and bishops occupied a separate chamber from the men who represented the cities, whose lowlier estate gave rise to the expression—the Commons. Thus there were two distinct assemblies, the House of Lords and the House of Commons.

Let us note briefly what was accomplished by these remarkable events. First, the nation was beginning to govern itself, for even in the reign of Edward I, 1272–1307, it was laid down that no tax could be levied by the king without the consent of Parliament; and the Commons, then sitting with barons or lords, began to petition the king to remove certain hardships, thus suggesting to him new measures to be made the basis of legislation.

In Edward III's reign the House of Commons became still more powerful, and in return for voting money to the king, or granting supplies as it was termed, obtained from him laws which helped the people. But as yet the Commons could only get laws as a favour from the sovereign, although even in those days the people were not entirely governed by him.

In the reign of Henry VII, 1485–1509, England was a limited monarchy. This means that the king, although head of the State, was limited in his power by Parliament, and could not govern as he wished. His son, Henry VIII, reigned 1509–47, seized great power and practically ruled alone, as did Charles I, reigned 1625–49, whose abuse of authority led to his being tried for treason and beheaded. But during Charles's reign several very important rights were established, such as the famous Petition of Rights, whereby Charles was asked to agree to levy no taxes without consent of Parliament. He did so, but later broke his promise. The Bill of Rights of 1689 established further reforms.

As time went on the people called for a greater share in the government of the country. There were large districts which did not have a member of Parliament, while for what were called pocket or rotten boroughs, with hardly any people in them, there was an M.P. This demand was met by the Reform Bill of 1832, which extended the vote more widely among the middle classes. Since that date the franchise, or right to vote, has been greatly extended, until in 1928 the privilege of voting in a

National Portrait Gallery

HOUSE OF COMMONS ELECTED UNDER THE REFORM ACT

The first of the Parliamentary reforms of modern times was the Reform Act of 1832, which extended the right to vote more widely among the middle classes and did away with the pocket boroughs—sparsely-populated districts which were represented in Parliament. At the same time the responsibility of Parliament to the nation began to be fully recognized. This painting by Sir George Hayter (1792–1871) shows the first House of Commons elected under the Reform Act.

parliamentary election was given to virtually all persons who had reached the age of twenty-one.

Parliament is the law-making branch of government. To carry out its behests there is the Executive, commonly called the Civil Service, a vast body of officials in our own day. Then there is the Judiciary, or body of judges who interpret the law and try offenders. Every man and woman possesses the right to a fair trial and to obtain justice. It may sometimes happen that Parliament passes a bad law, or the Executive enforces a law in a spirit quite different from what was intended by the Act. Under our system of government the citizens have a right to appeal to the courts of law. The latter are presided over by judges and magistrates appointed by the Lord Chancellor or in some cases by the Home Secretary. Note again how the whole of our national life is interwoven. We elect Members of Parliament ; Parliament makes our laws; and the judges, who are appointed by Ministers responsible to Parliament, interpret the law in the courts over which they preside.

There is another branch of the judicature known as the civil law. Courts exist for settling disputes, cases in which no crime is involved, but where people can bring what is called a civil suit against a person or body of people. The lowest is the County Court, presided over by a paid judge. There is the Chancery division, where cases dealing with property are heard. Then there is the King's Bench division, which consists of a number of courts, each presided over by a judge. You can go to one of these courts if you claim damages from a man who has wronged you, or to obtain payment of money due to you. Above these is a Court of Appeal to which you may carry your case.

Supposing you again fail, you can take your case to the House of Lords, where the highest court of appeal sits, presided over by the Lord Chancellor and seven Lords of Appeal and ex-Lord Chancellors. If you win your case there it means that the decisions in the two lower courts were wrong. Sometimes, when a man or a company has done this, what is in effect a new law has come about, for the decision reached by the highest court may upset earlier decisions ; fresh legislation is usually introduced in Parliament in such cases to straighten out the law.

Basis of the British Constitution

Britain is peculiar in having no exact, written Constitution. But certain very important Acts which go to the making of our government are clearly laid down in writing, such as the Bill of Rights, the Habeas Corpus Act, the Act of Settlement which decided the succession to the throne of Great Britain after Queen Anne's death, Magna Carta, already referred to, and in later times the two Parliament Acts of 1911, which curtailed the powers of the House of Lords. The greater part of our Constitution, however, is based on custom, experience and legal decisions, not simply on Acts of Parliament. A king who rules without reference to any Constitution is called an absolute monarch, and one who observes the Constitution of his country is said to be a constitutional ruler.

The Constitution of Britain makes no provision for a Cabinet or a Prime Minister. Yet the latter and his Cabinet or inner circle of Ministers are really the most important people in the government of the country. The King is the recognized head of the nation, but he governs only through his advisers—that is, through the Cabinet or the Government, as it is called.

Some mention must be made of what is known as party government in order to understand what is very typical of Britain. In the earlier days of Parliament the members were united as one party, though naturally there were differences of opinion on certain questions, but in the 17th century the idea of two distinct parties grew up. These were Whigs and Tories, from which later arose Liberals and Conservatives. These two main parties were again divided up into groups, and since 1900 the Labour or Socialist party has arisen. Let us assume there are only the Liberal and Conservative parties, to illustrate our point.

How Party Government is Carried On

We will suppose there is a general election, when Members of Parliament are elected in all the constituencies or districts throughout the country. In each district a Liberal and a Conservative candidate for Parliament appear, and in his election address and speeches each asks the people to vote for him. The Liberals win in 400 out of the 600 constituencies, and the Conservatives win in 200. This means that the Liberals have a clear majority of 200 over their opponents. Next the Sovereign sends for the leader of the Liberal party, and asks him to form a Government. The leader accepts the invitation and then chooses his Ministers, one to look after Foreign Affairs, another (the Home Secretary) to look after Home matters, and so on. From among his chief Ministers the Liberal leader, who is now known as Prime Minister, selects a number to act with him in a sort of council. Together they are known as the Cabinet, and, with a few other Ministers not having seats in the Cabinet, are called the Ministry or Administration. Once the Ministry or Government of the day is formed the Sovereign calls Parliament together.

The Liberals, being in the majority, are able to impose their measures on the country; that is, they can pass Acts of Parliament to suit their own views. These may be good or bad, but all the same they pass the House of Commons because there are more Liberals to vote for them than Conservatives to oppose them. However much the latter dislike the Liberal measures, and no matter how much the Conservative voters in the country object to them, they become law after being also passed by the House of Lords and receiving the Royal Assent. We assume that all—or nearly all—the Liberal members vote for the measure introduced by their leader, but there is nothing to compel them to do so. And we also assume that most of the Conservatives (who now constitute the " Opposition ") vote against the Government measure.

A corrective is that, should the Government of the day try to push through a very unpopular measure, there is an outcry in the country, voiced by people at public meetings, and by the newspapers. Liberal members (in the assumed case which we are considering) may even feel constrained to vote *against* their own party. Support may fall so low that the Government suffers a defeat in the voting in the Commons. In the last extreme the Prime Minister, feeling that his government has

LONDON'S COUNTY COUNCIL IN SESSION

On the south bank of the River Thames, just below Westminster Bridge, is the handsome building which houses the London County Council. This photograph shows a meeting of the Council. The members' seats are arranged in a horseshoe, and on a dais at the farther end sits the Chairman who presides over meetings. The Council deals with local government affairs, such as housing, rates, roadways, sanitation, and street lighting. It can also pass laws known as by-laws.

" lost the confidence of the country," may resign. The King will then send for another political leader and ask him to form a government. If a Liberal leader is unable or unwilling to do so, then an " Opposition " leader may be asked to form a Cabinet. It would be futile for any leader to take on the task unless he were sure of enough support in Parliament and in the country. It may be that the only solution is to hold a general election, by means of which the country can give its " mandate " on any grave points at issue.

While party government is a distinctive and recognized feature of the British Constitution, and probably in all the circumstances the best that can be devised, yet it has some defects. One of these defects is that if one party is in power for, say, five years, the legal duration of a British Parliament, there is a tendency for the Cabinet to acquire too much power, and the country to be governed by the Cabinet without consulting the people. The House of Lords can delay the passing of an Act of which they disapprove, but they cannot prevent it eventually being enacted. Sometimes, in a serious crisis, both parties unite to form what is called a Coalition government. This happened during the two World Wars of 1914–18 and 1939–45.

Another very important part of the government of present-day Britain is that known as local government. Each county has a lord-lieutenant representing the Sovereign, and England and Wales are divided into administrative counties, and county boroughs, in each of which is a council elected by the votes of the people. Then, again, the administrative counties are divided into districts, urban or rural, each with its council. Then there are the non-county boroughs, some of very ancient foundation. London is divided into boroughs, and each has a borough council also popularly elected. Great cities like Liverpool, Manchester, Leeds, Glasgow, Cardiff, and others, also have their elected councils. Unlike members of the House of Commons, who are paid £1,000 per annum, local councillors receive no payment for their services. Their work is of very great importance to the everyday life of the community.

Local government deals with affairs such as rates, roadways, sanitation, street lighting, refuse collection, and many other matters of everyday concern to the locality. It is related to parliamentary government in that it carries out the laws affecting health, housing, etc., passed by Parliament. Local governments are also permitted to make laws, known as by-laws. For example, a borough council can pass a law relating to such matters as the disposal of refuse, which all householders have to obey. Or the council can make by-laws and regulations concerning buildings in its area. In reality, we are nevertheless governed by Parliament because the local authorities actually carry out its laws, modified to suit the needs of individual districts. The power so to act is conferred on the local authorities by numerous Local Government Acts of Parliament. Many towns perform their local government under ancient charters which have been granted by various kings, and modified and confirmed by Acts of Parliament.

The British Commonwealth of self-governing Nations includes Canada, Australia, New Zealand, the Union of South Africa, Ceylon and Pakistan. All these are self-governing countries—that is, they manage their own affairs through their elected parliaments. But they are linked together, and to Great Britain, by ties of kinship and association and, above all, by their allegiance to the King. He is represented in each country by a Governor-General who acts in his place. Affairs between them and Great Britain are transacted through the Secretary of State for Commonwealth Relations, who is usually a Cabinet Minister. In addition the Commonwealth includes the Union of India, which although a republic recognizes in the King the symbol of Commonwealth unity.

The Crown Colonies are largely controlled by the British Government through the Colonial Office. Unlike the Dominions, they are only in part self-governing. Thus we see that the British Commonwealth is a federation of states united by a common purpose, namely the defence of freedom and the advancement of civilization.

All the Dominions have constitutions based on that of England. From time to time there are Imperial Conferences (sprung from a conference held in London in 1887). The British Prime Minister, the Secretary of State for Commonwealth Relations, and the Prime Ministers of the countries concerned constitute their membership. Questions such as defence and trade are discussed. A conference of Commonwealth Foreign Ministers, attended by Mr. Bevin, Britain's Secretary of State for Foreign Affairs, took place in Colombo, Ceylon, in 1950.

When you enjoy a visit to a museum or an art gallery, or receive a letter from a friend, you should give thanks to the organizations administered as government and public offices. These are institutions that are owned and managed by the State for the general education, pleasure, or welfare of the public and for the administration of the business affairs of the Government. The staff of these offices consists of members from the various ranks of the Civil Service.

Then we have public corporations such as the British Broadcasting Corporation, the staff and equipment of which were taken over in 1927 and is now administered by a government-nominated board in the spirit of a public service. Another example is the British Electricity Authority, which controls the production of electricity and supplies current to all the authorized concerns in Great Britain. The coal mines, railways, road transport, the Bank of England, and the gas industry are other examples of State-owned organizations. Among other establishments administered as government and public offices are many museums—including the British Museum and the great assembly of museums at South Kensington, London. Besides these there are art galleries, libraries, and certain observatories, including the Royal Observatory, Hurstmonceux. H.M. Stationery Cffice supplies books and stationery to Government departments, and publishes official pamphlets and books.

Offices occupied with the business affairs of the Government are such as the Colonial Office, the Crown Agents for the Colonies—who are the financial agents in this country for the governments of the Colonies—the Commonwealth Relations Office, the Board of Customs and Excise, the Inland Revenue, and others.

There are many large and important departments, such as the Ministry of Agriculture and Fisheries, the Board of Trade (which, among other things, organizes the British Industries Fairs), the Ministry of Education, the Ministry of Health, the Home Office, the Ministry of National Insurance. and the Post Office.

Goya y Lucientes, FRANCISCO JOSÉ

DE (1746–1828). Among the world's great painters. there are some who owe their reputation to their technical skill pure and simple, and others whose popularity depends largely on the appeal of the subjects they painted. Goya (pron. gō′-ya) belongs to neither of these groups, for he is one of those artists who by sheer brilliance and unconventionality forced themselves upon the world of their day; even now his pictures are almost startling in their cleverness, their originality and in some cases their bitterness, while they still look as " modern " as the latest works of living painters.

Goya was born of peasant stock at Fuendetodos. near Saragossa, Spain, on March 30, 1746. He was forced to leave Saragossa after a street fight, and fled to Madrid, arriving finally in Rome, where he studied art. Returning to Spain he was invited to provide the cartoons for the famous tapestries in the Prado Art Gallery at Madrid, and by 1780 he had completed the score of cartoons which revolu-

W. F. Mansell

FROM GOYA'S BRUSH
In his portraits the Spanish artist Goya showed acute understanding of character and ability to reveal it in strong lines and brilliant colouring. This portrait of Doña Isabel Cobos de Porcel, now in the National Gallery, London, was painted in 1806. Goya was also notable as an etcher.

tionized that branch of art. Made director of the Academy of Arts in 1785, he became court painter in the following year. He visited Bordeaux in 1825, but he was in failing health, and died there, on April 16, 1828.

For the Prado tapestries Goya drew scenes from contemporary life in the fields and streets of Spain, works of extreme realism, such as the Washerwoman, or Child Riding a Sheep. Later, as a court painter, he declined to allow riches or favours to obscure his cynical vision; his portraits of the king and queen and their courtiers show acute understanding of character and ability to reveal it in strong lines and brilliant colouring. Everyone of note sat to Goya, including the Duke of Wellington, whom he portrayed with particular brilliance. In addition he painted many fine frescoes.

Moreover, Goya, as versatile as he was facile, occupies a high place among etchers ; his three most famous sets of etchings, Los Caprichos, exposing the abuses of society, the Tauromaguia, bull-fighting scenes, and Los Desastros de la Guerra, inspired by the atrocities of Napoleon's invading army, express his satirical genius almost better than his paintings.

Gracchus, TIBERIUS SEMPRONIUS (163–133 B.C.) and GAIUS (153–121 B.C.). These two Roman brothers, known in history as the Gracchi, who played a prominent part in the history of ancient Rome, were the sons of Tiberius Sempronius Gracchus (pron. grak'-us), a distinguished citizen

Giraudon

THE GRACCHI BROTHERS
In the Luxembourg Museum, Paris, is this fine group of statuary showing the two famous Roman democrats, Tiberius and Gaius Gracchus, with their mother.

of Rome, who was twice Consul. Their mother, Cornelia, was the daughter of the elder Scipio Africanus, the Roman general.

Tiberius won military renown first at the siege of Carthage, and later in Spain, and it was on his journeys to and from the latter country that he first observed the deplorable condition of Roman agriculture.

As one of the tribunes (officials chosen by the people to protect them from oppression) for the year 133 B.C., he brought forward a measure providing that the public lands should be distributed in small holdings among the poor, and that a certain proportion of free labourers should be employed on all large farms. Another tribune, who was named Octavius, opposed the proposed legislation. Tiberius, thereupon, prevailed upon the assembly of the people to deprive Octavius of his office, and the bill was passed.

Threatened with accusation at the end of his term of office for his illegal proceedings, Tiberius set himself to obtain the tribunate for another year. The elections were held, but the Senate declared them illegal, and in ensuing riots Tiberius was killed.

Ten years after his death, his younger brother Gaius reached the position of tribune. During a second tenure of this office he succeeded in making his brother's law operative to a considerable extent. He was, however, in constant opposition to the Senate, and in another riot the followers of Gaius were slain or scattered and their leader, in his despair, caused his own servant to kill him.

The BASIC RULES *of* 'GOOD ENGLISH'

Every time you open your mouth to utter a sound you are using a part of speech, even if it is only an interjection. How we build sentences on these foundation-stones is told in this chapter.

Grammar. Everyone desires to be " understood," in the wider sense as well as in the narrower one. The first and the essential step is to acquire the art of speaking and writing your own language correctly. Good English is easy to acquire if only we learn how to construct and use the simple sentence. If you do not use sentences properly— that is, if you speak or write ungrammatically— people may mistake your meaning.

A sentence is a group of words expressing a complete thought. For example, *Old King Cole* is not a sentence, but *Old King Cole was a merry old soul* is a complete sentence.

A printed or written sentence must always begin with a capital letter.

At the end of every sentence there is always a full stop or period (.), or an interrogation mark (?), or a note of exclamation (!). It is always a safe rule to put a full stop at the end of a sentence, except when

you ask a question, as *Where is my hat ?* or when you utter a cry such as *The house is on fire !*

With these last two rules one can go through a book and count the sentences very easily. But you cannot be sure about these rules in some compositions written by young people. For instance:

" I got my first pair of skates on my seventh birthday they were more fun than anything else I ever had. It began to thaw the day before my birthday. so that I had to wait nearly a week for the river to freeze again before I could try them."

The boy who wrote this was not careful to indicate where one sentence ended and the next began. The first complete statement ends with the word *birthday*, so he should have put a full stop after that word and started *they* with a capital letter.

He was perfectly right in putting a full stop after *had* and starting the next word with a capital, because the second complete statement ended with *had;* but the next complete statement runs all the way to the end of the paragraph, and so the writer was wrong in putting a full stop between the second *birthday* and the *so.*

Sometimes sentences have what seem like two or more sentences in them, but these are not exactly sentences; they are called *clauses.* For instance, I may say: *I have a pain. I ate too much ice cream.* But it would perhaps be better to say: *I have a pain because I ate too much ice cream.* Here the two clauses are joined by the word *because,* and together they form a completed sentence.

These words that join sentences are called conjunctions. They also join words and phrases. In the sentence, *Jack and Jill went up the hill,* the word *and* is a conjunction joining two other words. And in the sentence, *It is in the kitchen or under the table,* the conjunction *or* joins the two phrases, *in the kitchen* and *under the table.*

The most common conjunction is *and.* This word some people use too frequently, joining all their ideas together. For instance:

" I woke early and dressed and found the bait and went fishing and caught eight trout and I came home and gave them to mother and she asked me to clean them and she fried them for us and they tasted fine."

This looks like one sentence; but it is not really one, for it would sound much better to break up this long statement and say :

" I woke early, and after I had dressed I found the bait and went fishing. I caught eight trout. After a while I came home and gave them to mother, who asked me to clean them. Then she fried them for us. They tasted fine."

Many persons try to make a single sentence do the work of many. Very often an untidy or involved piece of prose can be made clear merely by splitting up long sentences into shorter ones. But we must point out—although it has nothing to do with grammar—that the first thing to do, before you begin to write, is to sort out and to marshal your *ideas* in their logical order. Unless you *think* clearly, you cannot *write* clear prose.

Main Parts of a Sentence

All sentences can be divided into two main parts. —subject and predicate. The subject is the thing we talk about, and the predicate indicates what is said about it. No matter how long or complicated a sentence may be, this is true. In the sentence " The largest city in Great Britain is London," the subject is, *The largest city in Great Britain.* The predicate is, *is London.*

In the sentence " My finger hurts," *finger* is the name of something, just as city, Great Britain, and London are names of places. These name words are called nouns. They may name some particular person or place, or merely a group of things. Most nouns begin with small letters in English, but the names of all persons and places begin with capital letters. The first of these classes we call common nouns, and the second proper nouns.

In the sentence " Baby is hungry," the word *is* is what we call an " existence " word. Such a word does not show action; it merely links *baby* and *hungry.* The words which show action, and those that link the subject to something said about it, are verbs. *Run, jump, play, eat, sleep, read, write* are all action verbs. *Is, are, were,* are all linking verbs.

A ten-year-old boy named James in talking to his mother would not say, " James is hungry. James wants an apple." He would have noticed that people do not speak of themselves by name, but use the words *I, me,* and the like. He would say " *I* am hungry. *I* want an apple." If he were a generous boy he might say, " John is hungry; *he* wants one too." The word *he* would stand for John. These substitute words are called pronouns, because they are used for nouns, and the Latin word meaning " for " is *pro. I, he, you,* are all pronouns.

The imaginary James might have said " Oh! I am hungry," using the interjection " Oh! " to give more force to his request. Other interjections, which we hope to never need to use, are " Fire! " " Police! " and so on. But we may have to interject the call " Help! " if we get into trouble.

Adjectives and Adverbs

So far we have talked about five of the eight kinds of words, or parts of speech—nouns, pronouns, verbs, conjunctions, and interjections. One can build many sentences with only these five kinds of words, but if there were no other parts of speech we should not be able to say many things that we should like to say. For example, suppose you had lost your coat and were trying to reclaim it at the lost property office. If you said " Have you found a coat? " nobody could help you very much, because perhaps other people had also lost coats. But if you said, " I have lost a *blue* coat," there would be more chance of your finding it. *Blue* adds to the meaning of coat—it describes it. You might have used *large,* or *old,* or *shabby,* or *new,* in place of, or with *blue.* All such words as these, that add to the meaning of nouns, are called adjectives.

If only one blue coat had turned up, you would not have much trouble in claiming your own. But suppose that four coats, and four blue coats, were awaiting their owners. You might have to give the man in charge other details—the *time* you lost the coat, the *place* in which you left it, or *why* you were so long claiming it. You might say, " I lost a blue coat yesterday in a tram." Then *yesterday* and in a *tram* would tell time and place. They would make the verb *lost* clearer, and would add to its meaning. The coat found in that place (*in a tram*) and at that time (*yesterday*) would be recognized as belonging to you.

Such words or groups of words that narrow down or add to the meaning of verbs are called adverbs or adverbial phrases.

In the sentence " Very heavy clouds rolled quickly across the sky " we shall discover a new way of using a helping word, if we look closely. We have had adverbs modifying or changing the meaning of verbs, but now we have a word modifying an adjective. The writer was not satisfied with saying that the clouds were heavy. He added the word *very* to make *heavy* more intense. *Very* is an adverb modifying an adjective. If the writer had wanted to make *quickly* more intense, he might have said *very quickly,* just as he said *very heavy.* In that case the modifying adverb would have helped out the meaning of another adverb. Adverbs, then, may modify verbs, adjectives or other adverbs.

In some of the little groups of words used so far, as in *a tram,* there are expressions which have not as yet been explained. In the sentence, " I lost my coat in a tram," *in* is a new kind of word. It is a preposition, or " relation " word, which shows a connexion between *lost* and *tram*, but does not mean anything alone. Thus in " The boy in the playground has a new bat," *in* is a preposition which shows the relation between *boy* and *playground*. These prepositions always have nouns or pronouns for objects.

Those are the names of the eight parts of speech, and all the hundreds of thousands of words in the dictionary belong to one or another of these eight classes. We often use one part of speech in a manner which makes it serve as another part: for example, there are verbal nouns, and verbal adjectives. And of course there is a great deal more in grammar than we have mentioned in this brief account.

Uneducated persons often have great difficulty in making others understand just what they want to say, because they do not know enough about words and sentences and how to use them. That is why it is important thoroughly to learn grammar, which tells you how to use these valuable tools.

You will learn many other interesting and important facts about the parts of speech, and how to use them correctly, if you will turn to the articles in this work under the headings Adjective; Adverb; Conjunction; Noun; Preposition; Pronoun; Punctuation; Sentence; Verb.

The real value of grammar may be stated thus: All thought is expressed chiefly through language, and, at bottom, the rules of correct thinking are involved in the study of grammar.

Correct language indeed is the expression of logical thinking. To analyse sentences, to examine the structure and arrangement of the parts, to study the various modes of expressing thought and shade of thought grammatically—these activities have always been regarded as the very best way of learning to think correctly. But, as we said earlier, you must sort out your ideas, and make up your mind just what you want to say or write, before you utter or write your sentences.

Gramophone. If you have read our story of the Ear and its mechanism you will know that sound is the sensation which our ears receive as air vibrations, and which the ear and the brain interpret as noise, speech or music, according to the character of the originating sound. You have banged the tightly stretched skin of a drum, and have sent out low-pitched vibrations; you may have done something of the sort merely by bending a flexible sheet of tin, or by flexing the middle part of a metal teatray, without striking it. Probably you have at some time or other plucked or twanged the string of a violin or guitar or mandolin, and sent out high-pitched vibrations. Whenever you did any of these things you set up air movements which the air carried as waves, and which anyone in the range of the waves might receive with their ears.

You may read a fuller explanation of sound propagation in the story of Sound; sufficient has been said here to show you that the problem of reproducing sound is one of utilising the air vibrations to write their own signature in some suitable recording substance, and to devise mechanism for playing back that record, as we should term it today. Scientists had found out a good deal about sound waves by the 1870s; Graham Bell had made a workable telephone by 1875, and telegraph inventors were

seeking some way of getting a record of the " longs and shorts " sounded by the Morse instrument.

Twenty years earlier, Leon Scott had, it is true, caused sound waves to write their autograph, but this record was made by a needle on smoked paper, in the form of a wavy line; there was no known means of reversing the process. Scott's device was a sort of large ear-trumpet, over the bell of which was tightly stretched a membrane. Attached to the membrane was a light stylus (a bristle), and near this was a cylinder on which the smoked paper was wound. Any sound made near the opposite open end of the trumpet made the membrane vibrate, and the shape of the vibrations was traced on to the cylinder by the stylus. Scott called his machine the phonautograph.

In 1877 Thomas Alva Edison produced his phonograph, which is used almost in its original form for recording dictated letters and messages,

Science Museum, London

EDISON'S FIRST PHONOGRAPH

In the centre is a grooved cylinder, covered with tinfoil ; turning the handle moved the cylinder along past the stylus or needle of the diaphragm. Words spoken into the mouthpiece vibrated the diaphragm, so that the stylus made a corresponding track on the tinfoil. To play back the record, it was again traversed past the stylus, this time causing the diaphragm to vibrate and repeat the original sounds.

and for playing them back. The machine had a small trumpet, with a membrane made of a thin glass plate and bearing a steel needle. The cylinder was grooved, and covered with a sheet of tinfoil— soft enough to be indented by the gentle pressure of the needle, and yet hard enough to retain the " sound track." In this first phonograph the cylinder had to be turned slowly by a handle; later ones were moved by clockwork. When anyone spoke into the mouthpiece, the glass plate vibrated and the point traced an indented line on the cylinder; the latter not only revolved, but moved sideways so that continually a new portion of the tinfoil was presented to the needle.

Now for the play-back—which really " made " the talking-machine. After the needle had written its record on the cylinder the latter was moved along again to the starting point, the needle set in the groove it had already made, and the handle turned to rotate the cylinder. Now the grooved track in the tinfoil pushed the needle up and down over the inequalities in the floor of the groove; thus

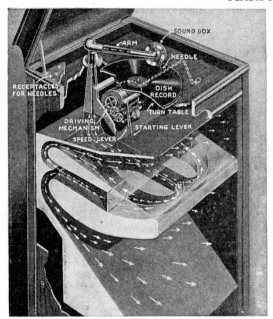

HOW A GRAMOPHONE WORKS

By cutting away a portion of the cabinet and other parts in the above drawing the mechanism of the gramophone is displayed. The arrows leading out of the sound-box at the end of the arm trace the course of the sound waves through the folded horn that is used in this type of machine.

the needle imparted vibrations to the glass membrane; the membrane pushed against the column of air in the horn and set up air vibrations. Edison's first machine gave out a weak and feeble reproduction of the words which had been spoken into the horn to make the original record on the tinfoil. The inventor himself did something to improve its performance; he used a wax-coated cylinder instead of the tinfoil, and the mechanism

was made better. But it fell to other workers to do most of the development which has given us the modern gramophone.

Emile Berliner, German-born but later a naturalised American, applied himself to making a more permanent record. He used a disk, at first made of glass and later of zinc. The needle impression was taken on special paper, and next this tracing was etched out on the glass or zinc with acid in the same manner as photo-engraving is done (*see* Engraving). Berliner's further problem was to make reproductions of the zinc disk so that many " records "—we now use the word in the sense in which we understand it today—could be produced cheaply. He did this by a process of electrotyping not unlike that used for making printing plates of illustrations. A mould was obtained from the zinc original disk, and a hard metal master-record was thus got by casting in the mould. Now Berliner had a die from which records in vulcanite could be stamped out. Later he used shellac for the records made, and in due time many other mixtures of plastic materials came to be employed.

Disk-shaped records were much more convenient than cylindrical ones; they took up less room, and could be manufactured easily and cheaply. The needle in Berliner's machine moved from side to side as the diaphragm vibrated—not up and down as Edison's had done. The two systems rivalled each other for many years, until at last the side-to-side one became established. In order to guide the recording needle gradually towards the middle of the disk, in a spiral of decreasing radius, a screw-thread mechanism was used at first. In playing the commercially produced records, the groove itself guided the needle. By now we had obtained a gramophone resembling that of today, and further improvements were in the diaphragm and needle, and in the horn or some other amplifying device.

Much study was given to types of horn which should allow the sound waves to become larger

A GRAMOPHONE RECORD IN THE MAKING

Two essentials of gramophone records are that they must not be brittle and that they must have long life. The modern disk is made of a composition in which resin plays a large part, minerals and fibre being added to give greater strength. These photographs show three stages in the making of a record. On the left a cake of plastic material, which will form a record, is being scraped from a hot plate. In the centre the cake is being placed beneath the matrix or die which will impress the sound track upon it. Right, a completed record is removed from the press after being moulded.

WONDERLAND OF THE GRAND CANYON MADE BY THE MIGHTY COLORADO RIVER

The incomparable glory of the Grand Canyon in the United States is spectacular enough without the added beauty of the varied colouring of the cliffs. Here the River Colorado cuts through the plateau of Arizona between rocky banks. This photograph from the air shows the scene after a rainstorm has transformed the dull red of the sandstone into a vivid vermilion. Fleecy clouds are still scudding above the flat-topped plateaux. Those who have visited the Grand Canyon say that the colours shown above are not in the least exaggerated.

To face page 1496

THE GREATEST CLEFT IN THE GLOBE'S SURFACE

ONE of the world's scenic wonders is the Grand Canyon of the Colorado. The photograph on the previous page shows some of the beauty of its colouring, but the vivid scarlet of the rain-soaked sandstone is not the only beauty of colour that it offers, for there are cream-coloured cliffs, spaces of varied green, and rocks of sombre black. In the previous photograph the distance is obscured by the rain clouds that have just passed, but in that above, taken under a cloudless sky, the awe-inspiring area of this great waste land cut in two by the hundreds of miles of canyon can be realized. As far as the eye can see, folded ranges of rock tower into the air, for all the world like a giant tablecloth rucked into pleats by a supernatural hand. Down at the bottom of the gorge runs the Colorado river, which is still cutting deeper and deeper into the rocky mass.

To face page 1

while keeping their original structural form. Then manufacturers very cleverly tucked the horn away inside the cabinet of the instrument, folding and curving it upon itself but still obtaining the length and breadth needed for good reproduction. In making the first record, from which the " master " was to be formed, the soloist sang near a large horn connected with the recording diaphragm and needle; the players of the orchestra had to be grouped around the horn, and it was difficult to get the best results from a musical point of view.

All this was changed when electrical recording was perfected. Microphones like those used for broadcasting (they are essentially improvements of the simpler microphones used in telephone apparatus) took the place of the horn. The sound vibrations were converted into electrical current pulses; by means of an apparatus corresponding in p r i n c i p l e to the telephone receiver these pulses were made to vibrate the needle of the recording machine which cut the original record. Thermionic valve apparatus for amplifying the impulses was interposed between the recording machine and the microphone, and control panels resembling those used in a broadcasting studio enabled the recording to be supervised so as to get the most faithful reproduction.

Henceforth what may be called the musician's gramophone was possible—one in which real musical reproduction was effected, giving a result comparable with the playing of a live orchestra or the performance of a soloist as heard in the concert hall.

The older type of gramophone now began to give place to the electrical reproducer; instead of the horn, in which sound waves were set up directly by the reproducing diaphragm, a little electromagnetic device called a pickup took the vibrations of the record-playing needle. The pick-up vibrated a metallic diaphragm near the poles of an electro-magnet, somewhat as the diaphragm of a microphone does in the telephone transmitter. The electrical pulses were fed to a valve-amplifier like that of a wireless receiver, and operated a loud-speaker. Often a radio-receiver and an

Courtesy, His Master's Voice
A MODERN RADIOGRAM
When a wireless set and an electric gramophone are combined in the same cabinet the instrument is called a radiogram. Here the front panel is open to show the record-changing mechanism.

electric gramophone are combined in a cabinet—the radio-gramophone—and part of the radio-receiver apparatus is used for amplifying and reproducing the sound from the pick-up. Portable gramophone players are made for plugging in at a radio-receiver.

Many ordinary (acoustic) gramophones are still made, and are handy as portable instruments where a radio set is not available. Such small ones are still worked by a spring motor; larger gramophones of any kind are generally turned by an electric motor, and include mechanism for changing the records automatically. Thus a long symphony can be listened to, once we have arranged the records on the machine, without breaking off to attend to the apparatus.

Broadcasting studios use gramophones for playing recorded programmes, repeating performances which have been given at some previous time as "live" broadcasts, or giving complete programmes of recorded favourites. Then there are other sound-recording machines which are not strictly gramophones. Some of these use as the record a wire or a ribbon of steel or some ferro-magnetic alloy (one susceptible to magnetism). This wire or ribbon is impressed with the changing electro-magnetic quality resulting from the action of a kind of pick-up; it preserves

British Broadcasting Corporation
GRAMOPHONES IN A BROADCASTING STUDIO
For playing recorded programmes or to give a concert of records, broadcasting studios use a number of electrical gramophones placed side by side in a bank (above). This arrangement enables a series of records to be played without an interval occurring while the disks are changed. Tone and volume can be controlled by the operators.

this character unless de-magnetized, and on feeding it through a suitable reproducing apparatus the magnetic variations are made to effect electric pulses and to operate a loud-speaker. Another use of gramophones is in connexion with talking-picture systems. (*See* Microphone; Radio; Sound; Telephone).

Granada. (Pron. gran-ah'-da). One of the most important events in the history of Europe was the conquest of Spain by the Moors. After the departure of the Romans in the 5th century after Christ, Spain was without any strong or stable government, until in 711, an invading army of Moors from Northern Africa, probably not more than 12,000 in number, landed in Spain, and defeated the very much larger armies of the Gothic king who opposed them. Before long the whole of Spain was held by the Moors, or Saracens, and when the country was re-conquered by the Christians, the kingdom of Granada was the last territory to be recovered; it was not until 1492 that the Moors lost the last remnants of Granada.

It was as late as 1609 that Philip III drove the remaining descendants of the Moors, who then numbered about a million, back to Africa. Few things in European history are more astonishing than the hold which this race of Mahomedans, possessing a civilization and a culture far superior to the European people they had conquered, maintained in Spain for so many centuries.

Granada was founded by the Moors in the 8th century, and in the 13th century, when it was the capital of the Moorish kingdom of Granada, it had a population of 700,000, and was one of the most splendid cities in the world.

The history and monuments of this one city are in themselves eloquent proof of the remarkable achievements of the Moors in Spain. It contains the Alhambra (*q.v.*), a unique memorial of Moorish power and art; and there are remains of Moorish walls, towers and water conduits. The modern city has many educational institutions and manufactures textiles, soap, liqueurs and paper. The population is 162,000.

Grand Canyon. Anyone standing on the rim of the 200-miles gorge, cut by the Colorado river through the high plateau of northern Arizona in the United States, cannot help being overwhelmed with awe, because the canyon is the longest and deepest in the world.

Look across the yawning depths of the stupendous chasm to the opposite wall, ablaze with bands of glowing colours! Peer over the edge, and far below you see what appears to be a tiny silver thread! It is the swift-flowing Colorado, one of the large rivers of North America. It looks very small because it is a mile below. At the top, the Canyon is two to 18 miles wide.

From the rim to the river's brink the walls descend in a succession of cliffs and terraces, like a giant's staircase, each step several hundred feet high. The barren rocks of white, buff, dull red, and green have been carved into a bewildering variety of shapes and forms. (*See* colour plate facing page 1496).

Few have seen more than a fraction of the canyon's wonders, for the journey through the length of the gorge is made extremely dangerous by the many rapids, in some of which the river attains a speed of nearly 25 knots.

The first authenticated passage through the canyon was made by Major J. W. Powell (1869). Even the hardiest frontiersmen shunned the unknown perils of whirlpools, underground passages, and giant falls which Indian legend attributed to the canyon, until Major Powell organized a party to explore the gorge from end to end. Dangerous enough the adventure proved, even though the underground channels and giant waterfalls were found to be nothing but myths.

Granite. If you look closely at a piece of granite, you will see that it is made up of more than one kind of material, and if you could crush it to powder, you would be able easily to pick out tiny fragments of the separate substances that compose it. The chief minerals are quartz, feldspar, and mica. The colour of granite depends on the proportions and varieties of the minerals present. The prevailing colour is grey—light grey if dark minerals are few, dark grey if they are abundant. Greenish, pink, and red hues are frequently seen, usually due to different kinds of feldspar.

Granite belongs to the group of igneous rocks—that is, it was formed ages ago by the cooling of molten magma (fluid rock-matter) far below the earth's surface.

Dorien Leigh

GRANADA : LAST MOORISH CITY IN SPAIN
Founded by the Moors in the 8th century, Granada, capital of the Spanish province of Andalusia, was not captured by the Spaniards until 1492, being the last Moorish stronghold to fall into their hands. Besides possessing the Alhambra, the greatest relic of the Moors in Spain, the city contains many other memorials of their culture. In the old quarter (above), known as the Albaicin, the streets are narrow, and some of the houses have high latticed windows.

GRANTHAM'S OLD CHURCH
In the market town of Grantham, Lincolnshire, the chief building is the church of St. Wulfram, which was built mainly in the 13th century. It is noted for its window tracery and chained library. Grantham's principal industry is the manufacture of agricultural implements and machinery.

This cooling took place very slowly, thus giving plenty of time for the formation of crystals. Granite belongs mainly to periods of active mountain-building in the geological record, but it is likely that the lower part of the earth's crust beneath the continents—though not beneath the great oceans—consists of granitic rocks.

Fresh granite is a hard stone, but like other rocks it may have been altered; one of the products so formed is the kaolin, or china clay (q.v.), so extensively used today. Because of its hardness, granite is difficult to work, and so is an expensive building stone. It is used chiefly for road metal, or as paving blocks, for monuments, and for large buildings where great strength and durability or beauty of finish are required. Many varieties are exceedingly beautiful in colouring, e.g. the red Peterhead granite, and take a high polish.

Aberdeenshire, Kirkcudbrightshire, Cornwall, and Cumberland supply us with much of our granite.

Grantham. Sir Isaac Newton was educated at the King Edward VI Grammar School at Grantham, before going to Cambridge University. This fact is sufficient to entitle this Lincolnshire market town to an honourable position in English history.

Grantham is situated 25 miles south of Lincoln, and 105 miles north of London. The chief industries are the manufacture of agricultural implements and engines, plastics, malting and basket-making. There are granite quarries near the town. The most notable building in Grantham is the church of

St. Wulfram, which was completed in 1300 and has a chained library. Another ancient structure is the Angel Inn, dating from the 14th century. The estimated population is 22,500.

Grape-fruit. Closely related to the orange, lemon and citron, the grape-fruit is a native of the Malayan Archipelago; its scientific name is *Citrus decumana*. The tree is small, growing to a height of only 25 feet, and has downy shoots and oval leaves, with winged leaf stalks. The fruits, called grape-fruit from their habit of growing in bunches, are four to six inches in diameter and have a yellow rind. The pulp, which has a slightly acid and bitter flavour, resembles that of the lemon.

The grape-fruit was not cultivated until the 17th century, when some trees were transported from Malaya to the West Indies, the fruit being first imported into Europe in 1707. It became very popular as a breakfast food in the West Indies and the United States, but it found little favour in Great Britain until the beginning of the 20th century. The largest producers of grape-fruit are the United States, Palestine, Cuba, South Africa and Jamaica. (*See* illustration below.)

Grapes. It is believed that the grape was the first fruit to be cultivated, and certainly grape seeds have been found with mummies in Egyptian tombs at least 3,000 years old. The original home of the vine was Asia, whence it was brought to Europe, probably by the Phoenicians.

The grape-vine (*Vitis vinifera*) was probably introduced into Britain about the first or second century of the Christian era, but it may have arrived even

CLUSTER OF GRAPE-FRUIT
Comparatively unknown in Britain until the beginning of the 20th century, grape-fruit was introduced from Malaya into the West Indies by the Spaniards in the 17th century. The fruit grows in grape-like bunches on trees 25 feet high.

earlier. In some parts of England, chiefly in the south-west, grapes ripen in the open, but usually they are grown under glass.

Many varieties of this luscious fruit are produced, among them being White Sweetwater, Miller's Burgundy, Chasselas Vibert, Muscat, Black Hamburg, Diamond Jubilee, Black Alicante and Gros Maroc. The distinctive colours are entirely in the outer skin, which may be green, red, yellow, purple, or even variegated. Sometimes grape-vines remain fruitful for a century or more.

Wines are made by fermenting the juice of the grape. During fermentation a greyish or reddish crust forms in the vat, and this, a crystalline substance called argol, becomes, when refined, the cream of tartar used in medicine, in effervescent drinks, and in baking-powders.

Graphite.

In appearance graphite, also known as black lead or plumbago, is so different from the diamond that it is at first difficult to believe that the black, opaque, soft mineral is chemically identical with the colourless, transparent, precious stone, the hardest of all known substances. But, like the diamond, graphite is one of the crystalline forms in which the useful element carbon is found. It also occurs naturally as amorphous or non-crystalline graphite, a softer form.

One of the familiar uses of graphite is for the "leads" of black pencils. Its name comes from the Greek *grapho*, "I write." Because it is a good conductor of electricity it is also much used in electrotyping and electrical apparatus. Graphite makes an excellent lubricant, since the countless minute flakes of which it consists easily adhere to rough metal, producing a smooth surface and so reducing friction. In the special form known as colloidal graphite, it is used as a mechanical lubricant in motor-cars. Most of the world's graphite, however, is mixed with clay and sand to make heat-resisting crucibles and retorts in which metals are melted. Graphite is also used for paints and for stove-polish.

Ceylon, that most wonderful gem-producing country, produces large quantities of mined graphite. Mexico, the United States, and Cumberland (noted for pencil graphite) are among other producers.

Graphite can also be made artificially, *e.g.* by melting, and allowing to cool slowly, cast iron containing a high percentage of carbon.

Pure graphite is now manufactured and employed in constructing the "piles" used for producing atomic energy and material for atomic bombs. The graphite acts as a moderator; it slows down neutrons, so that they more easily split uranium atoms. This graphite must be very pure indeed, otherwise it absorbs neutrons needed for the atomic reaction. (*See* Atom).

Fox

GRAPE-VINE AT HAMPTON COURT PALACE

Perhaps the most famous grape-vine in England is the one planted at Hampton Court Palace, Middlesex, in 1768, which still produces Black Hamburg grapes of the finest quality (above). It is most unusual for a vine to remain fruitful for so long. In England grapes are usually grown under glass, though in the south-west, given favourable conditions, they will ripen in the open.